Giinaquq Like a Face / Comme un visage

Giinaquq Like a Face
Comme un visage

Sugpiaq Masks of the Kodiak Archipelago
Sven D. Haakanson Jr. and Amy F. Steffian, editors

Les masques sugpiat de l'archipel de Kodiak
Sous la direction de Sven D. Haakanson Jr. et Amy F. Steffian

A project of

The Alutiiq Museum & Archaeological Repository, Kodiak, Alaska, USA

The Château-Musée, Boulogne-sur-Mer, France

Un projet de l'Alutiiq Museum & Archaeological Repository de Kodiak (Alaska), aux États-Unis, et du Château-Musée de Boulogne-sur-Mer, en France

UNIVERSITY OF ALASKA PRESS

FAIRBANKS, ALASKA

University of Alaska Press
P.O. Box 756240
Fairbanks, AK 99775-6240

ISBN 978-1-60223-049-1

Library of Congress Cataloging-in-Publication Data

Giinaquq = Like a face : Sugpiaq masks of the Kodiak archipelago / Sven D. Haakanson Jr. and Amy F. Steffian, editors.
  p. cm.
"A project of The Alutiiq Museum & Archaeological Repository, Kodiak, Alaska, USA & The **Château-Musée**,
Boulogne-sur-Mer, France." Includes bibliographical references and index. ISBN 978-1-60223-049-1 (pbk. : alk. paper)
1. Pacific Gulf Yupik Eskimos—Material culture—Alaska—Kodiak Island—Exhibitions. 2. Eskimo masks—Alaska—
Kodiak Island—Exhibitions. 3. Kodiak Island (Alaska)—Social life and customs—Exhibitions. I. Haakanson, Sven D.
II. Steffian, Amy F. III. Alutiiq Museum & Archaeological Repository. IV. **Château-Musée** de Boulogne-sur-Mer.
V. Title: Like a face. VI. Title: Sugpiaq masks of the Kodiak archipelago.
E99.E7G375 2009
979.8'40899714—dc22
                    2008049089

Révision-Correction : Francys Gramet

Cover design by Dixon Jones, University of Alaska Fairbanks, Rasmuson Library Graphics
Cover illustrations: Front cover, 988-2-156 and 988-2-165; back cover, 988-2-145. All from the Château-Musée Pinart
Collection. Photographs by Will Anderson.

This publication was printed on acid-free paper that meets the minimum requirements for ANSI / NISO Z39.48–1992
(R2002) (Permanence of Paper for Printed Library Materials).

Quyanaasinaq, our sincerest thanks, to Koniag, Inc., the Kodiak Island Housing Authority, and the Château-Musée for
funding to make this book possible.

In memory of
À la mémoire de

Larry Matfay, 1907–1998

Sven David Haakanson Sr., 1934–2002

Dr. Lydia T. Black 1925–2007

Thank you for helping to keep the Sugpiaq culture alive.
Pour les remercier d'avoir œuvré à garder vivante la culture sugpiaq.

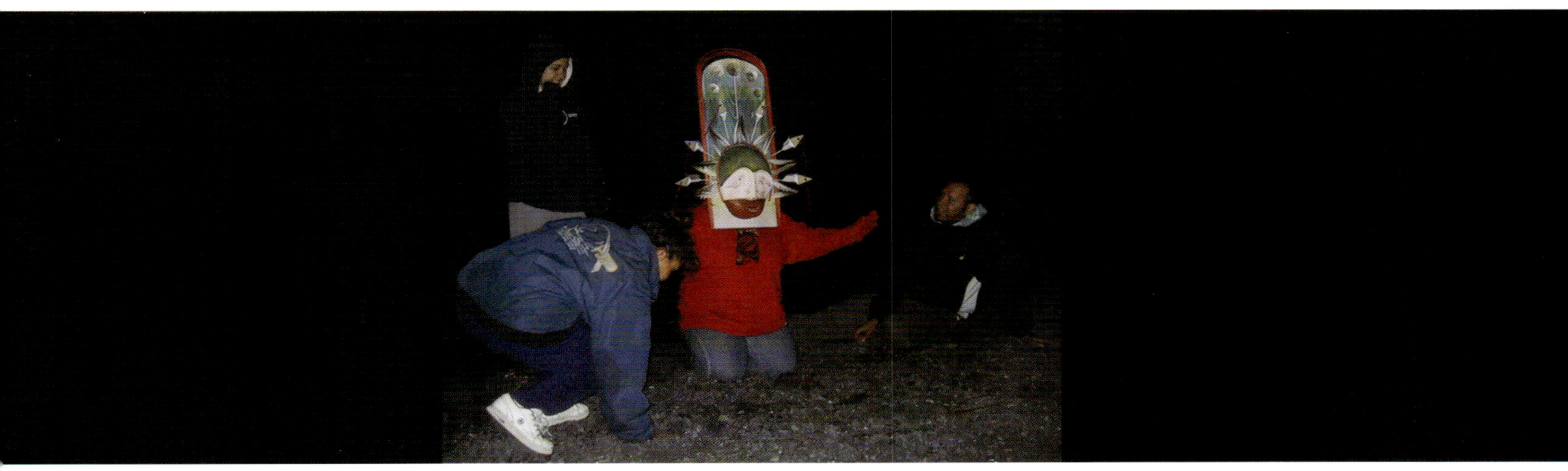

Figure 1. Phyllis Clough dances a memorial mask carved by
Perry Eaton in honor of her late father Sven Haakanson Sr.
PHOTO BY SVEN HAAKANSON JR.

Illustration 1. Phyllis Clough porte un masque sculpté par
Perry Eaton lors d'une danse en l'honneur de son père décédé,
Sven Haakanson Sr.
PHOTOGRAPHIE DE SVEN HAAKANSON JR

Contents
Sommaire

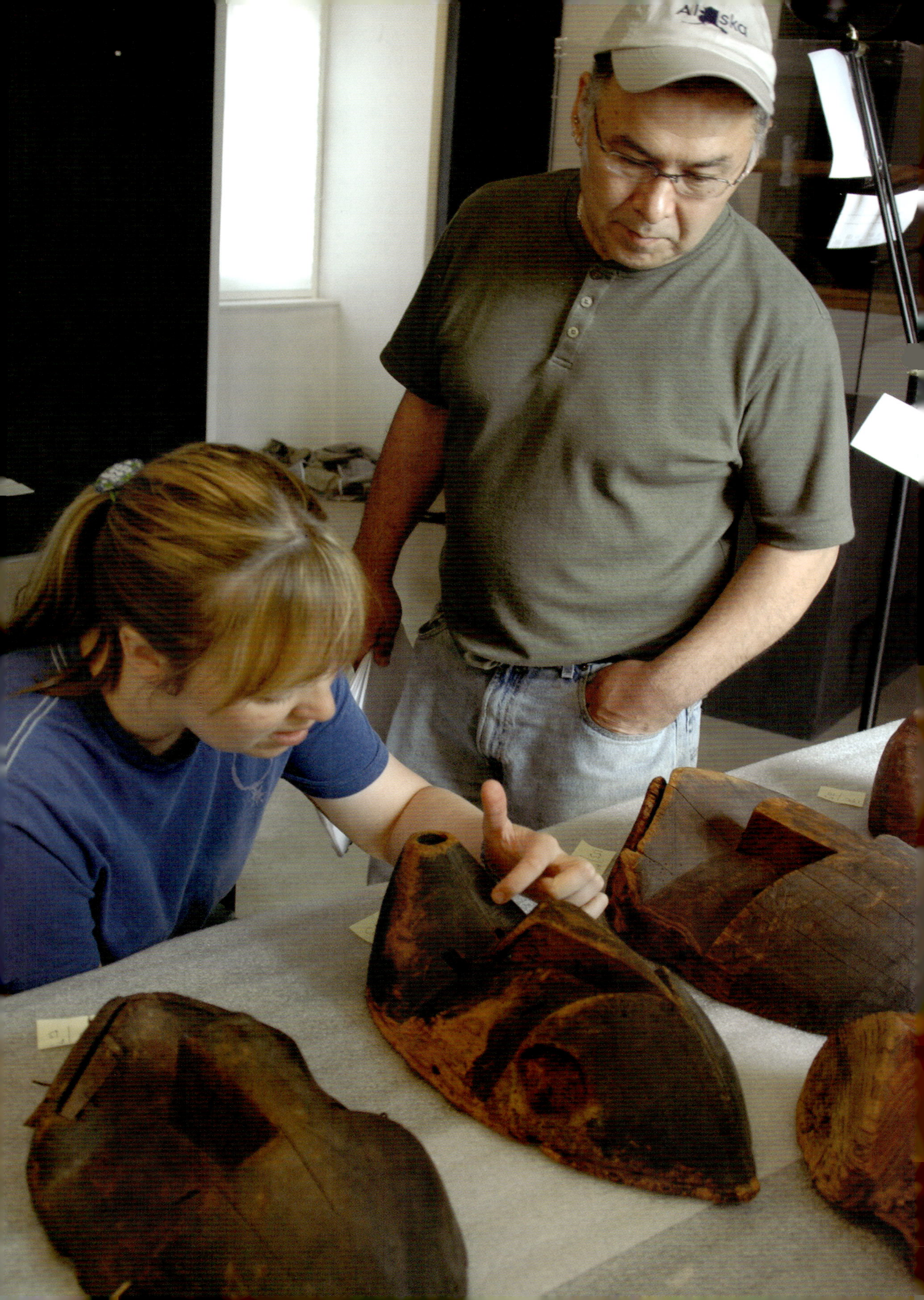

Invocation

Essence
Doug Inga

Excited to go to France. Got there, fell on my back. All the art on buildings, the streets, and the place we stayed in was fun. We got to the other town called Boulogne. More excited. Getting closer to the building. By now I wanted to see the objects of my heart. Now we went through meeting people. My heart was racing. Now we were climbing the stairs. I felt something. My heart was stirring. Got to the top of the stairs. I looked in the room and there was an essence. I could not put my finger on what that was for a little bit. But it came to me—home. Home was the feeling. All these thousands of miles to feel that. It was strange to feel that, but when I went in, it was not.

J'avais attendu avec impatience ce voyage en France et, arrivé sur place, ce fut l'émerveillement. Tout cet art m'enchantait, l'architecture, les rues, l'endroit où nous logions. J'étais encore plus impatient de connaître Boulogne-sur-Mer. Comme nous approchions du bâtiment, j'avais hâte de découvrir ces objets auxquels j'étais tellement attaché. On commença par nous présenter des gens. Mon émotion était à son comble. Comme je gravissais enfin la dernière marche, la salle s'offrit à mes yeux et je ressentis à cet instant la présence d'une essence. Il me fallut un bon moment pour saisir de quoi il s'agissait : nous nous retrouvions chez nous. Nous avions fait des milliers de kilomètres et, finalement, c'est cela que nous ressentions. Sur le moment, la sensation me parut étrange, mais dès que nous pénétrâmes à l'intérieur, ça ne le fut plus du tout.

Figure 2. Lena Amason and Doug Inga study Sugpiaq masks at the Château-Musée, Boulogne-sur-Mer, France.
PHOTOGRAPH BY WILL ANDERSON.

Illustration 2. Lena Amason et Doug Inga examinent des masques sugpiat au Château-Musée de Boulogne-sur-Mer.
PHOTOGRAPHIE DE WILL ANDERSON.

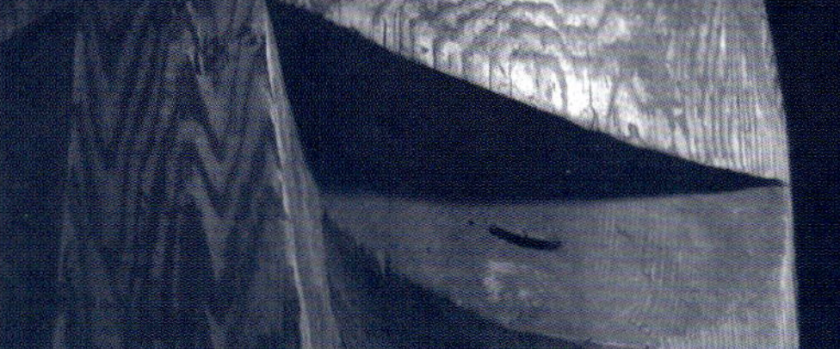

Foreword

Will Anderson

Chair, Alutiiq Heritage Foundation Board of Directors

In June of 2006 I had the privilege of traveling with nine artists from the Kodiak region to visit the Château-Musée in Boulogne-sur-Mer, France, to examine their collection of Sugpiaq masks. Early contact with explorers from Russia and other parts of the world had a profound impact on the Sugpiaq people who inhabited the Kodiak Island area. As a result, by the early 1870s, the period when these masks were collected, the Sugpiaq people no longer viewed these objects as a priceless part of their heritage. However, the Sugpiaq people of today are gaining a new perspective on the value of preserving our language, rekindling ancient traditions, and reawakening the dances and other art forms that are distinct and important elements of the Sugpiaq culture.

The effort to rediscover our culture has been ongoing for a number of years. However, in the last decade interest in the Sugpiaq culture has reached a new level of intensity. Numerous communities in the region have traditional dance groups, and efforts to preserve the Alutiiq language through a program spearheaded by the Alutiiq Museum and Archaeological Repository are producing very positive results. I believe the trip to France by the nine Sugpiaq artists, the creation of this exhibit catalog, and the Château-Musée's agreement to allow a portion of the collection to travel from

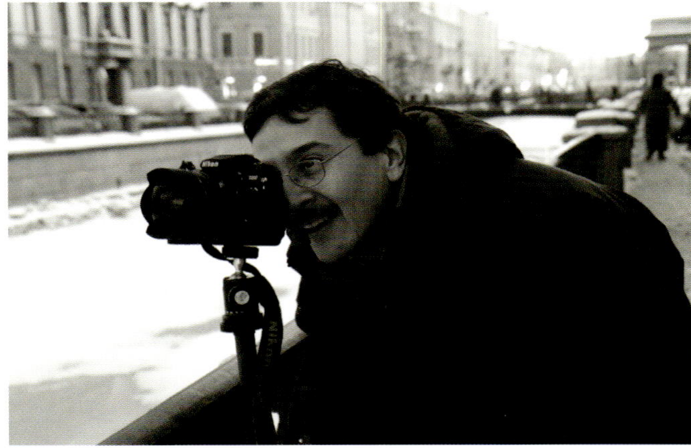

Figure 3. Will Anderson in St. Petersburg, Russia.
PHOTOGRAPH BY SVEN HAAKANSON JR.

Illustration 3. Will Anderson à Saint-Pétersbourg.
PHOTOGRAPHIE DE SVEN HAAKANSON JR.

France back to Alaska are watershed moments in the path the Sugpiaq people are following in the effort to reconnect with our culture.

Prior to visiting France, I had a great interest in the Château-Musée's Sugpiaq mask collection and had studied numerous photographs taken by others on prior visits. As a result, I went to France with a very analytical mind-set, with a focus on studying the masks' design, proportions, and color schemes. I expected to feel a sense of familiarity when I finally had the opportunity to work with the masks firsthand. I was surprised to find that when it came time to see the masks pictured in this exhibit catalog for the first time I was literally overcome with emotion. Since returning from France, I've spent a considerable amount of time trying to understand why I felt such strong emotions. I believe that in recent years people of Sugpiaq descent like me have come to realize a sense of loss when we come to fully understand that many of the traditions and stories that are an integral part of our culture are gone. Perhaps seeing so many objects from our culture in one place and at one time helped to bring this sense of loss into greater focus.

It's also possible that the emotions I felt in France came from a sense of awe, since the objects lying before me could have been crafted by a long-forgotten relative. On one level, having the opportunity to look at these masks provided me a glimpse of the physical remnants of my heritage. But on another level, knowing these masks were used as part of dances, ceremonies, and storytelling, I couldn't help but feel that in a very real sense I was getting an opportunity to look into the faces of my ancestors.

Regardless of the reasons why viewing these masks struck such an emotional chord with me, I'm also left with a great sense of appreciation for the staff at the Château-Musée and the community of Boulogne-sur-Mer for the care that has been taken to ensure these important examples of Sugpiaq culture are preserved. Perhaps these masks left the Kodiak region at a time when their value was established by the amount of trade goods they could provide. Now these masks have a much greater value, and the Sugpiaq people are fortunate they have been preserved so that they might play a part in sparking the reawakening of our culture.

So as you look through the pages of this book, I hope there is an understanding that while these masks are beautiful and aesthetically pleasing, they are not mere art objects. These masks are part of Sugpiaq culture, and they play a role in an effort by the Sugpiaq people to regain an understanding of our ancient practices and traditions.

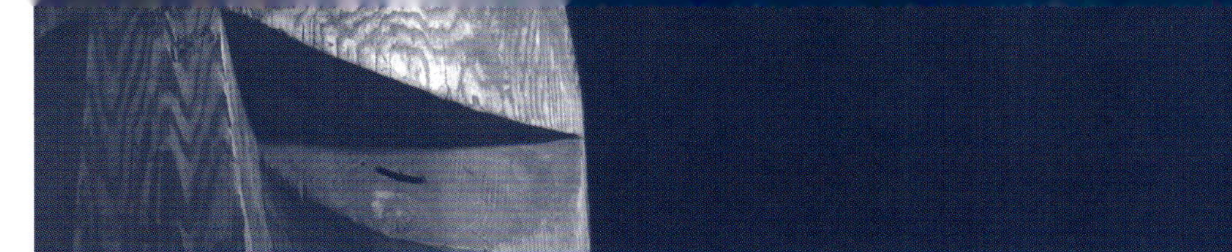

Avant-propos

Will Anderson

Directeur du conseil d'administration de l'Alutiiq Heritage Foundation

Au mois de juin 2006, j'ai eu le privilège d'accompagner neuf artistes de la région de Kodiak dans leur voyage en France, au Château-Musée de Boulogne-sur-Mer. Il s'agissait d'étudier la collection des masques des Sugpiat, une population des environs de l'île de Kodiak. Les premiers contacts avec le peuple sugpiaq que les explorateurs russes puis ceux d'autres régions du monde ont établis amenèrent de profondes modifications dans leur culture. Déjà, au début des années 1870, au moment où ces masques furent collectés, le peuple sugpiaq ne les considérait plus comme un élément essentiel de sa culture. De nos jours, cependant, les Sugpiat prennent de plus en plus conscience de l'importance pour eux de conserver leur langue, de se réapproprier leurs anciennes traditions, de faire revivre leurs danses et tous leurs autres arts.

Depuis de nombreuses années déjà, nous nous efforçons de redécouvrir notre culture, et cet effort s'est amplifié au cours de ces dix dernières années. Nombreuses sont les communautés qui participent à des groupes de danse traditionnelle ou au programme de langue alutiiq de l'Alutiiq Museum & Archaeological Repository, avec d'excellents résultats. Je suis convaincu que ce voyage des neuf artistes sugpiat en France, la création du catalogue de l'exposition, ainsi que la décision de la ville de Boulogne-sur-Mer d'autoriser le retour en Alaska d'une partie de sa collection sont autant d'étapes importantes dans l'effort que fait ce peuple pour renouer avec sa culture.

Avant même de me rendre en France, poussé par mon intérêt profond pour ces masques sugpiat du Château-Musée, j'avais étudié les nombreuses photographies déjà parues de ces masques. Aussi, arrivé en France, je possédais déjà une vision très analytique, centrée sur l'étude particulière de leur conception, de leurs proportions et des combinaisons de couleurs. Je m'attendais à ressentir une certaine familiarité une fois mis en leur présence. Je fus surpris de découvrir qu'au moment où j'aperçus pour la première fois les masques photographiés dans ce catalogue d'exposition, je fus littéralement submergé par l'émotion. Depuis mon retour de France, j'ai longuement réfléchi, essayant de comprendre pourquoi j'ai ressenti de tels sentiments. Je pense qu'au cours de ces dernières années les personnes d'origine sugpiaq, comme moi, ont soudain éprouvé une impression de perte lorsqu'ils ont vraiment réalisé que de nombreux pans de nos traditions et de notre histoire, parties intégrantes de notre culture, avaient disparu. Peut-être que de voir tant d'objets de notre culture rassemblés en même temps au même endroit a contribué à renforcer ce sentiment de perte.

Il est possible également que les émotions que j'ai ressenties en France soient nées d'un sentiment de respect et d'admiration du fait que les objets que j'avais sous les yeux ont pu être fabriqués par un parent éloigné et inconnu. D'un certain côté, cette opportunité de contempler ces masques me permettait d'avoir une vision de mon héritage culturel. D'un autre côté, l'idée que ces masques avaient participé à des danses, à des cérémonies et à des récits me permettait de ressentir la chance que j'avais là de regarder le visage de mes ancêtres.

À côté de ces raisons émotionnelles provoquées par la vision de ces masques, je garde aussi un immense sentiment de gratitude envers le personnel du Château-Musée et la commune de Boulogne-sur-Mer pour les soins portés à ces éléments de la culture sugpiaq afin d'en assurer la préservation.

Ces masques ont peut-être quitté la région de Kodiak à une époque où ils représentaient une valeur d'échange, mais à présent ils possèdent une valeur autrement plus importante, et le peuple sugpiaq est heureux qu'ils aient été préservés afin de jouer un rôle dans la renaissance de sa culture.

Ainsi, tout en regardant les pages de ce catalogue, j'espère que le lecteur aura conscience qu'au-delà de leur beauté, ces masques ne sont pas de simples objets d'art. Ils font partie de la culture sugpiaq, ils jouent un rôle dans la quête du peuple sugpiaq pour retrouver le sens de ses anciennes pratiques et traditions.

Foreword

Frédéric Cuvillier

Deputy and Mayor of Boulogne-sur-Mer

Claude Allan

Mayor Cuvillier's First Deputy, in charge of the Cultural Heritage

Translated from French by Sarah Froning

Since 1875, the Sugpiaq masks collected and donated by Alphonse Pinart have constituted one of the most remarkable assemblages of objects in the Château-Musée of Boulogne-sur-Mer. Along with the exceptional Egyptian, Greek, Peruvian, Oceanic, and Boulonnais collections, the Pinart masks represent one of the most stunning symbols of the city's nineteenth-century intellectual wealth and prosperity.

In 2001 and 2002, two separate exhibitions approached the history of Sugpiaq masks from unique standpoints: *Looking Both Ways*, presented in Anchorage and Kodiak, Alaska, as well as in Washington, D.C., and *Kodiak, Alaska*, organized by the Musée du quai Branly in Paris. The *Like a*

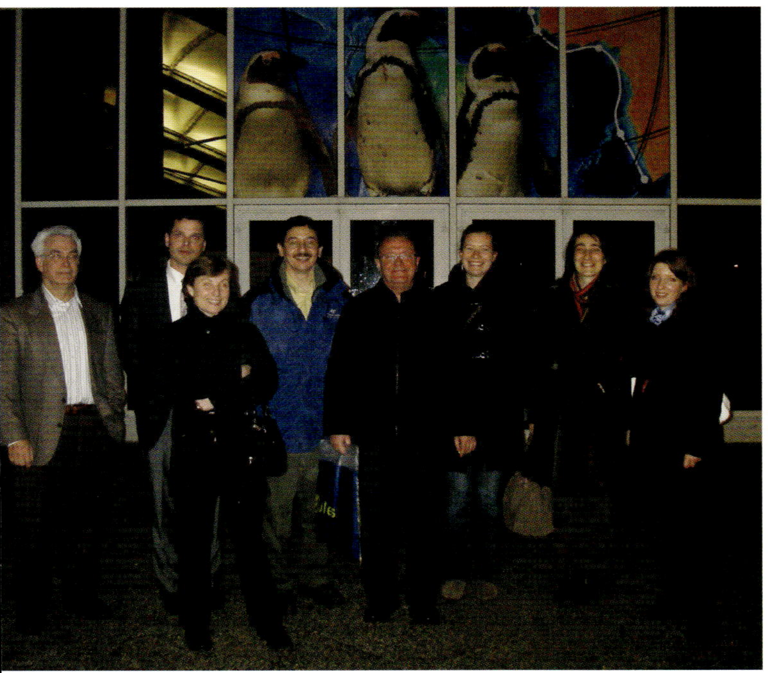

Figure 4. Claude Allan, Mayor Cuvillier's First Deputy, in charge of the Cultural Heritage (*front row, center*), and Sylvie Becquelin, Head of Cultural Affairs of Boulogne-sur-Mer (*front row, left*), with Perry Eaton, Andy Teuber, Will Anderson, Éneline Chartier, Céline Ramio, and Anne-Claire Laronde (*back row from left*).

PHOTOGRAPH BY SVEN HAAKANSON JR.

Illustration 4. Claude Allan, premier adjoint au maire de Boulogne-sur-Mer, en charge du patrimoine (*premier rang, au centre*), et Sylvie Becquelin, directrice des Affaires culturelles de la Ville de Boulogne-sur-Mer (*premier rang, à gauche*), en compagnie de Perry Eaton, Andy Teuber, Will Anderson, Éneline Chartier, Céline Ramio et Anne-Claire Laronde (*dernier rang, à partir de la gauche*).

PHOTOGRAPHIE DE SVEN HAAKANSON JR.

Face exhibition proposes an innovative approach to the interpretation of the masks by establishing a close collaboration between Native American and European museums. The exhibition has brought together researchers from both French and Sugpiaq cultures to study and present this collection—the only one of its kind in the world. This unprecedented partnership has allowed the objects to return temporarily to their country of origin for the first time after being housed for more than a century on French soil.

The City of Boulogne-sur-Mer is proud to associate with the Alutiiq Museum and Archaeological Repository in Kodiak, Alaska, as well as with Alutiiq corporations in this pioneering and ambitious effort. Indeed, the *Like a Face* exhibition is the first publicly visible element of what promises to be a profound and lasting alliance between our two cultural communities, which are henceforth permanently linked by this unparalleled collection.

After the 2008 display of the collection in Kodiak and Anchorage, a similar exhibition will be presented in Boulogne in 2009. The scientific cooperation between researchers is thus only beginning; continued joint efforts will demonstrate the extent to which objects in museum collections are actors that facilitate the mutual sharing of knowledge between different cultures. In the end, this ongoing partnership will provide the most relevant context for fostering a widespread understanding of the Pinart collection. As the years go by, let us hope that the masks of the Pinart collection continue to reveal more and more about who we are—members of the Sugpiaq and Boulonnais communities.

Préface

Frédéric Cuvillier

Député-maire de Boulogne-sur-Mer

Claude Allan

Premier adjoint au maire de Boulogne-sur-Mer, en charge du patrimoine

Depuis 1875, la collection de masques sugpiat offerte par son collecteur Alphonse Pinart est l'un des ensembles les plus remarquables du Château-Musée de Boulogne-sur-Mer. Aux côtés des exceptionnelles collections égyptienne, grecque, péruvienne, océanienne et boulonnaise, elle constitue l'un des plus beaux témoignages de la richesse intellectuelle et de la prospérité de la ville au XIXᵉ siècle.

En 2001 et 2002, deux expositions distinctes, « Looking Both Ways », aux États-Unis (présentée à Anchorage, Kodiak et Washington), et « Kodiak, Alaska », organisée par le musée du Quai-Branly à Paris, abordaient chacune de leur côté l'histoire des masques sugpiat. À l'inverse, l'exposition « Giinaquq: Like a Face », présentée dans la ville de Kodiak, en Alaska, inaugure une réelle et nouvelle collaboration entre musées américains et européens, car c'est ensemble cette fois que les chercheurs des deux cultures, française et sugpiaq, étudient et présentent cette collection unique au monde. C'est aussi pour ces objets un premier retour temporaire au pays après plus d'un siècle d'histoire sur le sol français.

La Ville de Boulogne-sur-Mer est fière de pouvoir s'associer à l'Alutiiq Museum et aux corporations alutiiq pour un nouveau projet ambitieux. En effet, l'exposition « Giinaquq: Like a Face » est le premier volet visible d'une coopération profonde et suivie entre nos deux communautés culturelles, liées désormais de façon indéfectible par cette formidable collection.

Après Kodiak et Anchorage, une exposition similaire est présentée à Boulogne-sur-Mer en 2009. La coopération scientifique, qui a déjà commencé mais n'en est qu'à ses débuts, démontre que les objets des musées sont des acteurs de connaissance mutuelle entre les peuples. La collection Pinart ne peut se comprendre sans cette coopération. Souhaitons que ces masques continuent à nous révéler encore un peu plus chaque année qui nous sommes, nous membres des communautés sugpiaq et boulonnaise.

Quyanaa—We Thank You

The *Giinaquq: Like a Face* project benefited from the assistance of many generous people and organizations. A grant from ConocoPhillips Alaska supported a project planning conference in January 2007, allowing community advisors, artists, educators, scholars, and museum professionals to meet for two days in Kodiak. Participants included Nick Alokli, Will Anderson, Ruth Dawson, Dixie Dayo, Sarah Froning, Mary Haakanson, Doug Inga, Tanya Inga, Suzi Jones, Dennis Knagin, Gary Knagin, Julie Knagin, Anne-Claire Laronde, Ivan Lukin, Marti Murray, Alfred Naumoff, Florence Pestrikoff, Gordon Pullar, Teri Schneider, Helen Simeonoff, Speridon Simeonoff, Herman Squartsoff, Jack Wick, and the entire staff of the Alutiiq Museum. The outline of the exhibition and its catalog evolved from this important gathering.

The City of Boulogne-sur-Mer generously provided permission for this project with support from the Honorable Frédéric Cuvillier, Mayor and deputy of the city and a deputy of the national parliament, and the Honorable Claude Allan, Mayor Cuvillier's First Deputy, in charge of the Cultural Heritage. These busy officials took the time to understand how the unique Alaskan artwork in their city's museum could reawaken the hearts of a community halfway around the world. We are profoundly grateful for their willingness to embrace this international cultural exchange.

We extend our deepest gratitude to curator Anne-Claire Laronde and the staff of the Château-Musée in Boulogne-sur-Mer for their assistance with everything from collections access to project photography, translations, and understanding the history of the collection in France. The Château-Musée provided the Alutiiq Museum with unparalleled access to the Pinart collection and committed itself enthusiastically to this project. *Giinaquq: Like a Face* was truly a collaborative effort. In addition to Anne-Claire Laronde, Château-Musée staff members Philippe Girot, Stéphane Delpierre, Francis Donval, Céline Ramio, and Deputy Director Eneline Guette deserve special recognition for their many contributions. Registrar Céline Ramio provided summary information on the Pinart collection used in Chapter 4, kindly shared during her monthlong stay in Kodiak to install the exhibition.

We also extend our sincere appreciation to the Musée du quai Branly for access to their collection, their hospitality in Paris, and their permission to publish our photographs of the seven Sugpiaq masks in their care. They have allowed us to reunite Pinart's collection in a single publication and we are most grateful for this opportunity. We recognize Director Stephane Martin and staff members Hélène Cerutti-Fulgence, André Delpuech, and Paz Núñez-Regueiro for their kind assistance.

Support for catalog photography came from Koniag, Inc., and the Old Harbor Native Corporation, which paid for Sven Haakanson Jr., Will Anderson, Perry Eaton, and Andy Teuber to travel to France to systematically document each mask, as well as from a private donation that purchased a professional digital camera. The Château-Musée retains copyright for the images of the seventy masks pictured from its collections, and the Musée du quai Branly maintains the copyright for the images of the seven masks pictured from its holdings. In Kodiak, graphic artist and technical consultant Janelle Peterson provided assistance sizing the photographs.

Understanding Pinart's field notes required assistance from speakers of Russian, French, and Alutiiq. Céline Wallace translated and transcribed copies of Pinart's notes stored in the University of California's Bancroft Library with funding from ConocoPhillips Alaska. Mark Rusk volunteered his time to investigate Pinart's drawings and correspondence in the Bancroft's holdings, and Alutiiq Museum staff member Rose Kinsley translated documents, inventories, and emails. University of Alaska Fairbanks linguist Jeff Leer generously assisted with the translation of the Alutiiq and Russian portions of Pinart's field notes, working from his own notes and those provided to him by our friend and mentor, the late Russian American scholar Dr. Lydia Black, to create a new translation. Elders Mary Haakanson, Florence Pestrikoff, and Nick Alokli and speaker Sperry Ash assisted with Alutiiq language translations of songs and names—helping to decode Pinart's phonetic spellings of Alutiiq words and develop modern Alutiiq names for masks with no known title. April Laktonen Counceller provided assistance with the spelling of Alutiiq words. Their contributions helped to bring the masks to life in the exhibition and on these pages. They are gratefully acknowledged.

The Alutiiq Museum's board and staff worked tirelessly to support all aspects of the *Giinaquq: Like a Face* project, from planning to implementation. The exhibition and this catalog reflect their leadership, expertise, determination, and teamwork. Our many thanks to board members Will Anderson, Margie Bezona, Fred Coyle, Ruth Dawson, Tanya Inga, Loretta Nelson, Nick Pestrikoff, Margaret Roberts, Andy Teuber, and Donene Tweten for their support, and to staff members Carol Austerman, Valen Bishop, Peter Boskofsky, April Laktonen Counceller, Jennifer Dickinson, Clare Fulp, Tanya Glaspell, Sarah Kennedy, Rose Kinsley, Jill Lipka, Annie Lund, Patty Mahoney, Marnie Leist, Katie St. John, Annie Salsman, Patrick Saltonstall, and Tricia

Squartsoff for rising to the many challenges of this complex project. Walt Ebell of the Old Harbor Native Corporation deserves special recognition for his enthusiastic assistance with fund-raising. We also commend our project volunteers Nick Alokli, Claudia Anderson, Karen Andreasen, Alisha Blondin, Isabella Blatchford, Catherine Chichenoff, Ruth Dawson, Brittney Hinther, Tanya Inga, Dennis Knagin, Jill Lipka, Florence Pestrikoff, Dale and Marie Rice, and Donene Tweten for their service.

We thank Erica Hill, Elisabeth Dabney, Amy Simpson, and the University of Alaska Press for their patient support of the project; Sarah Froning and Céline Wallace for thoughtful translations both from French to English and English to French; Katie St. John for assistance organizing the mask data; and our reviewers Don Clark and Aron Crowell who strengthened this publication with insightful comments. The Alutiiq Heritage Foundation, the Château-Musée, Koniag, Inc., the Kodiak Island Housing Authority, and the University of Alaska Press provided funding for the production of this catalog.

Support for the larger *Giinaquq: Like a Face* exhibition project came from many generous people and organizations. They include the Afognak Native Corporation, Alutiiq Heritage Foundation, Anchorage Museum at Rasmuson Center, Château-Musée, ConocoPhillips Alaska, First Alaskans Institute, Institute for Museum and Library Services, Kodiak Area Native Association, Kodiak Island Housing Authority, Koniag, Inc., Natives of Kodiak, Inc., Old Harbor Native Corporation, Rasmuson Foundation, Akhiok-Kaguyak, Inc., Alaska Army National Guard—Kodiak, Alaska State Museum, Will and Jill Anderson, Sven and Balika Haakanson, Koncor Forest Products, National Museum of the American Indian, Northern Air Cargo, Alaska Fresh Seafoods, Nick Alokli, Anonymous, Don Argetsinger and Lynda Hadley, Ruth Dawson, Jim and Bonnie Dillard, Tony and Sandee Drabek, Perry and Ardene Eaton, Walt Ebell and Dianna Gentry, Ben Fitzhugh and Lada Bilaniuk, Charlotte Fox and Mike Stinebaugh, Patty Ginsburg and Steve Lindbeck, Mary Haakanson, Willie and

Kathy Hall, Dick and Andrea Hobbs, Mary K. Hughes and Andrew Eker, John C. Hughes Foundation, Julie Kaiser, Rick Knecht, Jeff Leer, Susan Malutin, Bob and Denise May, Michael O'Connor, Tom Panamaroff, Rick Pelasara, Florence Pestrikoff, LeRoy Pettijohn, Gordon Pullar, Kim and Cameron Reitmeirer, Rotary International—Kodiak Club, Patrick and Zoya Saltonstall, Amy Steffian and Steven Hall, Steve and Linda Suydam, Sugpiaq, Inc., Andy Teuber and Natasha Kutchick, Jana and Richard Turvey, Donene and Arnold Tweten, Eric and Jennifer Waltenbaugh, Laurel Jean Zampa, and all those who continue to support the Alutiiq Museum. We honor their contributions. Their investment in preserving the past has created lasting resources for the future. *Quyanaasinaq*—we thank you most sincerely.

Quyanaa : Remerciements

Le projet « Giinaquq: Like a Face » a bénéficié de l'assistance et de la générosité de nombreuses personnes et organisations. Grâce au mécénat de ConocoPhillips Alaska, une conférence de planification du projet a permis en janvier 2007 aux conseillers, aux artistes et au personnel éducatif des communautés ainsi qu'à des universitaires et professionnels des musées de se réunir pendant deux jours à Kodiak. Parmi les participants figuraient Nick Alokli, Will Anderson, Ruth Dawson, Dixie Dayo, Sarah Froning, Mary Haakanson, Doug Inga, Tanya Inga, Suzi Jones, Dennis Knagin, Gary Knagin, Julie Knagin, Anne-Claire Laronde, Ivan Lukin, Marti Murray, Alfred Naumoff, Florence Pestrikoff, Gordon Pullar, Teri Schneider, Helen Simeonoff, Speridon Simeonoff, Herman Squartsoff, Jack Wick, et le personnel au complet de l'Alutiiq Museum. Le projet détaillé de l'exposition et du catalogue est né lors de cet important rassemblement.

La Ville de Boulogne-sur-Mer a généreusement permis la réalisation ce projet grâce au soutien de MM. Frédéric Cuvillier, maire de la ville et député, et Claude Allan, premier adjoint au maire de Boulogne-sur-Mer, en charge du patrimoine. Ces représentants officiels, dont l'agenda est pourtant particulièrement chargé, ont pris le temps de comprendre comment des œuvres uniques venant d'Alaska et conservées dans le musée de la ville pourraient aider à faire renaître une communauté à l'autre bout du monde. Nous leur sommes profondément reconnaissants d'avoir permis avec enthousiasme cet échange culturel international.

Nous souhaitons exprimer notre profonde gratitude envers Anne-Claire Laronde, conservatrice, et envers tout le personnel du Château-Musée de Boulogne-sur-Mer pour leur assistance, depuis l'accès aux collections jusqu'à la couverture photographique du projet, en passant par la traduction et la diffusion de l'histoire française de la collection. Le Château-Musée a fourni à l'Alutiiq Museum un accès sans précédent à la collection Pinart et s'est engagé avec enthousiasme dans ce projet. « Giinaquq: Like a Face » est le fruit d'un véritable travail collectif. En plus d'Anne-Claire Laronde, nous tenons particulièrement à remercier pour leurs nombreuses contributions les membres suivants du personnel du Château-Musée : Philippe Girot, Stéphane Delpierre, Francis Donval, Céline Ramio et la directrice adjointe, Éneline Chartier. La responsable des collections Céline Ramio nous a aimablement fourni le résumé des informations concernant la collection Pinart, utilisé dans la quatrième contribution de ce catalogue, lors de son séjour d'un mois à Kodiak pour installer l'exposition.

Nous remercions également le musée du Quai-Branly, à Paris, qui a autorisé l'accès à ses collections, pour son hospitalité et pour l'autorisation de publier les photographies de sept masques sugpiat conservés dans ses collections. Il nous a ainsi permis de réunir la totalité de la collection Pinart en une publication, ce dont nous lui sommes particulièrement reconnaissants. Notre gratitude s'adresse aussi à Stéphane Martin, directeur, et aux membres du personnel, Hélène Cerutti-Fulgence, André Delpuech et Paz Nuñez-Regueiro, pour leur aimable assistance.

Le soutien apporté par Koniag, Inc. et The Old Harbor Native Corporation au travail de photographie du catalogue a permis de financer le voyage en France de Sven Haakanson, Will Anderson, Perry Eaton et Andy Teuber. Ils y ont documenté chaque masque de façon systématique, un don privé ayant servi à l'achat d'un appareil photo numérique professionnel. Le Château-Musée conserve les droits à l'image sur les soixante-dix masques photographiés dans ses collections et le musée du Quai-Branly sur les sept masques de ses collections. À Kodiak, l'artiste graphique, consultante technique, Janelle Peterson a effectué la mise en forme photographique.

La compréhension des notes de terrain de Pinart impliquait l'assistance de personnes parlant couramment russe, français et alutiiq. Céline Wallace a traduit et transcrit les copies des notes de Pinart conservées par la Bancroft Library de l'université de Californie grâce à un financement apporté par ConocoPhillips Alaska. Mark Rusk a mené des recherches bénévoles sur les dessins et la correspondance de Pinart conservés par la Bancroft Library, et Rose Kinsey, employée de l'Alutiiq Museum, a traduit divers documents, inventaires et courriels. Le linguiste Jeff Leer de l'université d'Alaska, à Fairbanks, a généreusement apporté sa contribution en traduisant les parties alutiiq et russes des notes de terrain de Pinart, travaillant à partir de ses propres notes et de celles fournies par notre amie commune et mentor, feu-Dr. Lydia Black, spécialiste des études russo-américaines, pour produire une nouvelle traduction. Mary Haakanson, Florence Pestrikoff et Nick Alokli, Anciens de culture alutiiq, et Sperry Ash, conversant alutiiq, ont aidé à traduire les chants et noms en langue alutiiq, décodés à partir des mots écrits en phonétique par Pinart. Ils ont ainsi élaboré des noms alutiiq modernes donnés aux masques sans titre. April Laktonen Counceller a aidé à préciser l'orthographe des mots alutiiq. Leurs contributions ont aidé à donner vie aux masques à la fois dans l'exposition et dans ces pages. Nous leur en sommes reconnaissants.

Le conseil d'administration et le personnel de l'Alutiiq Museum ont travaillé sans relâche à accompagner le projet « Giinaquq: Like a Face », de sa planification jusqu'à sa réalisation. L'exposition et le catalogue reflètent leur savoir-faire, leur détermination et leur travail d'équipe. Tous nos remerciements vont aux membres du conseil d'administration, Will Anderson, Margie Bezona, Fred Coyle, Ruth Dawson, Tanya Inga, Loretta Nelson, Nick Pestrikoff, Margaret Roberts, Andy Teuber et Donene Tweten, pour leur soutien, ainsi qu'aux membres du personnel, Carol Austerman, Valen Bishop, Peter Boskofsky, April Laktonen Counceller, Jennifer Dickinson, Clare Fulp, Tanya Glaspell, Sarah Kennedy, Rose Kinsley, Jill Lipka, Annie Lund, Patty Mahoney, Marnie Leist, Katie St. John, Annie Salsman, Patrick Saltonstall et Tricia Squartsoff, qui se sont montrés à la hauteur des nombreux défis rencontrés sur le parcours de ce projet complexe. Walt Ebell, de la Old Harbor Native Corporation, mérite des remerciements particuliers pour son enthousiasme et son aide à lever des fonds. Nous félicitons également nos bénévoles Nick Alokli, Claudia Anderson, Karen Andreasen, Alisha Blondin, Isabella Blatchford, Catherine Chichenoff, Ruth Dawson, Brittney Hinther, Tanya Inga, Dennis Knagin, Jill Lipka, Florence Pestrikoff, Dale, Marie Rice et Donene Tweten pour leur précieuse aide.

Nous remercions Erica Hill, Elisabeth Dabney, Amy Simpson et University of Alaska Press pour leur patience et leur soutien de ce projet ; Sarah Froning et Céline Wallace pour leurs traductions attentives du français à l'anglais et de l'anglais au français ; Katie St. John pour son assistance dans l'organisation des données concernant les masques ; et nos relecteurs, dont la correctrice éditoriale Sue Mitchell, dont les précieux commentaires ont bénéficié à cette publication. L'Alutiiq Heritage Foundation, le Château-Musée, Koniag, Inc., Kodiak Island Housing Authority et l'University of Alaska Press ont financé la publication de ce catalogue.

De nombreuses personnes et organisations ont généreusement apporté leur soutien au projet d'exposition « Giinaquq: Like a Face », dont : Afognak Native Corporation, Alutiiq Heritage Foundation, Anchorage Museum au Rasmuson Center, le Château-Musée, ConocoPhillips Alaska, First Alaskans Institute, Institute for Museum and Library

Services, Kodiak Area Native Association, Kodiak Island Housing Authority, Koniag, Inc., Natives of Kodiak, Inc., Old Harbor Native Corporation, Rasmuson Foundation, Akhiok-Kaguyak, Inc., Alaska Army National Guard-Kodiak, Alaska State Museum, Will et Jill Anderson, Sven et Balika Haakanson, Koncor Forest Products, National Museum of the American Indian, Northern Air Cargo, Alaska Fresh Seafoods, Nick Alokli, des donneurs anonymes, Don Argetsinger et Lynda Hadley, Ruth Dawson, Jim et Bonnie Dillard, Tony et Sandee Drabek, Perry et Arden Eaton, Walt Ebell et Dianna Gentry, Ben Fitzhugh et Lada Bilaniuk, Charlotte Fox et Mike Stinebaugh, Patty Ginsburg et Steve Lindbeck, Mary Haakanson, Willie et Kathy Hall, Dick et Andrea Hobbs, Mary K. Hughes et Andrew Eker, John C. Hughes Foundation, Julie Kaiser, Rick Knecht, Jeff Leer, Susan Maltin, Bob et Denise May, Michael O'Connor, Tom Panamaroff, Rick Pelasara, Florence Pestrikoff, LeRoy Pettijohn, Gordon Pullar, Kim et Cameron Reitmeirer, Rotary International-Kodiak Club, Patrick et Zoya Saltonstall, Amy Steffian et Steven Hall, Steve et Linda Suydam, Sugpiaq, Inc., Andy Tuber et Natasha Kutchick, Jana et Richard Turvey, Donne et Arnold Tweten, Eric et Jennifer Waltenbaugh, Laurel Jean Zama et tous ceux qui continuent à apporter leur soutien à l'Alutiiq Museum. Nous rendons hommage à leurs contributions. Leur investissement dans la préservation du passé a généré des ressources durables pour l'avenir.

Quyanaasinaq : nous vous remercions sincèrement.

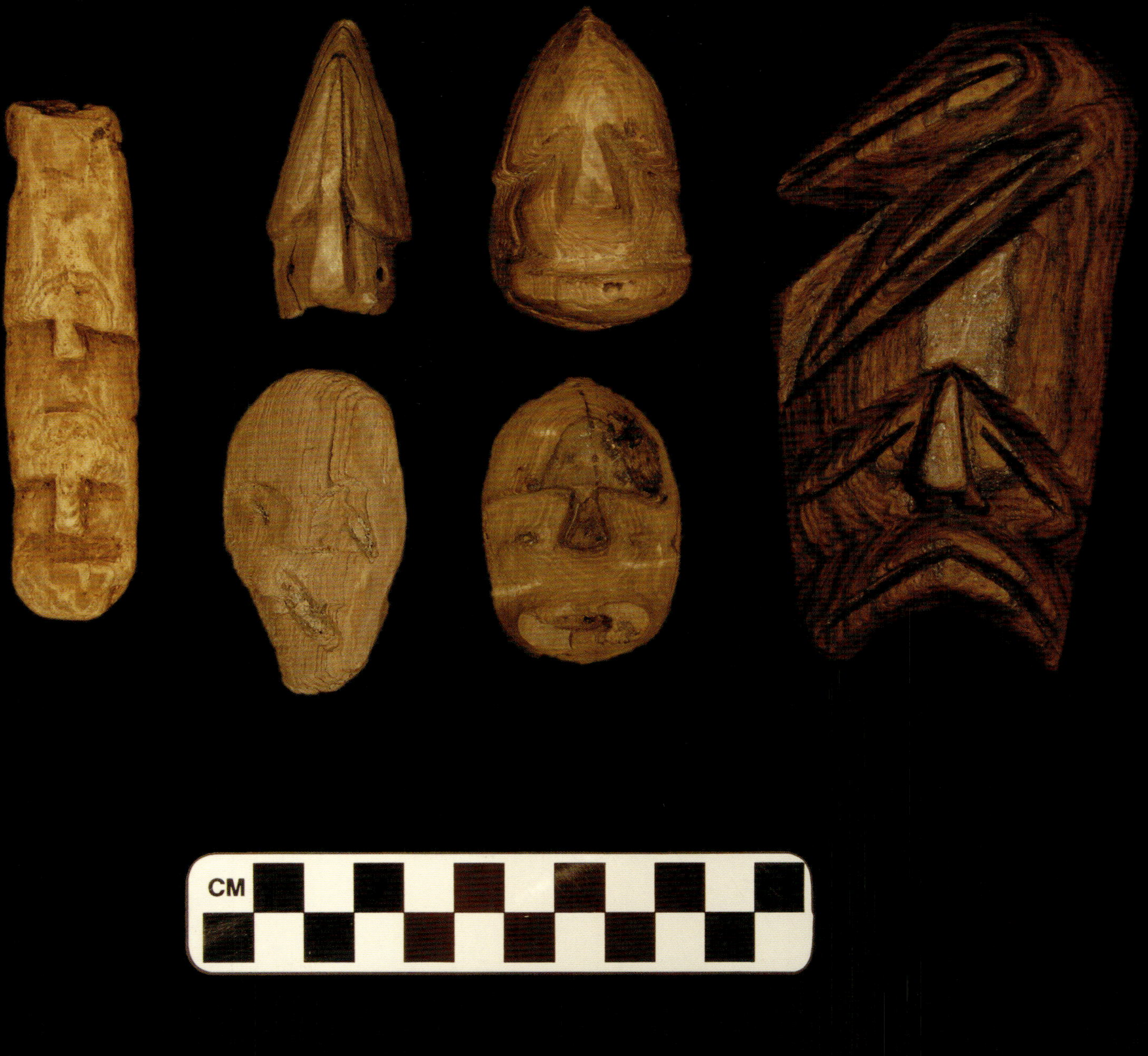

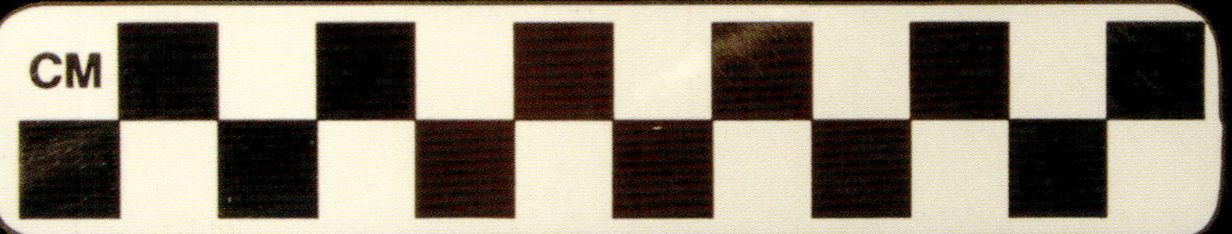

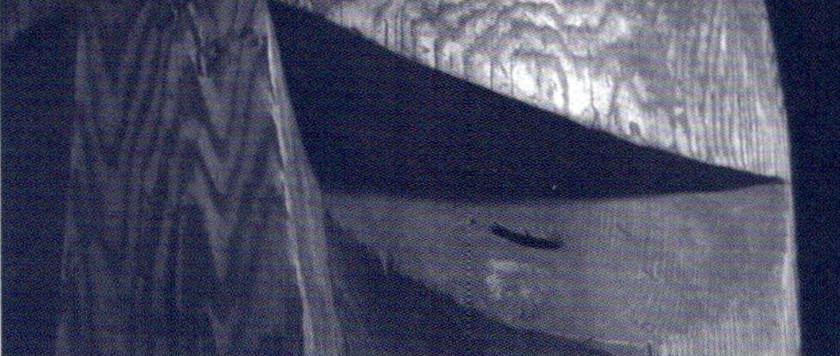

CHAPTER ONE

Giinaquq—Like a Face

Sven D. Haakanson Jr. and Amy F. Steffian

The Alutiiq word for mask—*giinaquq*—means "like a face, but not really." This term reflects the mystical place that carved faces held in classical Sugpiaq culture.[1] Carefully crafted and ornately decorated masks were both works of art and powerful religious objects. Made to share history, teach values, and represent the spirit world, they were also used in hunting ceremonies to allow Sugpiaq people to communicate with the unseen world. Through masked dancing at winter festivals, Sugpiaq people maintained balance with the forces that controlled daily life and ensured that spring would return with fish to catch and seals to hunt. To the Sugpiat, masked dancing was a path to spiritual and physical sustenance, and masks were *agayullqutaq,* "something to hold sacred."

In the past two centuries, Sugpiaq culture and its views of masks have changed dramatically. Kodiak's Native people lost many of their traditions in the clash of cultures that followed the Russian conquest of the archipelago in 1784.[2] Sugpiaq objects, customs, language, beliefs, and cultural dignity disappeared from the landscape, forcibly stripped away, hidden by humiliation, or forgotten because they no longer served their primary role—the perpetuation of the Sugpiaq world. Precontact religious practices faded in the late nineteenth century,[3] concealed from the disapproving view of colonizers and replaced by Christianity. Despite these profound changes, Sugpiaq people never forgot their masks. There is still knowledge of the spirit faces carved in wood.

In the 1980s, when archaeologists began recovering expertly crafted wooden masks, dolls, feast bowls, and other ceremonial gear from a prehistoric, waterlogged Sugpiaq settlement in Karluk,[4] Elders confirmed the finds (Figure 5). They shared stories about masks and how they disappeared. They also offered words of caution.[5] Many knew about the power of masks but had been taught to feel shame about the old religion. Masks had been branded as examples of primitive behavior and a belief in evil gods. They were not to be talked about or touched. To a younger generation, however, archaeological data offered proof of a Sugpiaq way of seeing the world and a chance to reconsider interpretations of the Sugpiaq past imposed by outsiders.

Opportunities to reconsider Sugpiaq heritage and the meaning of its spiritual traditions grew with Kodiak's heritage revitalization movement. Archaeological investigations, ethnographic studies, and collections research continued to bring Sugpiaq traditions into focus and illustrate the power

Figure 5. Prehistoric miniature wooden masks, Karluk One Site, AD 1400–1750, Koniag, Inc. Collection, Alutiiq Museum. PHOTOGRAPH BY SVEN HAAKANSON JR.

Illustration 5. Masques préhistoriques miniatures en bois, provenant du site de Karluk One, entre 1400 et 1750, collection Koniag, Inc., Alutiiq Museum. PHOTOGRAPHIE DE SVEN HAAKANSON JR.

of cultural exploration.[6] Then in the 1990s, Dominique Desson, an anthropology student at the University of Alaska Fairbanks, shared her pioneering study of ancestral carvings stored in France.[7] In a small coastal seaport known for its fishing economy—a place not unlike Kodiak, Alaska—the shelves of a municipal museum held Alaskan treasure. Stored amid collections of Greek vases and Egyptian funerary objects was the largest known assemblage of Sugpiaq masks. Where did these pieces come from?

In 1871, a wealthy young Frenchman named Louis Alphonse Pinart left the comfort of his family home in northern France to study the indigenous languages of coastal Alaska. As he traveled through the Aleutian Islands, Bristol Bay, and finally the Kodiak archipelago, he collected ethnographic objects. During the winter of 1872, Pinart journeyed by *qayaq* to Kodiak's Sugpiaq communities, documenting stories, songs, and dances and collecting objects, especially masks.[8] Three years after returning to France, Pinart donated the bulk of his collections to the municipal museum in Boulogne-sur-Mer, the largest repository near his home in Marquise. Today, this museum is known as the Château-Musée and Pinart's collection remains the largest single assemblage of Sugpiaq masks in the world.

Over the years, anthropologists remained aware of Pinart's collection,[9] but the Sugpiat did not. As knowledge of the masks spread through Kodiak's Native community in the 1990s, so did questions. How could Pinart have collected so many spiritually powerful Sugpiaq artifacts? What could these pieces tell today's Sugpiat about their heritage? Could the masks ever come home? Discussions of these issues renewed interest in ancestral masks, and gradually a new perception of their meaning to the Sugpiaq people emerged.

This catalog of masks from the Pinart collection[10] explores the evolving meaning of Sugpiaq masks. In addition to providing a comprehensive set of data on the collection, this publication considers the cultural context of the masks both past and present. In this chapter we begin this exploration with an introduction to masks in Sugpiaq society, a summary of the work that led to an Alaskan exhibition of masks from the Pinart collection, and an outline of the articles we've assembled to tell the fuller story of these remarkable artifacts.

Masks in Sugpiaq Society

During his six-month stay in the Kodiak archipelago, Pinart recorded a great deal of information about Sugpiaq masks. Consultation of his field notes,[11] as well as historic accounts of Sugpiaq culture[12] and archaeological data from Sugpiaq settlements,[13] provide a broad view of masks in classical Sugpiaq society—from their creation to their use and meaning.

Among the Sugpiat, carving, woodworking, and mask making were typically the domain of men.[14] Boys learned to work wood by watching and working with male relatives, a tradition that continued in Kodiak Sugpiaq villages into the twentieth century.

As spruce forests are a relatively recent addition to the archipelago, and cover only its northern islands,[15] most carvers obtained their wood from the sea, gathering drift logs of Pacific yew, Douglas fir, red and yellow cedar, and spruce from Kodiak's beaches. They also harvested alder, dwarf birch, and cottonwood from coastal thickets.[16] For the production of tool handles, household objects, and artwork, wood may have been cured—left to dry before working. (Modern Sugpiaq carvers will allow wood to age in their yards or workshops to improve its workability.)

Tools and wooden artifacts recovered from archaeological sites reveal ancient carving techniques. The carving process began by cracking open logs with resilient whale bone and spruce wedges (Figures 6a and 6b),[17] which craftsmen pounded into logs with weighty stone mauls to create lengths of workable wood. Round holes drilled in the wedges may have been filled with fat to reduce friction and keep a wedge from getting stuck.[18] Carvers cut the resulting pieces of wood to length, forming blanks or plugs, which they shaped with a variety of stone adzes, tied to handles made of flexible alder branches.[19]

Handheld carving implements, particularly rodent incisors (marmot, beaver, or porcupine) hafted in the side of

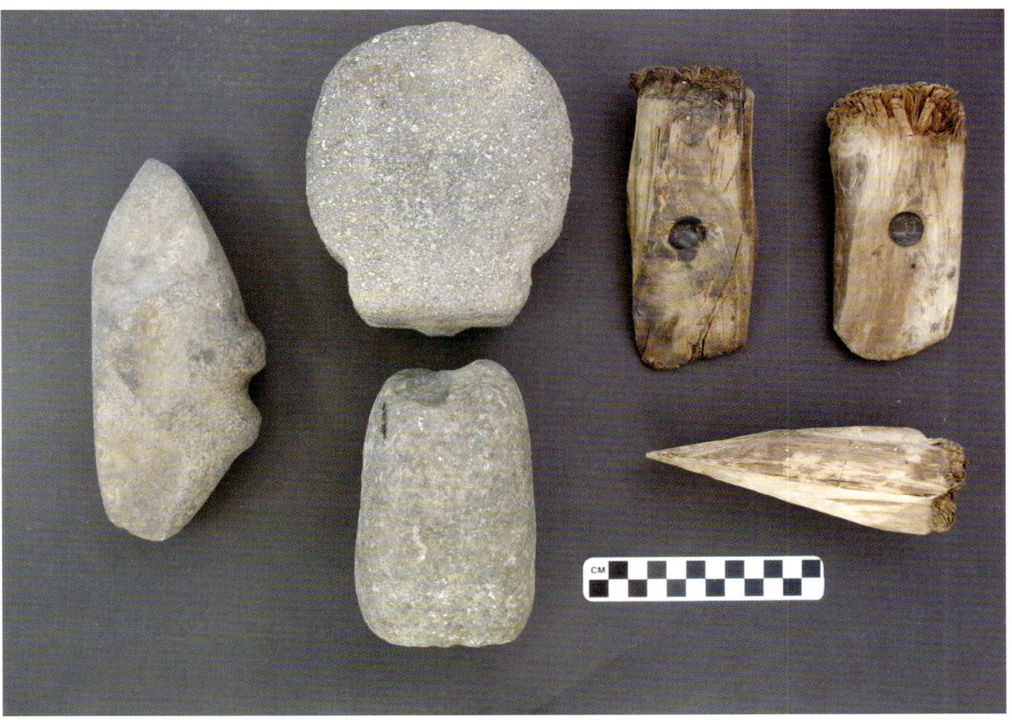

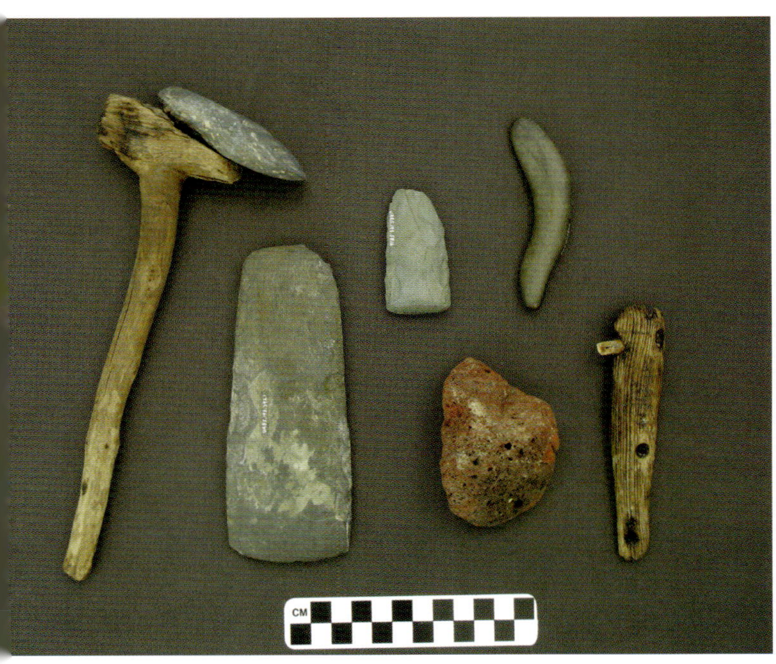

Figure 6a. Tools for woodworking, Karluk One Site, AD 1400–1750, Koniag, Inc. Collection, Alutiiq Museum. From left: grooved splitting adze of graywacke, grooved mauls of graywacke, wooden wedges.

Figure 6b. Tools for fine carving, Karluk One Site, AD 1400–1750, Koniag, Inc. Collection, Alutiiq Museum. From left: wooden adze handle with small planing adze, large planing adze, small planing adze, burnishing stone, scoria abrader, wood-handled carving tool with a tooth bit.

PHOTOGRAPHS BY PATRICK SALTONSTALL.

Illustration 6a. Outils utilisés pour le travail du bois, provenant du site de Karluk One, entre 1400 et 1750, collection Koniag, Inc., Alutiiq Museum. De gauche à droite : doloire usée en grauwacke destinée à éclater le bois, mailloches usées en grauwacke, coins en bois.

Illustration 6b. Outils utilisés pour la gravure fine, provenant du site de Karluk One, entre 1400 et 1750, collection Koniag, Inc., Alutiiq Museum. De gauche à droite : manche de doloire en bois avec petite doloire à aplatir, grande doloire à aplatir, petite doloire à aplatir, pierre à polir, scorie à poncer, couteau à manche en bois portant un morceau de dent.

PHOTOGRAPHIES DE PATRICK SALTONSTALL.

small wooden handles, permitted finer carving—the shaping of features.[20] The narrow bits of these tools left gouges[21] that carvers likely sanded away with gritty abraders of pumice, scoria, and sandstone. A burnishing stone, a water-worn pebble rubbed over the carving to create a polished, splinter-free surface, probably provided the finishing touch.[22]

Classical craftsmen carved masks in a variety of styles and sizes, all depicting faces.[23] Face masks are the most common

style in both historic and archaeological collections. These masks feature a hollowed back and eyeholes. Some face masks approximate the size of a human head. Others are much larger. One striking aspect of Pinart's collection is the size and weight of some of the face masks, which can be up to 60 cm long and 33 cm wide and weigh as much as 9 kilos (20 lbs.). Although some large face masks may have been suspended from the ceiling of the ceremonial house during performances, others may have been worn.

In addition to face masks, the Sugpiat created two styles of plank masks. Some plank masks are largely two-dimensional. They are large, shaped and painted boards with slits cut for eyeholes and occasionally other carved facial features.[24] An archaeological example from Karluk has a painted leather covering (Figure 7).[25] Other plank masks feature a small three-dimensional face mask carving lashed to a large deco-rated plank.[26]

Figure 7. Plank mask (back) with painted leather covering for front, Karluk One Site, AD 1400–1750, Koniag, Inc. Collection, Alutiiq Museum.

PHOTOGRAPH BY WILL ANDERSON.

Illustration 7. Masque-planche (vue de dos) recouvert de cuir peint sur la face extérieure, provenant du site de Karluk One, entre 1400 et 1750, collection Koniag, Inc., Alutiiq Museum.

PHOTOGRAPHIE DE WILL ANDERSON.

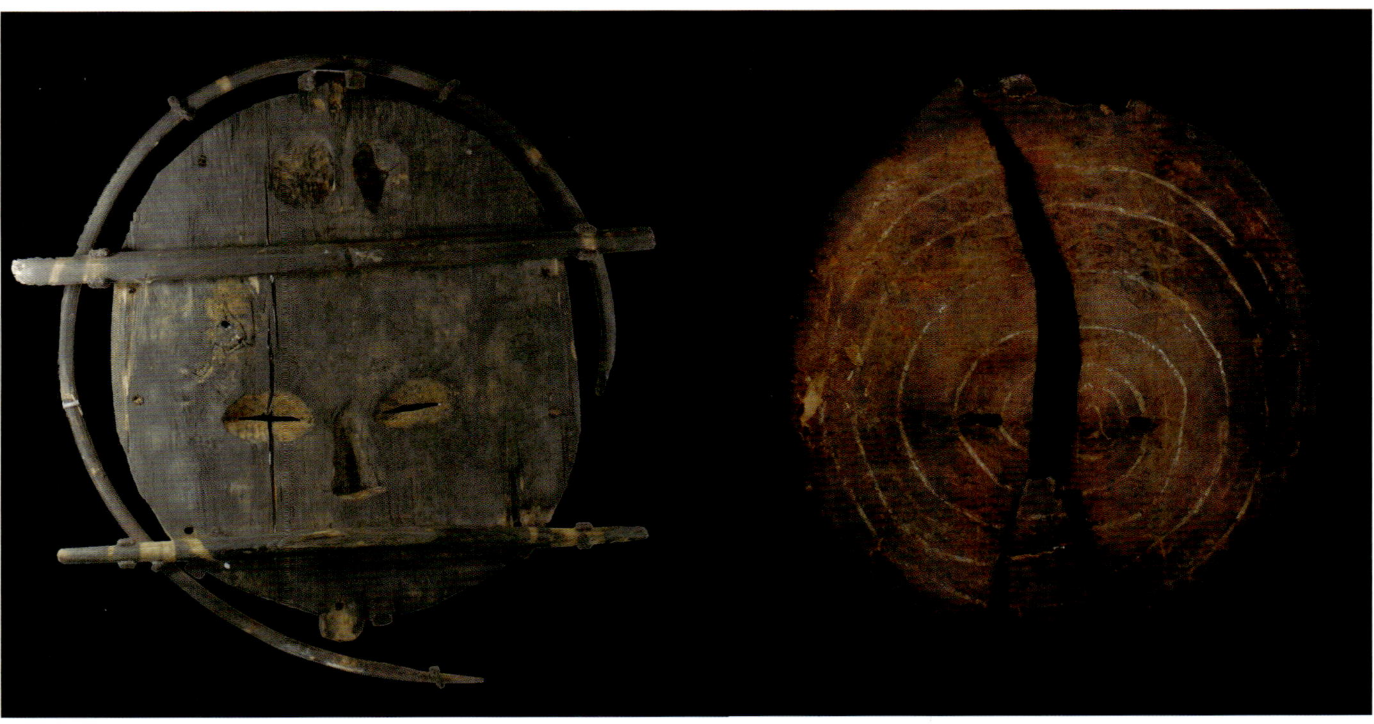

In contrast to these large pieces, miniature masks are a common find in well-preserved, late prehistoric Sugpiaq settlements. Although the function of these pieces is unknown, they strongly resemble full-sized masks and include both face masks and plank masks.[27] Some of these miniature carvings may have been tied to drum handles. Ethnographic collections illustrate that some Sugpiaq drum handles were embellished with carved human faces.[28]

Decoration was an essential part of every mask, as finely made objects demonstrated respect for the spirits that provided for people. Thus, mask makers collected a variety of feathers, leather, animal hair, and plant materials to enhance their carvings. These included eagle feathers, down, gutskin, baleen, kelp, twigs, grass, and other highly perishable materials.[29] To attach these materials to a mask, carvers created encircling hoops, bending narrow lengths of wood with steam—perhaps working in the steambath rooms often attached to Sugpiaq homes.[30] Archaeological examples of mask hoops have an oval cross section,[31] and ethnographic collections indicate that hoops occurred in a variety of sizes and configurations. Some hoops completely encircled a mask, others did not, and some masks had multiple hoops.[32]

To secure a hoop to his mask, a carver might first attach cross braces to the back of his mask, drilling small holes in

Figure 8. Mask attachments, Karluk One Site, AD 1400–1750, Koniag, Inc. Collection, Alutiiq Museum.
PHOTOGRAPH BY SVEN HAAKANSON JR.

Illustration 8. Éléments décoratifs de masques, site de Karluk One, entre 1400 et 1750, collection Koniag, Inc., Alutiiq Museum.
PHOTOGRAPHIE DE SVEN HAAKANSON JR.

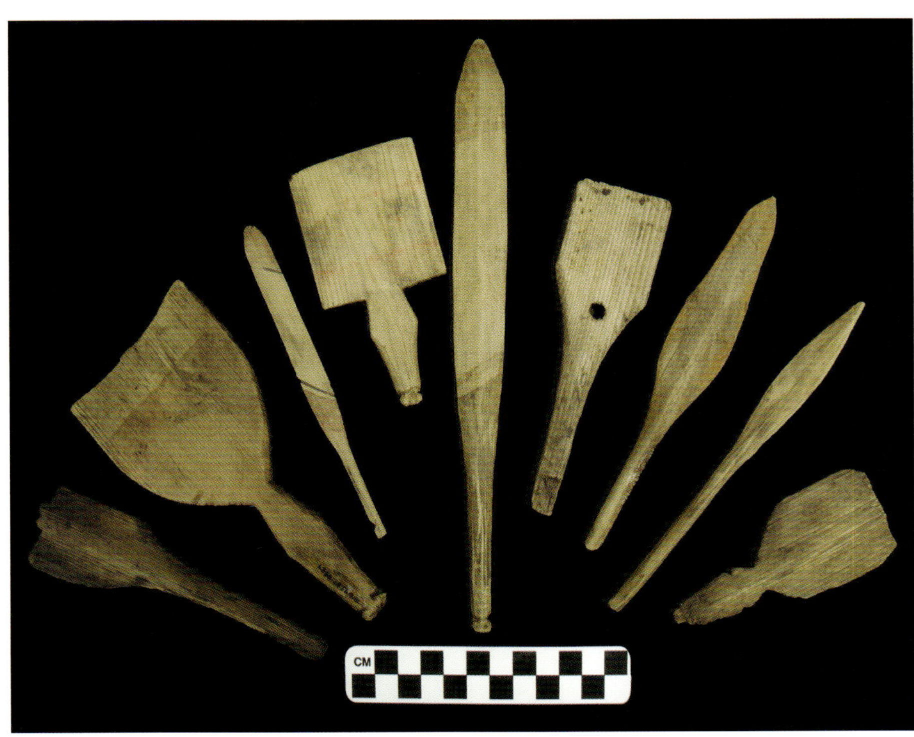

the sides of the mask for lashing. Then the hoop could be lashed to the ends of the brace and embellishments lashed to the hoop. Examples of this technique appear in the Pinart collection (Chapter 4). Some masks also have small holes in their edges, places where embellishments may have been added directly.[33]

Carved wooden attachments complemented those made from natural materials. Examples from Kodiak archaeological sites occur in a variety of shapes, including feathers, crescents, squares, circles, whale tails, and even people (Figure 8).[34] Each features a cylindrical shaft with a notched end for lashing to a mask hoop, and some are painted with bands or geometric designs of red and black pigment.[35] Many of these carvings are strikingly similar to the wooden attachment on historic masks collected by Voznesenskii in 1842[36] and those pictured here from the Pinart collection.

Another common attachment to Sugpiaq masks, seen in the Pinart collection, was a bite bar. This piece of wood, lashed horizontally across the back of a mask, allowed a dancer to grasp the carving in his teeth, keeping his hands free to carry props and perform motions.[37] Similarly, some masks featured head straps.

For paint, artists extracted colors from bark, grasses, and berries, or created colorful powders by crushing minerals—limestone, copper ore, and iron oxide—with a mortar and pestle.[38] They mixed these pigments with a binder of oil or blood[39] and then applied them with their fingers, a small stick, or a paintbrush made by securing animal hair to a small handle.[40]

Inspiration for mask designs came from many places. Pinart's field notes include a legend about the origins of Kodiak masks that suggests mask makers learned of their masks in dreams.[41]

> The origin of these masks is the following as given by the Aleutes of Orlovski. They say that a hunter among the rich was not able to kill anything. Once he sailed to the end of the Ugak Bay, came on shore and pulled his baidarka onto the cliff. There he fell asleep and slept for two nights

and two days. In his sleep he dreamt of these various masks.[42]

In general, mask makers crafted images of humanlike faces. Portraits of animals were rare although not unknown. A prehistoric mask from Karluk depicts the face of an owl,[43] and some historic masks show animal features on a human face—a pair of crablike pincers or a beak-shaped mouth. This focus on human forms and on faces sets Sugpiaq masks apart from those made by their culturally related Yup'ik neighbors. A number of Yup'ik masks depict animals, including animal bodies.[44] Some have a human face carved in the creature's back or belly, or peering out of its mouth to represent its *yuit*—or inner spirits.[45] Despite strong ties between Yup'ik and Sugpiaq spiritual beliefs and similarities in the ways masks were incorporated into festivals, Sugpiaq masks show the spirits, with rare references to the animals some represent.

Among the spirit faces depicted by Sugpiaq masks, none are identical. Yet, there is a stylized quality uniting the portrayals that suggests carvers worked within a well-defined design tradition. The masks are not portraits but representations of humanlike beings with identifiable characteristics. For example, some masks show long, pointed-head figures. According to Sugpiaq tradition, a figure with this head shape is an *iyaq*, literally, "one that is hidden."[46] Today Elders translate this word as "devil," a term that captures its powerful, negative connotation. Pinart recorded that the soul of an evil person could become such a spirit. Similarly, a number of Sugpiaq masks have whistling mouths or puckered mouths tied closed with strips of gutskin.[47] Among the Sugpiaq, whistling was the way spirits talked and how people could call them to festivals.[48]

Despite the prevalence of spirit masks, a few masks appear to have been portraits of people, with only two represented in Pinart's collection. Archaeologists found one such mask in a prehistoric burial in Karluk, suggesting that it was part of the individual's funerary rites.[49]

Who were the spirits depicted in masks? Many were the owners of living things.[50] In the Sugpiaq universe everything is alive. The mountains, the wind, every fish, and each blade of grass has an inner consciousness or *sua* (literally "its person") that is aware of human action. Like a person, a *sua* could take human form, speak, and act with great intelligence, but it could not be reincarnated. At death it was the animal's soul—a distinct spiritual entity without human characteristics—that could be reborn. For the Sugpiat the reincarnation of animals' souls was essential for a future supply of game, and it required care for the soul and the *sua* of every animal harvested.[51]

In this system, animals gave themselves to people who continually demonstrated their worth through responsible acts. The whaler's wife gave the dead whale a drink of fresh water to satisfy its thirst before butchering.[52] People dressed neatly, decorated their clothing, and never wasted scraps of fur to show respect for the animals whose skins they wore.[53] Fishermen returned salmon intestines to the water so that the soul of the animal could live to propagate.[54] Through thoughtful action, thrift, care for one's belongings, and observance of rituals, the Sugpiat encouraged reincarnation and requested assistance with this process from the human-like spirit inside every animal. Masked dancing was part of the ritual behavior that perpetuated a person's ability to harvest animals. By depicting the animal spirits, carvers revealed the beings that controlled life on earth, communicated with these spirits, and ensured future prosperity.

Mask dancing occurred during certain winter festivals, those dedicated to future hunting success.[55] Dancing was not a part of other festivals, the Bladder Festival or the Feast of the Dead for example. Held in early winter, following fall salmon fishing, community hunting celebrations recounted recent events, celebrated the deeds of ancestors, and honored the spirit world. Mask dances were hunting ceremonies. Through performance, people called the animal *suas* to festivals, showed their respect for the gifts of the previous year, and ensured a future supply of game. As such, masks functioned as religious objects. They were spirit representations used to communicate with the unseen world, acknowledge the dependent relationship of people, and promote prosperity.

Historic accounts indicate that winter festivals occurred in a *qasgiq*, a large structure built for community affairs.[56] Owned and maintained by a wealthy member of the elite class, the *qasgiq* functioned as a men's house during most of the year—a place for repairing tools, discussing politics, and preparing for war.[57] In the fall, however, community members assisted in the refurbishment of this large rectangular structure, filling it with fresh grass and patching its roof in preparation for festivals to be attended by all. With the assistance of a ritual specialist known as a *kas'aq*,[58] a community leader would organize a gathering, perhaps inviting friends from neighboring communities as well as members of his own village.[59] In preparation, the *qasgiq* would be fumigated with smoke and hunting gear hung from its rafters. Weaponry, animal skins, and even boat models might be suspended from the ceiling and tied together so that a person with a rope could make this gear sway during performances to mimic the movement of the ocean.[60]

People wore their finest clothing for festivals, donning elaborately decorated parkas and painting their faces. Festival guests arriving by boat were met in the water, and then carried ashore and into the *qasgiq*.[61] Here they sat by social status on benches that lined the walls, or on the floor, in a room lit by oil lamps.[62] Food, games, and visiting opened the festivities, followed by dances that enacted hunting scenes. As drummers beat rhythmically on large, circular, skin-covered drums, one or more masked dancers appeared to tell a story.[63] Dancing naked or nearly naked, men performed movements choreographed specifically for the festival and their masks. Many masked dances were accompanied by stories and songs and might include a set of masks. Three masks might illustrate a song, with one mask for each verse. Alternatively, a pair of different masks might dance together to tell one story (see Appendix). Women also danced, performing in lines and singing songs to the dead.[64] Desson argues that these performances were an integral part of the hunting ceremony, as they recalled the skills and success of ancestors and called on the spirits of the dead for assistance in future hunts.[65] As the festivities progressed, the dances and songs became more mystical as performers began calling the animal spirits to the *qasgiq* with shouting and whistling.

Figure 9. The Russian Orthodox Church in Kodiak, 1869. Watercolor by Vincent Colyer.

Illustration 9. L'église orthodoxe de Kodiak, 1869. Aquarelle de Vincent Colyer.

Individual festivals lasted days, with continuous activity and guests napping in the *qasgiq* as they tired. At the end of gatherings, the host offered visitors gifts of clothing, beads, and food.[66] The festival season progressed into midwinter until food stores from the previous summer were exhausted.[67] Following festivals, masks were often burned, broken, and discarded, or stored in secluded caves to protect people from their power.[68]

Sugpiaq winter ceremonies and the production of ceremonial objects lasted well into the nineteenth century, as evidenced by the notes of observers and the collections they made. Voznesenskii witnessed masked dancing on Kodiak

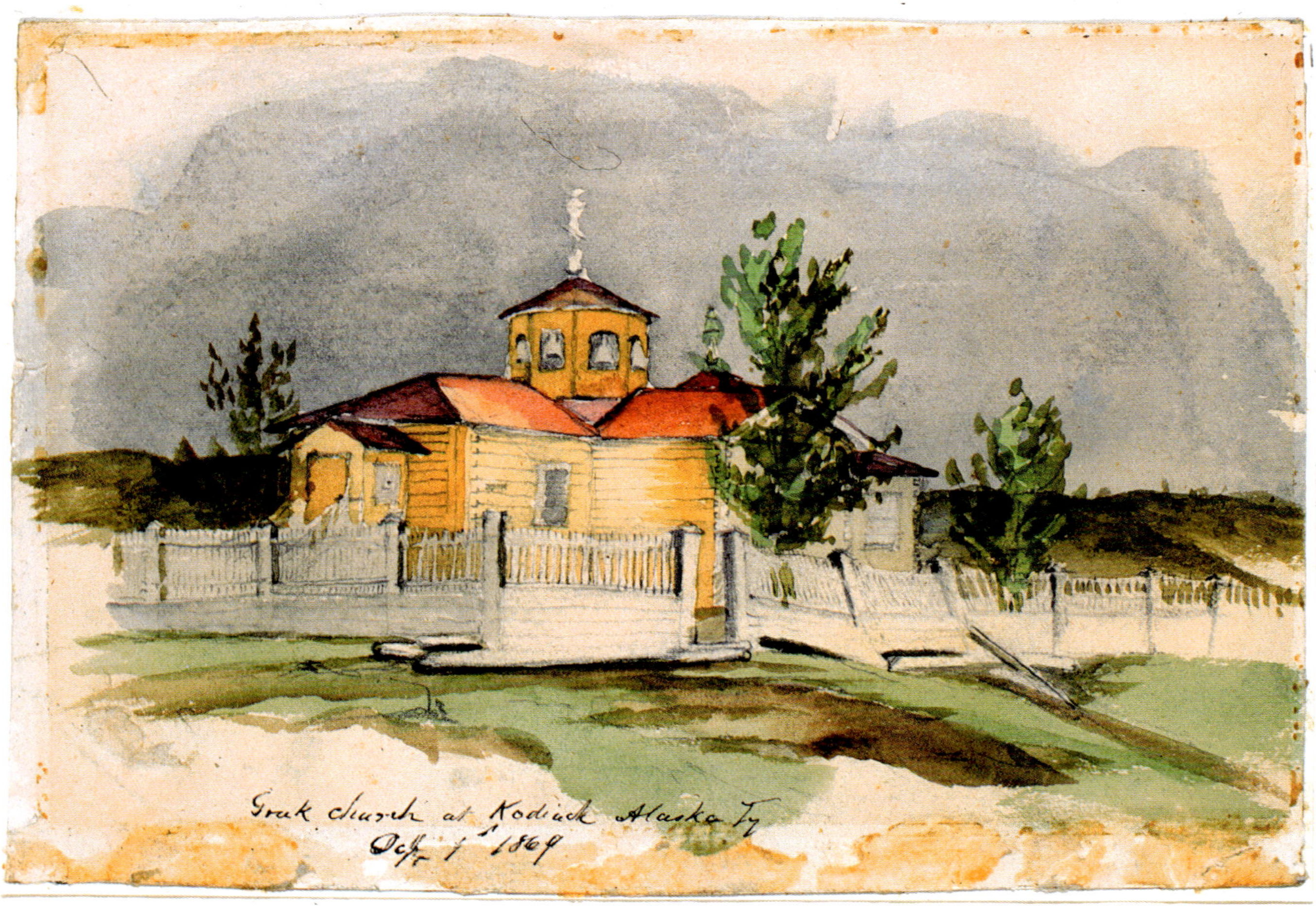

Island in 1842, recording dances and collecting masks and their associated Alutiiq names.[69] Similarly, Pinart's field notes describe a festival he attended in the village of Uyak on February 3, 1872.[70] With his collection of ceremonial objects and texts (Chapter 4), these observations indicate that winter festivals were still known and at least occasionally practiced thirty years after Voznesenskii's visit. In contrast, William Fisher's notes, made a decade after Pinart's, are less clear about the status of festivals. Although Fisher, who lived in St. Paul from 1879 to 1885, collected Sugpiaq ceremonial gear—including dance masks, rattles, a beaded headdress, and shamans' paraphernalia—he never witnessed their use.[71] His correspondence indicates that he heard of ritual performances but that they were rare.[72]

The ethnographic record of Russian Orthodox practices among the nineteenth-century Sugpiat is clearer. In 1821, the second charter of the Russian-American Company required the provision of religious and educational services to Sugpiaq communities under its jurisdiction.[73] In the decades that followed, the company built churches and chapels and hired clergy (Figure 9). The influence of the church grew as a result. For the Sugpiat it was both socially and economically advantageous to convert to Christianity. Affiliation with the church offered access to power and opportunities for education. Moreover, Christian beliefs were not necessarily at odds with Sugpiaq beliefs and could even help to explain some of the failure of the Sugpiaq spirits to act in predictable ways in the face of colonial atrocities.[74] Thus, substantial elements of the old faith coexisted with the growing influence of Russian Orthodoxy until the later decades of the century. At this time, communities also began to feel the influences of American Protestantism, whose explicit goals were conversion and acculturation.[75]

What happened to masks and masked dancing? Anthropologists suggest that as the nineteenth century progressed, Sugpiaq masking blended with Russian folk traditions under the safety of Christian celebrations.[76] Mishler notes that while the Sugpiat lost their masks, they did not lose masking. They adapted the tradition to fit the accepted

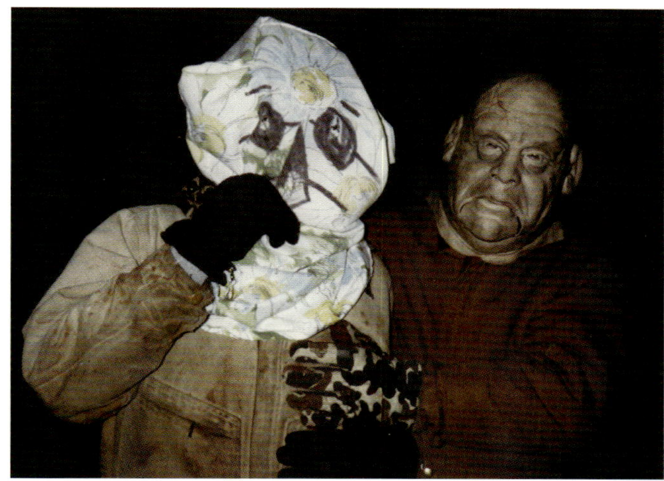

Figure 10. Masked revelers in Old Harbor, ca. 1985.
PHOTO BY SVEN HAAKANSON JR.

Illustration 10. Personnes masquées faisant la fête à Old Harbor, vers 1985.
PHOTOGRAPHIE DE SVEN HAAKANSON JR.

celebrations of church holidays—particularly Russian Christmas and New Year's.[77]

Elements of this masking persist, particularly in Kenai Peninsula and Alaska Peninsula Sugpiaq communities. During the Russian Christmas season, which runs from Christmas Eve on January 7 to the Eve of Theophany on January 18 following the Julian calendar, some Sugpiaq people still participate in *maskalataq*—masking.[78] The first masking events occur in conjunction with starring. From January 7 to 9, Russian Orthodox carolers visit homes in their communities carrying a large decorated, twirling star. With songs in Alutiiq, Slavonic, and English, they announce the birth of Jesus and enjoy refreshments provided by their hosts.[79] In some communities, people begin masking after the evening's caroling sessions are over.[80] In others, masking starts on the fourth day of the season, when all of the caroling is complete.[81] During masking, groups of fully disguised men and women travel from house to house to dance and see if people can guess their identities. They cover themselves with old clothes, including rubber masks or masks made out of pillowcases, and alter their voices (Figure 10). If they are identified, they must unmask and stop for the evening.[82]

In addition to the masking that follows Christmas starring, Sugpiaq people participate in New Year's Eve masquerade parties. People dress in costumes to disguise their identities and participate in parties. In the past, one element of such parties was a New Year's play, known in some places as a devil dance.[83] In this play, a masked person dressed as the new year vanquished a masked person dressed as the old year, with the help of other revelers.[84]

Like the masking of old, modern disguised characters are still associated with the supernatural world, although these associations are biblical. The maskers who visit homes after starring processions represent King Herod's murderous soldiers searching for the baby Jesus.[85] After masking, participants typically purify themselves by attending church services, swimming in cold water, or taking a *banya*—a Sugpiaq-style steambath. While masking traditions are no longer widely practiced in Kodiak Sugpiaq communities, they are still known.[86]

The *Giinaquq: Like a Face* Project

Although small pieces of the ancestral masking tradition remain in Kodiak's Sugpiaq communities, the rediscovery of Pinart's classically crafted collection led to a period of cultural exploration. Sugpiaq artists Helen Simeonoff, Perry Eaton, and Sven Haakanson Jr. made personal journeys across the Atlantic to study the masks and returned with information.[87] Haakanson, an anthropologist, educator, and museum professional, knew at once that the collection should be seen in Kodiak. Although photographs of the pieces could provide inspiration for the Sugpiaq community, he saw that it was not possible to share their full impact in pictures. He also understood that Sugpiaq people could tell the story of the masks in a fresh, culturally grounded way—reuniting their own cultural knowledge with the collection.

In 2001 Haakanson began working to bring a selection of the Château-Musée's Sugpiaq masks to Kodiak for exhibition. At the time, the new Musée du quai Branly in Paris was working on an exhibition featuring the masks. Curator Emmanuel Désveaux invited Haakanson to write an article for the exhibition catalog on the meaning of the collection to the Sugpiat in return for his assistance developing an Alaskan exhibition.[88] However, plans for the exhibition failed to gain approval in France due to fear of the Native American Graves Protection and Repatriation Act, a law that protects sacred objects belonging to Native peoples, but only in the United States. Ironically, misunderstanding of a law designed to reunite people with the objects of their ancestry was actually making it more difficult for Haakanson to negotiate an international exhibition.[89]

A chance meeting with American anthropologist and French resident Sarah Froning opened the door for a new exhibition effort. At a conference in Belgium, Haakanson spoke about the value of European ethnographic collections to Native American people and the frustrations he faced attempting to form trustworthy relationships that would allow such objects to be exhibited in the United States. Listening in the audience, Froning realized she could help. She had just completed a doctoral study of French museums and understood how to develop a project proposal the City of Boulogne-sur-Mer would be likely to support. She introduced herself to Haakanson and they began work on a proposal.

At the same time the Château-Musée was in transition to new leadership, with French museum professional Anne-Claire Laronde assuming the role of curator.[90] Committed to making the Château-Musée's collections more accessible to the peoples whose heritages they reflected, Laronde listened earnestly to Haakanson's ideas for an Alaskan exhibition of the Pinart masks and agreed to support a proposal to the City of Boulogne-sur-Mer, the owner of the Château-Musée and its collections.

As French authorities began to consider the exhibition anew, Haakanson was working to share the collection through photographs in Alaska. The Alutiiq Museum, Kodiak's Sugpiaq-governed cultural center and repository, had an annual outreach program to rural villages called Traveling Traditions.[91] Each spring the museum created a small exhibit on a Sugpiaq art form, then traveled the show to Sugpiaq communities during heritage weeks—periods of community exploration and celebration of Native traditions set in area schools. Artists would accompany the show and teach an intensive hands-on, five-day workshop on the featured art to middle and high school students. With limited funding for the program and few artists with the knowledge to teach classical Sugpiaq carving, Haakanson stepped up to teach mask-making workshops. He used photos of the Pinart collection as inspiration for student carvers, creating notebooks of images to share in schools. Mask making became more popular than any other Traveling Traditions program, and the demand for Haakanson's time grew to be overwhelming. He realized that he needed to train the current generation of carvers in classical styles and manufacturing techniques to develop additional instructors.

With no agreement for an Alaskan exhibition of Pinart's masks yet in place, Haakanson knew that it could be years before pieces from the collection were able to visit Kodiak. So, in June of 2006, he took Sugpiaq carvers to France. A federal grant for economic development, provided by the Institute for Museum and Library Services, paid for their travel. Accompanied by Haakanson, nine Sugpiaq artists traveled the eight thousand miles to Boulogne-sur-Mer to see their ancestors' work and absorb the details of tool use, design, proportion, and color that could not be fully appreciated in the few published photographs of the collection.[92] In return for their participation, each artist agreed to share the knowledge he or she gained by teaching carving back home in Kodiak and producing an original work for the Alutiiq Museum's permanent collections.[93]

This trip cemented the *Giinaquq: Like a Face* exhibition. In just three days, representatives of both nations learned the value of the collection to the other and developed a sense of trust. French officials witnessed the deep emotional ties

Sugpiaq people felt for the masks and the opportunities they provided for continued cultural exploration and artistic expression. Stereotypes of Native Americans seeking repatriation melted as the artists expressed their sincere respect for the Frenchman who had preserved their patrimony and gratitude for the care the French people provided the collection. For Sugpiaq visitors, touring Boulogne and learning its history brought the French commitment to the collection into sharper focus as well. Located at the narrow southeastern entrance to the English Channel, where the northern tip of France meets the North Sea, Boulogne-sur-Mer was of great strategic importance in World War II. Allied forces seeking to flatten occupying German troops destroyed 85 percent of the city during the conflict. With their families in peril and the community literally collapsing around them, the museum's staff saved the collection. They moved it to safety and then reassembled it after the war. Without their efforts, there would be no Pinart collection today. Sugpiaq artists, particularly those who remembered the hardships of World War II in Alaska, were moved. They saw the French pride in the collections and understood how it represented a part of French history. It was evident that Sugpiaq carvings had a meaningful home in the Château-Musée.

During the trip, Haakanson called Kodiak to say that, over lunch, the Deputy Mayor of Boulogne had agreed to the loan. Masks from the Pinart collection could travel to Alaska—soon.[94] Planning for the exhibition began immediately. First, the Alutiiq Museum obtained funding for a community conference. Staff members developed an exhibition concept, then assembled a team of Elders, artists, educators, community leaders, and museum professionals to evaluate and enhance their ideas. The two-day meeting, held in Kodiak in January of 2007, kicked off sixteen months of preparation and intense fund-raising. The French would loan thirty-five pieces to the exhibition—thirty-four masks and a bird-shaped feast bowl—for a total of nine months. The planning team decided to open the exhibition in Kodiak in late May 2008, to coincide with the annual community Crab Festival, which would be celebrating its fiftieth anniversary.

The show would stay in Kodiak for four months, then travel to the Anchorage Museum at Rasmuson Center for an additional four months before the objects returned to France.

While exhibition preparations were under way, the artists who had traveled to France taught mask making and created their own works for the Alutiiq Museum (Figure 11). To generate excitement for the *Giinaquq: Like a Face* exhibition, and to illustrate the powerful links between ethnographic collections and modern Native peoples, the Alutiiq Museum created *Making Faces*. This small preview exhibit featured photos from the France trip, quotes from the artists, and artwork inspired by the experience. It drew uncharacteristically large crowds, and signaled an eagerness to reconsider the heritage of Sugpiaq masks. Exhibition advisors had warned that it might be difficult for some people to talk about or visit the masks collected by Pinart and that the museum should be prepared for powerful emotional reactions to the project. Yet the mood surrounding *Making Faces* and the anticipation of the *Giinaquq* exhibition was celebratory.

As wet snow fell on Kodiak airport in April of 2008, a jet landed with five crates and Château-Musée registrar Céline Ramio. Staff members and Elders gathered to open the crates in the Alutiiq Museum's laboratory, smiling and laughing as each revealed its contents of Sugpiaq masks. The exhibit opening and its weeklong series of events were equally cheerful. Elders gathered for a preview followed by tea and conversation. Sugpiaq community leaders participated in a dinner fund-raiser for educational projects. Four dance groups welcomed the masks with performances, and hundreds of Kodiak residents visited the exhibition. The show moved people of many heritages, and it was evident that the Sugpiaq masks could be openly explored and celebrated in Kodiak (Figure 12). Attitudes toward Sugpiaq culture and its spiritual heritage had changed.

Further evidence of this new climate came during the summer of 2008. During the exhibition in Kodiak, the Alutiiq Museum hosted Future Masters, a two-week mask-making workshop for youth. Artists Perry Eaton, Coral Chernof, and Haakanson worked with twelve Alaskan students to learn the art of Sugpiaq mask carving, using the exhibited pieces for information and inspiration. Over twelve days, teens transformed blocks of rough-cut Sitka spruce into full-sized masks, carved, painted, and decorated in the Sugpiaq tradition. Elders joined the project, helping each student compose a song for his or her mask and ensuring that the entire process was accurately completed—that each mask could tell its story with accompanying words in the Alutiiq language.

A Fuller Picture

This catalog of Sugpiaq masks from Pinart's collection is an extension of the *Giinaquq: Like a Face* exhibition. It is designed to provide a comprehensive view of the collection and a lasting resource for exploration. However, unlike most previous scholarly publications,[95] it is intended not as an analysis but as a reference to the objects and a summary of their cultural context. As such, this research builds on the work of Desson, Désveaux, and others. By assembling historic observations, cultural information, linguistic data, physical details, museum records, and photos for all the Sugpiaq masks cared for by the Château-Musée and the Musée du quai Branly, we offer a comprehensive view of the collection. We also place this unparalleled assemblage of Sugpiaq religious artifacts within the framework of Kodiak's Native culture—past and present.

In recent decades, authors and exhibitors have tended to view the masks as examples of Native American artwork,[96] and less as an archive of Sugpiaq information. In part, this situation reflects the eight thousand miles and 136 years that have separated the collection from Alaska and the people whose heritage it most closely reflects. The masks preserved in France were unknown to the Sugpiat until the 1990s, making it impossible for the descendents of their makers to share in interpretation.[97]

This artistic view also reflects historical circumstances. The Sugpiat remain one of Alaska's least-known peoples due to far-reaching cultural changes and limited documentation of their traditions. The profound influences of an early, brutal,

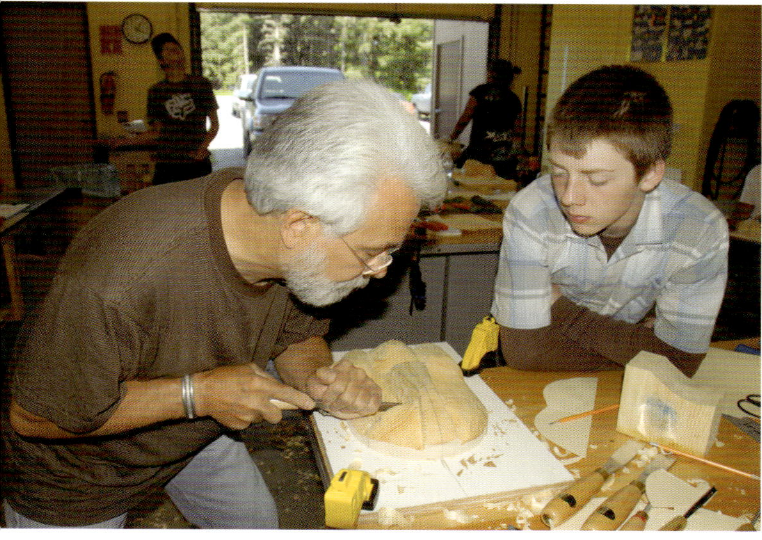

Figure 11. Perry Eaton works with student carver Lucas Gerlitz.

PHOTOGRAPH BY SVEN HAAKANSON JR.

Figure 12. The *Giinaquq: Like a Face* exhibition on display in Kodiak.

PHOTOGRAPH BY SVEN HAAKANSON JR.

Illustration 11. Perry Eaton travaillant en compagnie de l'apprenti sculpteur Lucas Gerlitz.

PHOTOGRAPHIE DE SVEN HAAKANSON JR.

Illustration 12. L'exposition « Giinaquq: Like a Face » présentée à Kodiak.

PHOTOGRAPHIE DE SVEN HAAKANSON JR.

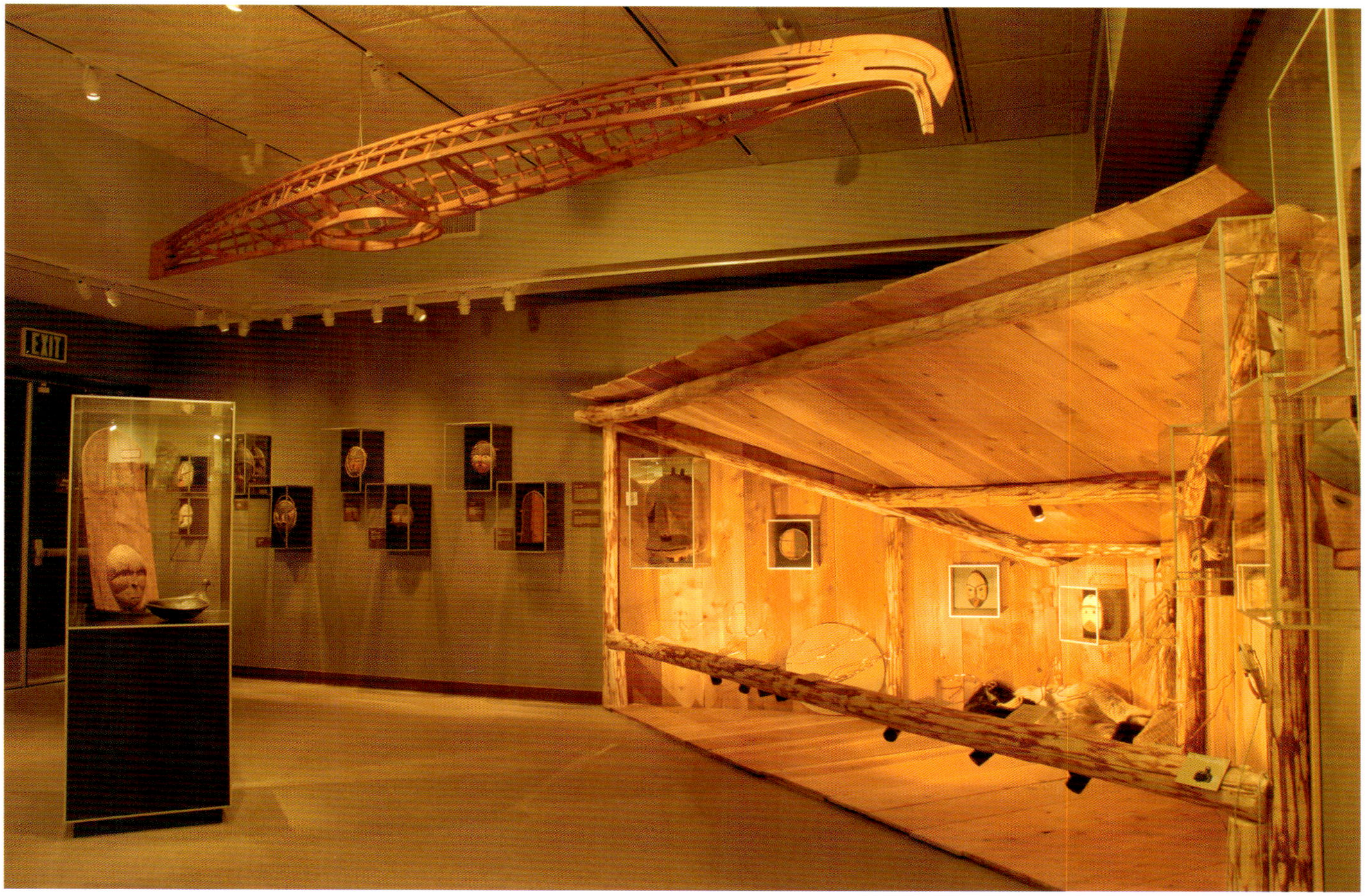

and sustained period of Western colonization led to the suppression of traditions beginning with Russian conquest in the 1780s and continuing with American rule.[98] The masks left Kodiak just as the Sugpiaq people were encountering American culture and the unrelenting push of acculturation brought by American schools, religious traditions, and economic practices. Pinart was one of the few anthropologists to hear Sugpiaq songs or to witness a winter festival. He arrived on the eve of a cultural transition, as the spiritual, artistic, and linguistic traditions of the Sugpiat were about to be swamped by those of another. Ethnographers who came to Alaska in the following decades passed by Kodiak, believing its Native culture too altered for meaningful study. As a result, there is no traditional ethnography of the Kodiak Sugpiaq people,[99] and only one systematic account of the neighboring Prince William Sound Sugpiaq people.[100] Researched in 1933, this account documents Sugpiaq culture 150 years after Russian conquest.

It is not surprising that the Pinart mask collection has not been widely interpreted in cultural terms. Scholars have not had access to reliable information about Sugpiaq traditions, which until recently[101] resided in relatively inaccessible places—Sugpiaq Elders, archaeological sites, historic manuscripts, and distant museum collections. Even Pinart's notes, handwritten in at least five languages, including a phonetic version of Alutiiq, are extremely difficult to read and translate. This publication seeks to correct this situation. By creating a framework for understanding the collection, the following chapters offer insight on the collection's origins, importance, contents, and continuing impact, as well as its great artistry.

Chapter 2 outlines Alphonse Pinart's journey, exploring the circumstances that brought a wealthy young Frenchman to Alaska and took the world's largest collections of Sugpiaq masks back to France. Château-Musée curator Anne-Claire Laronde considers Pinart's family background, education, and mentorship in revealing his motivations for studying Alaska Natives, and provides a detailed history of the collection in France. This history is a valuable addition to the collection. It illustrates that historic objects are as much a part of the present as they are of the past, and that cultural values, museum practices, and even world politics have a profound influence on what is passed to future generations. Laronde's essay reveals the enormous pride the French have taken in caring for the collection, and how the collection has become an honored part of French history. In addition to Sugpiaq spirituality, the collection represents French intellectual history and the outstanding contributions of this European nation to the preservation of world heritage.

In Chapter 3, Sugpiaq historian Gordon Pullar reaches back to 1872 to examine Kodiak Island and Sugpiaq life in Pinart's time. He describes the political, economic, and social landscape of the decade immediately succeeding the transfer of Alaska to American rule and provides sketches of the communities that Pinart visited. Pullar's summary reveals the stresses the Sugpiaq community faced living under a new governing power. It also illustrates the blending of Native and European traditions that Pinart encountered and foreshadows cultural changes to come. Although we do not know how Pinart obtained the masks in his remarkably large collection, Pullar's summary reveals the climate in which growing cultural marginality might have influenced Sugpiaq people to part with the artifacts of an older faith.

A review of the Château-Musée's Pinart collection appears in Chapter 4. Here we examine the importance of the collection by considering Pinart's approach to collecting, characterizing the contents of his collection, and discussing its documentation. In this chapter, Sugpiaq anthropologist and carver Sven Haakanson Jr. shares data he assembled from the seventy-seven masks in the Château-Musée and Musée du quai Branly collections. He pairs this information with detailed images of each piece, skillfully taken by Sugpiaq carver Will Anderson. Photographs from different angles illustrate mask proportions, the depth of facial features, and construction details, as well as the artistry evident in the carvings.

The final chapter of this catalog considers the impact of the Pinart collection on contemporary Sugpiaq artists. Sugpiaq carver Perry Eaton shares the Kodiak cultural heritage movement and discusses how the discovery of Pinart's Sugpiaq mask collection is helping to fuel a period of cultural revitalization and exploration. Eaton examines the influence of the masks on individual Sugpiaq artists and traces how the knowledge preserved in these pieces surfaces in the work of contemporary carvers, painters, and jewelers.

The catalog ends with an appendix of Alutiiq texts culled from Pinart's anthropological field notes by Haakanson and linguist Jeff Leer. Here readers will find examples of mask songs, dances, and legends. Some of these texts relate to pieces illustrated in Chapter 4. Others are not associated with a known mask. The carvings made to grace these words have not survived the hardships of time. Translated for this project with the assistance of Elder Alutiiq speakers, the songs enliven the masks and remind us of the chain of traditions that links today's Sugpiat to the masterful works of ancestors.

With the *Giinaquq: Like a Face* project, the masks of the Pinart collection have assumed a new role in Sugpiaq society. In the twenty-first century the seventy-seven faces are no longer envoys to the spirit world. Nor are they objects that people look at with shame. Today, they are again respected spiritual artifacts. This restored power comes from the opportunity they afford to study the past, the connections they provide to ancestors, and their ability to uplift and inspire.[102] These changing views of masks reflect the periods of cultural perception through which Sugpiaq people have passed. As the Sugpiat begin to relearn and embrace ancestral knowledge, collections like Pinart's become priceless cultural ambassadors.

Alphonse Pinart could not have imagined the role his collection would play in modern Native Alaska. Yet his efforts to create a comprehensive assemblage of Sugpiaq masks, record mask songs, dances and legends, and deposit these materials in reputable repositories suggest that he understood their value to history. Pinart must have seen that Sugpiaq culture was changing and that the masks were artifacts of a fading tradition. Had he not collected them, it is likely they would have been lost—intentionally destroyed or left to decompose. Pinart's work is a great gift to many people. For the French, his collection is a testament to intellectual achievement and an unwavering commitment to the stewardship of world art. For Americans it is documentation of a once populous and flourishing but now little-known Native society. For Kodiak Islanders it reveals a forgotten chapter in local history and fosters a more inclusive dialogue on community culture. For the Sugpiat the collection is irrefutable confirmation of a complex and beautiful heritage. In the *Giinaquq* exhibition comment book, a Kodiak visitor summarized this feeling. She wrote, "reassurance and awe."

Giinaquq: Like a Face

Sven D. Haakanson Jr. et Amy F. Steffian

Le mot alutiiq pour traduire « masque », *giinaquq*, signifie « comme un visage, mais pas vraiment ». Ce terme montre la place mystique tenue par les visages sculptés au sein de la culture sugpiaq classique[1]. Ces masques, fabriqués et décorés avec un soin particulier, étaient à la fois des œuvres d'art et d'importants objets religieux. Fabriqués à des fins de récits, d'enseignement des valeurs et de représentation du monde spirituel, ils étaient aussi utilisés lors de cérémonies de chasse et permettaient au peuple sugpiaq de communiquer avec le monde de l'invisible. Lors des festivals d'hiver, les danses masquées permettaient aux Sugpiat de maintenir l'équilibre des forces régulant la vie quotidienne et le retour du printemps, avec son lot de poissons à pêcher et de phoques à chasser. Pour les Sugpiat, les danses masquées donnaient à la fois accès aux nourritures spirituelles et à l'alimentation proprement dite, et les masques étaient *agayuullqutaq* : « quelque chose à respecter comme étant sacré ».

Au cours des deux derniers siècles, la culture sugpiaq et sa vision des masques ont radicalement changé. Le peuple natif de Kodiak a perdu nombre de ses traditions au moment de la confrontation des cultures intervenue à la suite de la conquête de l'archipel par les Russes en 1784[2]. Les objets, les coutumes, la langue, les croyances et les valeurs culturelles sugpiat disparurent, arrachés de force, cachés, victimes d'humiliations ou oubliés puisque ne remplissant plus leur rôle

essentiel de perpétuation du monde sugpiaq. Les pratiques religieuses traditionnelles déclinèrent à la fin du XIXe siècle[3] du fait du regard désapprobateur des colonisateurs russes et furent remplacées par le christianisme. Malgré ces profondes transformations, le peuple sugpiaq n'a jamais oublié ses masques et la signification de ces visages d'esprits de bois sculpté perdure encore.

Dans les années 1980, des archéologues ont redécouvert ces masques, ainsi que des poupées, des bols de banquet et autres parures cérémonielles, façonnés par des mains habiles, sur le site d'un campement préhistorique sugpiaq englouti sous les eaux, à Karluk[4]. Les Anciens reconnurent ces objets retrouvés *(ill. 4)* et se mirent à raconter l'histoire des masques, de leur disparition, non sans émettre en même temps quelques réserves[5]. Plusieurs en connaissaient les pouvoirs, mais ils avaient aussi été habitués à avoir honte de leur ancienne religion : ces masques étaient considérés comme des manifestations de comportements primitifs, de croyance en des dieux maléfiques. Personne n'avait le droit d'en parler ni de les toucher. Pour la génération suivante, cependant, ces données archéologiques confirmaient la façon qu'avaient les Sugpiat de voir le monde. Ils étaient l'occasion d'une remise en cause des interprétations que les étrangers avaient imposées à leur culture passée.

Les remises en cause de l'héritage culturel sugpiaq et de la signification de ses traditions religieuses se multiplièrent, parallèlement au mouvement grandissant qui faisait renaître la vie culturelle de Kodiak. Les fouilles archéologiques, les études ethnographiques et les travaux sur des collections se poursuivirent, mettant en lumière les traditions sugpiat et accentuant ainsi les effets positifs suscités par l'exploration approfondie d'une culture[6]. Par la suite, dans les années 1990, Dominique Desson, alors étudiante en anthropologie à l'université d'Alaska, à Fairbanks, présenta les recherches novatrices qu'elle avait effectuées sur des sculptures ancestrales conservées en France[7]. En effet, dans un port côtier français renommé pour son économie basée sur la pêche (et pas si différent de Kodiak, en Alaska) existait un musée municipal dont les rayons recelaient des trésors provenant d'Alaska. Entreposé parmi des collections de vases grecs et d'objets funéraires égyptiens dormait le plus grand ensemble connu de masques sugpiat. D'où provenaient donc ces pièces ?

En 1871, un jeune homme français issu d'un milieu aisé, Alphonse Louis Pinart, avait quitté le confort de sa maison familiale du nord de la France pour étudier les langues autochtones de la côte de l'Alaska. Tout au long de son voyage qui le menait à travers les îles Aléoutiennes, la baie de Bristol, et se terminait par l'archipel de Kodiak, il collecta des objets ethnographiques. Durant l'hiver 1872, Pinart visita en *qayaq* les communautés sugpiat de Kodiak, recueillant des chants, des récits et des danses ainsi que des objets, en particulier des masques[8]. Trois ans après son retour en France, Pinart fit don de la plupart de ses collections au musée municipal de Boulogne-sur-Mer, qui était alors le lieu de conservation le plus important à proximité de Marquise, son lieu de résidence. Ce musée porte aujourd'hui le nom de Château-Musée et la collection Pinart demeure le plus grand ensemble cohérent de masques sugpiat du monde.

Année après année, si l'existence de la collection Pinart se fit connaître parmi les anthropologues[9], ce ne fut pas le cas parmi les Sugpiat. Cependant, dans les années 1990, l'existence des masques commença enfin à se répandre dans les communautés autochtones de Kodiak, et bientôt on commença à se poser des questions. Comment Pinart avait-il pu collecter autant d'artefacts sugpiat d'une telle valeur spirituelle ? Quels enseignements les Sugpiat d'aujourd'hui pouvaient-ils en retirer concernant leur héritage culturel ? Les masques pourraient-ils un jour revenir chez eux ? En discutant autour de ces thèmes, on relançait l'intérêt suscité par ces objets ancestraux et, petit à petit, le peuple sugpiaq se forgea une nouvelle vision quant à leur signification.

Ce catalogue de masques de la collection Pinart[10] expose les recherches actuelles concernant les différents sens que revêtent les masques sugpiat. À côté d'informations techniques complètes concernant la collection, cette publication aborde le contexte culturel des masques, celui d'hier et celui d'aujourd'hui. Dans ce chapitre, nous commencerons cette exploration par une introduction dans laquelle on explicite la place que les masques occupaient dans la société sugpiaq, puis nous donnerons un résumé du travail qui a abouti à l'exposition des masques d'Alaska de la collection Pinart, et, enfin, nous donnons un aperçu d'articles que nous avons rassemblés afin de retracer l'histoire complète de ces remarquables artefacts.

Les masques dans la société sugpiaq

Au cours des six mois qu'il a passés dans l'archipel de Kodiak, Alphonse Louis Pinart a accumulé une grande quantité d'informations concernant les masques sugpiat. La consultation de ses notes de terrain[11], ajoutée à celle des récits historiques sur la culture sugpiaq[12] et aux données archéologiques provenant des sites sugpiat[13], permet de se forger une vision globale de la place qu'occupaient ces masques dans la société sugpiaq traditionnelle, depuis leur création jusqu'à leur utilisation et leur signification.

Chez les Sugpiat, la sculpture sur pierre, le travail du bois et la fabrication de masques étaient, en règle générale, des activités réservées aux hommes[14]. Les jeunes garçons apprenaient à travailler le bois par l'observation en travaillant avec des parents de sexe masculin. Cette tradition s'est poursuivie dans les villages sugpiat de Kodiak jusqu'au XXe siècle.

Les forêts d'épicéas n'ont été plantées sur l'archipel que récemment et ne couvrent que les îles du nord[15]. La plupart des sculpteurs se procuraient autrefois du bois en récupérant des bois d'essences variées sur les plages de Kodiak : l'if du pacifique, le sapin de Douglas, le cèdre rouge ou jaune, et l'épicéa. Ils ramassaient également du bois d'aulne, du bouleau nain et du peuplier de Virginie dans les fourrés en bord de côte[16]. La fabrication de manches d'outils, d'objets courants et d'objets d'art pouvait nécessiter de préparer le bois en le mettant à sécher avant de le travailler. De nos jours encore, les sculpteurs sugpiat mettent le bois à vieillir dans leur jardin ou leur atelier pour le rendre plus facile à travailler.

Les outils et artefacts en bois provenant de fouilles archéologiques témoignent des anciennes techniques de sculpture et de gravure. On tronçonnait d'abord le bois à l'aide d'un grand os de baleine très dur et des coins d'épicéa *(ill. 5a et 5b)*[17] que l'artisan enfonçait dans la bûche avec une lourde mailloche de pierre afin d'obtenir des morceaux de bois d'une longueur plus maniable. On creusait peut-être des trous arrondis dans les coins d'épicéa, ensuite remplis de gras d'animal, pour réduire la friction et empêcher ces coins de rester coincés[18]. Les sculpteurs coupaient en long les morceaux de bois obtenus afin d'en faire des ébauches ou des pièces à assembler, qu'ils taillaient alors à l'aide de toutes sortes de doloires en pierre, dont les manches étaient faits de branches souples d'if[19].

Des outils manuels, en particulier ceux à base d'incisives de rongeurs (marmotte, castor ou hérisson) montés sur de petites poignées en bois, permettaient d'inciser les traits plus finement[20]. Les pointes acérées de ces outils laissaient des empreintes[21], que les sculpteurs effaçaient probablement en les ponçant avec des objets abrasifs, pierre ponce, scories ou grès. On frottait la surface gravée avec une pierre lisse, un galet érodé, pour apporter la touche finale, donner un aspect poli, une surface sans aspérités[22].

Les artisans traditionnels sculptaient des masques de taille et de style variés, représentant tous des visages[23]. Les masques représentant des visages sont les plus courants dans les collections historiques ou archéologiques. Ils présentent la particularité d'avoir le dos et les yeux creux. Certains masques ont approximativement la taille de visages humains, d'autres sont beaucoup plus grands. La collection Pinart est remarquable par la taille et le poids de certains de ces masques : ils peuvent atteindre soixante centimètres de long et trente-trois centimètres de large, et peser jusqu'à neuf kilos. Alors que certains de ces grands masques pouvaient être suspendus au plafond des lieux de cérémonies pour des spectacles, d'autres ont peut-être été portés.

En dehors de ces masques de visages, les Sugpiat fabriquaient aussi deux sortes de masques-planches. Certains d'entre eux se limitent quasiment à deux dimensions. Ils sont constitués de grandes planches taillées et peintes, avec des fentes pour les yeux et, parfois, d'autres traits du visage sculptés[24]. L'un d'eux, provenant d'un site archéologique de Karluk, se présente recouvert simplement de cuir peint *(ill. 6)*[25]. D'autres masques-planches montrent un visage sculpté en trois dimensions, rivé à une grande planche décorée[26].

À côté de ces œuvres de taille importante, dans les campements préhistoriques tardifs on trouve fréquemment des masques miniatures bien conservés. Bien que l'on ne connaisse pas la fonction de ces œuvres, elles ressemblent beaucoup aux masques de grande taille et on y trouve à la fois des masques de visages et des masques-planches[27]. Certaines de ces sculptures miniatures étaient peut-être attachées aux poignées des tambours : des collections ethnographiques montrent que les poignées de certains tambours étaient effectivement décorées de visages humains sculptés[28].

La décoration constituait un élément essentiel des masques, car les objets finement décorés témoignaient du respect que les personnes portaient aux esprits qui les aidaient. Pour ce faire, les sculpteurs de masques collectaient toutes sortes de plumes, de cuir, de poils d'animaux et de plantes destinés à mettre en valeur leurs sculptures. Les masques pouvaient être ornés de plumes et de duvet d'aigle, de peau d'intestins, d'os de baleine, de varech, de brindilles, d'herbes et d'autres matériaux périssables[29]. Pour fixer ces matériaux sur les masques, les sculpteurs fabriquaient des anneaux qui encerclaient ceux-ci. Ils recourbaient à la vapeur de minces lamelles de bois, en utilisant peut-être les pièces des maisons sugpiat où l'on prenait des bains de vapeur[30]. Les exemples archéologiques d'anneaux de masques présentent des points d'attache ovales[31], tandis que les collections ethnographiques nous montrent des anneaux de taille et de configuration variées. Certains anneaux encerclaient la totalité du masque, alors que d'autres non, et certains masques possédaient plusieurs anneaux[32].

Pour fixer l'anneau sur le masque, le sculpteur commençait sans doute par fixer une armature à l'arrière du masque en perçant des petits trous sur les bords de celui-ci. Il pouvait alors fixer l'anneau aux extrémités de l'armature et y accrocher les éléments décoratifs. On voit des exemples de cette technique dans la collection Pinart *(cf. chapitre 4)*. Certains masques présentent également des trous sur les bords pour fixer directement les éléments décoratifs[33].

Aux éléments pris dans la nature s'ajoutaient ceux sculptés dans du bois. Les sites archéologiques de Kodiak nous en montrent différents exemples, en forme de plume, de croissant, de carré, de cercle, de queue de baleine et même de personnages *(ill. 7)*[34]. Tous présentent une tige cylindrique terminée par un crochet pour le fixer à l'anneau du masque et certains sont couverts de dessins géométriques peints en rouge et noir à l'aide de pigments[35]. Beaucoup présentent une ressemblance frappante avec les masques historiques collectés par Voznesenski en 1842[36], photographiés ici dans la collection Pinart.

La collection Pinart nous montre un autre élément que l'on attachait souvent aux masques sugpiat : une barre servant de mors. Ce morceau de bois, fixé horizontalement au revers du masque, permettait au danseur de maintenir la sculpture entre ses dents. Il gardait ainsi les mains libres pour manier des accessoires et se mouvoir[37]. Dans le même but, certains masques présentaient des lanières à attacher derrière la tête.

Pour peindre, les artistes utilisaient des couleurs extraites d'écorces, d'herbes ou de baies. Ils pouvaient aussi obtenir des poudres de couleur vive en écrasant des minéraux (pierre calcaire, minerai de cuivre et oxyde de fer) dans un mortier à l'aide d'un pilon[38]. Ils mélangeaient ensuite ces pigments à un liant à base d'huile ou de sang[39] et appliquaient la couleur avec les doigts ou avec un petit bâton, ou encore avec un pinceau constitué de poils d'animal fixés sur un petit manche[40].

La conception des masques provenait de diverses sources d'inspiration. Dans ses notes prises sur place, Pinart a consigné une légende qui concerne l'origine des masques de Kodiak, selon laquelle les sculpteurs voyaient les masques dans leurs rêves[41] :

> L'origine de tous les masques, donnée les Aléoutes d'Orlovic, est la suivante selon : ils disent qu'un chasseur de parmi les riches ne pouvait rien tuer ; une fois, il alla dans le fond de la baie d'Ijouk et il aborda le rivage et tira sa *baïdarka* sur la falaise : là il s'endormit pour deux nuits et deux jours, et durant ce sommeil il vit en songe ces différents masques[42].

Les sculpteurs de masques représentaient en général des visages aux traits humains et les portraits d'animaux restaient rares. Un masque préhistorique de Karluk représente le visage d'un hibou[43], tandis que certains masques historiques qui montrent des visages humains présentent des caractères zoomorphes (pinces similaires à celles d'un crabe, bec en guise de bouche…). Cette constance dans la représentation de visages humains caractérise les masques sugpiat par comparaison avec ceux que fabriquaient leurs voisins yup'ik, qui appartiennent pourtant à la même culture. En effet, de nombreux masques yup'ik représentent des animaux ou des corps d'animaux[44]. Certains de ces animaux présentent un visage humain gravé sur leur dos ou leur ventre, ou même à l'intérieur de la bouche, d'où il regarde vers l'extérieur, représentant le *yuit* ou esprit intérieur de l'animal[45]. En dépit du lien entre les croyances spirituelles yup'ik et sugpiat, et leur même façon d'intégrer les masques au sein des festivals, les masques sugpiat représentent les esprits sans aucune référence ou presque à l'animal que certains d'entre eux peuvent symboliser.

Parmi les masques sugpiat, aucun visage d'esprit ne ressemble à un autre. Ces visages montrent cependant une unité de style qui laisse penser que les sculpteurs respectaient une tradition esthétique bien établie. Ce ne sont pas des portraits, mais plutôt des représentations d'êtres à l'aspect humain et que l'on peut différencier grâce à leurs traits particuliers. Certains masques, par exemple, représentent un personnage à tête longue et pointue. Or, selon la tradition sugpiaq, quand un être présente une tête ayant cette forme, il s'agit d'un *iyaq*, « celui qui est caché[46] ». Les Anciens traduisent aujourd'hui ce mot par « diable », terme qui exprime bien à la fois sa connotation négative et son évocation d'être puissant. Pinart note ainsi que l'âme d'une personne malfaisante pouvait se muer en un tel esprit. De la même façon, certains masques sugpiat avaient des bouches sifflantes ou proéminentes, maintenues fermées par des lanières de peau d'intestin[47]. Chez les Sugpiat, le sifflement était la façon de s'exprimer des esprits et c'est ainsi qu'on les appelait lors des festivals[48].

Si la plupart des masques représentent des esprits, quelques-uns semblent cependant bien être des portraits. C'est le cas de deux masques appartenant à la collection Pinart. Des archéologues ont découvert un masque pouvant être un portrait sur le site d'une tombe préhistorique à Karluk, ce qui indiquerait qu'il avait participé aux rites funéraires d'un défunt[49].

Quels étaient ces esprits que l'on représentait par des masques ? Beaucoup d'entre eux possédaient des caractéristiques d'êtres vivants[50]. Dans la croyance sugpiaq, tout est vivant. Les montagnes, le vent, le moindre poisson, le moindre brin d'herbe sont dotés d'une conscience, ou *sua*, sa « personne », qui peut percevoir les actions humaines. À l'image d'une personne, une *sua* pouvait prendre une forme humaine, parler ou agir avec intelligence, mais elle ne pouvait se réincarner. Lorsqu'elle mourait, c'est l'âme de l'animal (une entité spirituelle distincte de ses caractéristiques humaines) qui, seule, pouvait renaître. Pour les Sugpiat, la réincarnation de l'âme de l'animal était essentielle afin d'assurer le renouvellement du gibier. Ainsi était-il important de prendre soin de l'âme et de la *sua* de chaque animal capturé[51].

En vertu de cette conception, les animaux s'offraient plus volontiers aux personnes qui accomplissaient régulièrement des actes responsables. La femme du chasseur de baleine donnait un verre d'eau à la baleine morte pour la désaltérer avant de la découper[52]. Les gens s'habillaient avec soin,

ornaient leurs vêtements et ne gaspillaient jamais un morceau de fourrure, afin de respecter l'animal dont ils portaient la peau[53]. Les pêcheurs remettaient à l'eau les intestins de saumon pour permettre à l'âme de l'animal de continuer à vivre et à se reproduire[54]. Par leurs actions réfléchies, leur frugalité, l'attention qu'ils portaient à leurs biens et leur respect des rituels, les Sugpiat favorisaient la réincarnation et attendaient le soutien, dans ce processus, des esprits à forme humaine habitant tout animal. En dansant avec les masques, on perpétuait sa propre habilité à chasser. La représentation des esprits animaux permettait aux sculpteurs de faire vivre les êtres qui contrôlaient la vie sur la terre, de communiquer avec eux, et d'assurer la prospérité.

Les danses masquées avaient lieu au cours de certains festivals d'hiver, dédiés au succès des parties de chasse à venir[55]. Les danses étaient exclues d'autres festivals, tels le festival de la Vessie ou la fête des Morts. Ces célébrations avaient lieu au début de l'hiver, après la pêche d'automne du saumon. Elles étaient organisées par la communauté pour célébrer la chasse et elles étaient l'occasion d'évoquer les récents événements, de célébrer les hauts faits accomplis par les ancêtres et de rendre hommage aux esprits. Les danses masquées étaient des cérémonies de chasse. Par la création de ces spectacles, les gens demandaient aux *sua* d'animaux de venir participer aux festivals, ils manifestaient leur reconnaissance pour les bienfaits reçus l'année précédente et assuraient le renouvellement du gibier. En ce sens, les masques remplissaient bien une fonction religieuse. Ils étaient la représentation des esprits et permettaient de communiquer avec le monde de l'invisible, de reconnaître l'interdépendance des personnes et de favoriser la prospérité.

Dans des récits historiques, on mentionne que les festivals d'hiver se déroulaient dans un *qasgiq*, un grand bâtiment construit pour accueillir les activités de la communauté[56]. Propriété d'un membre aisé de la classe supérieure qui en assurait l'entretien, ce *qasgiq* fonctionnait comme la maison des hommes pendant la plus grande partie de l'année, un lieu où l'on réparait les outils, où l'on discutait de politique et où l'on préparait les guerres[57]. À l'automne, en revanche, les membres de la communauté procédaient aux réparations du grand bâtiment rectangulaire, on le remplissait d'herbe fraîchement coupée et on colmatait les trous du toit en prévision des festivals à venir, auxquels tous participaient. Avec l'aide du responsable des rituels, le *kas'aq*[58], un dirigeant de la communauté organisait une réunion à laquelle il pouvait inviter des amis membres de communautés voisines et des membres de son propre village[59]. Pour préparer le *qasgiq*, on l'enfumait et on suspendait à ses chevrons du matériel de chasse. On pouvait suspendre au plafond des armes, des peaux d'animaux et même des modèles réduits d'embarcations, attachés ensemble pour pouvoir les agiter en tirant une corde durant les spectacles et imiter ainsi le mouvement des vagues[60].

À l'occasion de ces festivals, les gens revêtaient leurs plus beaux atours, des parkas richement ornées, et se peignaient le visage. On allait à la rencontre des invités qui arrivaient par bateau et on les escortait jusqu'au rivage, puis jusqu'au *qasgiq*[61]. Là, selon leur statut social, ils étaient assis sur des bancs le long des murs ou par terre, dans une salle éclairée par des lampes à huile[62]. On débutait les festivités par des mets et des jeux, tout en se rendant visite. Puis, on continuait par des danses et par la reconstitution de scènes de chasse. Tandis que des percussionnistes battaient le rythme sur de grands tambours circulaires tendus de peau, un ou plusieurs danseurs munis de masques se présentaient pour raconter une légende[63]. Les danseurs, des hommes nus ou quasiment nus, effectuaient les mouvements chorégraphiques propres au festival et à chaque masque. De nombreuses danses masquées s'accompagnaient de récits et de chants, parfois à plusieurs masques. Ces masques pouvaient illustrer un chant, accompagnant chacun son tour un couplet. Ou bien deux masques différents pouvaient danser ensemble pour raconter un même conte (*cf. Annexes*). Les femmes dansaient elles aussi, alignées, et entonnaient des chants pour les morts[64]. Desson émet l'hypothèse que ces spectacles faisaient partie de la cérémonie de chasse, du fait qu'ils rappelaient l'habileté et le succès des ancêtres et qu'ils en appelaient aux esprits des morts pour leur soutien lors des parties de chasses à venir[65].

Au fur et à mesure que les festivités progressaient, les danses et les chants devenaient plus mystiques, les danseurs commençaient à appeler les esprits animaux en criant et en sifflant pour qu'ils viennent au *qasgiq*.

Le festival durait chaque fois plusieurs jours. L'activité se déroulant de façon ininterrompue, les invités fatigués pouvaient faire des siestes dans le *qasgiq*. À la fin des rassemblements, l'hôte offrait des vêtements, des perles et des mets aux visiteurs[66]. La saison des festivals se poursuivait jusqu'au milieu de l'hiver, jusqu'à ce que les réserves de nourriture de l'été précédent soient épuisées[67]. Le temps des festivals terminé, les masques étaient souvent brûlés, ou cassés et jetés, ou bien conservés dans des grottes éloignées pour préserver les gens de leurs pouvoirs[68].

Les cérémonies hivernales sugpiat et la production d'objets cérémoniels se perpétrèrent longtemps au XIXe siècle, comme le prouvent les notes des observateurs et leurs collections. Voznesenskii assista à des danses masquées sur l'île de Kodiak en 1842, époque où il nota les détails des danses et recueillit les masques ainsi que leurs noms alutiiq[69]. De même, dans ses notes de terrain, Pinart décrit un festival auquel il a assisté dans le village d'Uyak, le 3 février 1872[70]. Il accompagne ses notes de collections d'objets cérémoniels et de textes (*cf. chapitre 4*), et observe que les festivals d'hiver étaient encore connus et avaient lieu, du moins occasionnellement, trente ans après le passage de Voznesenskii. En revanche, les notes de William Fisher, prises dix ans après celles de Pinart, sont moins explicites concernant l'existence des festivals. Fisher, qui vécut à Saint-Paul de 1879 à 1885, recueillit des objets cérémoniels (dont des masques de danse, des maracas, une coiffe décorée de perles et le matériel d'un chaman), mais il n'assista jamais à leur utilisation[71]. Il note, dans sa correspondance, qu'il a entendu parler de spectacles rituels mais qu'ils semblaient rares[72].

Les archives ethnographiques qui ont trait aux pratiques des Russes orthodoxes chez les Sugpiat au XIXe siècle sont plus claires. En 1821, la seconde charte de la Compagnie russo-américaine stipulait que des services religieux et éducatifs soient mis à la disposition des communautés sugpiat sous sa juridiction[73]. Durant les dix années qui suivirent, la compagnie construisit des églises et des chapelles, et mit en place un clergé *(ill. 8)*. Il s'ensuivit un accroissement de l'influence de l'Église. Les Sugpiat avaient intérêt à se convertir au christianisme, tant socialement qu'économiquement. Appartenir à l'Église permettait plus facilement d'accéder au pouvoir et de recevoir une éducation. De plus, les croyances chrétiennes n'entraient pas nécessairement en contradiction avec les croyances sugpiat et pouvaient même aider à comprendre pour quelle raison les esprits sugpiat n'avaient pas réussi, du fait de leur comportement, à empêcher les exactions coloniales[74]. Des éléments importants de l'ancienne religion coexistèrent ainsi avec l'afflux grandissant de l'orthodoxie russe jusqu'aux dernières décennies du xixe siècle. À ce moment-là, les communautés commencèrent également à subir l'influence du protestantisme américain qui, lui, visait explicitement la conversion et l'acculturation[75].

Que sont devenus les masques et les danses masquées ? Les anthropologues émettent l'hypothèse qu'au cours du xixe siècle la tradition des masques sugpiat s'est confondue avec les traditions populaires russes lors de fêtes chrétiennes où ils étaient protégés[76]. Mishler remarque que, bien que les Sugpiat aient abandonné leurs anciens masques, ils n'en perdirent pas la tradition. Ils adaptèrent leur tradition aux célébrations orthodoxes des jours de fête, en particulier le Noël russe et le Nouvel An[77].

Des éléments de cette tradition des masques subsistent, notamment dans les communautés sugpiat de la péninsule de Kenai et de la péninsule d'Alaska. Au moment du Noël russe qui, selon le calendrier julien, dure de la veille de Noël, le 7 janvier, jusqu'à la veille de la Théophanie, le 18 janvier, quelques membres de la communauté sugpiaq participent encore au *maskalataq*, la tradition des masques[78]. Celle-ci se déroule, au début, conjointement avec les nuits de processions des étoiles *(starring)*. Entre le 7 et le 9 janvier, les chorales orthodoxes russes, portant une grande étoile décorée qu'elles font tourner, se rendent de maison en maison dans leurs communautés. En chantant en alutiiq, en slave et en anglais, elles annoncent la naissance de Jésus, puis leurs hôtes leur offrent des rafraîchissements[79]. Dans d'autres communautés, on commence la tradition des masques en fin de journée, lorsque la chorale a fini sa tournée[80]. Chez d'autres encore, la tradition des masques commence le quatrième jour de la fête, quand les chorales sont toutes passées[81]. Des groupes d'hommes et de femmes, entièrement déguisés, passent de maison en maison en dansant pour voir si les gens devinent qui ils sont. Ils s'habillent de vieux vêtements, portent des masques en caoutchouc ou mettent une taie d'oreiller sur la tête, et déguisent leur voix *(ill. 9)*. Si quelqu'un devine qui est sous le masque, la personne doit alors ôter son déguisement et cesser ce jeu pour la soirée[82].

Outre cette tradition des masques qui suit les processions des étoiles à Noël, les Sugpiat participent aux fêtes masquées du Nouvel An. Les gens portent des déguisements qui dissimulent leur identité et se rendent à des fêtes. Autrefois, au cours de celles-ci, on jouait une pièce de théâtre du Nouvel An, appelée, en certains endroits, « danse du diable[83] ». Une personne masquée, représentant la nouvelle année, devait vaincre une autre personne masquée, représentant l'année écoulée, aidée des autres participants de la fête[84].

De la même façon que le port du masque d'antan, le déguisement d'aujourd'hui fait toujours référence au monde du surnaturel, bien que cette association soit à présent liée au monde biblique. Les personnes masquées qui passent dans les maisons après les processions nocturnes des étoiles représentent les soldats du roi Hérode à la recherche de l'Enfant Jésus[85]. Puis, après avoir porté les masques, les participants se purifient, soit en assistant à la messe, soit en nageant dans l'eau froide, soit en prenant un *banya*, le bain de vapeur sugpiaq. Bien que la tradition des masques ne soit plus vraiment pratiquée dans les communautés sugpiat, elle continue néanmoins d'y être connue[86].

Le projet « Giinaquq: Like a Face »

Même si la tradition des masques, par certains aspects, survit en partie au sein des communautés sugpiat de Kodiak, la découverte de la collection de facture classique rassemblée par

Alphonse Pinart a amené l'ouverture d'une phase de recherches sur cette culture. Les artistes sugpiat Helen Simeonoff, Perry Eaton et Sven Haakanson Jr. ont entrepris de traverser l'Atlantique afin d'aller étudier les masques et sont revenus chez eux avec des informations[87]. Haakanson, anthropologue, éducateur et professionnel de musée, a notamment tout de suite pensé que la collection Pinart devait venir à Kodiak. Certes, les photographies des œuvres constituent une source de réflexion pour la communauté sugpiaq, mais il restait persuadé que les images ne pouvaient pas remplacer totalement leur présence réelle. Il savait aussi que le peuple sugpiaq pourrait réellement retrouver l'histoire de ces masques, nés au sein de leur culture, et qu'ainsi ils pourraient faire le lien entre leurs propres connaissances culturelles et cette collection.

En 2001, Haakanson envisagea de faire venir à Kodiak une sélection de masques sugpiat du Château-Musée en vue d'une exposition. À ce moment-là, le musée du Quai-Branly, récemment inauguré, préparait lui aussi une exposition dans laquelle figuraient ces masques. Le conservateur, Emmanuel Désveaux, proposa à Haakanson d'écrire un article pour le catalogue de l'exposition, qui expliciterait quelle signification revêtait cette collection pour les Sugpiat. En échange, il proposait son aide pour préparer une exposition en Alaska[88]. Mais le projet d'exposition ne put aboutir : la France ne l'autorisa pas, par crainte de la loi américaine de protection des objets sacrés d'origine amérindienne, le *Native American Graves Protection and Repatriation Act*, qui pourtant ne s'applique qu'aux États-Unis. L'interprétation erronée de cette loi rendit la tâche plus difficile à Haakanson pour monter une exposition internationale[89].

Sa rencontre fortuite avec l'anthropologue Sarah Froning, qui résidait en France, rouvrit la possibilité d'envisager l'exposition. Lors d'une conférence en Belgique, Haakanson fit un exposé sur la valeur des collections ethnographiques européennes aux yeux des Amérindiens et fit part des difficultés qu'il rencontrait dans l'établissement de relations confiantes qui permettraient la venue de ces objets aux États-Unis. Présente parmi les auditeurs, Froning pensa pouvoir apporter son aide afin de débloquer la situation. Elle venait de terminer son doctorat dont la recherche portait sur les musées français, et elle savait comment il était nécessaire de s'y prendre pour monter un projet susceptible d'être accepté par la Ville de Boulogne-sur-Mer, propriétaire du Château-Musée et de ses collections. Elle se présenta à Haakanson et ils se mirent à travailler ensemble sur une proposition de projet.

Au même moment, à la direction du Château-Musée, une jeune femme en début de carrière, Anne-Claire Laronde, prenait le poste de conservatrice[90]. Elle s'était notamment engagée à rendre les collections plus accessibles aux populations dont elles montraient la culture. Elle écouta attentivement Haakanson qui lui exposa son projet et promit d'apporter son soutien afin de soumettre la proposition à la Ville de Boulogne-sur-Mer.

Tandis que les autorités françaises examinaient à nouveau la possibilité d'une exposition, Haakanson entreprit de faire connaître la collection en Alaska grâce à des photographies. L'Alutiiq Museum, centre culturel et lieu de conservation de la culture sugpiaq de Kodiak, organisait chaque année un programme destiné aux communautés villageoises rurales, appelé « Traveling Traditions[91] » Chaque année, au printemps, le musée montait une petite exposition sur l'art sugpiaq, qui ensuite voyageait parmi les communautés sugpiat pendant les semaines où se tenaient les fêtes culturelles sugpiat. Ces fêtes ont pour but d'explorer et de célébrer les traditions autochtones au sein des écoles locales. Des artistes accompagnent l'exposition et animent un atelier de cinq jours sur le thème de l'art exposé. L'enseignement, intensif et basé sur la pratique, s'adresse aux enfants de primaire et de collège. Étant donné le financement limité de ce programme et le nombre restreint d'artistes possédant les connaissances nécessaires pour pouvoir enseigner la sculpture classique sugpiaq, Haakanson se mit à animer lui-même des ateliers de sculpture de masques. Il utilisait les photos de la collection Pinart pour inspirer les apprentis sculpteurs et constitua ainsi des albums qu'il mit à la disposition des écoles. La création de masques devint le volet le plus populaire du programme

« Traveling Traditions » et les demandes d'ateliers commencèrent à submerger Haakanson. Il comprit alors qu'il lui fallait former une nouvelle génération de sculpteurs aux styles et techniques de fabrication classique afin qu'ils puissent les enseigner à leur tour.

Cependant, Haakanson n'avait toujours pas obtenu l'accord pour l'exposition des masques de Pinart en Alaska. Il savait que cela pourrait prendre des années avant que la situation se débloque. Aussi, en juin 2006, décida-t-il de venir en France avec des sculpteurs sugpiat. Leur voyage fut financé par une aide au développement économique versée par l'Institute for Museum and Library Services. Accompagnés d'Haakanson, neuf artistes sugpiat franchirent les douze mille kilomètres qui les séparaient de Boulogne-sur-Mer pour étudier le travail de leurs ancêtres et assimiler les techniques concernant l'utilisation des outils, la conception, les proportions et le choix des couleurs qu'ils n'avaient pu encore jusqu'alors apprécier dans toute leur finesse sur les quelques photos de la collection [92]. En retour, pour avoir le privilège de participer à ce voyage, les artistes s'engageaient à partager les connaissances nouvellement acquises en enseignant la sculpture à Kodiak et en faisant don d'une œuvre originale à l'Alutiiq Museum [93].

Ce voyage constitua le point de départ de l'exposition « Giinaquq: Like a Face », car il suffit de trois jours aux représentants des deux pays pour comprendre la valeur que chacun d'entre eux attachait à la collection et pour établir une relation basée sur la confiance. Les représentants officiels français découvrirent les liens émotionnels profonds qui unissaient les Sugpiat et leurs masques, et ils saisirent l'opportunité d'explorer ainsi de leur côté une culture et son expression artistique. L'image de l'Amérindien préoccupé uniquement par la restitution des objets s'effaça devant la sincérité d'artistes qui manifestaient un grand respect pour ce Français qui avait préservé leur héritage culturel et qui exprimaient leur gratitude envers les personnes qui avaient pris soin de la collection en France. Pour les visiteurs sugpiat, la visite de Boulogne et la découverte de son histoire les aidèrent aussi à découvrir certains aspects du dévouement des

Boulonnais à cette collection. Située à l'entrée de la Manche, à un endroit où l'extrémité nord de la France touche presque la mer du Nord, Boulogne-sur-Mer avait été une place stratégique importante durant la Seconde Guerre mondiale. Les Alliés, qui souhaitaient affaiblir les troupes allemandes d'occupation, détruisirent la ville à 85 % durant cette période. En dépit des dangers que couraient leurs familles et des drames que vivait leur pays à ce moment-là, les membres du personnel du musée sauvèrent la collection. Ils la mirent en sécurité puis, après le conflit, la reconstituèrent. Sans leurs efforts, la collection Pinart n'existerait plus aujourd'hui. Les artistes sugpiat, surtout ceux qui avaient encore eux-mêmes le souvenir des épreuves de la Seconde Guerre mondiale vécues en Alaska, en furent très touchés. Ils constataient que les Français étaient fiers de ces collections qui représentaient aussi un épisode de leur propre histoire nationale. L'hébergement des sculptures sugpiat au Château-Musée prenait ainsi tout son sens.

Au cours de son séjour, Haakanson put téléphoner à Kodiak pour annoncer que lors d'un déjeuner avec le député-maire de Boulogne, ce dernier avait donné son accord pour le prêt : les masques de la collection Pinart pourraient voyager en Alaska… sous peu [94]. On commença immédiatement à planifier. Tout d'abord, l'Alutiiq Museum leva des fonds pour organiser une conférence avec les membres de la communauté, puis le personnel du musée étudia un projet d'exposition qui rassemblerait un groupe d'Anciens, des artistes, des éducateurs, des responsables de la communauté et des professionnels des musées afin qu'ils puissent réfléchir et confronter leurs idées. La réunion se déroula à Kodiak durant deux jours, en janvier 2007, et marqua le point de départ d'une intense période de seize mois de préparatifs et de levée de fonds. Les Français acceptaient de prêter trente-cinq œuvres pour l'exposition : trente-quatre masques et un bol de banquet en forme d'oiseau, le tout pour une durée de neuf mois. L'équipe chargée de la planification fixa la date d'ouverture de l'exposition à la fin mai 2008, ce qui coïncidait avec la cinquantième édition de la Fête annuelle du Crabe organisée par la communauté. L'exposition devait rester quatre mois à Kodiak, avant de rejoindre l'Anchorage Museum, au Rasmuson Center, où elle resterait à nouveau quatre mois avant de revenir en France.

Parallèlement à ces préparatifs, les artistes qui s'étaient rendus en France enseignaient la sculpture des masques et créèrent tous une œuvre originale pour l'Alutiiq Museum *(ill. 10)*. En avant-première à l'ouverture de l'exposition « Giinaquq: Like a Face », et afin de souligner les liens intenses qui existaient entre les collections ethnographiques et les peuples autochtones d'aujourd'hui, l'Alutiiq Museum organisa « Making Faces », une petite exposition qui dévoilait des photos du voyage en France, citait des artistes et montrait des œuvres d'art que cette expérience avait inspirées. Elle attira un nombre de visiteurs inhabituel et fit naître le désir de prendre en compte l'héritage culturel représenté par les masques sugpiat. Les organisateurs de l'exposition avaient prévenu que certaines personnes trouveraient peut-être difficile de parler des masques recueillis par Pinart, ou même de venir les voir, et que le musée devait s'attendre à une forte réaction émotionnelle du public vis-à-vis de ce projet. Cependant, l'ambiance autour de « Making Faces » s'avéra festive, préfigurant celle qui entourerait l'exposition « Giinaquq ».

En avril 2008, une neige mouillée tombait sur l'aéroport de Kodiak lorsqu'atterrit l'avion qui transportait les cinq caisses et la responsable des collections du Château-Musée, Céline Ramio. Ce furent les membres du personnel et les Anciens qui, dans le laboratoire de l'Alutiiq Museum, procédèrent à l'ouverture des caisses. Ils souriaient ou riaient même au fur et à mesure qu'on en dévoilait le contenu : les masques sugpiat. Le vernissage de l'exposition, puis la semaine de manifestations qui s'ensuivit se déroulèrent dans la joie. On organisa une avant-première, réservée aux Anciens, autour d'un thé et de discussions. Des responsables de communautés sugpiat organisèrent un dîner de charité pour lever des fonds destinés à financer des activités pédagogiques. Quatre groupes de danse fêtèrent les masques en montant un spectacle et des centaines d'habitants de Kodiak vinrent visiter l'exposition. Celle-ci souleva l'émotion de nombreuses personnes d'origines différentes et il devint évident que l'on pourrait étudier et célébrer ouvertement les masques sugpiat à Kodiak *(ill. 11)*. Les comportements envers la culture sugpiaq et son héritage spirituel avaient décidément changé !

D'autres témoignages de cette modification d'attitude se firent jour au cours de l'été 2008. Durant l'exposition à Kodiak, un atelier de fabrication de masques à destination des jeunes, intitulé « Future Masters », se déroula sur deux semaines à l'Alutiiq Museum. Les artistes Perry Eaton, Coral Chernof et Sven Haakanson enseignèrent à douze étudiants d'Alaska l'art de sculpter les masques sugpiat à partir des œuvres exposées, qui fournissaient informations et inspiration. Durant douze jours, les adolescents firent émerger, à partir de blocs grossiers d'épicéa de Sitka, des masques de taille réelle, qu'ils gravèrent, peignirent et décorèrent selon la tradition sugpiaq. Des Anciens participaient au projet, aidant chaque stagiaire à composer un chant pour son masque et s'assurant que le processus dans son ensemble se déroulait dans le respect de la tradition. À chacun des masques correspondait une légende en langue alutiiq.

Une image plus complète

Ce catalogue de masques sugpiat, qui proviennent tous de la collection Pinart, prolonge l'exposition « Giinaquq: Like a Face ». Il est destiné à fournir un panorama plus complet de la collection et à servir de base de recherche. Cependant, contrairement à la plupart des publications savantes publiées avant lui[95], il n'a pas pour objectif l'analyse des masques, mais de permettre plutôt de se référer aux œuvres au sein de leur environnement culturel. En tant que tel, ce résultat de recherches s'appuie sur les travaux de Desson, Désveaux et d'autres. En rassemblant ici des notes historiques, des informations sur la culture, des données linguistiques, des détails matériels, des documents d'archives fournis par les musées et des photos de chacun des masques conservés par le Château-Musée et par le musée du Quai-Branly, nous proposons un aperçu complet de cette collection. Nous replaçons enfin cet ensemble exceptionnel d'artefacts religieux sugpiat dans son contexte, celui de la culture autochtone de Kodiak, d'hier et d'aujourd'hui.

Depuis des dizaines d'années, les auteurs universitaires et les conservateurs d'expositions ont eu tendance à considérer les masques comme des exemples d'art amérindien [96] plutôt que comme des archives riches d'informations sur les Sugpiat. Cette attitude est due, en partie, à la distance de douze mille kilomètres et à la durée de cent trente-six ans qui séparaient la collection du peuple d'Alaska, dont elle est l'héritière directe. Les masques conservés en France ne furent connus des Sugpiat qu'au cours des années 1990, d'où l'impossibilité de les interpréter pour les descendants de ceux qui les avaient fabriqués [97].

Cette conception exclusivement artistique est également due au contexte historique. Le peuple sugpiaq demeure l'un des peuples d'Alaska les plus méconnus, en raison notamment des profonds bouleversements culturels qui l'ont affecté et de l'insuffisante documentation concernant ses traditions. Ce peuple a été très fortement marqué par la colonisation occidentale survenue très tôt, à commencer par la conquête russe dans les années 1780, suivie par la domination américaine [98], qui fut brutale et ininterrompue, entraînant la suppression des traditions. Les masques ont quitté le territoire de Kodiak au moment même où les Sugpiat se voyaient confrontés à la culture américaine, qui les poussait sans relâche à l'acculturation en exerçant une forte pression dans les écoles américaines, au sein des traditions religieuses et par les pratiques économiques. Pinart fut l'un des rares anthropologues à entendre des chants sugpiat ou à assister à un festival d'hiver. Il arriva à l'aube d'une mutation culturelle, au moment où les traditions spirituelles, artistiques et linguistiques des Sugpiat allaient être submergées par celles d'une autre culture. Les ethnographes qui se rendirent en Alaska dans les années suivantes ne s'arrêtèrent plus à Kodiak, convaincus que les Sugpiat étaient trop acculturés pour faire l'objet de recherches fructueuses. C'est pourquoi il n'existe aucune ethnographie traditionnelle du peuple sugpiaq de Kodiak [99]. Il n'existe qu'une description systématique du peuple sugpiaq voisin, dans le détroit du Prince-William [100], et cette étude, qui date de 1933, documente la culture sugpiaq cent cinquante ans après la conquête par les Russes.

Il n'est pas surprenant qu'on n'ait pas analysé la collection de masques de Pinart en termes culturels : les chercheurs n'avaient pas accès à des informations fiables sur les traditions sugpiat. Jusqu'à une période récente [101], il fallait chercher ces informations auprès de sources relativement inaccessibles : les Anciens de culture sugpiaq, les sites archéologiques, les manuscrits historiques et les collections de lointains musées. Même les notes de Pinart, rédigées à la main en cinq langues différentes au moins, dont une version phonétique de l'alutiiq, se sont révélées extrêmement difficiles à déchiffrer et à traduire. Cette publication cherche à dénouer cette situation, à créer un ensemble de données qui permettent d'analyser la collection. Ainsi, au fur et à mesure des chapitres, s'ouvrent de nouvelles perspectives qui abordent les origines de la collection, son importance, son contenu et son impact, qui n'a pas cessé, ainsi que sa grande qualité artistique.

Le deuxième chapitre retrace le parcours d'Alphonse Pinart et expose les circonstances qui ont amené un jeune homme français, issu d'un milieu aisé, à se rendre en Alaska pour y recueillir la plus grande collection de masques sugpiat du monde et à la ramener en France. Anne-Claire Laronde, conservatrice du Château-Musée de Boulogne-sur-Mer, étudie les origines familiales de Pinart, ainsi que son éducation et les raisons qui l'ont poussé à étudier les autochtones d'Alaska. Elle relate également, dans le détail, l'histoire de la collection Pinart en France. Cet aspect historique donne sa grande valeur à la collection et montre bien que les objets historiques appartiennent autant au présent qu'au passé. Il souligne aussi combien les valeurs culturelles, les pratiques muséales et même la politique mondiale ont d'impact sur ce qui est transmis aux générations futures. L'essai d'Anne-Claire Laronde met en lumière combien les Français sont fiers d'avoir prodigué leurs soins à cette collection et d'en avoir fait un épisode glorieux de l'histoire de leur pays. Au-delà de la spiritualité sugpiaq, la collection fait partie de l'histoire intellectuelle française et constitue une contribution remarquable de cette nation européenne à la préservation du patrimoine mondial.

Dans le troisième chapitre, l'historien sugpiaq Gordon Pullar revient sur l'année 1872, à l'époque de Pinart, sur ce qu'étaient alors l'île de Kodiak et la vie des Sugpiat. Il évoque le climat politique, économique et social des dix années qui ont suivi le passage de l'Alaska sous l'autorité américaine, et il dépeint les communautés que Pinart a visitées. Le résumé qu'en fait Gordon Pullar évoque les pressions subies chaque jour par la communauté sugpiaq sous la domination du nouveau gouvernement. Il expose, par ailleurs, l'imbrication des traditions autochtones et européennes que Pinart rencontra sur place, et les bouleversements culturels qu'elle annonçait. Bien que l'on ignore comment Pinart s'est procuré les masques de sa collection remarquablement complète, le résumé que nous donne Gordon Pullar dénote le sentiment de marginalité qui se développait dans la culture des Sugpiat, les incitant à se défaire de ces artefacts, témoins de leurs anciennes croyances.

Le quatrième chapitre dresse un panorama de la collection Pinart du Château-Musée. Nous en évaluons l'importance au vu de la façon dont a procédé Pinart pour la réunir, de la qualité des œuvres rassemblées et de la documentation qu'il nous a laissée. Au fil de ce chapitre, l'anthropologue et sculpteur sugpiaq Sven Haakanson nous confie la documentation qu'il a rassemblée sur les soixante-dix-sept masques qui appartiennent aux collections du Château-Musée et du musée du Quai-Branly. Il illustre ces informations par des images détaillées de chacune des œuvres, grâce aux photographies remarquables prises par le sculpteur sugpiaq Will Anderson. Ces photographies, prises sous différents angles, permettent d'appréhender les proportions de chaque masque, la profondeur des traits du visage et l'élaboration des détails, autant que le talent artistique manifeste du graveur.

Enfin, dans le cinquième et dernier chapitre du catalogue, nous abordons le retentissement que connaît la collection Pinart auprès des artistes sugpiat d'aujourd'hui. Le sculpteur sugpiaq Perry Eaton évoque le mouvement de défense du patrimoine culturel de Kodiak et explicite de quelle manière

la découverte de la collection de masques sugpiat de Pinart a contribué à la renaissance de cette culture ainsi qu'à son étude. Par ailleurs, il examine l'influence qu'exercent ces masques sur certains artistes sugpiat et revient sur la signification de ces objets, préservés jusqu'à aujourd'hui et que les artistes contemporains se sont appropriés, qu'ils soient sculpteurs, peintres ou bijoutiers.

À la fin du catalogue, en annexe, nous reprenons des textes alutiiq sélectionnés par Sven Haakanson et Jeff Leer, linguiste, parmi les notes anthropologiques que Pinart a consignées. Le lecteur y découvrira un ensemble de chants, de danses et de légendes associés aux masques. Certains de ces textes concernent des œuvres figurant au chapitre 4, tandis que d'autres ne sont associés à aucun masque connu. Grâce aux traductions des Anciens parlant la langue alutiiq, les chants font revivre les masques, nous rappelant comment les traditions permettent d'établir des liens entre les Sugpiat d'aujourd'hui et les chefs-d'œuvre que réalisaient leurs ancêtres.

Grâce au projet « Giinaquq: Like a Face », les masques de la collection Pinart remplissent à nouveau leur rôle dans la société sugpiaq. Au XXIe siècle, ces soixante-dix-sept visages ne sont plus désormais de simples messagers vers le monde des esprits, ni des objets dont on a honte. Aujourd'hui, ils sont à nouveau des artefacts spirituels que l'on respecte. S'ils ont retrouvé ce rôle important, c'est qu'ils offrent l'opportunité d'étudier le passé, qu'ils permettent de renouer avec les ancêtres, et qu'ils arrivent à élever les esprits et à les inspirer[102]. Cette façon de regarder ces masques, qui évolue avec le temps, est liée à l'image que portent les Sugpiat sur leur culture. Tandis qu'ils commencent à s'ouvrir et à s'intéresser aux savoirs de leurs ancêtres, une collection comme celle de Pinart sert de véritable ambassadeur de leur culture.

Alphonse Pinart n'aurait sans doute jamais imaginé qu'un jour sa collection revêtirait autant d'importance auprès des populations autochtones d'Alaska. Cependant, l'énergie qu'il dut déployer pour constituer un ensemble complet de masques sugpiat, mettre par écrit les chants des masques, les danses et les légendes, puis confier ces trésors à des institutions reconnues, laisse penser qu'il avait compris la valeur historique qu'ils représentaient. Il s'était sans doute rendu compte que la culture sugpiaq était en train de changer et que la tradition des masques allait disparaître. S'il n'avait pas recueilli ces masques, ceux-ci auraient probablement été perdus, volontairement détruits, ou abandonnés jusqu'à leur décomposition. Pour beaucoup, le travail que Pinart a accompli se révèle être un merveilleux cadeau : pour les Français, sa collection est un exemple de réussite intellectuelle et confirme l'engagement de la France dans la protection des arts dans le monde ; pour les Américains, elle constitue un document sur une société autochtone autrefois vaste et florissante mais tombée aujourd'hui dans l'oubli ; pour les habitants des îles Kodiak, elle redonne vie à un épisode oublié de l'histoire de cette région et permet des échanges plus ouverts sur la culture de leur communauté ; pour les Sugpiat, enfin, la collection constitue un témoignage irréfutable que leur culture est là en possession d'un héritage magnifique et complexe. Et dans le livre d'or de l'exposition « Giinaquq », une visiteuse originaire de Kodiak résume ce sentiment par ces simples mots : « Je ressors confortée et admirative. »

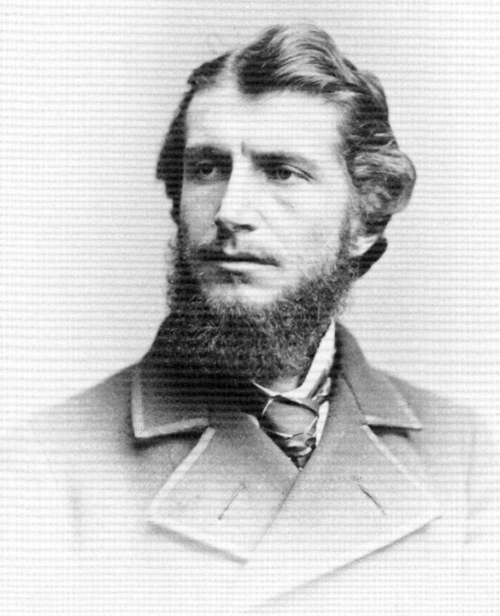

A. G. (signature)
Bancroft Library
San Francisco December 20/75

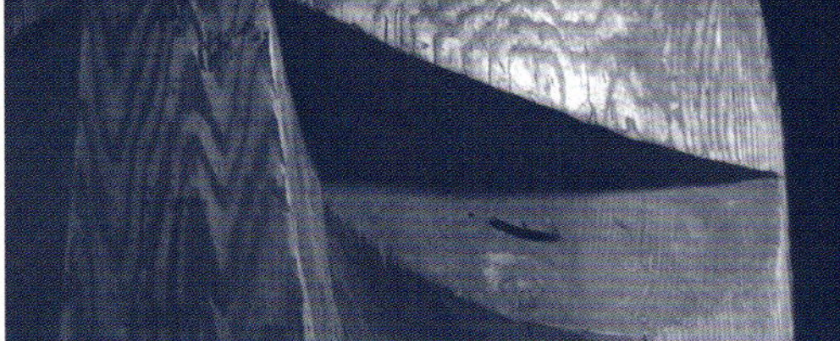

The Atypical History of Collector Alphonse Pinart (1852–1911) and the Sugpiaq Masks of Boulogne-sur-Mer in France

Anne-Claire Laronde

Based on the research of Géraldine Bouterin and Anne-Laure Gerbert
Translated from French by Sarah Froning and Céline Wallace

This article retraces the path of Alphonse Pinart during his collecting foray through the Kodiak archipelago to provide a better understanding of the history of his collections in France, from their first arrival in Paris in 1872 and transfer to Boulogne in 1875. The article draws on archival sources, some of which have never been revealed. It builds on the foundations of the exhibition *Kodiak, Alaska,* organized by the Musée du quai Branly in Paris in 2002, as well as on the research of Evelyne Lot-Falck and Dominique Desson.[103] Following their lead, the Ecole du Louvre and the Château-

Figure 13. Alphonse Pinart.
PHOTOGRAPH COURTESY OF THE BANCROFT LIBRARY.

Illustration 13. Alphonse Pinart.
PHOTOGRAPHIE REPRODUITE AVEC L'AIMABLE AUTORISATION DE LA BANCROFT LIBRARY.

Musée of Boulogne-sur-Mer joined forces to explore the treatment of the collection up to the present day.[104]

Thus will be revealed the early professional activities of the mask collector Alphonse Pinart, an explorer and voyager whose scientific passion for the peoples of the Americas resulted in a collection of Sugpiaq masks that, while typical in the context of its nineteenth-century origin, is totally exceptional by its nature and history.

Alphonse Pinart, Collector

Alphonse Louis Pinart was born in Marquise, in the northern region of France near Boulogne-sur-Mer, in 1852 (Figure 13). He died in Boulogne-Billancourt, near Paris, in 1911. Pinart's family owned the Metallurgic Factories of Marquise, and Alphonse helped run the prosperous business with his two brothers, Prosper and Alexandre, after the death of their father in 1859.[105] Alphonse thus benefited from both financial stability as well as the freedom that allowed him to envision his journeys to the American continent at a young age.

Due to the city's location, facing England and linked to Paris by rail, Boulogne-sur-Mer has long been one of France's ports and seaside resorts, a status it maintains today.[106] In Pinart's time, Boulogne was in the midst of an economic boom, and the city boasted a rich artistic, intellectual, and cultural life. Alphonse, who left at a young age to study in Paris, in the bosom of his father's family, thus grew up in two very stimulating intellectual environments.[107]

Early on, young Alphonse was interested in linguistics. At the Paris Universal Exposition in 1867, where the Pinart Frères Company was exhibiting its products, Alphonse met the Abbé Brasseur de Bourbourg (1814–1874), a fellow northerner who was also an ethnologist.[108] This meeting spurred Alphonse's interest in American languages,[109] an interest that would set him on the path toward the American continent. Alphonse was only fifteen years old at the time. After this meeting, he oriented his studies toward American languages in order to demonstrate, via their comparison with the languages of the Far East, that the Native populations of the Americas originated from Asia. He organized his first voyage in 1869, traveling to California and then Arizona.[110] The following year, he returned to North America, this time to Alaska.

While it is not clear why Alphonse chose to visit Alaska in 1871, it is undeniable that this journey, during which he made the most remarkable collection of his career, left a profound mark on him. All his life, he would attempt to return to this region of the world, albeit without success, as circumstances always deterred him from this central project. His stay in Alaska lasted just over a year, from April 1871 until May 1872.[111] At this time, Alphonse began to correspond regularly with a fellow citizen of Boulogne, Ernest-Théodore Hamy, who, as president of the Society of Americanists in Paris, did much to centralize research in the discipline. Today, this correspondence provides some insight into Alphonse's intentions; notably, in a letter he wrote to Hamy on July 4, 1872, upon his arrival in California, Pinart described the sudden change of heart that had brought him to Alaska: "when I got the idea to take a trip to Russian America I was in Tucson in the interior . . . and I left my entire journey behind me."[112]

The articles published by Pinart upon his return to France and his field notes that he transmitted to the American Hubert Bancroft allow us to understand the different stages of his Alaskan journey with some precision.[113]

The Trip to Alaska

In the spring of 1871, Pinart arrived in the Aleutian Islands at Ounalashka,[114] where he stayed several days before departing on May 31 for Bristol Bay (Figure 14). Thus began a summer spent making short jaunts from bay to bay. Apart from a few photographs, little information exists today about this leg of his journey; however, we do know that Pinart traveled by *qayaq*.[115] He returned to Ounalashka only to leave there again on September 4, 1871, accompanied, it appears, by six Aleuts and headed for the Kodiak archipelago. It would take the crew more than two months to reach their destination.

On the way to Kodiak, Pinart visited villages, dwellings, and Orthodox chapels. He collected geographical information that would later allow him to revise the map of Alaska. However, perhaps the most important element of this Aleutian expedition for the present purpose is that it was the context for Pinart's first collection of objects. During his stay on the island of Ounga, an old man named Lazarus led Pinart into a cave that was used for funerary purposes: the cave of Aknanh. Here, Pinart took masks, arms, instruments, and bones—these masks are today part of the collections of the Château-Musée in Boulogne-sur-Mer.[116] Then he continued his voyage, arriving on November 10, 1871, at the village of St. Paul on the island he called "Kadiak." [117]

During the winter he spent on Kodiak, Pinart undertook his first ethnographic fieldwork, collecting Sugpiaq legends and songs.[118] He also began his first major collection of objects, that of the present-day collection of the Château-Musée of Boulogne-sur-Mer.[119]

On March 24, 1872, Pinart set off to continue his exploration of the archipelago. Accompanied by men whom he called "Aleuts," Pinart left to study the geography of Afognak and

Shouiak islands. He left the archipelago on May 8, headed back toward the Aleutian Islands and Ounalashka, then on to San Francisco, where he arrived on May 21. It was here, during the end of spring 1872, that Pinart wrote the reports he would send to the Smithsonian and met Hubert Howe Bancroft.[120] He returned to France during the summer.[121]

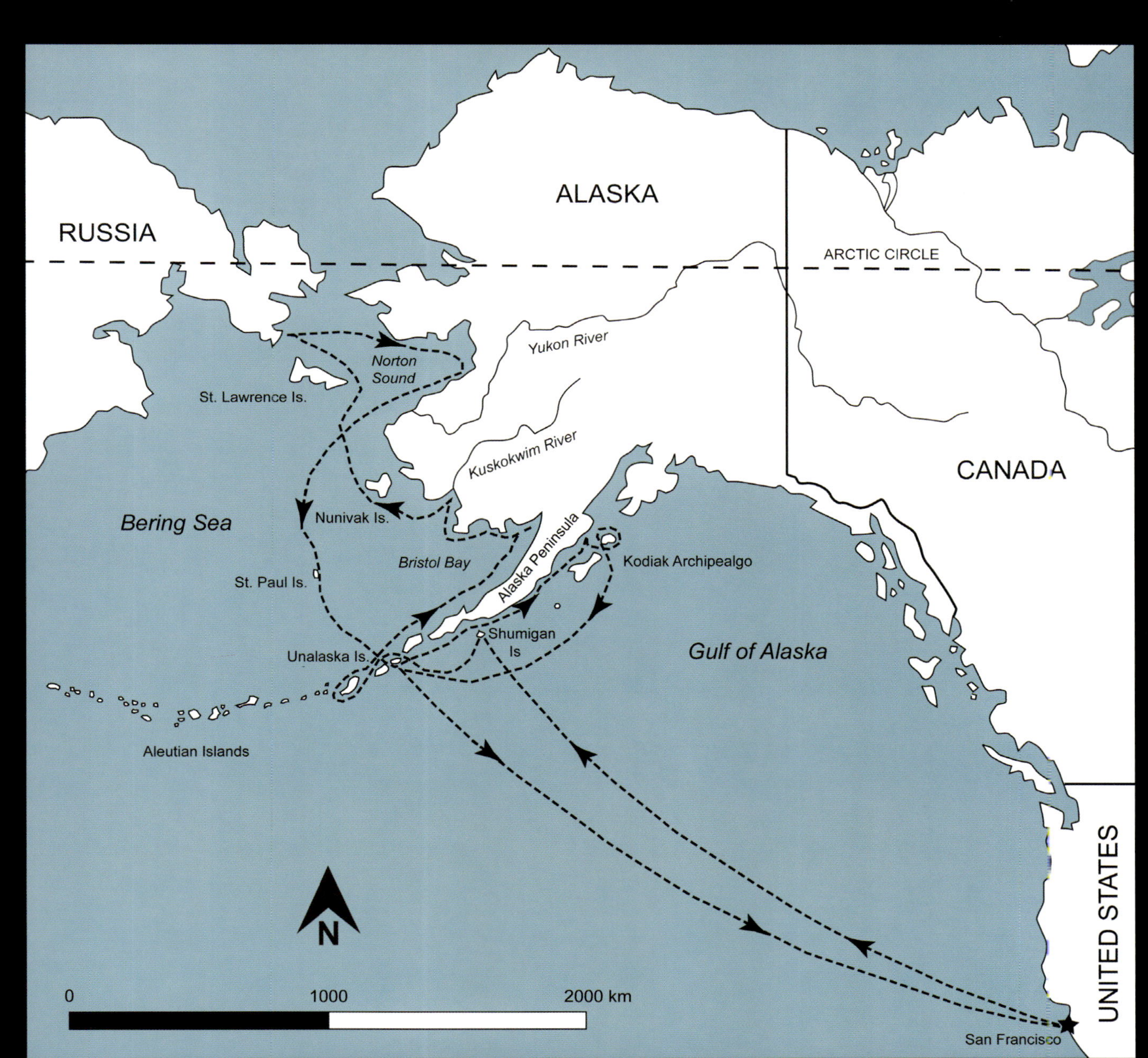

Figure 14. Pinart's Alaska travels.
ADAPTED FROM ROBERT-LAMBLIN 1976.

llustration 14. Les voyages de Pinart en Alaska.
ADAPTÉ DE ROBERT-LAMBLIN, 1976.

Return to France[122]

Back in Paris, Pinart drafted his observations regarding his Alaskan journey and—perhaps more unusual for the time—sought to deepen his knowledge of the objects he had brought back and the cultures he had encountered. He then communicated his observations and knowledge publicly, publishing articles in the journals of scholarly societies in Paris of which he was now a member. With Ernest-Théodore Hamy, he organized the first exhibition of his collection in the anthropology gallery of the Musée national d'histoire naturelle (Natural History Museum) in Paris and visited other European collections from Alaska.[123] Through this transmission of knowledge to his peers, and the public showing of the products of his first voyage, Alphonse Pinart acquired the status of *voyageur-collecteur* in France.

Even though the project to develop a grammar of American languages[124] seemed to be the basis of his career as an explorer, and although he embarked on several voyages after his Alaskan trip, he would never again undertake such a thorough analysis of his field notes as he did upon returning from Kodiak. New constraints were imposed on Pinart following the sudden bankruptcy of the family business in 1877[125] and his entry into the system of missions financed by the Ministry of Public Instruction. He could no longer choose his destinations freely and was obliged to regularly send back reports and crates of collections to Paris. After 1875, Pinart was working much like other French explorers of his time, following instructions that were given to him by the sponsors of his missions. He tried to obtain another mission to Alaska, but for reasons that seemed to have been beyond his control, he never succeeded. Instead, his missions led him to other parts of the American continent, between California and Mexico, with a detour to Oceania.

Apart from the picturesque account of a French marine who accompanied Pinart on one of his voyages, which describes him as an original "jack of all trades,"[126] and aside from his short marriage to American ethnologist Zelia Nuttal,[127] there is little information revealing Pinart's personality aside from what we know regarding the way he conducted his missions.

Two characteristics stand out: first, Pinart's personality was built around the Alaskan experience that he tried in vain to re-create; second, despite his abundant research efforts, Pinart had great trouble completing his projects. In the end, the collection of Aleutian and Sugpiaq masks remains the only ensemble of such number and importance that Pinart would acquire in his entire career in the field.

Pinart's Collection in France[128]

As mentioned previously Pinart's collection was made public as soon as it arrived in France via an exhibition in the anthropology gallery of the Natural History Museum, the only museum in which ethnographic objects could find a place at that time in Paris, and through the catalog that was published soon thereafter.[129] Following this first exposure, the interest that ethnologists, museologists, and artists would take in the collection would only continue to grow.

In a letter to the mayor of Boulogne dated January 3, 1875, Pinart donated the collection to the largest museum of his home region; the mayor readily accepted.[130] In 1875, Hamy served on the board of the Boulogne museum and certainly could have encouraged Pinart to make the donation while simultaneously urging the museum to accept it. However, after founding the Musée d'Ethnographie du Trocadéro in Paris in 1878, Hamy no doubt became torn between his attachment to the Boulogne museum and his commitment to the Paris one.[131] In September 1886, Hamy submitted a request to the Boulogne museum, asking that twelve "exact reproductions" (objects that he thought were copies) in the Pinart collection be transferred to the new Trocadéro. Although the request was eventually granted, it certainly did not happen smoothly.[132]

In this regard Pinart and Hamy's actions, by choosing which museums this collection would go to, resulted in the division of the Pinart collection between the Château-Musée of Boulogne-sur-Mer and the Musée du quai Branly of Paris, the latter having inherited the Trocadéro collections (it now owns seven masks from the Pinart collection).

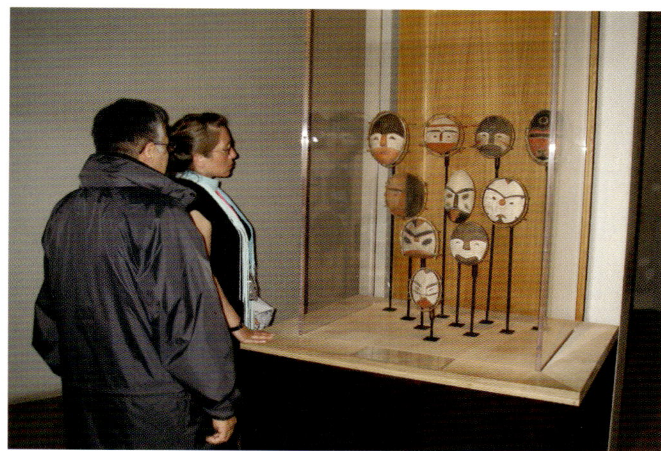

Figure 15. Sugpiaq masks from the Pinart collection on display at the Château-Musée.

Illustration 15. Masques sugpiat de la collection Pinart exposés au Château-Musée de Boulogne-sur-Mer.

This transfer of collections is one reason that it is today impossible to know the exact number of masks Pinart brought back.[133] Several different systems were used to inventory the masks upon their arrival in France, and Pinart himself never provided a precise count—for example, he lists 266 Aleut and Sugpiaq objects for the 1872 exhibition but assigns only 198 inventory numbers. Throughout the twentieth century, the Château-Musée would conduct several different inventories that are evidence of the interest in the collections but also of the incertitude surrounding the collection that persists to this day. In 2008, the collection verification run by the Château-Musée counted 224 objects and fragments from the Pinart collection (Figures 15 and 16).[134]

In addition, in the course of the collection's tumultuous life,[135] the physical appearance of the masks changed, as they lost some of their mobile parts such as feather borders. That the masks have been restored only a few times in the past, and that restorers working on the collection have exercised stringent precautions with regard to the collection,

demonstrates that the masks have been both misunderstood and highly respected. These interventions have for the most part been limited to consolidating masks that were in pieces, and removing dust.[136]

In conclusion, it is worth noting that the French approach to the Pinart collection that came after Pinart and Hamy was more and more aesthetic. One reason for this is perhaps the incomprehension and poor knowledge of the cultural context of the creation of the masks, for Pinart's notes are sparse and were ignored for a long time. In addition, the contemporary Sugpiat were not aware of the collection's existence until recently, starting with the work of ethnologist Dominique Desson in the early 1990s. Today, the Pinart collection has been revealed, studied, and exhibited by the descendents of the masks' creators. As such, the implicit project of Pinart to better understand this collection is finally coming to fruition.

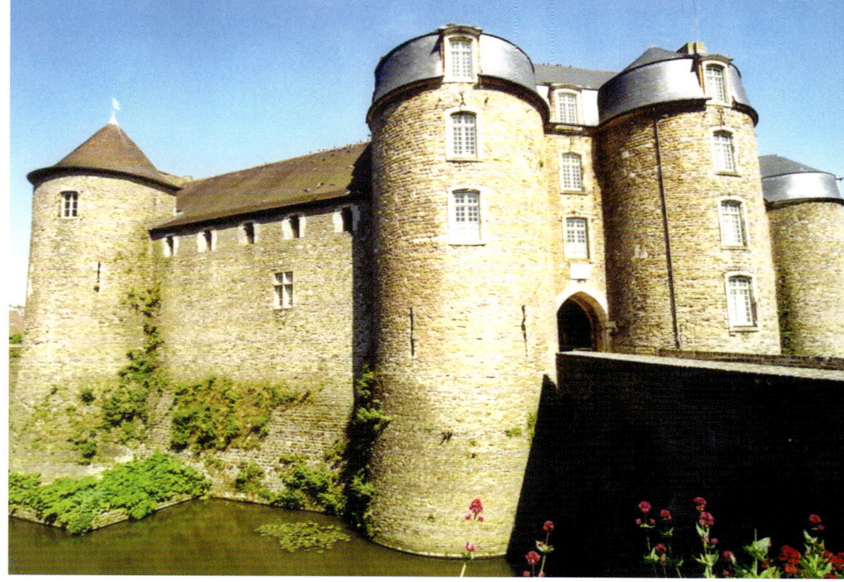

Figure 16. The Château-Musée, Boulogne-sur-Mer, France.

Illustration 16. Le Château-Musée de Boulogne-sur-Mer.

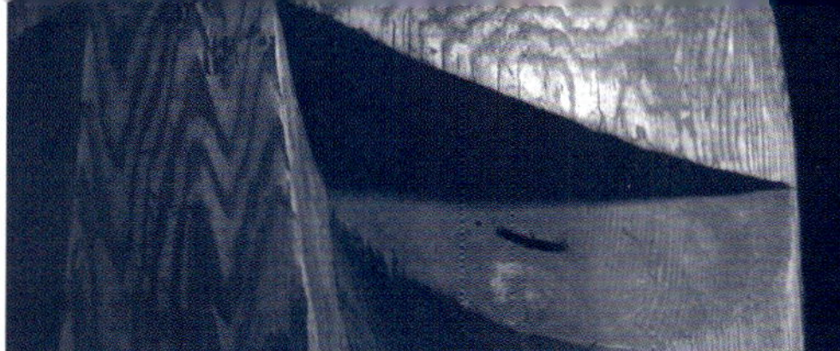

L'histoire atypique du collecteur Alphonse Pinart (1852-1911) et de la collection de masques sugpiat de Boulogne-sur-Mer (France)

Anne-Claire Laronde

Conservatrice du Château-Musée de Boulogne-sur-Mer, d'après les recherches de Géraldine Bouterin et Anne-Laure Gerbert, étudiantes en master I à l'école du Louvre (Paris)

Cet article a pour but de retracer le parcours d'Alphonse Pinart et de sa collecte sur l'archipel de Kodiak et surtout de comprendre quelle a été l'histoire de la collection depuis son arrivée en 1872 à Paris, puis à Boulogne en 1875, en s'appuyant sur des sources archivistiques en partie inédites. Pour cela, à la suite des premiers jalons posés lors de l'exposition « Kodiak, Alaska » organisée par le musée du Quai-Branly à Paris en 2002 et des recherches d'Évelyne Lot-Falck puis de Dominique Desson [103], le musée du Quai-Branly, l'école du Louvre et le Château-Musée de Boulogne sur Mer ont uni leurs forces pour retrouver le devenir de la collection jusqu'à aujourd'hui [104].

Nous découvrons ainsi l'action primordiale du collecteur des masques Alphonse Pinart, explorateur et voyageur qui, par sa passion scientifique envers les peuples du continent américain, a légué cet ensemble de masques sugpiat, une collection ethnologique typique du XIXe siècle de par son contexte de collecte, mais totalement exceptionnelle de par sa nature et de par son histoire.

1. Un explorateur boulonnais qui organise sa vie autour de ses recherches sur le continent américain

Alphonse Louis Pinart (Marquise, 1852-Boulogne-Billancourt, 1911) est issu d'une famille d'industriels du nord de la France, de la région de Boulogne-sur-Mer. Sa famille est propriétaire des Usines métallurgiques de Marquise, entreprise prospère qu'il dirige en partie avec ses deux frères, Prosper et Alexandre Pinart, depuis la mort de leur père en 1859 [105]. Cette situation lui procure une assise financière solide ainsi qu'une certaine liberté d'action qui lui permet d'envisager très tôt des voyages vers le continent américain.

Boulogne-sur-Mer, encore aujourd'hui l'un des plus grands ports français [106], était alors en plein essor économique. Grâce à sa situation en bord de mer, face à l'Angleterre et reliée à Paris par une voie de chemin de fer, Boulogne est aussi devenue l'une des premières et plus importantes stations balnéaires françaises. La vie intellectuelle, artistique et mondaine y est foisonnante. Alphonse Pinart, parti tôt vivre et étudier dans la famille de son père à Paris, évolue donc entre deux milieux intellectuels stimulants[107]. L'intérêt du jeune garçon se porte très tôt sur l'étude de la linguistique. Suite à la rencontre avec l'abbé Brasseur de Bourbourg (1814-1874), l'un de ses compatriotes nordiste, lui aussi ethnologue[108], à l'Exposition universelle de Paris en 1867 où la société Pinart Frères expose le produit de son industrie, Alphonse s'intéresse aux langues américaines[109]. Il a alors quinze ans, et c'est son premier pas vers les cultures du continent américain. Il oriente dès lors l'ensemble de ses études et recherches vers les langues américaines, cherchant à démontrer par leur comparaison avec les langues extrême-orientales, que les populations natives d'Amérique sont originaires d'Asie. Il organise un premier voyage en 1869 : il se rend en Californie, puis en Arizona[110]. L'année suivante, il retourne sur le continent américain, en Alaska.

Si l'on perçoit difficilement les raisons pour lesquelles il choisit dès 1871 de se rendre en Alaska, nous pouvons constater que ce voyage, durant lequel il constitue la collection la plus remarquable de sa carrière, le marque profondément. Toute sa vie, il cherchera à retourner vers cette région du monde, sans succès cependant car une multitude de contingences l'éloigneront toujours de ce projet central. Le séjour alaskien dure d'avril 1871 à mai 1872, soit un an[111]. Pinart commence alors à correspondre régulièrement avec un autre Boulonnais, Ernest-Théodore Hamy, qui, en tant que président de la Société des américanistes, centralise les actions des collecteurs français depuis Paris. Les vestiges de leurs échanges épistolaires permettent aujourd'hui de connaître les intentions d'Alphonse Pinart. C'est notamment à Hamy que Pinart, de retour en Californie, exprime le 4 juillet 1872 son brusque changement de cap qui le mène en Alaska :

> Quand j'ai eu l'idée de faire mon voyage dans l'Amérique russe je me trouvais à Tucson, dans l'intérieur du territoire [...] et j'ai laissé tout mon voyage derrière moi[112].

Les publications de Pinart à son retour en France et les notes de terrain qu'il transmet par la suite à l'Américain Hubert Bancroft apportent une relative précision quant aux différentes étapes de son séjour alaskien[113].

2. Le séjour en Alaska : un circuit en kayak dans les îles Aléoutiennes, puis un hivernage dans l'archipel de Kodiak, qui donneront lieu à des collectes d'objets

Au printemps 1871, Pinart débarque dans les îles Aléoutiennes, à Ounalashka[114], où il séjourne quelques jours avant de partir le 31 mai pour la baie de Bristol. Commence alors un été de courts séjours de baie en baie. Il ressort peu d'information de ce circuit, hormis quelques photographies ; nous savons au moins que Pinart voyageait alors en *kayak*[115]. De retour à Ounalashka, il en repart le 4 septembre 1871, accompagné semble-t-il de six Aléoutes, en direction de l'archipel de Kodiak. Il faudra à cet équipage plus de deux mois pour arriver à destination.

En route pour Kodiak, Pinart visite les villages, les habitations et les chapelles orthodoxes. Il collecte des informations géographiques qui lui permettront par la suite de rectifier la carte de l'Alaska. Ce que nous retenons cependant aujourd'hui de cette expérience aléoutienne est la première collecte d'objets de Pinart. Pendant son séjour sur l'île d'Ounga, un vieil homme aléoute prénommé Lazare le conduit dans une caverne à usage funéraire : la caverne d'Aknanh. Pinart y prélève masques, armes, instruments et ossements (les masques sont aujourd'hui conservés au Château-Musée de Boulogne sur Mer)[116]. Il reprend ensuite le cours de son voyage et arrive le 10 novembre 1871 au village de Saint-Pau[117], sur l'île qu'il nomme « Kadiak ». Durant l'hiver passé à Kodiak, Pinart fait un premier travail de terrain ethnographique : il recueille des légendes et chants sugpiat[118], et procède à sa seconde collecte de grande ampleur, celle de la collection actuelle du Château-musée de Boulogne sur Mer[119].

Le 24 mars 1872, Pinart reprend son exploration de l'archipel. Accompagné d'hommes qu'il dit « Aléoutes », il part étudier la géographie des îles d'Afognak et de Shouiak. Il quitte l'archipel le 8 mai, en direction à nouveau des îles

Aléoutiennes et Ounalashka, puis revient à San Francisco le 21 mai. C'est là, à la fin du printemps, qu'il rédige ses rapports pour l'Institut Smithsonian et qu'il rencontre Hubert Howe Bancroft[120]. Il rentre en France durant l'été[121].

3. L'expérience alaskienne permet à Pinart d'initier une carrière de collecteur[122]

Revenu à Paris, Pinart, rédige des observations de son séjour en Alaska et, fait plus inhabituel, approfondit ses connaissances sur les objets rapportés et les cultures qu'il a rencontrées. Il fait des communications publiques et publie des articles dans le cadre des sociétés de chercheurs parisiennes dont il devient membre. Avec Ernest-Théodore Hamy, il organise une première exposition de sa collection dans la galerie d'Anthropologie du muséum d'Histoire naturelle en 1872 et visite les autres collections européennes portant sur l'Alaska[123]. En portant à la connaissance de ses pairs les produits de ce premier voyage, Alphonse Pinart accède en France au statut de voyageur-collecteur.

Bien que le projet qui sous-tend toute sa carrière d'explorateur semble être de concevoir une grammaire des langues américaines[124], jamais au cours des autres missions qu'il effectuera par la suite il n'approfondira autant son travail de mise en valeur de ses résultats de terrain qu'il ne l'a fait avec son expérience alaskienne. Son entrée dans le système des missions financées par le ministère de l'Instruction publique, puis la brusque faillite de l'entreprise familiale en 1877[125] lui imposent de nouvelles contraintes : il n'est plus tout à fait libre dans ses choix de destination pour ses missions et se doit d'envoyer rapports écrits et collectes d'objets régulièrement à Paris. À partir de 1875, comme bien d'autres explorateurs français de son temps, Pinart travaille donc à partir d'instructions dictées par les instances qui l'envoient en mission. Il tente toujours de retourner en Alaska, mais, pour diverses raisons qui semblent indépendantes de sa volonté, il n'y parvient jamais. Ses missions le mènent dans d'autres parties du continent américain, entre la Californie et le Mexique, avec un détour par l'Océanie.

Outre un pittoresque récit d'un accompagnateur de la marine française qui le dépeint comme un original « touche-à-tout[126] » et le court mariage qu'il fait avec une ethnologue américaine, Zélia Nuttal[127], la personnalité de voyageur de Pinart peut se déceler à travers la façon dont il mène ses missions. Deux caractéristiques semblent se dessiner. Premièrement, Pinart s'est construit autour de son expérience alaskienne, qu'il cherche en vain à renouveler. Deuxièmement, malgré sa démarche foisonnante de recherche d'informations, Pinart a bien du mal à mener à terme ses projets. Toutefois, la collection de masques aléoutiens et sugpiat reste le seul ensemble d'objets aussi important, en nombre et en qualité, qu'il rassemble sur le terrain durant toute sa carrière.

4. Depuis leur arrivée sur le sol français, les masques collectés par Pinart ont suscité un intérêt particulier[128]

Nous avons vu que dès son arrivée, grâce à l'action de Pinart et d'Hamy, la collection est mise en lumière en France. L'ensemble bénéficie rapidement d'une exposition parisienne dans le principal musée à caractère ethnologique, dans la galerie d'Anthropologie du muséum d'Histoire naturelle, et de la publication d'un catalogue dans les mois qui suivent son arrivée sur le sol français[129]. Par la suite, l'intérêt porté par les ethnologues, muséologues et artistes ne faiblira pas.

Dans une lettre du 3 janvier 1875, Pinart fait don de sa collection au plus important musée de sa région natale, le musée de Boulogne. Le maire l'accepte de suite[130]. En 1875, Hamy faisait partie de la commission du musée de Boulogne et, à ce titre, il a peut-être pu encourager Pinart à faire don de sa collection et pousser le musée à l'accepter. Mais, plus tard, après avoir fondé le Musée d'ethnographie du Trocadéro, en 1878, ses loyautés entre le musée de Boulogne et son nouveau musée de Paris seront plus partagées[131]. En septembre 1886, Hamy demande ainsi au musée de Boulogne le transfert de douze « reproductions exactes » dans la collection Pinart (il s'agissait d'objets qu'il pensait être des duplicatas ou des copies) au Trocadéro. Bien que la réponse à sa demande ait été positive, il s'ensuivra nombre de tribulations administratives avant que le transfert finisse par s'effectuer[132].

En conséquence, les actions de Pinart et de Hamy, qui ont choisi eux-mêmes à quels musées appartiendrait cette collection, ont pour résultat actuel la répartition des objets ramenés par Pinart entre le Château-Musée de Boulogne-sur-Mer et le musée du Quai-Branly, héritier actuel des collections du Musée d'ethnographie du Trocadéro, qui possède aujourd'hui sept masques issus de cette collection.

Mais ce transfert est également une des circonstances qui nous empêche de connaître le nombre exact de masques et d'objets rapportés par Pinart[133]. Dès son retour en France, différents systèmes d'inventaires sont utilisés et Pinart lui-même ne donne jamais un nombre exact d'objets (ainsi, il dénombre 266 objets aléoutes et sugpiat exposés en 1872, auxquels il attribue 198 numéros). Tout au long du XXe siècle, différents inventaires se sont succédé au musée de Boulogne-sur-Mer : leur nombre témoigne à la fois de l'intérêt porté à ces objets, mais également de l'incertitude dans la démarche d'étude à adopter à leur égard. En 2008, le récolement effectué par le Château-Musée dénombre 224 objets et fragments provenant de la collection Pinart[134].

Aussi, au fil de leur histoire somme toute mouvementée[135], les masques ont pour certains changé d'aspect, perdant certaines de leurs parties mobiles (notamment les ramures de plumes). Pour autant, le faible nombre de restaurations dans le passé et les précautions affichées par les restaurateurs à leur égard démontrent l'incompréhension mais aussi le respect qui leur a été accordé. La plupart de ces interventions se limitent ainsi à des consolidations et des dépoussiérages[136].

On note que le regard français porté sur la collection Pinart, après l'action de leur collecteur et de Hamy, va devenir toujours plus esthétisant. L'une des raisons en est peut-être l'incompréhension et la méconnaissance croissantes du contexte culturel de création des masques, car les écrits de Pinart, épars, ont longtemps été oubliés et l'existence de la collection a longtemps été elle-même ignorée par la culture sugpiat contemporaine. Ce fait ayant été réparé par l'action de l'ethnologue Dominique Desson au début des années 1990, les objets de la collection Pinart sont désormais éclairés d'un nouveau jour, étant étudiés et exposés par les héritiers de ceux qui les ont créés. Le projet implicite de Pinart de comprendre au mieux cette collection semble donc enfin pouvoir se réaliser.

CHAPTER THREE

Historical Ethnography of Nineteenth-Century Kodiak Villages

Gordon L. Pullar

When Alphonse Pinart arrived on Kodiak Island in November of 1871, Kodiak Sugpiaq villages were undergoing dramatic changes, adjusting to new ways of living brought by the Americans. The Treaty of Cession had been ratified by the United States just over four years earlier, on May 28, 1867, transferring control of Alaska from Russia to the United States.[137] We know that Pinart visited the villages of Kodiak (*Sun'aq/Pavlovsk Gavan*, "Paul's Harbor"), Afognak (*Ag'uaneq/Derevnia*), Eagle Harbor (*Igatsk/ Orlova*), and Karluk (*Kal'uq*), but it is also highly likely that he visited the villages of Woody Island (*Tangirnaq/ Ostrov Leisnoi*) and Ouzinkie (*Uusenkaaq/Seleniye Ruskiy I Kreolovy*) (Figure 17).[138] It has been reported that Pinart visited other villages as well. These included Katmai, Starie Gavan, Kattani (near Afognak village), Uyak, Kiliuda, and Selezoffsky (Little Afognak).[139]

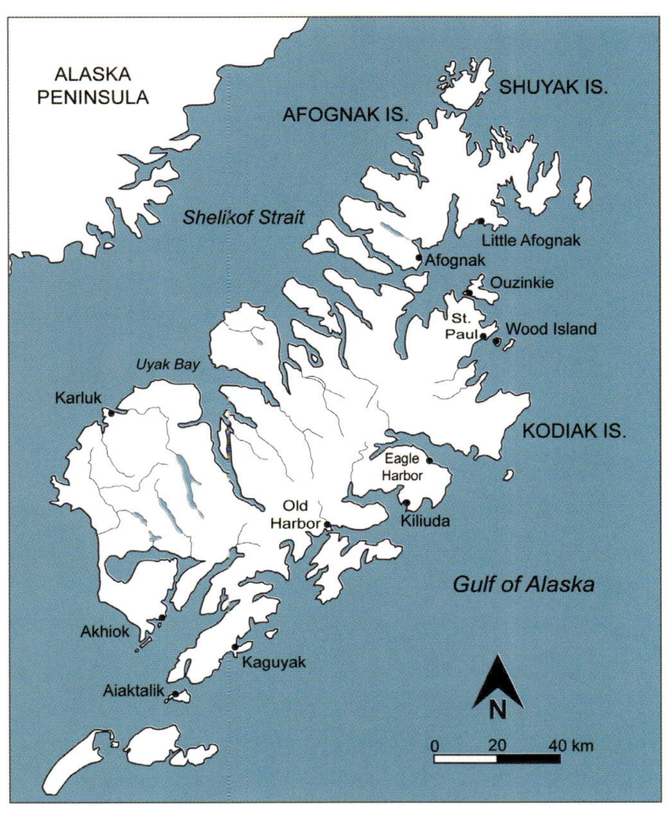

Figure 17. Kodiak archipelago communities of the late nineteenth century.

ADAPTED FROM LUEHRMANN 2008:48.

Illustration 17. Les communautés peuplant l'archipel de Kodiak à la fin du xixe siècle.

ADAPTÉ DE LUEHRMANN 2008, P. 48.

By 1868, there were fewer than five hundred Russians remaining in all of Alaska, many of whom were headed to their homeland.[140] Consequently, there were few full-blooded ethnic Russians on Kodiak Island by 1871.[141] There were, however, well over a thousand Creoles, who were usually people of mixed Russian and Sugpiaq blood.[142] This does not complete the picture, though, as some Creoles had no Russian blood and some had a mixture of Siberian Native and Sugpiaq blood.[143] There were more than twelve hundred Sugpiat (or "Aleuts" as they were listed) in the Kodiak archipelago in 1870.[144] Oleksa points out that, by 1867, 90 percent of the residents of the town of Kodiak had Native blood. "As generations passed, all or most Native Alaskans in an area came to be Creole, although their genetic relationship to any Caucasian ancestor may have been slight, or even nonexistent."[145]

By 1867, the Kodiak Sugpiaq population (including Creoles) was primarily bicultural. The Sugpiat ate traditional foods such as dried and boiled fish, sea mammals, and wild plants and spoke their own language, but most also spoke Russian and ate Russian foods such as *pirok, piroshki, borsch, blini*, and breads. Imported fruits such as apples, pears, and grapes were also well known to everyone.[146] Many Sugpiat were engaging in agricultural activities introduced by the Russians and now grew such foods as potatoes, turnips, and rutabagas.[147] Whale hunting still occupied an important place in the Sugpiaq culture, and the first whale of the summer was a festive event that drew residents from all the surrounding villages to help butcher it.[148] While living off the land and sea they also participated in wage labor in various Russian-American Company enterprises, most notably sea otter hunting.[149]

A complex social system, introduced decades earlier, also blended traditional ways with Russian customs. Pinart would have seen Kodiak Sugpiaq villages with traditional, semisubterranean sod houses called *ciqlluaq* (*barabara* in Russian) alongside log houses built in the Russian style (Figure 18). He would have heard people speaking both in the Native language, *Sugt'stun*,[150] and in Russian. However, it is doubtful he would have heard English spoken by anyone other than the newly arrived Americans. The Russian language and Russian customs were already firmly in place on Kodiak with the introduction of formal education nearly a century earlier in the 1790s.[151] Bilingual schools were the norm in Kodiak-area villages by the nineteenth century, with books published in the Sugpiaq language as well as Slavonic.[152]

While living under Russian rule, the Sugpiat were not allowed to wear or own clothing made of sea otter, ground squirrel, bears, or other furs considered valuable to the Russians.[153] This rule necessitated that they either wear Russian-style clothing or use other materials. For parkas, previously made from sea otter and ground squirrel skins, bird skins were substituted. Cormorant skins were the most popular for a fine parka but were very time-consuming to make, as it took forty birds to make one garment.[154] The most valuable of the parkas were made from just the necks of the cormorant, and it took from 150 to 200 birds to make a single parka.[155] The Russian-American Company eventually allowed garments to be made from ground squirrel skins, and these would have been visible during Pinart's visit to Kodiak Island.[156] When the Finn Heinrich Johann Holmberg visited Kodiak in 1851, he noted traditional-style parkas decorated with "red wool and strips of cloth" as well as European-style clothing consisting of calico men's shirts, cloth pants, and bright-colored vests and women's chintz dresses.[157] Holmberg described the process of preparing the bird skins for parkas:

> After the birds were carefully skinned, the women sucked out the fatty parts of the skins and left them standing for a while, covered in soured fish roe. Later, the skins were cleaned and kneaded by hand till completely dry. Instead of fish roe, urine often was employed, in which the skins had to lie two or three days. The hides thus prepared were sewed together with a needle (made from bones of smaller birds) and thread, which was painfully made from grated, dried whale sinews twisted together.[158]

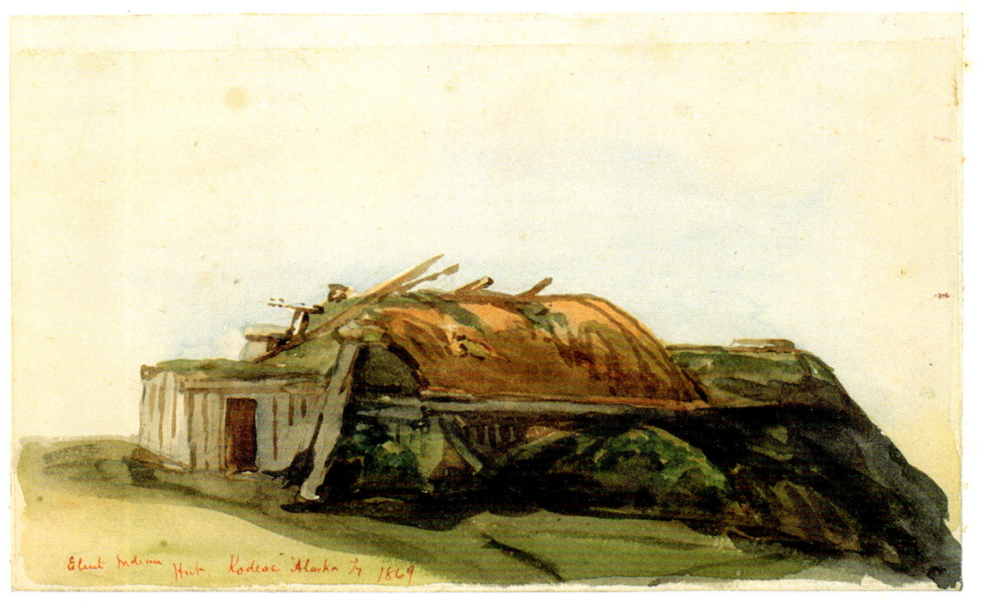

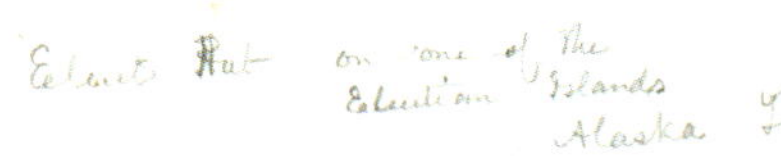

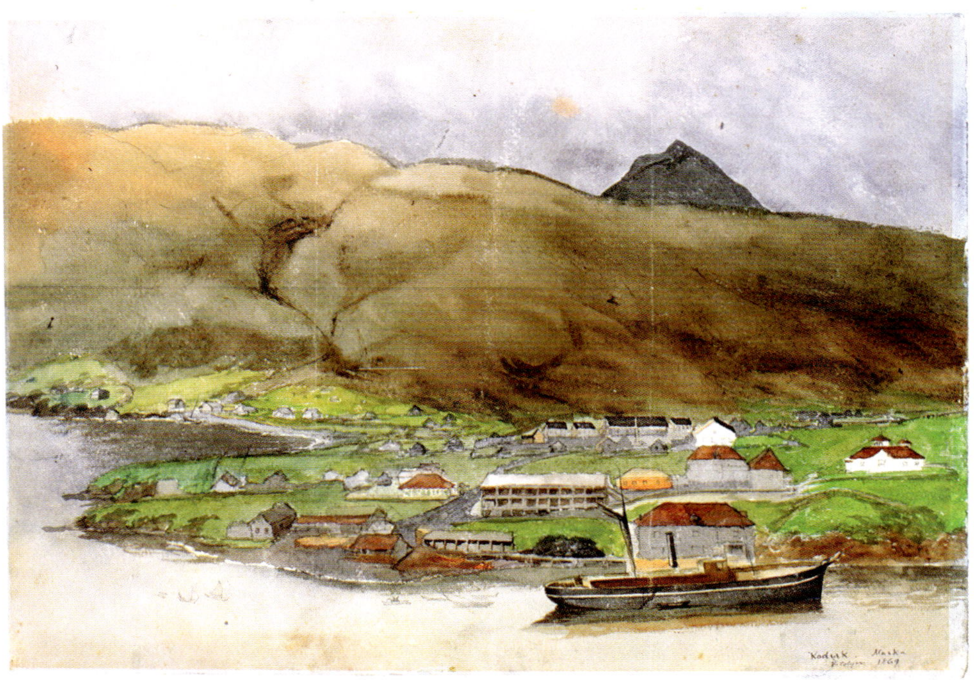

Figure 18. Sugpiaq sod house, 1869. Watercolor by Vincent Colyer.

Figure 19. Kodiak in 1869. Watercolor by Vincent Colyer.

COURTESY OF THE BEINECKE RARE BOOK AND MANUSCRIPT LIBRARY, YALE UNIVERSITY.

Illustration 18. Maison sugpiaq traditionnelle recouverte de terre et d'herbes, 1869. Aquarelle de Vincent Colyer.

Illustration 19. Kodiak en 1869. Aquarelle de Vincent Colyer.

AVEC L'AIMABLE AUTORISATION DE LA BEINECKE RARE BOOK AND MANUSCRIPT LIBRARY, YALE UNIVERSITY.

Most Sugpiat were active members of the Russian Orthodox Church, and some young men joined the priesthood.[159] Other Sugpiat still practiced their traditional religion and spirituality recognizing their "supreme being," *Llam Sua*,[160] or followed both religions. This is not surprising, as some scholars, such as Russian Orthodox priest Michael Oleksa, believe that the primary reason that the Sugpiat adopted Russian Orthodoxy was that its tenets paralleled their traditional religious beliefs.[161] "The structures of precontact worldview and the Orthodox Christian vision paralleled and complemented each other in many significant ways," Oleksa said.[162]

Traditional ceremonies involving dances and the use of carved wooden masks were still being performed in Pinart's day, but it is unlikely that they were as prominent as they had been in the early part of the nineteenth century when a young Russian naval lieutenant, Gavril Davydov, visited Woody Island village. Although Davydov did not understand the meanings of the ceremonies he witnessed, he described them in great detail and referred to "magnificent masks" used in dances.[163]

The first Americans to arrive on Kodiak Island after the United States took possession of Alaska were U.S. Army troops and Navy vessels cruising the coasts (Figure 19). The military force sailed from San Francisco for Kodiak in May of 1868 and arrived at Kodiak after twenty-six days at sea.[164] The expedition consisted of a company of army troops, some civilian employees, and a Smithsonian naturalist.[165]

When Pinart arrived in Alaska, Native people, including the Sugpiat, were about to join a whole new political system with specific federal policies regarding interaction with Native Americans. In 1867, the year of the U.S. takeover of Alaska, the U.S. Congress was debating whether the United States should be "feeding or fighting" the Indians.[166] In 1871, Congress passed a law ending treaty making between the United States and American Indian nations.[167] Although the Treaty of Cession covered many areas, it was vague concerning the U.S. government's relationship with Alaska Natives.[168] Even though they had been classified as

"truly dependent" by the Russian-American Company, the Sugpiat of Kodiak Island were at least semi-self-governing at the village level at the time of the transfer. The Sugpiat lived in a system that mixed traditional ways with the needs of the company and the structure of the Russian Orthodox Church.[169]

Pinart witnessed the Kodiak Sugpiat in the early stages of transition to American ways and may have sensed that the traditional masks and other representations of Sugpiaq culture were about to be lost. This may have inspired him to gather as much as he could to save for future generations to learn from. It is doubtful, however, that he could have imagined that more than 135 years in the future the items he collected would play a significant role in the revitalization of Sugpiaq culture and inspire Sugpiaq artists to resurrect the art of mask carving and making of other traditional items. There were some things that were impossible to preserve, however, such as the Sugpiaq women's practice of tattooing their chins. Only Elder women still had tattoos during the time of Pinart's visit.[170]

The first Americans to live in Kodiak were mostly members of the U.S. military. Before long, new outsiders, especially individuals from the Scandinavian countries, began to arrive to seek both adventure and fortune in the newly opened Alaska. In 1874, shortly after Pinart's visit, a group of Icelanders, with U.S. government help and approval, visited Kodiak and considered establishing a colony but quickly changed their minds when a measles epidemic broke out among the Sugpiaq population.[171]

Economy

After living many millennia in a subsistence lifestyle, hunting and gathering, and trading with other groups, the Kodiak Sugpiat were introduced to capitalism with the arrival of the Russian *promyshlenniki*, or fur traders. They were at first enslaved but then forced to work for "pay," which usually took the form of food, clothing, or other items.[172] According to Davydov:

The Russian-American Company does not buy animals from the Koniagas or other peoples subject to it, but sends them off hunting on long journeys far away. It rarely pays them in European goods (i.e. tobacco, axes, knives, needles, nankeens, varicolored stones, silks or other trinkets). In the main they are rewarded with evrashka or birdskin parkas, kamleikas, seal skins, nets, various objects woven from gut and even sometimes with fat. All these are used by the wives and children of the Americans (Natives) who hunt animals, so that the payment for a pelt is very small.[173]

The years of Russian rule on Kodiak Island had not been administered directly by the Russian government but rather by the Russian-American Company with government authorization. The Russian-American Company was a private enterprise whose managers were determined to make the most profit, whatever the social cost to the people. In a mixture of government and private business, the Russian government assigned the Russian-American Company "ever-increasing responsibility for social service duties in return for the sole right to exploit Alaska's economic resources. The company was obligated to maintain the church, schools, and medical services."[174] The Alaska operations of the Russian-American Company grew such that by the 1860s there were thirty-two subsidiary enterprises, including such varied operations as sawmills, coal mines, brick-making complexes, and shipbuilding.[175] All of the company's ventures required labor that came primarily from the Sugpiat and Creoles.

One of the businesses in operation during the time of Pinart's visit was the Woody Island Ice Company, an operation that employed Sugpiat, Creoles, and Russians to cut and pack freshwater ice for shipment to California. The Woody Island Ice Company had been in operation in Woody Island village for twenty-eight years prior to the 1867 transfer, and had been shipping ice to San Francisco since 1852. Two ice houses were built there, each capable of holding three thousand tons of ice.[176] The ice was cut with a horse-powered saw and transported by way of a wooden plume from the lake above the village down to the pier, where it was stored in the ice houses and later loaded onto sailing ships at the wharf.[177] The ice company workers were mostly Sugpiat and Creoles who worked for one ruble per day with food and vodka.[178] The regular company workers, primarily Russians, were paid an annual salary of 350 to 500 rubles and a daily issue of a glass of vodka.[179]

With the 1849 gold rush in California came a great demand for ice and a new market for the Woody Island Ice Company. Until 1852, the ice came to California from Boston around Cape Horn at a price of $75 per ton.[180] Due to the much shorter shipping distance, ice was first sent from Sitka to San Francisco at a price of $35 per ton; however, mild winters caused the ice quality to be inconsistent and unsatisfactory.[181] Ice was then produced at Woody Island, where the production capacity was between five thousand and six thousand tons per year. Ice from this more dependable source could be sent to San Francisco and sold for $25 per ton.[182] There were years, however, when mild winters hampered the production of ice even at Woody Island.[183] Throughout the life of the ice company labor was provided primarily by Creoles and Sugpiat and the jobs provided an important source of income, even if modest in size.

Historian Stephen Watrous described the role of the Russian-American Company in the colonization of Alaska:

> The Russian-American Company, like other European joint-stock companies (Dutch East India Company, Hudson's Bay Company, Northwest Fur Company, British East and West India Companies), was given tasks to perform that went beyond the realm of trade. It was authorized to use the coastal areas of North America south to 55° north latitude (near Alaska's current southern boundary) and to explore and colonize unoccupied lands. It was also given the right to exploit surface and mineral resources in the areas settled by Russians. In effect, it became the "right arm" of the Russian government in the

American hemisphere. Members of the Tsar's family, the court nobility, and high officialdom held shares in the Company, and it was understood that the Company would henceforth control all Russian exploration, trade, and settlement in North America.[184]

Immediately after taking control of Kodiak Island in 1784 by way of the massacre of hundreds of Sugpiat at *Awa'uq* (Refuge Rock),[185] Russian merchant Grigorii Shelikhov took children of Sugpiaq leaders as hostages so he could control them and thus all of the people.[186] He needed the local Sugpiaq population to hunt and gather sea otter pelts for him while not being a military threat. His objective was to collect as many furs as possible, especially sea otter pelts, and to develop a monopoly on the fur hunting grounds in Alaska.[187] Shelikhov was brutal in his subjugation of the Sugpiat and was clear to his subordinates on what he expected from them.[188] Shelikhov, in written instructions to his chief manager, Konstantin Alekseevich Samoilov, in 1786, said:

> When the abovementioned natives are subjugated, every one of them must be told that people who are loyal and reliable will prosper under the rule of our Empress, but that all rebels will be totally exterminated by Her strong hand . . . They must be told to stop wars and robbery among themselves, murderous plotting against the Russians, and all their inconstancy and disobedience.[189]

After the American takeover, entrepreneurs and others seeking economic benefit arrived on Kodiak Island. As the waters around Kodiak had an abundance of salmon, fish soon became the focus of economic ventures. The Russian-American Company had tried unsuccessfully to market salted salmon packed in barrels prior to the U.S. takeover.[190] By 1870, at least two American companies had begun to market salt salmon, and their activities provided some employment opportunities for Kodiak Sugpiat.[191]

The backs of some of the dried salmon became a staple food for Sugpiaq sea otter hunters working for the Alaska Commercial Company.[192] The commercial canned-salmon industry would become a huge industry on Kodiak Island, but it would not take off until the 1880s, a decade after Pinart's visit to the region.[193]

The Alaska Commercial Company, established in 1868 as a consortium of San Francisco businessmen, largely took over Russian-American Company activities on Kodiak Island after the transfer of Russian interests to the United States.[194] While it did not have the same monopoly status or power over Alaskan people, the Alaska Commercial Company assumed the responsibility of providing schools and medical services to some communities.[195] This company established trading posts and stores in Kodiak Island villages, and many believed that it had more power in Alaskan affairs than the military during this time period.[196] Inspection of the Alaska Commercial Company records from this time period reveals that the Sugpiat continued to consume many of the Western-style foods and goods that they had become accustomed to under Russian rule. These included such items as pilot bread, candles, tobacco, suspenders, and hip boots.[197] Other new items appeared in ACC stores as well. There were the first cartridge-loaded guns (Henry .44s) and an increase in bottled and canned foods, patent medicines, ceramics, and new types of beads.[198]

Sea Otter Hunting

The most common "job" for Sugpiaq men in the mid-nineteenth century was that of sea otter hunter. The Russian-American Company maintained an active sea otter hunting business throughout its years of Alaskan operations. In the Kodiak area, sea otter hunting parties were composed of "details" made up of ten "baidarkas" or *qayaqs* (Figure 20). As an example of the size of this operation, ninety-two *qayaqs*, or nine details, were sent out to hunt sea otters in the "Kodiak Department" in 1861. Each detail was under the command of an elder or *zakashchik* (overseer). The entire hunting party fell under the leadership of the chief *baidarsh-chik* or "hunt leader."[199] Because of the often-violent weather in the Kodiak Island area, this hunting generally took place in the summertime. This took men away from their communities at the time of year they should have been gathering their own subsistence foods for their families. It was a difficult time for entire families as the Sugpiaq women were expected to perform work for the benefit of the company as well. They sewed such items as *qayaq* covers and waterproof clothing as a "part of the commodity production organized by the companies."[200] The majority of traditional ceremonies took place during the winter months, making it possible for the hunters to be home for those festivities.

Following the takeover of the Russian-American Company operations in Alaska by the Alaska Commercial Company, the sea otter hunting continued. By the time of the U.S. takeover, the Sugpiat required at least some cash

Figure 20. Men in *qayaqs*, ca. 1900.

PHOTOGRAPH COURTESY OF THE CAROLYN ERSKINE COLLECTION, KODIAK HISTORICAL SOCIETY, BARANOV MUSEUM.

Illustration 20. Des hommes à bord de *qayaqs*, vers 1900.

PHOTOGRAPHIE REPRODUITE AVEC L'AIMABLE AUTORISATION DE CAROLYN ERSKINE COLLECTION, KODIAK HISTORICAL SOCIETY, BARANOV MUSEUM.

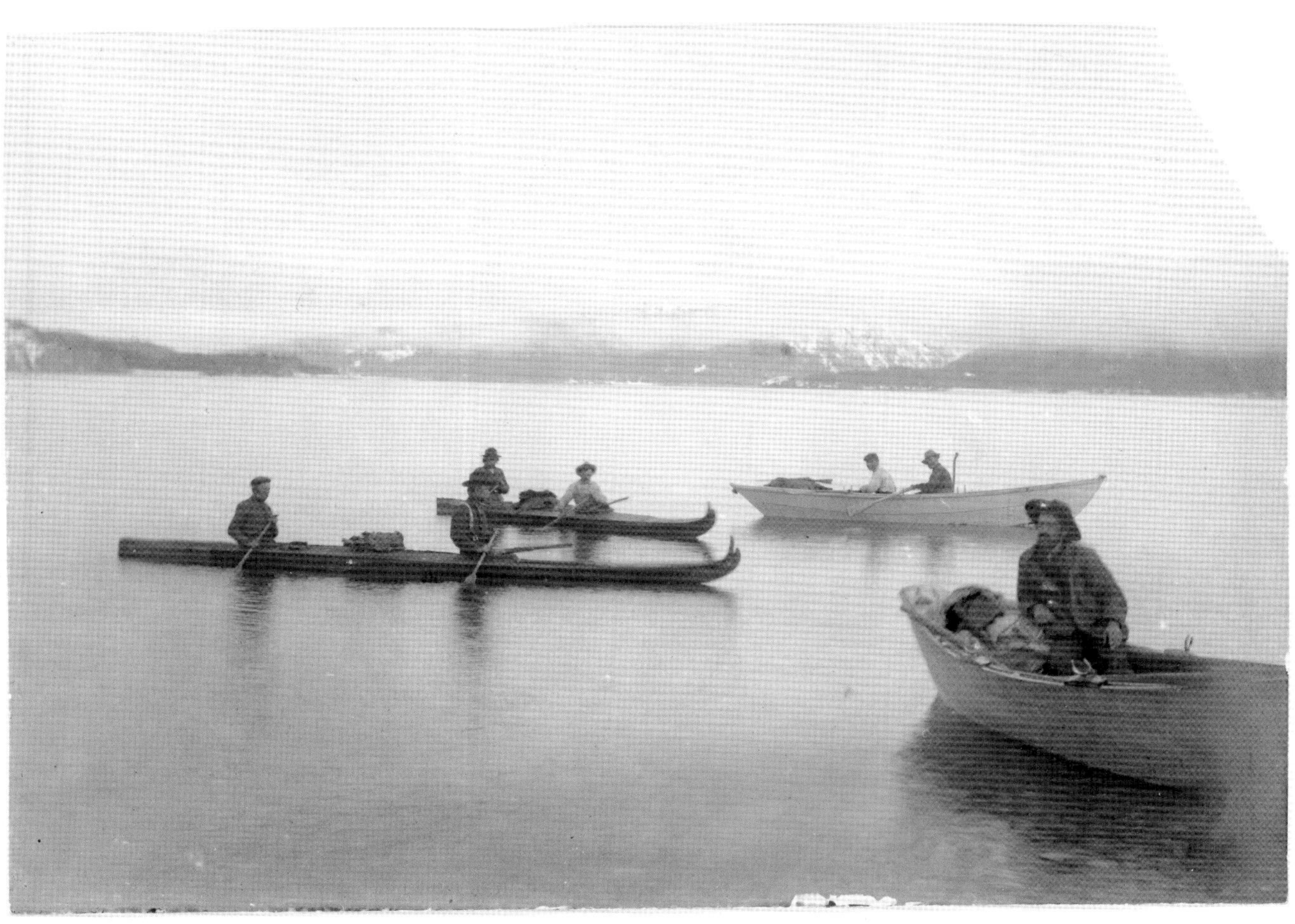

income in order to survive, and thus the Sugpiaq men continued working in their sea otter hunting jobs. The hunters loaded their *qayaqs* on board Alaska Commercial Company schooners, which took them great distances to more abundant sea otter hunting areas. Not all sea otter hunters were dependent on the schooners, however, and some worked independently. For a time, the pay was good, as the company bought sea otter pelts from the hunters for $80 to $100 each through the 1880s. Without regulation, however, a free-for-all atmosphere developed, and by the 1890s the stocks were greatly depleted.[201] Though the sea otter population was diminished, hunting continued. Even as late as the taking of the 1900 census, sea otter hunting parties from the villages of Afognak and Wood Island were counted while on an Alaska Commercial Company ship docked at Kodiak.

Social Structure

During the years following the Treaty of Cession, many social changes took place in Kodiak Sugpiaq villages. Russian colonists had been in political control of the Kodiak archipelago for more than eighty years, mandating the social and political structure of the Sugpiat. The period of Russian fur trader atrocities against the Sugpiat essentially ended in 1818 with the reforms by the new governor of Alaska, naval captain Leontii Hagemeister.[202] It is likely, however, that the psychological trauma wrought on the Sugpiat by the ruthless Russian conquest of Kodiak Island was still being felt barely fifty years later, even if unidentified. Now, for the first time in over eight decades, the Sugpiat had the freedom to decide for themselves how they wanted to organize. Were they too acculturated to Russian ways to fully return to traditional ways? That seems likely, but as a strong, resilient, and adaptive people who had lived on Kodiak Island for seventy-five hundred years, they would adapt again, finding ways to combine parts of three cultures into a workable system.

One foundation of the Russian system was a rigid division of social classes. The 1841 Third Charter of the Russian-American Company mandated this social order. Black says,

"In this third charter, the government recognized five social categories under colonial administration: contract employees, colonial citizens (voluntary settlers), creoles, settled foreigners (Natives, *inorodtsy*), and foreign settlers of religious faiths other than Orthodox not fully dependent on the company (*inovertsy*)."[203] None of these categories was familiar to or recognized by the newly arrived Americans.

The category that caused much confusion for the Americans was that of "Creole." Creoles were initially the children of Russian *promyshlenniki* ("frontiersmen") and Alaska Native mothers.[204] Charters of the Russian-American Company further defined this designation, making it possible for a Sugpiaq to become a "Creole" without having any Russian blood.[205] "By 1821, all Native Alaskans who pledged their political allegiance to the tsar and became thereby 'naturalized citizens' were considered 'Creoles,'" explains archpriest Michael J. Oleksa.[206] "Creoles combined elements of two cultures, often spoke two languages, and later could read and write two or more, but were not necessarily biologically 'mixed.' To be a Creole was more a matter of the spirit, a state of mind, a question of self identity," Oleksa adds.[207] He also says, "A Creole was not only a person of mixed Russian-Native ancestry, but any Native who was a permanent resident of a town. It was a social rather than a racial designation."[208] Well over a third of the population of Kodiak Island were Creoles in 1870, and the only Russians remaining were eleven living in the village of Afognak, down from forty-nine living in the Kodiak area in 1867.[209]

Lührmann says that Creoles "were Russian citizens equal to the burgher estate, but free from state taxation as long as they lived in Alaska. Creoles educated at the expense of the RAC [Russian-American Company] were obligated to serve the Company for at least ten years. Creoles free of that obligation . . . and registered as 'colonial citizens' were encouraged to establish agricultural settlements."[210] Black points out that "neither the term 'creole' nor the term 'colonial citizen' were racial categories."[211]

According to Fedorova, the company believed that the Creoles would eventually "predominate over the Aleuts, if not entirely replacing them."[212] In the last days of the Russian-American Company in Alaska, Russian naval captain Pavel N. Golovin reported, "One can predict that in a few decades the creole population will become dominant in the colonies and completely replace the Aleuts, whose number is gradually diminishing."[213]

To a newcomer such as Pinart, the visual difference between Creoles and Natives was most likely often indiscernible, other than the Creoles were more likely to be dressed in Russian-style clothing. Their physical appearances would have been, of course, influenced by the actual biological makeup of each Creole, which could vary greatly. Elliott provided a description of Creoles:

> The original Creole was the offspring of a Russian father and an Aleutian or Kaniag mother. He inherited the strong thickset frame and bushy, curly beard and brown hair of his father; in many cases his eyes were as blue (and his hair sometimes red), his skin as white, and his bearing just as good as was his Russian progenitor's. The aggressive energy, however, of the sire seldom was transmitted, the Creole being indolent and very pacific in disposition. If this original Creole, in his time and turn, married a full-blooded Aleutian or Kaniag girl, then the offspring would show a marked dominance of the mother's race—indeed, the child would be as much like other Aleutian babies as they are related in looks among themselves; but if this original Creole marries an original Creole girl, sired like himself, then we have a type which cannot be distinguished at all from the full-blooded Slavonian, only much less demonstrative, alert, and pugnacious. Most of these old colonial citizens of this district of Kadiak are therefore full-blooded Russian quadroons and octoroons, and in every physical aspect are as much like Russians as if of pure origin. Those early Creoles, male and female, who mated, as they matured, with the native males and females, in so doing caused all their offspring long ago, to revert to the savage types, and we cannot distinguish them to-day.[214]

Klimovskii, a Russian-American Company official, made a series of recommendations concerning Creoles, although many were not adopted. He saw them as important because "They constitute a link between the Russians and the islanders, between people and savages, and between education and ignorance."[215] He proposed rules requiring that Creoles could only marry other Creoles or Natives and that they should all be provided with houses and vegetable gardens in Kodiak. He also suggested that Creoles should be given cattle "on the condition that they are able to get hay for them with their own effort, but they cannot keep more than two milk cows and one bull. The surplus calves are to be given to the company at set prices."[216] Klimovskii also thought that Creoles should receive assistance from the company to breed pigs, goats, and chickens and be taught skilled trades.[217] Perhaps most notable to the Sugpiaq political structure, however, was his successful suggestion that the company choose leaders from the Creole population to watch over Natives, settling internal disputes and reporting any absences.[218]

Karl Armstrong Jr. (1927–1983), a Sugpiaq leader of the 1960s, '70s, and '80s and the son of Afanasiia Rysev of Woody Island, a Creole, and Karl Armstrong, the longtime deputy U.S. Marshal for the Kodiak area, had this to say about Creoles:

> The Creoles, who were said to be "half as good as a Russian and twice as good as a Native," quickly became the most numerous and successful group in the colony. It did not take long for this relatively pampered class (though without citizenship status, they were not taxed and were guaranteed education, land, farm animals and pensions) to decide that they were God's specially blessed and "twice as good as anyone." This racial arrogance

persisted, and was especially pronounced among Creole youths selected by the church and sent to Russia for special education. While their ranks were decimated by diseases in Russia, those who survived became the leadership elite in Russian America upon their return as surveyors, ship captains, navigators, army officers and technicians. They were resourceful, skilled, competent and often cruel in their domination and rule.[219]

Over time Creoles were placed in many management and professional positions of the Russian-American Company. Despite this, Russians still often viewed them as inferior, similar to how they viewed all Natives. Dall described a meeting he had with Ivan Pavloff, a Creole and manager of the Nulato Trading Post on the Yukon River. The meeting included both Russians and Americans and took place shortly after the American takeover of Alaska. "A disagreeable servility marked his intercourse with the Americans and full-blooded Russians, the latter regarding him with unconcealed contempt on account of his Indian blood, notwithstanding his responsible position," Dall said.[220] Golovin's negative description of Creoles included the following:

> The mothers' blood expressed itself in the children in their inclination toward hooliganism, primitivism, dishonesty and laziness. However, although creoles are all likely to be sensitive, proud, and quick to take offense, they do have good qualities, notably an aptitude in mechanical crafts. For the most part they are well proportioned and very good looking, especially the second and third generations; but they early acquire an inclination toward a carefree life, and this has a tragic effect. They soon become weak. Between the ages of 30 and 35 nearly all suffer from a chest disorder which often develops into consumption. The result is that very few creoles live to an advanced age. Drink, especially, is their ruination.[221]

Black pointed out that under the Russian system, "an Alaskan native, educated in Russia and occupying a managerial position, became first a creole, then a 'man' (i.e. a Russian of relatively low rank)."[222] Fedorova said that both Russians and Aleuts showed the Creoles "disrespect and even contempt."[223] "The Company wanted the Creoles to be a link between the Russians and the aborigines. However their separation into a special class made them neither one nor the other," she said.[224] Golovin said the Russians looked upon Creoles "with great contempt" and used the word "'creole' as a pejorative."[225] He continued with this description:

> Even the Aleuts have no respect for the creoles, and say that they are lower than Aleuts because their mothers were immoral women. This contempt, this constant oppression, is very destructive to the sensitive nature of the creoles. They are ashamed of being called creoles . . . They consider themselves men of the land and of course want to retain some stature, but they are downtrodden and forced to submit to Russian influence . . .
>
> Obviously there are very fine persons among the creoles, but they are the exceptions, and I am speaking about the group as a whole. Even education and rank do not always benefit their crude natures. Thanks to the efforts of the Company many creoles receive an education; some obtain the rank of noncommissioned officers; others command ships or hold various responsible positions in the colonies. But in the group as a whole, there are only a few gratifying exceptions. Under strict supervision they behave acceptably, but when left to their own devices they revert to their natural behavior and become embittered drunkards.[226]

By the time the Russians officially left Kodiak, 90 percent of the citizens of the town of Kodiak were Creoles.[227] It seems probable at this time that a majority of Kodiak

Sugpiat possessed at least some Russian blood and were thus Creoles.[228] The Creoles wanted to maintain their superior social status but to the Americans they were considered either "half-breeds" or Natives, both considered inferior classes.[229] In an effort to maintain the appearance of a higher status to the Americans, many Creoles began referring to themselves as "Russians." Many were sensitive about being called "Native," as an early twentieth-century American schoolteacher found when she referred to Creoles as "Natives" and was fired by the local school board in Kodiak, which was made up of Creoles.[230] The term "Creole" continued to show up on birth certificates and Russian Orthodox Church records well into the twentieth century.[231] Having lost their superior social status under American rule, many Kodiak Creoles looked back to the Russian period as a kind of "Golden Age."[232] This separation of classes within the Sugpiaq community would become a contentious issue and cause hard feelings and resentments for well over a century after the American takeover of Alaska.[233]

Epidemics and Healthcare

In 1871 the Kodiak Sugpiat were still facing serious health issues despite improvements in healthcare under the Russian-American Company. The early days of Russian occupancy of Kodiak Island were marked not only by physical atrocities against the Sugpiat but by numerous deaths from newly introduced diseases to which they were particularly vulnerable.[234] The Russians noted devastating epidemics among the Sugpiat even before 1800.[235] The first documented epidemic of respiratory disease hit Kodiak in 1804.[236] Another epidemic, now considered to have been a particularly virulent strain of the influenza virus, hit in 1819–1820 and resulted in forty-eight deaths.[237] Yet another epidemic suggestive of influenza struck Kodiak in the winter of 1827–1828, killing 158 Sugpiat across the island.[238]

As the Sugpiat were a crucial part of the Russian-American Company workforce, it was in the company's best interests to attempt to keep them physically healthy. In 1832, a twenty-five-bed hospital was established in Kodiak, and the head physician for the colonies, Mr. Meier, visited all the villages on Kodiak Island treating the sick and sending some to the new hospital.[239] The hospital had only ten beds, yet 550 patients were treated there during the year of 1861.[240]

The Kodiak Sugpiat suffered heavy loss of life when the smallpox epidemic that swept through Alaska between 1835 and 1840 reached Kodiak, despite efforts by the Russian-American Company to combat the disease. The company sent five batches of vaccine to Kodiak Island in 1835, but most of the vaccine had already lost its potency by the time it arrived. The first cases of smallpox broke out in Kodiak on July 8, 1837. A medical team from Sitka arrived in October, but 265 Sugpiat had already died. Many Sugpiat refused to be vaccinated or accept any medical advice from the company doctors.[241] By the time the epidemic burned itself out in January of 1838, another 473 people had died.[242] At the time of the smallpox epidemic there were a reported sixty-five villages on Kodiak Island. Russian-American Company officials, led by Chief Manager Etholen, consolidated these villages into just seven in order to more efficiently provide medical care.[243] These seven were existing villages into which survivors from other communities were incorporated, thus changing their social and political structure as well. The seven villages were St. Paul (*Sun'aq*, present-day Kodiak), Three Saints (near present-day Old Harbor), Orlova (also known as Eagle Harbor), Afognak (*Ag'waneq*, relocated as Port Lions after the 1964 earthquake and tsunami), Woody Island (*Tangirnaq/Leisnoi*), Karluk (*Kal'uq*), and *Ukamok* (Chirikof Island).[244] This consolidation undoubtedly made these seven communities more like relocation centers or refugee camps than villages.[245] The smallpox epidemic changed the face of Kodiak Island villages forever. The disease took many village leaders and heads of households, leaving the Russian-American Company with the task of providing food and shelter to children, widows, and the elderly.[246]

Epidemics continued to have a severe impact on Kodiak Sugpiaq villages up to and after the transfer of Alaska from Russia to the United States in 1867. Medical care was sparse directly after the transfer, and people and communities were still reeling from recent epidemics. After the transfer, "the Russian health care system, so painstakingly developed, was rapidly dismantled."[247] A measles epidemic struck Kodiak Island in 1860, causing eighty-one deaths, and in 1861, a

typhus epidemic hit Afognak. Kodiak villages experienced an outbreak of scarlet fever in 1865 and of mumps in 1868. An outbreak of "bilious pneumonia" struck Kodiak in 1870 with fifty people becoming ill, although no deaths were reported. In the winter of 1874–1875 a severe form of measles struck Sugpiaq villages and, by one account, claimed the lives of "515 Kodiak Natives and Creoles."[248] There were "many deaths" reported from influenza in Kodiak villages in outbreaks in 1881 and 1889.[249] Other illnesses, none of which were present prior to the first Russian contact, including, tuberculosis, venereal diseases, and various other respiratory diseases, claimed many lives in Kodiak villages.[250] These many serious outbreaks were an immense challenge for Alaska Commercial Company physicians, who had inherited

Figure 21. Census taker and Sugpiaq children in the village of Aiaktalik, ca. 1930.

PHOTOGRAPH COURTESY OF THE KODIAK HISTORICAL SOCIETY, BARANOV MUSEUM.

Illustration 21. Recenseur et enfants sugpiat dans le village d'Aiaktalik, vers 1930.

PHOTOGRAPHIE REPRODUITE AVEC L'AIMABLE AUTORISATION DE LA KODIAK HISTORICAL SOCIETY, BARANOV MUSEUM.

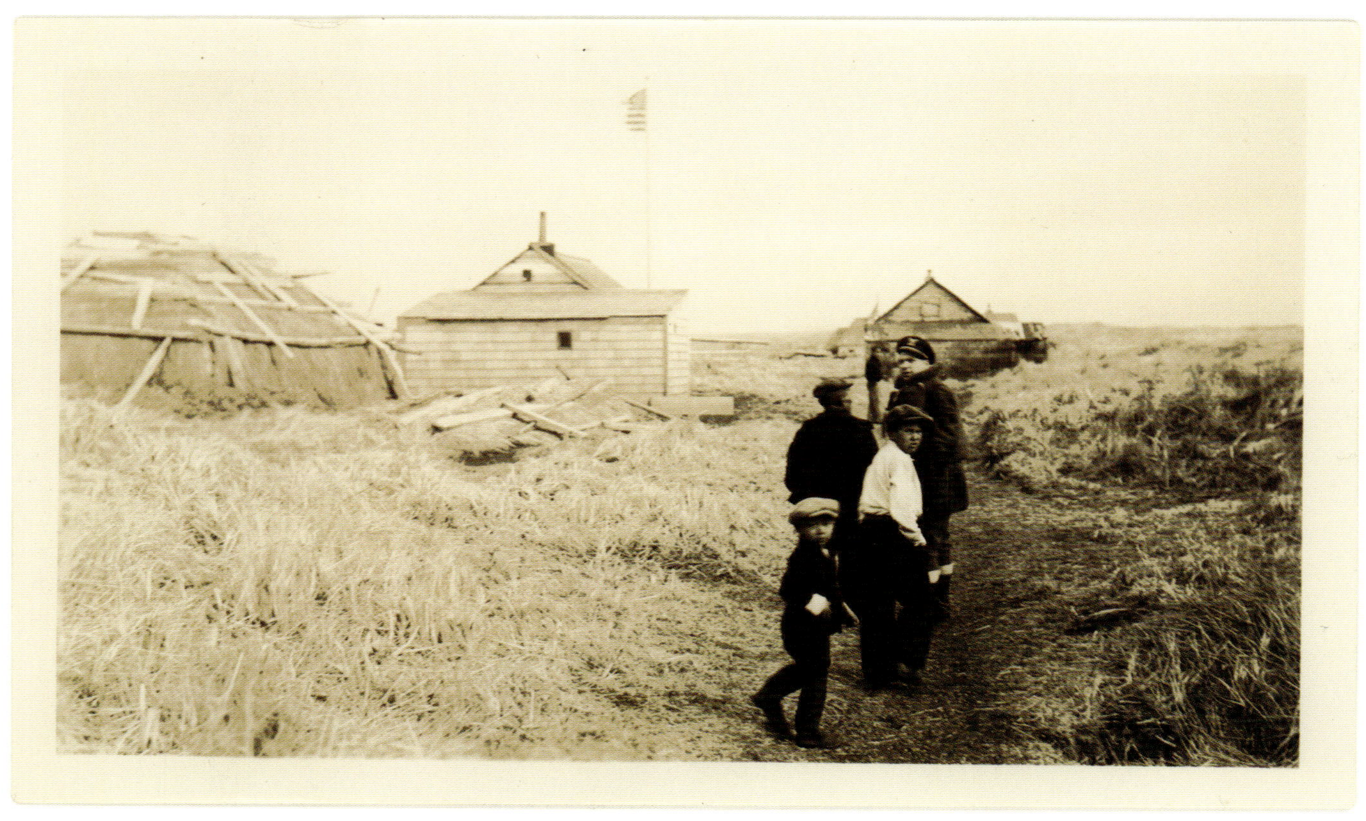

from the Russian-American Company the responsibility for Kodiak Island healthcare.[251]

While the Russians had introduced Western medicine, traditional healthcare was also being practiced. Describing traditional healthcare practices in nearby Alaska Peninsula Sugpiaq communities, anthropologist Patricia Partnow said:

> Both male and female practitioners were skilled at massage and bleeding for the treatment of conditions as varied as heart ailments, boils and arthritis. Midwives skillfully assisted women in childbirth. But perhaps the most important healing tool was the steam bath, locally called a *banyu*,[252] where therapy was generally performed.[253]

The use of the steambath, or *banya,* continues in Kodiak villages today. While it has been used for many years by traditional healers for a variety of ailments including childbirth problems,[254] it is now usually used in place of a regular bath or shower and as a place where each sex can have conversations without fear of being interrupted by the other.[255] There is little doubt, however, that there is a spiritual component to the use of this ancient practice. With a revival of Sugpiaq culture on Kodiak Island some are forsaking the Russian word *banya* for the Sugt'stun word *maqiq*. It has been suggested that the Sugpiat did not have the steambath until it was introduced to them by the Russians, but archaeological and historical evidence has shown that the *maqiq* long predated the *banya*.[256] As Partnow said:

The steam bath itself is therapeutic both as an aid to physical health and cleanliness, and as a necessary step in spiritual health. In fact, in traditional Alutiiq thinking the states of physical and spiritual health are closely related: physical ailments were often signs of a mental or spiritual imbalance, while moral or ritual mistakes often resulted in physical afflictions. Even today, both before and after hunts and important religious rituals, participants take a steam in the *banyu*.[257]

It is most likely that Pinart collected in the villages that were most convenient for him to get to due to their close proximity to Kodiak. There is, however, the possibility that he was also aware that traditions and cultural practices such as mask making, dancing, and storytelling in these communities were in the most danger of disappearing. These were the villages that were consolidated after the smallpox epidemic less than thirty years before. These villages, perhaps more

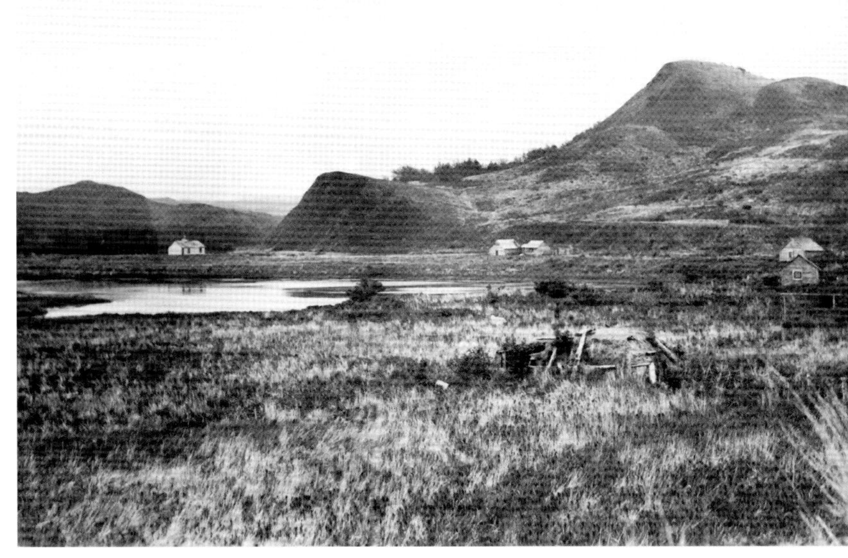

Figure 22. Eagle Harbor around the turn of the twentieth century.

Illustration 22. Eagle Harbor à l'aube du xxᵉ siècle.

than others, had suffered extreme psychological trauma, most recently from the smallpox epidemic, but also from the lasting effects of the ruthless Russian conquest.

Political Structure and Leadership

Prior to Russian contact, the Kodiak Sugpiat had a well-developed system of village governance. Each village had a chief, called an *angayuqaq,* whose position of influence was not necessarily what might be expected. The *angayuqaq* did not exert strong power over the village citizens but acted in more of a servant leader role. Individuals had influence in specific areas such as hunting, fishing, or warfare and served as leaders for those functions. There was a hereditary method of passing on the chieftainship, usually from a man to his nephew.[258] The *angayuqaq* chose his successor prior to his own death, and did so formally in a special ceremony in the *qasgiq,*[259] the ceremonial men's house. Women were not allowed to attend these ceremonies but joined the festivities and feasting that followed.[260] There were no guarantees that an *angayuqaq* would be allowed to maintain his position or that his chosen successor would be accepted.[261]

The traditional system of governance and leadership changed under Russian rule, where the leaders were appointed by Russian-American Company officials and called *toions* (indigenized to *toyuq*), becoming salaried employees of the company.[262] The *toions'* "duties included assigning men to hunting parties and planning the hunt in consultation with company employees, but also mediating disputes in the village and taking care of orphans and poor people."[263] In order to maintain order, the Russian-American Company tried to select leaders who were "from families in which chieftainship had been hereditary."[264] By the time of the American takeover, the Russian Orthodox Church influence had changed the system even more by combining village leadership with church leadership. Under this system, the *toyuq* was the chief. The second chief, called a *sukashiq,* was also the church lay reader. The third in command was the *staristaq,* also a church lay reader and church warden.

The *staristaq* was often a lifetime position and carried the responsibility for maintaining church property, lighting and extinguishing candles, serving as an usher, painting crosses for the graves of the newly deceased, and recording vital statistics, such as baptisms, marriages, and deaths, as well as handling other church administrative duties.[265]

After the Russians left power, the village leaders were chosen by a council of Elders.[266] This system of mixing church and state and relying on Elders' wisdom seemed to be very effective in governing Sugpiaq communities.[267] This was the primary system until the U.S. government mandated that Alaska Native tribal governments establish a political and administrative structure that resembled that of the U.S. government. This first happened in the 1930s and 1940s when the federal Indian Reorganization Act (IRA) was applied to Alaska.[268] Villages that chose not to organize under the IRA were forced into a more "American structure" in the 1970s when the U.S. government began funding village programs. The U.S. government required that tribal governments have written constitutions and bylaws in order to be eligible for federal funding.[269] The system that was in effect when Pinart visited Kodiak Island stayed largely in place for the next hundred years, and was longed for decades after it was forcibly changed.

Agriculture

Early in the Russian occupation period the Sugpiat were introduced to agriculture and the raising of livestock. These practices made them quite different from any other indigenous group in Alaska. The first cattle were brought to Kodiak in 1795. By 1833, the herd had increased to more than 220, but by the 1880s it had shrunk to about 60.[270]

Agriculture became a focus for the Russian-American Company early in its occupation of Kodiak Island. The company's chief agricultural settlement was at *Chiniatsk* (Chiniak), located on the coast about eight or nine miles from St. Paul's Harbor (Kodiak). This company settlement maintained more cattle than any other and grew wheat and barley to feed the herd. Initially, cattle raising was done only at *Igatsk* (*Orlova* or Eagle Harbor), but as the need expanded cattle were kept on many of the small islets in the area as well as at Woody Island.[271] The cattle herds declined, however, and by 1843 all cattle on the island were consolidated into three herds totaling no more than 250 head at *Chiniatsk, Kalsinsk* (Kalsin Bay), and Igatsk.[272]

Eagle Harbor was considered an excellent spot for agriculture, with the best vegetables, especially potatoes, grown there of any Kodiak settlement.[273] By 1847, every house at St. Paul's Harbor (Kodiak) had a vegetable garden.[274]

Petroff particularly notes the agriculture taking place in Kodiak Sugpiaq villages:

> The climatic conditions of the island are more favorable than most other sections of Alaska, the cultivation of potatoes and turnips and the rearing of cattle being among the general industries of the people. At the creole settlement of Afognak there is quite extensive acreage, fenced in, under cultivation; and at the village of Saint Paul, on Wood Island, and on Spruce Island these farming operations are extending every year. The crops are by no means abundant, and cannot be counted upon as a certainty every year; but there is enough to add much to the comfort of life and a pleasant and wholesome variety to the dietary of the people. Experiments in sheep-raising have also been made with encouraging results.[275]

Villages

By the time of the American takeover of Alaska, Sugpiaq villages had been realigned a number of times. Throughout their long history, the Sugpiat had moved their villages when conditions required. This situation changed with the Russian occupation when the Russians required the relocation of some villages. New villages emerged as retirement communities for Russian-American Company employees, populated by retired company workers and their Sugpiaq wives. Thus, many, if not most, of the residents were Creoles and thus Sugpiaq themselves. The first retirement communities were established in the 1830s at Afognak and Spruce Island.[276] As there are not many nineteenth-century photographs of Kodiak Sugpiaq communities, especially during the time surrounding Pinart's visit, one must rely on the written record for descriptions. Henry W. Elliott, a Smithsonian Institution colleague of William H. Dall, published some descriptions in 1886 that help create a picture of the Kodiak villages.

Eagle Harbor *(Orlova; Igatsk)*

The deep recess of Eagle Harbor, which lies between this point of earliest Russian occupation (Three Saints Harbor) and Kadiak village, affords the location of another large native village, and its region is called the best grazing group in all Alaska. On the surf-beaten islets at the mouth of the inlet a great many sea-lions are always found, and thus yield to these hunters of Orlova a rich return in hides and sinews so essential for the construction of the "bidarka." A few families of Creoles also reside here, who attend to a small herd of cattle, keep fowls, and generally look after their commissions as middle-men in the sea-otter revenues.[277]

Wood Island *(Tangirnaq; Leisnoi)*

Looking down the bay, we observe a thickly timbered and a somewhat more level island than usual—it is the famous Wood Island, where the largest spruce-trees in all this section grow; upon it is a small village of one hundred and fifty-six souls, living in thirteen log houses, thickly clustered together; they are all sea-otter hunters during the summer. This village is also the depot of that mysterious San Francisco corporation which has regularly cut up and stored tons of ice here every winter since 1856, and never has shipped a pound of it away![278] and when the bright hearty agent of this corporation asks you to come out with him to the stable and advises you to mount one of the three or four horses sheltered therein, so that you can gallop round the island with him, your astonishment is perfect.

Sure enough, there is a road, incredible as it first seemed; for, in order that the horses might be exercised, a good track has been made upon the entire tide-level circuit of the island, about twelve miles in length, over which the ice company's stock is trotted every summer at frequent intervals; in the winter these unwonted animals are busy hauling ice. You may well improve this opportunity, for it will not occur again as you travel in Alaska—you will not be able to ride else where on a road worthy of the name.

A number of small trading-sloops and schooners have been built here in a boatyard, fashioned by the skill of some Creole ship-carpenters, who were trained in the yards of Sitka when Russian authority was dominant, and who have taken up their permanent abode in the "Leesnoi" settlement. A few small, tough Siberian cattle, such as we saw at Neelshik, Cook's Inlet, are roaming about here, cared for by the natives who prize milk; also several of these same bovines are to be seen in Kadiak, where they are limited also to a few head, on account of the trouble of winter attendance and loss from bears in the summer pasturage.[279]

Elliott also notes, "On Wood Island . . . a small field of rye, oats, or barley, is planted every year for use of the horses kept there; here a plough is used."[280]

Karluk *(Kal'uq)*

From the earliest colonial time to the present the little village of Karlook, on the north side of the island, has been the busiest spot in the country. Here is a salmon-fishing settlement right on the coast at the mouth of a small river, where from the ancient date of Russian occupation there has been a salt house and packing establishment, in which dried fish used throughout the entire Alaskan region was annually secured and

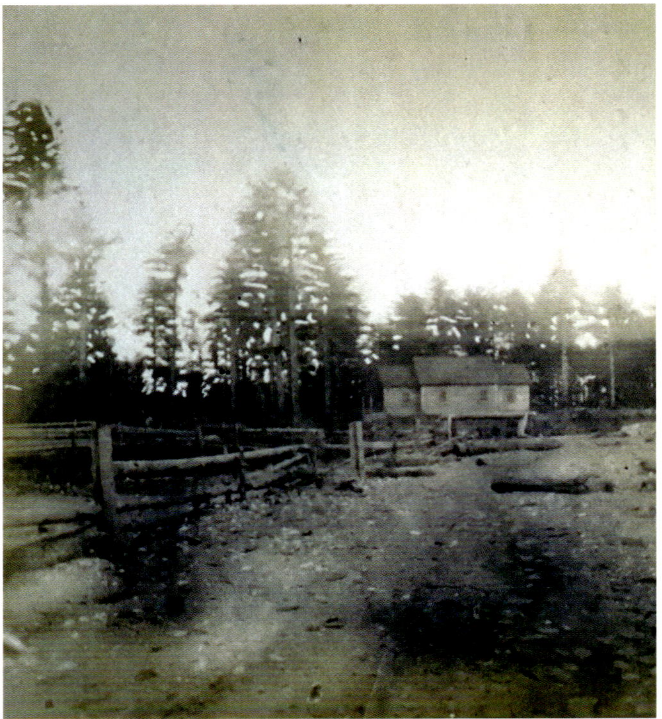

Figure 23. Russian Orthodox Church in Afognak Village, 1872.

PHOTOGRAPH BY ALPHONSE PINART. COURTESY OF THE BANCROFT LIBRARY, UNIVERSITY OF CALIFORNIA, BERKELEY.

Illustration 23. L'église orthodoxe russe du village d'Afognak en 1872.

PHOTOGRAPHIE PRISE PAR ALPHONSE PINART. AVEC L'AIMABLE AUTORISATION DE LA BANCROFT LIBRARY, UNIVERSITÉ DE CALIFORNIE, BERKELEY.

prepared. . . . The run of salmon into this river of Karlook at the height of the season is so great that it interferes with the free movement of canoes crossing the stream . . . [281]

Ouzinkie *(Uusenkaaq)*

An odd, weather-beaten faded little building is pointed out by the natives with pride and animation, as the house in which a "soul-like" man—a Russian monk (St. Herman) made his abode for thirty consecutive years, teaching the children of the village and those of neighboring towns, who flocked here in great numbers to be instructed. . . . This unique shrine is in the heart of the next village closely adjoining and which is located on Spruce Island, or "Yealovnie," as the seventy odd Russian Creoles who live here call it. It is a little hamlet of only fifteen small log houses, very neat and clean; and the prettiest of flower-pots within the scant windows give you a far-away thought as you observe them. Here is also one of the tiniest of Greek chapels, in which the natives are regularly joined by the small number of those of Oozinkie village (a little way off) and just across the straits; there people have no church, are also pure Creoles, and unite in perfect accord with those of Spruce town.[282]

Afognak *(Ag'uaneq* and *Derevnia)*

on the southern shore of Afognak Island, is the largest settlement of the "old colonial citizens" in the Territory; three hundred and thirty of these people are living here in a very picturesque and substantial village; a large chapel, which is also used as a school-house, is the distinguishing architectural feature, while a number of newly-built row-boats for fishermen, on the stocks, in a miniature shipyard, point to an industry worthy of attention. The town is spread over a large landed extent, which in many places between the dwellings is devoted to vegetable gardens. More land is under cultivation here than all the rest so treated in Alaska to-day; the crops of potatoes, cabbages, turnips, and garden-salads, like radishes, etc., seldom fail except in the very backward years. No ploughing is done; the earth prepared for potatoes is thrown with spades, picks, and hoes up as small ridges or tumuli, in the surface of which the seed is planted. A few of those shaggy little bulls and cows, which we have noticed before at Wood Island and Kadiak, are also roaming about, and a great many domestic fowls, such as chickens and ducks are raised by the women and children, who take the poultry into the attics or lofts above their living rooms during the inclemencies of winter.[283]

Afognak consisted of two communities living side-by-side. The original Sugpiaq village, called *Ag'uaneq*, was on one side while a community called *Derevnia*, originally established by the Russian-American Company for retired Russian workers and their Sugpiaq wives, was on the other. These two villages came to be known as Aleut Town and Russian Town (Figure 23).

Robert P. Porter, superintendent for the 1890 U.S. Census in Alaska, provided descriptions of both sides of Afognak village beginning with the Russian Town side:

Afognak village, consolidated for enumerating purposes, really consists of a series of settlements lining a long, curving beach. At the eastern mouth of Afognak straits and opposite Whale Island begins the creole village of Afognak, extending in a single row of dwellings, somewhat widely scattered, about three fourths of a mile along the beach. This settlement was founded during the first quarter of the present century under the name of Rutkovsky village by superannuated and pensioned employees[284] of the Russian-American Company, who were encouraged to keep cattle and engage in agriculture upon a limited scale. Their descendents have always lived on a plane of civilization somewhat higher than that of their neighbors. Their representatives could always be found among the local officials of the Russian company in various districts and among the petty officers of their numerous fleet. The Afognak mechanics were prominent in the company's shops, and even now we find several families that furnish competent carpenters and boat builders. The men of the village are much away from home hunting or trapping, or laboring at the canneries and employed on schooners or larger craft, or during the winter cutting cordwood and logs for the fishing and trading establishments; and in their absence the women and old men take care of the cattle and dig, plant, and weed their potato gardens, or cure the fish which were caught by the boys. Near the northern end of the creole village there is a neat chapel built by the people and a handsome school building erected by the United States government, and a trading store of the Alaska Commercial Company. A few white men, sea-otter hunters married to Afognak women, have settled here also, finding a safe and convenient harbor for their small schooners in a cove opening into Afognak straits.[285]

Porter goes on to describe the Aleut Town side of Afognak:

Proceeding northward a few hundred yards over a well-beaten trail we find the native village of Afognak, inhabited by Kadiak Eskimo. In contrast to the well-constructed log and frame houses of the creoles we find here a large number of sod and log huts, all covered with earth and scattered irregularly over a piece of swampy ground, protected from inroads of the sea by a high ridge of bowlders and shingle.[286]

Ivan Petroff, who wrote the 1880 U.S. census report, also offered his descriptions of Kodiak-area villages. His impression was that by 1880, "A century of uninterrupted presence of Christianizing influences among them has so transformed these natives that not a vestige of their former fierce and savage nature can now be found, and their settlements will compare favorably in neatness and domestic comfort with most of the fishing villages of northern Europe."[287]

Treatment of the Dead

The Sugpiat held their dead in high reverence, especially shamans, important leaders, or others of high social status. This status determined how they would be buried. One traditional way of dealing with the dead was to leave them in the sod house, seal it up, and move to a new location; in other cases the deceased were placed in a side room of a sod house, the room was sealed, and the people continued to reside in the house.[288] Yet another traditional burial practice of the Sugpiat involved interring the dead in the ground, covering them with stones, and erecting poles in the vicinity.[289] The bodies of whale hunters, considered powerful and very important, were kept in secret caves where they mummified.[290] These mummies were provided offerings, including the "first berries, oil, and fish of the season." The bodies were removed from the caves prior to a whale hunt and placed in streams from which the living whale hunters then drank to develop success in their upcoming hunt.[291] This practice is consistent with indigenous worldviews in which time is considered circular and those who lived in the past continue to be members of the living group.[292]

William H. Dall, the noted naturalist, was in Kodiak in 1874 and focused on securing the remains of dead Sugpiaq whalers buried in secret caves to take to the Smithsonian Institution. Dall was well aware of Pinart's unsuccessful attempts, three years earlier, to secure remains from the Kodiak Island cave burials.[293] "M. Alphonse Pinart, while in Kadiak, attempted to discover the retreat of one which was particularly spoken of, but was not successful," Dall said.[294] Dall was successful, however, in collecting one of the mummies from L. Sheeran, the U.S. Deputy Collector of Customs stationed in Kodiak, and transferred it to the Smithsonian Institution.[295]

Many ceremonial items, including masks, were placed with the deceased in the caves. "The Kadiak natives made great use of masks in their dances and festivals, especially those in which Shamans took part. They are said to be deposited in many places with the dead," Dall said.[296] He described the deceased Sugpiat as being dressed in "elaborately ornamented clothing sometimes with wooden armor, and carved masks."[297] Dall continued:

> it was not an uncommon practice to dry the bodies of the dead in some natural attitude, and to place them in a cave or rock-shelter dressed in gay attire, and arranged as if in some occupation characteristic of the individual's pursuits in life. Thus, women were placed as if sewing, or nursing children; noted hunters, in bidarkas engaged in transfixing the effigy of a seal or otter; or old men as occupied in beating a tambourine, their recognized occupation in the dances and festivals of the Innuit. By them were placed the masks which they wore in life, or sometimes an individual was dressed in his wooden armor, arrayed in his mask, and supplied with wooden models of his implements or the game of fur animals which were his favorite pursuit. For some reason or other, actual weapons or implements were rarely placed with the dead, but were represented only by wooden models.[298]

Dall described his perceptions of the importance of masks in funeral ceremonies:

> During the mystic dances, formerly practiced before a stuffed image, the dancers wore a wooden mask which had no eye-holes, but was so arranged that they could only see the ground at their feet. At a certain moment they thought that a spirit, whom it was death or disaster to look upon, descended into the idol. Hence the protection of the mask. A similar idea led them to protect the dead man, gone to the haunts of spirits, from the sight of the supernatural visitor. After their dances were over the temporary idol was destroyed.[299]

Under Russian rule, however, the local Sugpiat took on the customs of the Russian Orthodox Church and began developing cemeteries, usually near the Russian Orthodox chapel. This practice continues to the present day.

Conclusion

Pinart was on Kodiak Island a short time, arriving on November 8, 1871, after a two-month *qayaq* trip from Unalaska, and leaving sometime in the spring of 1872.[300] For most, this would not have been enough time to learn much about a culture or to collect many cultural items such as traditional masks. His principal purpose for visiting Kodiak Island was to study the Sugpiaq language, but he gathered much more information on customs and items representing Sugpiaq material culture. He not only described Sugpiaq villages but recorded many traditional activities, including stories, whaling rituals, cosmology, dancing, songs, mask use, and ceremonies that helped him understand the Sugpiaq worldview.[301] During this period of intense transition for the Sugpiat, Pinart was able to witness both traditional ceremonies and the beginnings of the painful transition for the Creoles, a large segment of the Sugpiaq community, who had just lost their privileged status enjoyed under the Russians. He was able to witness a society under stress, which, after nearly eight thousand years of cultural development, had experienced genocide, assimilation, acculturation, and massive epidemics during the previous eighty-five years, and was now forced to make new adjustments in order to survive. Had Pinart not visited Kodiak Island, the Sugpiat of today would have far less information to go on in reconstructing their culture and history from this time period. It is clear that the Kodiak Island Sugpiat continue to be very grateful that a visionary nineteen-year-old from France visited their homeland more than 135 years ago.

Ethnographie historique des villages sugpiat de Kodiak à la fin du XIXe siècle

Gordon L. Pullar

Quand Alphonse Pinart débarque sur l'île de Kodiak, en novembre 1871, les villages sugpiat de Kodiak sont en plein bouleversement, obligés qu'ils sont de se plier au mode de vie des Américains. Le traité de cession, ratifié à peine quatre ans auparavant, le 28 mai 1867, stipulait pour l'Alaska le transfert d'autorité de la Russie aux États-Unis[137]. Nous savons quels furent les villages alors visités par Pinart : Kodiak (*Sun'aq/ Pavlovsk Gavan*, « Paul's Harbor »), Afognak (*Ag'uaneq/ Derevnia*), Eagle Harbor (*Igatsk/Orlova*) et Karluk (*Kal'uq*). Il s'est probablement aussi rendu dans les villages de Wood Island (*Tangirnaq/Ostrov Leisnoi*) et Ouzinkie (*Uusenkaaq/ Seleniye Ruskiy I Kreolovy*) (*ill. 16*)[138]. Selon certains témoignages, Pinart aurait également visité d'autres villages : Katmai, Starie Gavan, Kattani (près du village d'Afognak), Uyak, Kiliuda et Selezoffsky (Little Afognak)[139].

Trois ans auparavant, en 1868, il restait en Alaska moins de cinq cents Russes, dont la plupart s'apprêtaient à rentrer dans leur pays[140]. On comptait donc peu de Russes de sang pur sur l'île de Kodiak en 1871[141]. En revanche, plus d'un millier de créoles y vivaient, des descendants pour la plupart d'unions entre Russes et Sugpiat[142], mais aussi des descendants d'unions entre autochtones de Sibérie et Sugpiat[143].

En 1870, la population sugpiaq recensée sur l'archipel de Kodiak sous le nom d'« Aléoutiens » s'élevait à mille deux cents personnes[144]. Selon Oleksa, dès 1867, 90 % des habitants de la ville de Kodiak comptaient au moins un autochtone parmi leurs ascendants. « Au fil des générations, la plupart, voire la totalité des Indiens d'Alaska (*Alaska Natives*) étaient devenus créoles, même si leur lien de parenté avec un ancêtre d'origine caucasienne était parfois lointain, voire inexistant[145]. »

En 1867 la population sugpiaq de Kodiak, en y incluant les créoles, est majoritairement biculturelle. Les Sugpiat se nourrissent alors de poisson séché ou bouilli, de mammifères marins et de plantes sauvages. Ils parlent leur propre langue, mais la plupart d'entre eux parlent aussi le russe et ils mangent des mets typiquement russes, tels le *pirok*, les *pirojki*, le *bortsch*, les *blinis* et du pain. Ils connaissent aussi les fruits importés, comme les pommes, les poires et le raisin[146]. De nombreux Sugpiat participent à des activités culturelles introduites par les Russes et cultivent désormais des pommes de terre, des navets et des rutabagas[147]. La chasse à la baleine tient toujours une grande place dans la culture sugpiaq et la capture de la première baleine de l'été prend les allures d'une fête qui attire tous les habitants des villages environnants, venus pour la découper[148]. Bien qu'ils continuent à vivre des produits de la terre ou de la mer, ils sont aussi employés par diverses entreprises de la Compagnie russo-américaine, en particulier dans le domaine de la chasse à la loutre [149].

La structure sociale complexe, mise en place depuis plusieurs décennies, résultait de l'imbrication entre traditions sugpiat et coutumes russes. Pinart a dû voir des villages sugpiat traditionnels où les habitations semi-enterrées sont recouvertes d'une fine couche de terre plantée d'herbes sauvages, appelées *ciqlluaq* (*barabara* en russe), mais il a dû voir aussi, à côté, des maisons en rondins de bois de style russe *(ill. 17)*. Il a dû entendre les gens parler tantôt en langue locale, le *sugt'stun* [150], tantôt en russe. Toutefois, il est peu probable qu'il ait entendu parler anglais, si ce n'est auprès des nouveaux arrivants américains. La langue et les coutumes russes étaient déjà solidement implantées à Kodiak, introduites dans le système éducatif officiel dans les années 1790, soit presque un siècle auparavant [151]. Au XIXe siècle, les écoles bilingues étaient la règle dans les villages de la région de Kodiak et les livres étaient publiés à la fois en langue sugpiaq et en langue slave [152].

Sous l'administration russe, les Sugpiat n'avaient le droit ni de porter ni de posséder de vêtements confectionnés en peau de loutre, en peau d'écureuil, en peau d'ours ni en aucune des peaux qui avaient la faveur des Russes [153]. Ils étaient donc obligés de porter des vêtements de style russe ou bien d'utiliser d'autres matières. Pour les parkas, qu'ils avaient fabriquées jusque-là en peau de loutre ou d'écureuil, ils utilisaient dorénavant des peaux d'oiseaux. Les plus recherchées étaient les peaux de cormorans qui servaient à réaliser des parkas fines, mais leur fabrication était longue et pouvait nécessiter jusqu'à quarante oiseaux par vêtement [154]. Les parkas les plus appréciées étaient faites uniquement de cous de cormorans et il fallait entre cent cinquante et deux cents oiseaux pour en fabriquer une seule [155]. La Compagnie russo-américaine finit par autoriser le port de vêtements en peau d'écureuil, ce qui était le cas au moment du séjour de Pinart à Kodiak [156]. Lors de sa visite en 1851, le Finlandais Heinrich Johann Holmberg remarqua que les parkas traditionnelles étaient décorées « de bandes de laine et de tissu rouges », et que les gens portaient des vêtements de style

européen, des chemises en calicot et des pantalons en tissu pour les hommes, et des vestes et des robes en chintz de couleurs vives pour les femmes [157].

Holmberg décrit comment on préparait les peaux d'oiseaux pour la confection des parkas :

> On dépeçait soigneusement les oiseaux, puis les femmes ôtaient les parties grasses de la peau et la laissaient tremper un moment dans un mélange d'œufs de poisson caillés. Ensuite, on nettoyait la peau et on l'assouplissait à la main jusqu'à ce qu'elle soit bien sèche. On utilisait alors de l'urine, dans laquelle on faisait tremper la peau pendant deux ou trois jours. Une fois les peaux préparées, on les cousait à l'aide d'une aiguille en os de petit oiseau et d'un fil qu'on fabriquait à partir de tendons de baleine raclés, séchés et filés, ce qui demandait beaucoup de travail [158].

La plupart des Sugpiat étaient membre de l'Église orthodoxe russe, et certains jeunes hommes entraient dans les ordres [159]. D'autres continuaient à pratiquer leur religion traditionnelle et à vénérer leur « Être suprême », *Llam Sua* [160]. D'autres encore étaient adeptes des deux religions, ce qui n'avait rien de surprenant puisque, selon certains spécialistes comme le prêtre orthodoxe russe Michael Oleksa, la principale raison qui poussait les Sugpiat à adopter la religion orthodoxe russe était qu'ils trouvaient une analogie entre ses principes et ceux de leurs croyances religieuses traditionnelles [161]. « L'organisation du monde précédant le contact et la vision du monde orthodoxe chrétienne étaient parallèles et complémentaires à bien des égards, et de façon significative », affirme Oleksa [162].

À l'époque de la visite de Pinart, on organisait encore des cérémonies traditionnelles avec des danses et des masques en bois sculpté, mais ces cérémonies n'étaient probablement plus aussi répandues qu'elles avaient pu l'être au début du XIXe siècle, lorsqu'un jeune lieutenant de la marine russe, Gavril Davydov, visita le village de Woody Island. Même si Davydov ne comprit pas le sens des cérémonies auxquelles il assistait, il les décrivit de façon très précise et mentionna des « masques magnifiques » utilisés lors des danses[163].

Les premiers Américains à atteindre l'île de Kodiak, lorsque les États-Unis eurent pris possession de l'Alaska, étaient des militaires de l'armée américaine venus sur des navires de la marine qui longeaient la côte *(ill. 18)* : en mai 1868, le premier convoi militaire quitta San Francisco à destination de Kodiak, où il arriva après vingt-six jours de mer[164]. L'expédition était composée d'une compagnie de militaires, de quelques employés civils et d'un naturaliste de la Smithsonian Institution[165].

Au moment où Pinart arrivait en Alaska, les autochtones, dont les Sugpiat, s'apprêtaient à accepter une nouvelle organisation politique conforme à la politique fédérale spécifique d'interaction avec les Amérindiens. Au moment où les États-Unis prenaient possession de l'Alaska, en 1867, le Congrès américain était agité par un débat sur l'attitude des États-Unis vis-à-vis des Indiens : fallait-il « les nourrir ou les combattre[166] » ? En 1871, le Congrès vota une loi mettant fin à la signature des traités entre les États-Unis et les nations amérindiennes[167]. Si le traité de cession régulait par ailleurs de nombreux domaines, il restait flou quant à la relation entre le gouvernement américain et les autochtones de l'Alaska[168]. Alors que ces derniers étaient qualifiés de « complètement dépendants » par la Compagnie russo-américaine, les villages sugpiat de l'île de Kodiak avaient des gouvernements locaux semi-autonomes au moment du transfert. Les Sugpiat fonctionnaient selon une organisation qui admettait leurs traditions, à côté des besoins de la Compagnie ou de la structure de l'Église orthodoxe russe[169].

Pinart, qui fut le témoin du mode de vie des Sugpiat de Kodiak au début de leur passage sous administration américaine, avait sans doute pressenti que les masques traditionnels, comme d'autres aspects de la culture sugpiaq, étaient sur le point de disparaître. Cela l'incita peut-être à sauvegarder tout ce qu'il pouvait de ces connaissances dans le but de les transmettre aux générations futures. Toutefois, il n'avait sans doute pas imaginé que, cent trente-cinq ans plus tard, les objets et récits qu'il avait recueillis pourraient jouer un rôle majeur dans le mouvement de revitalisation de la culture sugpiaq, ni qu'ils inciteraient des artistes sugpiat à faire renaître l'art de la sculpture des masques ou la fabrication d'objets traditionnels. Certains aspects furent malheureusement impossibles à préserver, comme par exemple la tradition du tatouage sur le menton des femmes. Seules les femmes âgées portaient encore ces tatouages au moment de la visite de Pinart[170].

Les premiers Américains à s'installer à Kodiak appartenaient pour la plupart à l'armée américaine. Peu de temps après arrivèrent d'autres étrangers, venus en particulier des pays scandinaves pour tenter l'aventure et essayer de faire fortune dans cette contrée récemment ouverte qu'était l'Alaska. En 1874, peu après la visite de Pinart, un groupe d'Islandais se rendit à Kodiak grâce à l'aide et avec l'accord du gouvernement américain. Ils envisageaient d'y installer une colonie, mais ils changèrent rapidement d'avis en raison d'une épidémie de rougeole qui se déclara dans la population sugpiaq[171].

Économie

Après des millénaires d'un mode de vie basé sur la pêche, la chasse, la cueillette et le troc avec d'autres groupes, les Sugpiat de Kodiak se sont vus confrontés au capitalisme avec l'arrivée des *promyshlenniki* russes, des négociants en peaux. Dans un premier temps, on les réduisit en esclavage, avant de les forcer à travailler pour un « salaire » qui consistait en général en nourriture, vêtements ou autres biens[172]. Davydov raconte :

> La Compagnie russo-américaine n'achète pas d'animaux aux Koniagas ni aux autres populations soumises, elle expédie les hommes à la chasse dans de lointaines et très longues expéditions. Parfois, elle les rétribue en objets européens, comme du tabac, des haches, des couteaux, des aiguilles, du nankin, des pierres multicolores, de la soie ou d'autres babioles. Mais la plupart du temps, ils sont récompensés en *evrashka* ou

parkas en peau d'oiseau, en *kamleïkas*, en peaux de phoque, en filets, en objets variés à base d'intestins, parfois même en graisse animale. Tous ces objets sont utilisés par les femmes et les enfants de ceux qui sont allés à la chasse, si bien que le montant de l'échange de chaque fourrure est dérisoire [173].

L'organisation russe en vigueur sur l'île de Kodiak n'avait pas été organisée directement par le gouvernement russe, mais bien plutôt par la Compagnie russo-américaine, avec l'autorisation du gouvernement russe. Cette compagnie était une entreprise privée dont les dirigeants ne cherchaient qu'à faire le plus de profit possible, quelles qu'en soient les conséquences pour les populations locales. Dans le cadre d'une organisation où intervenaient gouvernement public et entreprise privée, le gouvernement russe confia à la Compagnie russo-américaine « la haute responsabilité de servir le peuple en échange de l'exclusivité du droit d'exploiter les ressources économiques de l'Alaska. La compagnie était tenue d'entretenir les églises, les écoles et les services médicaux [174]. » Les activités de la Compagnie russo-américaine en Alaska devinrent si florissantes que, dans les années 1860, elle disposait de trente-deux succursales qui déployaient des activités aussi variées que des scieries, des mines de charbon, des usines de fabrication de briques et des chantiers navals [175]. Toutes ces activités nécessitaient une main-d'œuvre constituée principalement de Sugpiat et de créoles.

Au moment de la visite de Pinart, l'une des entreprises installées sur Woody Island était une usine qui fabriquait de la glace. La Compagnie glaciaire de Woody Island employait des Sugpiat, des créoles et des Russes qui coupaient et empaquetaient de la glace d'eau douce que l'on expédiait ensuite par bateau en Californie. Elle fonctionnait depuis vingt-huit ans dans le village de Woody Island lors de la date du transfert de 1867, et elle expédiait de la glace à destination de San Francisco depuis 1852. Deux entrepôts à glace y avaient été construits, pouvant chacun contenir jusqu'à trois mille tonnes de glace [176]. La glace était découpée à l'aide d'une scie tirée par des chevaux, puis elle était transportée sur un radeau de bois depuis le lac près du village jusqu'à une jetée, où on la gardait dans des entrepôts avant de la charger sur des navires dans le port [177]. Les ouvriers de l'usine à glace, essentiellement des Sugpiat ou des créoles, recevaient un rouble par jour, avec un repas et de la vodka [178]. Les autres employés de l'usine, surtout des Russes, recevaient un salaire annuel compris entre trois cent cinquante et cinq cents roubles, ainsi que la distribution quotidienne d'un verre de vodka [179].

La ruée vers l'or de 1849 en Californie entraîna une importante demande en glace, ce qui représenta un nouveau débouché pour la Compagnie glaciaire de Woody Island. Jusqu'en 1852, la glace fournie à la Californie venait de Boston en passant par le cap Horn, et coûtait soixante-quinze dollars la tonne [180]. Pour réduire ce coût, dans un premier temps on l'expédia à San Francisco depuis Sitka, au prix de trente-cinq dollars la tonne, mais lorsque les hivers étaient trop doux, la qualité de la glace n'était plus régulière ni satisfaisante [181]. On se mit alors à fabriquer de la glace à Woody Island où la capacité de production pouvait atteindre cinq mille ou six mille tonnes par an. On pouvait expédier cette glace, d'origine plus fiable, vers San Francisco, puis la vendre vingt-cinq dollars la tonne [182]. Toutefois, certaines années, les hivers doux pouvaient affecter l'état de la glace jusqu'à Woody Island [183]. Pendant longtemps, la main-d'œuvre de la compagnie qui fournissait la glace resta surtout constituée de créoles et de Sugpiat, pour qui ce travail représentait une source de revenue essentielle même si elle restait modeste.

L'historien Stephen Watrous décrit le rôle colonisateur qu'a joué la Compagnie russo-américaine en Alaska :

> La Compagnie russo-américaine, tout comme d'autres sociétés par actions européennes (comme la Dutch East India Company, la Hudson's Bay Company, la Northwest Fur Company, les compagnies British East et West India), s'occupait d'activités qui dépassaient le simple commerce de fourrures. Elle avait le droit d'utiliser les zones côtières de l'Amérique du Nord jusqu'au 55ᵉ degré de latitude nord (près de la frontière actuelle de l'Alaska), d'y explorer

et d'y coloniser les terres inoccupées. Elle avait aussi le droit d'exploiter les ressources superficielles ou minières des terres autour des colonies russes. En fait, elle était devenue le bras droit du gouvernement russe dans les territoires américains. Plusieurs membres de la famille du tsar, les nobles de la cour et les hauts fonctionnaires possédaient tous des titres de la Compagnie. Il était donc évident que, pour ce qui concernait l'Amérique du Nord, la Compagnie exerçait un contrôle sur les expéditions, sur les échanges commerciaux et sur les colonies russes[184].

En 1784, peu après la prise de contrôle de l'île de Kodiak par les Russes qui avait entraîné le massacre de centaines de Sugpiat à *Awa'uq* (Refuge Rock)[185], le marchand russe Grigorii Shelikhov prit en otage les enfants de responsables sugpiaq pour les avoir sous son contrôle et, ainsi, contrôler tout leur peuple[186]. Il lui fallait mettre la population locale sugpiaq sous son joug pour l'obliger à aller à la chasse et à lui rapporter des peaux de loutre sans risque d'affrontement armé. Il voulait amasser le plus de fourrures possible, surtout des fourrures de loutre, et instaurer un monopole du commerce de fourrures sur les terres de chasse d'Alaska[187]. Shelikhov soumit brutalement les Sugpiat et il exposa clairement à ses subordonnés ce qu'il exigeait d'eux[188]. En 1786, il envoya par écrit à son contremaître Konstantin Alekseevich Samoilov les instructions suivantes :

Lorsque les indigènes que je vous ai indiqués ci-dessus se seront soumis, veuillez dire à chacun d'entre eux que les sujets qui se montreront loyaux et obéissants seront riches sous le règne de notre Impératrice, mais que les rebelles seront tous exterminés par Sa poigne de fer… Il faut leur dire de cesser tous ces combats et ces vols entre eux, ainsi que les complots contre les Russes, leur manque de fidélité et leur désobéissance[189].

Avec la souveraineté des États-Unis, on vit arriver sur l'île de Kodiak des entrepreneurs et d'autres personnes préoccupés elles aussi de faire des profits. Comme les eaux entourant Kodiak étaient riches en saumon, ce poisson devint rapidement une nouvelle source de développement économique. La Compagnie russo-américaine avait déjà tenté, sans succès, de commercialiser des barils de saumon salé avant le traité de transfert du pays aux États-Unis[190]. En 1870, deux entreprises américaines au moins s'étaient mises à commercialiser le saumon salé, et cette activité devint une source d'emploi pour les Sugpiat de Kodiak[191]. Une partie des dos de saumon séché servit alors d'aliment courant aux chasseurs de loutres sugpiat qui travaillaient pour la Compagnie commerciale d'Alaska[192]. La conserve de saumon allait devenir l'industrie principale de l'île de Kodiak, mais il fallut pour cela attendre les années 1880, soit presque dix ans après la visite de Pinart dans la région[193].

La Compagnie commerciale d'Alaska, fondée en 1868 par des hommes d'affaires de San Francisco sous un statut de consortium, s'empara de la majeure partie des activités de la Compagnie russo-américaine sur l'île de Kodiak après le transfert des intérêts russes aux États-Unis[194]. Si elle ne jouissait pas du même monopole ni du même pouvoir sur la population locale, elle était quand même chargée de construire et de gérer les écoles et les services médicaux dans certaines communautés[195]. La Compagnie établit des comptoirs de commerce et des magasins dans les villages de l'île de Kodiak, et on estime généralement qu'elle était plus puissante que l'armée à la même époque quand il s'agissait des affaires d'Alaska[196]. L'étude de ses archives concernant cette période nous montre que les Sugpiat continuaient à consommer de nombreux aliments et de biens du monde occidental. Ils s'y étaient habitués sous l'administration russe. C'était, entre autres, du pain, des bougies, du tabac, des bretelles de pantalon et des bottes montant jusqu'aux hanches[197]. De nouveaux produits apparurent aussi dans les magasins de la Compagnie commerciale d'Alaska. Les premiers pistolets à cartouches furent introduits (Henry 44s) et la quantité d'aliments sous verre ou en boîtes, de médicaments brevetés, de poteries et de nouvelles sortes de perles se mit à augmenter[198].

La chasse à la loutre de mer

Chez les Sugpiat au XIXᵉ siècle, le métier le plus courant était celui de chasseur de loutres de mer. Durant toutes ses années de fonctionnement en Alaska, la Compagnie russo-américaine a maintenu cette activité intense de chasse à la loutre. Dans la région de Kodiak, les expéditions de chasse à la loutre étaient constituées de « détails » comptant chacun une dizaine de *baïdarkas* ou *qayaqs (ill. 19)*. Pour donner une idée de la taille de telles opérations, quatre-vingt-douze *qayaqs*, autrement dit neuf détails, furent envoyés chasser la loutre au sein du « Département Kodiak » en 1861. Chaque détail était sous les ordres d'un Ancien ou *zakashchik* (un contremaître). L'expédition de chasse était commandée par le *baidarshchik*, le « meneur de la chasse [199] ». À cause du climat souvent très rigoureux dans la région, la chasse avait généralement lieu l'été. À cette époque de l'année, les hommes se trouvaient donc loin de leurs communautés au moment où, justement, ils auraient dû constituer des réserves de nourriture pour subvenir aux besoins de leur famille. Les temps étaient très difficiles pour nombre de familles puisque les femmes sugpiat étaient aussi appelées à travailler pour la Compagnie. Elles cousaient des objets, telles les membranes extérieures des *qayaqs,* des vêtements imperméables, considérés comme une « production de confort gérée par la Compagnie [200] ». Mais la plupart des cérémonies traditionnelles se déroulant pendant les mois d'hiver, les chasseurs se trouvaient donc de retour à la maison pour y participer.

Quand la Compagnie commerciale d'Alaska prit en charge les activités de l'ancienne Compagnie russo-américaine, la chasse à la loutre de mer se poursuivit. À l'époque de ce transfert, les Sugpiat avaient besoin d'au moins un salaire en espèces pour survivre, c'est la raison qui poussa les hommes sugpiat à garder leur emploi de chasseur de loutres. Ils chargeaient leurs *qayaqs* à bord de goélettes de la Compagnie et parcouraient de longues distances pour parvenir dans les régions où la chasse était plus abondante. Néanmoins, tous les chasseurs de loutres ne dépendaient pas des goélettes, certains travaillaient en indépendants.

Durant une brève période, jusqu'à la fin des années 1880, les revenus furent avantageux puisque la compagnie achetait les peaux aux chasseurs entre quatre-vingts et cent dollars la pièce. Mais il n'existait aucune régulation de cette activité, qui dégénéra bientôt en « massacre général ». Dès les années 1890, les réserves étaient quasiment épuisées [201]. Malgré la rareté de la population des loutres, la chasse continua encore. Jusqu'au recensement de 1900, les expéditions de chasse à la loutre se poursuivirent au départ des villages d'Afognak et de Wood Island, à bord des bateaux de la Compagnie commerciale d'Alaska amarrés à Kodiak.

Structure sociale

Dans les années qui suivirent le traité de cession, la structure sociale des villages sugpiat de Kodiak fut profondément remaniée. L'archipel avait vécu sous le joug des colonisateurs russes durant plus de quatre-vingts ans, ils avaient imposé leurs structures sociale et politique aux Sugpiat. La période des atrocités commises par les marchands de fourrures à l'encontre des Sugpiat avait pris fin pour l'essentiel en 1818, grâce aux réformes du gouverneur de l'Alaska de l'époque, le capitaine de marine Leontii Hagemeister [202]. Mais il est probable que le traumatisme psychologique subi par les Sugpiat au cours de cette colonisation russe impitoyable perdurait cinquante ans après dans la population, même si cela était de façon inconsciente. Et, pour la première fois depuis plus de quatre-vingts ans, les Sugpiat avaient enfin la liberté de choisir leur façon de s'organiser. Étaient-ils déjà trop imprégnés du mode de vie russe pour revenir à leur mode de vie traditionnel ? C'est possible, mais ce peuple vigoureux, qui avait montré ses grandes capacités d'adaptation, de résistance, et qui avait vécu sept mille cinq cents ans dans cet endroit, devait de nouveau s'adapter en trouvant la faculté d'intégrer les éléments de trois cultures différentes afin d'inventer une organisation qui fonctionne.

L'organisation sociale russe fonctionnait sur un principe fondamental, la division en classes rigides. La Troisième Charte de la Compagnie russo-américaine, qui datait de

1841, avait imposé cet ordre dans la société. Black écrit :
« Dans cette Troisième Charte, le gouvernement reconnaît
cinq catégories sociales sous l'administration coloniale : les
employés sous contrat, les colons citoyens (résidents volon-
taires), les créoles, les étrangers résidents (les autochtones,
inorodtsy), et les colons étrangers dont la religion n'était pas
celle de l'Église orthodoxe, qui ne dépendaient pas entièrement de la compagnie (*inovertsy*)[203]. » Les nouveaux arrivants américains n'étaient familiarisés avec aucune de ces
catégories, qu'ils ne reconnaissaient pas jusque-là.

La catégorie la plus nouvelle pour les Américains était celle
des « créoles ». Les créoles avaient d'abord désigné les enfants
de père *promyshlenriki*, « habitant de la frontière » russe, et
de mère autochtone d'Alaska, ainsi que leurs enfants[204]. Les
chartes de la Compagnie russo-américaine en proposaient
une définition plus large, permettant à un Sugpiaq de devenir
« créole » sans avoir de sang russe[205]. « En 1821, tous les
Indiens d'Alaska qui faisaient serment d'allégeance au tsar
devenaient, de ce fait, des "citoyens naturalisés", ils étaient
considérés comme "créoles" », explique l'archiprêtre Michael
J. Oleksa[206]. Selon lui, « les créoles combinaient les fonde-
ments de deux cultures, parlaient souvent les deux langues, et
pouvaient plus tard en lire et en écrire deux ou davantage, sans
être nécessairement biologiquement "mixtes". L'appartenance
créole était plus une question de mentalité, d'état d'esprit,
une question d'auto-identification[207] ». Oleksa ajoute : « Un
créole ne consistait pas uniquement en une personne de des-
cendance mixte russe-indigène, mais il pouvait aussi être un
indigène qui était résident permanent d'une ville. C'était une
définition sociale davantage que raciale[208]. » Plus d'un tiers
de la population de l'île de Kodiak se déclarait créole en 1870 ;
les seuls Russes qui restaient étaient au nombre de onze dans
le village d'Afognak, alors qu'ils avaient été quarante-neuf à
vivre dans la région de Kodiak en 1867[209].

Lührmann écrit à propos des créoles : « Ils étaient des
citoyens russes pour l'administration locale, ils ne payaient
pas d'impôt à l'État d'Alaska aussi longtemps qu'ils y rési-
daient. Les créoles qui avaient reçu une éducation aux frais
de la Compagnie russo-américaine étaient tenus par la suite

de servir la compagnie au moins dix ans. Les créoles libres
de cette obligation […] et enregistrés dans la catégorie des
"colons citoyens" étaient incités à fonder des colonies agri-
coles[210]. » Black remarque que « ni le terme de "créole" ni
le terme de "colon citoyen" ne constituaient des "catégories
raciales"[211] ».

Selon Fedorova, les dirigeants de la Compagnie pensaient
que les créoles « finiraient par supplanter les Aléoutes, voire
même par les remplacer complètement[212] ». Vers la fin de
l'hégémonie de la Compagnie russo-américaine en Alaska,
le capitaine de bateau Pavel N. Golovin commente : « On
peut déjà prédire que dans quelques décennies la population
créole deviendra la plus nombreuse des colonies et rempla-
cera les Aléoutes, dont le nombre décline peu à peu[213]. »

Pour un visiteur fraîchement débarqué comme l'était
Pinart, la différence entre un créole et un autochtone ne
devait pas à première vue être toujours facile à discerner, si ce
n'est que les créoles avaient plutôt l'habitude de s'habiller à
la mode russe. Leurs caractéristiques physiques dépendaient,
bien évidemment, des origines biologiques de chaque créole,
et elles étaient très variées. Elliott donne cette description
des créoles :

> Le créole de la première génération est le fruit
> de l'union d'un père russe et d'une mère aléoute
> ou kaniag. Il tient de son père sa solide sil-
> houette, sa barbe broussailleuse et ses cheveux
> châtains bouclés. Il a souvent les yeux bleus (et
> parfois les cheveux roux), la peau blanche et il a
> bonne allure, comme son géniteur russe. Mais
> il hérite rarement de l'agressivité de son père,
> il est d'un naturel nonchalant et très pacifique.
> Si ce créole de la première génération épouse
> une femme purement aléoute ou kaniag, leurs
> enfants auront les traits dominants de leur mère,
> et ainsi ils ressembleront tout à fait aux autres
> bébés aléoutes puisqu'ils sont issus de la même
> famille de traits. Mais si ce créole de la première
> génération épouse une femme également créole,
> d'ascendance russe comme lui, leurs enfants

auront des traits absolument identiques à ceux des purs Slaves, mais leur tempérament sera beaucoup moins démonstratif, moins alerte et moins pugnace. La plupart des colons âgés qui sont citoyens du district de Kodiak sont ainsi des quarterons et "octorons" de purs Russes, et cependant leur apparence physique passe parfaitement pour celle de purs Russes. Ces premiers créoles, hommes et femmes, qui ont eu des enfants avec des conjoints indigènes depuis plusieurs générations, ont, de cette façon, amené tous leurs descendants à retrouver les traits physiques des sauvages d'origine, si bien qu'on ne peut aujourd'hui les en distinguer[214].

Klimovskii, membre de l'administration de la Compagnie russo-américaine, proposa une série de mesures concernant les créoles, mais très peu d'entre elles furent adoptées. Il accordait de l'importance aux créoles car « ils représentent un lien entre les Russes et les habitants originaires de l'île, entre les gens civilisés et les sauvages, et entre l'éducation et l'ignorance[215] ». Il proposa des règles qui n'autoriseraient les créoles à se marier qu'avec des créoles ou des « indigènes », et attribueraient à chacun d'eux une maison avec un jardin potager dans Kodiak. Il suggérait également d'attribuer du bétail aux créoles « à condition qu'ils puissent fournir eux-mêmes la paille dont les animaux ont besoin, mais ils doivent se limiter à deux vaches à lait et un bœuf. Les veaux doivent être cédés à la compagnie à un prix fixé[216] ». Klimovskii était aussi d'avis d'attribuer aux créoles l'aide de la Compagnie pour qu'ils élèvent des cochons, des chèvres et des poules, et pour qu'on leur enseigne des métiers techniques[217]. Sa suggestion la plus intéressante quant à l'élaboration d'une politique sugpiaq, d'ailleurs retenue par la direction de la Compagnie, était celle de désigner des leaders au sein de la population créole pour superviser les « indigènes », régler les disputes internes et relever les absences[218].

Karl Armstrong Jr. (1927-1983), leader sugpiaq entre les années 1960 et les années 1980, fils d'Afanasiia Rysev, originaire de Wood Island, une créole, et de Karl Armstrong, capitaine adjoint de la police américaine, installé depuis longtemps dans la région de Kodiak, disait ceci à propos des créoles :

Les créoles, que l'on disait "moitié aussi bien qu'un Russe et deux fois mieux qu'un autochtone", devinrent rapidement le groupe le plus nombreux et celui qui réussissait le mieux au sein de la colonie. Il ne fallut pas longtemps pour que cette classe privilégiée (ils n'avaient pas le statut de citoyen, mais ils étaient exempts d'impôt et bénéficiaient d'une éducation, de terres, d'animaux d'élevage et de pensions) réalise qu'elle était particulièrement bénie des dieux et "deux fois mieux que tout le monde". Cette arrogance raciale persistante était particulièrement prononcée chez les jeunes créoles que l'Église sélectionnait pour les envoyer en Russie recevoir une éducation particulière. Bien que leur groupe soit décimé par des maladies en Russie, ceux qui en réchappaient formaient à leur retour l'élite dirigeante de l'Amérique russe, en occupant les postes de géomètres, capitaines de navire, navigateurs, officiers de l'armée et techniciens. Ils étaient inventifs, qualifiés, compétents et étaient souvent cruels dans leur appétit de domination et de pouvoir[219].

Au fil du temps, les créoles occupèrent de nombreux postes d'employés ou de directeurs au sein de la Compagnie russo-américaine. Mais même quand ils réussissaient, les Russes continuaient à les traiter souvent en inférieurs, à la manière dont ils traitaient les « indigènes ». Dall rendit compte d'une réunion à laquelle il assista avec Ivan Pavloff, un créole responsable du comptoir commercial de Nulato, au bord de la rivière Yukon, qui comptait à la fois des Russes et des Américains depuis que les États-Unis avaient pris le pouvoir en Alaska : « Dans la discussion qu'il eut avec les Américains, comme avec les Russes de race pure, il manifesta une servilité désagréable. Les Américains et les Russes le traitèrent ouvertement avec mépris à cause de son sang indien, et sans tenir compte de sa position de responsabilité », raconte Dall[220]. Dans une description négative, Golovin parlait ainsi des créoles :

> Le tempérament de sa mère se manifestait chez son enfant par une tendance à la violence, à la cruauté, à la malhonnêteté et à la paresse. Bien que les créoles aient tous un penchant à la susceptibilité, à l'orgueil et à s'offusquer facilement, ils ont néanmoins des qualités, et en particulier un don pour l'artisanat. La plupart sont bien proportionnés et très beaux, surtout les créoles de la deuxième et de la troisième générations. Mais, très jeunes, ils manifestent une tendance à l'insouciance qui a des conséquences tragiques. Très vite, ils se montrent faibles. Entre trente et trente-cinq ans, presque tous souffrent de la poitrine et développent de la tuberculose. Finalement, peu de créoles vivent longtemps. L'alcoolisme, en particulier, les décime[221].

Black remarque que sous l'administration russe, « un Indien d'Alaska, éduqué en Russie puis placé à un poste de direction, se voyait dans un premier temps qualifié de créole, ensuite d'"homme" (qui est un statut relativement bas aux yeux des Russes)[222] ». Federova soulignait qu'à la fois Russes et Aléoutes « manquaient de respect aux créoles et leur montraient du dédain[223] ». « La Compagnie souhaitait que les créoles servent de lien entre les Russes et les indigènes. Mais leur appartenance à une classe à part faisait qu'ils n'appartenaient ni à un groupe ni à l'autre », dit-elle[224]. Golovin note que les Russes regardaient les créoles de haut, « avec un grand mépris », et qu'ils utilisaient le mot « créole » dans un sens péjoratif[225]. Il poursuit par cette description :

> Même les Aléoutes traitent les créoles sans aucun respect, et ils les tiennent pour inférieurs en disant que leur mère est immorale. Ce mépris,

cette oppression constante, sont dévastateurs pour la sensibilité des créoles. Ils ont honte d'être appelés créoles […]. Ils s'estiment des êtres humains, des fruits de cette terre, et veulent, bien sûr, garder une certaine dignité. Mais ils sont opprimés, forcés de se soumettre à la domination russe. […]

> De toute évidence il y a des personnes très bien parmi les créoles, mais ce sont des exceptions, tandis que je parle du groupe dans son ensemble. Même une éducation et un statut n'améliorent pas toujours leur naturel grossier. Grâce aux efforts de la Compagnie, de nombreux créoles reçoivent une éducation. Certains acquièrent le grade d'officier détaché, d'autres commandent des navires, ou occupent divers postes à responsabilité dans les colonies. Mais, sur l'ensemble du groupe, seuls quelques uns sont intéressants. Lorsqu'ils se sentent surveillés, ils se conduisent correctement, mais dès que l'on tourne le dos, leur nature reprend le dessus et ils s'avèrent alcooliques et pleins d'amertume[226].

Quand les Russes quittèrent officiellement Kodiak, 90 % des habitants de la ville de Kodiak étaient créoles[227]. On peut estimer qu'à cette époque la plupart des Sugpiat de Kodiak avaient au moins un peu de sang russe et qu'ils étaient donc des créoles[228]. Les créoles voulaient conserver leur statut et leur supériorité sociale, mais ils restaient, pour les Américains, soit des « sang-mêlé » soit des « indigènes », c'est-à-dire une classe inférieure[229]. Pour essayer de conserver, en apparence, leur statut supérieur auprès des Américains, beaucoup de créoles commencèrent à parler d'eux-mêmes en tant que « Russes. » Ils étaient généralement blessés qu'on les qualifie d'« indigène » (*Native*), comme le comprit une enseignante américaine, au début du XXᵉ siècle, lorsqu'elle fit référence aux créoles en tant qu'indigènes et qu'elle fut renvoyée pour cette raison par le conseil d'école local de Kodiak composé de créoles[230]. Le terme de

« créole » fut régulièrement mentionné sur les certificats de naissance et les archives de l'Église orthodoxe russe pendant toute une partie du xxᵉ siècle[231]. Comme l'administration américaine leur avait fait perdre leur statut social supérieur, beaucoup de créoles de Kodiak se mirent à penser avec nostalgie à la période russe comme à celle d'un « âge d'or[232] » Ce cloisonnement en classes au sein de la communauté sugpiaq allait s'avérer source de conflits et engendrer un grand ressentiment qui allait durer plus d'un siècle après la prise du pouvoir par les États-Unis en Alaska[233].

Épidémies et service de santé

En 1871, les Sugpiat de Kodiak étaient encore confrontés à de graves problèmes de santé malgré l'amélioration des services de santé apportée par la Compagnie russo-américaine. Au début de l'occupation russe de l'île de Kodiak, les Sugpiat subirent non seulement des atrocités physiques, mais ils souffrirent aussi de nouvelles maladies introduites par les Russes face auxquelles ils étaient particulièrement vulnérables, et ils furent nombreux à en mourir[234]. Les Russes faisaient état de grandes épidémies qui décimaient déjà les Sugpiat avant 1800[235]. La première épidémie documentée, due à une maladie respiratoire, s'abattit sur Kodiak en 1804[236]. En 1819-1820, une autre épidémie, sans doute provoquée par une souche particulièrement violente de grippe, fit quarante-huit morts[237]. Plus tard, c'est une autre épidémie, évoquant elle aussi la grippe, qui affecta Kodiak au cours de l'hiver de 1827-1828, et fit cent cinquante-huit victimes chez les Sugpiat à travers toute l'île[238].

Comme les Sugpiat constituaient la principale composante de la main-d'œuvre de la Compagnie russo-américaine, celle-ci avait tout intérêt à essayer de les garder en bonne santé. En 1832, un hôpital de vingt-cinq lits fut établi à Kodiak et le médecin en chef des colonies, M. Meier, visita tous les villages de l'île de Kodiak pour soigner les malades et en envoyer certains à l'hôpital[239]. En 1860, ce dernier n'avait plus que dix lits, mais cinq cent cinquante patients y furent tout de même soignés dans le courant de l'année 1861[240].

Les Sugpiat de Kodiak eurent à déplorer un grand nombre de morts au cours de l'épidémie de petite vérole qui perdura de 1835 jusqu'en 1840, malgré les efforts de la Compagnie russo-américaine pour lutter contre cette maladie. La Compagnie envoya cinq lots de vaccins à l'île de Kodiak en 1835, mais le vaccin avait perdu presque toute son efficacité pendant le voyage. Le premier cas de petite vérole se déclara à Kodiak le 8 juillet 1837. Une équipe médicale de Sitka arriva en octobre, mais deux cent soixante-cinq Sugpiat avaient déjà succombé. De nombreux Sugpiat refusaient les vaccins ou les recommandations des médecins de la Compagnie[241]. Quand l'épidémie commença à faiblir, en janvier 1838, on comptait quatre cent soixante-treize décès supplémentaires[242]. À l'époque de l'épidémie de petite vérole, on répertoriait soixante-cinq villages sur l'île de Kodiak. Les responsables officiels de la Compagnie russo-américaine, conduits par Etholen, regroupèrent ces villages pour n'en faire plus que sept afin que les soins médicaux apportés soient plus efficaces[243]. Il s'agissait de sept villages déjà existants qui accueillirent chacun les survivants de plusieurs villages. Du coup, leurs structures sociale et politique s'en trouvèrent modifiées. Ces sept villages étaient ceux de Saint-Paul (*Sun'aq*, devenu aujourd'hui la ville de Kodiak), Three Saints (aujourd'hui près de Old Harbor), Orlova (aussi connu sous le nom de Eagle Harbor), Afognak (*Ag'waneq*, qui fut déplacé et renommé Port Lions après le tremblement de terre et le tsunami de 1964), Woody Island (*Tangirnaq/Leisnoi*), Karluk (*Kal'ug*) et *Ukamok* (Chirikof Island)[244]. Ce regroupement donna sans aucun doute à ces sept communautés des allures de camps de déplacés ou de réfugiés plutôt que de villages[245]. L'épidémie de petite vérole transforma à jamais les villages de l'île de Kodiak. La maladie avait emporté de nombreux chefs de villages et chefs de famille, et la Compagnie russo-américaine dut prendre en charge la nourriture et les abris destinés aux veuves, aux orphelins et aux personnes âgées[246].

Les épidémies continuèrent d'avoir de terribles répercussions sur les villages sugpiat de Kodiak jusqu'au transfert de l'Alaska de la Russie aux États-Unis en 1867, et même au-delà. L'activité des services médicaux diminua après le transfert, alors que les habitants des communautés n'étaient pas encore remis des épidémies passées. Après le transfert, « l'organisation médicale russe, qu'on avait mise en place au prix de tant d'efforts, fut rapidement démantelée[247] ». Une épidémie de rougeole frappa l'île de Kodiak en 1860, entraînant la mort de quatre-vingt-une personnes, et en 1861 une épidémie de typhus s'abattit sur Afognak. Les villages eurent à affronter une épidémie de scarlatine en 1865, puis d'oreillons en 1868. En 1870, on dénombra cinquante cas de « pneumonie bilieuse » qui n'entraînèrent, semble-t-il, aucun décès à Kodiak. Durant l'hiver de 1874-1875, une forme aiguë d'oreillons se propagea dans les villages sugpiat, causant la mort de « 515 autochtones et créoles à Kodiak[248] ». De « nombreux décès » furent imputés à plusieurs vagues de grippe qui frappèrent les villages entre 1881 et 1889[249]. D'autres maladies, dont aucune n'était présente avant le premier contact avec les Russes, furent observées : la tuberculose, les maladies vénériennes et plusieurs maladies respiratoires qui firent de nombreuses victimes[250]. Ces graves épidémies, si fréquentes, représentaient un immense défi pour les médecins de la Compagnie commerciale d'Alaska qui, à la suite de la Compagnie russo-américaine, avaient pris en charge l'organisation médicale de l'île de Kodiak[251].

Même si les Russes avaient introduit la médecine occidentale, on continuait de pratiquer la médecine traditionnelle. Décrivant les soins traditionnels que pratiquaient des communautés sugpiat voisines de la péninsule d'Alaska, l'anthropologue Patricia Partnow relate :

> Le praticien, qui pouvait être un homme ou une femme, excellait dans l'art du massage et de la pratique des saignées pour le traitement de maux aussi variés que les affections du cœur, les furoncles ou l'arthrose. Les sages-femmes assistaient avec compétence les femmes qui accouchaient. Mais la méthode thérapeutique la plus répandue était peut-être le bain de vapeur, du nom local de *banyu*[252], où l'on dispensait généralement les soins[253].

Aujourd'hui encore, on continue de pratiquer le bain de vapeur, ou *banya,* dans les villages de Kodiak. Utilisé pendant des années par les médecins traditionnels pour traiter certaines maladies, dont les problèmes lors d'accouchements[254], il remplace souvent aujourd'hui le bain ou la douche et constitue le lieu où les hommes ou les femmes peuvent discuter tranquillement sans craindre d'être dérangés[255]. Cette pratique ancestrale, cependant, comporte probablement aussi un aspect spirituel. Certaines personnes rejettent le mot russe *banya* et préfèrent le mot sugt'stun *maqiq* qui rend compte du renouveau de la culture sugpiaq sur l'île de Kodiak. On prétend parfois que les Sugpiat ne connaissaient pas les bains de vapeur avant que les Russes les introduisent, mais il existe des preuves archéologiques et historiques qui montrent que le *maqiq* était utilisé bien antérieurement au *banya*[256]. À ce propos, Partnow écrit :

> Le bain de vapeur est en soi une thérapie, mais il contribue également au bien-être physique et à l'hygiène qui sont une condition essentielle de la santé spirituelle. De fait, la pensée traditionnelle alutiiq considère que la santé physique et la santé spirituelle sont intimement liées : les maux physiques étaient souvent des signes de perte de l'équilibre mental ou spirituel, et les dysfonctionnements d'ordre moral ou lors de rituels se traduisaient par des affections corporelles. Aujourd'hui encore, avant comme après la chasse ou les rituels religieux importants, les participants prennent un bain de vapeur dans le *banyu*[257].

L'hypothèse la plus probable est que Pinart a recueilli des objets dans les villages qui étaient les plus accessibles pour lui depuis Kodiak. Il est toutefois possible qu'il ait été conscient que c'était dans ces communautés que les traditions et les pratiques culturelles, comme la fabrication de masques, les danses ou les récits, risquaient davantage de disparaître. Les habitants des villages, regroupés après les épidémies de petite vérole un peu moins de trente ans auparavant, avaient peut-être dans une plus grande mesure qu'ailleurs souffert de traumatismes psychologiques extrêmes. Le plus récent était dû à l'épidémie de petite vérole, mais il y avait aussi le traumatisme dû à l'impitoyable conquête menée par les Russes dans les années précédentes.

Structure politique et leadership

Avant l'arrivée des Russes, les Sugpiat de Kodiak avaient mis sur pied une organisation très développée pour diriger le village. Cette organisation, de conception égalitaire, comprenait tout de même un chef de village appelé *angayuqaq*, dont l'influence n'était pas forcément ce auquel on pourrait s'attendre. En effet, ce chef ne disposait pas d'un pouvoir étendu sur les villageois, mais avait plutôt un rôle de leader serviteur du peuple. Certaines personnes particulièrement compétentes dans un domaine, comme la chasse, la pêche ou la guerre, remplissaient le rôle de chef de ces spécialités. La transmission héréditaire du rôle de chef se faisait en général d'un homme à son neveu[258]. L'*angayuqaq* désignait son successeur avant de mourir, au cours d'une cérémonie à la forme particulière qui se déroulait dans le *qasqiq*[259], la maison cérémonielle des hommes. Les femmes n'étaient pas admises lors de ces cérémonies, mais se joignaient aux festivités et banquets qui suivaient[260]. Il n'était pas acquis que la personne occupant la position d'*angayuqaq* y soit maintenue ni que le successeur qu'il avait désigné soit accepté[261].

L'organisation traditionnelle de gouvernement et de désignation des chefs changea sous l'administration russe. Les chefs, désormais désignés par les responsables de la Compagnie russo-américaine, étaient appelés *toions* (mot transformé en *toyuq* par les autochtones) et devenaient des salariés employés de la Compagnie[262]. Ces *toions* avaient pour « responsabilité la composition des équipes de chasse et l'organisation de la chasse en concertation avec les employés de la Compagnie, mais ils remplissaient aussi le rôle de médiateur dans les disputes au sein des villages et devaient s'occuper des orphelins et des pauvres[263] ». Afin de maintenir

l'ordre, la Compagnie russo-américaine essayait de sélectionner des leaders « issus de familles où le rôle de chef se transmettait de façon héréditaire[264] ». Au moment de la prise de pouvoir par les États-Unis, l'influence de l'Église orthodoxe russe modifia un peu plus encore l'organisation en faisant fusionner le rôle de chef de village avec le rôle de leader au sein de l'église. Dans cette organisation, le *toyuq* était le chef. Un chef adjoint, appelé *sukashiq*, remplissait le rôle de lecteur laïc à l'église. Le troisième responsable, appelé *staristaq*, remplissait également les rôles de lecteur laïc et de gardien de l'église. Le *staristaq* occupait souvent cette fonction à vie. Il était responsable de l'entretien des biens de l'église, allumait et éteignait les bougies, servait de placeur, peignait les croix destinées aux tombes récentes et tenait les registres des baptêmes, des mariages, des décès, à côté d'autres tâches administratives[265].

Quand les Russes partirent, les chefs des villages furent choisis par un conseil d'Anciens[266]. Cette organisation, mêlant Église et État, reposait sur la sagesse des Anciens et semble avoir été très efficace dans le gouvernement des communautés sugpiat[267]. Elle fonctionna bien jusqu'à ce que le gouvernement américain exige des gouvernements tribaux autochtones d'Alaska qu'ils mettent en place une structure politique et administrative à l'image de celle du gouvernement américain. C'était dans les années 1930 et 1940, lorsque la loi fédérale, appelée l'*Indian Reorganization Act* (IRA), fut appliquée en Alaska[268]. Les villages qui préférèrent ne pas se restructurer sur le modèle proposé par l'IRA furent obligés d'adopter une structure « plus américaine » dans les années 1970, au moment où le gouvernement américain décida d'allouer aux villages des sommes destinées à financer leurs programmes. Le gouvernement central exigea alors que les gouvernements tribaux se munissent d'une Constitution écrite et d'arrêtés municipaux s'ils voulaient bénéficier de ces financements publics[269]. L'organisation que Pinart avait trouvée en place au moment de sa visite sur l'île de Kodiak perdura en grande partie encore un siècle, et on s'en souvenait avec nostalgie des dizaines d'années après sa modification.

L'agriculture

Dès le début de l'occupation russe, les Sugpiat furent initiés à l'agriculture et à l'élevage de bovins. Ces activités les différencièrent beaucoup des autres groupes autochtones d'Alaska. Les premières bêtes furent amenées à Kodiak en 1795. En 1833, le troupeau avait augmenté, atteignant plus de deux cent vingt têtes, mais dans les années 1880 il se réduisit à soixante[270].

L'agriculture devint une source d'investissement pour la Compagnie russo-américaine dès le début de son occupation de l'île de Kodiak. Le responsable du développement agricole pour la compagnie résidait à *Chiniatsk* (aujourd'hui Chiniak), sur la côte, à environ treize kilomètres de Saint Paul's Harbor (aujourd'hui la ville de Kodiak). Cette colonie de la compagnie possédait plus de bétail que les autres et cultivait du blé et de l'orge pour nourrir le troupeau. Au départ, l'élevage était restreint à *Igatsk* (*Orlova* ou Eagle Harbor), mais au fur et à mesure que les besoins grandissaient on commença à élever du bétail sur de nombreuses petites îles des environs, ainsi que sur Woody Island[271]. Les troupeaux déclinèrent cependant, et en 1843 tout le bétail de l'île fut réuni en trois troupeaux ne comptant pas plus de deux cents cinquante têtes, à *Chiniatsk,* à *Kalsinsk* (Kalsin Bay) et à *Igatsk*[272].

Eagle Harbor avait la réputation d'être un excellent site pour l'agriculture, les meilleurs légumes des colonies y étaient cultivés, en particulier les pommes de terre[273]. En 1847, chaque maison à Saint Paul's Harbor (Kodiak) possédait son jardin potager[274].

Petroff a pu observer la pratique de l'agriculture dans les villages sugpiat de Kodiak :

> Les conditions climatiques sur l'île sont plus favorables que dans la plupart des autres régions d'Alaska. Les gens y cultivent généralement des pommes de terre et des navets, et ils pratiquent l'élevage de bétail. Dans la colonie créole d'Afognak, il y a un champ assez vaste, enclos, qui est actuellement cultivé. Au village de Saint Paul, à

Wood Island et à Spruce Island, les fermes prennent de l'ampleur chaque année. Les récoltes sont loin d'être abondantes, et la production n'est pas assurée tous les ans, mais le rendement est suffisant pour améliorer le confort et agrémenter l'alimentation des habitants. On tente également l'élevage de moutons, dont les résultats sont encourageants[275].

Les villages

Au moment de la prise de pouvoir par les Américains en Alaska, les villages sugpiat avaient subi plusieurs réorganisations. Durant leur longue histoire, les Sugpiat avaient dû déplacer leurs villages seulement lorsque les circonstances les y avaient forcés. Mais, avec l'occupation russe, la situation n'était plus la même, et les Russes ordonnèrent le déplacement de certains villages. On créa de nouveaux villages destinés aux populations d'employés à la retraite de la Compagnie russo-américaine. Les retraités habitaient ces communautés avec leur femme sugpiaq. Beaucoup d'entre eux étaient eux-mêmes créoles, et donc sugpiat. Les premières communautés de retraités furent établies dans les années 1830 à Afognak et à Spruce Island[276]. Comme il existe peu de photographies du XIXe siècle montrant les communautés sugpiat de Kodiak, en particulier au moment de la visite de Pinart, on doit avoir recours aux textes qui les décrivent. En 1886, Henry W. Elliott, un collègue de William H. Dall de la Smithsonian Institution, publia quelques descriptions de ces communautés, qui aident à se faire une image des villages de Kodiak.

Eagle Harbor (Orlova, Igatsk)

Eagle Harbor s'étend depuis l'endroit occupé par les Russes au tout début (Three Saints Harbor) jusqu'au village de Kadiak, dans un profond renfoncement de la côte qui a permis d'y établir un autre grand village autochtone. La région autour est connue pour concentrer les meilleurs pâturages de toute l'Alaska. À l'embouchure de la crique, sur des îlots battus par les vagues, séjournent en permanence de nombreuses otaries qui fournissent aux chasseurs d'Orlova une abondante production de peaux et de tendons qui sont indispensables dans la construction des *bidarka*. Quelques familles de créoles y habitent. Ils élèvent un petit troupeau et des volailles et, généralement, perçoivent des commissions en qualité d'intermédiaires dans le commerce de la peau de loutre[277].

Wood Island *(Tangirnaq, Leisnoi)*

Lorsqu'on regarde en direction de la baie, on remarque une île très boisée, au relief un peu plus plat que les autres. Il s'agit de la célèbre Wood Island, où poussent les plus hauts épicéas de la région. Sur l'île se trouve un petit village de cent cinquante-six âmes qui habitent des maisons en rondins de bois collées les unes contre les autres. Pendant l'été, tous se transforment en chasseurs de loutres. Le village accueille aussi l'entrepôt d'une mystérieuse corporation où, depuis 1856, on coupe et conserve des tonnes de glace chaque hiver, sans jamais en avoir expédié un kilo![278] Et quand l'agent de la corporation, un homme intelligent et généreux, vous invite à l'accompagner à l'écurie pour monter l'un des trois ou quatre chevaux qui y sont gardés, et à faire le tour de l'île au galop, alors votre étonnement est à son comble. [...]

Évidemment, il y a une route, aussi incroyable que cela puisse d'abord sembler. En effet, pour que les chevaux puissent s'entraîner, on a entièrement tracé une bonne piste qui suit la ligne régulière que dessine la marée. Cette piste parcourt environ vingt kilomètres, et sert de chemin au bétail de la compagnie que l'on sort par périodes régulières pendant l'été. Pendant l'hiver, ces animaux insolites servent à transporter la glace.

Profitez bien de cette opportunité, car elle ne se représentera pas au cours de votre voyage en Alaska : vous n'aurez nulle part ailleurs l'occasion de chevaucher sur une route digne de ce nom. [...]

Un certain nombre de sloops marchands et de goélettes ont été construits sur place dans un chantier naval, fabriqués par d'habiles charpentiers de bateaux créoles, formés dans les chantiers de Sitka à l'époque où l'autorité russe dominait, et qui vivent maintenant de façon permanente dans la colonie de "Leesnoi". Quelques petites vaches de race sibérienne, des animaux résistants, comme nous en avons vues à Neelshik près de Cook's Inlet, paissent non loin de là. Les autochtones en prennent soin car ils apprécient leur lait. On trouve aussi des spécimens de cette race à Kadiak, où ils sont également limités à quelques têtes, en raison des soins qu'ils demandent en hiver et des pertes occasionnées par les ours dans les pâturages d'été[279].

Elliott note également :

Sur Wood Island [...], un petit champ de seigle, d'avoine ou d'orge est planté chaque année à l'usage des chevaux. Ici on a recours à la charrue[280].

Karluk *(Kal'uq)*

Depuis le début de la colonisation et jusqu'à aujourd'hui, le village de Karlook, situé sur le versant nord de l'île, a toujours été le lieu le plus animé du pays. Dans cette colonie de bord de côte située à l'embouchure d'une petite rivière, spécialisée dans la pêche au saumon, s'élève un bâtiment destiné à la salaison et à l'empaquetage qui date de l'époque russe, dans lequel tout le poisson distribué en Alaska est préparé chaque année. [...] À Karlook, le flux des saumons qui remontent cette rivière est si dense qu'il gêne le mouvement des canoës qui traversent le courant[281].

Ouzinkie *(Uusenkaaq)*

Un curieux petit bâtiment délavé par les intempéries m'est indiqué avec fierté et admiration par les autochtones, car c'est dans cette maison qu'un homme "comme une âme", un moine russe (Saint Herman), a élu domicile pendant plus de trente ans, enseignant aux enfants du village et à ceux des villages avoisinants. Les enfants étaient nombreux à venir pour y être formés [...]. Ce vestige unique se trouve au cœur du village voisin, sur Spruce Island, ou "Yealovnie", comme l'appellent les soixante-dix créoles russes qui habitent ici. Le petit hameau compte seulement quinze maisons de rondins, très bien entretenues, avec de charmants pots de fleurs sur le rebord des fenêtres qui leur donnent l'air d'être d'un autre monde. C'est aussi là que se dresse une minuscule chapelle grecque dans laquelle se retrouvent souvent les autochtones, rejoints par les quelques habitants du village d'Oozinkie qui se trouve un peu plus loin, juste en face, de l'autre côté du détroit. Les gens de ce village n'ont pas d'église, ils sont de purs créoles et ils s'entendent très bien avec les habitants du village de Spruce[282].

Afognak *(Ag'uaneq* and *Derevnia)*

Sur le rivage nord de l'île d'Afognak s'est établi le plus grand groupe d'anciens "colons citoyens" du Territoire. Trois cent trente personnes habitent ce gros village très pittoresque. Une grande chapelle, qui fait aussi office d'école, y présente une architecture particulière, tandis qu'un certain nombre de bateaux à rames tout neufs, utilisés par les pêcheurs et mis sur cale dans le tout petit chantier naval, signalent une industrie intéressante. La ville se déploie sur une large étendue, présentant de nombreux espaces entre les habitations, consacrés à des jardins potagers. Ici, on cultive davantage la terre que dans tout le reste de l'Alaska, dont c'est pourtant la spécialité. Les cultures de pommes de terre, de choux, de navets, de salades vertes, de radis et autres ont de bons rendements chaque année, sauf quand l'hiver se prolonge tard. On ne laboure pas la terre. Pour la préparer à la culture des pommes de terre, on la retourne simplement à l'aide de pelles, de pics et de binettes pour former des petits amas ou tumuli, sur lesquels on plante les graines. Quelques petites vaches et taureaux au pelage broussailleux, comme ceux que l'on voit à Wood Island et à Kadiak, paissent aux environs, et de nombreuses volailles, des poulets et des canards, sont élevées par les femmes et les enfants qui, durant l'hiver, les mettent à l'abri des intempéries dans leurs greniers ou dans des soupentes installées au-dessus de leur salon[283].

Afognak faisait coexister deux communautés : d'un côté, le village sugpiaq d'origine, appelé *Ag'uaneq* ; de l'autre, une communauté appelée *Derevnia*, établie, à l'origine, par la Compagnie russo-américaine pour abriter les travailleurs retraités et leurs femmes sugpiat. Ces deux villages prirent les noms d'Aléoute-ville (*Aleut-town*) et Russie-village (*Russian-town*).

Robert P. Porter, directeur du recensement américain de 1890 sur le territoire d'Alaska, nous donne des descriptions de chacune des deux parties du village d'Afognak, en commençant par la partie russe :

Le village d'Afognak, restructuré pour différentes raisons, est constitué, en fait, d'une série de colonies qui se succèdent le long d'une grande plage en arc de cercle. À l'embouchure est du détroit d'Afognak, en face de Whale Island, commence le village créole d'Afognak, qui se déploie en une seule rangée d'habitations, quelque peu éparpillées le long de la plage, sur à peu près un kilomètre. Cette colonie avait été fondée au début du siècle sous le nom de Rutkovsky par des employés[284] mis à la retraite ou percevant une pension de la Compagnie russo-américaine, que l'on incitait à élever du bétail et à pratiquer l'agriculture en quantité raisonnable. Leurs descendants ont toujours bénéficié d'un niveau d'éducation un peu plus élevé que celui de leurs voisins. On en trouvait toujours quelques-uns parmi les dirigeants locaux de la compagnie russe dans divers domaines, ou parmi les quartiers-maîtres de leur grande flotte. Les mécaniciens d'Afognak étaient les plus nombreux dans les magasins de la Compagnie, et encore aujourd'hui on trouve des charpentiers et des constructeurs de bateaux compétents descendant de quelques-unes de ces familles. Les hommes du village quittent souvent le village pour aller à la chasse ou bien travailler dans les conserveries, ou encore travailler à bord des goélettes ou de bateaux plus grands. Pendant l'hiver, ils vont couper du bois et en faire des bûches pour les établissements de pêche et de commerce. Lorsqu'ils ne sont pas là, les femmes et les vieux s'occupent du bétail ou labourent, plantent et désherbent les plants de pommes de terre, ou encore mettent à sécher le poisson que les jeunes garçons ont pêché. À l'extrémité nord du village créole, il y a une jolie chapelle construite par les habitants, une belle école édifiée par le gouvernement des États-Unis, et un magasin appartenant à la Compagnie commerciale d'Alaska. Quelques hommes blancs, des chasseurs de loutres mariés à des femmes originaires d'Afognak, se sont aussi installés ici, où ils ont trouvé un abri sûr et agréable pour leur

goélette, dans une crique ouverte sur le détroit d'Afognak[285].

Porter décrit ensuite la partie aléoute d'Afognak :

En remontant quelques centaines de mètres vers le nord, on arrive au village autochtone d'Afognak, habité par des Eskimos de Kadiak. Contrastant avec les maisons solides, construites en rondins, des créoles, on trouve ici un grand nombre de cabanes en bois recouvertes de terre, dispersées de façon désordonnée sur un sol boueux, protégées des assauts de la mer par une haute barrière de rochers et de galets[286].

Ivan Petroff, chargé du rapport du recensement américain de 1880, y adjoignit une description des villages de la région de Kodiak. Son impression était qu'en 1880, « un siècle d'influence chrétienne a tellement transformé ces indigènes qu'on ne discerne plus chez eux aucun vestige de leur férocité ou de leur sauvagerie. Leurs villages sont certainement plus propres et leur intérieur plus confortable que la plupart des villages de pêche d'Europe du Nord[287] ».

Le respect des morts

Les Sugpiat manifestaient un grand respect pour leurs morts, en particulier lorsqu'il s'agissait de chamans, de leaders importants ou d'autres personnes de haut statut social. Ce statut déterminait la façon dont ils étaient enterrés. Une des façons traditionnelles de s'occuper des morts consistait à les laisser à l'intérieur de la maison en terre, à en boucher l'accès et à déménager ensuite dans un autre endroit. Dans d'autres cas, la dépouille était placée dans une chambre à part dans la maison de terre, la pièce était scellée et les gens continuaient à vivre dans la maison[288]. Une autre pratique funéraire traditionnelle chez les Sugpiat consistait à enfouir le mort dans la terre, où on le recouvrait de pierres, puis on érigeait des poteaux tout autour[289]. Les corps des chasseurs de baleines, puisque ces derniers étaient considérés comme puissants et très importants, étaient conservés dans des grottes secrètes où ils étaient momifiés [290]. On apportait des offrandes aux momies, notamment « les premières baies, la première huile et les premiers poissons de la saison ». Les corps étaient retirés des grottes avant chaque chasse à la baleine et placés dans des cours d'eau où venaient s'abreuver les chasseurs pour assurer le succès de leur chasse [291]. Cette pratique correspond bien à la vision du monde autochtone, selon laquelle le temps est un continuel recommencement et ceux qui vivaient auparavant continuent à faire partie du groupe vivant [292].

William H. Dall, un scientifique éminent, se trouvait à Kodiak en 1874 et s'efforça d'obtenir des restes de chasseurs de baleines sugpiat enterrés dans des grottes secrètes, dans le but de les ramener à la Smithsonian Institution. Dall était au courant des tentatives infructueuses qu'avait faites Pinart, trois ans auparavant, pour se procurer des restes humains provenant de grottes funéraires de l'île de Kodiak [293]. « M. Alphonse Pinart, pendant son séjour à Kadiak, a tenté de découvrir la cachette de l'une d'entre elles dont on parlait beaucoup, mais sans succès », raconte Dall [294]. Il réussit néanmoins à recueillir une des momies qui appartenaient à L. Sheeran, un officier de douane américain en poste à Kodiak, et il la fit transférer à la Smithsonian Institution [295].

De nombreux objets cérémoniels, dont des masques, étaient placés aux côtés des morts dans les grottes. « Les Inuits de Kadiak utilisaient merveilleusement les masques lors de leurs danses et de leurs festivals, en particulier lorsque les chamans y prenaient part. On dit que ces masques ont été déposés en de nombreux lieux auprès des morts », affirme Dall [296]. Il décrit les morts sugpiat portant des « vêtements décorés de façon élaborée et parfois une armure en bois et des masques sculptés [297] », et il poursuit :

> Il n'était pas rare que les corps des morts soient mis à sécher sur un promontoire naturel, avant d'être placés dans une grotte ou dans un abri fait de pierres, vêtus d'ornements de couleurs gaies et dans la position qu'ils auraient s'ils étaient occupés à une tâche qu'ils exécutaient de leur vivant.

Ainsi, on disposait les femmes dans des positions de couture ou d'allaitement d'un enfant ; on disposait les chasseurs réputés dans des bidarkas, occupés à transpercer l'effigie d'un phoque ou d'une loutre ; ou on mettait un vieillard en train de battre un tambour, ce qu'il était chargé de faire lors des danses et des festivals inuit. À leur côté, on plaçait les masques qu'ils avaient le plus souvent portés dans leur vie. D'autres fois, la personne était vêtue de son armure en bois, recouverte de son masque, et on la munissait de modèles réduits de ses outils en bois, ou des carcasses d'animaux à fourrure qu'il aimait le plus chasser. Pour une raison ou une autre, les armes et outils réels étaient rarement placés près du mort, mais représentés uniquement par des modèles en bois [298].

Dall relate comment il percevait l'importance des masques dans les cérémonies funéraires :

> Durant les danses mystiques, répétées officiellement en face d'une représentation empaillée de l'idole, les danseurs portaient un masque en bois qui ne présentait pas de trous pour les yeux, mais était porté de telle façon qu'on ne pouvait voir que le sol à ses pieds. Les danseurs pensaient qu'à un moment donné, un esprit, sur lequel porter le regard entraînait la mort ou une catastrophe, descendait sur l'idole et l'habitait. On portait donc un masque pour s'en protéger. C'est la même idée qui les incitait à protéger le mort, parti rejoindre le monde des esprits, de la vue de cet hôte surnaturel. Une fois les danses terminées l'idole temporaire était détruite [299].

Sous l'administration russe, cependant, les Sugpiat de la région adoptèrent les coutumes de l'Église orthodoxe russe et commencèrent à construire des cimetières, en général à proximité des chapelles russes orthodoxes. Cette pratique perdure de nos jours.

Conclusion

Pinart n'effectua qu'un court séjour sur l'île de Kodiak. Arrivé le 8 novembre 1871, après un voyage en *qayaq* de deux mois depuis Unalaska, il repartit peu après le printemps de 1872[300]. Pour la plupart des gens, ce séjour n'aurait pas été d'une durée suffisante pour en apprendre beaucoup sur une culture, ni pour recueillir beaucoup d'objets culturels, comme des masques traditionnels. Sa visite avait surtout pour but d'étudier la langue sugpiaq, mais, finalement, il réunit davantage d'informations sur les coutumes et sur les objets qui témoignent de la culture matérielle sugpiaq. Il ne se contenta pas de décrire les villages sugpiat, mais il consigna aussi, en détail, de nombreuses activités traditionnelles, dont les récits, les rituels accompagnant la chasse à la baleine, la cosmologie, les danses et les chants, l'utilisation des masques et les cérémonies, toutes activités qui l'aidèrent à mieux comprendre la vision du monde des Sugpiat[301]. À cette époque de transformation profonde pour les Sugpiat, Pinart a pu assister à la fois à des cérémonies traditionnelles et au début d'une période de transition douloureuse pour les créoles, cet important groupe de la communauté sugpiaq qui venait juste de perdre le statut privilégié dont il bénéficiait sous l'administration russe. Il put témoigner de la pression qui s'exerçait sur cette société qui, après presque huit mille ans de développement culturel, avait subi un véritable génocide, l'assimilation, l'acculturation et des épidémies dévastatrices au cours des quatre-vingt-cinq années précédentes, et devait à présent s'adapter pour survivre. Si Pinart n'avait pas visité l'île de Kodiak, les Sugpiat auraient aujourd'hui beaucoup moins d'informations à leur disposition pour reconstruire leur histoire et leur culture. Les Sugpiat de l'île de Kodiak sont très reconnaissants de la visite de ce jeune visionnaire de dix-neuf ans venu de France pour visiter leur pays, il y a plus de cent trente-cinq ans.

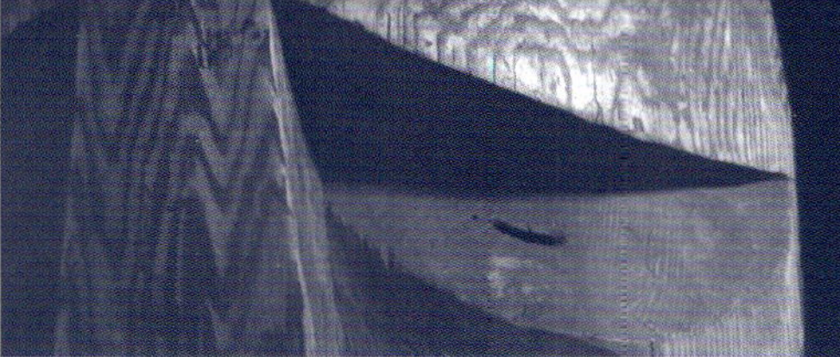

CHAPTER FOUR

Sugpiaq Masks from the Kodiak Archipelago

Sven D. Haakanson Jr. and Amy F. Steffian

Museums around the world preserve ethnographic collections from the Kodiak Sugpiaq people. At the Kunstkamera, the Peter the Great Museum of Anthropology and Ethnography in St. Petersburg, the legacy of Russia's Alaskan colonization is evident in hundreds of Sugpiaq tools and garments shipped home by naturalists and naval officers as early as 1780.[302] The expanding influence of Scandinavian seafarers in the Pacific Northwest can be seen in the National Museum of Finland, where the Alaskan collections of coastal surveyor Arvid Adolph Etholen document trade with the Sugpiat in the first decades of the nineteenth century.[303] Similarly, interest in the new Alaskan territory appears in the Smithsonian Institution's collections, where Sugpiaq items obtained in the 1880s by naturalist and tidal observer William Fisher became part of America's national museum.[304]

Together, these collections and many others[305] represent an unparalleled archive of Sugpiaq heritage, a connection to past cultural practices available from no other source. Today, Sugpiaq people equate studying these collections with apprenticing with master artists. Although an indirect result of cruel conquest and subjugation, ethnographic objects are gifts to the present. They are a source of modern cultural pride and a bridge to a shared world history.[306] Yet the ability of museum collections to tell the Sugpiaq story varies. Not all materials speak to the present with the same clarity. This is what sets Alphonse Pinart's Kodiak collections apart from others. As a linguist and a student of anthropology, Pinart collected systematically, recording the cultural context of the materials he gathered. He was not an amateur collector

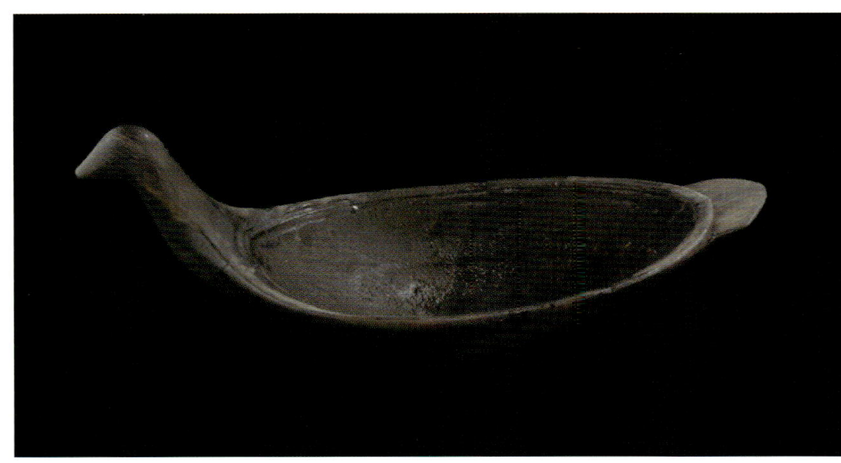

Figure 24. Bird-shaped feast bowl from Afognak Island. Pinart Collection, Château-Musée.

PHOTOGRAPH BY WILL ANDERSON.

Illustration 24. Bol de banquet en forme d'oiseau, provenant de l'île d'Afognak. Collection Pinart, Château-Musée de Boulogne-sur-Mer.

PHOTOGRAPHIE DE WILL ANDERSON.

picking up curios to fill the shelves of distant museums, but a scholar who developed an assemblage that reflected the spiritual practices of an Alaskan people. Pinart's collections reveal a little-known aspect of the nineteenth-century Sugpiaq world.

Several facts illustrate Pinart's holistic intent, particularly in comparison with others who made early ethnographic collections. First, as Anne-Claire Laronde details in Chapter 2, Pinart had no other job. He came to Alaska to study Native people. The collection of cultural information and objects was not a secondary endeavor but his primary intent. This distinguishes Pinart from many other collectors who obtained

objects sporadically during encounters with Native people or who collected ethnographic material as a postscript to their documentation of the natural world. With the notable exception of the Russian naturalist and ethnographer I. G. Voznesenskii, who collected on Kodiak in the 1840s for the St. Petersburg Academy of Sciences,[307] few collectors of Kodiak Sugpiaq objects had anthropological knowledge or training.

Additionally, Pinart collected from multiple Kodiak Sugpiaq communities, traveling with Native people in skin boats to reach remote villages. For roughly six months he journeyed around Kodiak, Afognak, and Shuyak islands, visiting St. Paul, Eagle Harbor, Karluk, Uyak,[308] and Afognak Island villages,[309] and most likely Woody Island and Ouzinkie (see Chapter 3). Thus, the objects and information he gathered reflect Kodiak Sugpiaq traditions broadly. They provide a snapshot of mid-nineteenth-century Kodiak Sugpiaq culture as known not just in the regional center but in the archipelago's Native villages.

The nature and volume of material in Pinart's collection are also notable. Pinart focused his research on Sugpiaq ceremonial practice. Although small numbers of tools and weaponry appear among the objects he obtained, the majority of artifacts are festival objects—items used in the practices of Sugpiaq ceremonies. A review of the Château-Musée's collections inventory illustrates this focus. The museum currently cares for 219 items from Pinart's Alaskan travels.[310] Of these, 115 can be attributed to the Sugpiaq people and 114 to the Kodiak archipelago.[311] Seventy masks from the Château-Musée, presented in this chapter, represent the bulk of these collections—64.2 percent of the Kodiak Sugpiaq objects held by the museum.[312] Other objects likely associated with

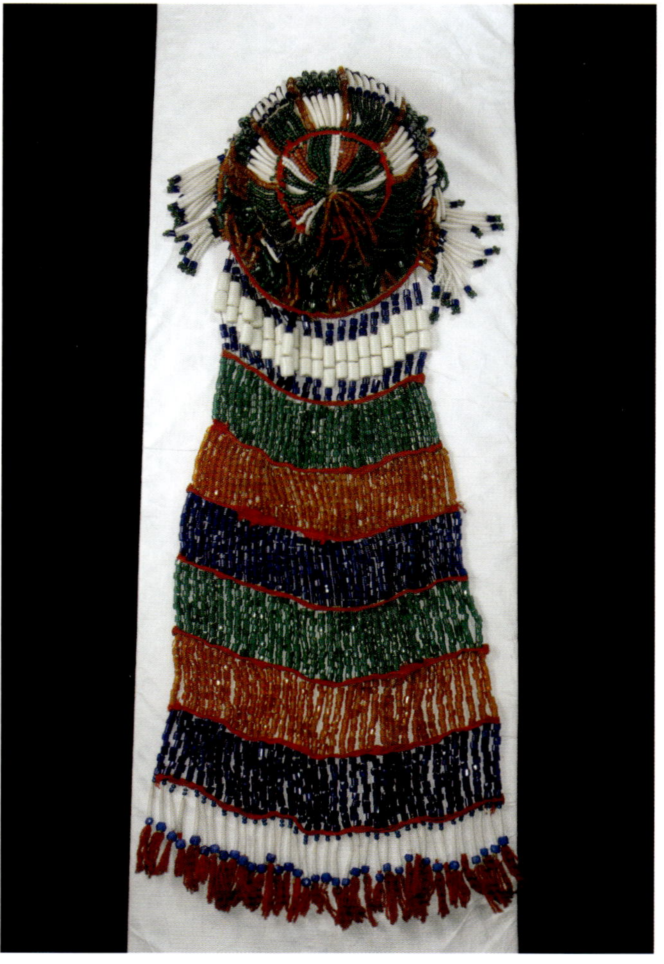

Figure 25. Beaded headdress from Afognak Island. Pinart Collection, Château-Musée.

PHOTOGRAPH BY WILL ANDERSON.

Illustration 25. Coiffe en perles provenant de l'île d'Afognak. Collection Pinart, Château-Musée de Boulogne-sur-Mer.

PHOTOGRAPHIE DE WILL ANDERSON.

ceremonies account for an additional eighteen items, or 16.5 percent of the Kodiak Sugpiaq collection. They include a drum, a drum handle, four decorated spoons, and three bowls (Figure 24), as well as nine pieces of festival regalia—three bracelets, three belts, and three beaded headdresses (Figure 25). The remaining objects are three lamps, three harpoon heads, six knife blades, six spear points, a spear, a bow, a knife, a scraper, an adze, an awl, a miniature *qayaq*, and a miniature *angyaq*.[313] Not only are there fewer of these objects, but in contrast with festival artifacts, many occur as individual specimens, indicating that they were not the focus of Pinart's attention.

This brief review illustrates that the Pinart collection contains a focused assemblage of festival gear. The presence of multiple examples of festival items, particularly the very large number of masks, provides a unique opportunity for comparative study. No other known assemblage of historic Sugpiaq items contains the quantity of masks found in the Pinart collection. Here, researchers can systematically investigate the characteristics of a nineteenth-century Sugpiaq mask. They can explore the dimensions of mask features, investigate concepts of Sugpiaq design, and examine the use of colors, attachments, and painted motifs.[314] They can also observe construction techniques. Tool marks record the movement of ancestral hands and the use of specific implements to transform wood into spirit. Pinart's large collection of Sugpiaq masks is as much an archive of manufacturing techniques as artistic conventions.

The collection is also a repository of cosmological information. Look closely at the assembled faces, and a Sugpiaq pantheon appears. Connections between the masks and the unseen world of Sugpiaq spirits are revealed further in Pinart's notes. Integral to the collection are his handwritten journal entries, which record mask names, songs, dances, and more than forty Sugpiaq legends. These rare examples of Sugpiaq oratory add context to the masks, placing them into their cultural setting and identifying their meaning to Sugpiaq people. Pinart's journals show the objects were still firmly connected to an active ceremonial culture. In addition

to the texts, Pinart's notes describe masked dancing at a festival in Uyak Bay in 1872.[315] Thus, the texts allow us to see the pieces as more than works of art—as religious artifacts. They also document the relationships between certain specimens. The masks were not necessarily collected individually, but as sets related to specific Sugpiaq performances or legends (see Appendix).[316]

In sum, the Pinart collection with its large and well-documented assemblage of masks provides a detailed look into the nineteenth-century Kodiak Sugpiaq world, its artistic customs, technological traditions, and spiritual beliefs. As with all collections, however, some key questions remain unanswered. One of these questions is how Pinart managed to collect so many masks. As outlined in Chapter 1 masks were among the most powerful objects in Sugpiaq culture. They were spiritually potent objects associated with the supernatural world and systematically separated from daily life to protect people. How could a young outsider obtain so many powerful religious artifacts? There are a number of possibilities. As Gordon Pullar reveals in Chapter 3 Pinart visited Kodiak just after the transfer of Alaska to American rule. He arrived before the influx of American missionaries and educators, and thus before the intense suppression of Sugpiaq spiritual practices and language. The objects he collected were still in use. Yet, they had also been marginalized by a century of Russian rule and the presence of new religion. As Pullar notes, most Sugpiat were members of the Russian Orthodox Church by the 1870s. Perhaps ambivalence about an old religion in changing times encouraged people to give or sell masks to Pinart, or to tell him where they were stored.

Another possibility is that Pinart commissioned some of the masks to take back to France. His collection includes a series of small painted masks made of white oak.[317] These masks are very different from the much larger, heavier masks that comprise the remaining collection. They don't display the wear typically found on larger pieces, and their painted surfaces are better preserved. In short, they do not appear to have been danced.[318] Interestingly, these are the pieces for which there are Alutiiq songs. Perhaps a Sugpiaq carver custom-made these smaller painted pieces to illustrate songs Pinart had already collected.

It is also possible that Pinart took some of the masks from caves where they were secluded. In September of 1871, Pinart collected six masks from a cave on Unga Island in the Shumagin Island group.[319] Sugpiaq people maintained similar caves where whalers prepared for the hunt[320] and people kept powerful ceremonial gear. We know that Pinart was aware of such caves, as his notes provide extensive descriptions of a cave and its contents.[321] The removal of masks from Kodiak caves would help to explain the puzzling lack of detailed provenance documentation for many of the pieces. Pinart took extensive notes on his travels. He recorded geographical and nautical data; described settlements; recorded legends; summarized rituals, dances, and shamanic practices; recorded Sugpiaq vocabulary and grammar; and even made artifact and landscape drawings,[322] yet he did not note how or where

Figure 26. Pinart collection masks on display at the Alutiiq Museum, Kodiak.

PHOTOGRAPH BY SVEN HAAKANSON JR.

Illustration 26. Masques de la collection Pinart exposés à l'Alutiiq Museum à Kodiak.

PHOTOGRAPHIE BY SVEN HAAKANSON JR.

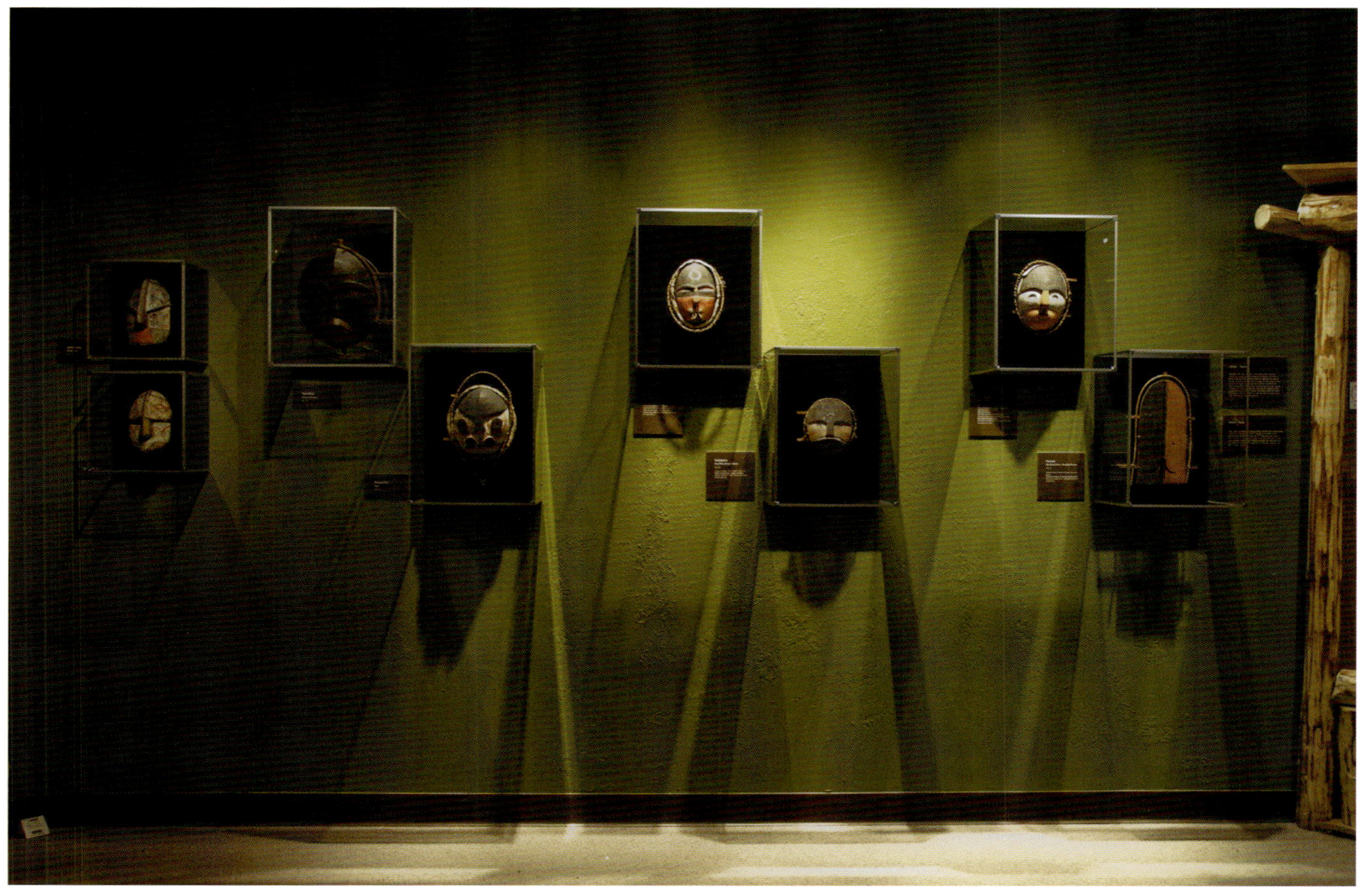

he obtained many of the masks, or how he transported such a large number of heavy pieces from remote areas. Taking objects reflecting the practices he was studying may have encouraged Pinart to remain silent about his procurement techniques. These details remain a mystery.

The following pages present the seventy-seven Kodiak Sugpiaq masks preserved in the Château-Musée and Musée du quai Branly collections. The pieces appear in five general groups that reflect age, carving styles, decoration techniques, and the cultural information preserved in Pinart's notes. The first group includes the oldest masks, those that show stone tool marks and distinctive signs of age—heavy wear and eroded wood. The next group includes the large, minimally decorated masks of a similar carving style. Again, these larger masks show wear, suggesting they have been danced. The masks for which Pinart collected songs appear in the third grouping, followed by the elaborately decorated masks, and finally, the set of small, painted white oak masks that Pinart may have commissioned to accompany the legends he recorded, primarily in Afognak village. Throughout the presentation we place related masks together.

For each mask we provide the current museum catalog number, a set of maximum dimensions in centimeters (length, width, and depth),[323] and a list of the raw materials present today. Sugpiaq artist, anthropologist, and hunter Sven Haakanson Jr. made the raw material identifications relying on his knowledge of the Kodiak environment, five years of research on the Pinart collection, and information in the Château-Musée's records. Experienced Alaskan carvers Perry Eaton and Jim Dillard helped Haakanson identify the wood types represented. However, as many of the masks have lost paint and organic attachments to the rigors of time,[324] these lists must be considered a minimal account of the materials once present. Faded pigments, tufts of animal hair, feather shafts, and bits of leather testify to the use of elaborate decorations on many pieces. Furthermore, because it is difficult to identify some materials with specificity, we provide a general identification of the raw materials, erring on the side of caution. For example, while we might suspect

that the sinew binding an element to a mask is made of porpoise tendons, as was often the custom in Sugpiaq communities, we simply identify the materials as sinew.[325] Similarly, although we suspect that red ochre is one of the red pigments applied to some masks, particularly the older, larger pieces in the collection, we identify all red pigment as red paint.

In addition to descriptive information, we provide a name in Alutiiq and English for most masks. Some of these names are original to the pieces. Pinart recorded names for twenty-seven of the masks he collected, both in his notes and by writing directly on the backs of some pieces.[326] Some of these names survived to the present. With the help of Sugpiaq Elders and linguist Jeff Leer, Haakanson worked to translate mask names. In the following presentation, we underline the original Alutiiq names for identification. These are presented even if they could not be translated. However, as the majority of masks did not have recorded Alutiiq names, Alutiiq speakers worked as a team to provide them with names. To differentiate the new Alutiiq mask names from those recorded by Pinart in the nineteenth century, we do not underline modern Alutiiq names. Alutiiq speakers offer these modern mask names in the spirit of reawakening that the *Giinaquq* project reflects. By naming the masks, Sugpiaq Elders helped to reunite them with the Kodiak Sugpiaq community and to breathe new life into sentient objects that have been asleep for over a century. There was one exception to this pattern. Unnamed masks among the set of small painted pieces were not subjected to this process. As the majority of named masks came from this group, and as Pinart's notes are difficult to read, the translation team felt that additional research might eventually yield names for these pieces.

Where possible, we also provide provenance information. As Desson discusses, not every mask has information about its origins.[327] Pinart's field notes and collection catalog[328] do not provide complete or consistent summaries of the origins of each mask, beyond the general attributions of Kodiak Island or Afognak Island. In some cases, however, there are records of a mask originating from the community of Eagle Harbor.

Similarly, only twenty-four of the masks have accompanying texts—songs, dances, or legends. While critical contributions to the collection and its interpretation, and ones that have not been widely shared, these limited but sometimes lengthy materials appear in the book's appendix. Where appropriate, they are presented along with information documenting the steps in their recent translation from Alutiiq into English and French. In the following pages we note which masks have accompanying texts to assist readers in connecting the pieces with their additional documentation. There is also a summary table of mask texts in the Appendix (Table 1).

Finally, for each mask we provide a set of color photographs showing front, side, back, and detail views. These images provide more information than the typical facial portraits found in previous publications.[329] The size and the depth of pieces often strike people viewing the mask collection for the first time. Many of the masks are quite large, with deeply carved features. The side and detail photographs offered here allow readers to sense the proportions of carved features, in addition to the arrangement of features and use of design elements offered by more standard portrait views. Other images show details of construction or decoration, to illustrate the subtle details of specific masks. These include pictures of the insides or backs of masks.

This presentation is intentionally technical. Others have published artistic descriptions of a selection of the masks[330] and completed detailed analyses of the masks' form and coloring.[331] The goal of this presentation is to reunite the masks with the cultural information Pinart collected and provide readers with a comprehensive set of images to show both their artistry and the details of their construction. With this data, and the articles in the book, we aim to place the masks back in their cultural context so they may be a source of ongoing illumination for those who wish to explore the cultural heritage of the Kodiak Sugpiat.

Les masques sugpiat de l'archipel de Kodiak

Sven W. Haakanson Jr. et Amy F. Steffian

Les collections ethnographiques du peuple supiaq de Kodiak sont conservées dans plusieurs musées répartis dans le monde entier. Au Kunstkamera, le musée d'anthropologie et d'ethnographie de Pierre le Grand à Saint-Pétersbourg, les objets hérités de la colonisation russe de l'Alaska sont présentés au travers de centaines d'outils et de vêtements sugpiat rapportés par bateau dès 1780 par des chercheurs en sciences naturelles et des capitaines de la marine [302]. La maîtrise des peuples scandinaves sur les mers dans le nord-ouest du Pacifique se fait sentir au Musée national de Finlande, où les collections d'Alaska recueillies par le géomètre Arvid Adolph Etholes, qui effectuait des relevés sur la côte, témoignent des échanges commerciaux avec les Sugpiat au début du XIXe siècle [303]. C'est ainsi que l'intérêt pour les nouveaux territoires d'Alaska apparaît dans les collections de la Smithsonian Institution, où les objets sugpiat obtenus dans les années 1880 par le biologiste marin William Fisher, spécialiste des crustacés et de l'observation des marées, ont rejoint le musée national américain [304].

Ces collections, parmi d'autres encore [305], représentent des archives exceptionnelles sur le patrimoine sugpiaq, un lien avec des pratiques culturelles ancestrales que l'on ne peut trouver auprès d'aucune autre source. Aujourd'hui, pour les Sugpiat, étudier ces collections équivaut à étudier auprès de grands maîtres. Bien qu'ils résultent indirectement d'une conquête cruelle et d'une soumission, ces objets ethnographiques représentent un cadeau. Ils sont source de fierté pour la culture de notre temps et constituent une histoire que nous partageons avec le monde [306]. Cependant, l'aptitude des collections muséales à nous raconter les histoires sugpiat est variable. Tous les objets ne nous parlent pas avec la même évidence. C'est ce qui fait de la collection koniag d'Alphonse Pinart une collection unique. Linguiste, étudiant en anthropologie, Pinart a fait une collecte systématique, consignant par écrit le contexte culturel des objets qu'il recueillait. Ce n'était pas un collecteur amateur qui aurait choisi par curiosité des objets à mettre sur les étagères d'un lointain musée, mais, en tant que chercheur, il a réuni un groupe d'objets qui témoignaient des pratiques spirituelles d'un peuple d'Alaska. La collection de Pinart révèle bien un aspect méconnu de la culture sugpiaq au XIXe siècle.

Plusieurs faits attestent l'intention de Pinart d'effectuer une étude complète, surtout quand on compare son travail avec celui des premiers auteurs qui réalisèrent des collectes ethnographiques. Pour commencer, comme le souligne Anne-Claire Laronde dans le chapitre 2, Pinart n'avait pas d'autre occupation. Il était venu en Alaska pour étudier ce peuple autochtone. La collecte d'informations et d'objets culturels ne représentait pas une activité annexe, elle était son intention première. En cela, il se distingue de beaucoup de chercheurs qui se procuraient des objets de façon sporadique à l'occasion de rencontres avec des autochtones, ou qui entreprenaient des collectes ethnographiques dans le but d'illustrer leur documentation sur l'environnement naturel. À l'exception notoire du naturaliste et ethnographe russe I. G. Voznesenskii, qui réalisa une collecte sur l'île de Kodiak dans les années 1840 pour l'Académie des sciences de Saint-Pétersbourg[307], peu de chercheurs qui recueillirent des objets sugpiat s'intéressaient ou étaient formés à l'anthropologie.

De plus, Pinart recueillit ces objets auprès de plusieurs communautés sugpiat de Kodiak, se déplaçant accompagné d'autochtones, dans des embarcations en peau, pour atteindre des villages éloignés. Pendant environ six mois, il parcourut les îles de Kodiak, d'Afognak, et de Shuyak, et visita Saint-Paul, Eagle Harbor, Karluk, Uyak[308], les villages de l'île d'Afognak[309] et, très probablement, Woody Island et Ouzinkie (*cf. chapitre 3*). C'est la raison pour laquelle les objets et les informations collectés témoignent de l'ensemble des traditions sugpiat de Kodiak. Ils dressent un panorama de la culture sugpiaq de Kodiak au XIXe siècle, non seulement telle qu'elle était dans la capitale régionale mais également dans les villages autochtones de tout l'archipel.

La nature et le volume de la collecte de Pinart sont également remarquables. Pinart centra ses recherches sur les pratiques cérémonielles sugpiat et même si un petit nombre d'outils et d'armes font partie des objets collectés, la majorité des artefacts proviennent de festivals où les objets étaient réellement utilisés au cours de cérémonies. On en a la confirmation en examinant l'inventaire des collections du Château-Musée. Celui-ci conserve aujourd'hui deux cent dix-neuf objets rapportés par Pinart lors de ses voyages en Alaska[310]. Parmi ceux-ci, cent quinze peuvent être attribués aux Sugpiat, dont cent quatorze à l'archipel de Kodiak[311]. Les soixante-dix masques conservés au Château-Musée et présentés dans ce chapitre constituent le cœur de cette collection, soit 64,2 % des objets sugpiat de Kodiak du musée[312]. On dénombre dix-huit autres objets associés, pense-t-on, à des cérémonies, soit 16,5 % de la collection sugpiaq de Kodiak. Ce sont : un tambour, une poignée de tambour, quatre cuillers décorées et trois bols (*ill. 23*), ainsi que neuf éléments ornementaux portés lors de festivals : trois bracelets, trois ceintures et trois coiffes de perles (*ill. 24*). Enfin, les derniers objets consistent en trois lampes, trois pointes de harpons, six lames de couteaux, six fers de lance, un arc, un couteau, un racloir, une doloire, un poinçon, un modèle réduit de *qayaq* et un modèle réduit d'*angyaq*[313]. Non seulement ces objets forment un plus petit groupe, mais, contrairement aux artefacts de festivals, ils sont isolés et on peut en déduire qu'ils n'étaient pas au centre de l'intérêt de Pinart.

Ce rapide inventaire montre que la collection Pinart réunit un ensemble centré sur les costumes et les accessoires de festivals. La présence de multiples objets de festivals, dont un grand nombre de masques, offre l'opportunité unique d'une étude comparative. Aucun autre ensemble connu d'œuvres sugpiat ne contient autant de masques que cette collection. Elle permet aux chercheurs l'étude systématique des masques sugpiat du XIXe siècle. Ils peuvent se pencher sur les dimensions de leurs traits, la conception de leurs formes, l'utilisation des couleurs, la réalisation des objets qu'on y adjoint ou les motifs peints[314]. Ils peuvent aussi analyser les techniques de fabrication, tandis que les empreintes laissées par les outils révèlent les mouvements des mains ancestrales et l'utilisation d'outils spécifiques pour transformer le bois en esprit. L'important rassemblement de masques sugpiat de Pinart permet de connaître les moyens de fabrication tout autant que les conventions artistiques de l'époque.

La collection est aussi un trésor d'informations cosmologiques. Si l'on observe attentivement l'ensemble des visages, le panthéon sugpiaq apparaît. Les liens entre les masques et le monde invisible des esprits sugpiat sont encore plus manifestes à l'examen des notes de terrain de Pinart. Ces notes consignées à la main dans son journal, qui font partie intégrante de la collection, mentionnent des noms de masques, des chants, des danses, et racontent plus de quarante légendes sugpiat. Ces exemples d'art oratoire viennent enrichir le contexte des masques, en les replaçant dans leur environnement culturel et en explicitant la signification qu'ils revêtaient pour les Sugpiat. Le journal tenu par Pinart montre que ces objets étaient alors fortement liés à une culture de cérémonies. Pinart décrit par ailleurs dans ses notes une danse masquée lors d'un festival tenu à Uyak Bay, en 1872[315]. Ces textes nous montrent que ces objets sont plus que des objets d'art : ce sont des artefacts religieux. Ils nous renseignent également sur les relations qui existaient entre certains objets. Les masques n'étaient pas toujours recueillis de façon isolée, mais parfois ils faisaient partie d'un ensemble participant d'un spectacle ou d'une légende particulière sugpiat (*cf. Annexes*)[316].

En définitive, la collection Pinart, parce qu'elle réunit un grand nombre de masques bien documentés, fournit une vision riche en détails du monde sugpiaq de Kodiak au XIXe siècle : ses pratiques artistiques, ses techniques traditionnelles et ses croyances spirituelles. Comme pour toute collection, néanmoins, certaines questions-clés demeurent sans réponse. L'une d'entre elle étant de savoir comment Pinart a pu se procurer autant de masques. Comme il est expliqué dans le premier chapitre de cet ouvrage, les masques faisaient partie des objets considérés comme les plus puissants de la culture sugpiaq. Ces objets au pouvoir spirituel redoutable étaient associés au monde du surnaturel et on les écartait systématiquement de la vie quotidienne pour s'en protéger. Alors, comment un jeune étranger a-t-il pu obtenir autant de puissants artefacts religieux ? On peut émettre un certain nombre d'hypothèses. Comme l'indique Gordon Pullar au chapitre 3, Pinart se rendit à Kodiak immédiatement après le transfert de l'Alaska sous l'administration américaine. Il arriva avant l'afflux de missionnaires et d'éducateurs américains, et donc avant l'interdiction des pratiques spirituelles et de la langue sugpiaq. Les objets qu'il collecta étaient encore utilisés, mais ils avaient été mis à l'écart pendant tout un siècle, sous la domination russe, et confrontés à la présence d'une nouvelle religion. En 1871, comme le remarque Pullar, la plupart des Sugpiat étaient devenus membres de l'Église orthodoxe russe. Peut-être les gens éprouvaient-ils alors un sentiment d'ambivalence envers leur ancienne religion en cette époque mouvementée, qui les a poussés à donner ou à vendre des masques à Pinart, ou à lui confier où ils étaient entreposés.

Une autre hypothèse serait que Pinart ait passé commande de certains masques afin de les rapporter en France.

Sa collection comprend une série de petits masques peints fabriqués en chêne blanc[317], qui s'avèrent très différents des masques considérablement plus grands et plus lourds qui forment le reste de la collection. Ils ne portent pas les signes d'usure que l'on observe sur les pièces plus grandes et leur surface peinte est mieux conservée. Bref, ils ne semblent pas avoir été portés lors de danses[318]. Il est intéressant de noter que ce sont les pièces auxquelles correspondent les chants alutiiq. Peut-être un sculpteur sugpiaq a-t-il fabriqué sur commande ces plus petites pièces peintes pour illustrer les chants collectés par Pinart auparavant.

On peut aussi envisager l'éventualité que Pinart ait pris certains de ces masques dans des grottes où ils avaient été placés pour les mettre à l'écart. En septembre 1871, Pinart collecta six masques dans une grotte sur l'île d'Unga, l'une des îles Shumagin[319]. Les Sugpiat entretenaient des grottes comme celle-ci qui servaient aux chasseurs de baleines à se préparer à la chasse[320] et dans lesquelles les gens conservaient un puissant équipement de cérémonies. On sait que Pinart connaissait l'existence de telles grottes, et ses notes fournissent des descriptions détaillées de l'une d'entre elles dont il indique le contenu[321]. La collecte de certains masques à l'intérieur de ces grottes de Kodiak peut expliquer pourquoi nous manquons étrangement de détails et de documentation sur la provenance de nombreuses pièces Pinart prenait beaucoup de notes lors de ses voyages. Il consignait des renseignements géographiques et nautiques, décrivait des colonies, recueillait des légendes, résumait des rituels, des danses, des pratiques chamaniques. Il enregistrait le vocabulaire et la grammaire sugpiat, et il réalisait même des dessins d'artefacts et de paysages[322]. Pourtant, il ne dit rien de la façon dont il obtint nombre de masques, ni de leur lieu d'acquisition, ni comment il transporta une telle quantité de lourds objets depuis des endroits certainement très isolés. Le fait de s'emparer d'objets qui révélaient des pratiques religieuses qu'il étudiait l'incita peut-être à rester discret quant à ses méthodes d'acquisition. Ces aspects restent une énigme.

Les pages qui suivent présentent les soixante-dix-sept masques sugpiat de Kodiak conservés dans les collections du

Château-Musée et du musée du Quai-Branly. Ces pièces sont répertoriées en cinq groupes distincts qui tiennent compte de leur âge, de leur style de gravure, de leur décoration et des notes culturelles de Pinart à leur sujet. Le premier groupe concerne les masques les plus anciens, qui présentent des marques d'outils en pierre et des signes qui témoignent de leur ancienneté : usure importante et érosion du bois. Le groupe suivant réunit les masques de plus grande taille dont la décoration est minimale mais dont le style de gravure est similaire. Eux aussi présentent des signes d'usure, qui laissent penser qu'ils ont servi lors de danses. Les masques liés à des chants collectés par Pinart constituent le troisième groupe, suivi d'un groupe de masques très ornementés. Vient enfin le groupe de masques de taille réduite en chêne blanc, que Pinart a peut-être commandés pour accompagner les légendes qu'il avait recueillies, pour la plupart dans le village d'Afognak. Nous présentons ensemble les masques qui sont regroupés sous un même critère.

Pour chaque masque, nous donnons son numéro de conservation dans la collection du musée, ses dimensions en centimètres (longueur, largeur, et épaisseur)[323], et la liste des matériaux bruts utilisés. Sven Haakanson Jr., artiste, anthropologue et chasseur sugpiaq, a identifié les matériaux bruts grâce à sa connaissance de l'environnement de Kodiak, grâce aussi à ses cinq années d'étude de la collection Pinart et aux informations qu'il a trouvées dans les archives du Château-Musée. Perry Eaton et Jim Dillard, deux sculpteurs d'Alaska qui ont une longue expérience, ont aidé Haakanson à identifier les essences de bois utilisés. Avec le temps, les masques ont perdu en partie leur peinture ou leurs accessoires décoratifs faits de matériaux naturels[324], aussi ces listes restent-elles un aperçu succinct des matériaux autrefois présents. Les pigments de couleur passée, les touffes de poils d'animaux, les tuyaux de plumes et les fragments de cuir montrent qu'on utilisait des décorations élaborées sur de nombreuses pièces. Par ailleurs, devant la difficulté que nous avons eue à identifier certains matériaux de façon précise, nous donnons par précaution une indication globale des matériaux bruts. Par exemple, même si nous

pensons qu'un lien en tendon appartenant à un masque est fait de tendon de marsouin, comme c'était souvent l'habitude dans les communautés sugpiat, nous préférons l'identifier simplement comme tendon[325]. De la même façon, bien que nous pensions qu'un ocre de couleur rouge composait les pigments rouges relevés sur un masque, en particulier s'il faisait partie des pièces les plus anciennes et les plus imposantes de la collection, nous l'identifions seulement comme peinture rouge.

En plus des informations techniques, nous indiquons le nom de chaque masque en alutiiq et en français. Certains noms sont ceux d'origine. Pinart a indiqué les noms de vingt-sept des masques qu'il a collectés, soit dans ses notes, soit directement au dos de certaines pièces[326]. Certains de ces noms sont parvenus jusqu'à nous. Avec l'aide d'Anciens sugpiat et du linguiste Jeff Leer, Haakanson s'est appliqué à traduire certains noms de masques. Dans la présentation qui suit, nous soulignons les noms alutiiq d'origine pour les identifier, même lorsqu'ils n'ont pas pu être traduits. Cependant, pour la plus grande partie des masques, le nom alutiiq n'est pas identifié, aussi une équipe de personnes parlant la langue alutiiq a-t-elle tâché de leur en trouver un. Pour différencier les nouveaux noms de masques en alutiiq de ceux du XIXᵉ siècle rapportés par Pinart, nous ne soulignons pas les noms modernes alutiiq, ce qui incarne bien l'esprit du projet « Giinaquq ». Les Anciens ont offert aux masques ces nouveaux noms en alutiiq dans le but de leur permettre de retrouver leur vitalité, toujours dans l'esprit du projet « Giinaquq ». En renommant ces masques, les Anciens sugpiat ont contribué à ce qu'ils puissent être à nouveau réunis à la communauté sugpiaq, à insuffler une nouvelle vie dans ces objets sensibles, restés endormis pendant plus d'un siècle. Nous avons cependant admis une exception pour les masques sans nom qui appartiennent au groupe de petites pièces peintes. Puisque la plus grande partie des masques portant un nom relevait de ce groupe, et que les notes de Pinart sont difficiles à déchiffrer, l'équipe traductrice a été conduite à penser que des recherches à venir permettraient peut-être de retrouver un jour les noms de ces pièces.

Lorsqu'elle était connue, nous avons aussi indiqué la provenance de la pièce. Comme le note Desson, nous n'avons pas nécessairement d'informations sur l'origine de tous les masques[327]. Ni les notes de terrain de Pinart ni le catalogue de la collection[328] n'offrent un aperçu complet ou cohérent concernant l'origine de chacun des masques. On ne connaît parfois que leur attribution d'ordre général à l'île de Kodiak ou à celle d'Afognak. Pour certains d'entre eux, néanmoins, les archives précisent que le masque est issu de la communauté de Eagle Harbor.

Par ailleurs, seuls vingt-quatre masques ont pu être associés à des textes : un chant, une danse, une légende. Ces textes sont des éléments essentiels de la collection, qui contribuent à son interprétation, mais qui n'ont guère été diffusés. Nous les avons placés ici en annexe. Bien qu'en nombre limité, ils s'avèrent parfois longs. Lorsque cela s'avère judicieux, nous les présentons accompagnés des informations qui montrent les étapes de leur récente traduction de l'alutiiq à l'anglais ou au français. Dans les pages qui suivent, nous signalons les masques assortis de textes, afin de permettre au lecteur de relier les œuvres à leur documentation supplémentaire. Un tableau propose également, en annexe, les textes associés aux masques *(tableau 1)*.

Enfin, chaque masque fait l'objet de photographies en couleur prises de face, de profil et de dos, ainsi que de détails, ce qui permet de donner davantage d'informations que les vues frontales habituellement présentées dans les publications précédentes[329]. En effet, les gens qui voient la collection de masques pour la première fois sont souvent surpris par la taille ou l'épaisseur des pièces. Beaucoup de ces masques sont très grands, et la gravure des traits est profondément marquée. Les photographies de profil et de détails permettent au lecteur de se faire une idée de la taille des traits gravés, ce qui n'était pas le cas dans les vues frontales qui ne montrent que la disposition des traits ou des éléments de dessin. D'autres vues révèlent des détails d'assemblage ou de décoration, qui sont différents pour chaque masque. Ces photographies des détails montrent également des vues de l'intérieur ou du dos des masques.

Cette présentation des masques est volontairement technique. Des publications artistiques d'une sélection de masques[330] qui offrent une analyse détaillée de leurs formes et de l'agencement de leurs couleurs ont déjà vu le jour auparavant[331]. L'objectif de cet ouvrage est de réunir les masques accompagnés de l'information culturelle collectée par Pinart, et d'offrir au lecteur une série complète de photographies qui dévoilent à la fois leur beauté et les détails de leur construction. Grâce à ces informations et grâce aux articles réunis dans ce livre, nous espérons avoir replacé les masques dans leur contexte culturel et qu'ils deviennent ainsi une inépuisable source d'enthousiasme pour ceux qui désirent explorer l'héritage culturel que nous ont légué les Sugpiat de Kodiak.

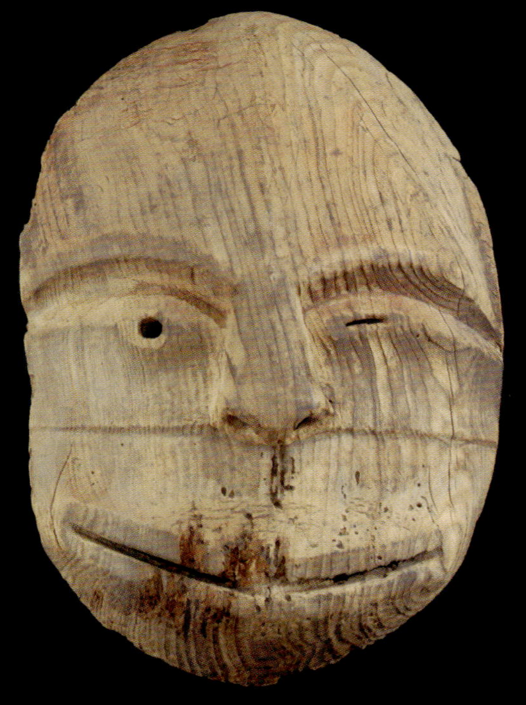
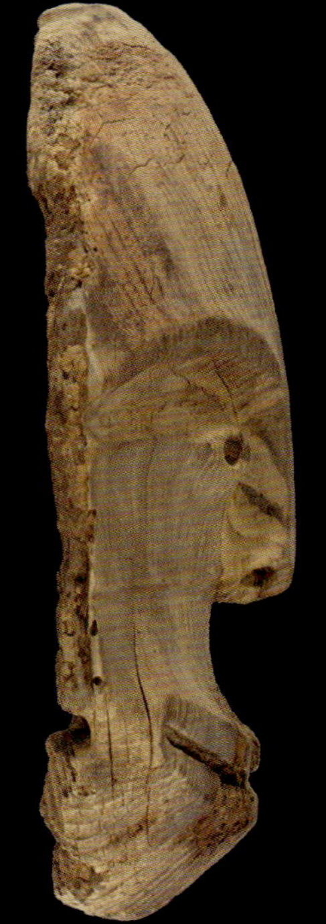
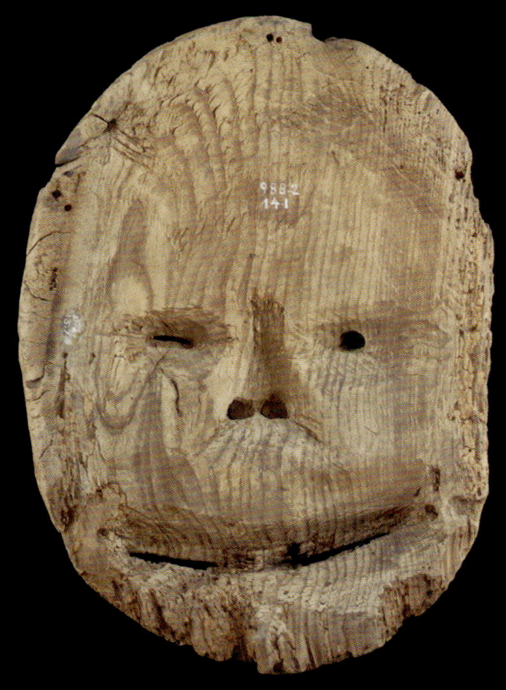

Figure 27
Temciyusqaq
Skeptical One

988-2-141
H. 40 cm
W. 29 cm
D. 11 cm
Spruce, red paint
Eagle Harbor

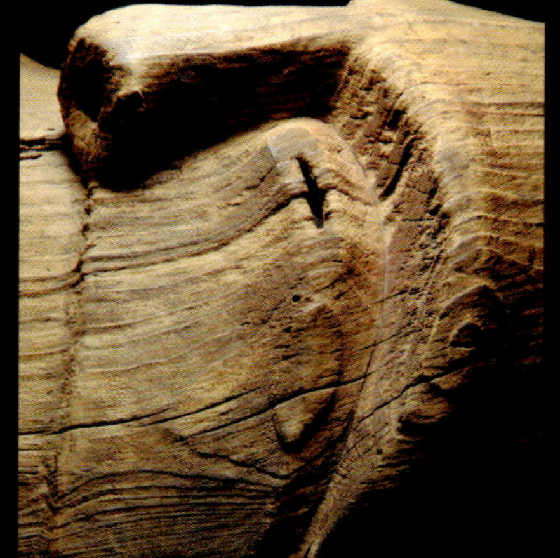
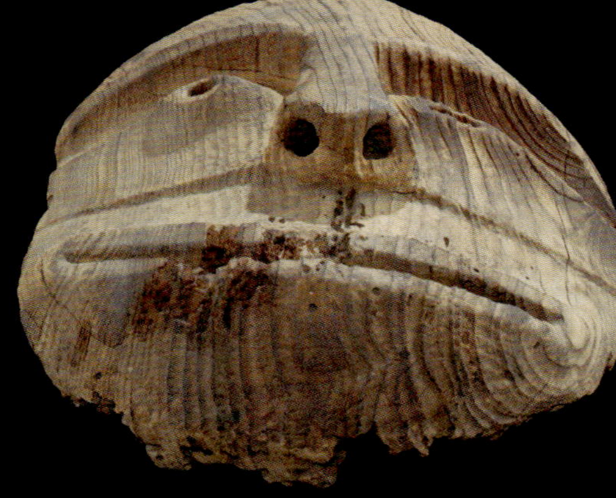

llustration 27
Temciyusqaq
Celui qui est sceptique

988-2-141
H. 40 cm
L. 29 cm
Ép. 11 cm
Épicéa, peinture rouge
Eagle Harbor

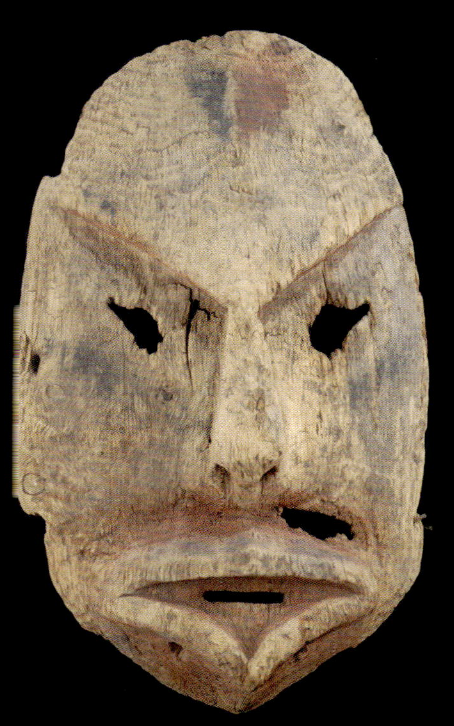
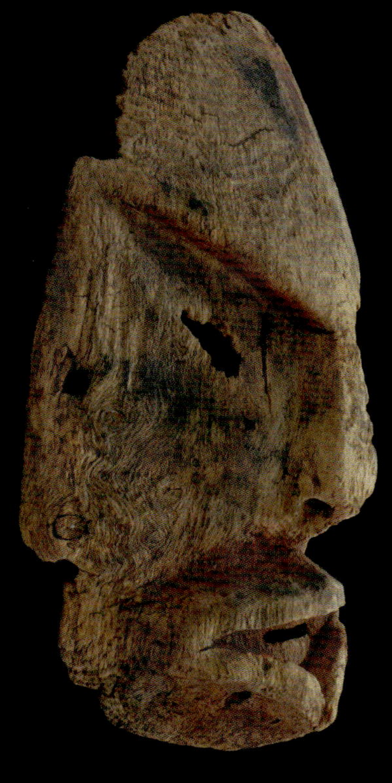
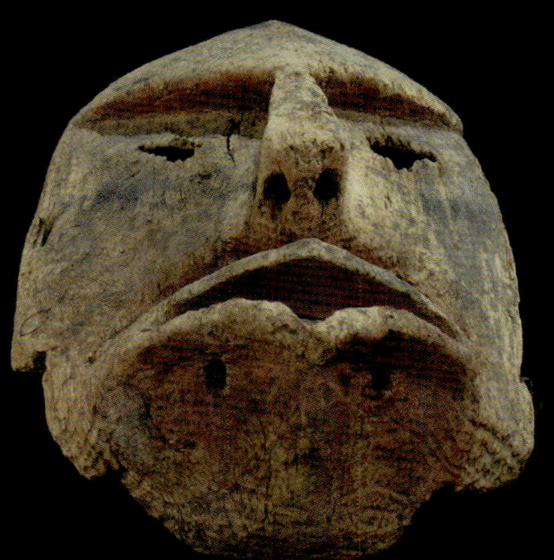
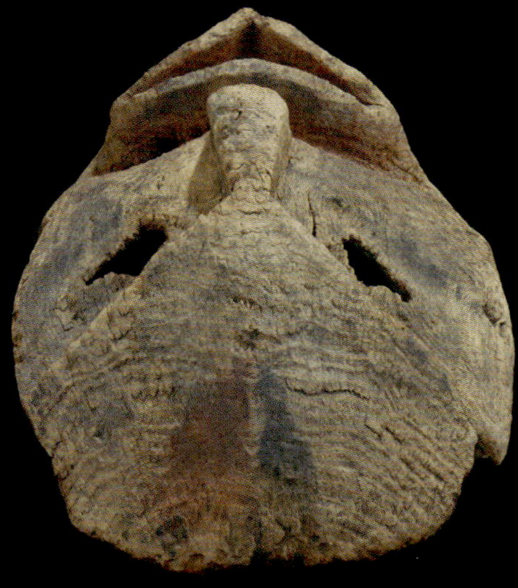

Figure 28
Alingnasqaq
Scary One

988-2-143
H. 34 cm
W. 20.5 cm
D. 10 cm
Spruce, red paint, black
paint
Kodiak Island

Illustration 28
Alingnasqaq
Celui qui fait peur

988-2-143
H. 34 cm
L. 20,5 cm
Ép. 10 cm
Épicéa, peinture rouge,
peinture noire
Île de Kodiak

Figure 29
Aitauwasqaq
Open-Mouth One

988-2-145
H. 30.5 cm
W. 16 cm
D. 8 cm
Douglas fir, baleen, red paint
Kodiak Island

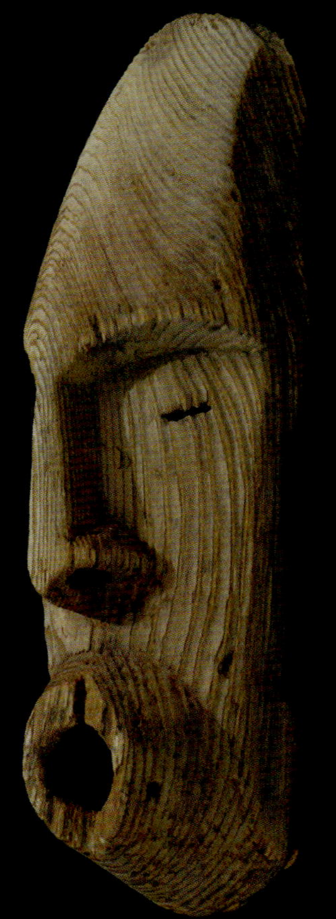
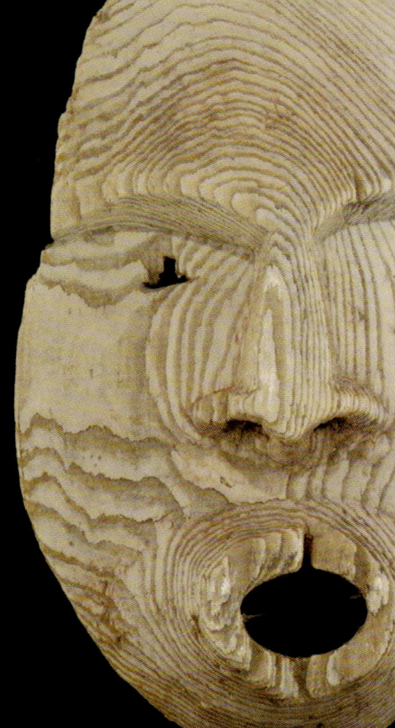
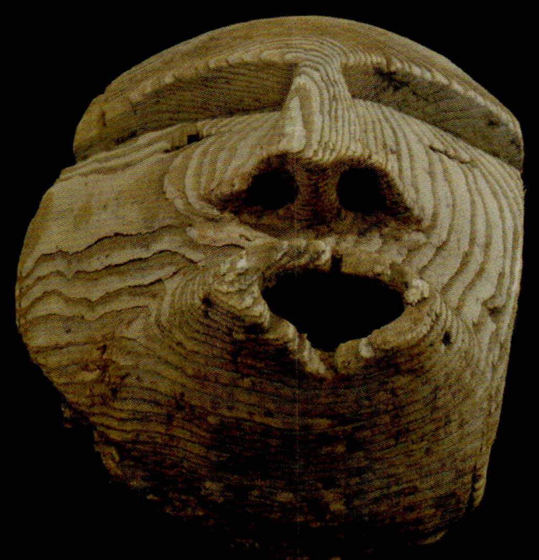

Illustration 29
Aitauwasqaq
Celui qui a la bouche ouverte

988-2-145
H. 30,5 cm
L. 16 cm
Ép. 8 cm
Sapin de Douglas, fanon de baleine, peinture
rouge
Île de Kodiak

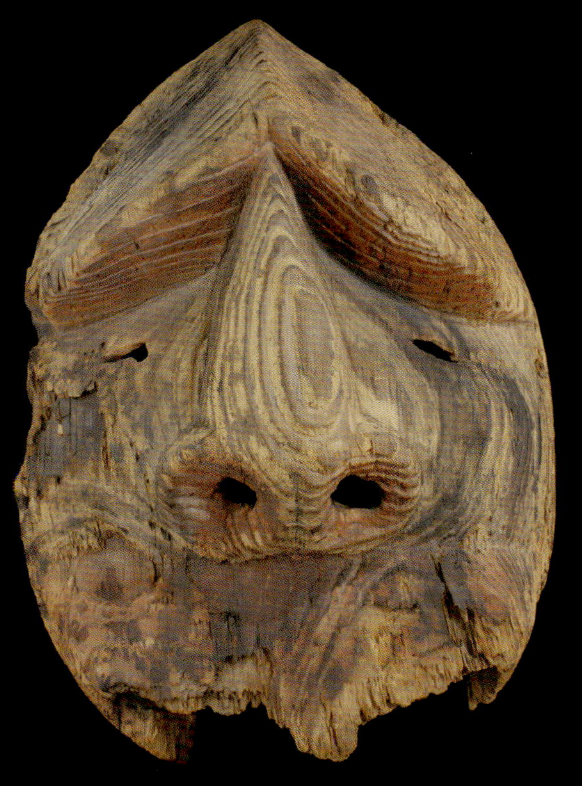
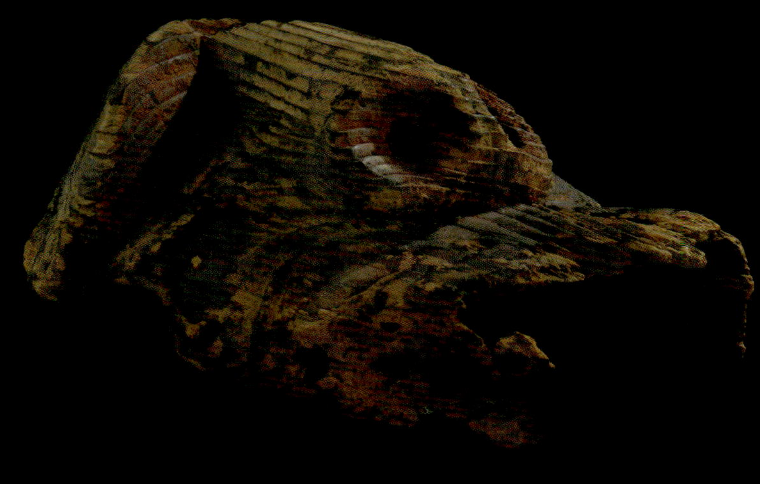
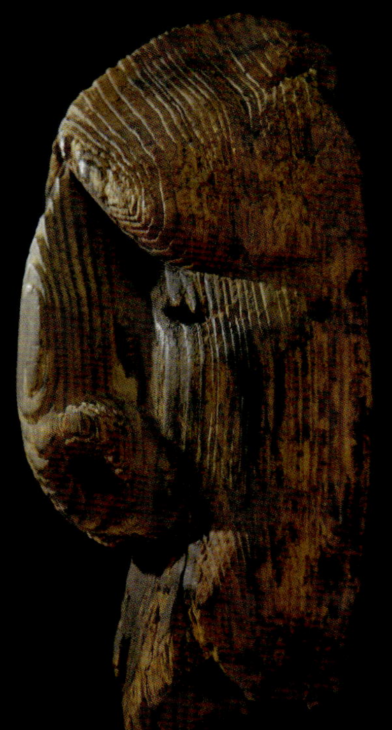

Figure 30
Qumsuugnasqaq
Ugly One

988-2-142
H. 31.5 cm
W. 22 cm
D. 11 cm
Spruce, red paint, black paint
Kodiak Island

Illustration 30
Qumsuugnasqaq
Celui qui est laid

988-2-142
H. 31,5 cm
L. 22 cm
Ép. 11 cm
Épicéa, peinture rouge,
peinture noire
Île de Kodiak

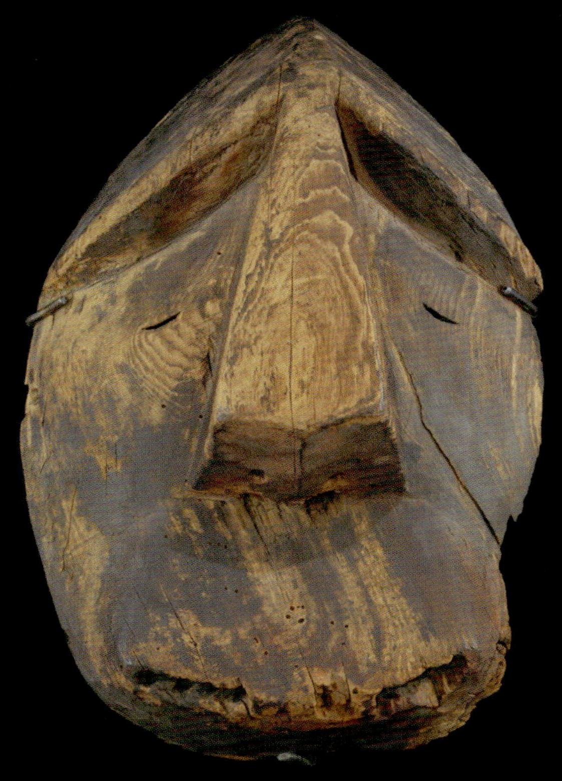
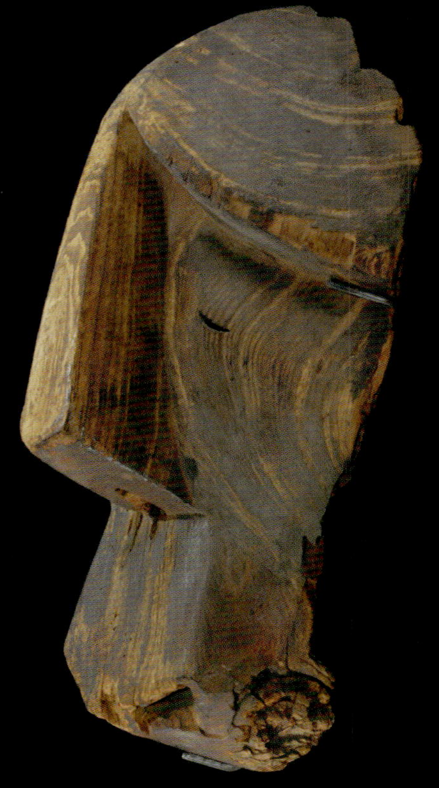
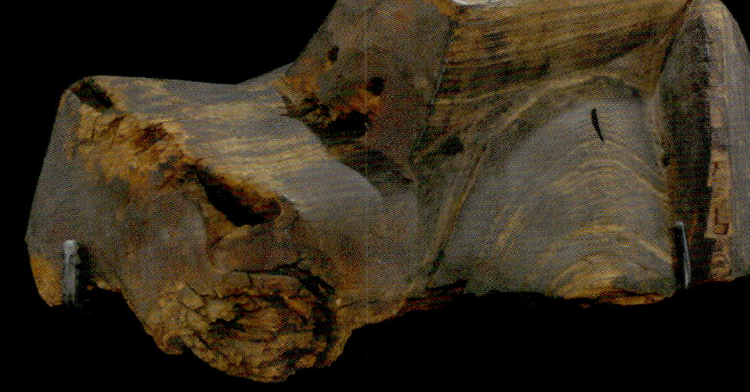

Figure 31
Ulluwatusqaq
Big Cheeks

988-2-164
H. 36 cm
W. 25 cm
D. 14 cm
Spruce, brown paint, black
paint, red paint
Kodiak Island

Illustration 31
Ulluwatusqaq
Grosses joues

988-2-164
H. 36 cm
L. 25 cm
Ép. 14 cm
Épicéa, peinture marron, peinture
noire, peinture rouge
Île de Kodiak

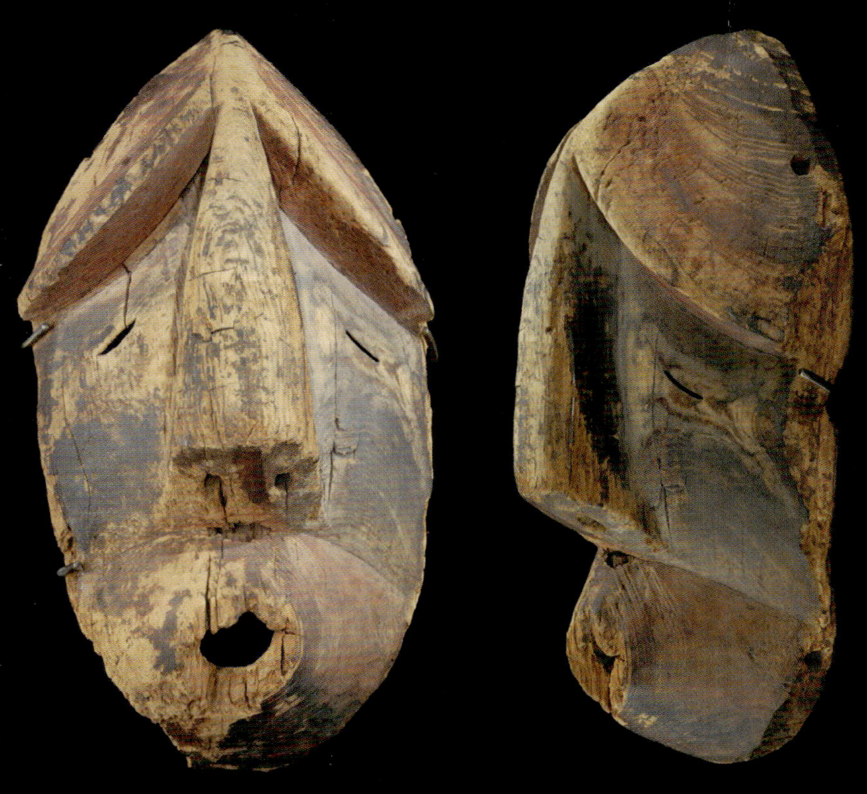
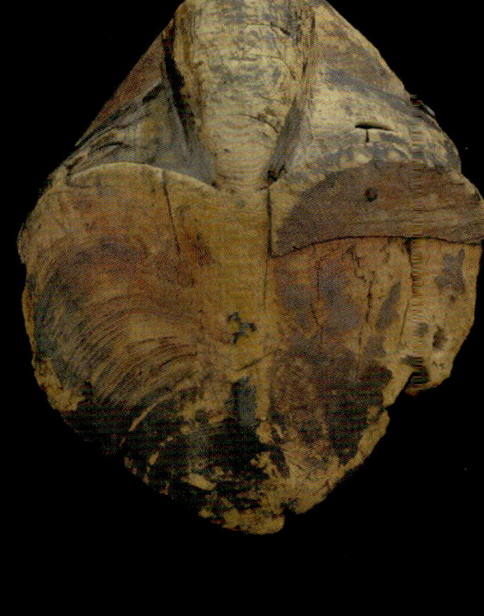

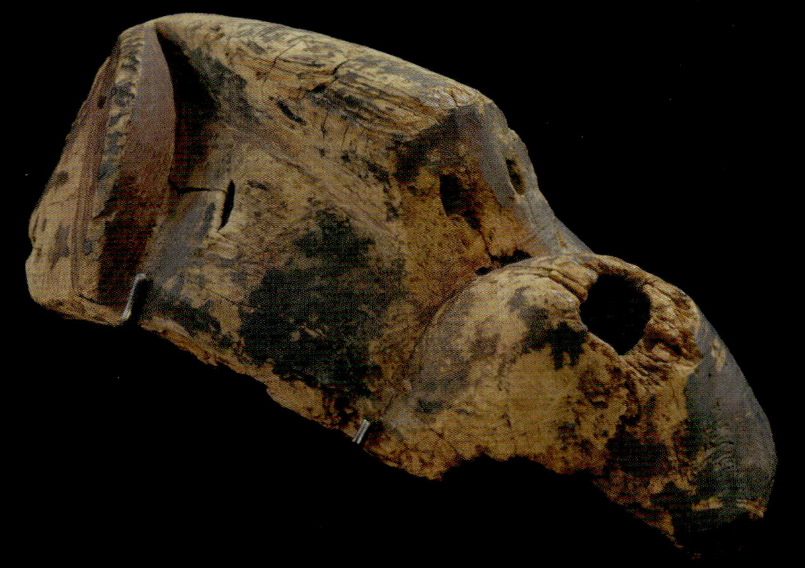
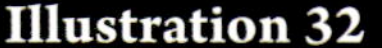

Figure 32
Umiartusqaq
Thinking One

988-2-147
H. 32 cm
W. 17 cm
D. 11 cm
Spruce, red paint, black paint
Kodiak Island or Afognak Island

Illustration 32
Umiartusqaq
Le penseur

988-2-147
H. 32 cm
L. 17 cm
Ép. 11 cm
Épicéa, peinture rouge, peinture
noire
Île de Kodiak ou d'Afognak

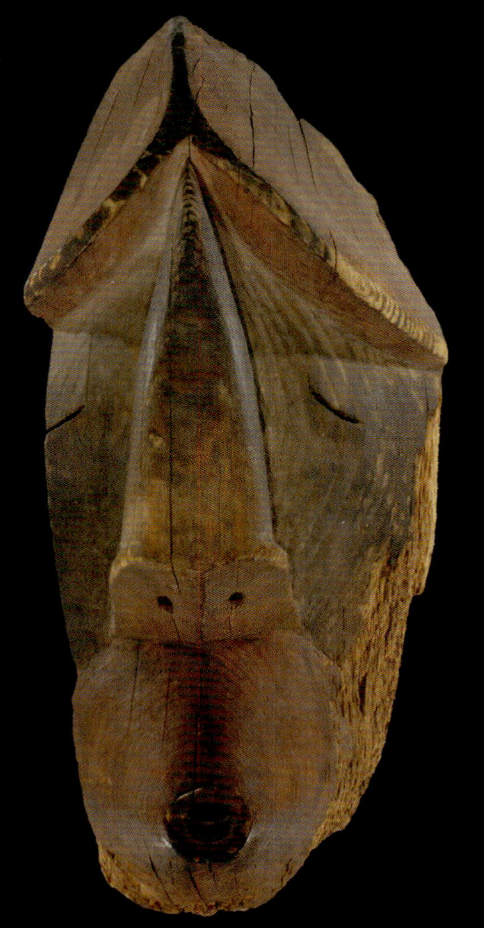

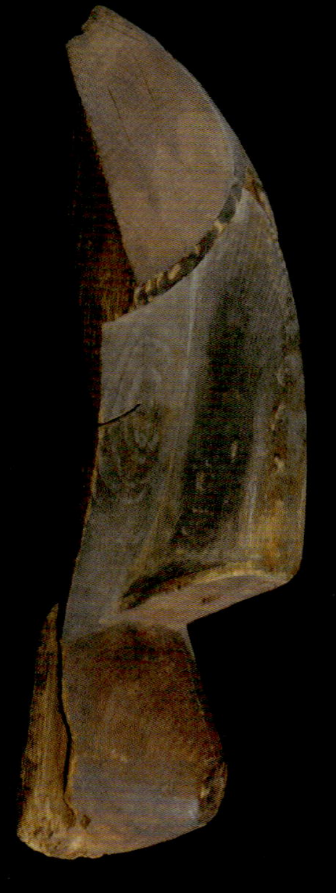

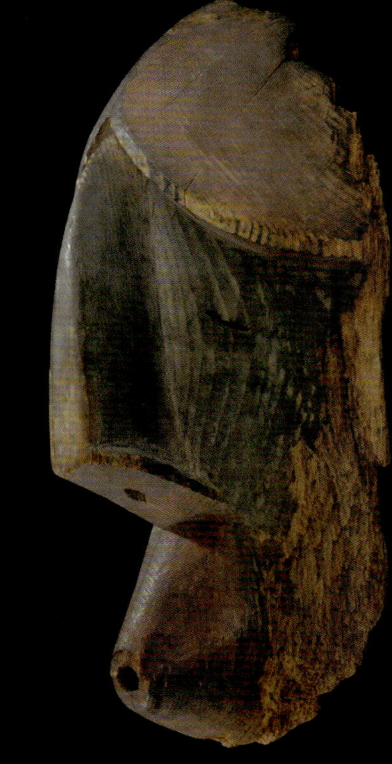

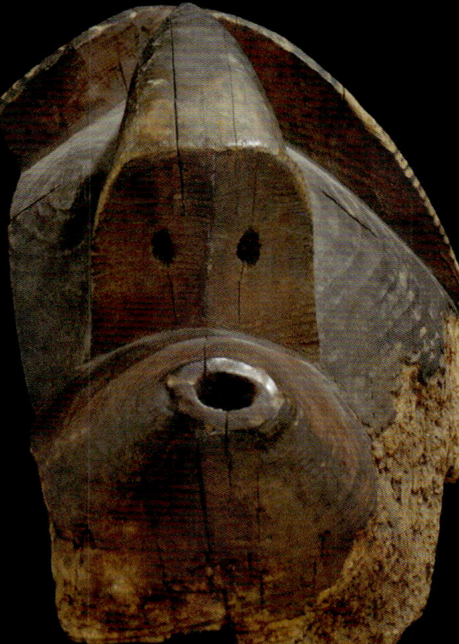

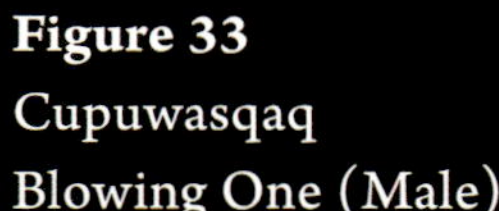

Figure 33
Cupuwasqaq
Blowing One (Male)

988-2-148
H. 31 cm
W. 13 cm
D. 9 cm
Spruce, red paint, black paint
Kodiak Island

Illustration 33
Cupuwasqaq
Celui qui souffle

988-2-148
H. 31 cm
L. 13 cm
Ép. 9 cm
Épicéa, peinture rouge, peinture noire
Île de Kodiak

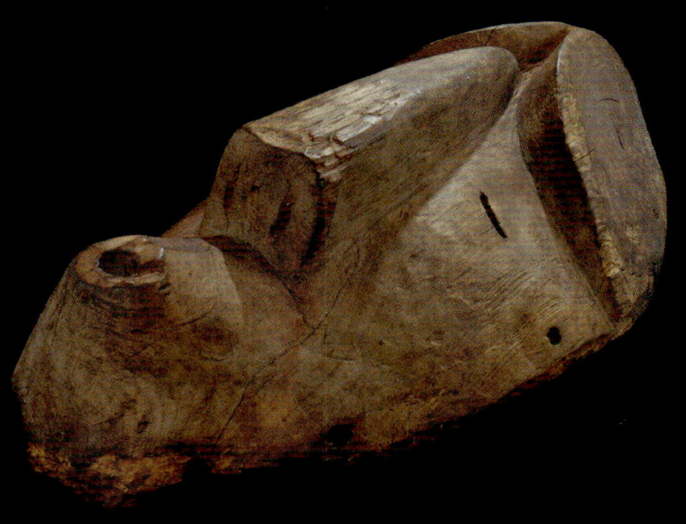
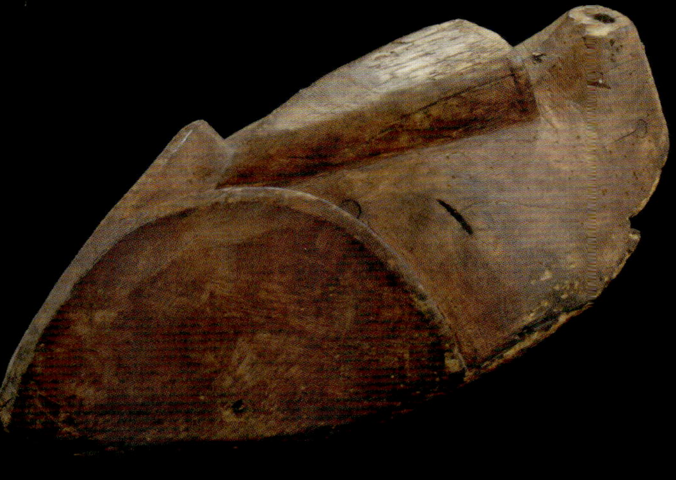
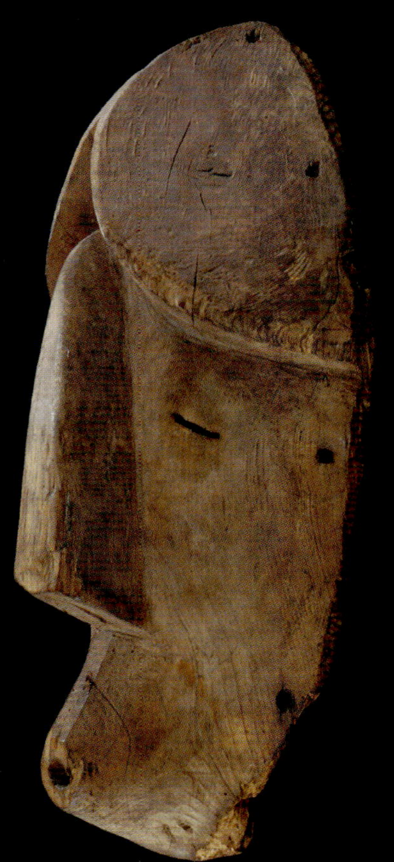
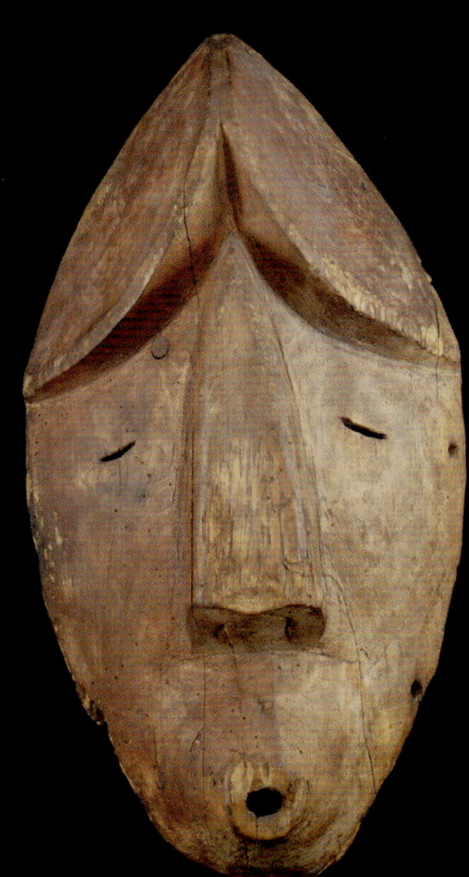

Figure 34
Cupuwasqaq
Blowing One (Female)

988-2-149
H. 38 cm
W. 19 cm
D. 10 cm
Spruce, red paint
Kodiak Island

Illustration 34
Cupuwasqaq
Celle qui souffle

988-2-149
H. 38 cm
L. 19 cm
Ép. 10 cm
Épicéa, peinture rouge
Île de Kodiak

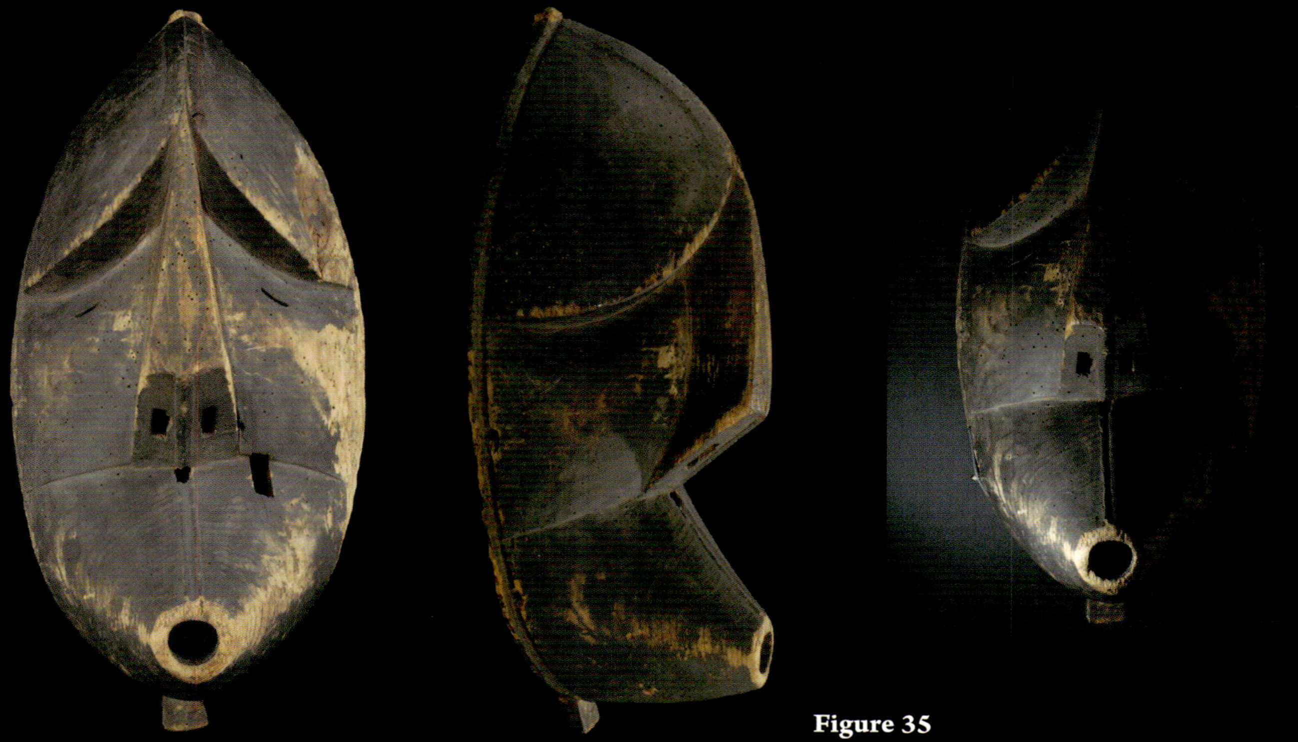

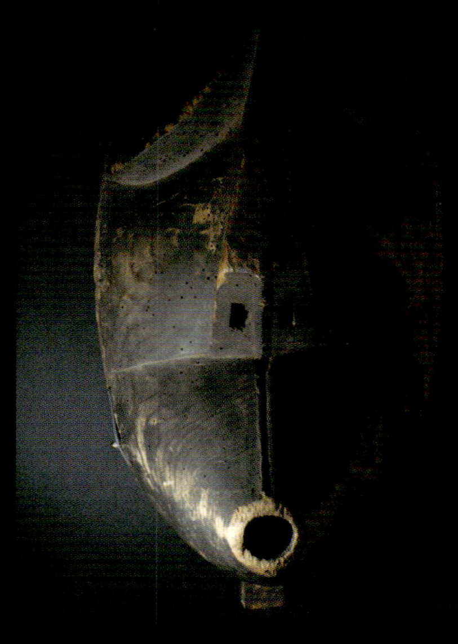

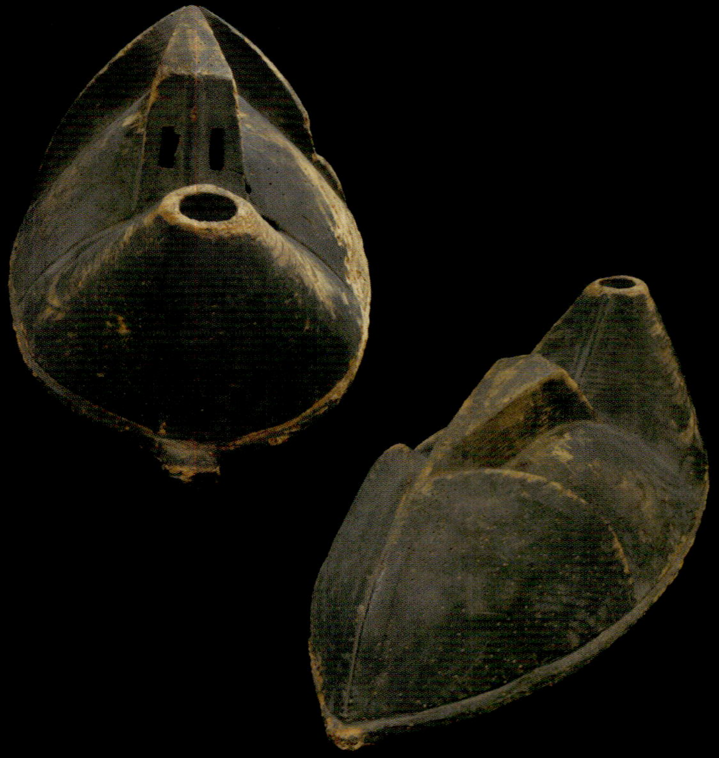

Figure 35
Kukumya'rngusqaq
Whistler, One Who Whistles All the Time

988-2-151
H. 43 cm
W. 20.5 cm
D. 13 cm
Spruce, black paint
Kodiak Island

Illustration 35
Kukumya'rngusqaq
Siffleur, celui qui siffle tout le temps

988-2-151
H. 43 cm
L. 20,5 cm
Ép. 13 cm
Épicéa, peinture noire
Île de Kodiak

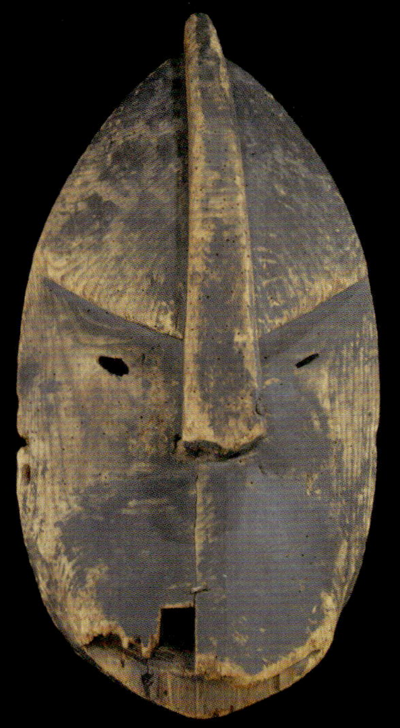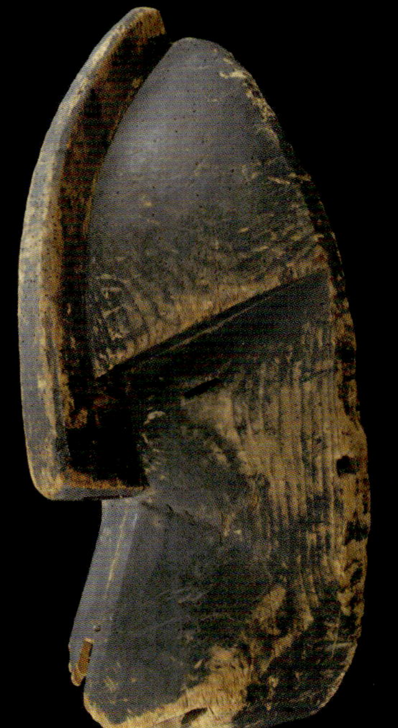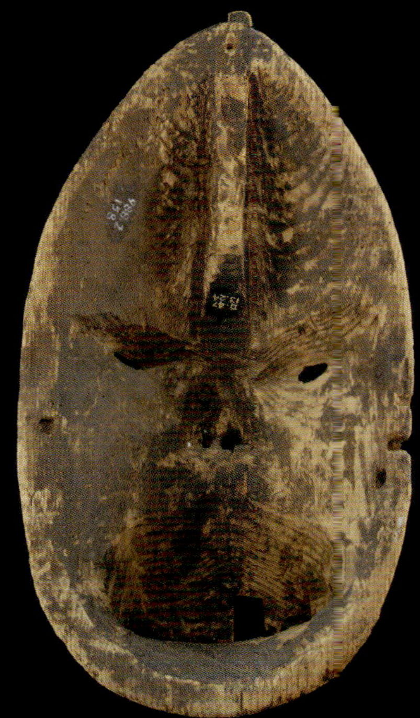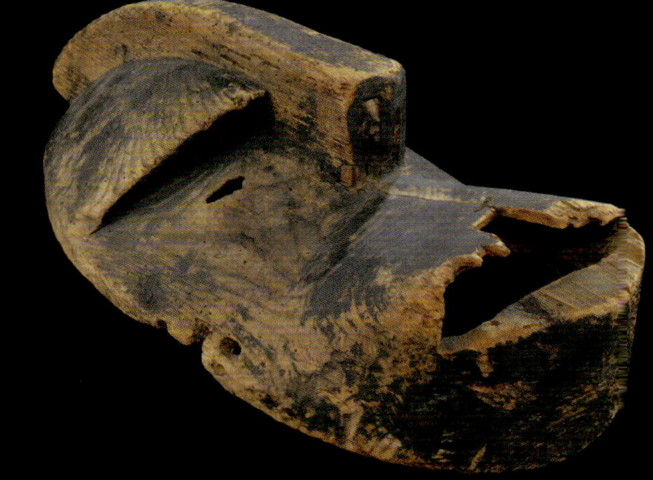

Figure 36
Nakllegnasqaq
Pitiful One

988-2-158
H. 44 cm
W. 23 cm
D. 15 cm
Spruce, baleen, brown paint, black paint
Kodiak Island

Illustration 36
Nakllegnasqaq
Le pitoyable

988-2-158
H. 44 cm
L. 23 cm
Ép. 15 cm
Épicéa, fanon de baleine, peinture marron, peinture
noire
Île de Kodiak

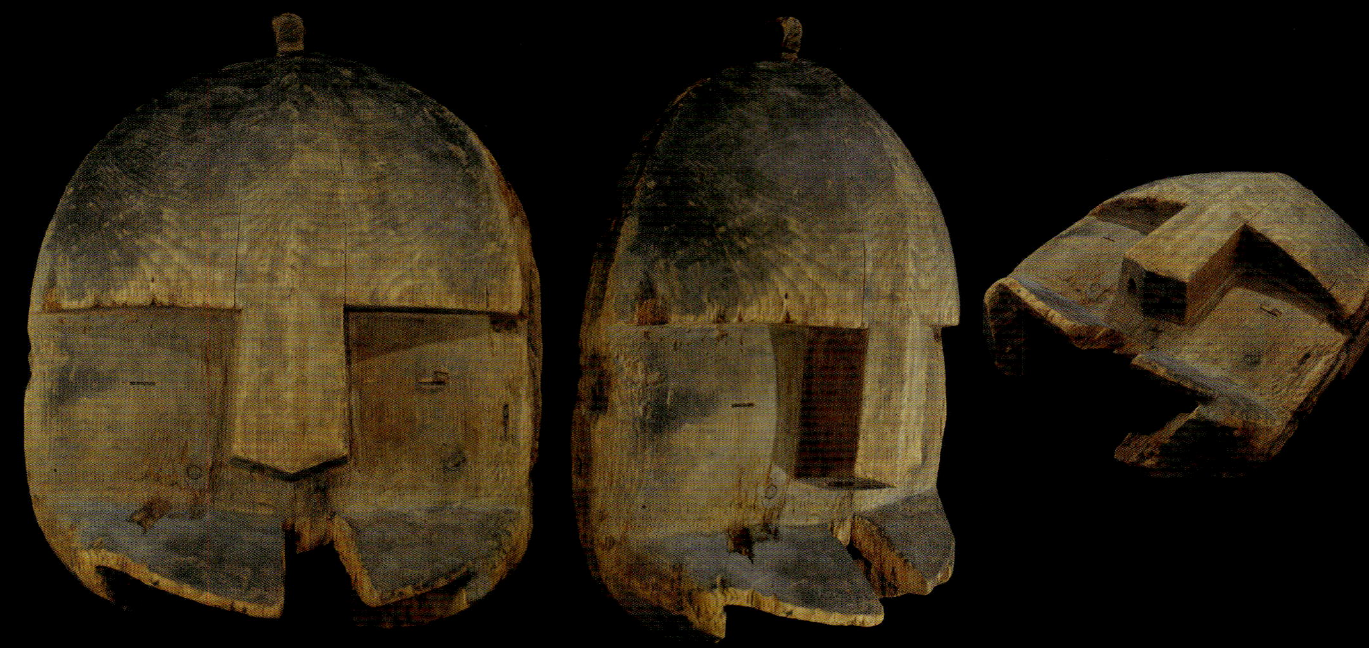

Figure 37
Lurtusqaq
Wide One

988-2-160
H. 54 cm
W. 44 cm
D. 16 cm
Spruce, sinew, brown paint, black paint, red paint
Kodiak Island

Illustration 37
Lurtusqaq
Celui qui est large

988-2-160
H. 54 cm
L. 44 cm
Ép. 16 cm
Épicéa, tendon, peinture marron, peinture noire,
peinture rouge
Île de Kodiak

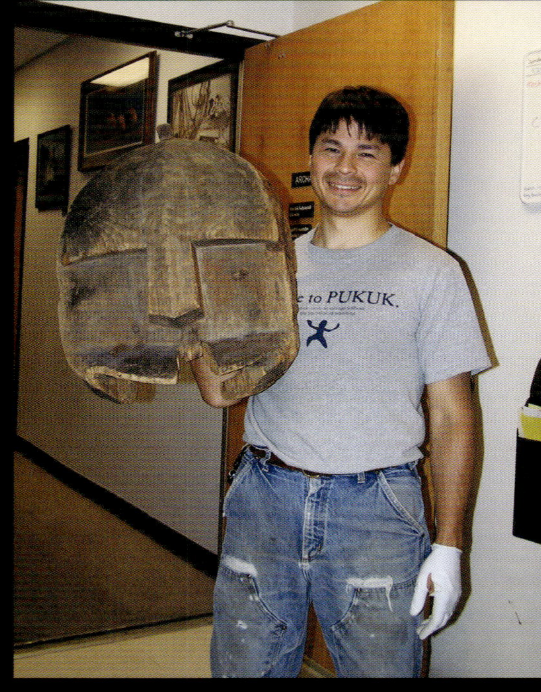

Sven Haakanson Jr. with mask.

Sven Haakanson Jr., masque.

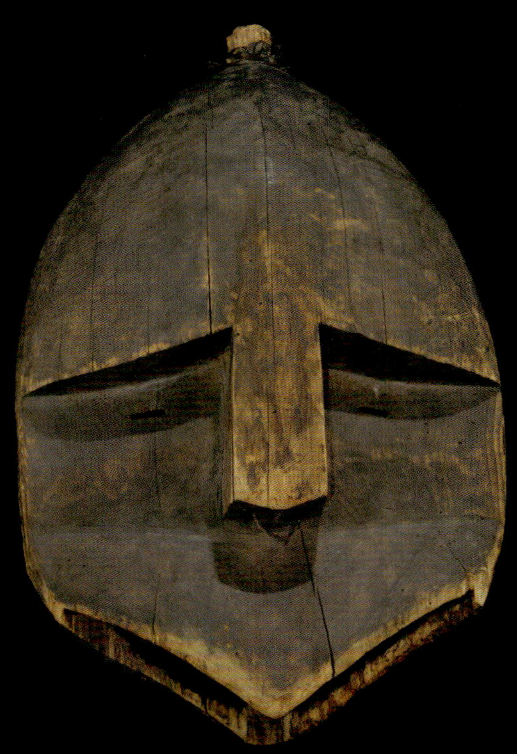

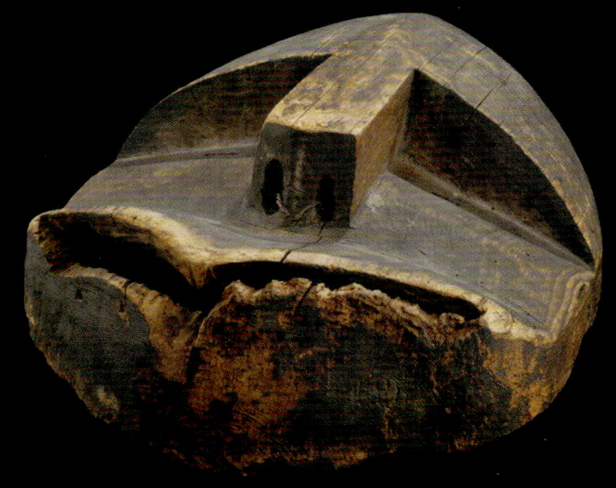

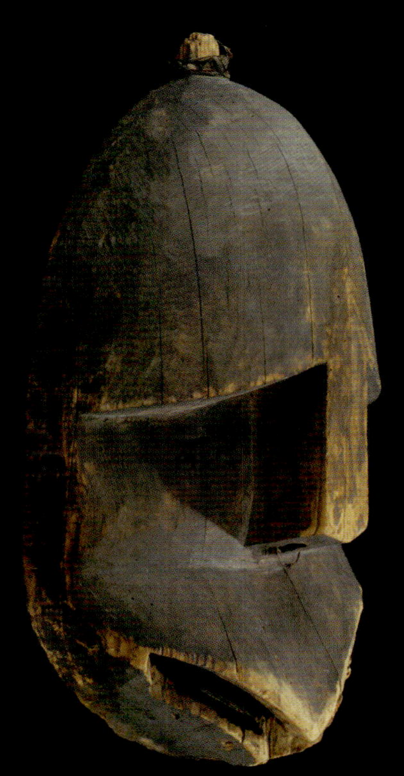

Figure 38
Qarua'at'stun Elnguq
Like a Crow

988-2-153
H. 48 cm
W. 32 cm
D. 14 cm
Spruce, brown paint, red paint, black paint
Kodiak Island

Illustration 38
Qarua'at'stun Elnguq
Comme un corbeau

988-2-153
H. 48 cm
L. 32 cm
Ép. 14 cm
Épicéa, peinture marron, peinture rouge,
peinture noire
Île de Kodiak

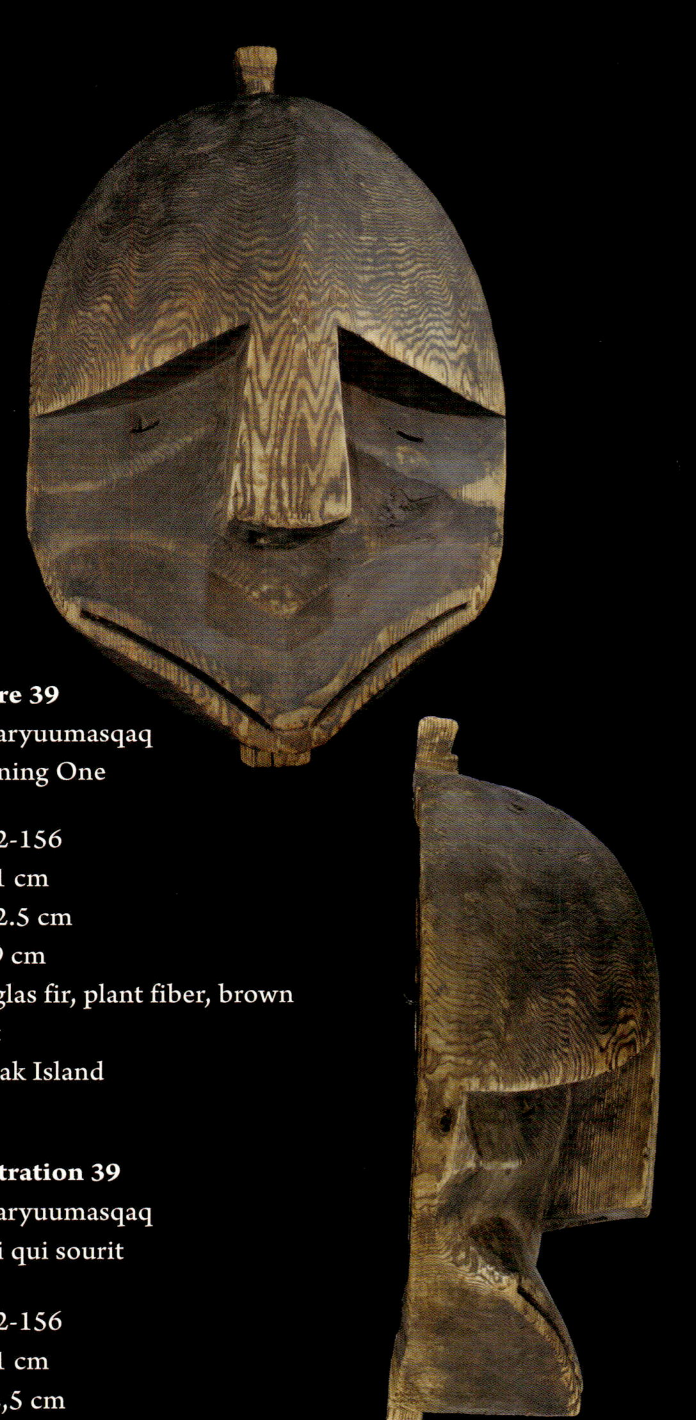
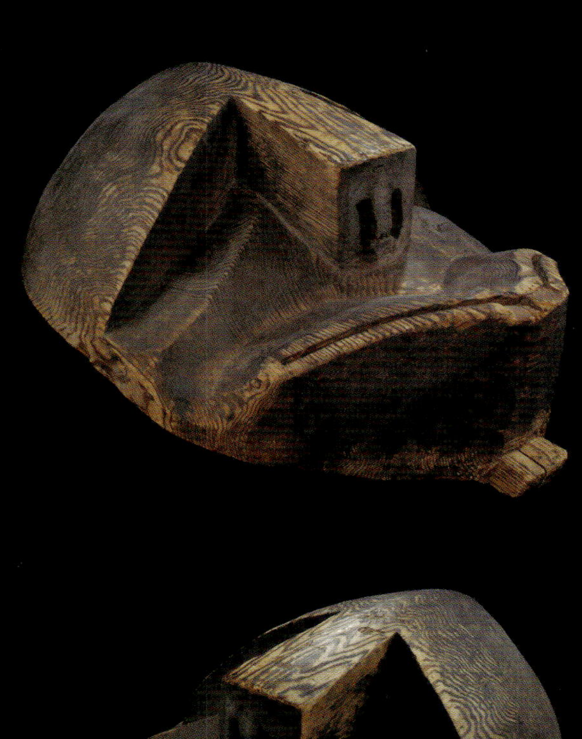
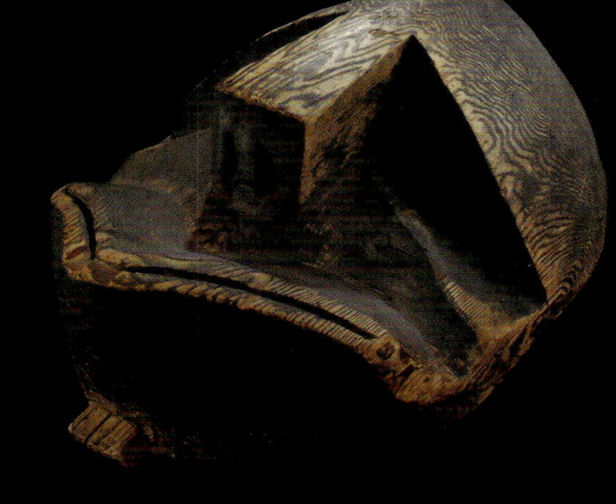
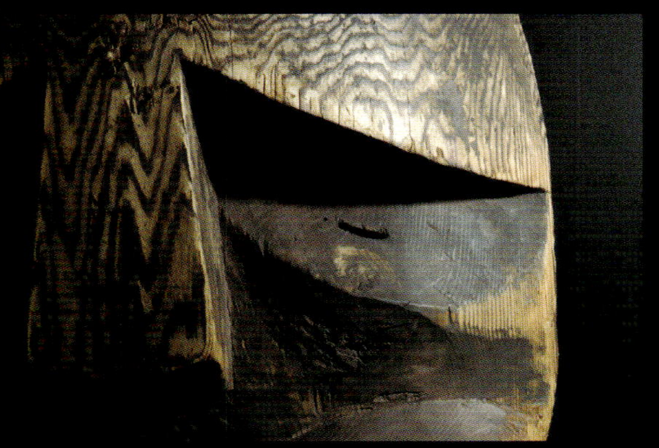

Figure 39
Englaryuumasqaq
Grinning One

988-2-156
H. 51 cm
W. 32.5 cm
D. 19 cm
Douglas fir, plant fiber, brown
paint
Kodiak Island

Illustration 39
Englaryuumasqaq
Celui qui sourit

988-2-156
H. 51 cm
L. 32,5 cm
Ép. 19 cm
Sapin de Douglas, fibres végétales,
peinture marron
Île de Kodiak

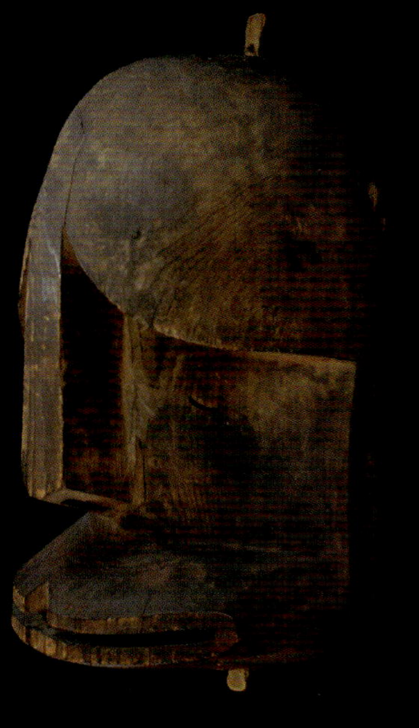

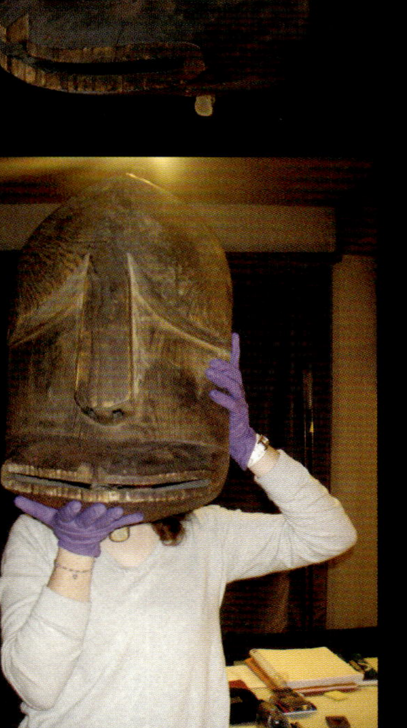

Director of the Château-Musée, Anne-Claire Laronde, holding one of the largest masks.

Anne-Claire Laronde, directrice du Château-Musée, tenant dans ses mains un des masques les plus grands.

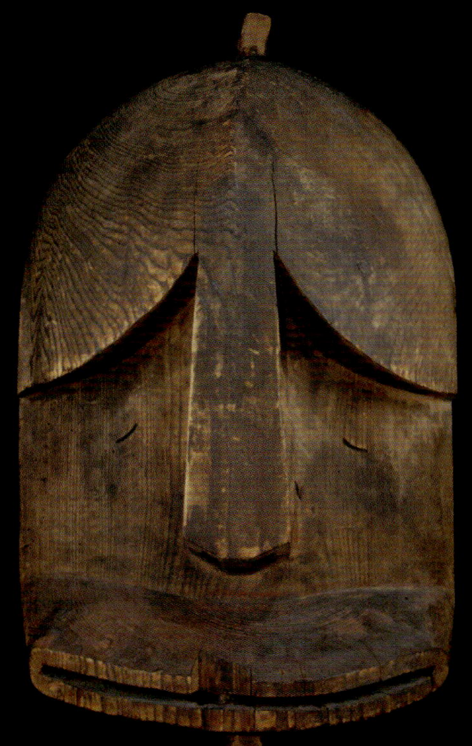

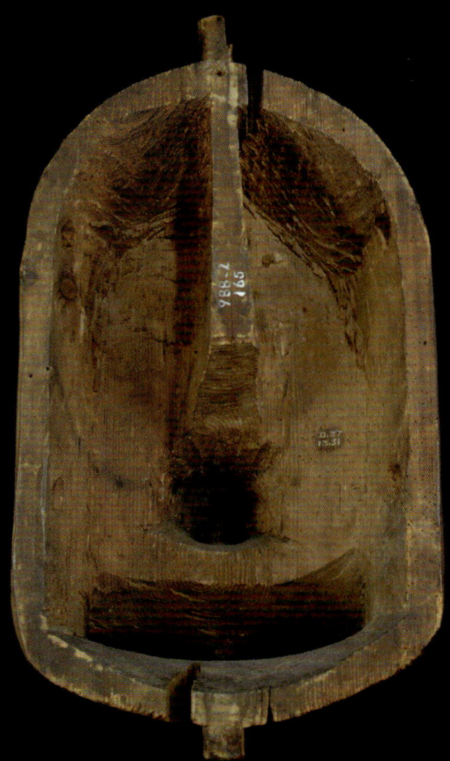

Figure 40
Giinasinaq
Big Face

988-2-165
H. 60 cm
W. 33 cm
D. 20 cm
Spruce or Douglas fir, leather, red paint, brown paint
Kodiak Island

Illustration 40
Giinasinaq
Grand visage

988-2-165
H. 60 cm
L. 33 cm
Ép. 20 cm
Épicéa ou sapin de Douglas, cuir, peinture rouge, peinture marron
Île de Kodiak

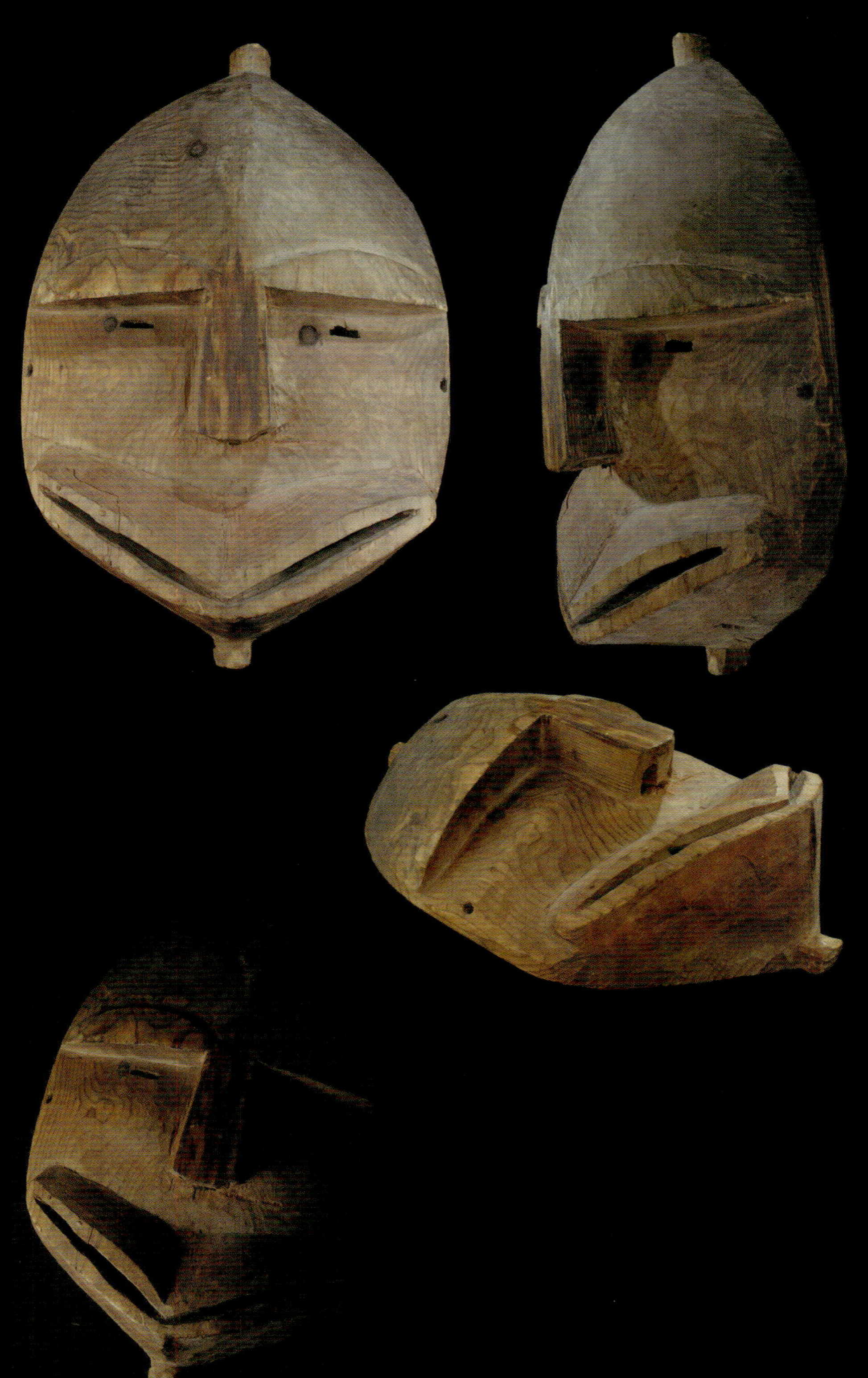

Figure 41
Nayurta
Watchman

988-2-157
H. 44.5 cm
W. 29 cm
D. 12 cm
Spruce, sinew, black paint
Kodiak Island

Illustration 41
Nayurta
Le veilleur

988-2-157
H. 44,5 cm
L. 29 cm
Ép. 12 cm
Épicéa, tendon, peinture noire
Île de Kodiak

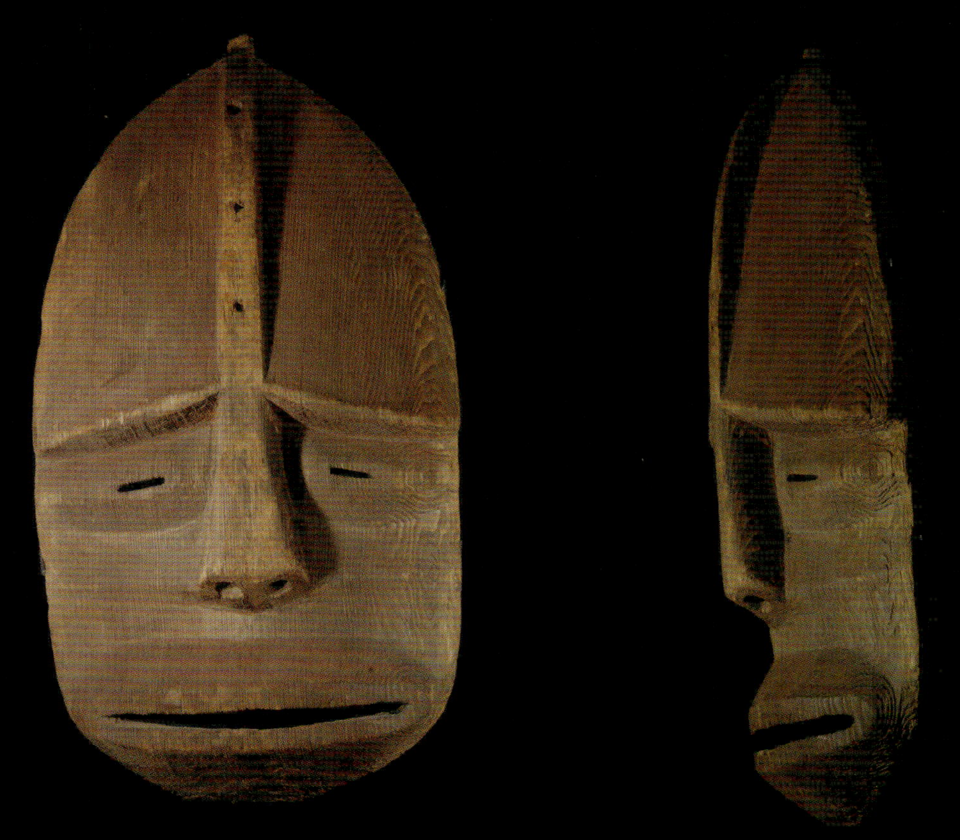
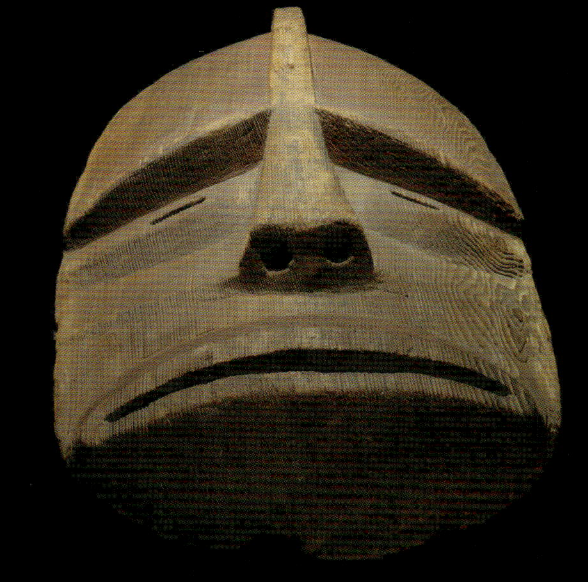

Figure 42
Name Unknown
71.1881.21.25
H. 57.3 cm
W. 31 cm
D. 11 cm
Spruce, red paint
Kodiak Island

Illustration 42
Nom inconnu
71.1881.21.25
H. 57,3 cm
L. 31 cm
Ép. 11 cm
Épicéa, peinture rouge
Île de Kodiak

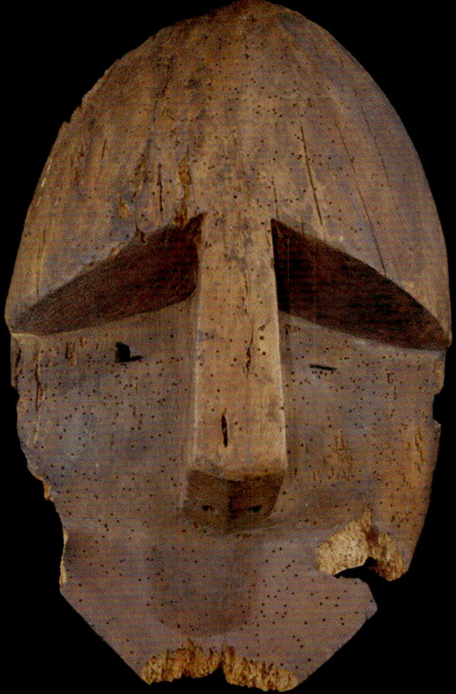

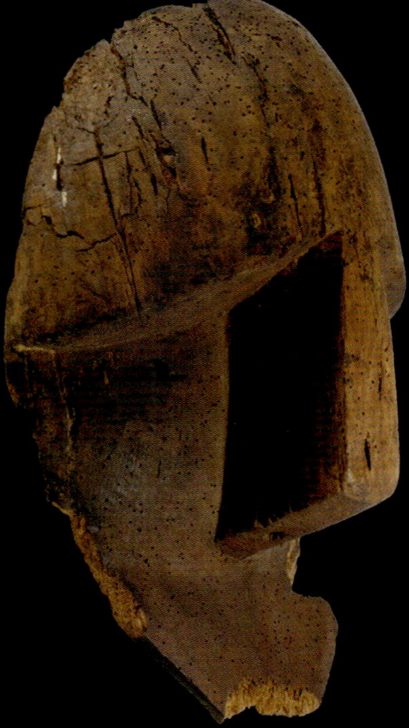

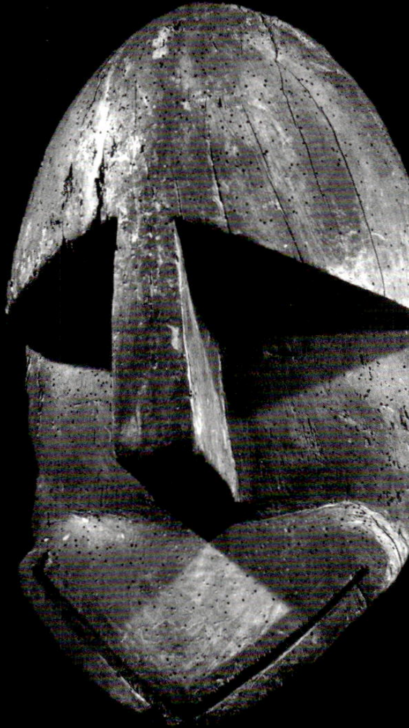

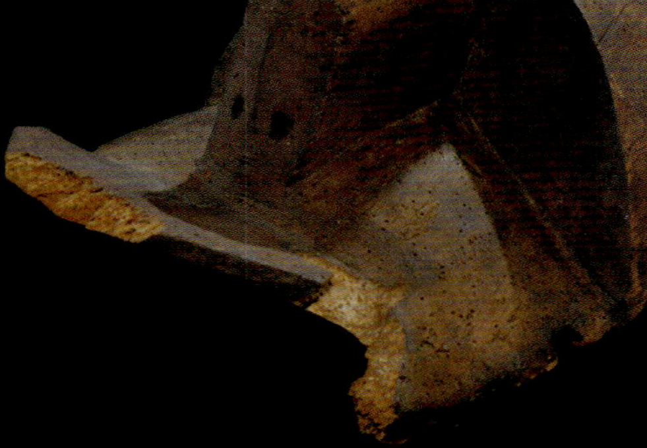

Mask as it appeared ca. 1940s
courtesy of Château-Musée.

Le masque tel qu'il était dans
les années 1940 (avec l'aimab[...]
autorisation du Château-Mus[...]

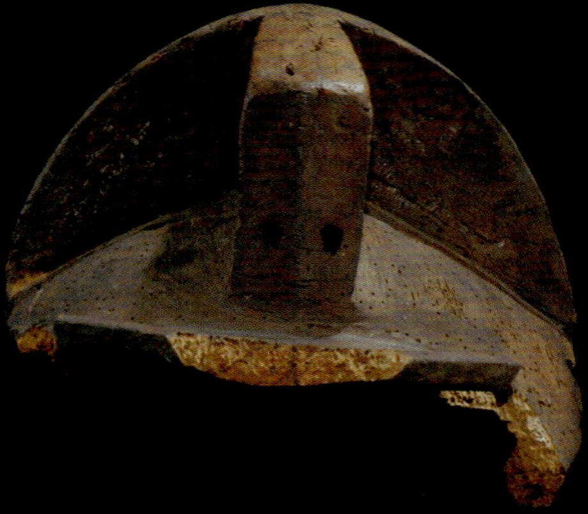

Figure 43
Qup'arngasqamek Qanlek
Broken Mouth

988-2-161
H. Incomplete
W. 29.5 cm
D. 10.5 cm
Spruce, brown paint
Kodiak Island or Afognak Island

Illustration 43
Qup'arngasqamek Qanlek
Bouche cassée

988-2-161
H. Incomplet
L. 29,5 cm
Ép. 10,5 cm
Épicéa, peinture marron
Île de Kodiak ou d'Afognak

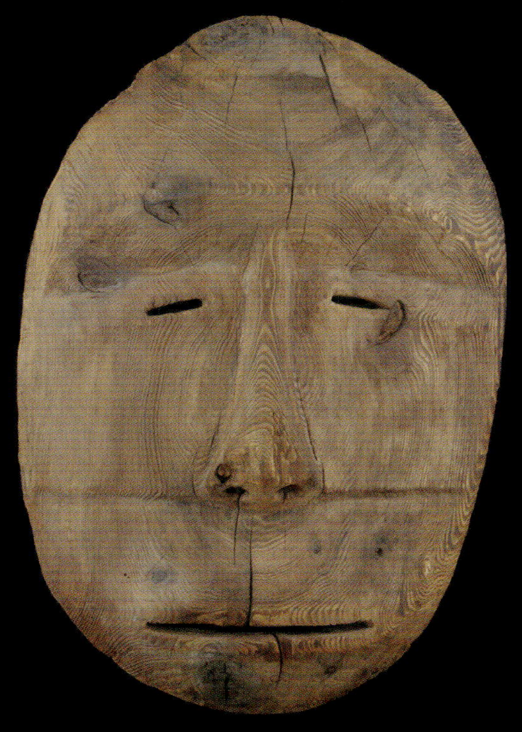

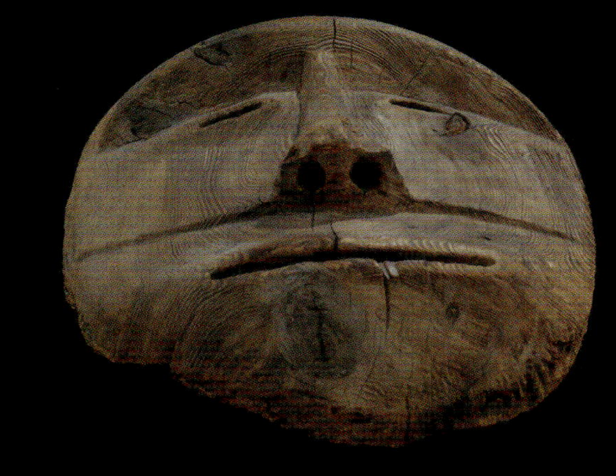

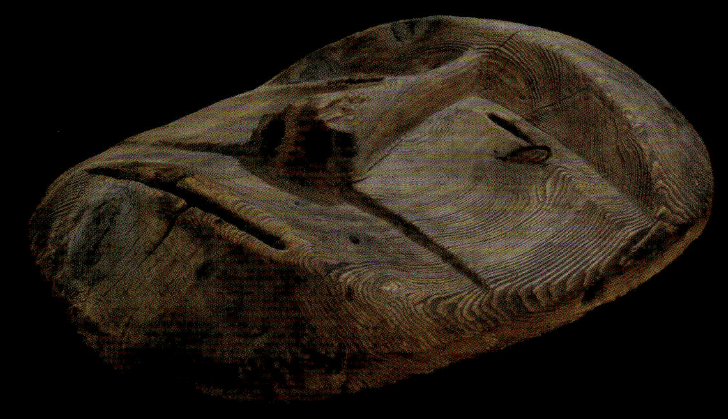

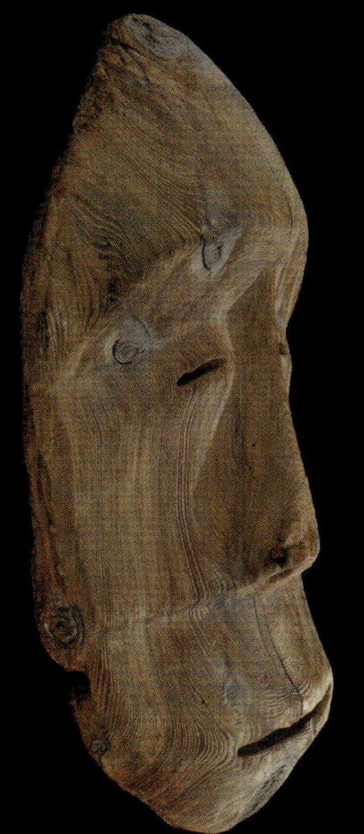

Figure 44
Putumasqaq
Pouting One

988-2-162
H. 38 cm
W. 25.5 cm
D. 8 cm
Spruce, light brown paint
Kodiak Island

Illustration 44
Putumasqaq
Celui qui fait la moue

988-2-162
H. 38 cm
L. 25,5 cm
Ép. 8 cm
Épicéa, peinture marron clair
Île de Kodiak

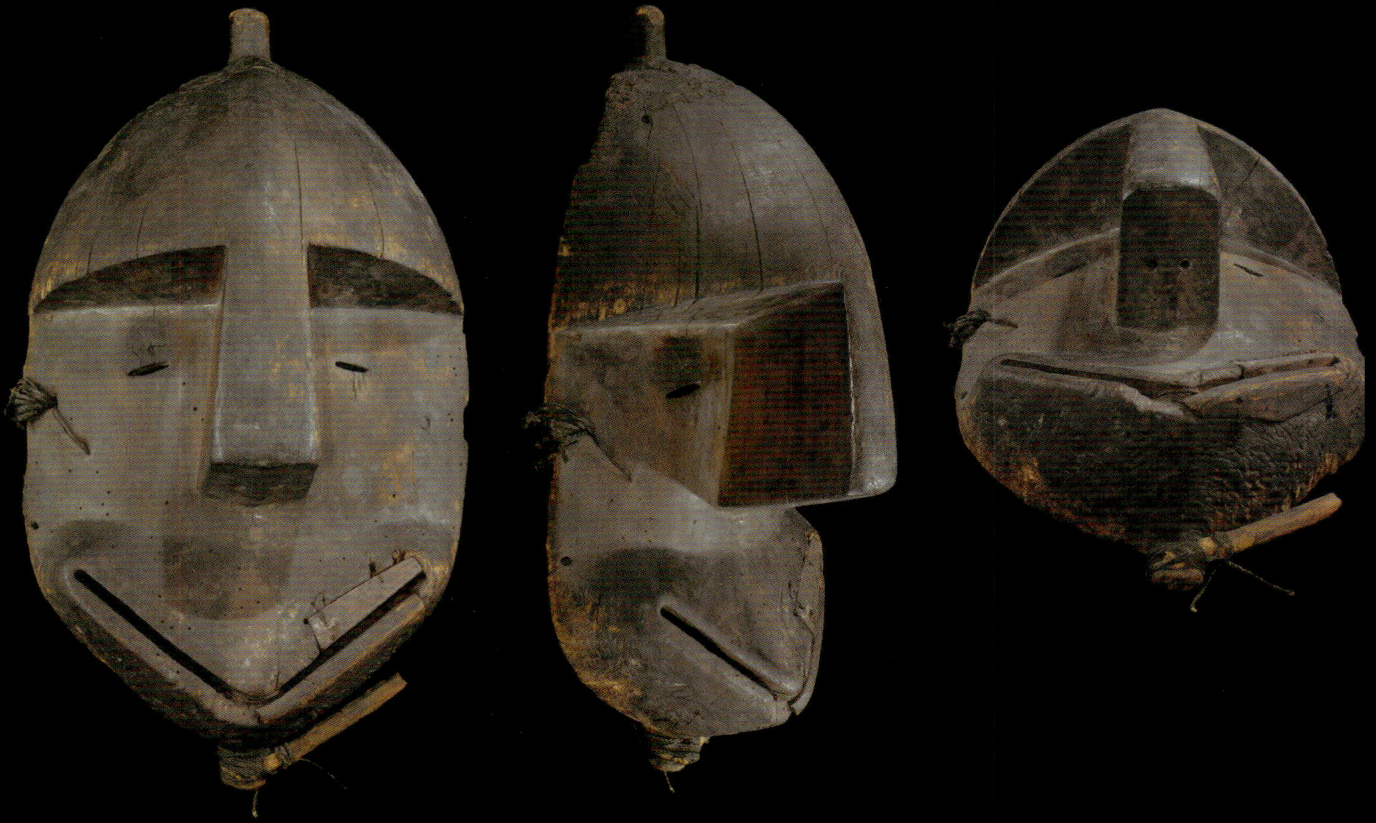

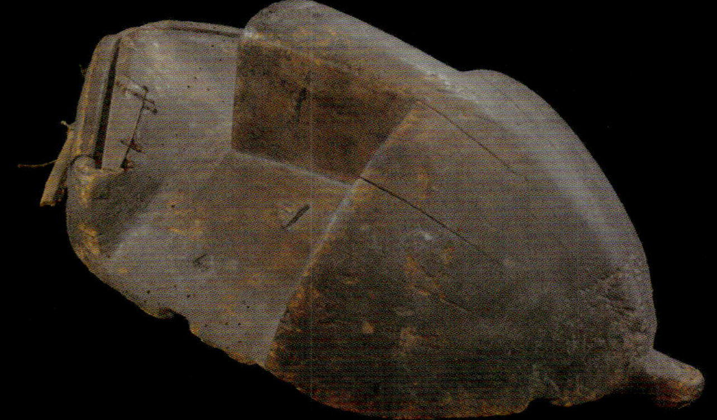

Figure 45
Nukallpiaq
Man

988-2-155
H. 42 cm
W. 23 cm
D. 13.5 cm
Spruce, sinew, brown paint,
black paint, white paint
Kodiak Island

Illustration 45
Nukallpiaq
Homme

988-2-155
H. 42 cm
L. 23 cm
Ép. 13,5 cm
Épicéa, tendon, peinture marron,
peinture noire, peinture blanche
Île de Kodiak

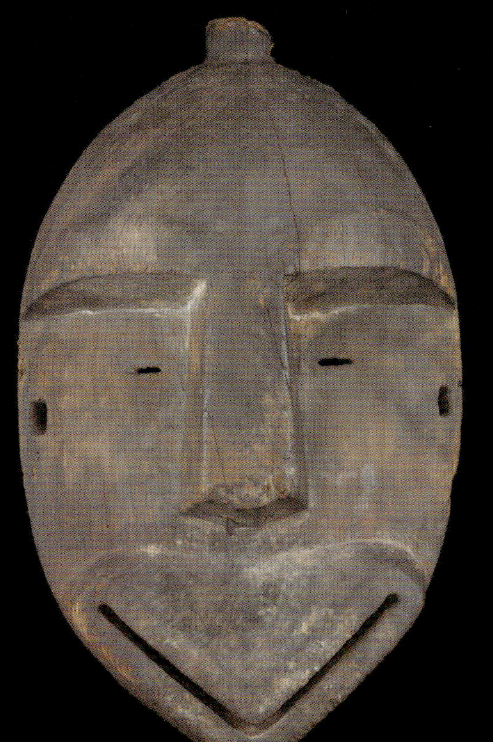

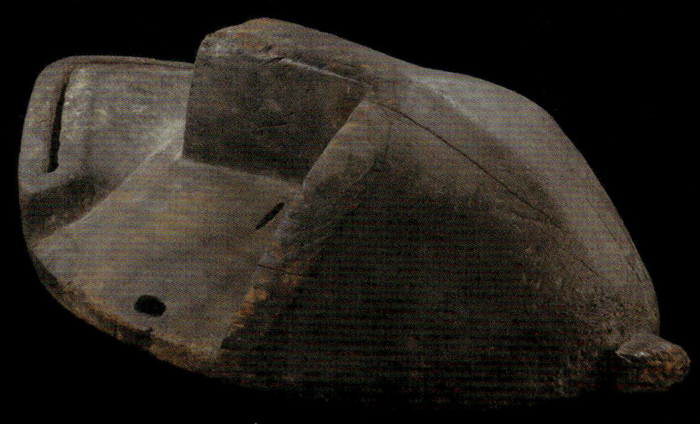

Figure 46
Arnaq
Woman

988-2-154
H. 41.5 cm
W. 23 cm
D. 13 cm
Spruce, black paint, white paint, red paint
Kodiak Island

Illustration 46
Arnaq
Femme

988-2-154
H. 41,5 cm
L. 23 cm
Ép. 13 cm
Épicéa, peinture noire, peinture blanche,
peinture rouge
Île de Kodiak

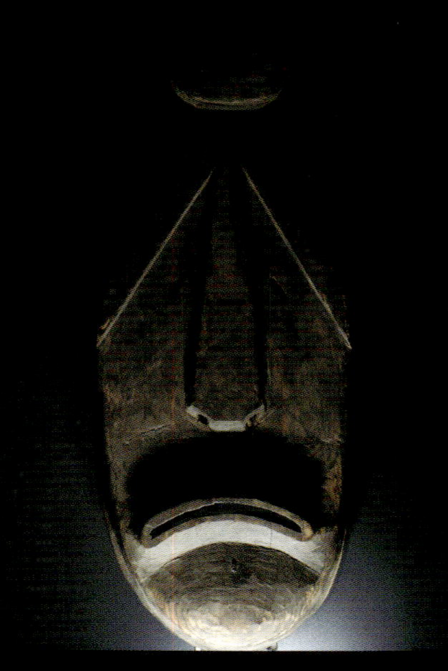

Figure 47
Angun Qiaculngusqaq
Old Man Who Feels Like Crying

988-2-166
H. 49 cm
W. 18 cm
D. 10 cm
Spruce, black paint
Kodiak Island

Illustration 47
Angun Qiaculngusqaq
Vieil homme qui a envie de pleurer

988-2-166
H. 49 cm
L. 18 cm
Ép. 10 cm
Épicéa, peinture noire
Île de Kodiak

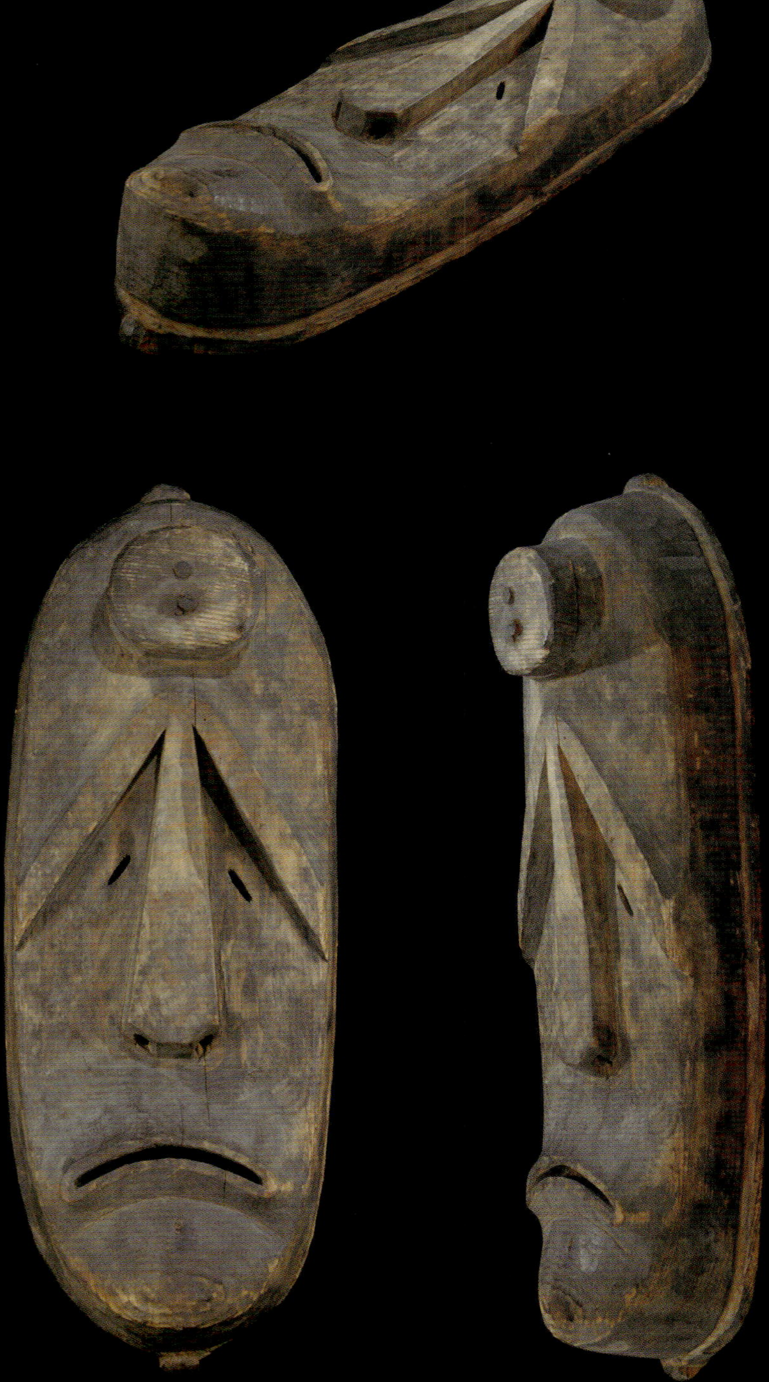

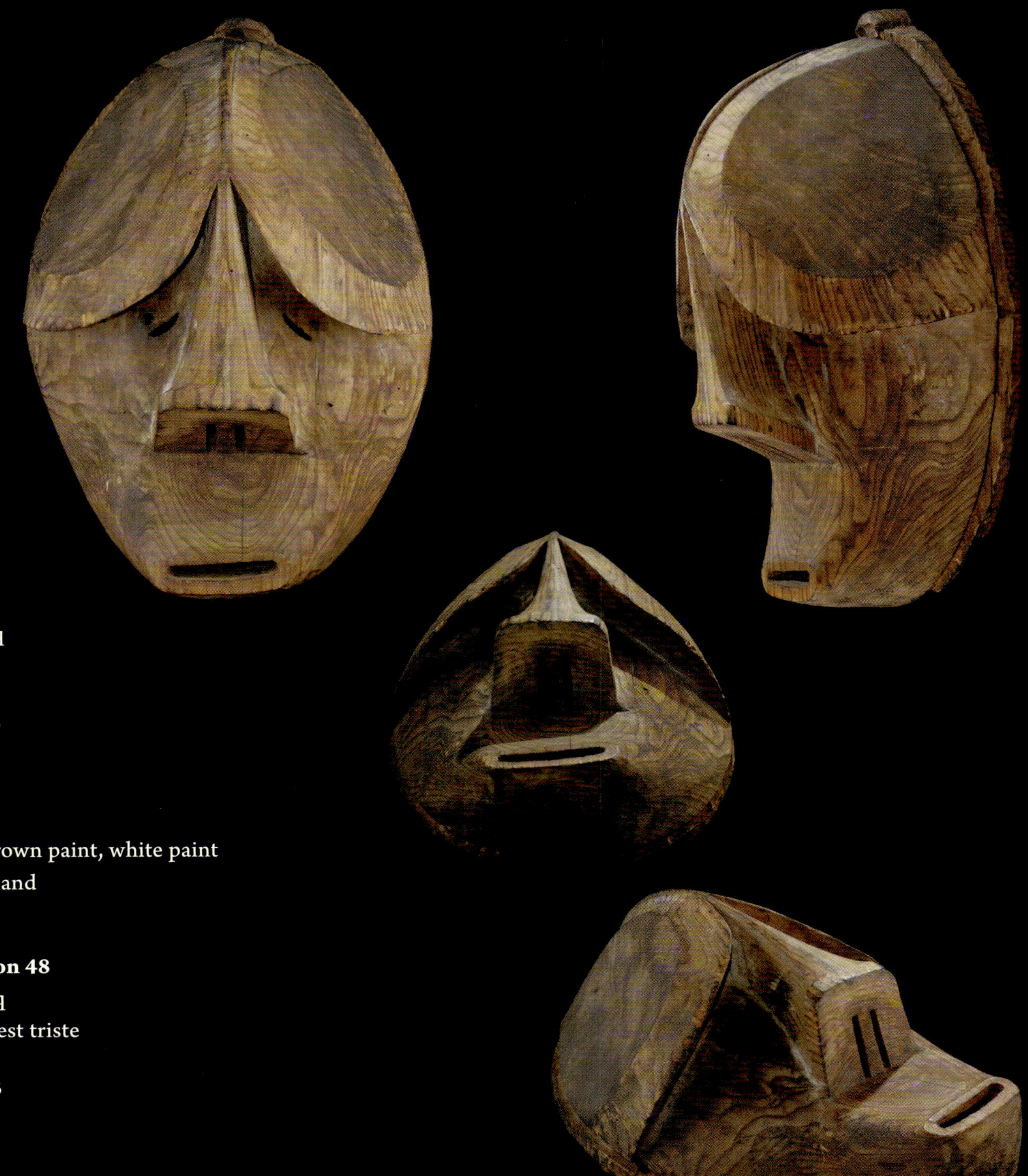

Figure 48
Imasusqaq
Sad One

988-2-163
H. 37 cm
W. 25 cm
D. 15 cm
Spruce, brown paint, white paint
Kodiak Island

Illustration 48
Imasusqaq
Celui qui est triste

988-2-163
H. 37 cm
L. 25 cm
Ép. 15 cm
Épicéa, peinture marron, peinture blanche
Île de Kodiak

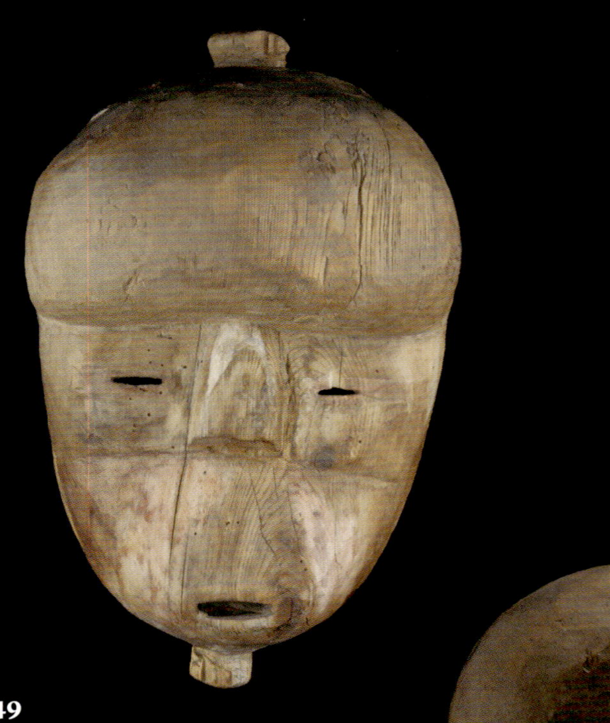

Figure 49
Cugyutusqaq
Big-Foreheaded One

988-2-167
H. 37 cm
W. 22 cm
D. 15 cm
Spruce, light brown paint, red paint, white paint
Kodiak Island

Illustration 49
Cugyutusqaq
Celui qui a un grand front

988-2-167
H. 37 cm
L. 22 cm
Ép. 15 cm
Épicéa, peinture marron clair, peinture rouge, peinture
blanche
Île de Kodiak

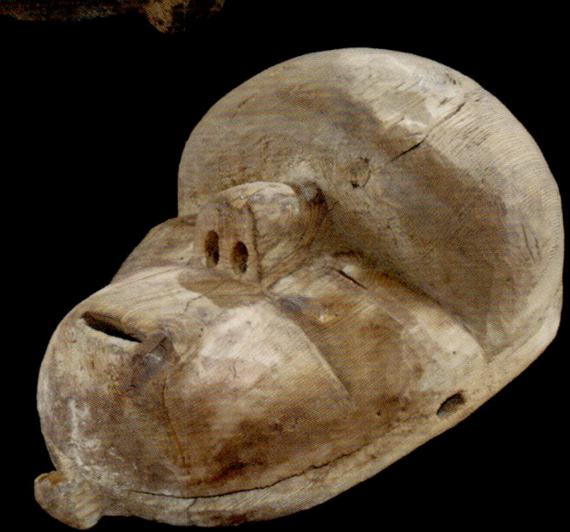

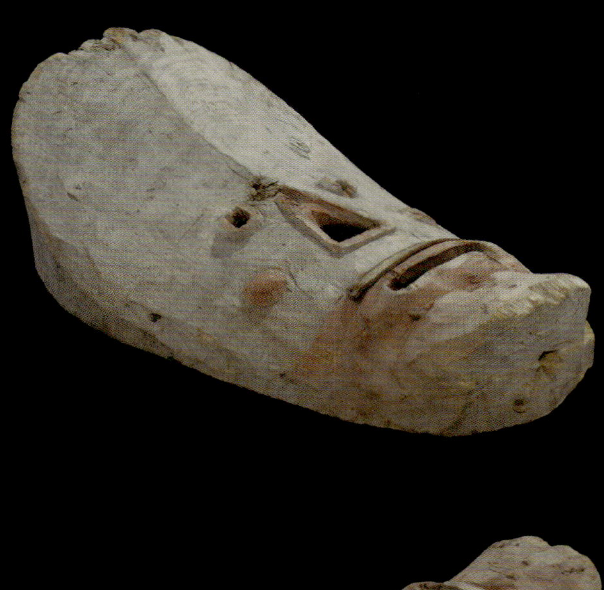

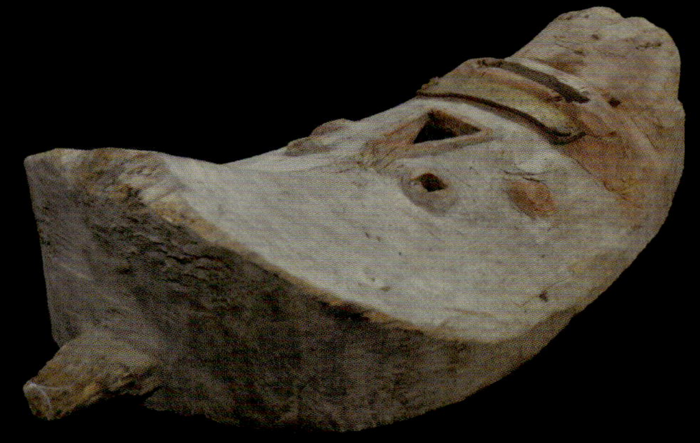

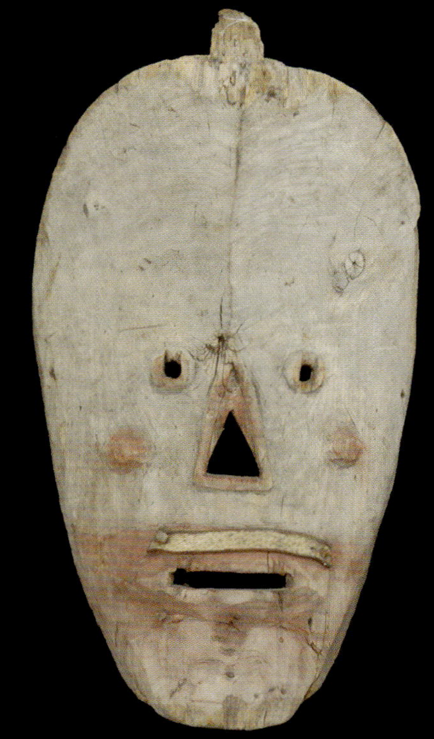

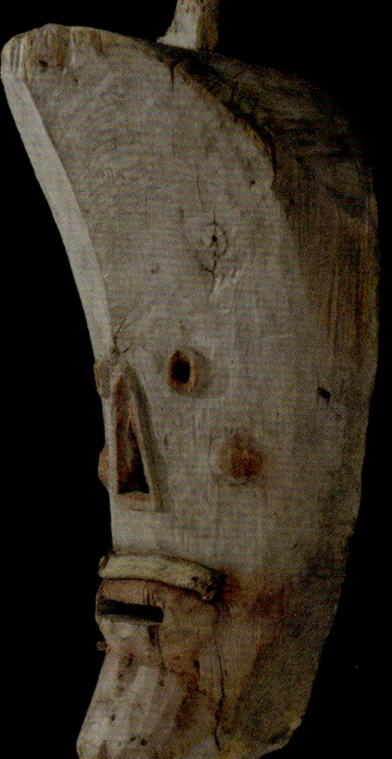

Figure 50
Qenasqaq
Sick One

988-2-210
H. 31 cm
W. 17 cm
D. 9 cm
Wood, leather, animal hair, white
paint, red paint
Kodiak archipelago

Illustration 50
Qenasqaq
Le malade

988-2-210
H. 31 cm
L. 17 cm
Ép. 9 cm
Bois, cuir, poils d'animal, peinture
blanche, peinture rouge
Archipel de Kodiak

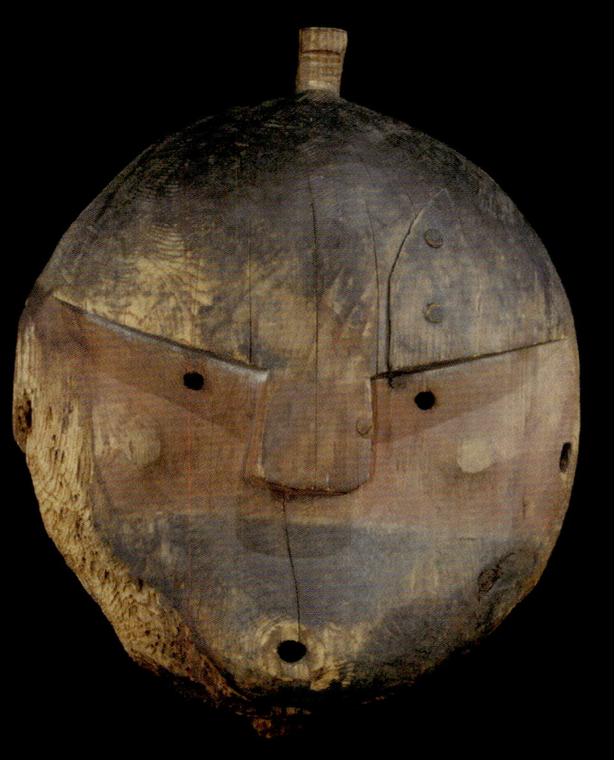

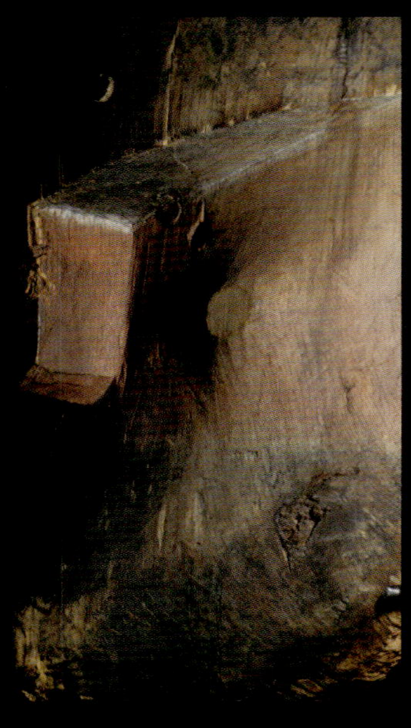

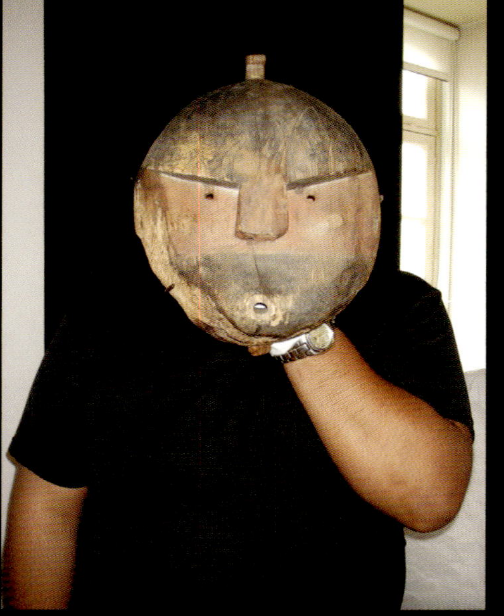

Speridon Simeonoff holds the mask.

Speridon Simeonoff, masque.

Figure 51
Akagngasqamek Giinalek
Round-Faced One

988-2-144
H. 35 cm
W. 27 cm
D. 10.5 cm
Spruce, red paint, black paint
Kodiak Island

Illustration 51
Akagngasqamek Giinalek
Celui qui a la tête ronde

988-2-144
H. 35 cm
L. 27 cm
Ép. 10,5 cm
Épicéa, peinture rouge, peinture noire
Île de Kodiak

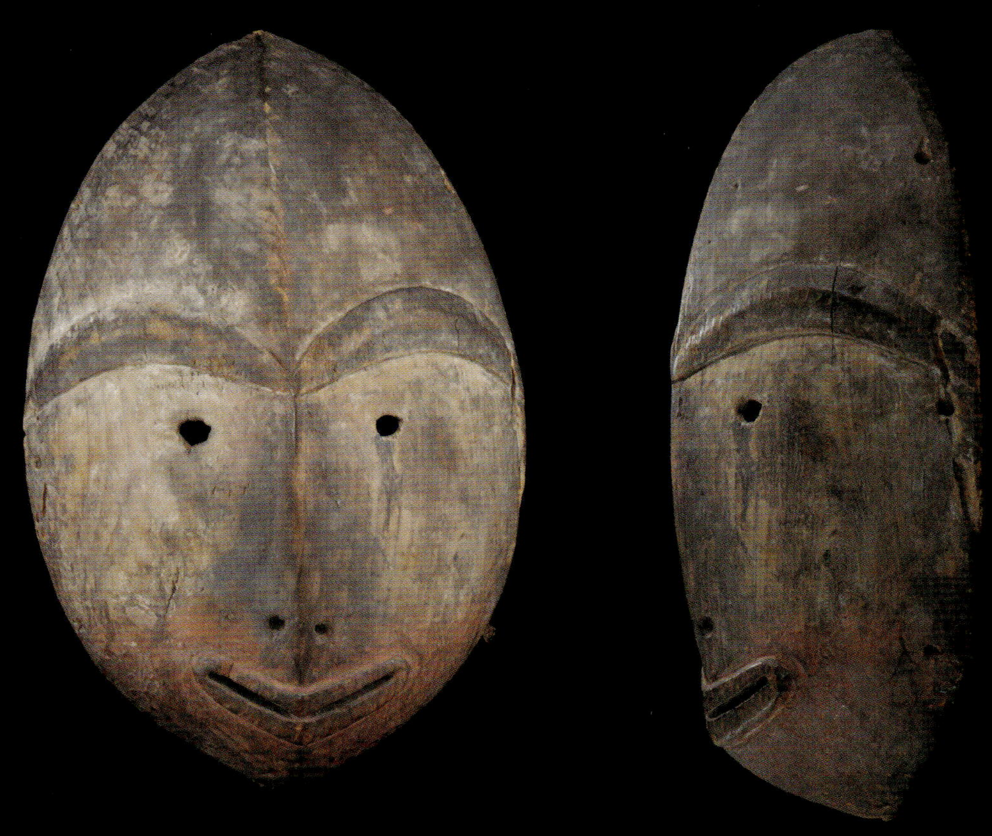

Figure 52
Saqullkaaq
Bird

988-2-174
H. 26 cm
W. 17 cm
D. 8 cm
Spruce, brown paint, red paint, black paint, white paint
Kodiak Island

Illustration 52
Saqullkaaq
Oiseau

988-2-174
H. 26 cm
L. 17 cm
Ép. 8 cm
Épicéa, peinture marron, peinture rouge, peinture noire,
peinture blanche
Île de Kodiak

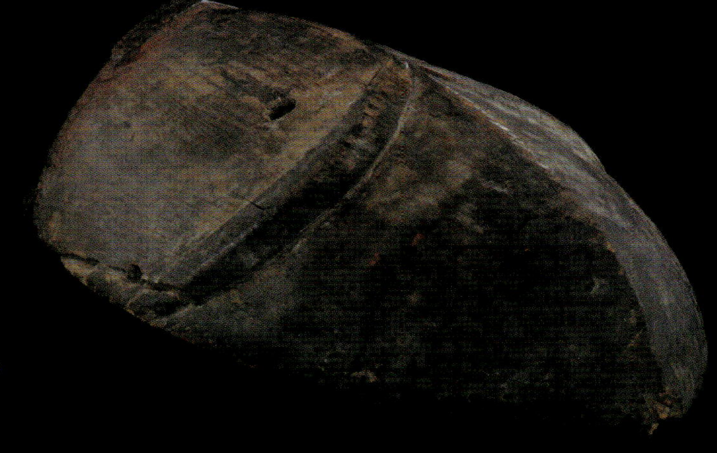

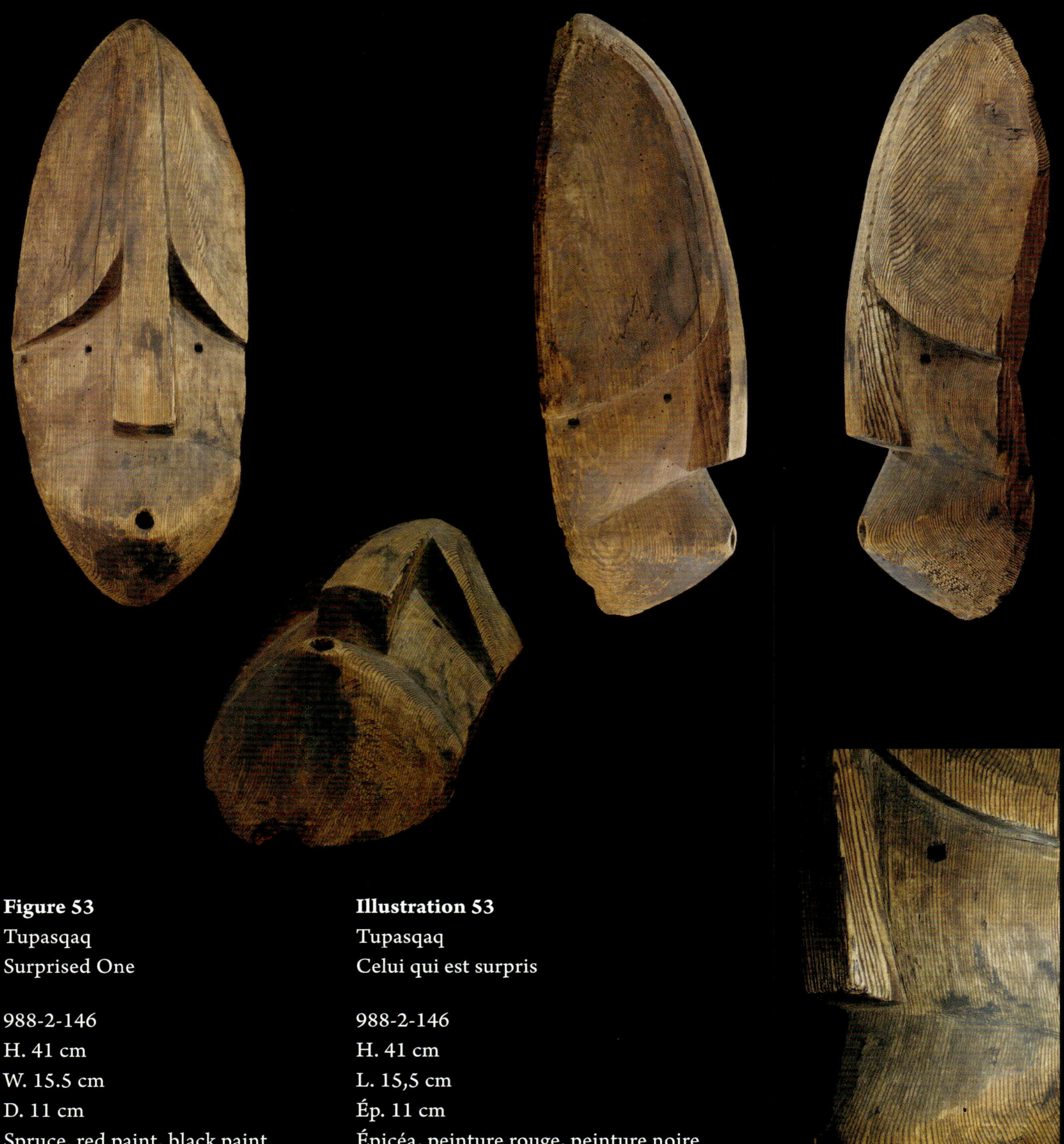

Figure 53
Tupasqaq
Surprised One

988-2-146
H. 41 cm
W. 15.5 cm
D. 11 cm
Spruce, red paint, black paint
Kodiak Island

Illustration 53
Tupasqaq
Celui qui est surpris

988-2-146
H. 41 cm
L. 15,5 cm
Ép. 11 cm
Épicéa, peinture rouge, peinture noire
Île de Kodiak

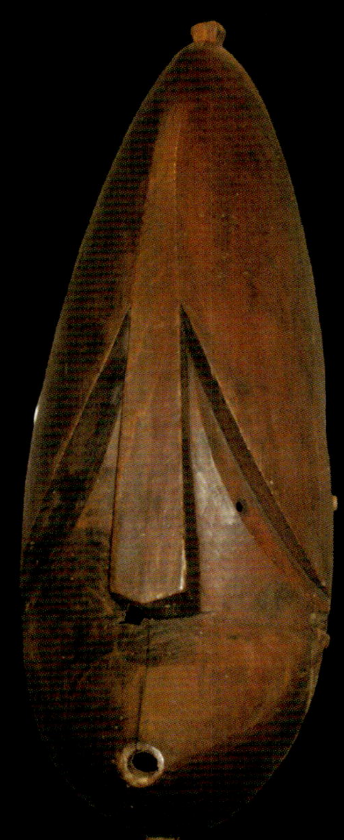

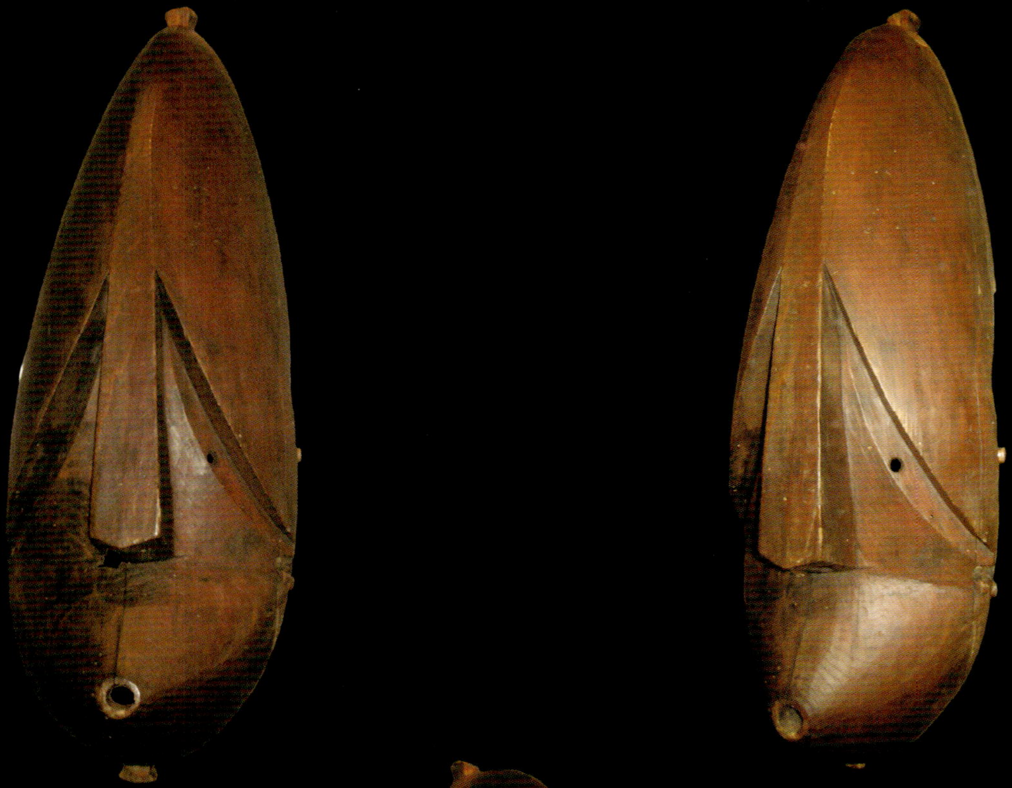

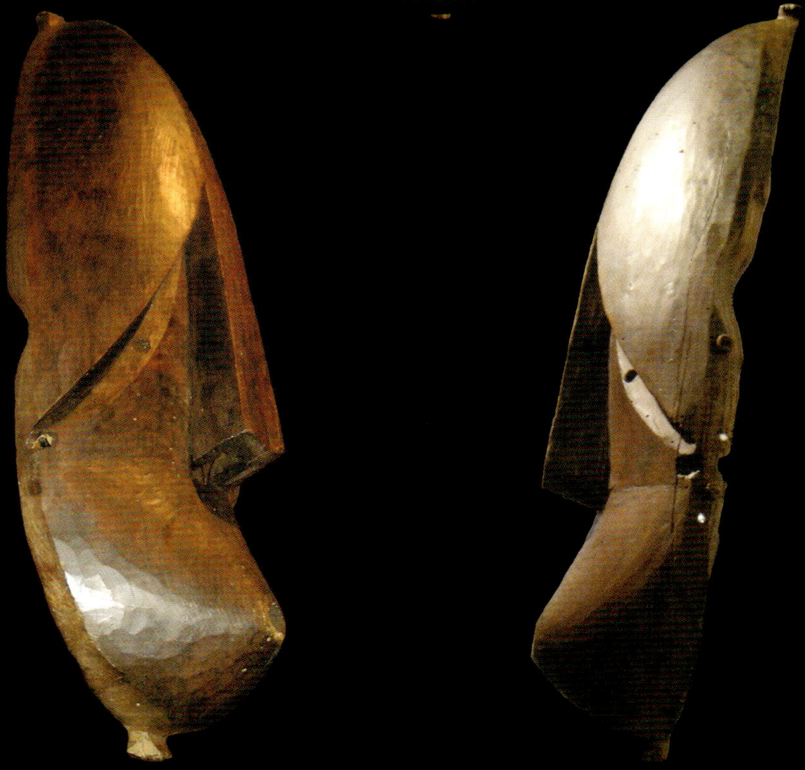

Figure 54
Name Unknown[332]

988-2-150
H. 49 cm
W. 17.5 cm
D. 9.5 cm
Spruce, red paint, black paint
Kodiak Island or Afognak Island

Illustration 54
Nom inconnu[332]

988-2-150
H. 49 cm
L. 17,5 cm
Ép. 9,5 cm
Épicéa, peinture rouge, peinture noire
Île de Kodiak ou d'Afognak

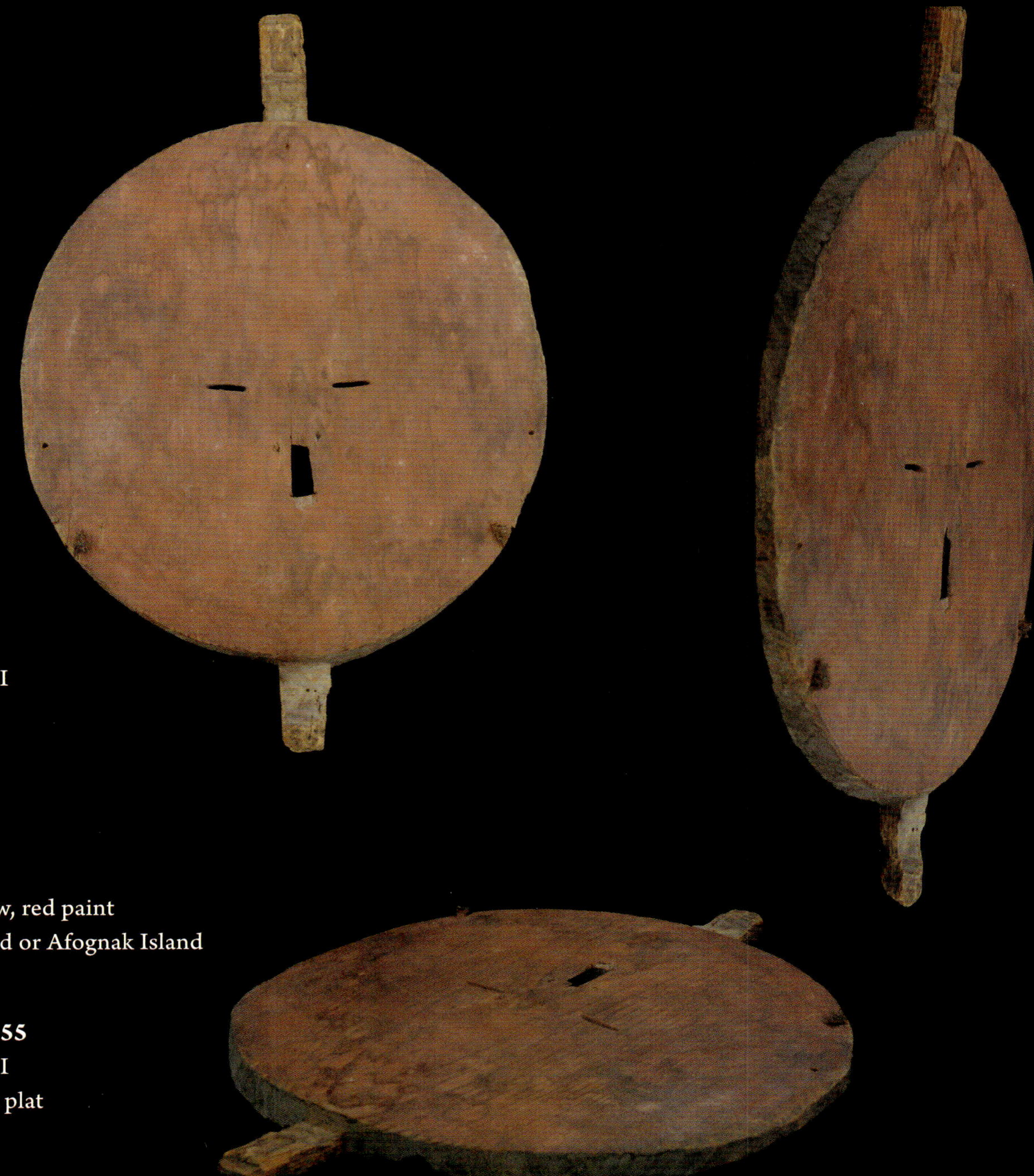

Figure 55
Pasisngaqaq I
Flat One

1988-2-178
H. 33 cm
W. 23 cm
D. 2 cm
Spruce, sinew, red paint
Kodiak Island or Afognak Island

Illustration 55
Pasisngaqaq I
Celui qui est plat

1988-2-178
H. 33 cm
L. 23 cm
Ép. 2 cm
Épicéa, tendon, peinture rouge
Île de Kodiak ou d'Afognak

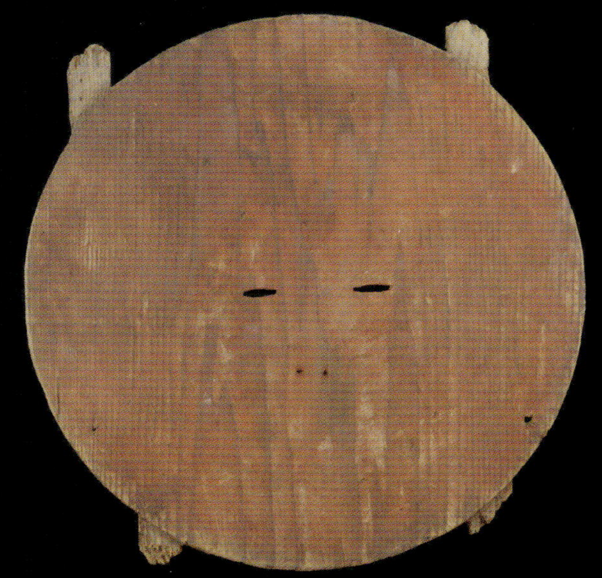
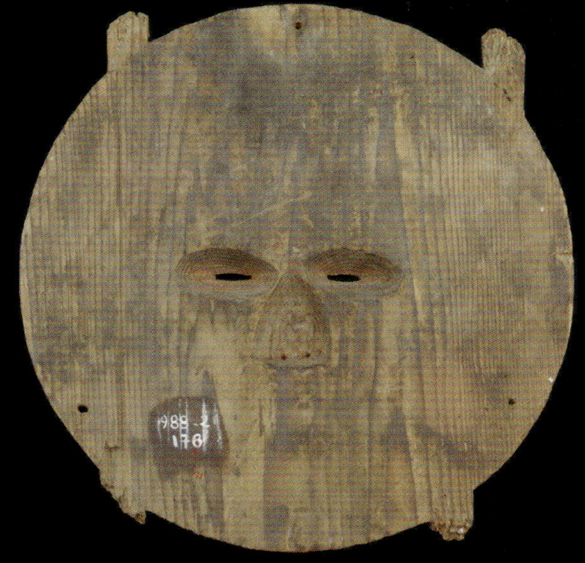
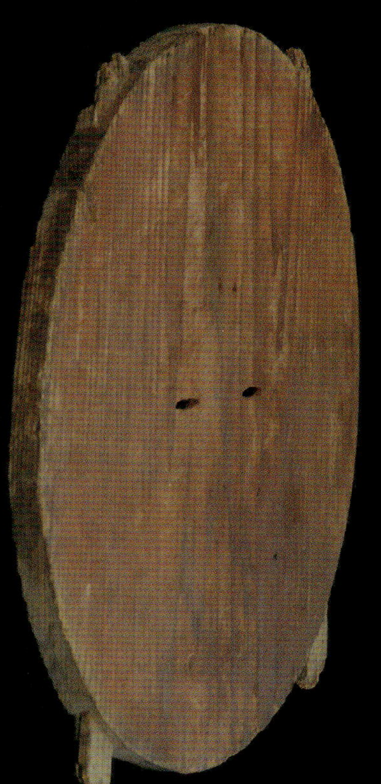
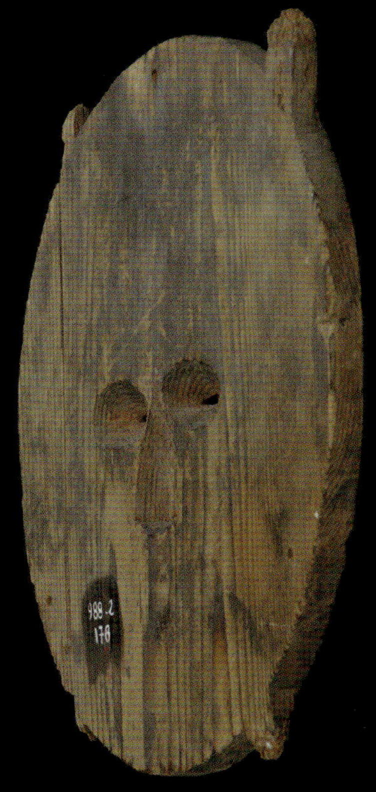

Figure 56
Pasisngaqaq II
Flat One

988-2-177
H. 23 cm
W. 22.5 cm
D. 1.2 cm
Spruce, red paint
Kodiak Island or Afognak Island

Illustration 56
Pasisngaqaq II
Celui qui est plat

988-2-177
H. 23 cm
L. 22,5 cm
Ép. 1,2 cm
Épicéa, peinture rouge
Île de Kodiak ou d'Afognak

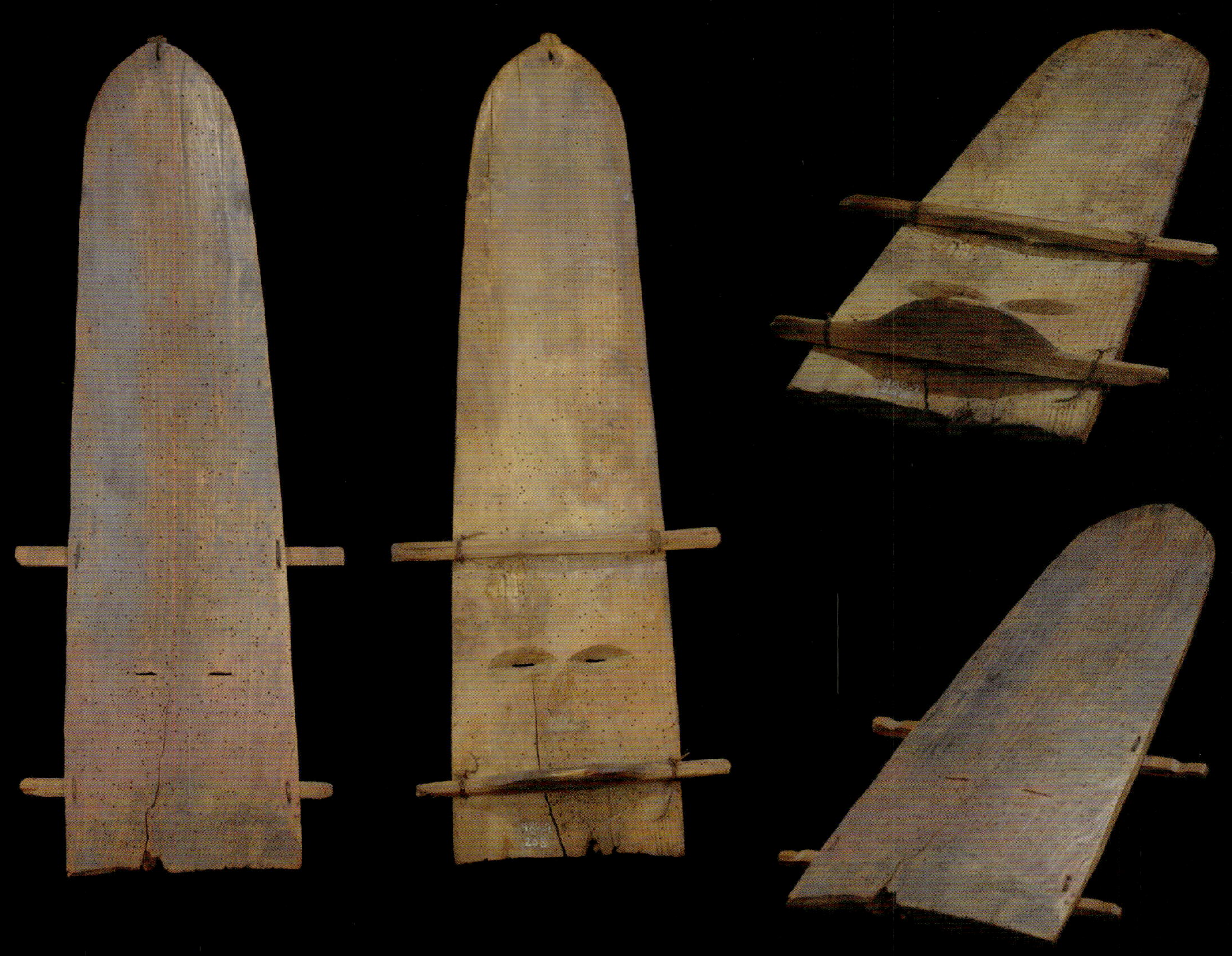

Figure 57
Tak'sqaq II
Long One

988-2-208
H. 61 cm
W. 23 cm
D. 5.5 cm
Spruce, sinew, brown paint, red
paint, black paint
Kodiak archipelago

Illustration 57
Tak'sqaq II
Celui qui est de forme allongée

988-2-208
H. 61 cm
L. 23 cm
Ép. 5,5 cm
Épicéa, tendon, peinture marron,
peinture rouge, peinture noire
Archipel de Kodiak

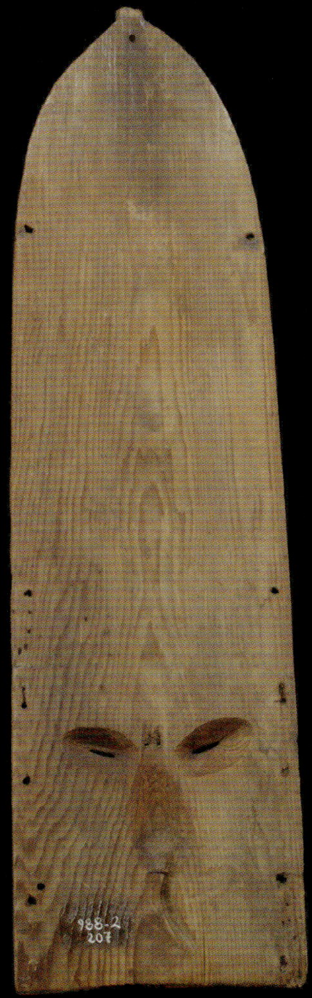
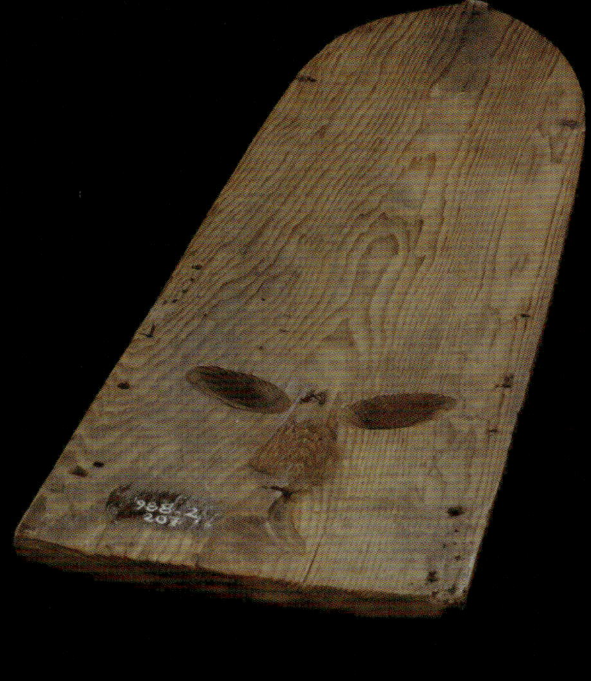
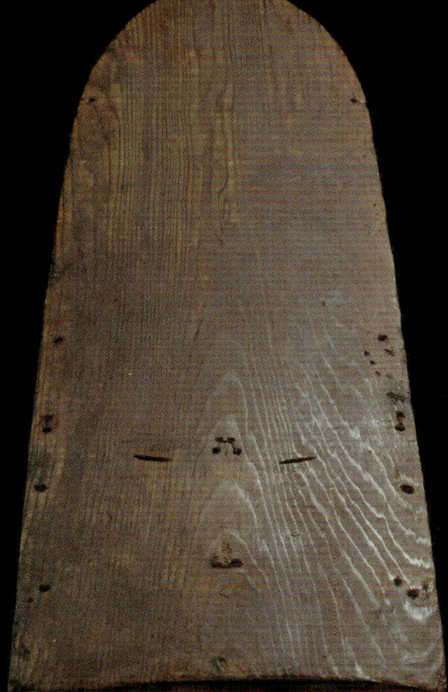

Figure 58
Tak'sqaq I
Long One

988-2-207
H. 60 cm
W. 16.7 cm
D. 1.2 cm
Spruce, sinew, red paint
Kodiak Island or Afognak Island

Illustration 58
Tak'sqaq I
Celui qui est de forme allongée

988-2-207
H. 60 cm
L. 16,7 cm
Ép. 1,2 cm
Épicéa, tendon, peinture rouge
Île de Kodiak ou d'Afognak

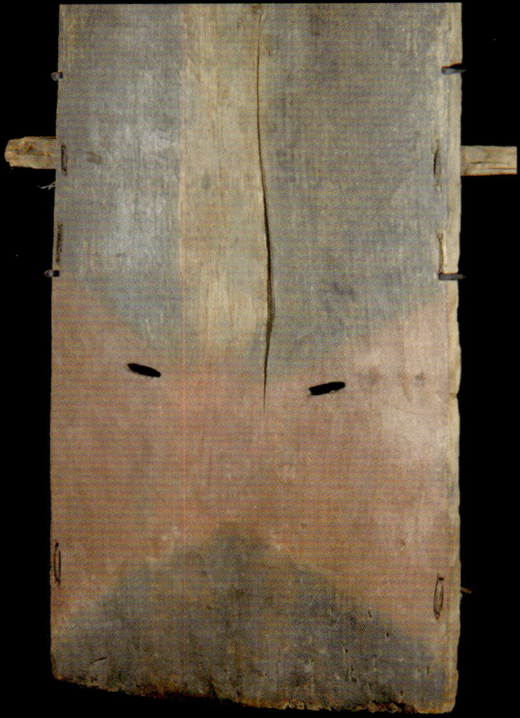

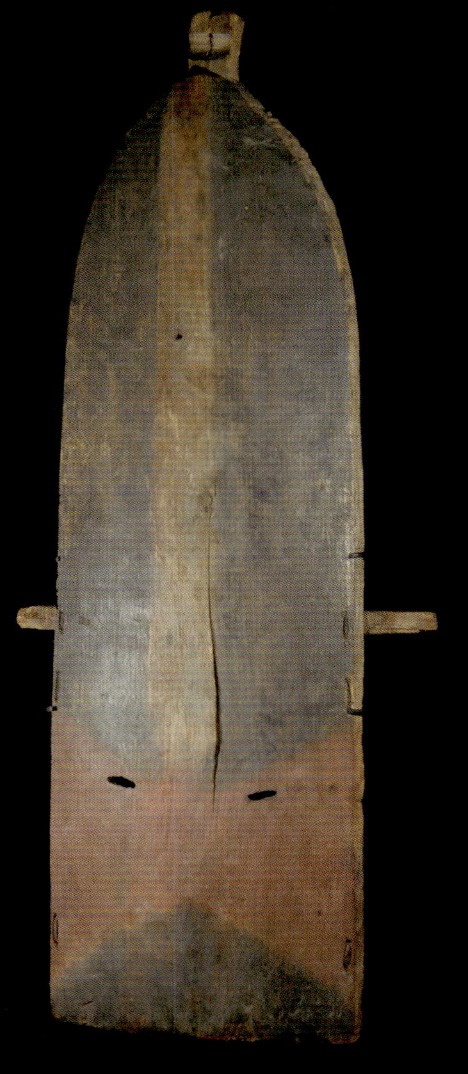

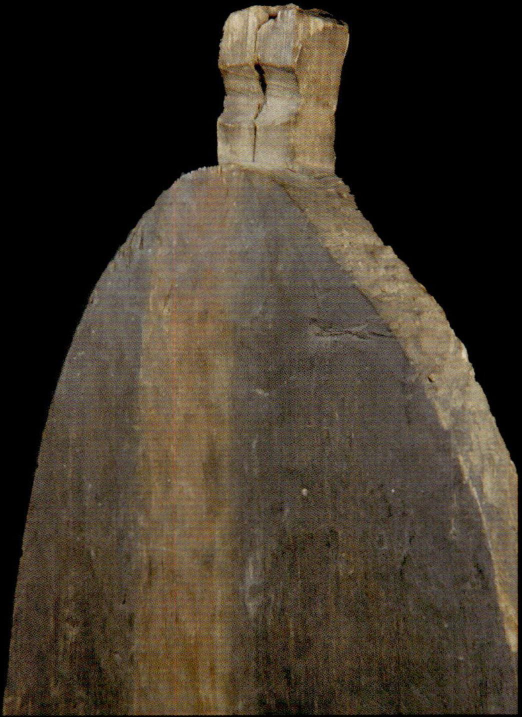

Figure 59
Tak'sqaq III
Long One

71.1881.21.29
H. 50 cm
W. 21 cm
D. 5 cm
Spruce, black paint, red
paint
Kodiak Island

Illustration 59
Tak'sqaq III
Celui qui est de forme allongée

71.1881.21.29
H. 50 cm
L. 21 cm
Ép. 5 cm
Épicéa, peinture noire, peinture
rouge
Île de Kodiak

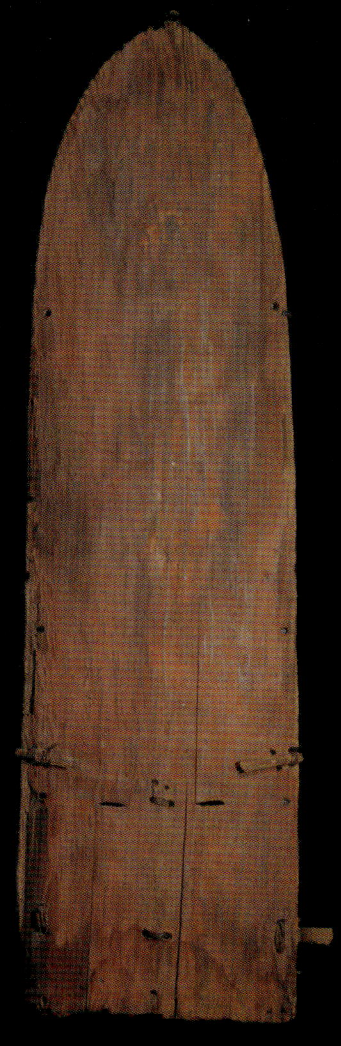

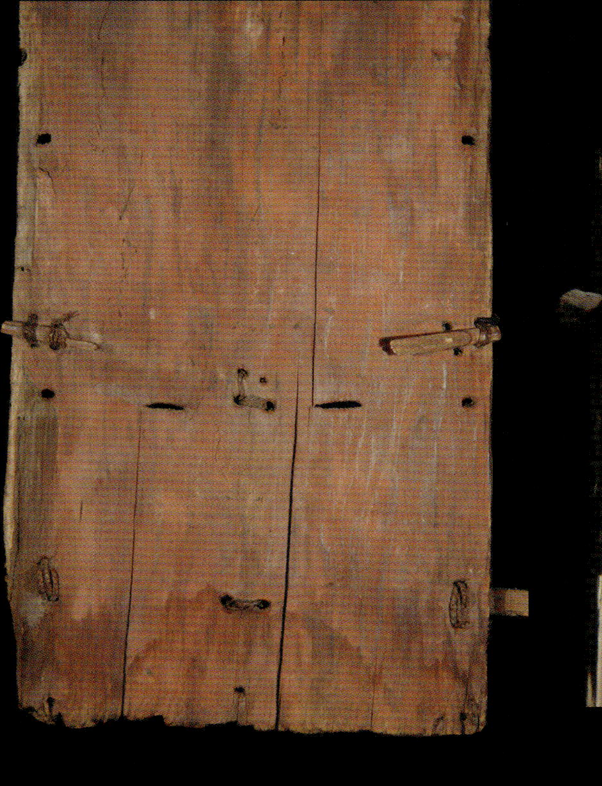

Figure 60
Tak'sqaq IV
Long One

71.1881.21.30
H. 60.5 cm
W. 19 cm
D. 5 cm
Spruce, black paint, red paint,
sinew
Kodiak Island

Illustration 60
Tak'sqaq IV
Celui qui est de forme allongée

71.1881.21.30
H. 60,5 cm
L. 19 cm
Ép. 5 cm
Épicéa, peinture noire, peinture rouge,
tendon
Île de Kodiak

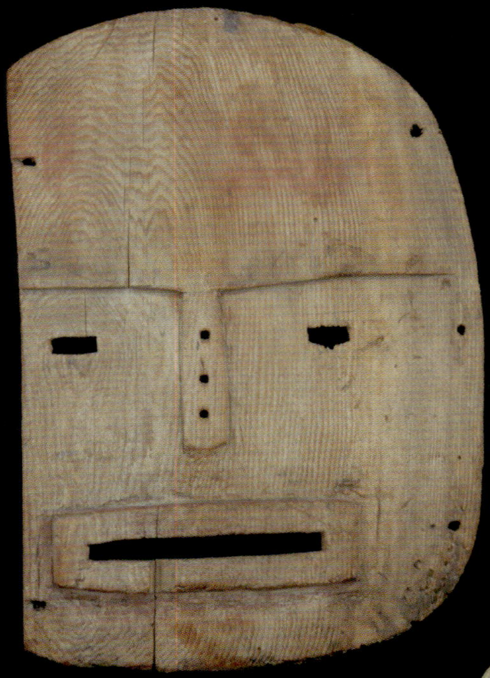

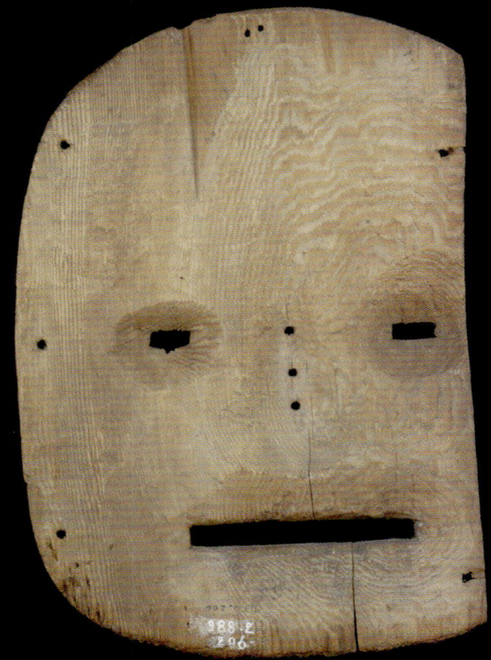

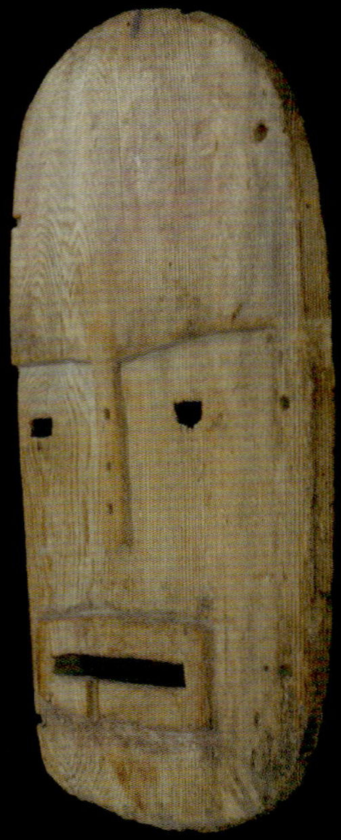

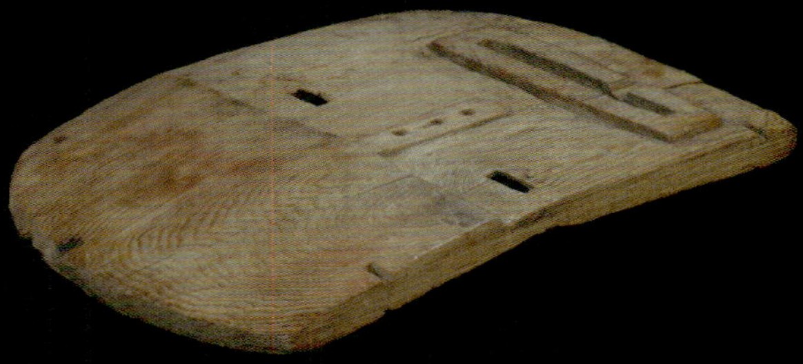

Figure 61
Awangasqaq
Spaced-Out One

988-2-206
H. 29 cm
W. 19.5 cm
D. 2.3 cm
Spruce, light brown paint, red paint
Kodiak Island or Afognak Island

Illustration 61
Awangasqaq
Celui qui a l'esprit ailleurs

988-2-206
H. 29 cm
L. 19,5 cm
Ép. 2,3 cm
Épicéa, peinture marron clair, peinture rouge
Île de Kodiak ou d'Afognak

Figure 62
Qanrilgnuq
Mouthless One

988-2-173
H. 26 cm
W. 15 cm
D. 5 cm
Douglas fir, brown paint, red paint,
black paint
Kodiak Island

Illustration 62
Qanrilgnuq
Celui qui est sans bouche

988-2-173
H. 26 cm
L. 15 cm
Ép. 5 cm
Sapin de Douglas, peinture marron,
peinture rouge, peinture noire
Île de Kodiak

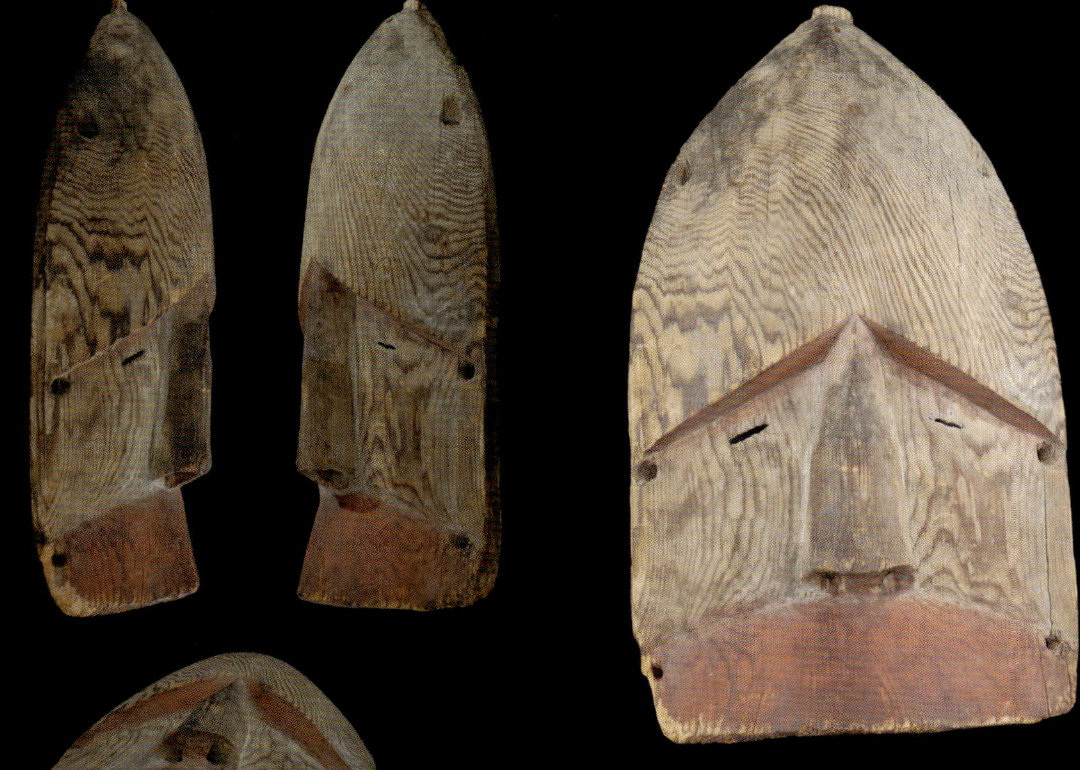

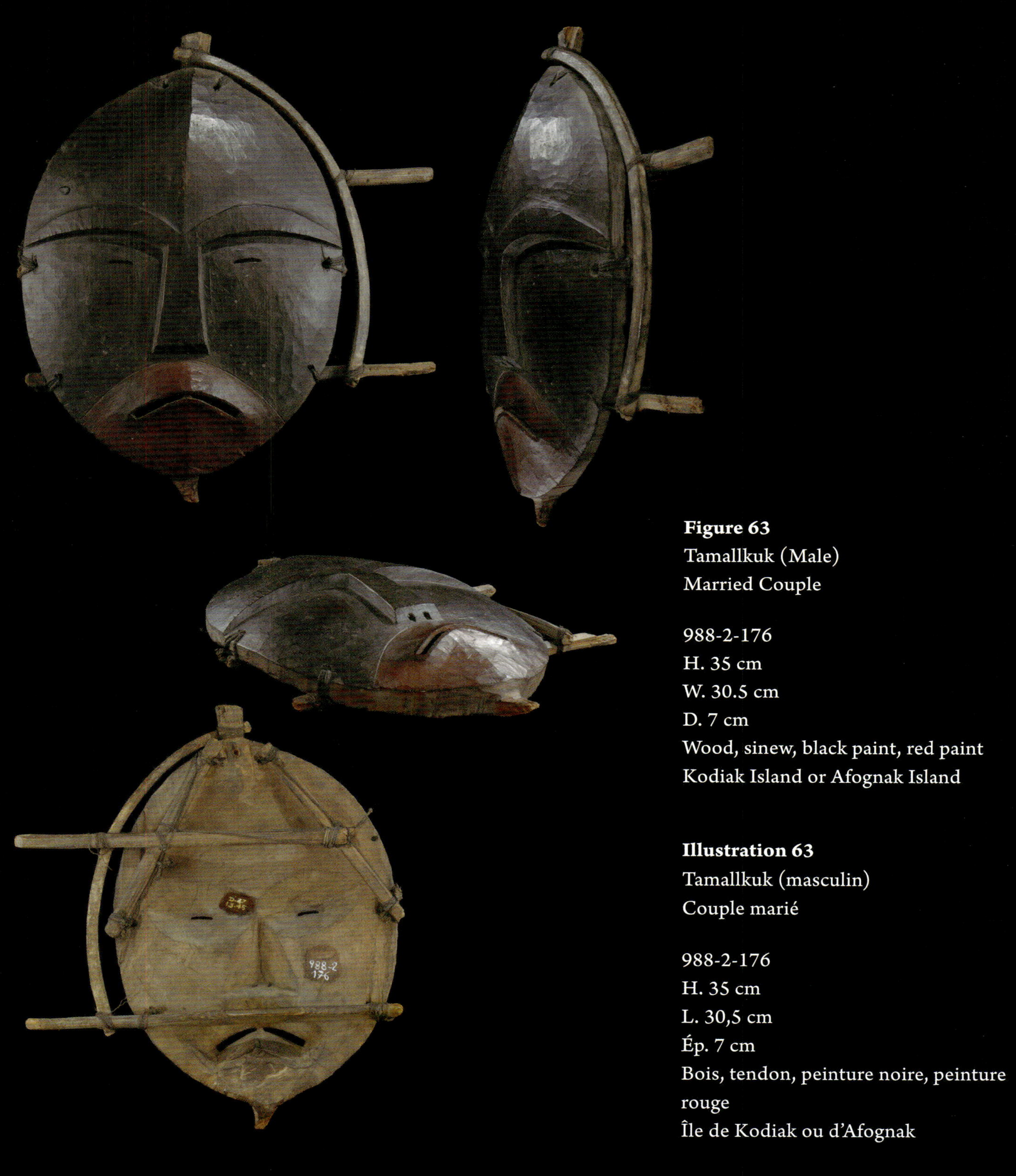

Figure 63
Tamallkuk (Male)
Married Couple

988-2-176
H. 35 cm
W. 30.5 cm
D. 7 cm
Wood, sinew, black paint, red paint
Kodiak Island or Afognak Island

Illustration 63
Tamallkuk (masculin)
Couple marié

988-2-176
H. 35 cm
L. 30,5 cm
Ép. 7 cm
Bois, tendon, peinture noire, peinture rouge
Île de Kodiak ou d'Afognak

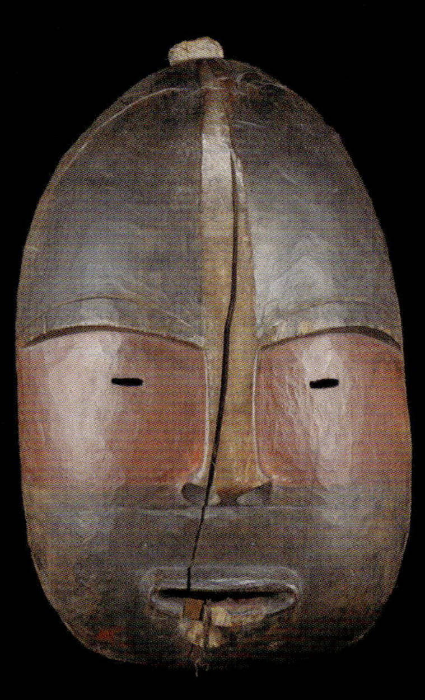
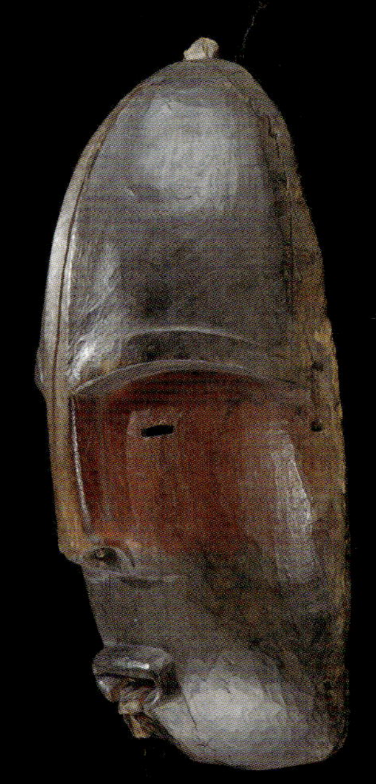
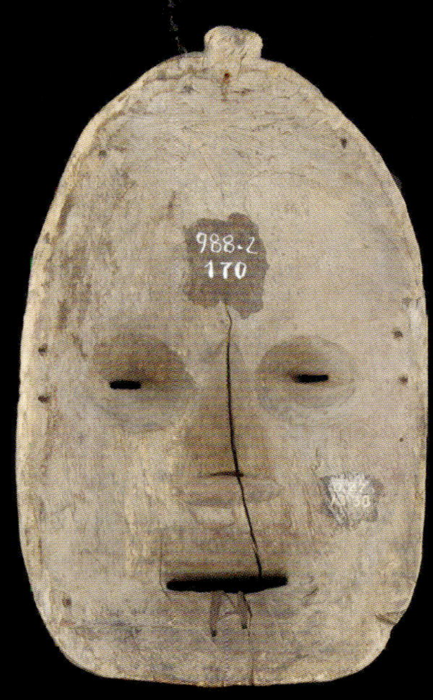

Figure 64
Tamallkuk (Female)
Married Couple

988-2-170
H. 26 cm
W. 16.5 cm
D. 7 cm
Spruce, brown paint, black paint, red paint
Kodiak Island

Illustration 64
Tamallkuk (féminin)
Couple marié

988-2-170
H. 26 cm
L. 16,5 cm
Ép. 7 cm
Épicéa, peinture marron, peinture noire,
peinture rouge
Île de Kodiak

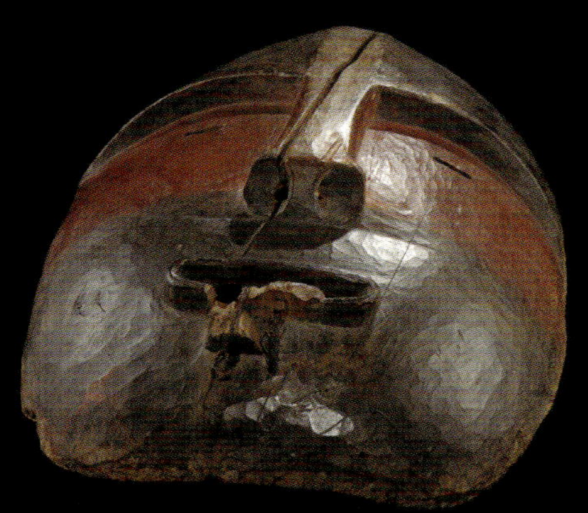
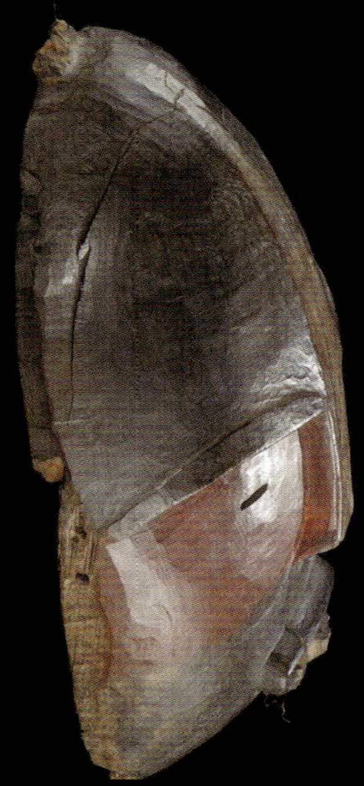

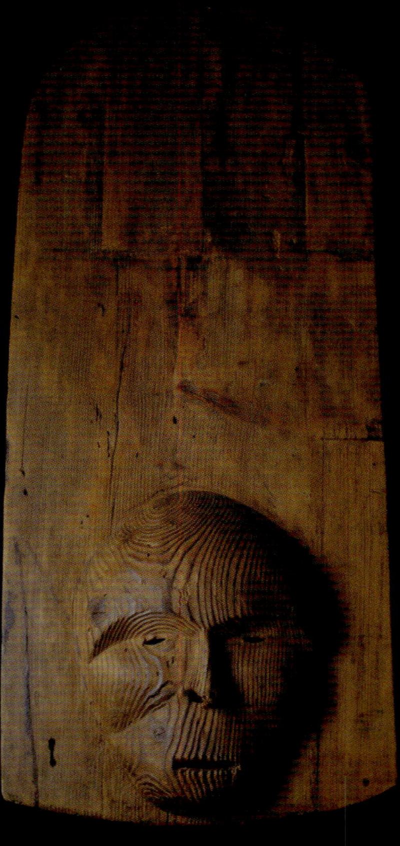
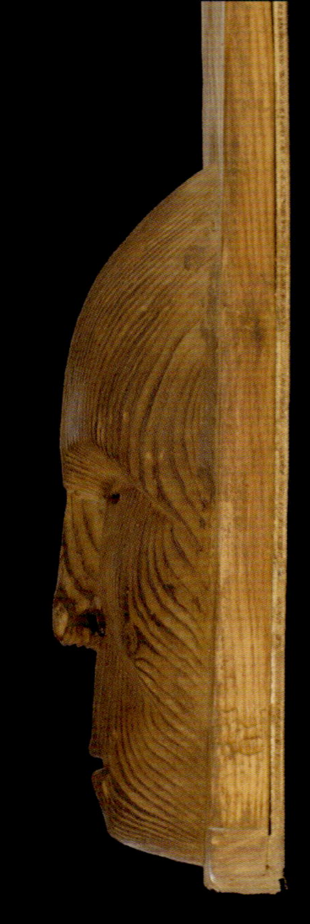
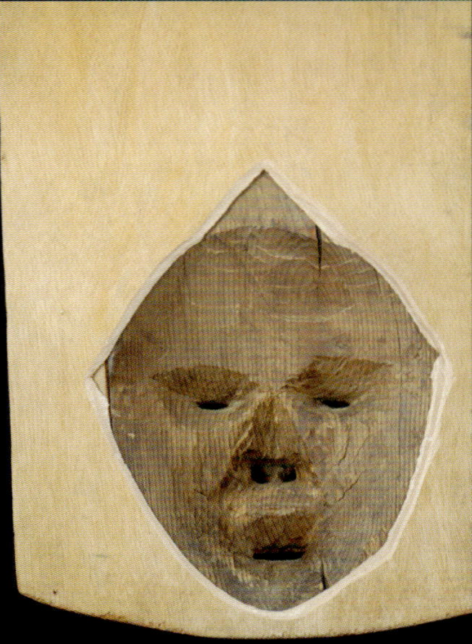

Figure 65
Umyaaqlluku Suumacillra
Remembering How They Lived

988-2-209
H. 80 cm
W. 33 cm
D. 8 cm
Douglas fir, brown paint
Afognak Island

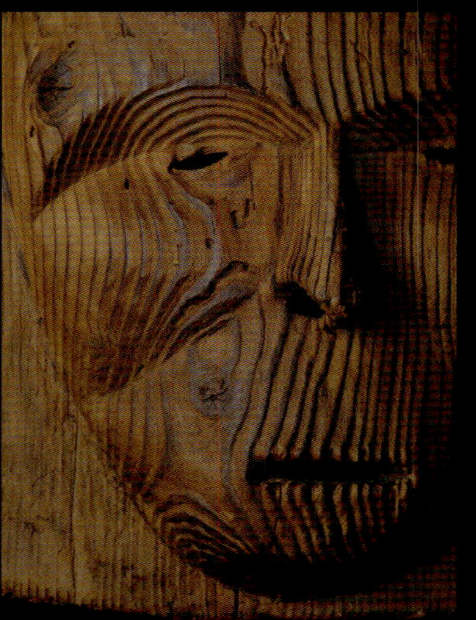
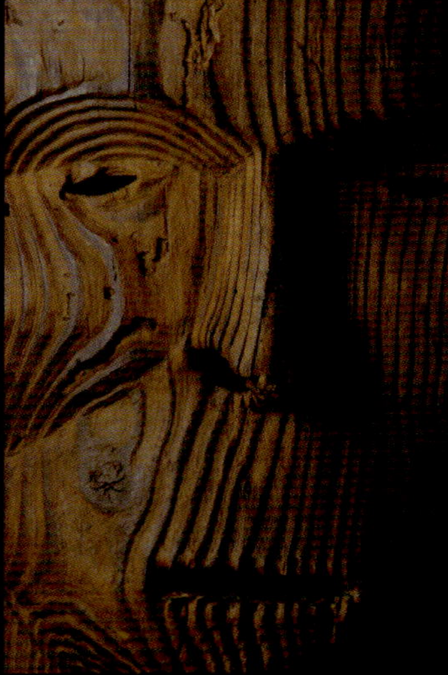

Illustration 65
Umyaaqlluku Suumacillra
Il (elle) se remémore comment il
(elle) vivait

988-2-209
H. 80 cm
L. 33 cm
Ép. 8 cm
Sapin de Douglas, peinture marron
Île d'Afognak

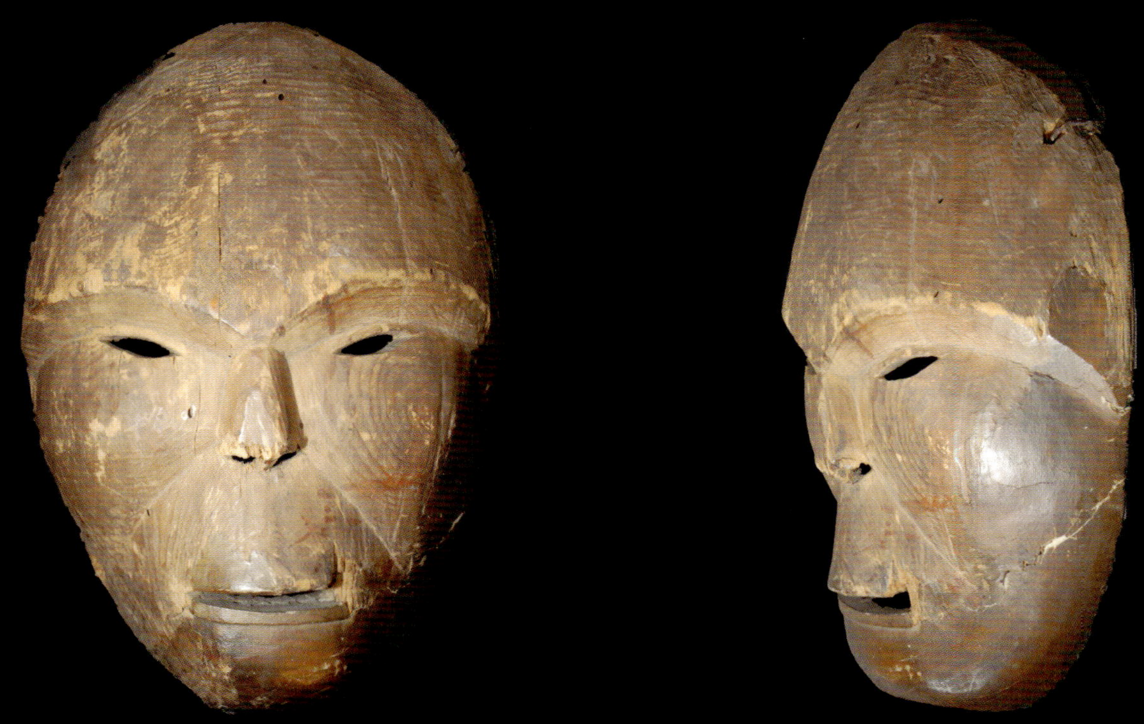

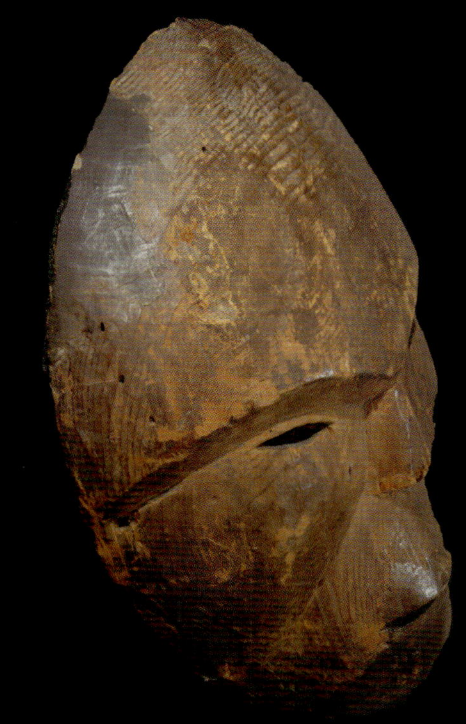

Figure 66
Name Unknown

71.1881.21.6
H. 31.5 cm
W. 20.5 cm
D. 9 cm
Wood
Afognak Island

Illustration 66
Nom inconnu

71.1881.21.6
H. 31,5 cm
L. 20,5 cm
Ép. 9 cm
Bois
Île d'Afognak

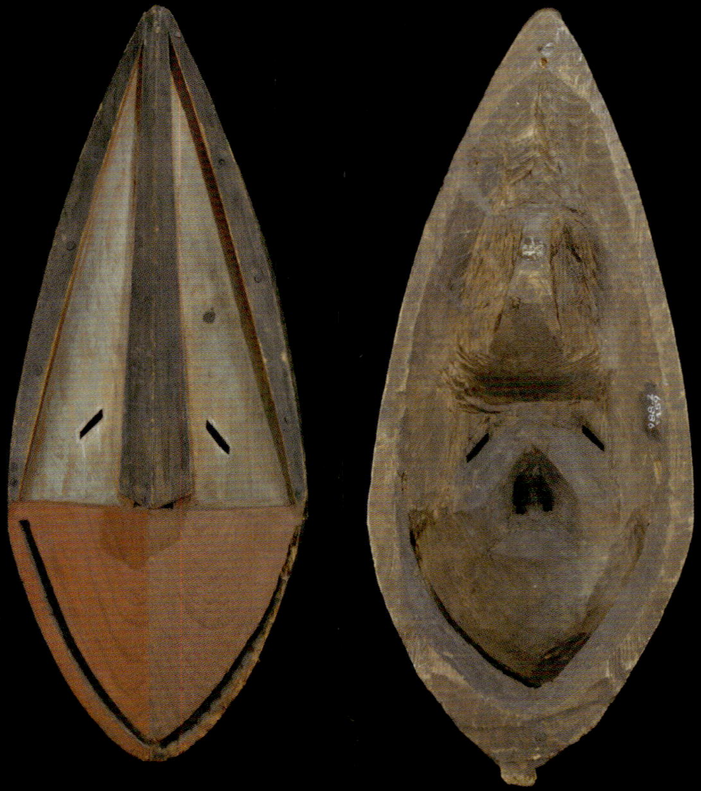

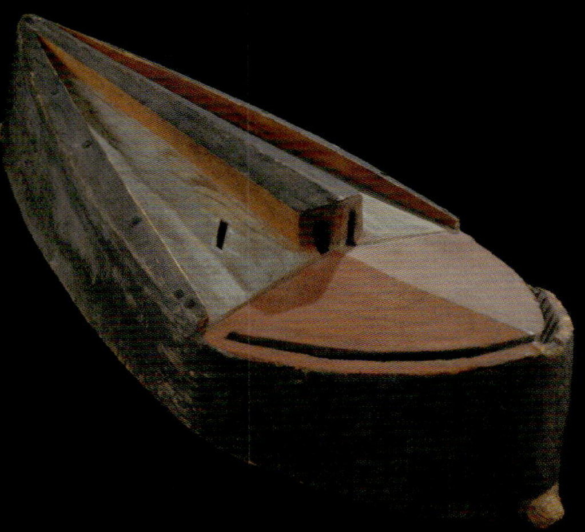

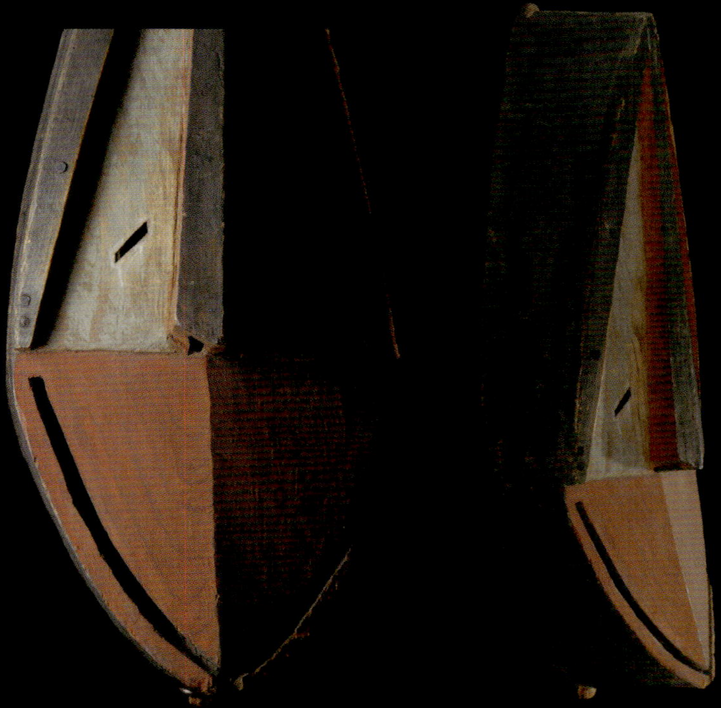

Figure 67

Igyuyrtuliksiinaq
Larger Searcher

988-2-159
H. 57 cm
W. 22.5 cm
D. 12.5 cm
Spruce, red paint, black paint, green paint, white paint
Kodiak Island or Afognak Island
See Appendix for mask song, dance, and legend.

Illustration 67

Igyuyrtuliksiinaq
Très grand chercheur

988-2-159
H. 57 cm
L. 22,5 cm
Ép. 12,5 cm
Épicéa, peinture rouge, peinture noire, peinture verte, peinture blanche
Île de Kodiak ou d'Afognak
Se reporter à l'Annexe pour le chant, la danse et la légende du masque.

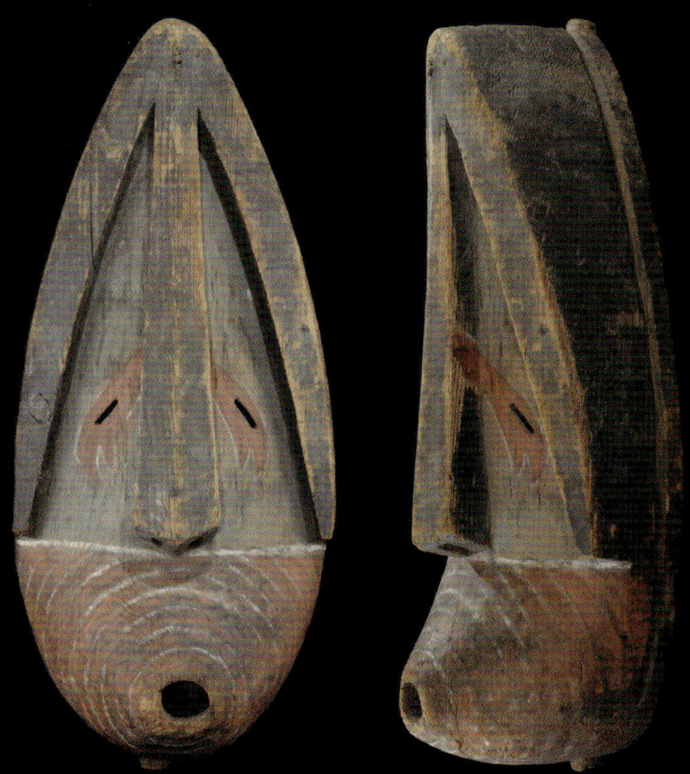
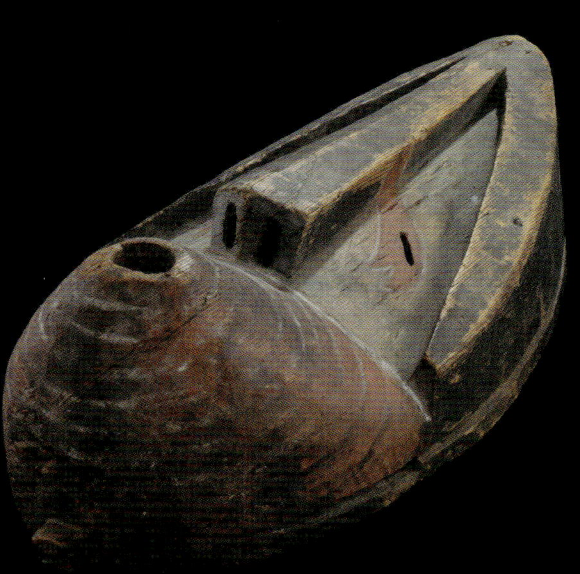
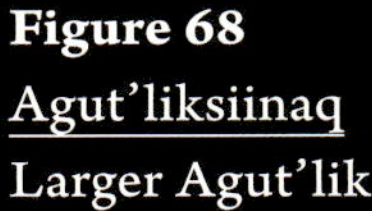

Figure 68
<u>Agut'liksiinaq</u>
Larger Agut'lik

988-2-152
H. 50 cm
W. 21 cm
D. 14 cm
Spruce, red paint, white paint, black paint, green
paint
Kodiak Island
See Appendix for mask legend.

Illustration 68
<u>Agut'liksiinaq</u>
Très grand Agut'liq

988-2-152
H. 50 cm
L. 21 cm
Ép. 14 cm
Épicéa, peinture rouge, peinture blanche, peinture
noire, peinture verte
Île de Kodiak
Se reporter à l'Annexe pour la légende du masque.

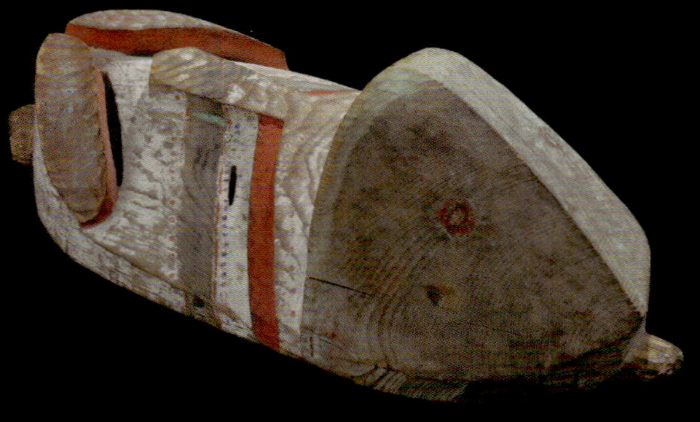

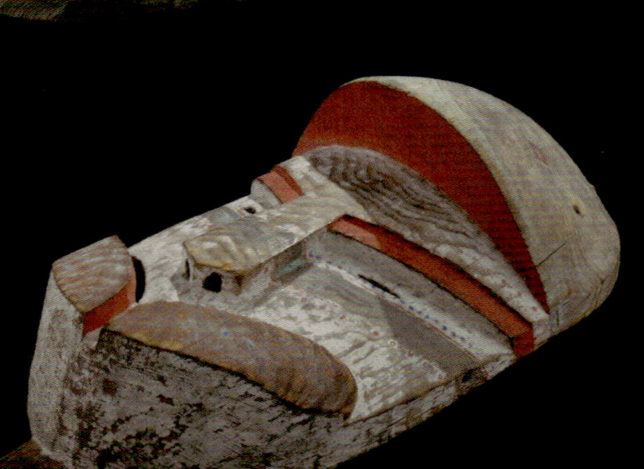

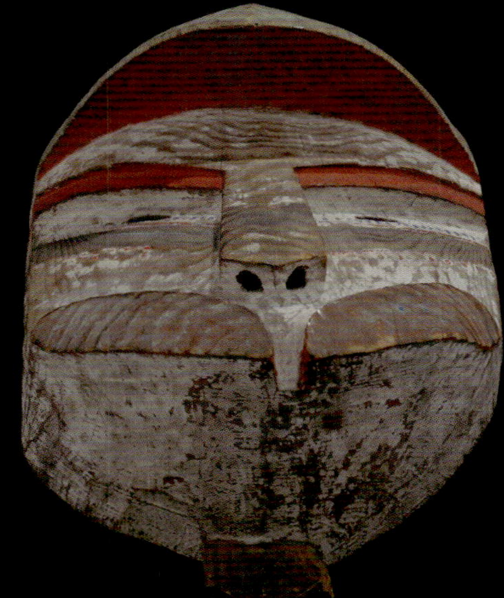

Figure 69
Cucunasqaq Giinaq
Pretty Face

988-2-184
H. 37 cm
W. 17 cm
D. 12 cm
Douglas fir, white paint, red paint,
green paint, blue paint
Kodiak Island or Afognak Island

Illustration 69
Cucunasqaq Giinaq
Joli visage

988-2-184
H. 37 cm
L. 17 cm
Ép. 12 cm
Sapin de Douglas, peinture blanche,
peinture rouge, peinture verte,
peinture bleue
Île de Kodiak ou d'Afognak

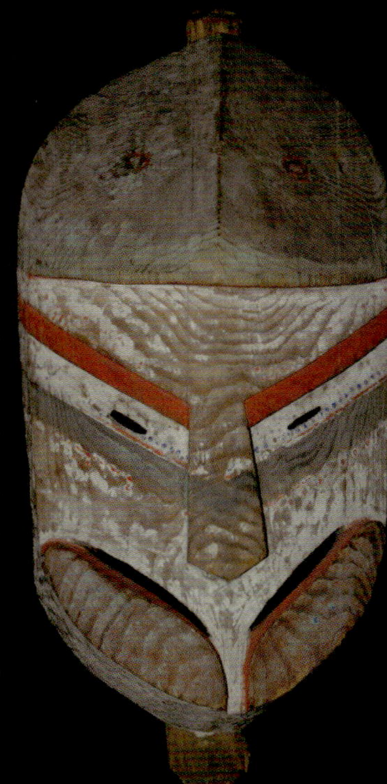

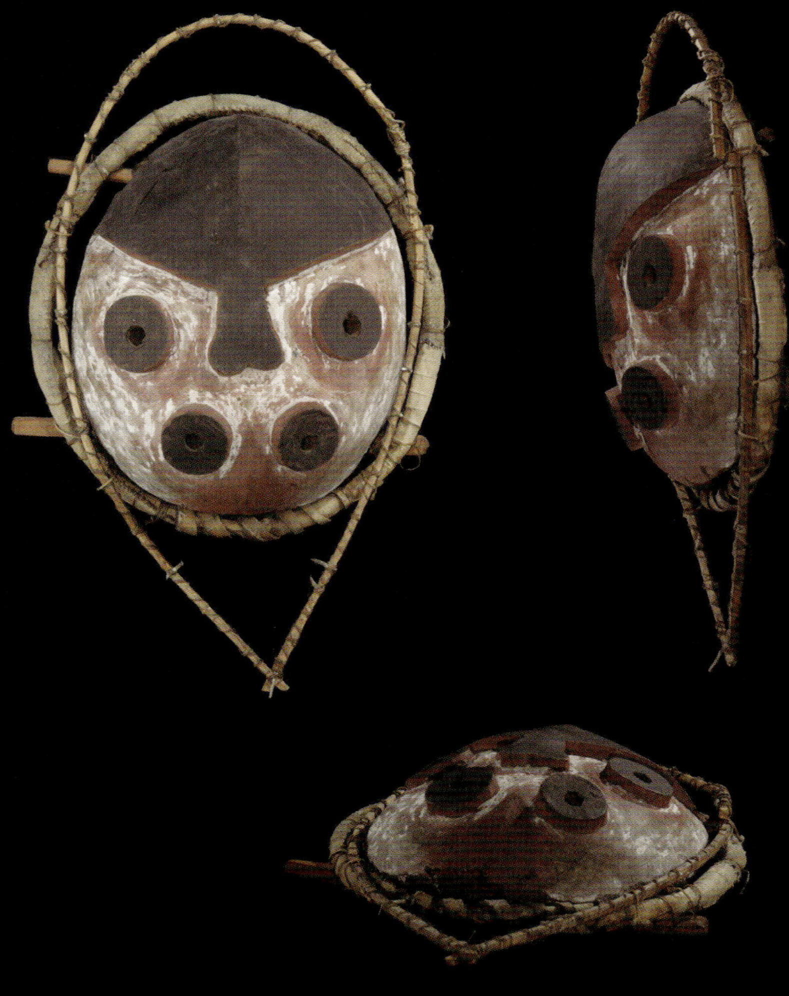

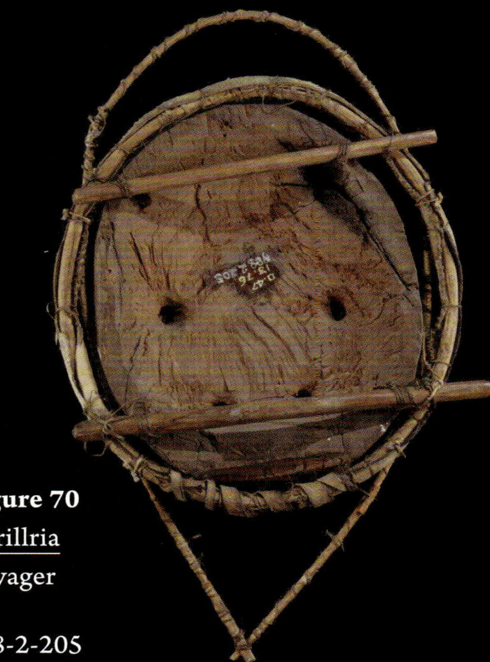

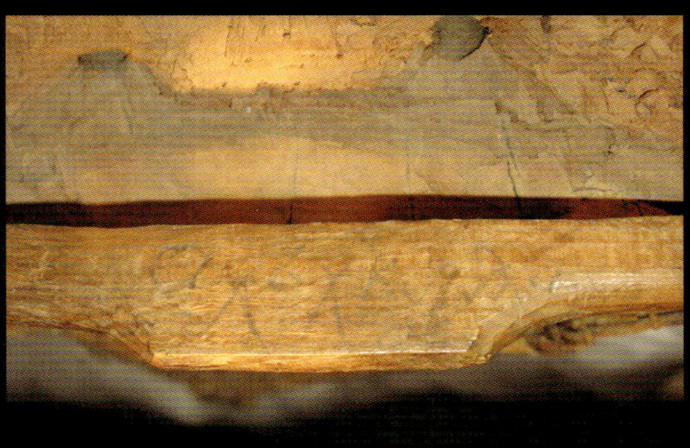

Mask name written on bite bar by Pinart.

Le nom de ce masque a été inscrit sur le mors par Pinart.

Figure 70
Akrillria
Voyager

988-2-205
H. 35 cm
W. 21 cm
D. 8.5 cm
Wood, sinew, leather, feathers, black paint,
red paint, white paint, light brown paint
Kodiak Island or Afognak Island
See Appendix for mask song.

Illustration 70
Akrillria
Voyageur

988-2-205
H. 35 cm
L. 21 cm
Ép. 8,5 cm
Bois, tendon, cuir, plumes, peinture noire,
peinture rouge, peinture blanche, peinture
marron clair
Île de Kodiak ou d'Afognak
Se reporter à l'Annexe pour le chant du
masque.

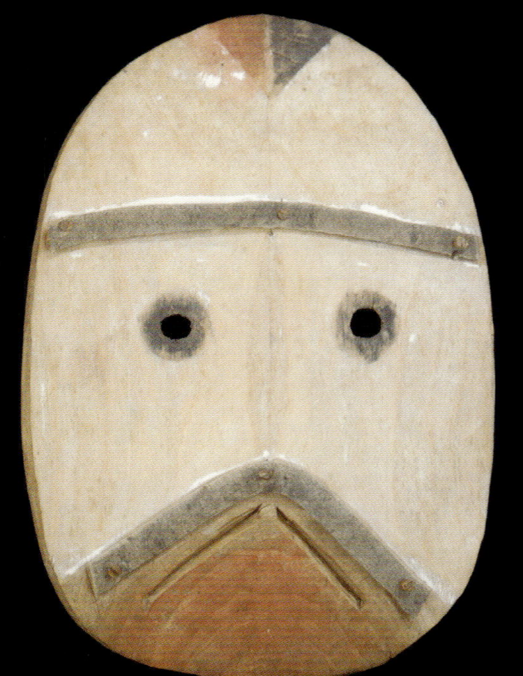

Figure 71
Payulik
Bringer of Food

988-2-169
H. 20.5 cm
W. 14.4 cm
D. 3 cm
Cottonwood, leather, white paint, red paint, black paint
Eagle Harbor
See Appendix for mask song and dance.

Illustration 71
Payulik
Celui qui apporte la nourriture

988-2-169
H. 20,5 cm
L. 14,4 cm
Ép. 3 cm
Peuplier de Virginie, cuir, peinture blanche, peinture
rouge, peinture noire
Eagle Harbor
Se reporter à l'Annexe pour le chant et la danse du
masque.

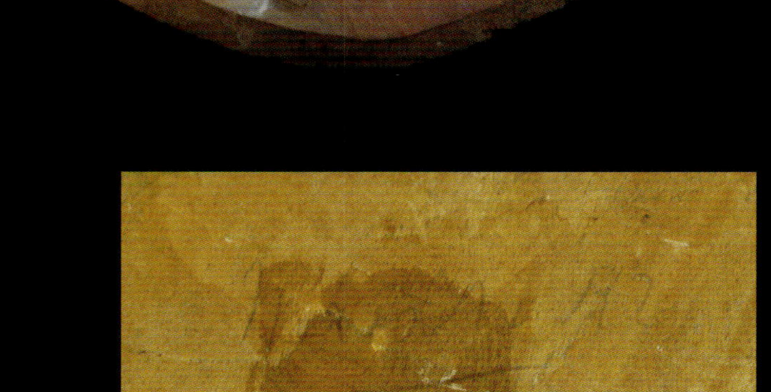

Mask name written on back of mask by Pinart.

Nom de masque écrit au dos du masque par
Pinart.

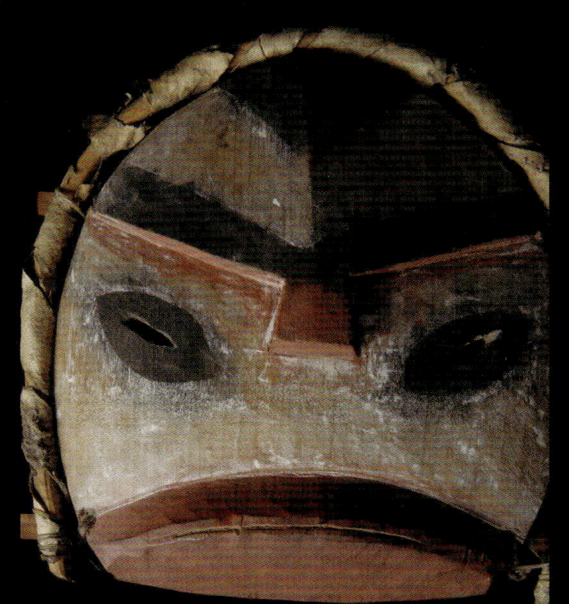
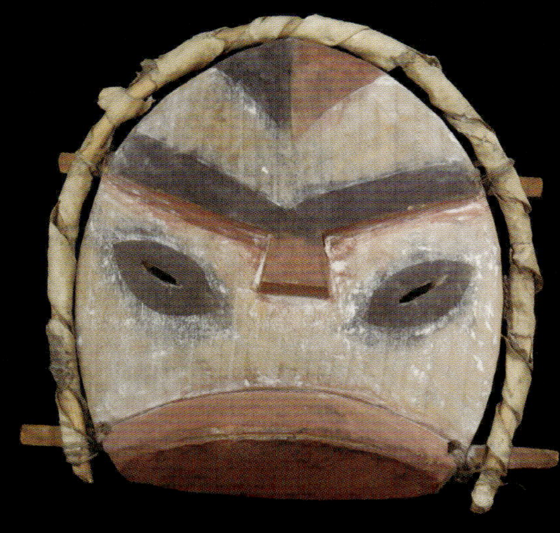
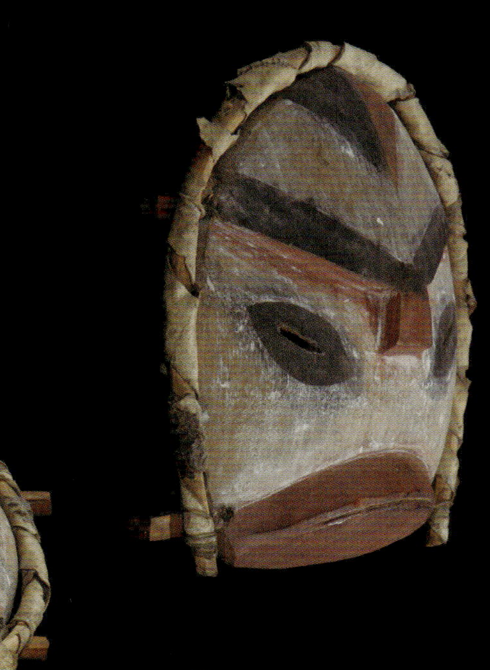
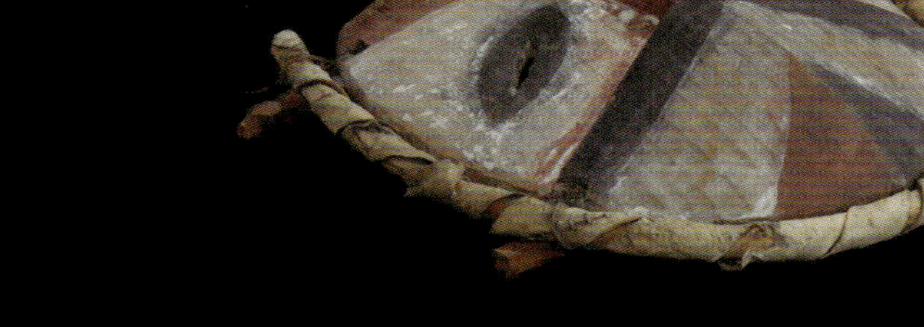

Figure 72
Unartuliq
Protector/Talisman

988-2-199
H. 16 cm
W. 17 cm
D. 4.5 cm
Wood, leather, sinew, black paint, red
paint, white paint
Eagle Harbor
See Appendix for mask song and dance.

Illustration 72
Unartuliq
Protecteur/Talisman

988-2-199
H. 16 cm
L. 17 cm
Ép. 4,5 cm
Bois, cuir, tendon, peinture noire,
peinture rouge, peinture blanche
Eagle Harbor
Se reporter à l'Annexe pour le chant et la
danse du masque.

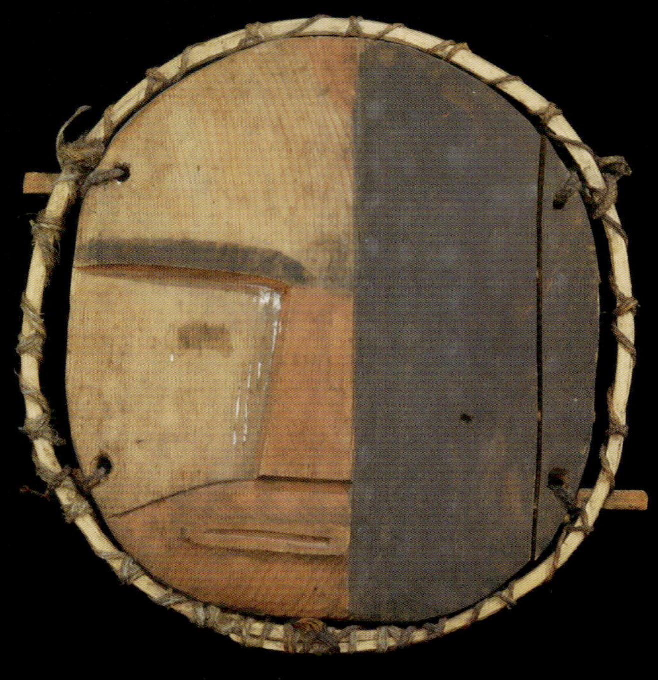

Figure 73
Unnuyayuk
Night Traveler

988-2-195
H. 19 cm
W. 19 cm
D. 2.5 cm
Wood, sinew, plant fiber, black paint, red paint, blue
paint
Eagle Harbor
See Appendix for mask song, legend, and dance.

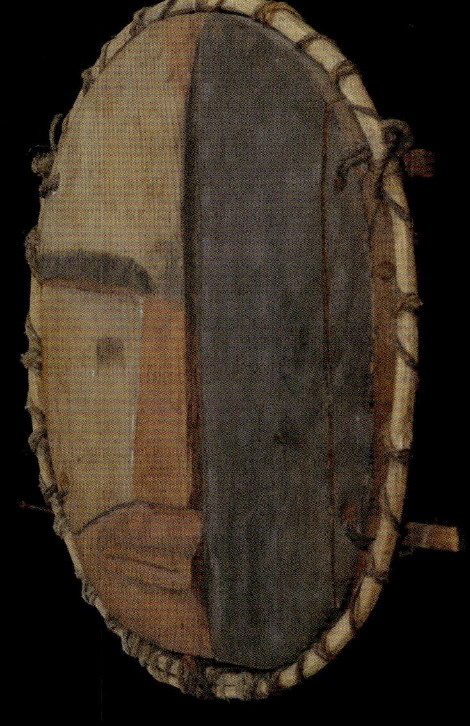

Illustration 73
Unnuyayuk
Voyageur nocturne

988-2-195
H. 19 cm
L. 19 cm
Ép. 2,5 cm
Bois, tendon, fibres végétales, peinture noire, peinture
rouge, peinture bleue
Eagle Harbor
Se reporter à l'Annexe pour le chant, la légende et la
danse du masque.

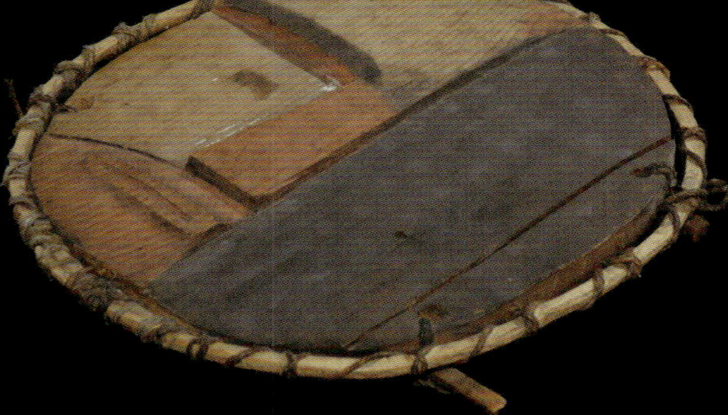

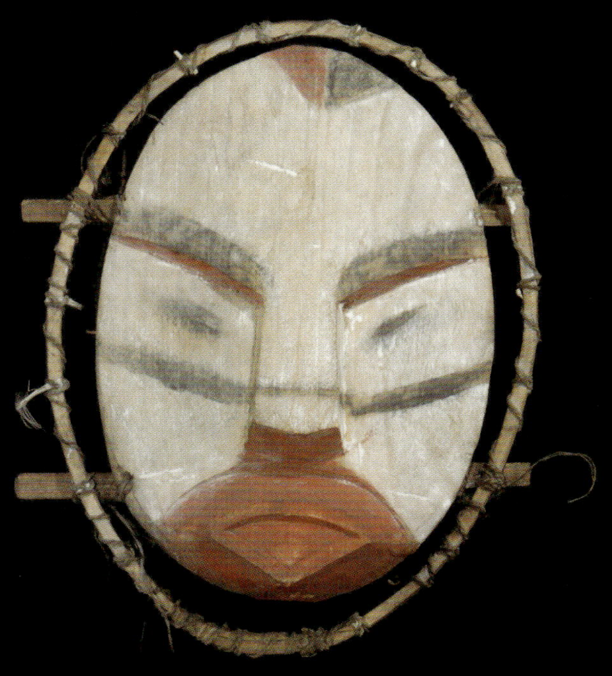

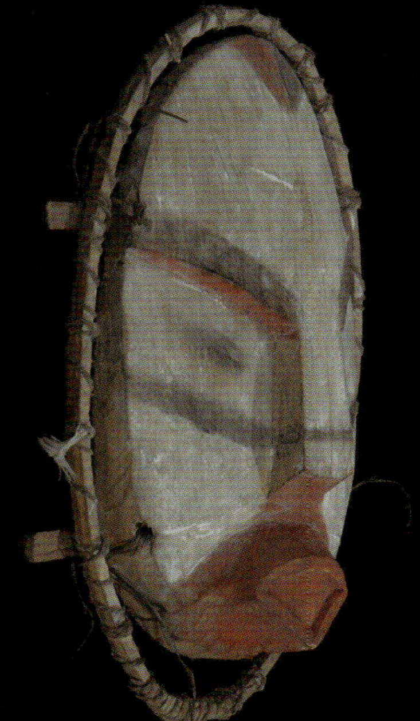

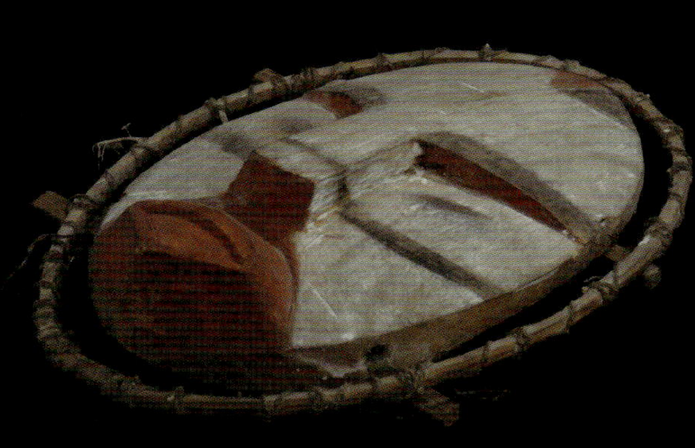

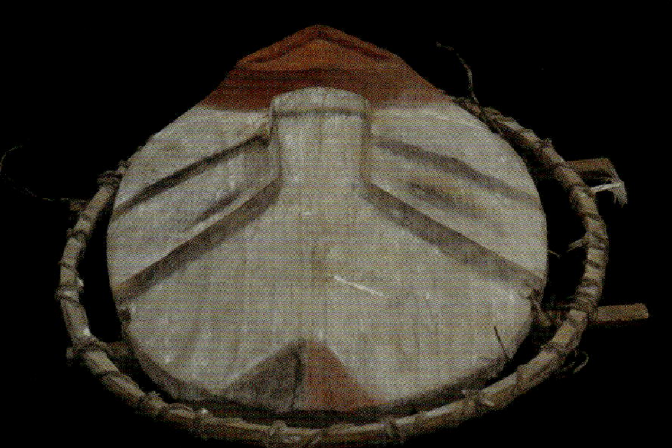

Figure 74
Agu'lik
Large Mask

988-2-200
H. 16.5 cm
W. 13.5 cm
D. 3.5 cm
White oak, sinew, white paint, red paint, black paint,
light brown paint
Kodiak Island or Afognak Island
See Appendix for mask song, legend, and dance.

Illustration 74
Agu'lik
Large masque

988-2-200
H. 16,5 cm
L. 13,5 cm
Ép. 3,5 cm
Chêne blanc, tendon, peinture blanche, peinture rouge,
peinture noire, peinture marron clair
Île de Kodiak ou d'Afognak
Se reporter à l'Annexe pour le chant, la légende et la
danse du masque.

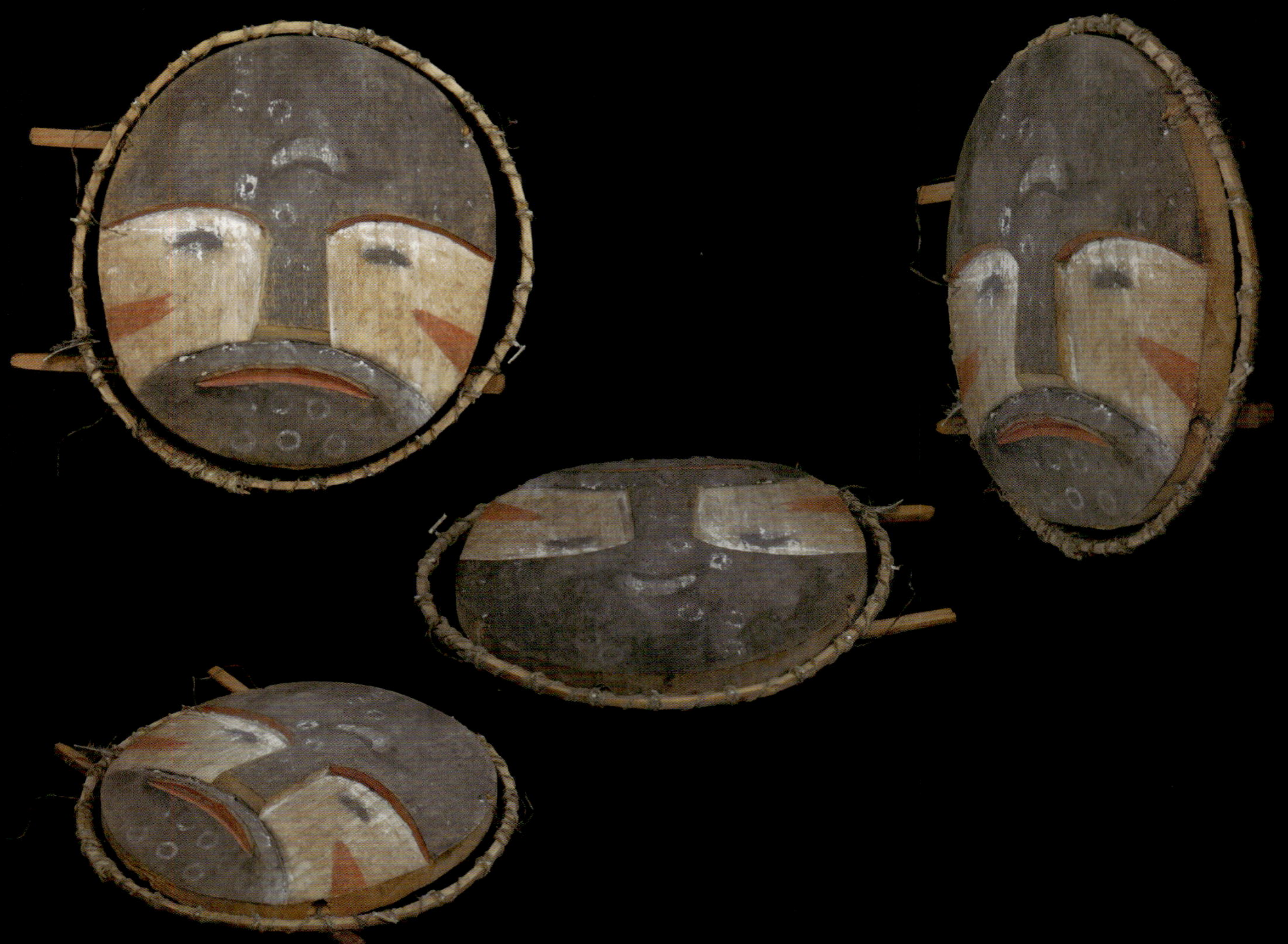

Figure 75

<u>Nallumalik</u>

One Who Doesn't Know

988-2-204
H. 17.5 cm
W. 18 cm
D. 3.5 cm
Wood, sinew, feathers, black
paint, white paint, red paint
Kodiak Island or Afognak Island
See Appendix for mask song and
dance.

Illustration 75

Nallumalik

Celui qui ne sait pas

988-2-204
H. 17,5 cm
L. 18 cm
Ép. 3,5 cm
Bois, tendon, plumes, peinture noire,
peinture blanche, peinture rouge
Île de Kodiak ou d'Afognak
Se reporter à l'Annexe pour le chant et
la danse du masque.

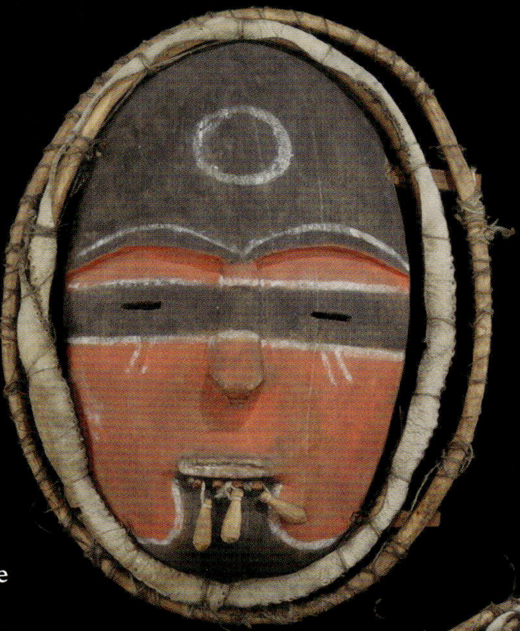

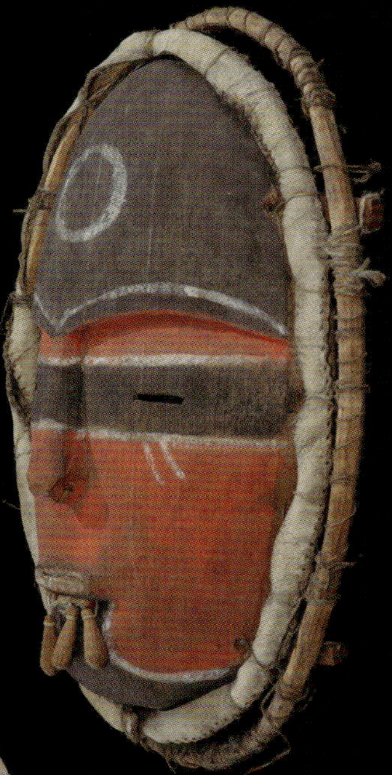

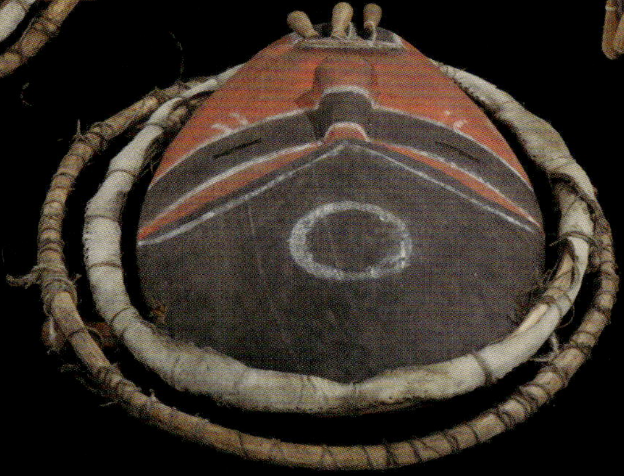

Figure 76
Ashigik
Fool/Lucky One

988-2-202
H. 22.5 cm
W. 17.5 cm
D. 5.5 cm
Wood, leather, sinew, cotton, feathers, red
paint, black paint, white paint
Kodiak Island or Afognak Island
See Appendix for mask song and dance.

Illustration 76
Ashigik
L'idiot/Celui qui a de la chance

988-2-202
H. 22,5 cm
L. 17,5 cm
Ép. 5,5 cm
Bois, cuir, tendon, peuplier de Virginie,
plumes, peinture rouge, peinture noire,
peinture blanche
Île de Kodiak ou d'Afognak
Se reporter à l'Annexe pour le chant et la
danse du masque.

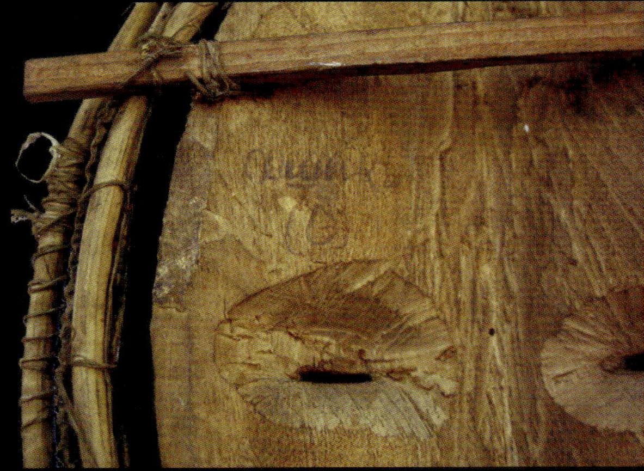

Mask name written on back of mask by Pinart.

Nom de masque écrit au dos du masque par Pinart.

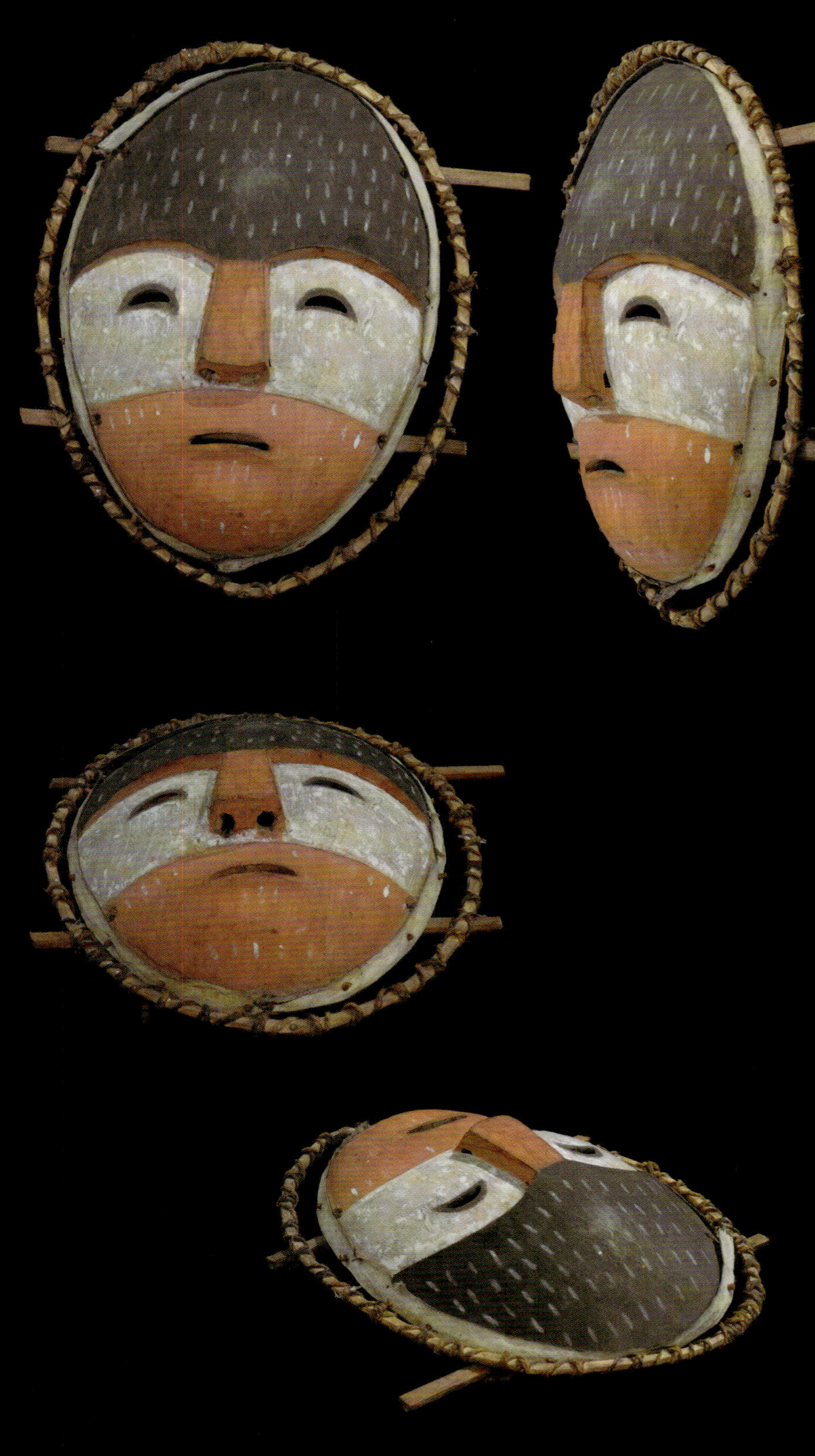

Figure 77
<u>Ingillagayak</u>
Weatherman

988-2-198
H. 23.5 cm
W. 20 cm
D. 5.5 cm
Wood, leather, sinew, plant fiber,
white paint, red paint, black paint
Kodiak Island or Afognak Island
See Appendix for mask song, legend,
and dance.

Illustration 77
<u>Ingillagayak</u>
Celui qui annonce le temps

988-2-198
H. 23,5 cm
L. 20 cm
Ép. 5,5 cm
Bois, cuir, tendon, fibres végétales,
peinture blanche, peinture rouge,
peinture noire
Île de Kodiak ou d'Afognak
Se reporter à l'Annexe pour le chant,
la légende et la danse du masque.

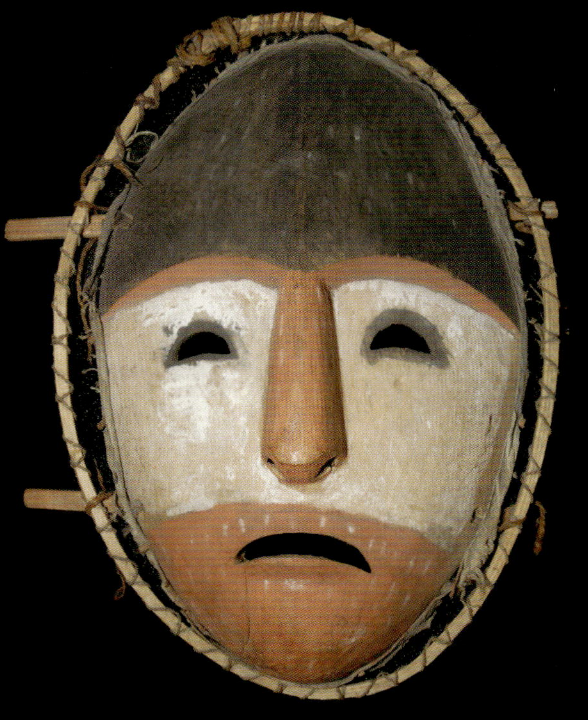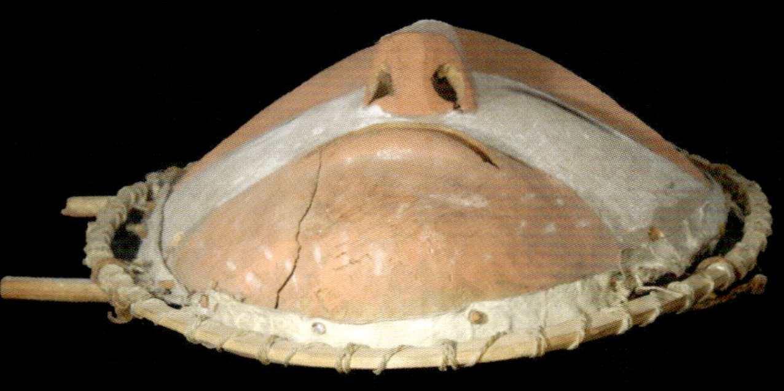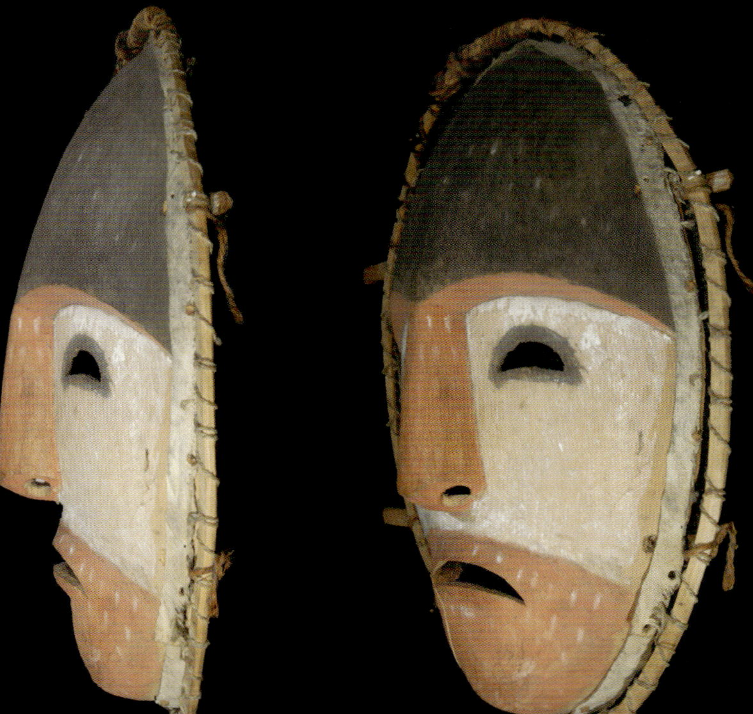

Figure 78
<u>Cummugiya</u> (alternative spelling Cummullria)
One That Went Ahead of Them

71.1881.21.27
H. 28 cm
W. 23 cm
D. 9 cm
Wood, leather, sinew, feather parts, black
paint, red paint, white paint
Kodiak Island

Illustration 78
<u>Cummugiya</u>
Celui qui est parti en éclaireur

71.1881.21.27
H. 28 cm
L. 23 cm
Ép. 9 cm
Bois, cuir, tendon, morceaux de plumes,
peinture noire, peinture rouge, peinture
blanche
Île de Kodiak

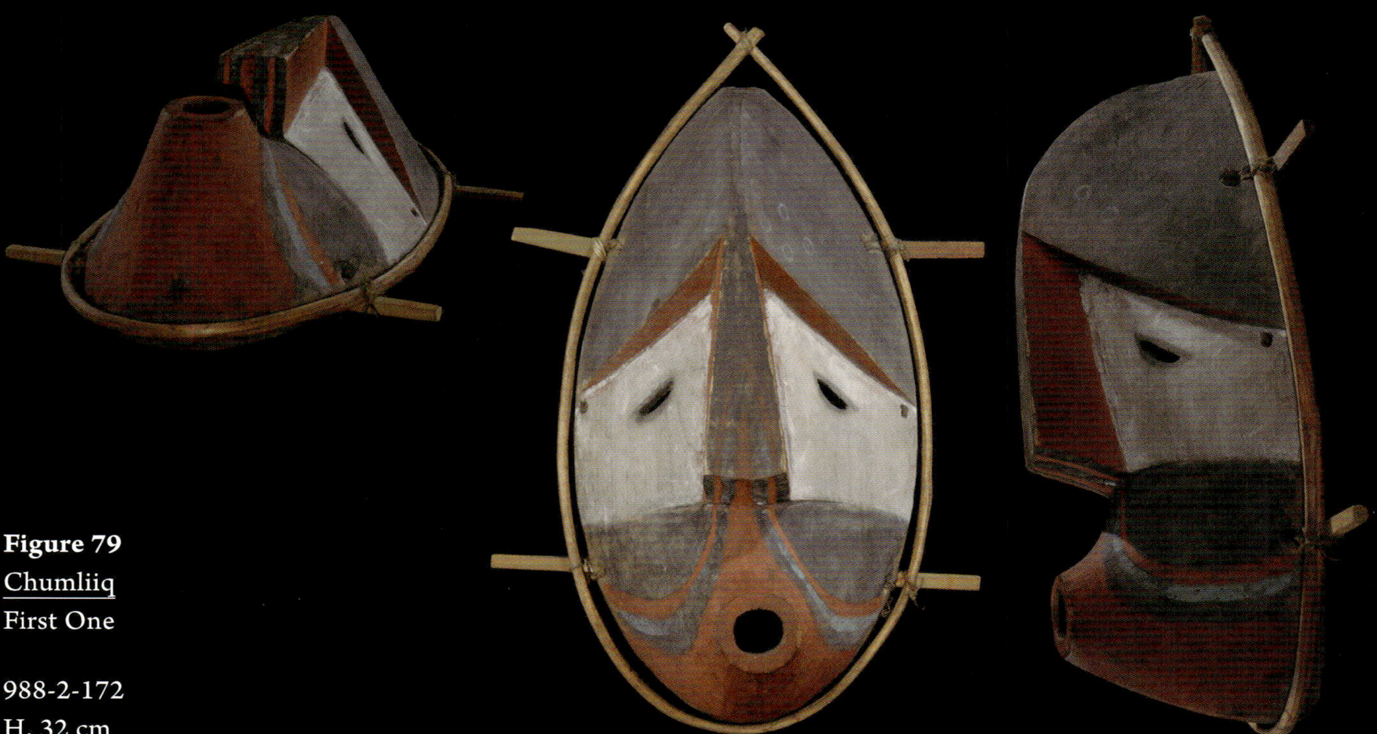

Figure 79
<u>Chumliiq</u>
First One

988-2-172
H. 32 cm
W. 21 cm
D. 10 cm
Cottonwood, sinew, black paint, red paint, white paint,
green paint
Kodiak Island or Afognak Island
See Appendix for mask song, legend, and dance.

Illustration 79
<u>Chumliiq</u>
Le premier

988-2-172
H. 32 cm
L. 21 cm
Ép. 10 cm
Peuplier de Virginie, tendon, peinture noire, peinture
rouge, peinture blanche, peinture verte
Île de Kodiak ou d'Afognak
Se reporter à l'Annexe pour le chant, la légende et la
danse du masque.

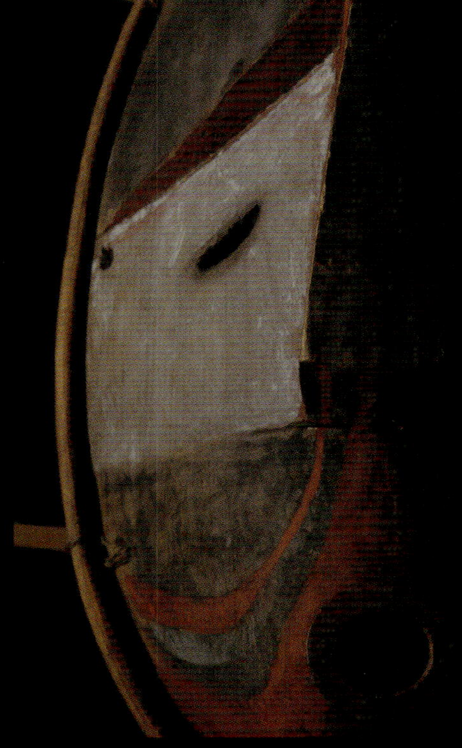

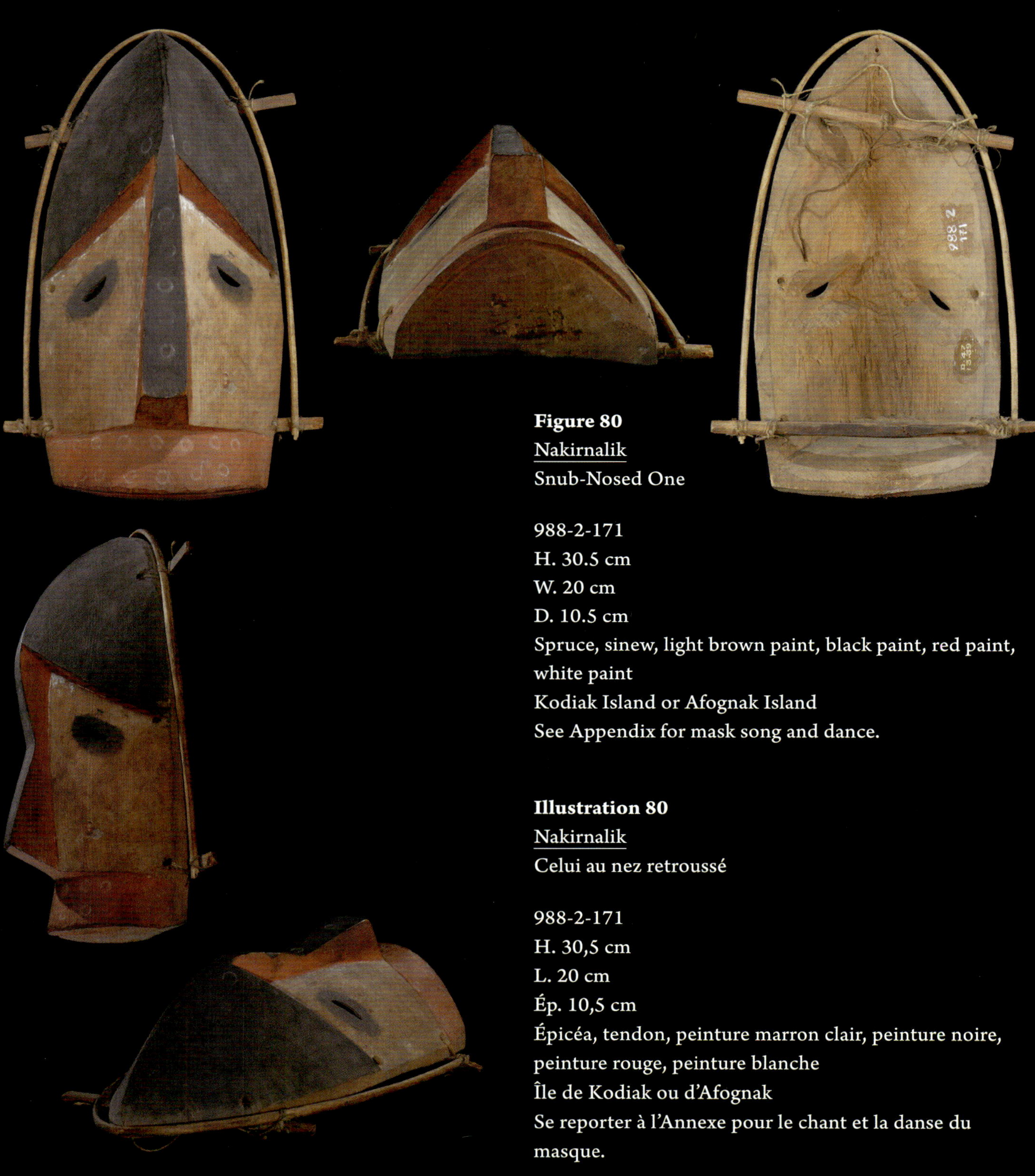

Figure 80
<u>Nakirnalik</u>
Snub-Nosed One

988-2-171
H. 30.5 cm
W. 20 cm
D. 10.5 cm
Spruce, sinew, light brown paint, black paint, red paint,
white paint
Kodiak Island or Afognak Island
See Appendix for mask song and dance.

Illustration 80
<u>Nakirnalik</u>
Celui au nez retroussé

988-2-171
H. 30,5 cm
L. 20 cm
Ép. 10,5 cm
Épicéa, tendon, peinture marron clair, peinture noire,
peinture rouge, peinture blanche
Île de Kodiak ou d'Afognak
Se reporter à l'Annexe pour le chant et la danse du
masque.

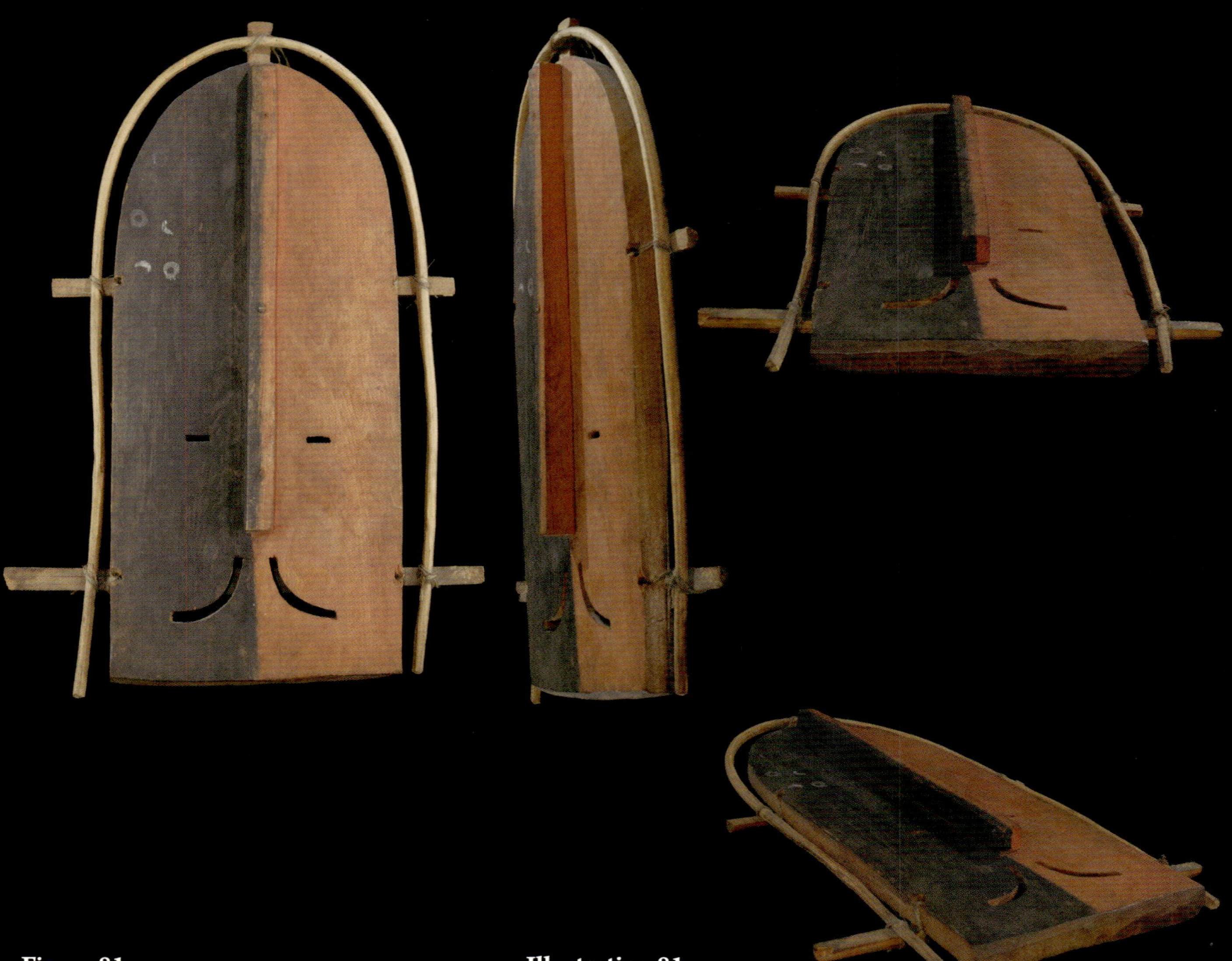

Figure 81

<u>Kuyauq</u>

Big-Nosed One/Thankful Person

988-2-175
H. 36 cm
W. 25 cm
D. 6 cm
Spruce, sinew, red paint, black paint,
white paint
Kodiak Island or Afognak Island
See Appendix for mask song and dance.

Illustration 81

<u>Kuyauq</u>

Celui au grand nez / Personne reconnaissante

988-2-175
H. 36 cm
L. 25 cm
Ép. 6 cm
Épicéa, tendon, peinture rouge, peinture noire, peinture
blanche
Île de Kodiak ou d'Afognak
Se reporter à l'Annexe pour le chant et la danse du masque.

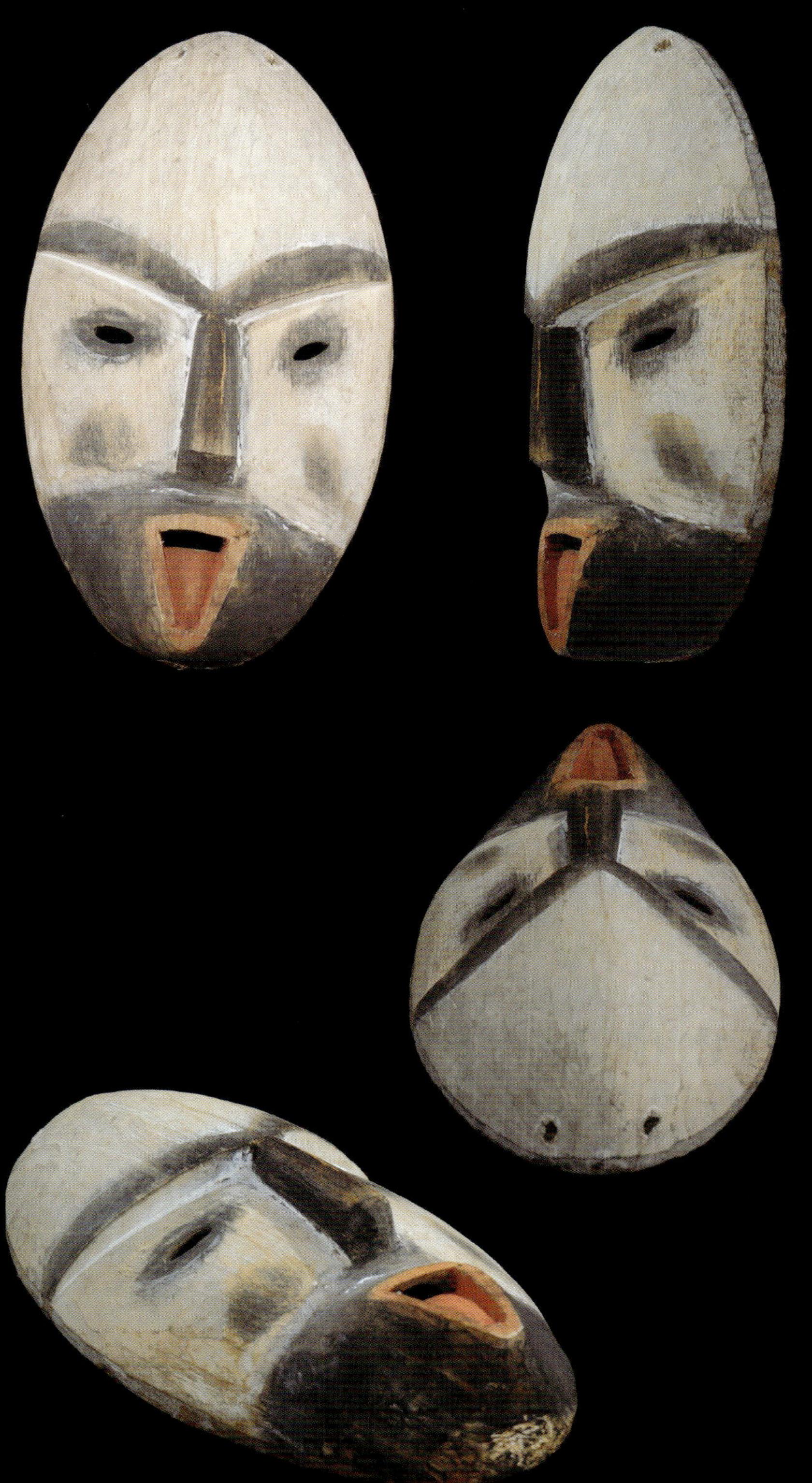

Figure 82
Angun
Old Man

988-2-168
H. 20.8 cm
W. 12 cm
D. 5.5 cm
White oak, white paint, red paint,
black paint
Eagle Harbor
See Appendix for mask song.

Illustration 82
Angun
Vieil homme

988-2-168
H. 20,8 cm
L. 12 cm
Ép. 5,5 cm
Chêne blanc, peinture rouge, peinture
noire
Eagle Harbor
Se reporter à l'Annexe pour le chant
du masque.

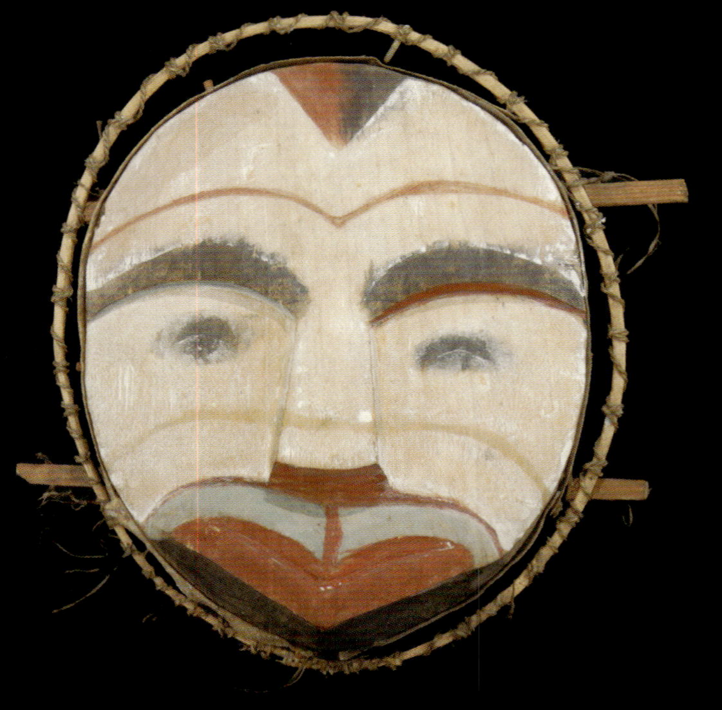

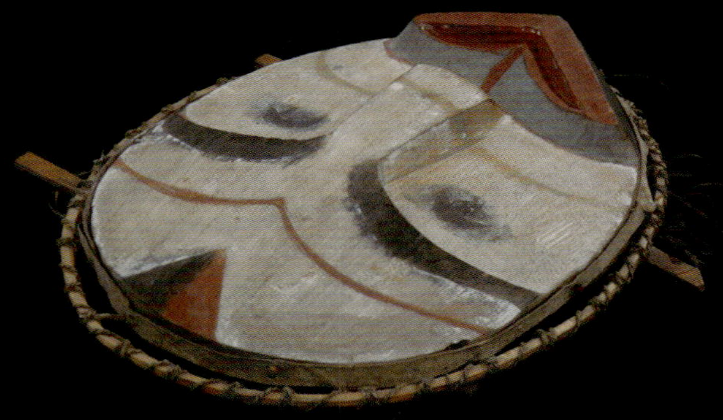

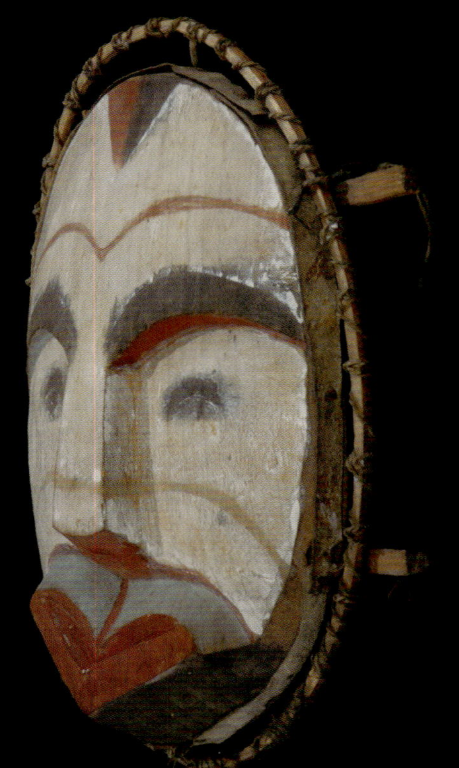

Figure 83
Name Illegible

988-2-196
H. 20 cm
W. 20 cm
D. 4.5 cm
White oak, leather, sinew, feathers, white
paint, red paint, black paint, green paint
Eagle Harbor

Illustration 83
Nom illisible

988-2-196
H. 20 cm
L. 20 cm
Ép. 4,5 cm
Chêne blanc, cuir, tendon, plumes, peinture
blanche, peinture rouge, peinture noire,
peinture verte
Eagle Harbor

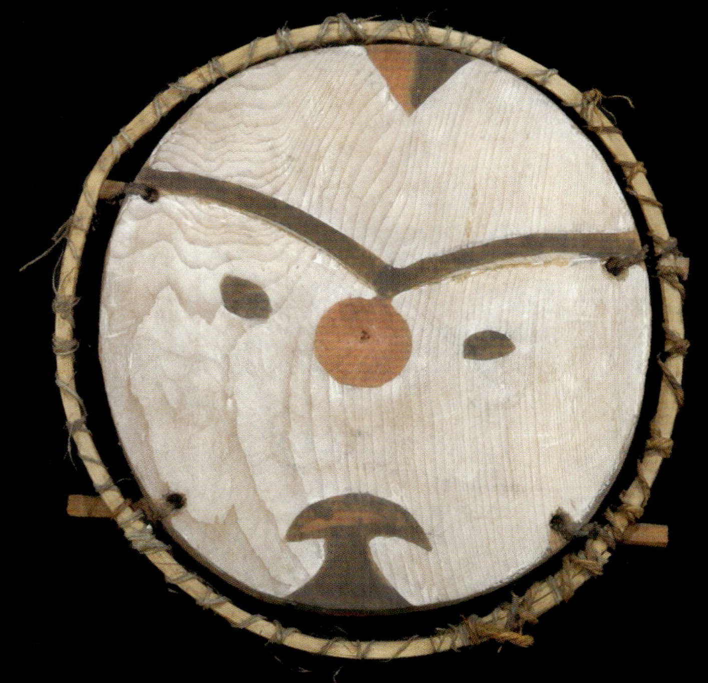
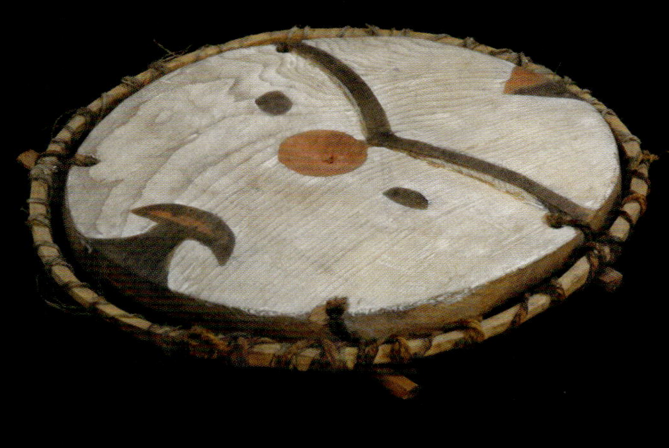

Figure 84
Name Unknown

988-2-203
H. 19 cm
W. 18.5 cm
D. 2 cm
Spruce, sinew, plant fiber, feathers,
white paint, black paint, red paint
Eagle Harbor

Illustration 84
Nom inconnu

988-2-203
H. 19 cm
L. 18,5 cm
Ép. 2 cm
Épicéa, tendon, fibres végétales,
peinture blanche, peinture noire,
peinture rouge
Eagle Harbor

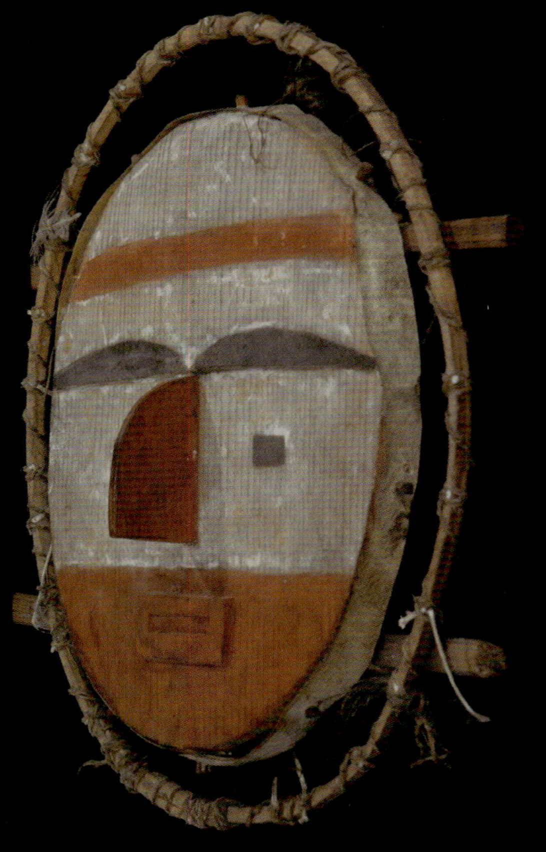

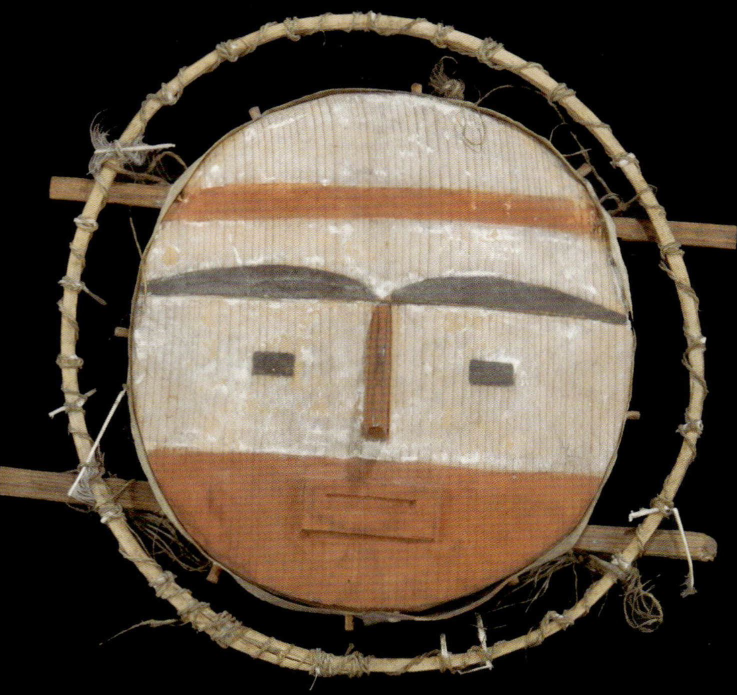

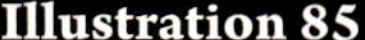

Figure 85
Name Illegible

988-2-197
H. 18 cm
W. 20 cm
D. 5 cm
Spruce, sinew, feathers, white paint, red
paint, black paint
Eagle Harbor

Illustration 85
Nom illisible

988-2-197
H. 18 cm
L. 20 cm
Ép. 5 cm
Épicéa, tendon, plumes, peinture blanche,
penture rouge, peinture noire
Eagle Harbor

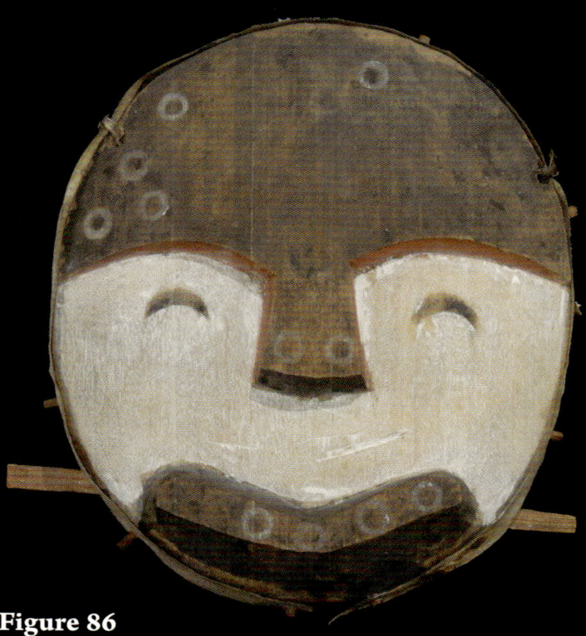

Figure 86
<u>Yuaulik</u>
Searcher

988-2-201
H. 16 cm
W. 15.5 cm
D. 4 cm
White oak, leather, sinew, black paint, white paint, red paint
Kodiak archipelago
See Appendix for mask song and dance.

Illustration 86
<u>Yuaulik</u>
Chercheur

988-2-201
H. 16 cm
L. 15,5 cm
Ép. 4 cm
Chêne blanc, cuir, tendon, peinture noire, peinture blanche,
peinture rouge
Archipel de Kodiak
Se reporter à l'Annexe pour le chant et la danse du masque.

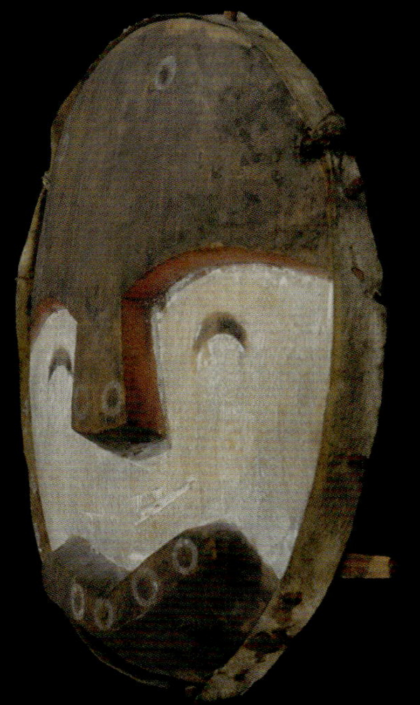

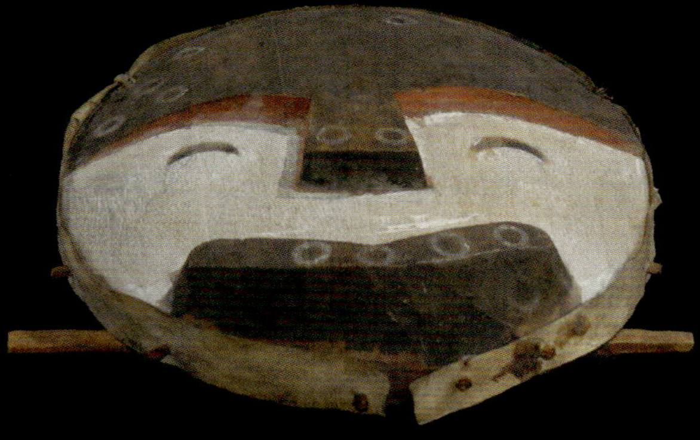

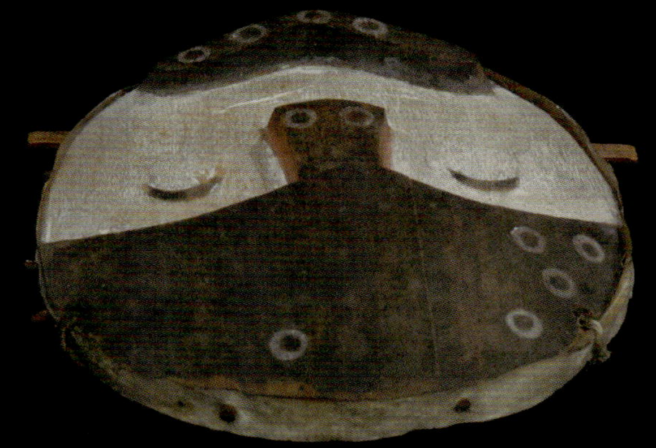

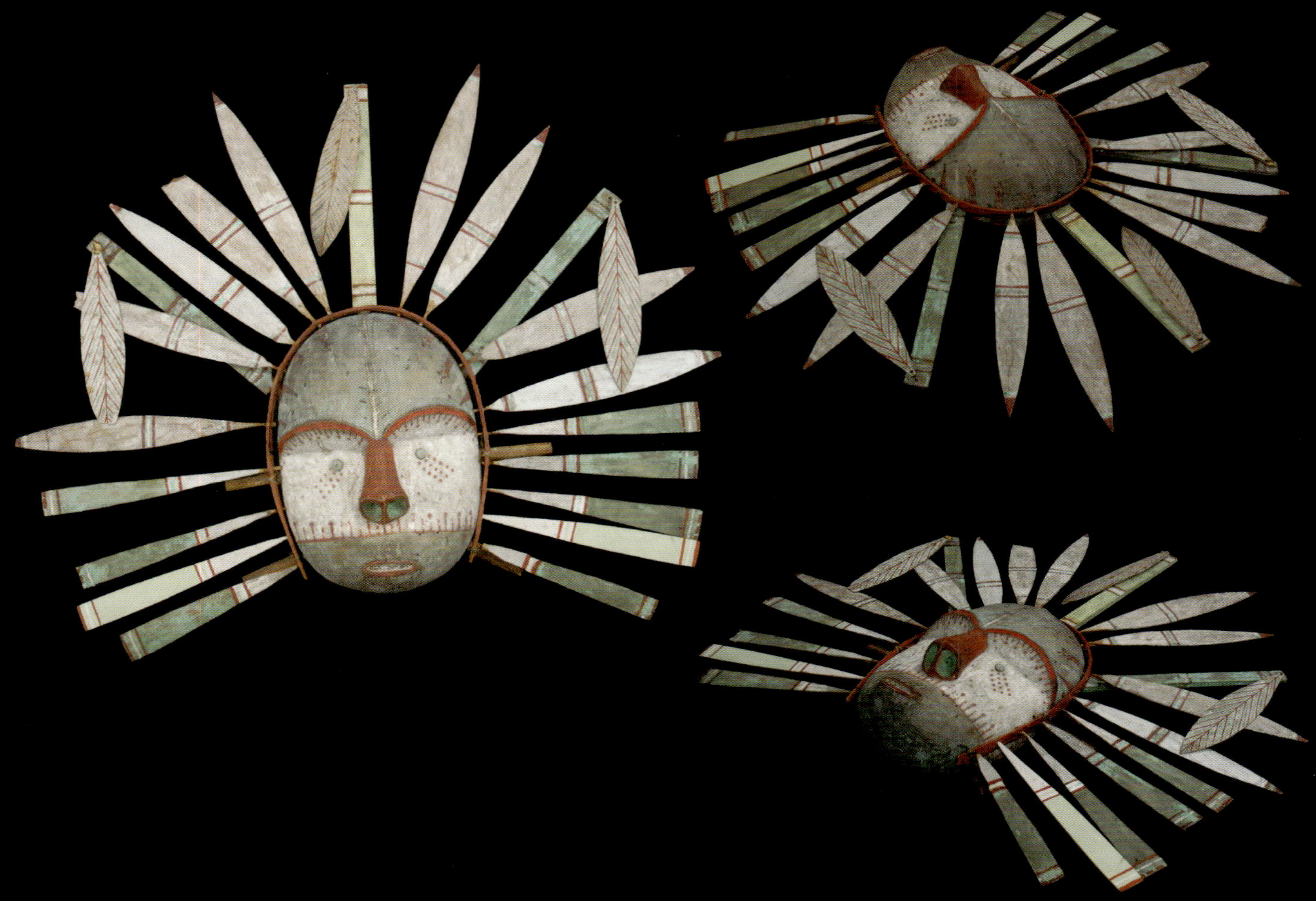

Figure 87

<u>Allayak</u>
Different, Not Like Us or Stingy/
Greedy One (Female)

988-2-193
H. 43 cm
W. 26 cm
D. 9 cm
Wood, fur, string, sinew, red paint,
green paint, white paint
Kodiak Island or Afognak Island
See Appendix for mask legend.

Illustration 87

<u>Allayak</u>
Différent, pas comme nous ou Pingre/Cupide
(féminin)

988-2-193
H. 43 cm
L. 26 cm
Ép. 9 cm
Bois, fourrure, ficelle, tendon, peinture rouge,
peinture verte, peinture blanche
Île de Kodiak ou d'Afognak
Se reporter à l'Annexe pour la légende du masque.

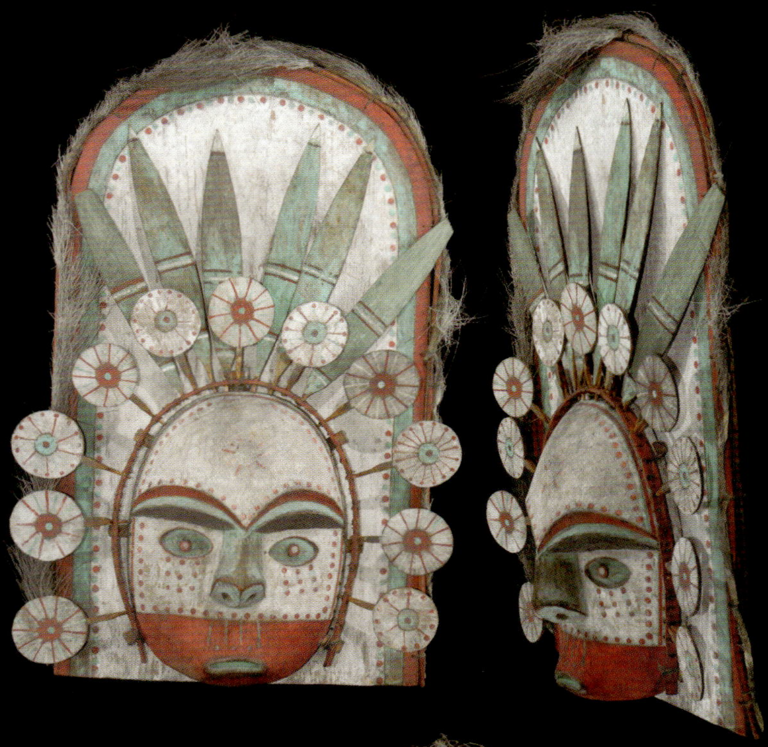

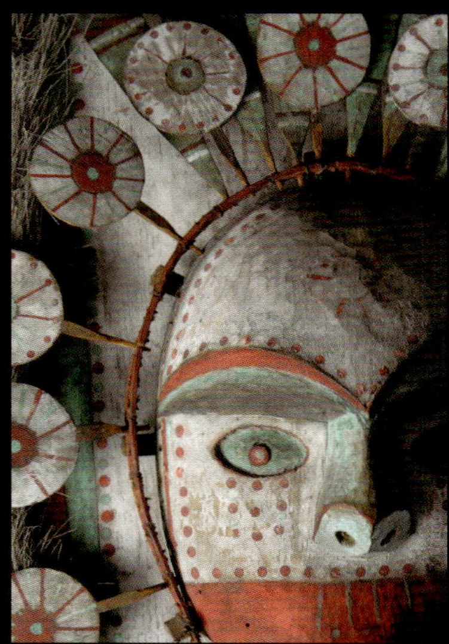

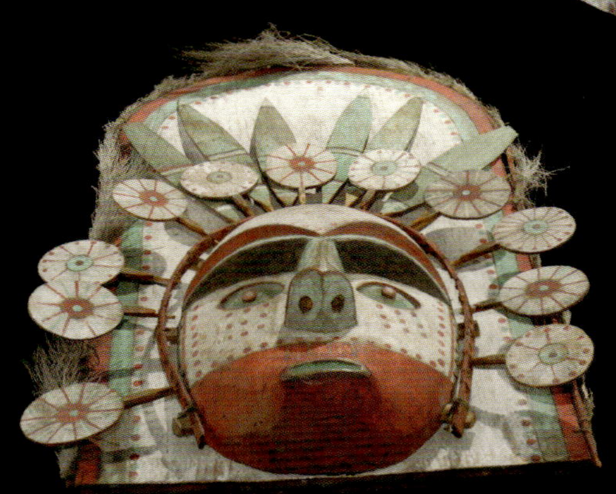

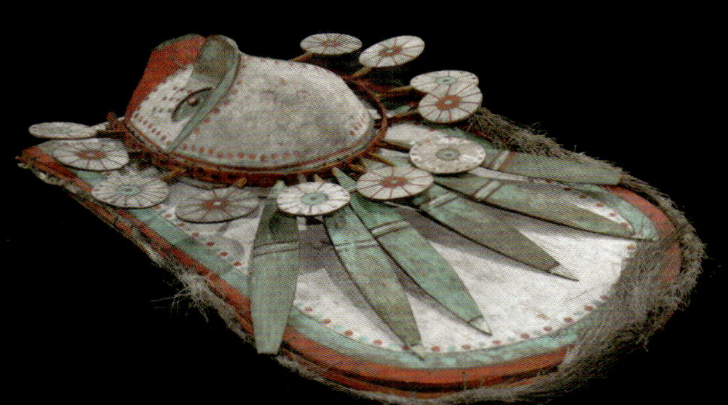

Figure 88
<u>Allayak</u>
Different, Not Like Us or Stingy/Greedy One
(Male)

988-2-194
H. 35 cm
W. 46 cm
D. 7 cm
Wood, string, sinew, green paint, white paint, red
paint, caribou hair
Kodiak Island or Afognak Island
See Appendix for mask legend.

Illustration 88
<u>Allayak</u>
Différent, pas comme nous ou Celui (celle) qui est
pingre/cupide (masculin)

988-2-194
H. 35 cm
L. 46 cm
Ép. 7 cm
Bois, ficelle, peinture verte, peinture blanche,
peinture rouge, fourrure de caribou
Île de Kodiak ou d'Afognak
Se reporter à l'Annexe pour la légende du masque.

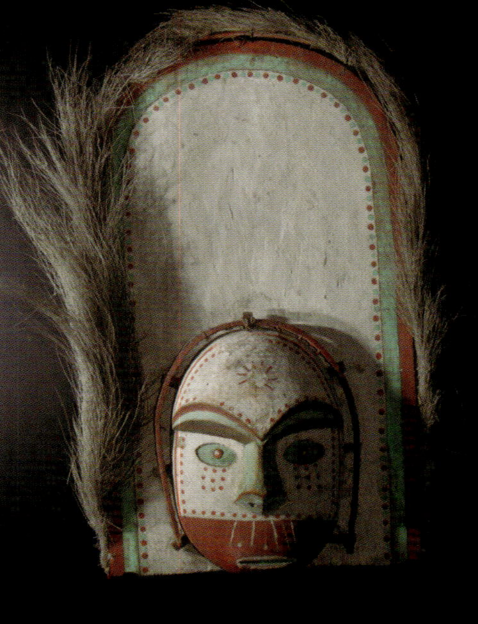 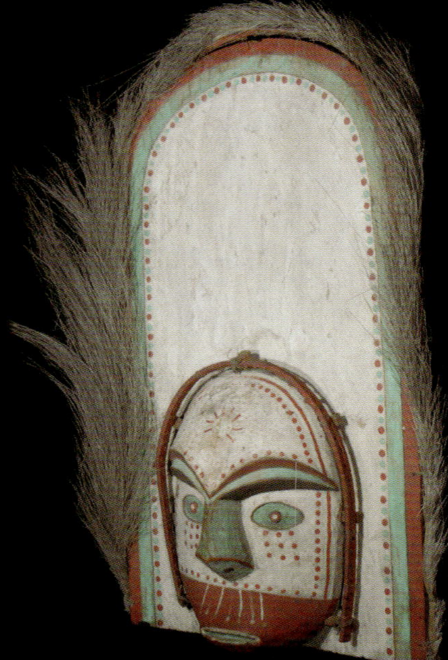

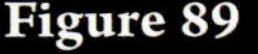

Figure 89

Allayak

Different, Not Like Us or Stingy/Greedy One (Male)

71.1881.21.28
H. 44 cm
W. 25 cm
D. 10 cm
Spruce, string, caribou hair, sinew, green paint, red paint, white paint
Kodiak Island or Afognak Island
See Appendix for mask legend.

Illustration 89

Allayak

Différent, pas comme nous ou Celui (celle) qui est pingre/cupide (masculin)

71.1881.21.28
H. 44 cm
L. 25 cm
Ép. 10 cm
Épicéa, ficelle, poils de caribou, tendon, peinture verte, peinture rouge, peinture blanche
Île de Kodiak ou d'Afognak
Se reporter à l'Annexe pour la légende du masque.

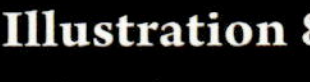

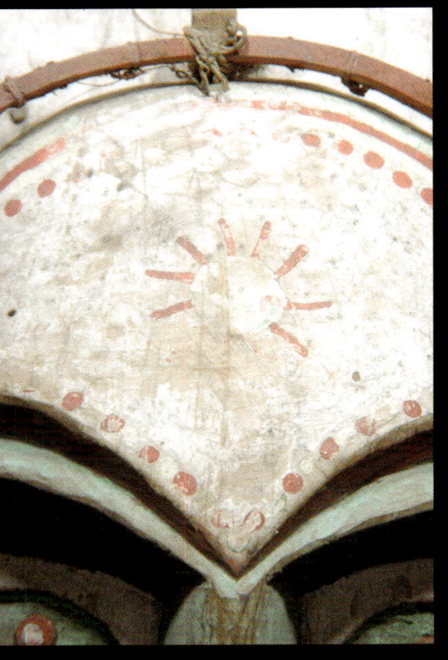 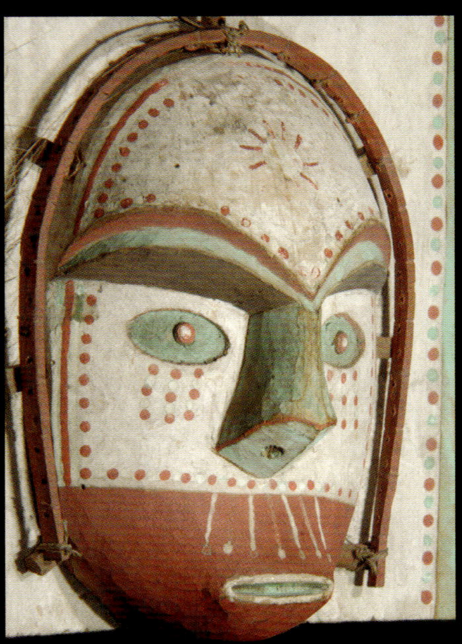

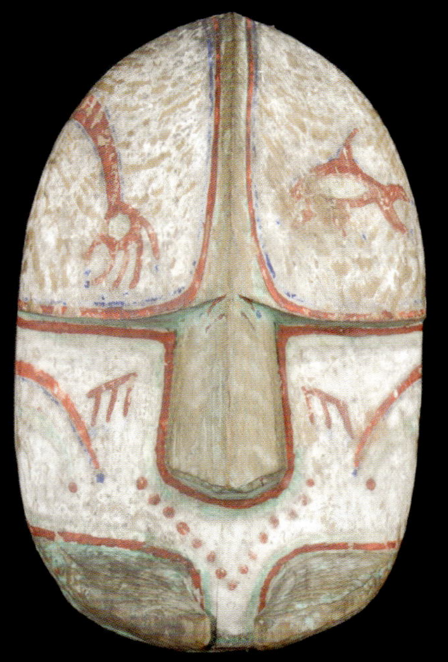
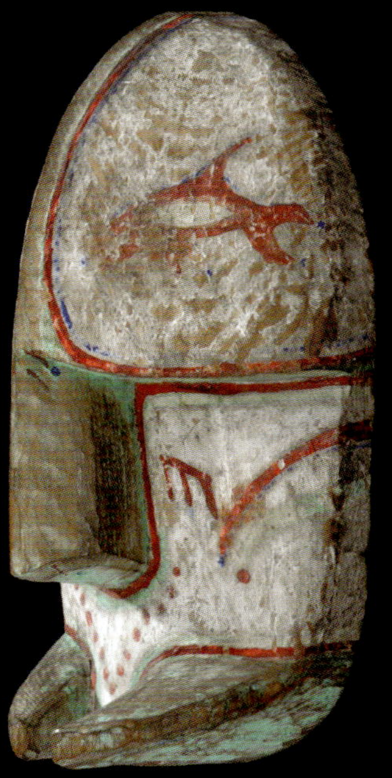
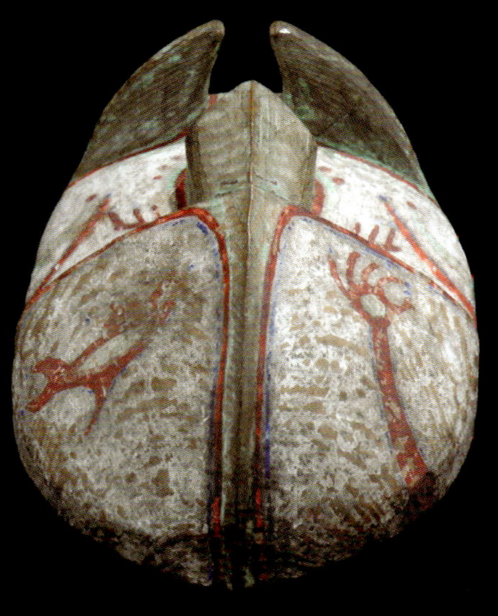
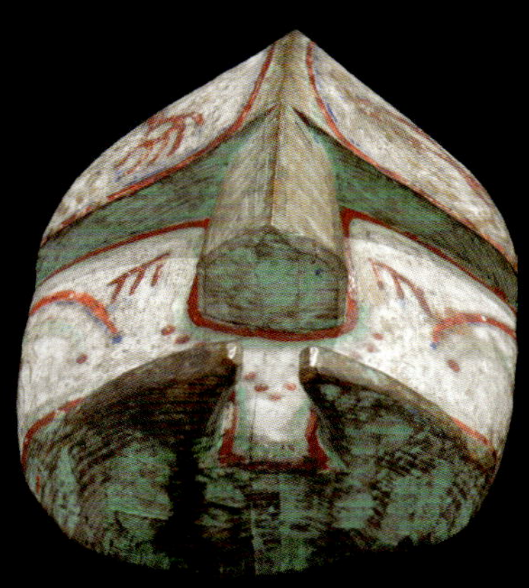
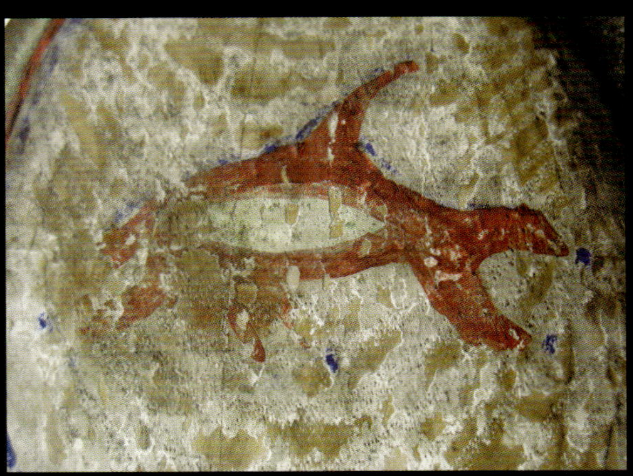

Figure 90
Spirit Taker[333]

988-2-187
H. 21 cm
W. 13.5 cm
D. 6.5 cm
White oak, white paint, red paint,
green paint, blue paint
Kodiak Island or Afognak Island

Illustration 90
Celui qui conduit les esprits[333]

988-2-187
H. 21 cm
L. 13,5 cm
Ép. 6,5 cm
Chêne blanc, peinture blanche,
peinture rouge, peinture verte,
peinture bleue
Île de Kodiak ou d'Afognak

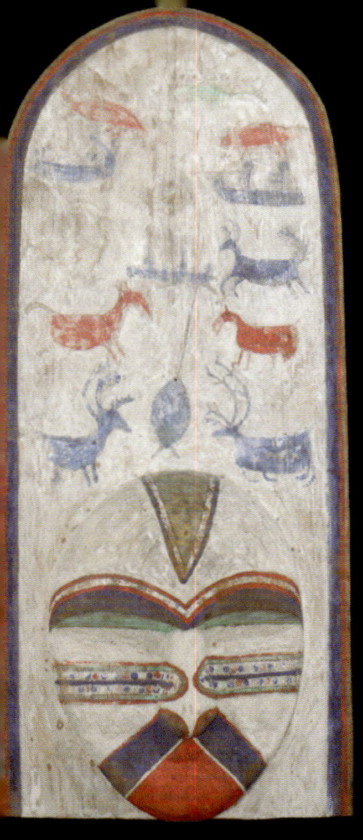

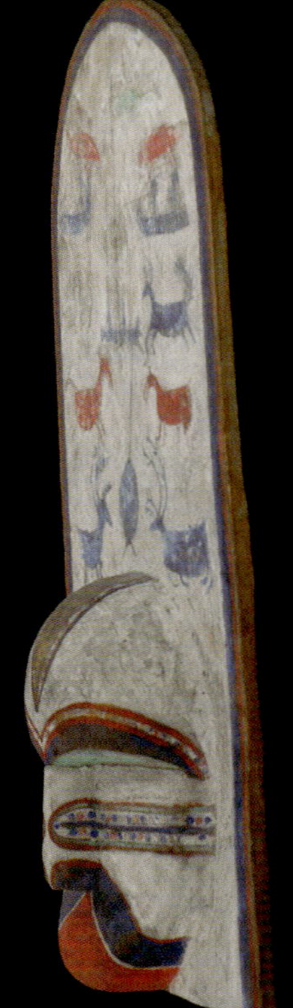

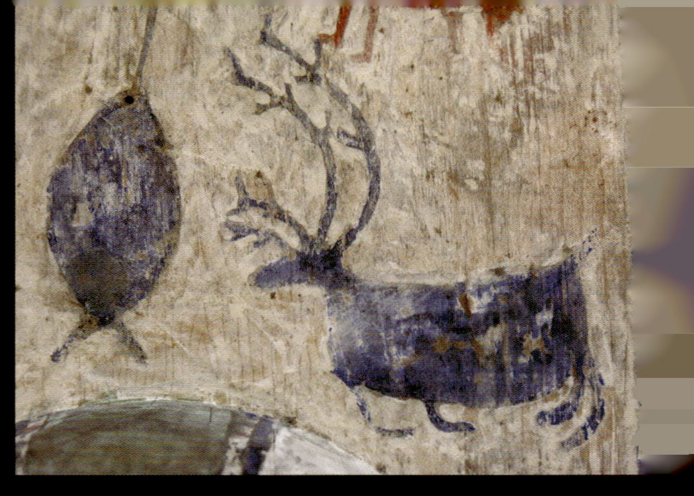

Figure 91
Suumacillra I
The Way They Lived

988-2-191
H. 48 cm
W. 20 cm
D. 6.5 cm
White oak, white paint, red paint, blue
paint, green paint, brown paint
Kodiak Island or Afognak Island

Illustration 91
Suumacillra I
La façon dont ils vivaient

988-2-191
H. 48 cm
L. 20 cm
Ép. 6,5 cm
Chêne blanc, peinture blanche, peinture
rouge, peinture bleue, peinture verte,
peinture marron
Île de Kodiak ou d'Afognak

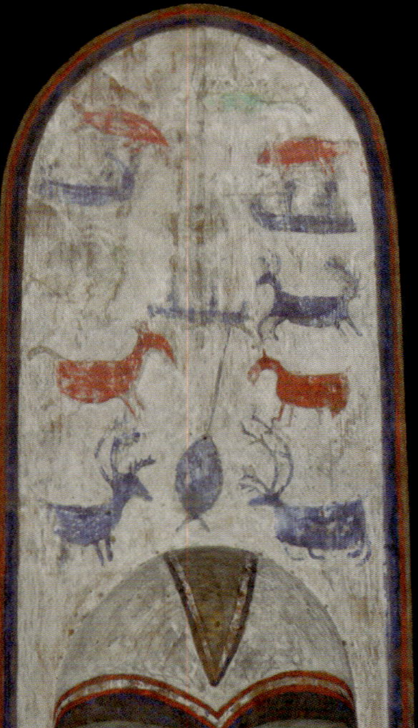

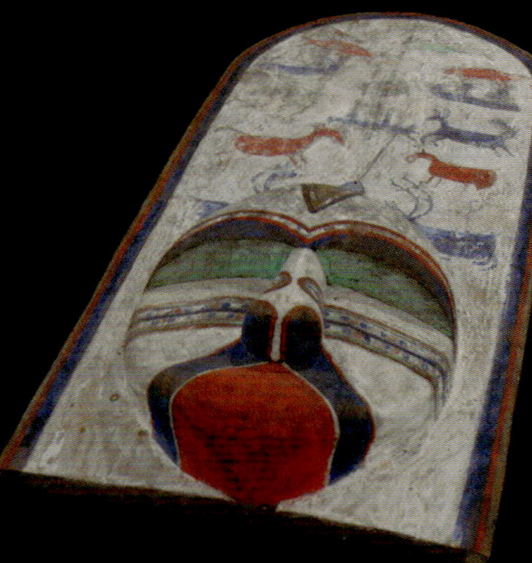

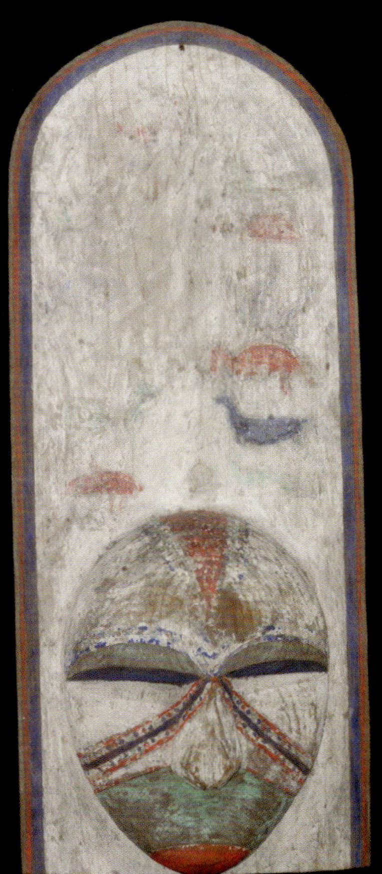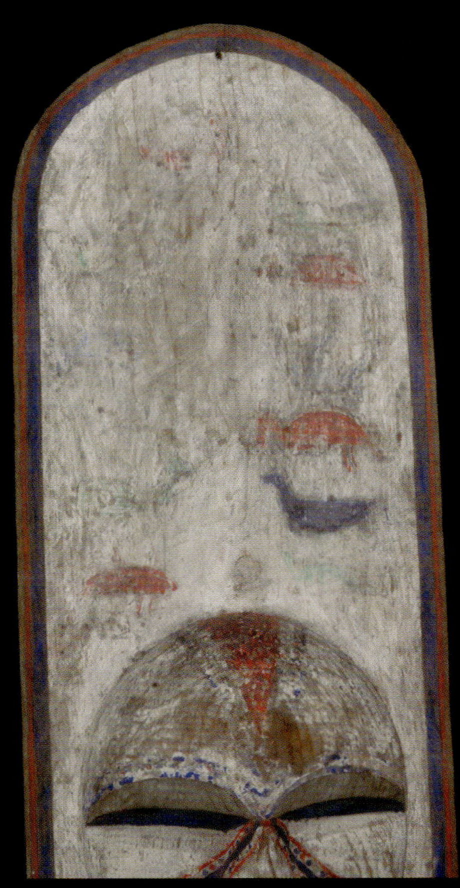

Figure 92
Suumacillra II
The Way They Lived

988-2-192
H. 48 cm
W. 19 cm
D. 6.5 cm
White oak, white paint, green
paint, red paint, blue paint,
brown paint
Kodiak Island or Afognak Island

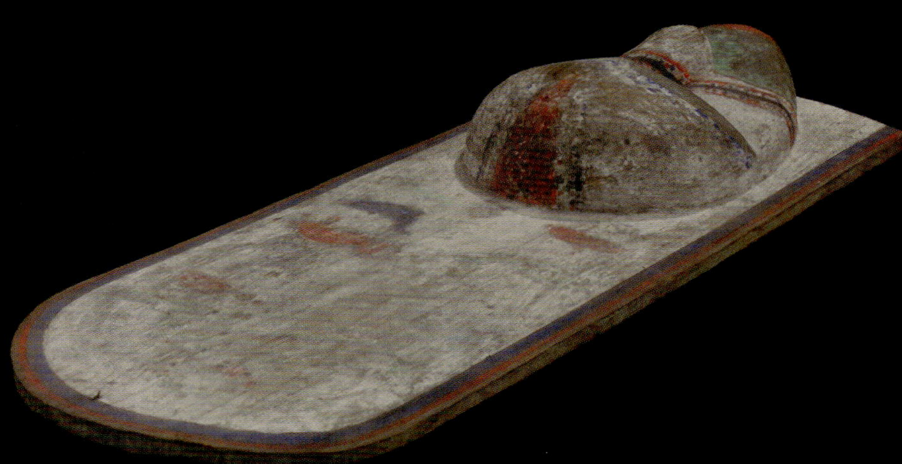

Illustration 92
Suumacillra II
La façon dont ils vivaient

988-2-192
H. 48 cm
L. 19 cm
Ép. 6,5 cm
Chêne blanc, peinture blanche,
peinture verte, peinture rouge,
peinture bleue, peinture marron
Île de Kodiak ou d'Afognak

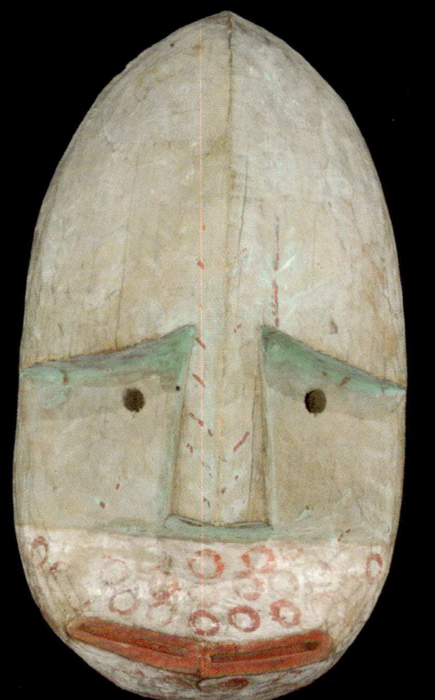

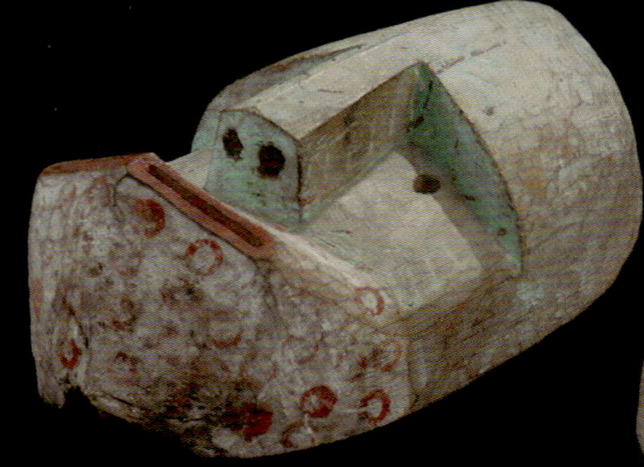

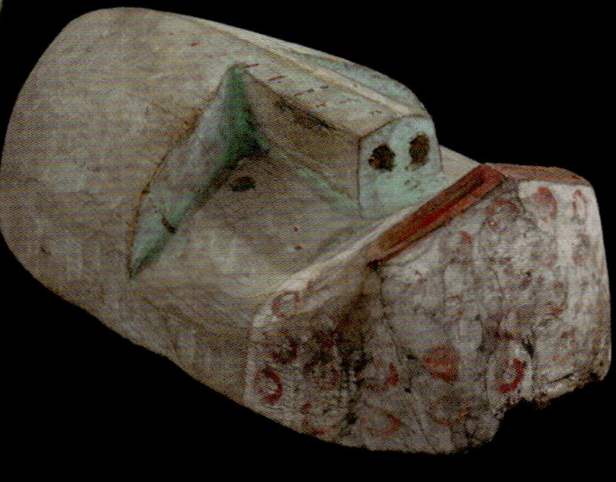

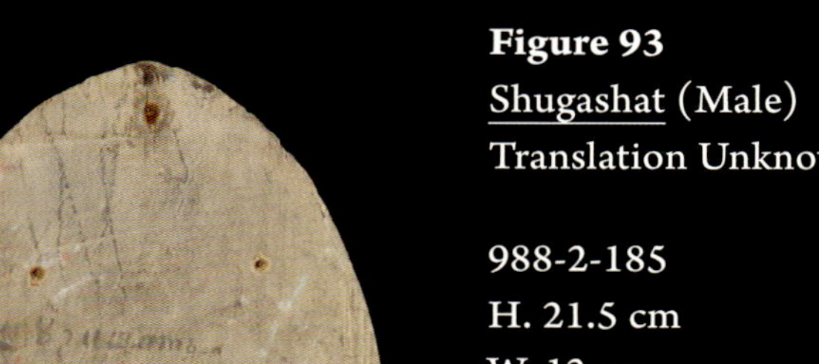

Figure 93
<u>Shugashat</u> (Male)
Translation Unknown

988-2-185
H. 21.5 cm
W. 12 cm
D. 7 cm
White oak, green paint, white paint, red paint
Afognak Island
See Appendix for mask legend and dances.

Illustration 93
<u>Shugashat</u> (masculin)
Traduction inconnue

988-2-185
H. 21,5 cm
L. 12 cm
Ép. 7 cm
Chêne blanc, peinture verte, peinture blanche, peinture rouge
Île d'Afognak
Se reporter à l'Annexe pour la légende et les danses du masque.

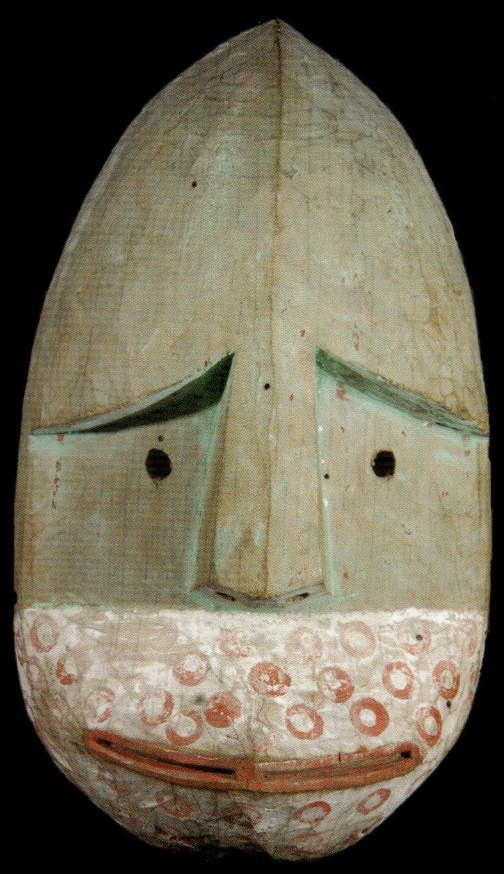 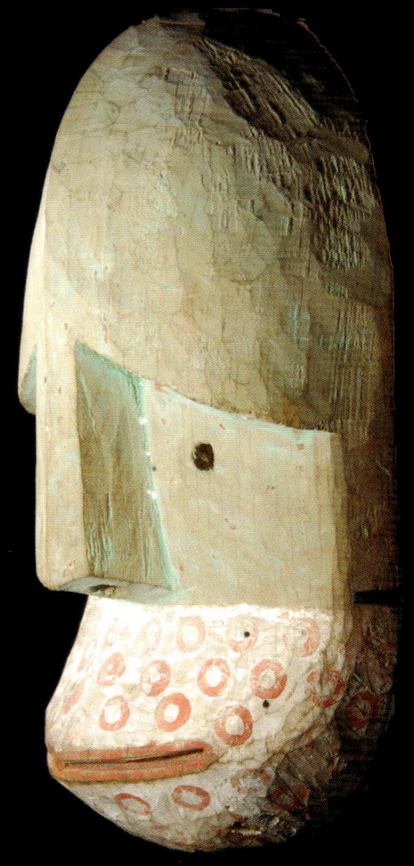

Figure 94
Shugashat
Translation Unknown

71.1881.21.31
H. 22.5 cm
W. 13.5 cm
D. 7.5 cm
White oak, green paint, red paint, white
paint
Afognak Island
See Appendix for mask legend and dances.

Illustration 94
Shugashat
Traduction inconnue

71.1881.21.31
H. 22,5 cm
L. 13,5 cm
Ép. 7,5 cm
Chêne blanc, peinture verte, peinture blanche
Île d'Afognak
Se reporter à l'Annexe pour la légende et les
danses du masque.

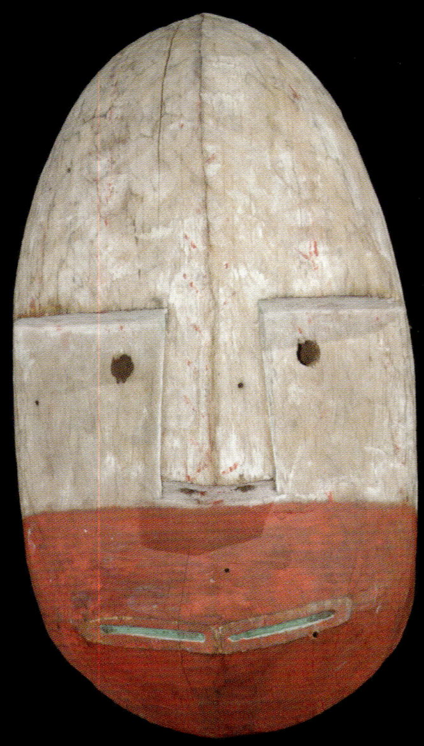

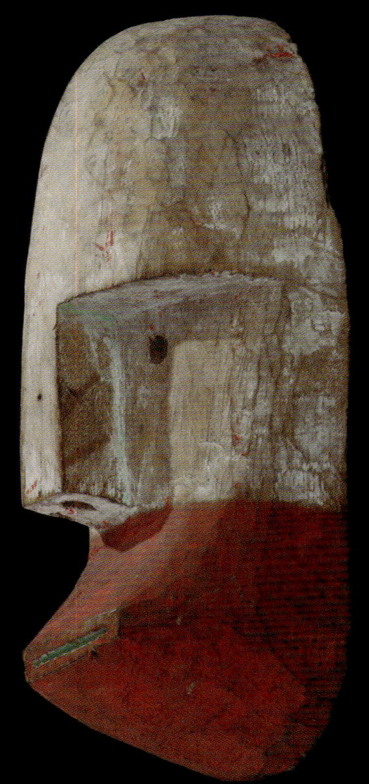

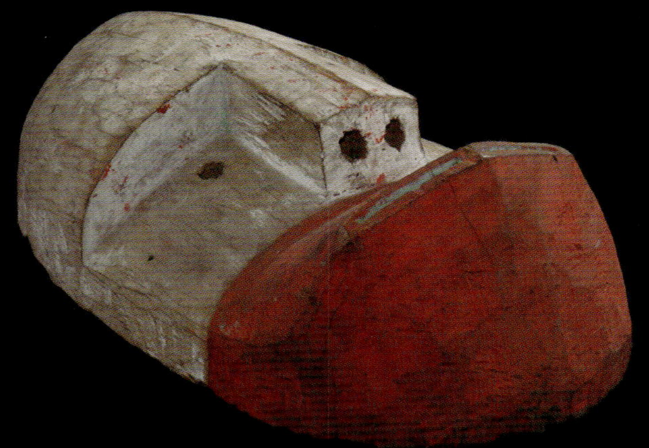

Figure 95
<u>Shugashat</u> (Female)
Translation Unknown

988-2-179
H. 21 cm
W. 11.5 cm
D. 6.5 cm
White oak, white paint, red paint, green paint
Kodiak Island or Afognak Island
See Appendix for mask legend and dances.

Illustration 95
<u>Shugashat</u> (féminin)
Traduction inconnue

988-2-179
H. 21 cm
L. 11,5 cm
Ép. 6,5 cm
Chêne blanc, peinture blanche, penture rouge, peinture verte
Île de Kodiak ou d'Afognak
Se reporter à l'Annexe pour la légende et les danses du masque.

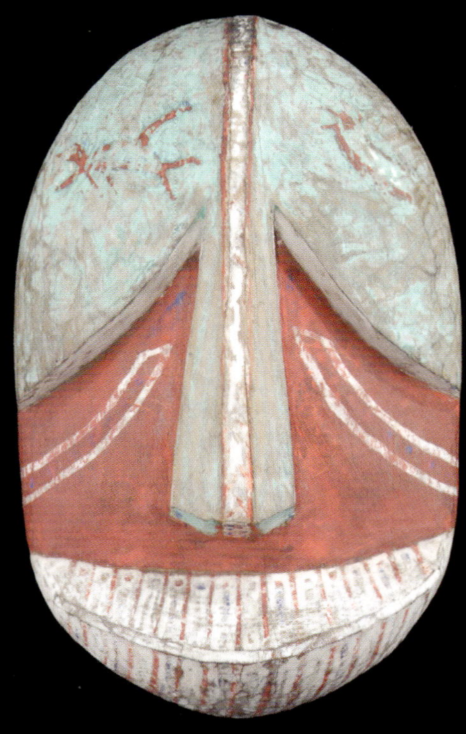

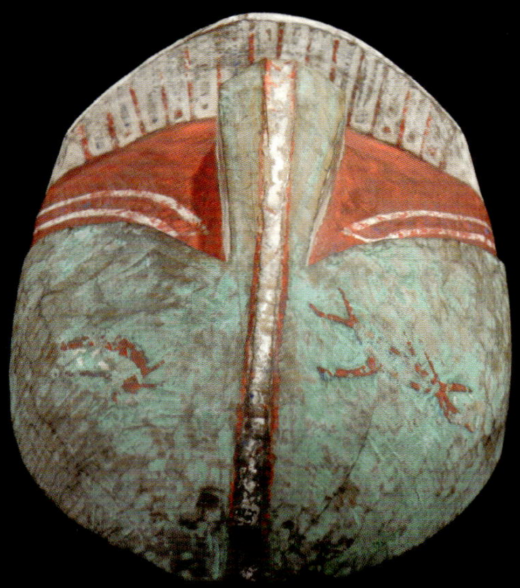

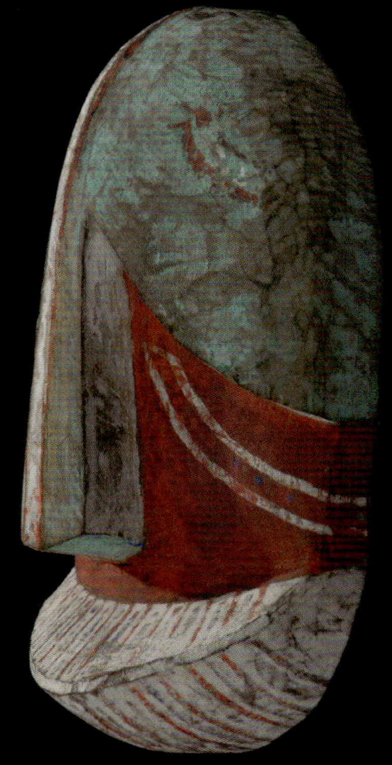

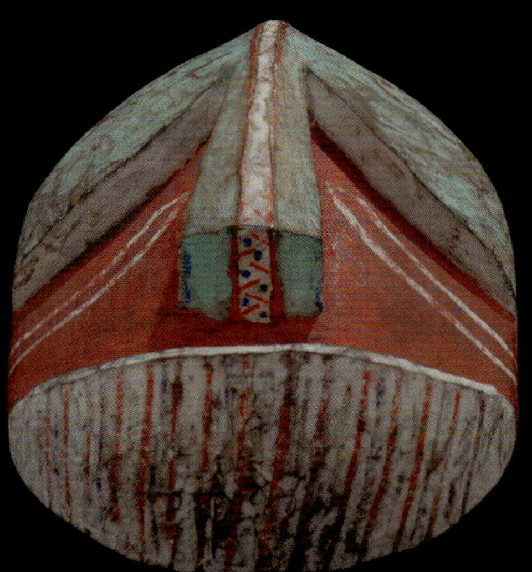

Figure 96
Name Unknown

988-2-186
H. 21 cm
W. 13.5 cm
D. 6.5 cm
White oak, green paint,
red paint, white paint, blue
paint
Afognak Island

Illustration 96
Nom inconnu

988-2-186
H. 21 cm
L. 13,5 cm
Ép. 6,5 cm
Chêne blanc, peinture verte,
peinture rouge, peinture
blanche, peinture bleue
Île d'Afognak

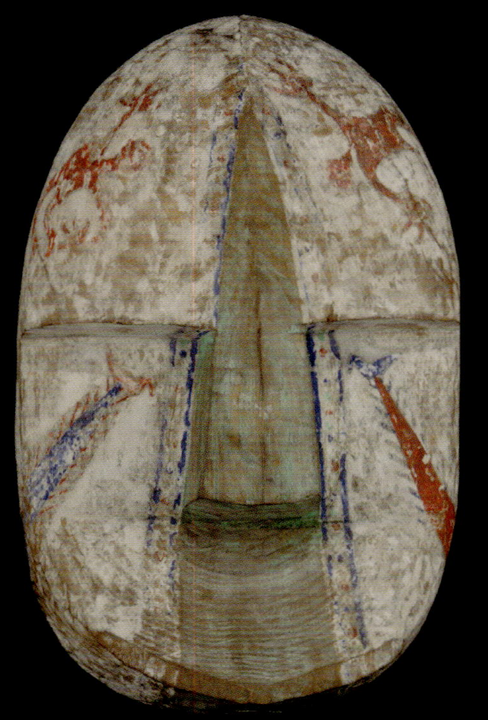
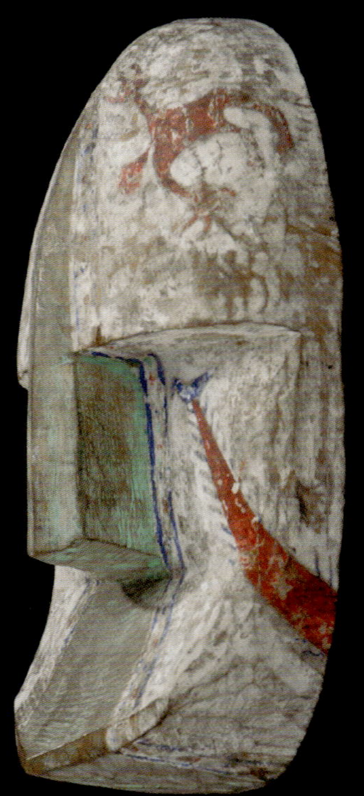
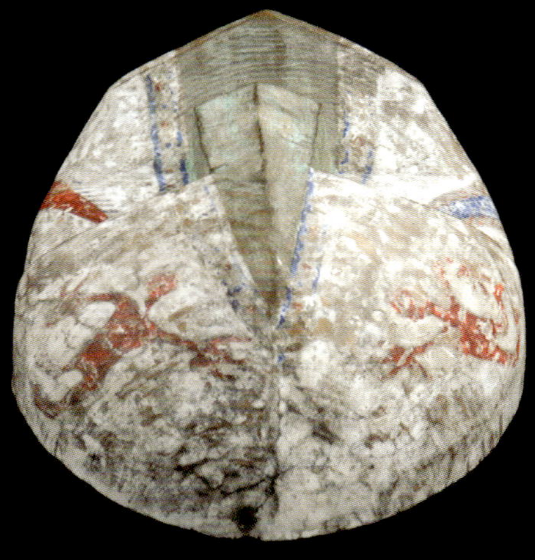
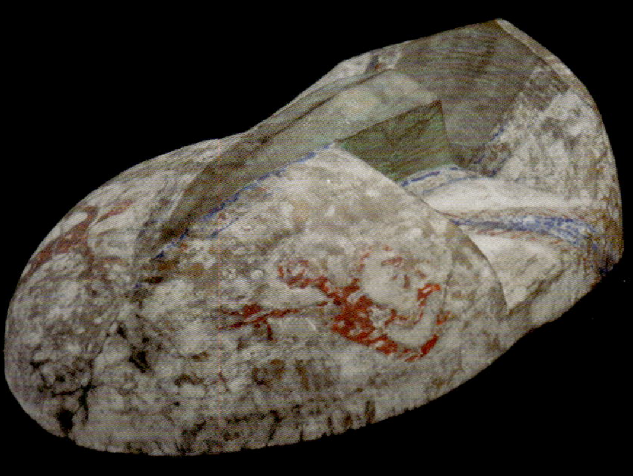
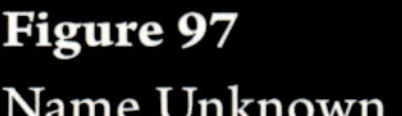
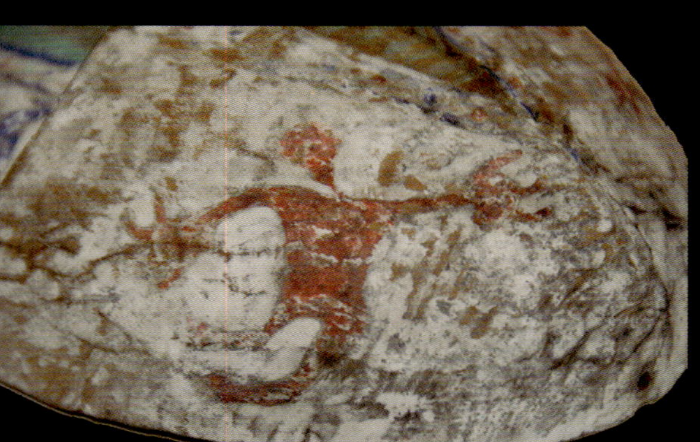

Figure 97
Name Unknown

988-2-188
H. 21 cm
W. 13 cm
D. 7 cm
White oak, white paint, green
paint, red paint, blue paint
Afognak Island

Illustration 97
Nom inconnu

988-2-188
H. 21 cm
L. 13 cm
Ép. 7 cm
Chêne blanc, peinture blanche,
peinture verte, peinture rouge,
peinture bleue
Île d'Afognak

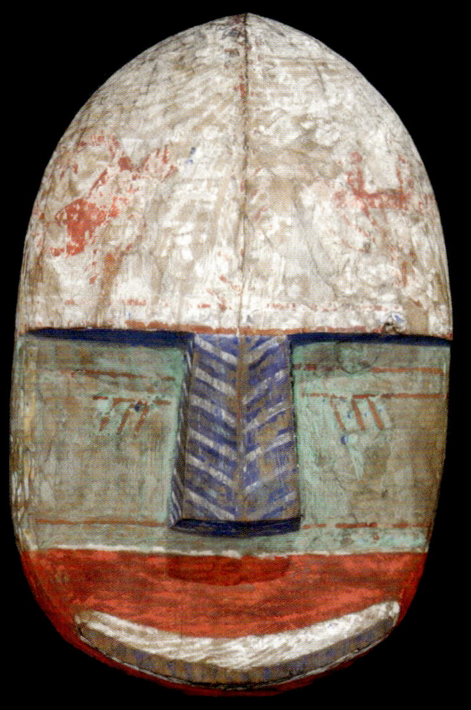
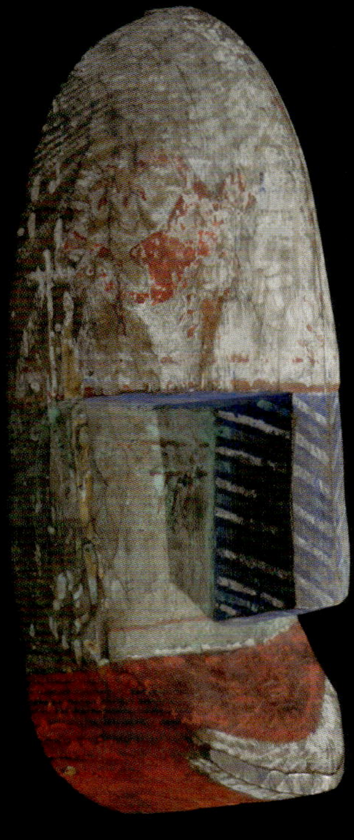
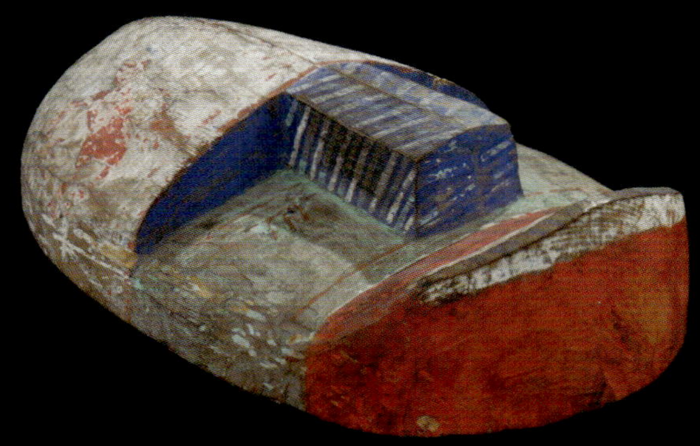
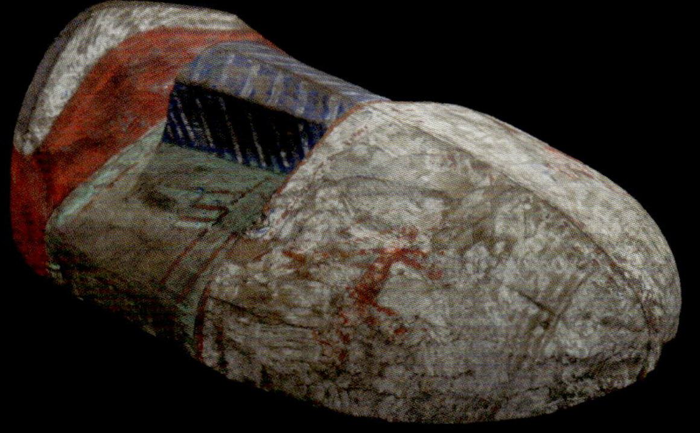

Figure 98
Name Unknown

988-2-180
H. 21 cm
W. 13 cm
D. 6 cm
White oak, white paint, blue paint,
green paint, red paint
Kodiak Island or Afognak Island

Illustration 98
Nom inconnu

988-2-180
H. 21 cm
L. 13 cm
Ép. 6 cm
Chêne blanc, peinture blanche,
peinture bleue, peinture verte,
peinture rouge
Île de Kodiak ou d'Afognak

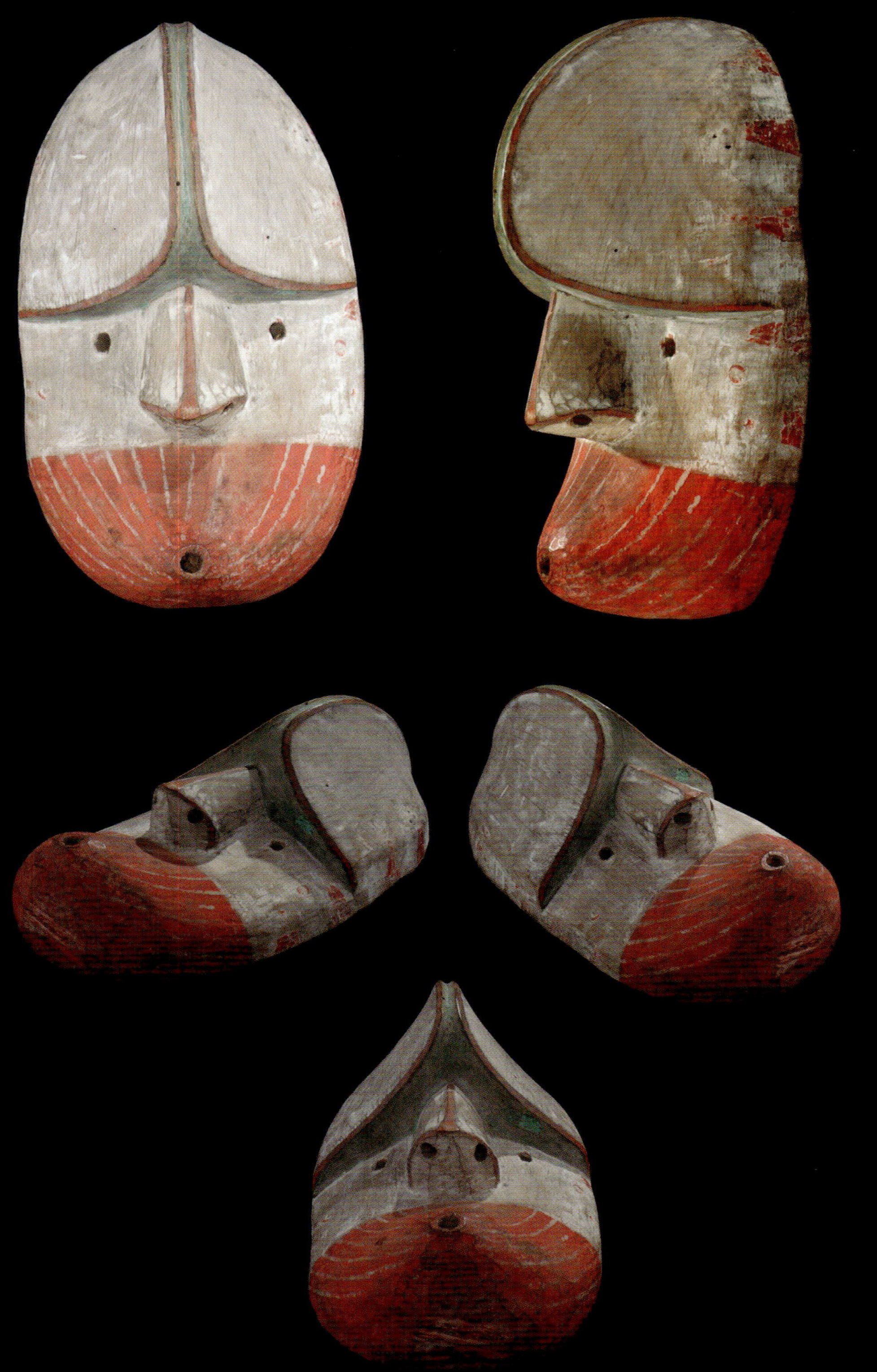

Figure 99

<u>Kugukauk</u>
Favorite One

988-2-181
H. 22 cm
W. 13 cm
D. 9.5 cm
White oak, white paint, red
paint, green paint
Afognak Island

Illustration 99

<u>Kugukauk</u>
Le préféré

988-2-181
H. 22 cm
L. 13 cm
Ép. 9,5 cm
Chêne blanc, peinture blanche,
peinture rouge, peinture verte
Île d'Afognak

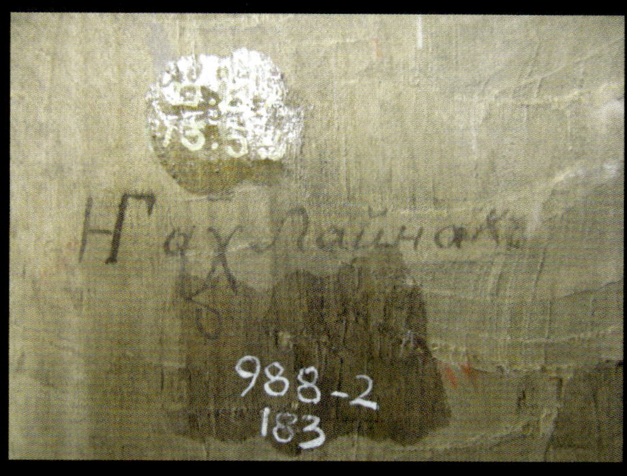

Mask name written on back of mask by Pinart.

Nom de masque écrit au dos du masque par Pinart.

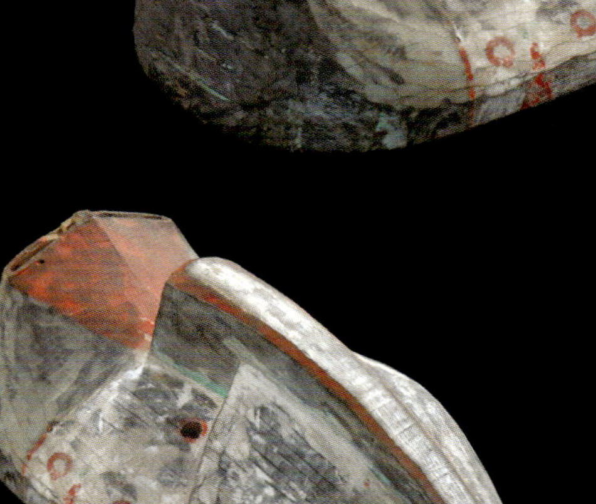

Figure 100
Nakllegnaq
Pitiful One

988-2-183
H. 22 cm
W. 12 cm
D. 9.5 cm
White oak, white paint, red
paint, green paint
Kodiak Island or Afognak Island

Illustration 100
Nakllegnaq
Le pitoyable

988-2-183
H. 22 cm
L. 12 cm
Ép. 9,5 cm
Chêne blanc, peinture blanche,
peinture rouge, peinture verte
Île de Kodiak ou d'Afognak

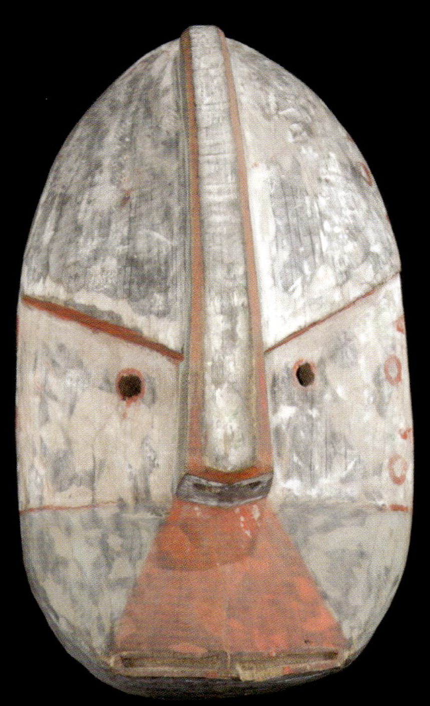

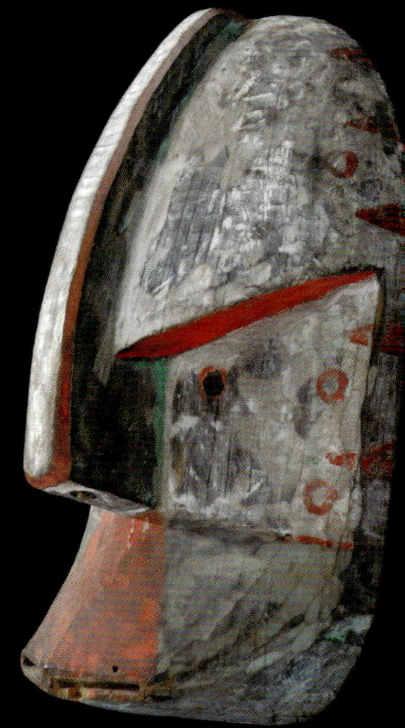

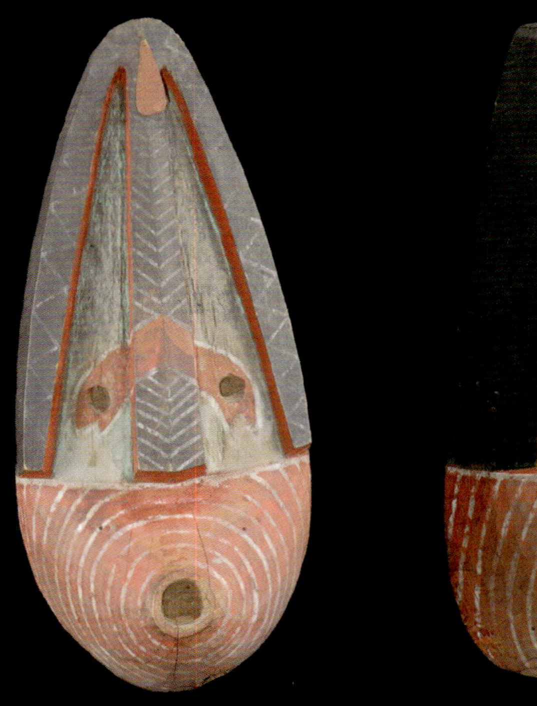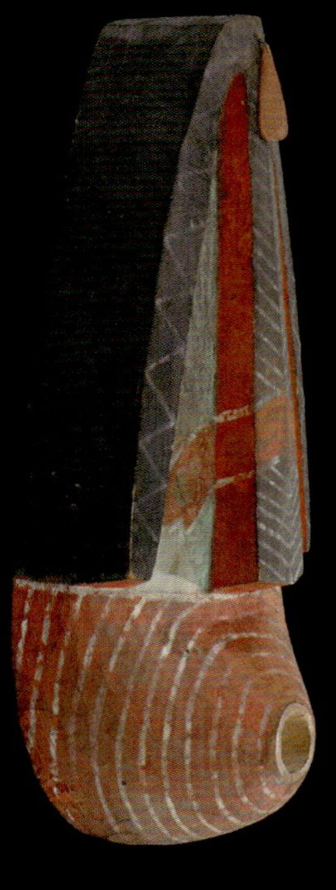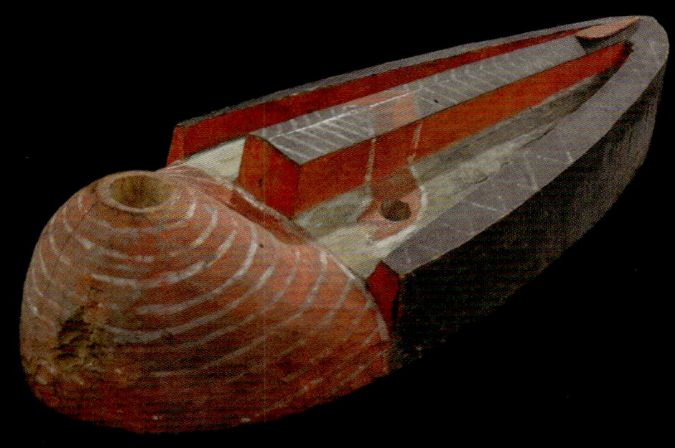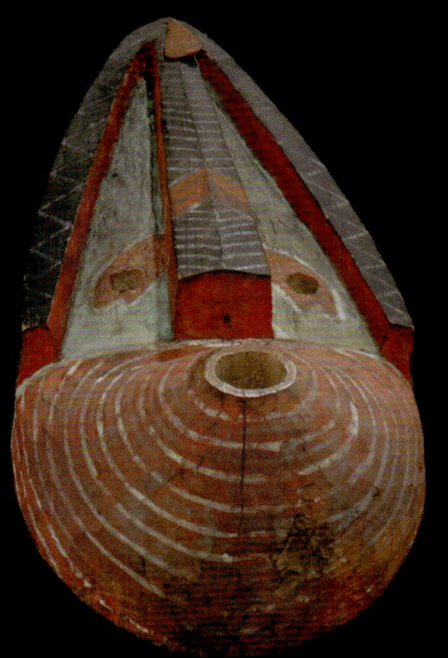

Figure 101
Agut'lik
Translation Unknown

988-2-189
H. 27 cm
W. 11.5 cm
D. 7.5 cm
White oak, sinew, black paint, red paint, green paint, white paint
Kodiak Island or Afognak Island
See Appendix for mask legend.

Illustration 101
Agut'lik
Traduction inconnue

988-2-189
H. 27 cm
L. 11,5 cm
Ép. 7,5 cm
Chêne blanc, tendon, peinture noire, peinture rouge, peinture verte, peinture blanche
Île de Kodiak ou d'Afognak
Se reporter à l'Annexe pour la légende du masque.

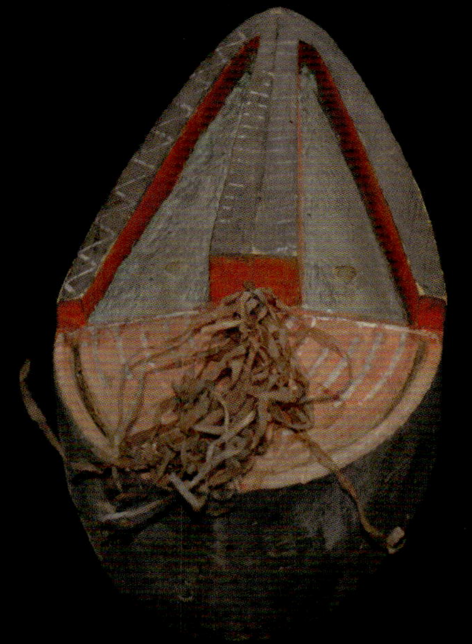

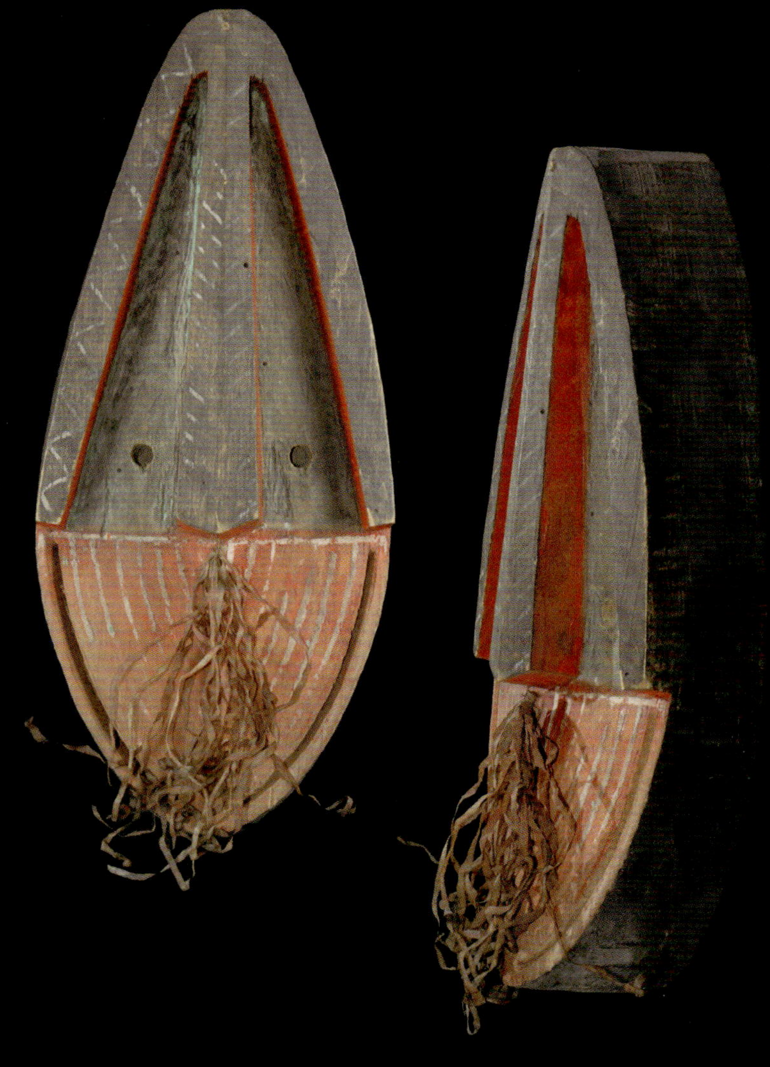

Figure 102

<u>Igyuyrtulik</u>
Searcher

988-2-190
H. 27 cm
W. 11 cm
D. 5 cm
White oak, sinew, gutskin, black paint, green
paint, red paint, white paint
Kodiak Island or Afognak Island
See Appendix for mask song, dance, and legend.

Illustration 102

<u>Igyuyrtulik</u>
Chercheur

988-2-190
H. 27 cm
L. 11 cm
Ép. 5 cm
Chêne blanc, tendon, peau d'intestin, peinture
noire, peinture verte, peinture rouge, peinture
blanche
Île de Kodiak ou d'Afognak
Se reporter à l'Annexe pour le chant, la légende et
la danse du masque.

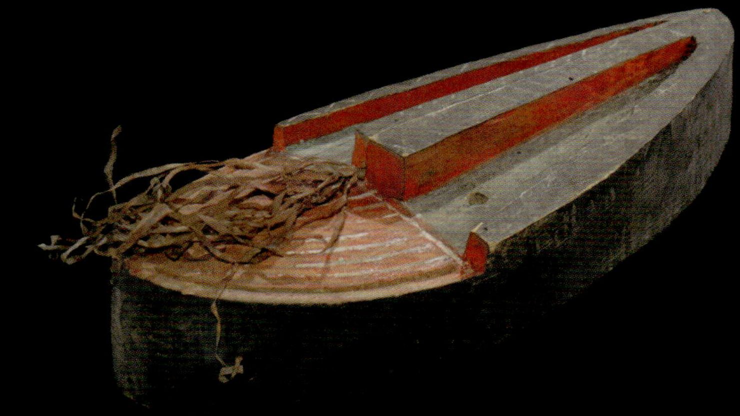

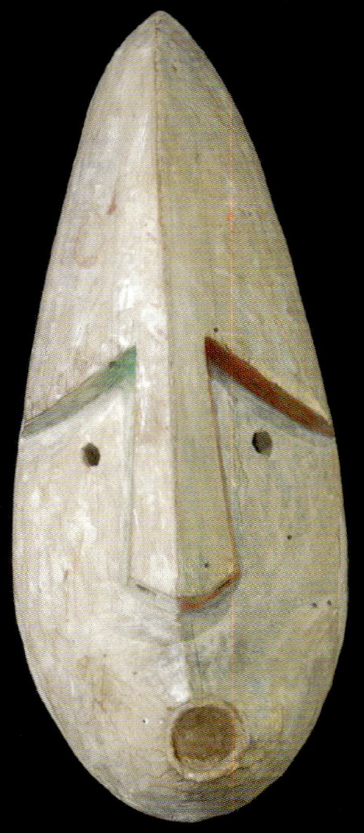
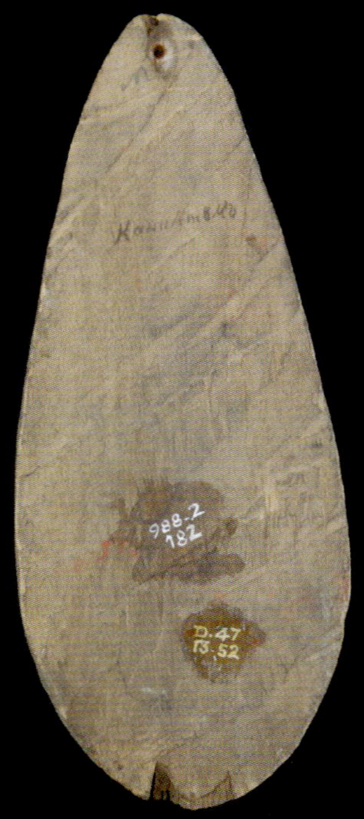
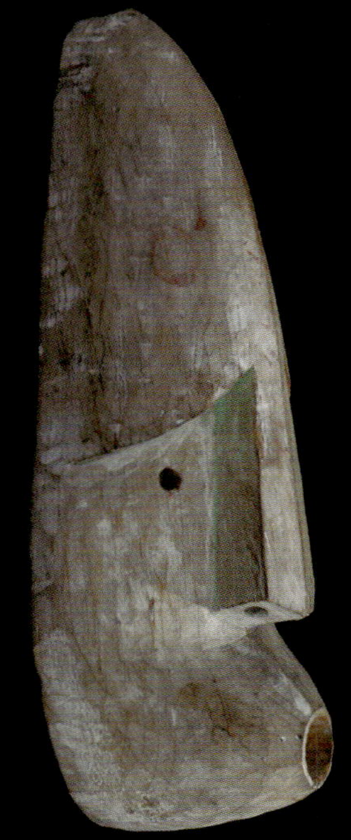
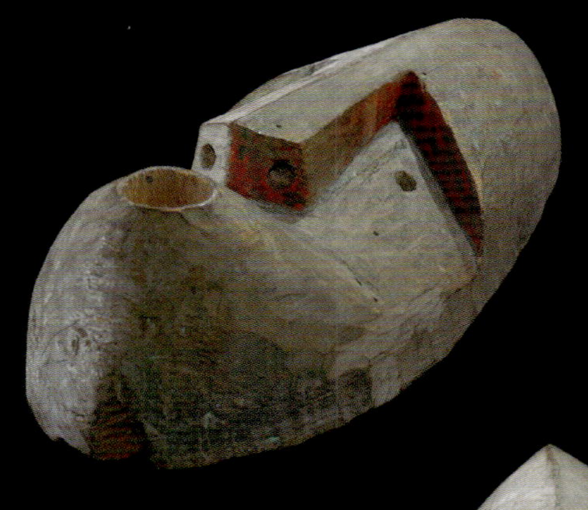

Figure 103

Kaniktuk

Snow?

988-2-182

H. 25.5 cm

W. 10.5 cm

D. 7 cm

White oak, white paint, green paint, red paint

Kodiak Island or Afognak Island

Illustration 103

Kaniktuk

Neige ?

988-2-182

H. 25,5 cm

L. 10,5 cm

Ép. 7 cm

Chêne blanc, peinture blanche, peinture verte, peinture rouge

Île de Kodiak ou d'Afognak

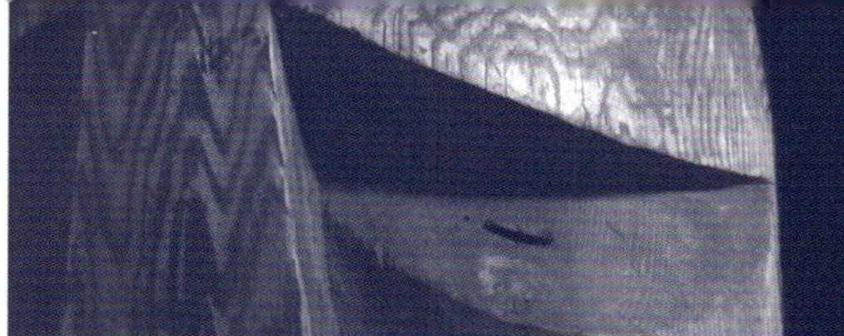

CHAPTER FIVE

From the Artist's Point of View

Perry Eaton

Following the political awakening of Sugpiaq identity that started in the late 1960s with the Alaska Native land claims, there developed a curiosity and then a passion for things Sugpiaq.[334] Our people were drawn to objects that anchored their newfound identity and cultural pride. The first efforts at cultural connection emerged as a few words of the old language, with the few speakers holding back and shyly correcting people's mumbled attempts. Simple words like *cama'i* (hello) held almost the status of passwords. Then dances reemerged, causing quite a stir. When a tribal group in Kodiak reintroduced dancing as a cultural connection, it was a visible leap from the safety of the sociopolitical framework corporations had established under the Alaska Native Claims Settlement Act. Some saw it as a giant step backward and were openly critical of the association of contemporary people with past practices. People also undertook research, or in many cases just a search for identity, for a connection with a tangible past. People pored through old books and manuscripts that had long been forgotten and had been of little interest to anyone before, eagerly looking for an old picture of their village or for accounts of visitors long forgotten and dormant. It is within the context of this Sugpiaq cultural renaissance that many modern Kodiak artists began examining the material culture of our ancestors.

There are few collections of Sugpiaq ethnographic materials, and the most significant are stored far from Alaska, even outside the United States. The Russian collections in the Kunstkamera of St. Petersburg,[335] the Etholen collection in

Figure 104. *Papa said, "No, no, no."* Oil painting by Alvin Amason.

PHOTOGRAPH BY PERRY EATON.

Illustration 104. Alvin Amason, *Papa a dit, « Non, non, non »*, peinture à l'huile.

PHOTOGRAPHIE DE PERRY EATON.

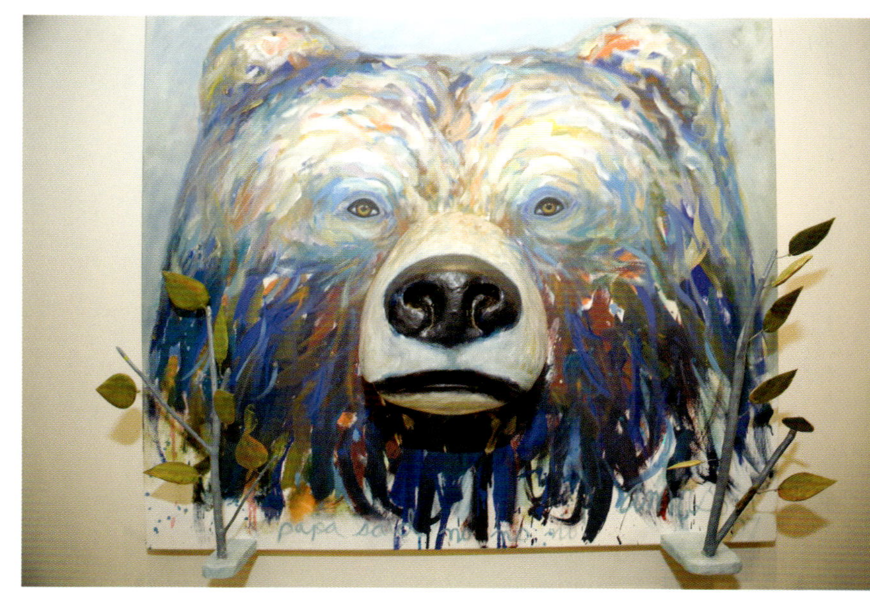

the National Museum of Finland,[336] France's Pinart collection in the Château-Musée,[337] and the Smithsonian Institution's Fisher Collection[338] are the backbone of material objects collected prior to 1900. For most artists, myself included, the collection that has had the most influence and the highest emotional impact is unquestionably the masks and objects collected by Alphonse Pinart in 1872.

Thanks to Dr. Lydia Black and her doctoral student Dominique Desson, the Pinart collection began to reemerge in 1986.[339] Professor Alvin Amason of the University of Alaska Fairbanks, an internationally recognized Sugpiaq artist, worked closely with Black and Desson in their study of the objects. By accompanying them on trips to Sugpiaq villages and introducing people who spoke the language, Amason helped smooth the way for research. He was probably the first to recognize the emotional and cultural impact the collection would have on the Sugpiaq Native arts community. He personally understood the cultural void that the physical presence of the masks would fill. While Amason's own artistic expression is far from traditional, the influence of the Pinart collection began to appear subtly in his work in the early 1990s. When asked about its impact, he said, "My work just took on a more Alutiiq look." Around 1987–1988 his work begins to display more symmetry, a hallmark of Sugpiaq masks, and a full-face look emerges as a strong and dominant theme in his work (Figure 104).

Prior to the completion of Desson's research, there was little for artists to study. There was only a scattering of published images of the objects from Pinart's collection.[340] The entire collection had not been photographed and the existing images were in black-and-white. Even when color reproductions became available in Desson's thesis in 1995, she provided only a portrait view—a straight, frontal photograph. This left no way for artists to judge the depth of an object's features. Even a mug shot has two views.

Jacob Simeonoff, considered by many to be the father of the modern Sugpiaq mask, was one of the first Sugpiaq artists whose work showed distinct impacts from the Pinart collection (Figure 105). Born in Old Harbor and raised traditionally, Jacob first saw photographs of the collection while studying art with Alvin Amason at the University of Alaska Fairbanks in the late 1980s. In the masks, he saw a way of conveying traditional Sugpiaq values to the younger generation through storytelling. The value of masks as props and costuming was important to him. When the Kodiak tribal group was formed and they brought back dancing, it was Simeonoff who produced the first mask to be danced on the island in

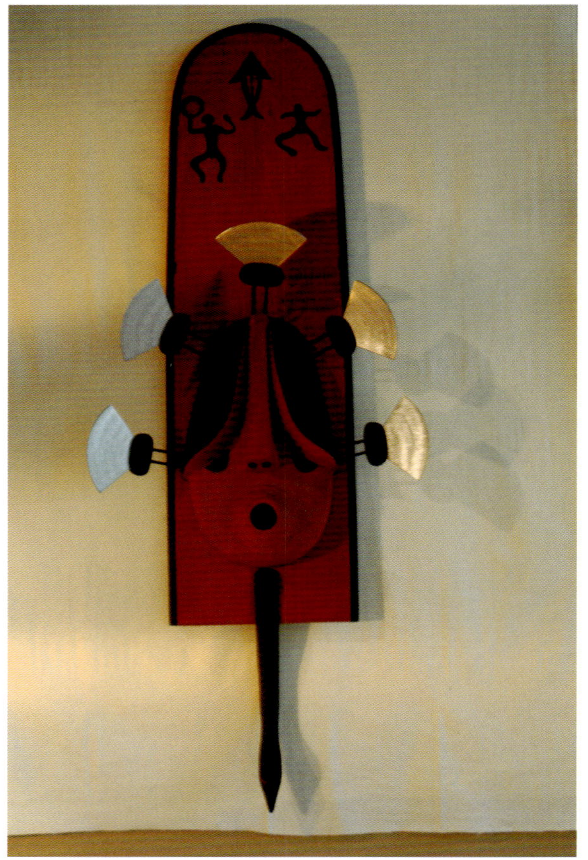

Figure 105. *Shaman*, plank mask by Jacob Simeonoff.

Illustration 105. *Chaman*, masque-planche de Jacob Simeonoff.

many scores of years. His body of work stood almost alone for a decade and inspired many of today's Sugpiaq artists.

For others, the Pinart collection has had significant emotional impact. Painter Helen Simeonoff[341] was the first Sugpiaq person to travel to France to visit the masks in person.[342] Like so many of today's Sugpiaq artists, Helen is forever hungry for things that ground her in her identity and validate the culture and history of Kodiak peoples. As an artist who draws inspiration from the indigenous world, Helen has brought obsessive passion to understanding the minutest details of our culture. Her visit to Boulogne-sur-Mer in 2000 became a high point in her artistic and cultural activist career. Being in the presence of so much collected work of the ancestors was emotionally overwhelming and left a deep and lasting impression on Helen and her work. On her return from France, she began a one-person crusade to expose other artists to the power of the collection. Since that first visit, she has returned to France several times and has worked tirelessly to expound the value of the collection to any and all who will listen. Her work has been forever changed by the exposure she has had to the masks and other artwork in the collection. Beyond offering the personal validation of coming from a culture that produced such significant works of art, the collection has proven to be a never-ending source of direct inspiration for her watercolors. She has created several series of paintings on the masks themselves and several others of costumed dancers (Figure 106).

The work of other artists—most notably Jerry Laktonen, Doug Inga, Alfred Naumoff Jr., and Sven Haakanson Jr.—also expresses a strong influence from the collection. Laktonen's work, which incorporates many influences from the modern world and a wide variety of materials, still depends on the basic form and shape defined in the collection for its fundamental spirit and soul. Many of Laktonen's works define current or "in the present" expressions of culturally grounded identity through the use of traditional form and shape. His "Joe Hazelwood"[343] and "Chugach Dude" masks are examples of his use of traditional form and shape to express current emotions.

Doug Inga and Alfred Naumoff Jr., traditional Native artists who grew up in Old Harbor, were both initially exposed to the collection through photographs; in 2006, they traveled to France to see the masks with a group of Kodiak Native artists sponsored by the Alutiiq Museum.[344] As it did for others, the collection left them momentarily stunned and speechless. To see so much of the past in one place, and to witness the variety and complexity of shape and form, was stunning (Figure 107). To say it left an indelible impression

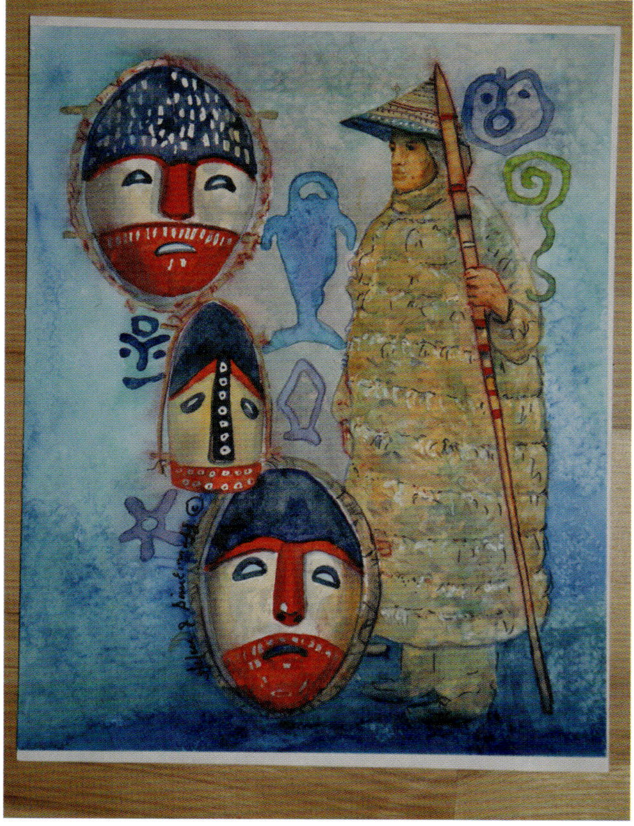

Figure 106. *Sugpiaq Man with Sugpiaq Masks*. Watercolor painting by Helen Simeonoff.
PHOTOGRAPH BY PERRY EATON.

Illustration 106. Helen Simeonoff, *Homme sugpiaq aux masques sugpiat*, aquarelle.
PHOTOGRAPHIE DE PERRY EATON.

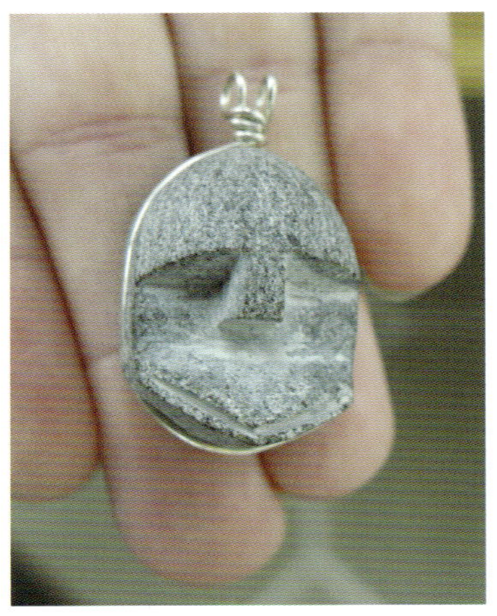

is an understatement. Naumoff summed it up when he said, "I'll never carve the same way again."

The carvings of Sven Haakanson Jr., also of Old Harbor, progressed from simple whittling to fine art over the course of a decade. In part, this transformation resulted from constant contact with the Pinart collection—its shapes, colors, proportions, and designs—as well as the influence of fellow artists highly impacted by the French collection.[345] Haakanson's efforts to photograph the masks, to document their fine-scaled details so they could be shared in Kodiak, led to an intimate knowledge of their construction. His efforts to teach carving in Sugpiaq communities[346] helped him refine his own carving style.

Lena Amason, raised in Port Lions and now a resident of Old Harbor, draws heavily on the shape and form found in traditional Sugpiaq masks for her artwork. While Amason does not represent herself as a mask maker, her sculptures enjoy many of the characteristics of masks (Figure 108). An excellent example is her piece *Whale 2003*, exhibited in a New York Museum of Arts and Design show titled *Changing Hands: Art Without Reservations 2*. This piece incorporates the traditional backboard and face at the bottom, surrounded by hoops and appendages.

Amason says, "For now, the majority of my pieces are wall sculptures rather than wearable masks. However, all of them are studies of the historical Kodiak dance masks, with

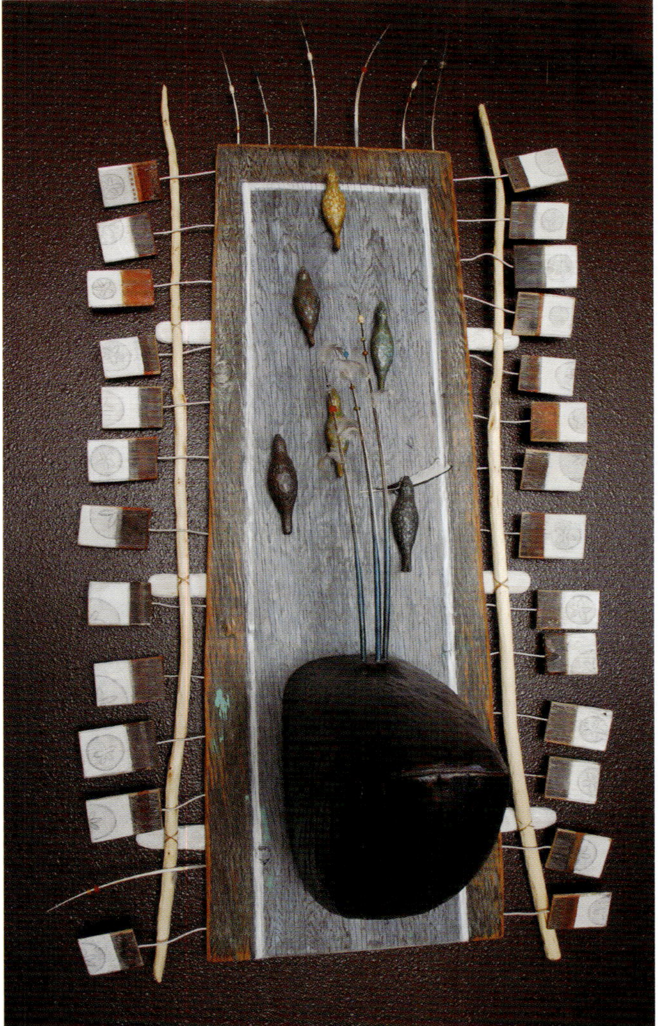

Figure 107. Stone mask pendant by Doug Inga.
PHOTOGRAPH BY PATRICK SALTONSTALL.

Figure 108. *Whale Jumper 1.* Sculpture by Lena Amason.
PHOTOGRAPH BY SVEN HAAKANSON JR. (THIS SCULPTURE IS THE COMPANION PIECE TO *WHALE 2003*.)

Illustration 107. Pendentif en pierre en forme de masque de Doug Inga.
PHOTOGRAPHIE DE PATRICK SALTONSTALL.

Illustration 108. Lena Amason, *Sauteur de baleine 1*, sculpture.
PHOTOGRAPHIE DE SVEN HAAKANSON JR. (CETTE SCULPTURE ACCOMPAGNE L'ŒUVRE BALEINE 2003.)

constant references to the life on the island, which surrounds me right now. Years spent commercial salmon fishing around the island have given me a wealth of sea life and boat life imagery from which to draw."

Other artists have been equally moved and have incorporated impressions of the collection throughout their work. Artists such as Coral Chernof and Elisabeth Peterson have used designs from the Pinart collection in jewelry and beadwork. The collection has also influenced artists beyond the Native community. Carver and former schoolteacher Jim Dillard used images of masks to teach mask carving to students in Port Lions in 1985, and Kodiak jewelers Helm Johnson[347] and Lisa McCormick have worked many of the Pinart mask designs into their beautiful pins, pendants, bracelets, and earrings (Figure 109).

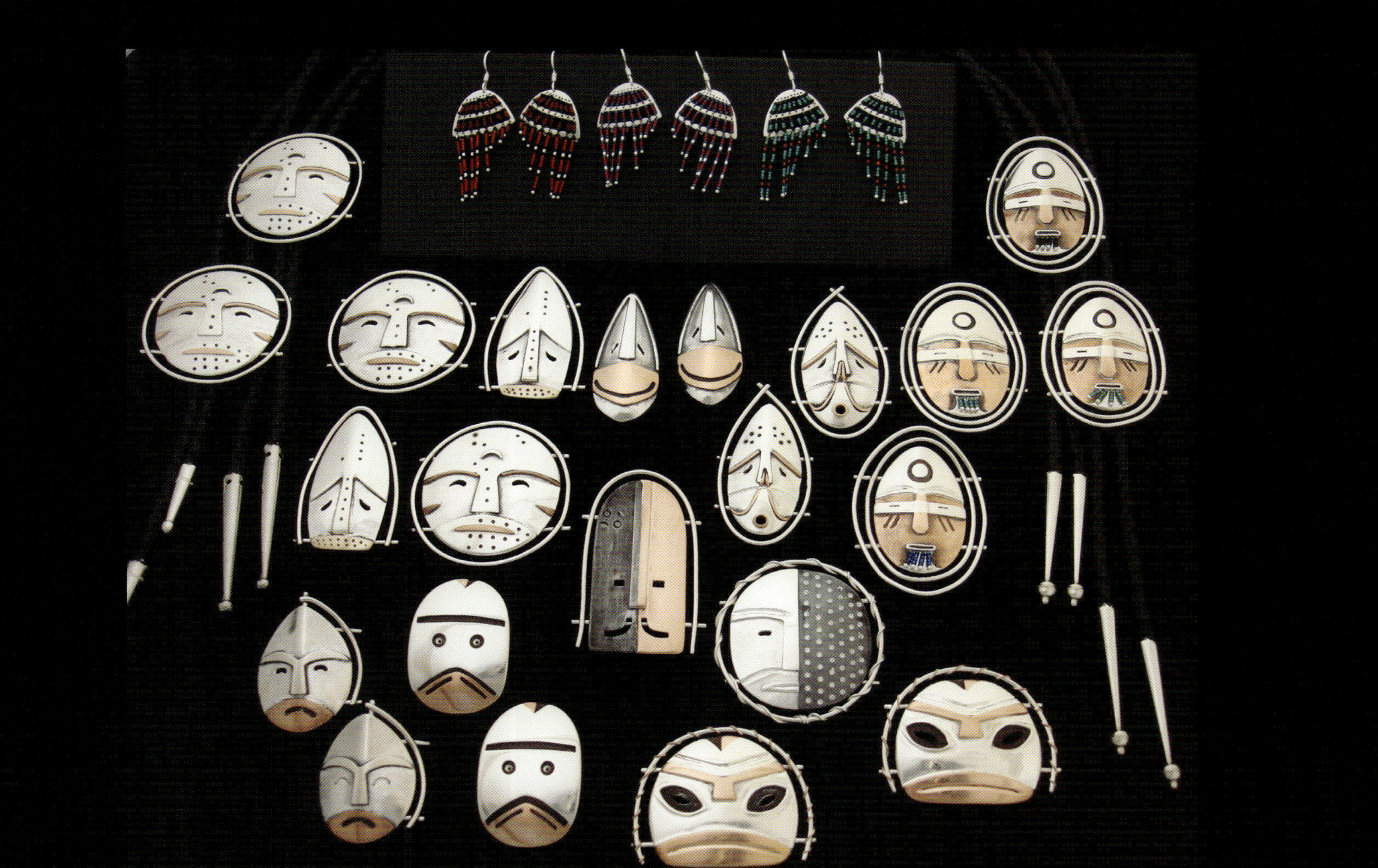

Figure 109. Silver mask pendants by Helm Johnson and Alisha Drabek.
PHOTOGRAPH COURTESY OF HELM JOHNSON AND ALISHA DRABEK.

Illustration 109. Pendentifs en argent en forme de masques réalisés par Helm Johnson et Alisha Drabek.
PHOTOGRAPHIE REPRODUITE AVEC L'AIMABLE AUTORISATION DE HELM JOHNSON ET ALISHA DRABEK.

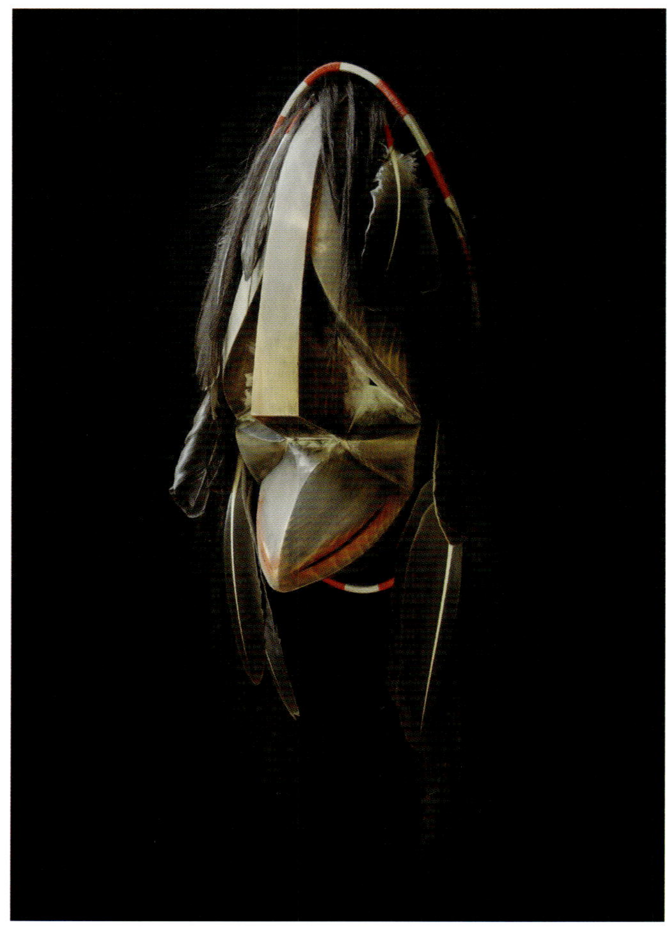

Like other artists, I too have been heavily influenced by the collection. I first heard of the collection in 1958. I was thirteen years old and fishing with my father. The season was a disaster and we were rehanging the seine for the third time to fish in deeper water when a relative, Charlie Christofferson, commented on a recent Native dance done in Karluk in an effort to influence the fish run. In the course of the short conversation, the question of whether the dance had been done with a mask arose. An elderly lady, Mrs. Joe Heitman, overhearing the conversation, interrupted and said with some force, "That mask stuff all end and they took them all away; they are all gone; there are none left on the island." Little did I know at the time that she may have been talking about Alphonse Pinart. For years I thought she was talking about the Russians. It turned out she was born in Afognak in 1885, just fourteen years after Pinart's visit, and may have learned of the masks from adults in the community who interacted with him.

For me, as a mask carver, the collection has become my baseline on shape and form. As with all artists, I take liberty with my interpretations, but my work never seems to fall far from the tree. The variety and variations represented in the masks collected by Pinart allow an almost endless mixing and matching for storytelling. I believe that the mask is but a tool for transformation through storytelling and dance. It is costuming for the play. In its purest form, the mask is paraphernalia for the greatest art form of all—the telling of our story, the thing that makes us human (Figure 110).

No single body of collected material has impacted the Sugpiaq Native arts community more significantly than the Pinart collection in the two decades since its reemergence. It has proven to be a fountain of inspiration and pride to the people of the island. Just as it did in the past and in our generation, it will continue to be a force of motivation, inspiration, and intrigue to people of all walks, on and off Kodiak Island, for generations to come.

Alone with the masks.
Quiet as a deserted museum . . .
but I could hear the songs.
Still as an unopened tomb . . .
but I could see the dance.
And we talked.

—PERRY EATON, SUGPIAQ ARTIST,
ON VIEWING THE PINART COLLECTION IN FRANCE

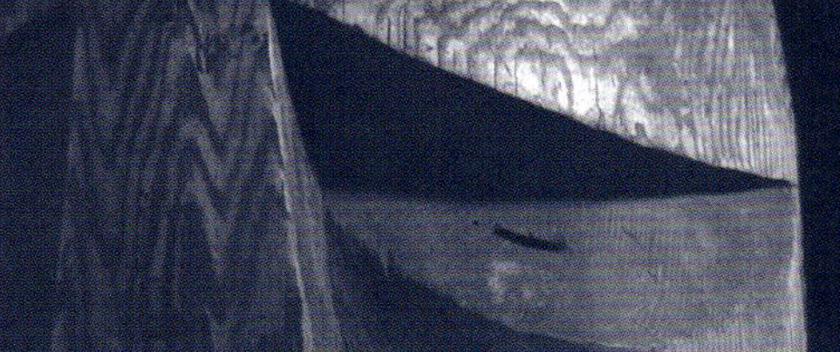

Le point de vue de l'artiste

Perry Eaton

À la fin des années 1960, le soulèvement politique et le renouveau de l'identité sugpiaq aboutirent aux réclamations territoriales des autochtones d'Alaska et à l'émergence d'une certaine curiosité, puis d'une véritable passion pour tout ce qui était sugpiaq[334]. Notre peuple se sentait attiré par les objets qui ancraient son identité et lui permettaient de retrouver avec fierté sa culture. Les premières tentatives destinées à lui permettre de renouer avec sa culture se manifestèrent sous forme de vocabulaire, quelques mots de la langue ancienne qu'on échangeait avec les personnes qui la parlaient encore, et qui osaient à peine corriger les balbutiements des gens. De simples mots comme *cama'i* (bonjour) servaient presque de mot de passe. Puis on redécouvrit les danses avec une certaine jubilation. Lorsqu'un groupe de Kodiak relança les danses pour rétablir un lien culturel, il était évident qu'on sortait brusquement des conventions du cadre sociopolitique que les corporations avaient instaurées au moment de l'accord sur les réclamations territoriales autochtones en Alaska (*Alaska Native Claims Settlement Act.*) Certains y virent un énorme retour en arrière et reprochèrent ouvertement aux associations d'aujourd'hui de vouloir instaurer des pratiques d'hier. Pour rétablir une communication concrète avec le passé, on entreprit des études, souvent en généalogie, à la recherche d'une identité. Les gens se plongeaient dans des vieux livres et des manuscrits oubliés depuis longtemps, qui n'avaient jamais intéressé personne jusque-là, essayant fébrilement de mettre la main sur une vieille photo de leur village ou des récits de visiteurs oubliés. C'est dans cet esprit de renaissance de la culture sugpiaq que de nombreux artistes vivants de Kodiak entreprirent d'étudier les objets légués par la culture de nos ancêtres.

Il existe peu de collections d'objets ethnographiques sugpiat, et les plus importantes sont conservées loin de l'Alaska, au-delà même des États-Unis. Les collections russes du Kunstkamera de Saint-Pétersbourg[335], la collection Etholen du Musée national de la Finlande[336], la collection française Pinart du Château-Musée de Boulogne-sur-Mer[337] et la collection Fisher de la Smithsonian Institution[338] constituent l'essentiel des objets collectés avant 1900. Pour la plupart des artistes, dont je fais partie, la collection qui a eu le plus d'influence, qui a eu le retentissement émotionnel le plus fort, est indubitablement celle qui réunit les masques et les objets collectés par Alphonse Pinart en 1872.

C'est grâce au Dr Lydia Black et à sa collaboratrice doctorante, Dominique Desson que la collection Pinart est réapparue en 1986[339]. Alvin Amason, professeur à l'université d'Alaska, à Fairbanks, et artiste sugpiaq internationalement reconnu, a travaillé en étroite collaboration avec Black et Desson pour en étudier les objets. Il les a accompagnées au cours de leurs voyages dans les villages sugpiat, facilitant leurs recherches en les présentant à des habitants qui parlaient la langue. Amason fut probablement le premier à se rendre compte des répercussions tant émotionnelles que culturelles que pourrait avoir la collection sur la communauté artistique autochtone sugpiaq. Il comprit combien la présence physique des masques pourrait combler le manque de culture. Bien que dans son travail artistique Amason soit loin d'être traditionnel, l'influence de la collection Pinart sur ses œuvres commença à se faire sentir de façon subtile au début des années 1990. Quand on lui demandait quelle sorte d'impact cette collection avait eu sur lui, il répondait : « Mon travail a simplement pris un air plus alutiiq. » Dans les années 1987-1988, ses œuvres commencèrent à présenter une plus grande symétrie, ce qui est une des caractéristiques des masques sugpiat, et on vit apparaître des visages entiers, un thème qui devint dominant dans son travail *(ill. 104)*.

Avant le travail de recherche entrepris par Desson, les artistes n'avaient pas beaucoup d'informations à leur disposition s'ils voulaient mener des études. On ne disposait que d'images des objets de la collection Pinart, publiées irrégulièrement[340]. La collection complète n'avait pas été photographiée et les images qui existaient étaient en noir et blanc. Même les reproductions en couleurs que publia Desson dans sa thèse en 1995 ne montraient que des vues de face, frontales, ce qui ne permettait guère aux artistes d'appréhender la profondeur des traits pour chacun des objets. C'est si vrai que même les photos d'identité prises par la police présentent deux clichés.

Jacob Simeonoff, que beaucoup considèrent être le père du masque sugpiaq moderne, fut l'un des premiers artistes sugpiat dont le travail se montra clairement inspiré par la collection Pinart *(ill. 105)*. Né à Old Harbor et élevé dans le respect de la tradition, Jacob découvrit les photos de la collection alors qu'il était étudiant en art avec Alvin Amason à l'université d'Alaska à la fin des années 1980. Il réalisa combien ces masques, par le récit de leurs histoires, pourraient tisser un lien avec les valeurs traditionnelles sugpiat auprès des jeunes générations. Pour lui, la valeur du masque, que l'on utilisait comme un accessoire et un élément de costume, revêtait toute son importance lors de sa réelle utilisation.

Lorsque le groupe tribal kodiak se constitua et que ses membres firent renaître la danse, c'est Simeonoff qui créa le masque qui fut le premier à participer à une danse sur l'île depuis bien des années. Son œuvre resta presque isolée pendant une dizaine d'années, mais elle a inspiré beaucoup d'artistes sugpiat d'aujourd'hui.

Pour d'autres artistes également, la collection Pinart fut un bouleversement important. Helen Simeonoff[341], qui est peintre, fut la première Sugpiaq à se rendre en France pour voir les masques[342]. Comme beaucoup d'artistes sugpiat d'aujourd'hui, Helen ne cesse de rechercher tout ce qui peut renforcer son identité ou enrichir la culture et l'histoire des peuples de Kodiak. Cette artiste, qui puise son inspiration dans le monde autochtone, tente passionnément de comprendre notre culture jusque dans ses moindres détails. Sa visite à Boulogne-sur-Mer en 2000 devint l'un des moments forts de sa carrière d'artiste et d'activiste culturelle. Elle fut extrêmement émue de se trouver en présence de toutes ces œuvres, recueillies il y a plus d'un siècle auprès de ses ancêtres. Cette visite laissa en elle une empreinte profonde et durable qui se refléta dans son travail. De retour de France, elle entama une véritable croisade pour exposer aux autres artistes la puissance de cette collection. Depuis cette première visite, elle est retournée plusieurs fois de l'autre côté de l'Atlantique et a œuvré sans relâche à faire reconnaître la valeur de cette collection. Son travail a été définitivement transformé depuis qu'elle a pu admirer les masques et les autres œuvres d'art de la collection. Au-delà de la fierté personnelle de se savoir issue d'une culture qui a produit des œuvres aussi remarquables, elle a puisé dans cette collection comme dans une source inépuisable d'inspiration pour ses aquarelles. Elle a peint plusieurs séries d'œuvres consacrées aux masques, d'autres encore sur le thème des danseurs en costume *(ill. 106)*.

La collection s'est effectivement révélée une source d'inspiration importante ayant influencé le travail d'autres artistes, en particulier Jerry Laktonen, Doug Inga, Alfred Naumoff Jr. et Sven Haakanson Jr. Le travail de Laktonen, même s'il révèle de nombreuses influences puisées dans le monde d'aujourd'hui et utilise les matériaux les plus divers, s'appuie sur les formes traditionnelles que l'on observe dans la collection, quant à leur profonde spiritualité et leur âme. Bien que nombre de ses œuvres soient ancrées « dans le présent » et reflètent des expressions identitaires actuelles, elles sont enracinées dans la culture à travers l'utilisation de formes traditionnelles. Ses masques intitulés *Joe Hazelwood*[343] et *Le Gars Chugach* sont des exemples de son recours aux formes traditionnelles pour exprimer des émotions contemporaines.

Doug Inga et Alfred Naumoff Jr., des artistes autochtones traditionnels qui ont grandi à Old Harbor, ont tous deux initialement pris connaissance de l'existence de la collection grâce à des photographies. En 2006, l'Alutiiq Museum parainna leur voyage en France pour voir les masques, accompagnés d'un groupe d'artistes autochtones de Kodiak[344]. Sur le moment, la collection les laissa, comme les autres artistes, abasourdis et sans voix. Il était extraordinaire de pouvoir contempler tant d'objets de leur passé réunis en un seul lieu, de pouvoir en admirer la variété, la complexité des formes *(ill. 107)*. Affirmer que cette expérience leur a laissé une impression inoubliable est peu dire. Naumoff résuma bien la situation lorsqu'il déclara, « Je ne sculpterai jamais plus le bois de la même façon. »

Les gravures de Sven Haakanson Jr., lui aussi originaire de Old Harbor, montrèrent une évolution, passant en une dizaine d'années d'objets simplement taillés au couteau à des objets d'art. Cette transformation s'est opérée en partie parce qu'il a été au contact permanent de la collection Pinart, avec ses formes, ses couleurs, ses proportions et ses dessins. Mais elle est due également à l'influence de ses amis artistes qui, eux aussi, ont été impressionnés par la collection française[345]. Les efforts qu'a déployés Haakanson pour photographier les masques, documenter leurs moindres détails afin d'en faire bénéficier les habitants de Kodiak, lui ont permis d'acquérir une profonde connaissance de leur conception. Son travail d'enseignement de la sculpture auprès des communautés sugpiat[346] l'a de plus amené à affiner son propre style.

Lena Amason, qui a grandi à Port Lions et habite aujourd'hui Old Harbor, s'inspire dans son œuvre directement de la forme des masques traditionnels sugpiat. Bien qu'elle ne se considère pas comme une femme sculpteur de masques, ses sculptures rappellent de nombreuses caractéristiques observées dans les masques *(ill. 108)*. Son œuvre *Baleine 2003*, actuellement montrée dans une exposition du New York Museum of Arts & Design intitulée « Changing Hands: Art Without Reservations 2 » (« Changement de mains : l'art sans réserve 2 »), en est un très bon exemple. Cette œuvre intègre des éléments traditionnels, tel le panneau, avec un visage dans la partie inférieure, entouré de cerceaux et d'accessoires. Amason explique ainsi sa démarche :

> Pour l'instant, la plus grande partie de mes œuvres est constituée de sculptures à accrocher au mur et non de masques que l'on porte. Mais elles sont toutes tirées de l'observation de masques associés à des danses historiques de Kodiak, et font constamment référence à la vie sur l'île, qui constitue mon environnement en ce moment. J'ai participé pendant des années à la pêche commerciale au saumon aux alentours de l'île, j'y ai connu l'expérience exaltante de la vie en mer et j'en conserve des images de la vie à bord d'un bateau, où je puise mon inspiration.

La collection a bouleversé d'autres artistes qui ont su exprimer leur émotion dans leurs œuvres. C'est le cas, par exemple, des artistes Coral Chernof et Elisabeth Peterson, qui ont utilisé le design des masques de la collection Pinart pour créer des bijoux ou des objets en perles. En dehors de la communauté autochtone, des artistes ont, eux aussi, pris leur inspiration dans la collection. Le sculpteur Jim Dillard, qui a été enseignant, s'est servi des images de masques lorsqu'il enseignait la sculpture des masques à ses étudiants de Port Lions en 1985. De même, les bijoutiers de Kodiak Helm Johnson[347] et Lisa McCormick ont incorporé nombre de designs de masques de la collection Pinart dans leurs magnifiques broches, pendentifs, bracelets, et boucles d'oreilles *(ill. 109)*.

Comme d'autres artistes, j'ai moi-même aussi été très impressionné par la collection. J'en ai entendu parler pour la première fois en 1958. J'avais treize ans et j'étais à la pêche avec mon père. La saison n'était pas bonne et nous étions en train d'accrocher nos filets pour la troisième fois afin de pouvoir pêcher en eaux plus profondes lorsqu'un membre de ma famille, Charlie Christofferson, parla d'une danse que les autochtones avaient récemment exécutée à Karluk dans l'espoir de modifier le parcours effectué par les poissons. Dans le courant de la conversation, nous nous sommes demandés si on avait exécuté la danse en portant un masque. Une femme âgée, Mme Joe Heitman, qui surprit la conversation, intervint pour déclarer avec conviction : « Ces histoires de masques c'est terminé, ils les ont tous emportés. Ils ont tous disparu, il n'en reste aucun sur l'île. » Je ne me doutais pas à l'époque qu'elle faisait peut-être allusion à Alphonse Pinart, et pendant des années j'ai cru qu'elle voulait parler des Russes. En fait, elle était née à Afognak, juste à l'époque de la visite de Pinart, et son père avait peut-être eu affaire à Pinart qui était à la recherche de masques dans le but de les rassembler.

Pour moi, qui suis sculpteur de masques, la collection a représenté peu à peu une référence quand je créais des formes. Comme tout artiste, je prends des libertés dans mes interprétations, mais sans jamais beaucoup m'éloigner de mon inspiration. La variété des masques collectés par Pinart, les variations qu'ils présentent, permettent de combiner et d'associer les éléments presque à l'infini pour dire des histoires. Je crois que le masque n'est qu'un outil qui accompagne l'évolution des récits et des danses. Il remplit le rôle de costume dans la pièce. Dans sa forme la plus pure, le masque est l'expression de la forme d'art la plus élevée qui soit : la narration de notre histoire, celle qui nous rend humains *(ill. 110)*.

Durant les vingt années qui ont suivi la réapparition de la collection Pinart, aucun autre ensemble d'objets collectés n'a eu une répercussion aussi importante sur la communauté artistique autochtone sugpiaq. Elle s'est révélée être une source d'inspiration et de fierté pour les habitants de l'île. Pour notre génération, comme elle l'a fait par le passé, elle continuera à représenter une source de motivation, d'inspiration et à intéresser toutes sortes de gens, qu'ils soient de l'île de Kodiak ou d'ailleurs, et cela pendant des générations encore.

Seul avec les masques.
Le silence comme dans un musée quand la foule est partie…
mais j'entendais les chants.
Comme une tombe encore fermée…
mais je voyais les danses.
Et nous avons parlé.

Perry Eaton, artiste sugpiaq,
sur sa vision de la collection Pinart en France

Mask Songs

Translated and transcribed by Jeff Leer and Sven D. Haakanson Jr. with assistance from Nick Alokli, Mary Haakanson, and Florence Pestrikoff

Alphonse Pinart not only collected Sugpiaq masks, he recorded the names, songs, dances, and legends associated with some.[348] His notes tie the carvings to Sugpiaq beliefs and to rare information from the Alutiiq language. Unfortunately, these notes are very hard to read and translate.[349] Pinart wrote his observations in many languages—including French, Russian, Alutiiq, Latin, and English. Moreover, as Alutiiq is traditionally a spoken, not a written, language, he spelled Alutiiq words phonetically, writing sounds with Russian Cyrillic characters. Translating his faded, handwritten notes required knowledge of the French, Russian, and Alutiiq languages, as well as assistance from Alutiiq speakers who could help to interpret the meaning of words. A number of the Alutiiq words Pinart recorded in 1872 either are not a part of common Alutiiq speech today or have several possible meanings. Fluent Elder Alutiiq speakers Nick Alokli, Mary Haakanson, and Florence Pestrikoff worked diligently with us for several months to develop translations for the mask songs, dances, and legends presented here, as well as the mask names used throughout the catalog and *Giinaquq: Like a Face* exhibition (see Chapter 4). We subjected each translation to multiple reviews until the project team—Alutiiq speakers, linguist, and anthropologists—was satisfied with

the result. Translator, educator, and museum professional Céline Wallace provided the transcription of Pinart's French notes, using his own words without any correction of his nineteenth-century French. As such, the translations presented here do not duplicate those offered by Desson,[350] but are a new attempt to interpret Pinart's notes.

For each mask we provide as much information as possible (Table 1). This typically includes a name and a song. These texts include an Alutiiq language translation, in Roman characters, of the Alutiiq words represented by Pinart's phonetically based Russian Cyrillic notes.[351] English and French versions follow the Alutiiq translations. In places, we added punctuation to enhance readability. Words presented in italics could not be translated. Additionally, where available, we provide English and French versions of Pinart's notes on the dances and legends that accompany specific masks. Pinart typically wrote these descriptions in French, so for these we offer no Alutiiq translations.

The mask texts provided below appear in the order in which each mask is first named in Pinart's journal. For the most part, this order follows the presentation of mask songs transcribed by Pinart during his travels to Sugpiaq villages, particularly Eagle Harbor. It is important to note that he described a number of the accompanying dances and legends in notes taken in the community of Kodiak, after returning from his village travels. In this later part of his journal, he provides a second list of mask songs, in an order distinct from that in which he initially recorded the verses.[352] He

Table 1. Mask Texts Available in Pinart's Kodiak Field Journal

Alutiiq Name—English Name	Catalog #	Song	Legend	Dance
Shugashat —Translation Unknown (F)[a]	988-2-179			
Shugashat —Translation Unknown (M)[a]	988-2-185		1	2
Shugashat —Translation Unknown (M)[a]	71.1881.21.31			
Payulik—Bringer of Food	988-2-169	1		1
Igyuyrtulik—Searcher	988-2-190			
Igyuyrtuliksiinaq—Larger Searcher	988-2-159	1	1	1
Unartuliq—Protector/Talisman[b]	988-2-199	1		1
Unnuyayuk—Night Traveler	988-2-195	1	1	1
Chumliiq—First One[c]	988-2-172	1	1	1
Ingillagayak—Weatherman[c]	988-2-198	1	1	1
Agu'lik—Large Mask	988-2-200	1	1	1
Shalgayak—Trader	None	1		1
Ashigik—Fool/Lucky One	988-2-202	1		1
Nallumalik—One Who Doesn't Know	988-2-204	1		1
Pugumalria—Woman Who Took	D47–13–75[d]	1		1
Nakirnalik—Snub-Nosed One	988-2-171	1		1
Kuyauq—Big-Nosed One/Thankful Person	988-2-175	1		1
Angalangyak—Good Mask[e]	None			
Chuyallik—The Big-Lipped One[e]	None	1		1
Angun—Old Man	988-2-168	1		
Akrillria—Voyager	988-2-205	1		
Ituryullria—One Who Arrived	None	1		1
Yuaulik—Searcher[b]	988-2-201	1		1
Yuilria—Voyager	None	1	1	1
Agut'lik—Translation Unknown	988-2-189			
Agut'liksiinaq—Larger Agut'lik	988-2-152		1[f]	
Kagukuak—Man Who Comes Back	None		1	
Agiyashik—Translation Unknown	None		1	1
Allayak—Different, Not Like Us (M)[g]	988-2-194			
Allayak—Different, Not Like Us (M)[g]	71.1881.21.28		1	
Allayak—Different, Not Like Us (F)[g]	988-2-193			

Notes:

(F) = Female, (M) = Male

The number of texts noted in this table does not equal the total number of texts presented in this appendix, as some masks shared a dance or a legend.

a. These masks share a legend.

b. These masks danced together. There is one dance for both masks.

c. These masks entered the *qasgiq* together and danced together. They share a dance.

d. This storage number was given in 1947 by the Musée de l'Homme. Although Lot-Falck illustrates this mask in her 1957 article (plate 5), it is now missing.

e. These masks danced together. They share a dance.

f. Igyuyrtulik—Searcher shares this legend.

g. On the back of these masks Pinart wrote "Allayak." Depending on the pronunciation of this word, it can mean "Different, not like us" in Alutiiq or "stingy one" or "greedy one" (Haakanson in press). Pinart's notes also associate the word "Kygumartaq" with the legend associated with the female version of this mask. In Alutiiq this means "bowlegged."

annotates this list with summaries of legends and descriptions of dances. In the presentation below, we reunited the texts associated with specific masks. Where available we include provenance, the name of the community in which Pinart collected the information.

Where possible, we also present linked sets of mask texts with catalog numbers (Table 1). This indicates that the texts can be linked to a specific mask or set of masks in the Château-Musée's collection based on Pinart's handwritten attributions on the backs of some masks and catalog information. In contrast, texts without a catalog number have no known surviving mask (e.g., Chuyallik—The Big-Lipped One). The text may be associated with an unidentified mask in the collection or it may relate to a mask that Pinart did not collect. In some cases, it appears that Pinart collected mask texts without an associated object.

Readers will note that some masks have pairs of texts—sets of legends and dances (Table 1). In these cases, we indicate which sets represent associated information. Finally, some masks have similar names. Although each mask has a distinct Alutiiq title, there are two masks whose Alutiiq name means Searcher and two whose name means Voyager. The repetition of these names is not surprising, as they evoke themes of travel and hunting common in Sugpiaq mask songs. Such names may have been widely used in titling masks. Additionally, it is possible that these names indicate the masks are related, or represent a specific, recurring character in the Sugpiaq pantheon. As Desson notes, stylistically similar masks with the same name occur in the Pinart collection, reflecting related male and female characters.[353]

Finally, we note that although the process of translating these texts across multiple languages was challenging, it helped to reawaken their Alutiiq meanings. Elders' interpretation of the word *ikayuqa* illustrates this point. In Russian this word became *d'yavol* or devil. However, the Elders and Dr. Leer translate it from Alutiiq to English as "helper spirit." This one difference significantly changes the meaning of the song in which *ikayuqa* appears and the interpretation of that song today.

Shugashat—Meaning Unknown

988-2-179 (F), 988-2-185 (M), 71.1881.21.31 (M)

DANCE 1. When the individual wearing it enters the *qasgiq*,[354] he holds, together with the rattles in his hands, a whaling spear, the tip of which is made of human bone. He walks to the center of the *qasgiq* and threatens those in attendance, until the *kasaq* stands up and intervenes. The mask wearer is considered a sort of devil. Afterwards, he does not eat for twenty days. He wears a parka made of sea parrots [puffins].

DANCE 2. (associated with the legend presented below, collected on Afognak Island, January 25, 1872):

Large mask which was supposed to have come from the sea. The individual who wears it enters the *qasgiq* with a flapper in his mouth.

He shows his elbows, first the right and then the left with his hand on the opposite hip each time. Then he runs forward.

Meanwhile two men and one woman are beating a drum and the man wearing the mask sings.

U-gu-u, o-go, u-gu-u. They feared him much.

LEGEND. (associated with dance 2 above, collected on Afognak Island, January 25, 1872):

One day while they were dancing in the *qasgiq* a fearless woman asked why during those games they did not go to the shore. Then she decided to go by herself, holding in one hand a wooden stick (of the kind used to dry the fish). She immediately saw something red on the sea, like fire. From it appeared two men and one woman. The two men wore *kaddaka* on their heads and the woman only her hair. The woman held a human hand in her mouth. They moved closer and were soon on the shore. The woman who had come out of the cabin holding a wooden spear had prepared to defend herself. They came out from the water in the direction of the mountains. They fell, and in their places were found only only skeletons. Their bellies were still [word unclear] and puffed up like bladders. Soon after, they got back up and flew over to

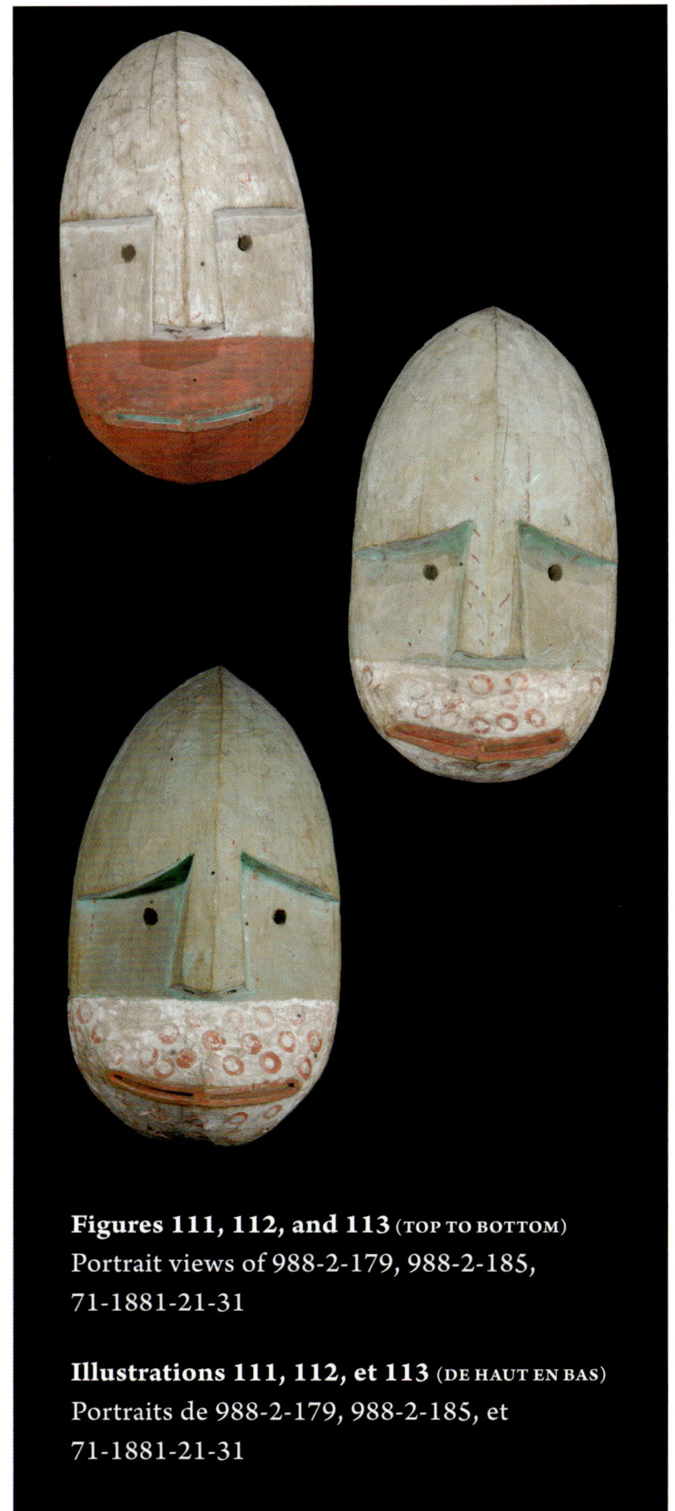

Figures 111, 112, and 113 (TOP TO BOTTOM)
Portrait views of 988-2-179, 988-2-185, 71-1881-21-31

Illustrations 111, 112, et 113 (DE HAUT EN BAS)
Portraits de 988-2-179, 988-2-185, et 71-1881-21-31

the mountains. A man then came out of the *qasgiq* after them. He soon went back and the three shapes followed. They did not stay long at the *qasgiq* and soon vanished completely.

Payulik—Bringer of Food

988-2-169

SONG.

Payulik

Ikayuqa alingenilu unani.
Agutamken ugwit puyuatni.
Unani agutamken.

Bringer of Food

My helper, don't be afraid down there.
I am going up to the smoke of the seal rocks.
I am taking you down there.

DANCE. When Payulliq arrives in the *qasgiq*, this mask holds a large bowl of *Beruske of chikcha* and Kamchatka lily roots. During the time this song lasts he dances holding this large bowl. When the song ends he passes the bowl amongst the elderly first and invites them to eat. Then he passes it to the young, etc.

Igyuyrtulik—Searcher

988-2-190

Igyuyrtuliksiinaq—Larger Searcher

988-2-159

SONG.

Igyuyrtulik

Nani imna sun'arausqaq nani imna iwa'anaaqa.
Piani-kiq iwa'inaaqa wiyullriani iwa'inaaqa imna.

Searcher

Where is that one, that young one, where is that one I am
　　trying to search for?

Perhaps, up above, the one I am trying to find is among
　　those who whirl about.
I am trying to find that one.

DANCE. He enters the *barabara*[355] searching through all the rows without finding what he wants. After having looked everywhere and the song is over he exits.

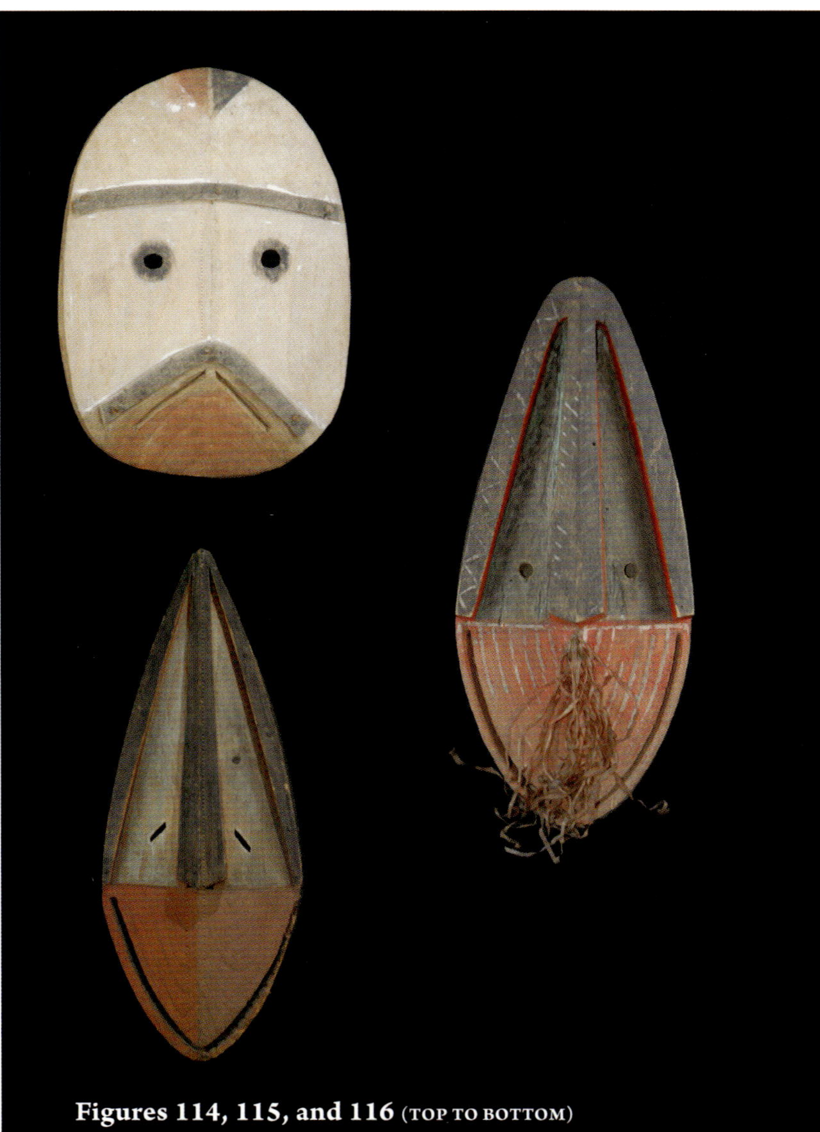

Figures 114, 115, and 116 (TOP TO BOTTOM)
Portrait views of 988-2-169, 988-2-190, and 988-2-159

Illustrations 114, 115, et 116. (DE HAUT EN BAS)
Portraits de 988-2-169, 988-2-190, et 988-2-159

A legend for these masks appears below, shared with Agut'lik and Agut'liksiinaq.

Unartuliq—Protector / Talisman

988-2-199

SONG.

Unartuliq

Qaiciina-gua ikayuaqa unani cing'urcaa unani cing'unilnga kia'ut agutamken llam ima'i iquanun.
Natgun maagun ag'it iluakun agumuukuk cauyang'arpetek kiugna (takuyaru).

Protector/Talisman

Why helper was he pushing down there? I was not pushing.
He is taking you North to the Universe's end.
From where? This way. Go inside the two are playing.
Even if you play music, answer me and go check on it.

DANCE. The two of them[356] dance sitting on their knees, moving from right to left, turning to one side and then to the other. During the second part they stand up and dance with a heavy motion [word unclear] around the *qasgiq*.

Unnuyayuk—Night Traveler

988-2-195

SONG.

Unnuyayuk

Qai-ciin ikayuqa, qai-ciin ulurakllua?
ugwini pitarkirnaya'amken.
Agellrianga llam iluakun; ikayuma kat'um tayatannga.
Aciqallrianga lliilerwiatnum gui.

Night Traveler

Why is it my helper spirit, why is it you are apprehensive of me on the seal rocks?
I will bring you game to be caught.
I went through the inside of the universe; my helper, that one made me afraid.
I went down where they are motioning.

LEGEND. They say that during a trip this mask looked at the devil and half of its face was burnt by the sight.

DANCE. He enters the *qasgiq*, goes to the left corner and, his back to the audience, he dances on his knees during the first part of the song. When the second song starts, he gets up

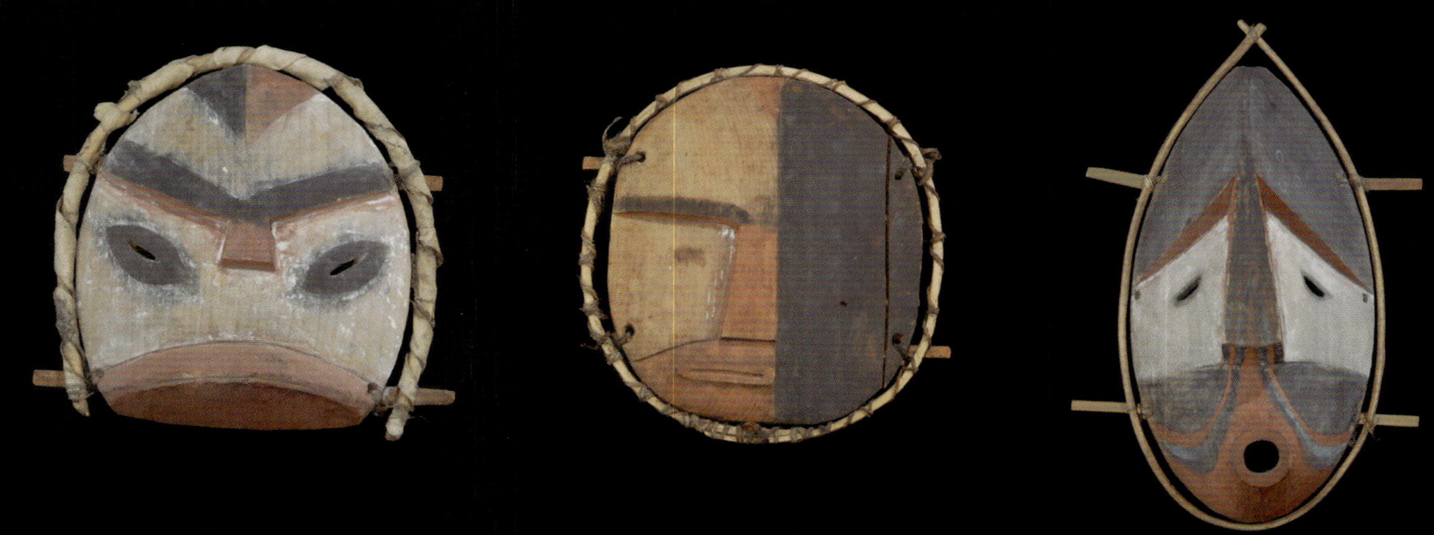

Figures 117, 118, and 119 (LEFT TO RIGHT)
Portrait views of 988-2-199, 988-2-195, and 988-2-172

Illustrations 117, 118, et 119 (DE GAUCHE À DROITE)
Portraits de 988-2-199, 988-2-195, et 988-2-172

with his back still turned, goes to the center and jumps and bounces before disappearing.

Chumliiq—First One

988-2-172

SONG.

Chumliiq

Engluqa pia'i, llam'i pia'i engluqa pia'i nallumaan.
Macam-qaa pik'um tunua pia'i?
Ikayuqa, ulla'amken piaken tailaryaaqamken.
Ikayuqa, nunam pik'um waamestainek.

First One

My house up there, in the Universe up there, you don't
    know it.
Is it behind the sun? Is it behind the one up above?
My helper, I am approaching you from up above. I keep
    trying to come.
My helper, that one's lands doesn't need performers.

LEGEND. The legend says that one day, a man who wanted
to become a shaman retreated in the woods. There he started
getting inspired, saw the devil, and turned into this mask.

DANCE. Two arrive with the following mask. The follower
goes to the left corner, hidden by a *kamlak*. He watches him
dancing on his knees during the first song. At the end of the
first song he gets up while holding rattles and dances and
hops around the *qasgiq*, falling down, getting up again and
dancing again.

Ingillagayak—Weatherman

988-2-198

SONG.

Ingillagayak

Naken-gwa ikayuqa tailuni itrumaakut ikaymta
Ug'um itrumaakut.
Ikayuqa ugna wiiyuhnaarpet.

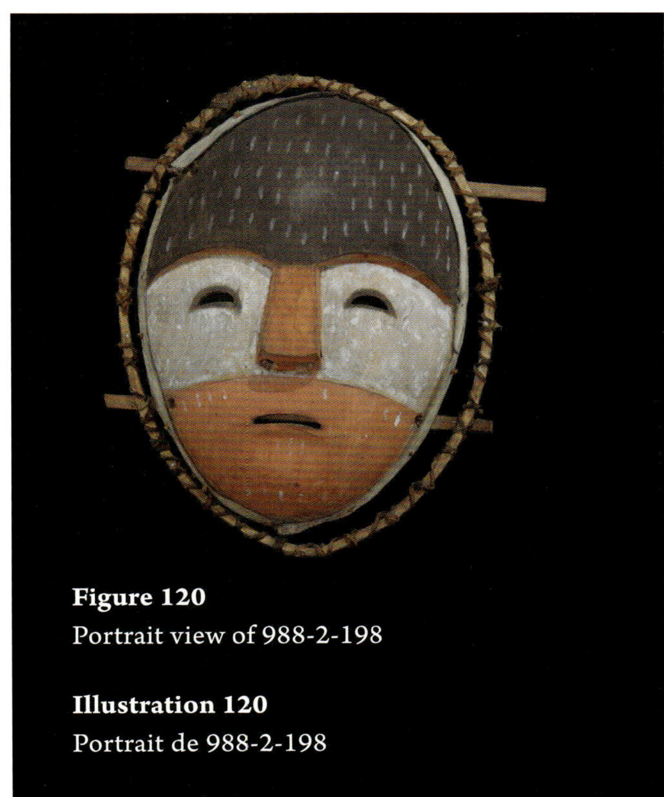

Figure 120
Portrait view of 988-2-198

Illustration 120
Portrait de 988-2-198

Unani ken'ami ken'am puyuani ikayuqa
Tan'rniq'gkia nani tang'rniq'gkia pitarkirnaamken tawamia.

Weatherman

From where now my helper is coming, he is entering in on
    us our helper
He came in on us.
My helper should we twirl this one?
Down [out] there in the tide flats, in the tide flat smoke my
    helper spirit
Watch me, somewhere, watch me I will catch the game over
    there.

LEGEND. They say that when the latter[357] was in the woods,
he (the devil) saw him from a distance and started laughing.
This mask represents him.

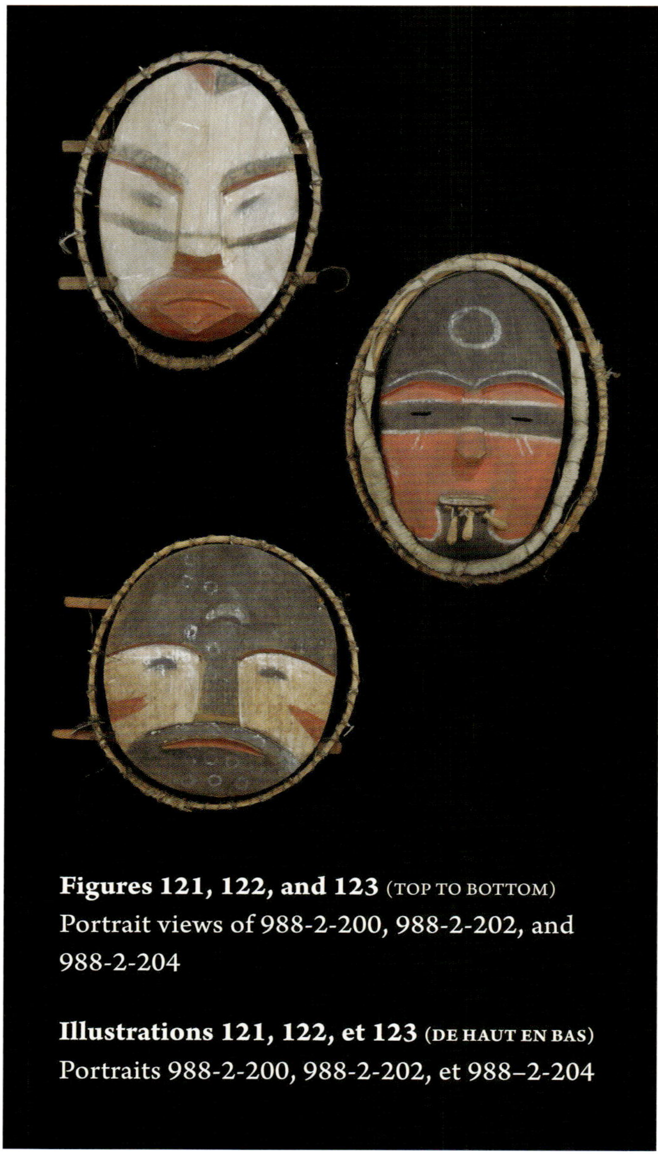

Figures 121, 122, and 123 (TOP TO BOTTOM)
Portrait views of 988-2-200, 988-2-202, and 988-2-204

Illustrations 121, 122, et 123 (DE HAUT EN BAS)
Portraits 988-2-200, 988-2-202, et 988–2-204

DANCE. He dances around, picks up the rattles, dances, and starts laughing. He dances around, stopping in the center between the four corners, and jumps. Meanwhile the other mask leaves.

Agu'lik—Large Mask
988-2-200

SONG.

Agu'lik

Awalaryaaqaqua ken'ami gui.
awalaryaaqaqua, puyulegnun gui.
Ikayuqa aguhnaamken utakinermen?
tus'uhnaamken pitarkanun?
tuqumallriamun aguhnaamken?

Large Mask

I am looking now where on the tide flats.
I am looking now where in the smoke.
My helper spirit should I take you to the place of waiting?
Should I take you to the game that will be caught?
Should I take you to the ones that are dead?

LEGEND. They talk about devils. . . . These masks say the devils are the dead.

DANCE. This mask wearer enters the *qasgiq* with a parka made of puffin skin. His arms are tucked inside the parka, a sleeve hanging on the front layer and the other on the back. He dances in place during the first part and then he goes outside. When he comes back in, he dances again, but this time he dances around the room with heavy movements, dancing in place after each leap.

Shalgayak—Trader
(No known mask)

SONG.

Shalgayak

Piaken ima aciwartua qiuryat pingkut nunaqlliitnek iiyur-
    wimnek aciwartua.
Lliilerwim sun'arai iiyuryuklluki aciwartua.

Trader

I descended from the Northern Lights, the land where they
    live, I whirl about as I descended.

I descended from where you put the young ones, who
thought they are whirling about.

DANCE. (Hunter of the aurora borealis) He enters the scene
wearing a kamleika with sleeves pulled up and arms covered
with blood. The lower part of the mask is also covered with
blood. He dances around the *qasgiq*, turning around briskly.

Ashigik—Fool/Lucky One
988-2-202

SONG.

Ashigik

Ikayuqa-gua taigua llam keg'um nallumasqaan-gua
tuuyaraaten.
Nallumasam pik'um ullakengama puyulget unkut neryugai.

Fool/Lucky One

I come my helper spirit. The one from the Universe doesn't
know, wants to take you.
That one over there, that one, even if he comes to me, those
over there in the smoke, he wants them.

DANCE. It takes a long time before this mask enters, and
the first part is sung while he is not in yet. He walks in with a
helper whose face is covered, and who sings the second part.

Nallumalik—One Who Doesn't Know
988-2-204

SONG.

Nalylgalan

Taingama taiqua ken'aq kan'a kewegluku.
Taiwimkun taigua tawa'i.
Qasgimen iterngama giinaruama uniqaqaanga.

One Who Doesn't Know

I came, I came, who is that, lift it up.
Where I came from, I came. So there.
When I entered the men's house, my mask keeps leaving
me.

DANCE. The man walks in without his mask, wearing only
eagle feathers on his head. The mask is hanging and swings
from one side of the *qasgiq* to the other. At a given time he
seizes the mask with his teeth, but it remains hooked. After
dancing for a while the mask flies away again moving in all
directions, at times falling to the ground, etc.

Pugumalria—Woman Who Took
D47-13-75[358]

SONG.

Pugumalria

Agwika ageng'arpet ikayuqa agwika
Nallumaan imam ima'i tagirnaa pugumawika.
Agellrianga llam iluakun ikayuqa tang'rhniqia.

Woman Who Took

Where I go, you go helper spirit.
You don't know where I come from, the sea or land.
As I travel the universe, helper spirit protect me.

DANCE. When he enters the *qasgiq* he kneels down on the
doorstep. He has a small oil lamp. He is covered by the others
with a large bag made of bear skin. While he is covered, he
burns birch roots inside (young roots) and an intense smoke
immediately fills up the *qasgiq*. The bag is removed and he is
still on his knees. His face is painted and he wears eagle feathers on his head. He holds a lamp in front of him in one hand,
and rattles behind him in the other. He exits and when the
second part is sung he puts on the mask and dances heavily
around the *qasgiq*.

Nakirnalik—Snub-Nosed One
988-2-171

SONG.

Nakirnalik

Atra'aqama atraryukua imam ima'i iluakun maagun.
Cagua kat'um ikayuma unani qia'utek'agu?
Giinaruaqa pitarkanun uulegtuq.

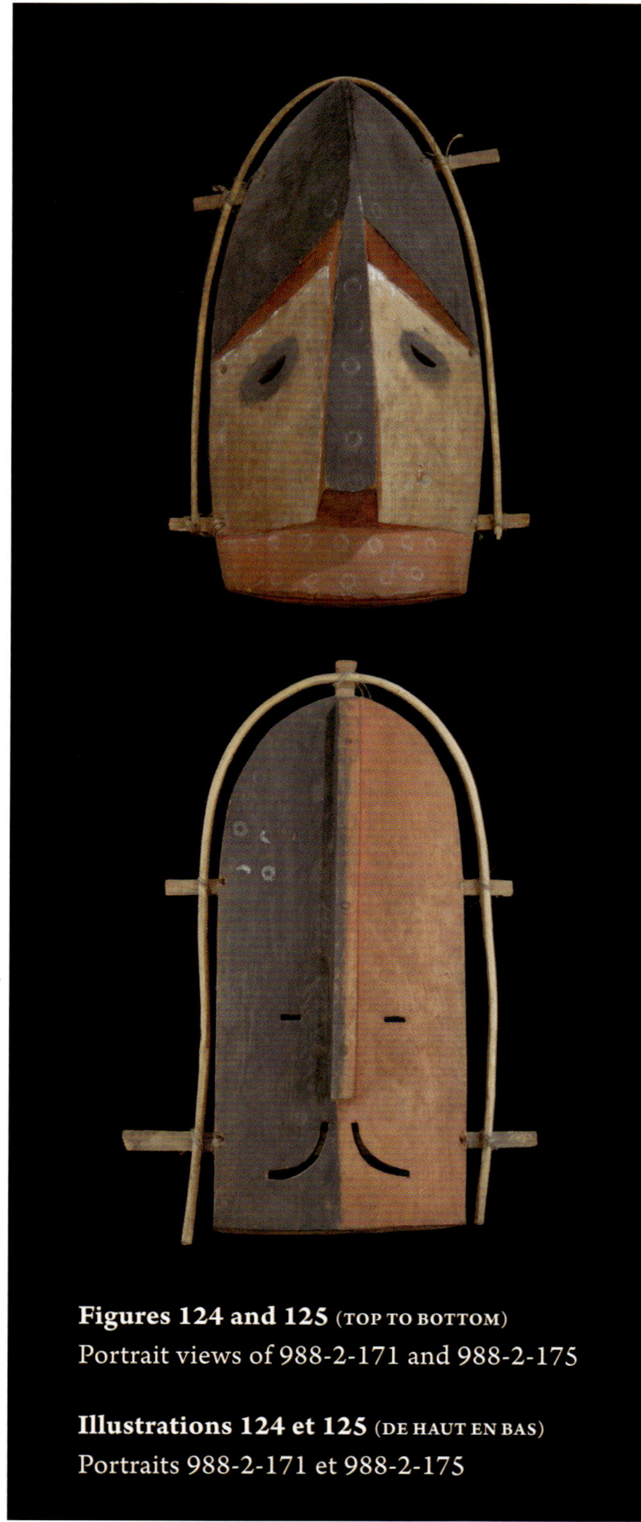

Figures 124 and 125 (TOP TO BOTTOM)
Portrait views of 988-2-171 and 988-2-175

Illustrations 124 et 125 (DE HAUT EN BAS)
Portraits 988-2-171 et 988-2-175

Snub-Nosed One

Whenever I descend I want to go down into the ocean's
    water.
Why is that one, my helper, crying down there?
My mask is trembling for the game that will be caught.

DANCE. During the first part, he walks into the *qasgiq* with
the mask and stands on his knees by the door, dancing with
rattles in one hand. When the second part starts he stands up
with his back to the audience. When the words of the second
part start, he turns around and goes around the *qasgiq*, looking at each person separately. He [words unclear] the door
and goes around again, dancing heavily in front of each seat,
and then exits.

Kuyauq—Big-Nosed One/Thankful Person
988-2-175

SONG.

Kuyauq

Naryam giinarua'a kana'I puyulegnun caulartuq.
Llam'ek gui aciwa'aqama amigenitua.
Man'a-kiq atkuk all'uku.
tugca'aryukua (aimqaryukua)

Big-Nosed One/Thankful Person

Naryam mask, below the volcano turned to face it.
From the Universe I come down without skin.
This one coat put it on.
I thought somebody grabbed me.

DANCE. He dances during the first part, his back to the
audience. During the second part he faces the audience, turning around from time to time while going once around the
qasgiq.

Angalangyak—Good Mask
No Mask Known

Chuyallik—The Big-Lipped One
No Mask Known

SONG.

(collected in Eagle Harbor, March 25, 1872)

Angalangyak

Nani una mingraka agayulluku kananisuq c'iami agaiullaku?

Nanai una agayuka nani una agayulluk kaninituk c'iami
pitarkanun Agayulluku?

Ayrutam aguya agauni yulara anguiagnun.

Good Mask

Where is your mask that you carried from below that you
danced with on the tide flats?

Where are these two masks that you danced with for the
game to be caught?

From the stars he keeps taking off his mask to the warriors.

DANCE. These two masks dance together beforehand, and
then they enter together to sing the second line.

Angun—Old Man

988-2-168

Akrillria—Voyager

988-2-205

SONG 1.

Angun

Nani una ikayuqa?

Aguhnaaqa, kanani?

Ken'ami pitarkanun aguhnaaqa?

Old Man

Where is my helper?

Will I find him down there?

Who should I take the catch to?

SONG 2.

Akrillria

Nallumawimnek llang'arcama (nuyarat) quagkut
kayakuwanka.

(Cayami) Ken'ami tuqumawimni inarngawimni agellrianga
gui ken'am puyuakun

unaagun.

Voyager

I did not know where I woke up.

They hide those ones I am really afraid of.

The tide flats where he was dead,

I laid down.

I went through the smoke of the tide flats down below.

Ituryullria—One Who Arrived

No Known Mask

SONG.

Ituryullria

Kana'i taiwika ikayuqa takuyaru imam ima'i ketllia takuyaru
taiwika.

Ageng'arpet ikayuqa agwika nallumaan kena'm kat'um
ul'urwia kan'a.

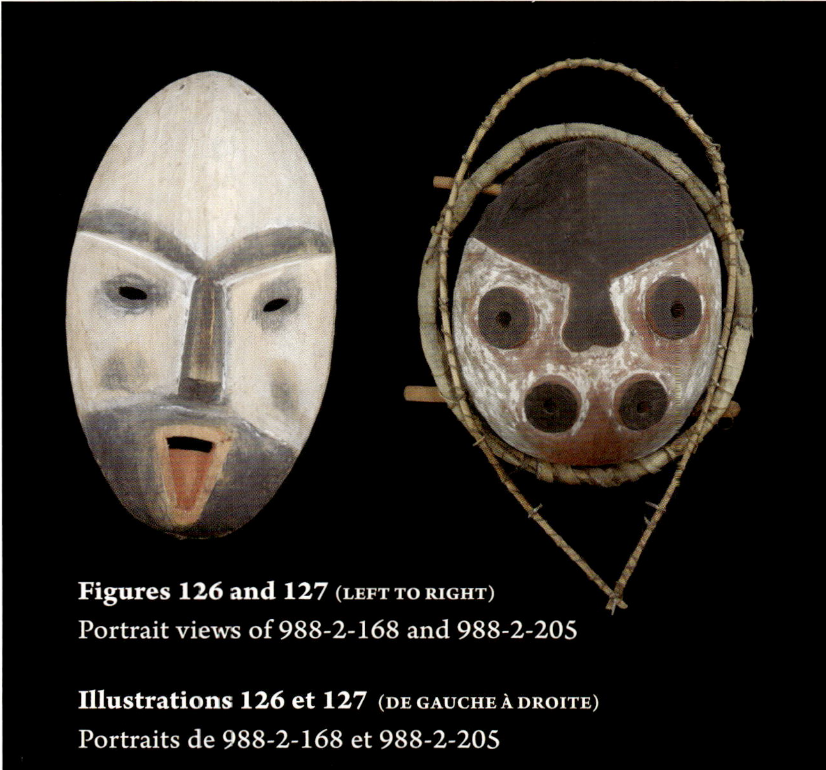

Figures 126 and 127 (LEFT TO RIGHT)
Portrait views of 988-2-168 and 988-2-205

Illustrations 126 et 127 (DE GAUCHE À DROITE)
Portraits de 988-2-168 et 988-2-205

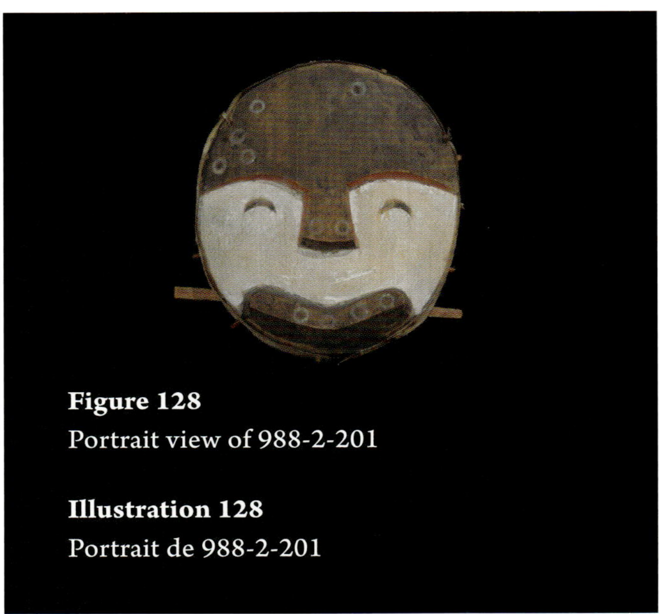

Figure 128
Portrait view of 988-2-201

Illustration 128
Portrait de 988-2-201

Naken ikayuma ug'um agutakut (?) Itert'shnaarpet qungah-
naarpet ciinuna kiugna.
Qungaquraarluten qangiq augkut lliilertet qayait
ketgwartai.
Naken ikayuma taitakut lliilert'hnek iiyullrianek.

One Who Arrived

Helper spirit look at the way you came from, the ocean in
front of you.
Helper spirit if you go where you are going, you won't know
who is the one who came here.
Helper spirit where are they taking us? When they went in
they dressed up like those ones over there.
Those dancers were dressed up for a long time and called
out to put them out in front.
Helper spirit where did the dancers who whirled about take
us to?

DANCE. During this dance in the back of the *qasgiq* two
people are seated playing on the drum in a corner. Between
them a man sits wearing a kamleika of bear and around his
head a reindeer skin aureole. When they sing the first part of
the song he flies in the air. He is held back by a rope, always
coming back to the same place. At some point he jumps from
the slanted upper part of the *qasgiq* and exits. Meanwhile, the
second song is sung. When it is over, he shows up with the
mask. Two men are in the corner next to the door, also with
an aureole. The three of them dance together.

Yuaulik—Searcher

988-2-201

SONG.

Yuaulik

Qaiciina-gua ikayuaqa unani cing'urcaa unani cing'unilnga
kia'ut agutamken llam ima'i iquanun.
Natgun maagun ag'it iluakun agumuukuk cauyang'arpetek
kiugna (takuyaru)

Searcher

Why helper spirit was he pushing me down there? I was not
pushing.
He is taking you North to the Universe's end.
From where, this way, go inside the two are playing. Even if
you two play drums answer me and go look at it.

DANCE. The two of them[359] dance sitting on their knees,
moving from right to left, turning to one side and then to the
other. During the second part they stand up and dance with
a heavy motion [word unclear] around the *qasgiq*.

Yuilria—Voyager

No Known Mask

SONG.

Yuilria

Atagwa ikayuqa engluqa takuyaru
Imam ima'I tangirnaa pitarkanun sulalarwika.
Una'I ken'am asgurt'stai tang'rhniq'gki
Pitarkanun sulalaquut pitarkirnia'amken.

Voyager

My good helper go check on my house.
At the ocean where they get food, where they ask for it,
He watched those over there going against the current.
Keep on asking where they get food and I will keep on
    bringing you some.

LEGEND. They say this mask told the man mentioned above while he was sleeping, "If you cannot kill anything, do not worry. I will provide you with a successful hunt."

DANCE. The mask wearer enters the *qasgiq* with an aureole around his face and dances during the first song. Meanwhile the mask is hung by a string and swings from one side of the *qasgiq* to the other. He steps forward asking where the mask is. When they start the second song, he seizes the mask with his teeth and dances.

Agut'lik—Translation Unknown
988-2-189

Agut'liksiinaq—Larger Agut'lik
988-2-152

Igyuyrtulik—Searcher
988-2-190

Igyuyrtuliksiinaq—Larger Searcher
988-2-159

LEGEND. (associated with four masks, collected on Afognak Island, April 10, 1872):

They say that these two masks represent some men who lived in a cave in a place very far away where the stream was very strong.

During one trip a man called Kugulak reached a place (in the North) where a large number of men lived. He went back often and for a while he spent the winter there, and the summer in other places. One day he got the idea to bring back these two masks to show his fellow citizens how the men were [word unclear]. On his way home he killed the first men on a baidarka he encountered and [word unclear]. In the same manner he killed two more men he met in the woods. Hence the masks show a man and a baidarka.

There were two men that drew masks in a large *qasgiq* who were natural brothers. They lived there for a few years.

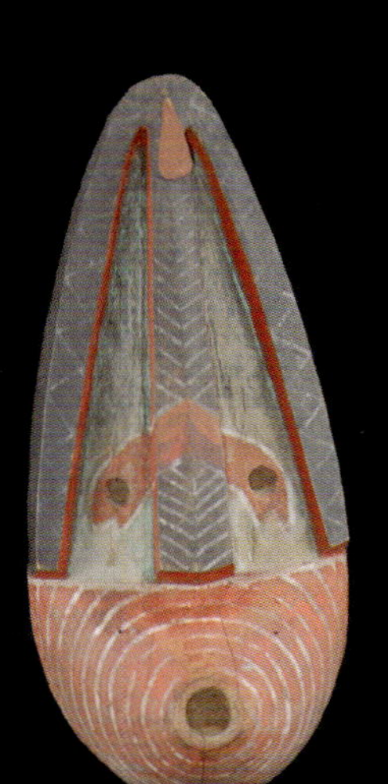
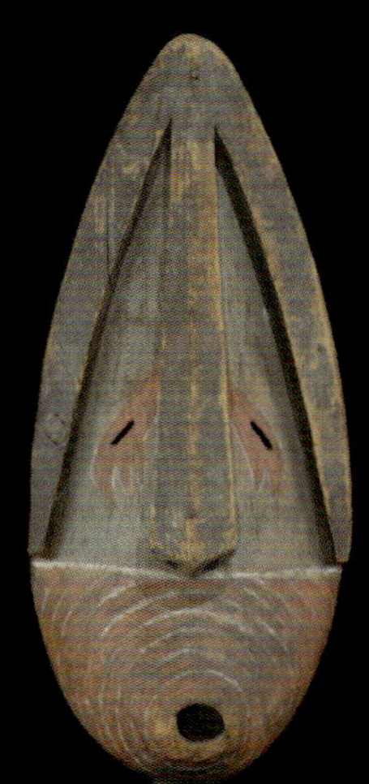
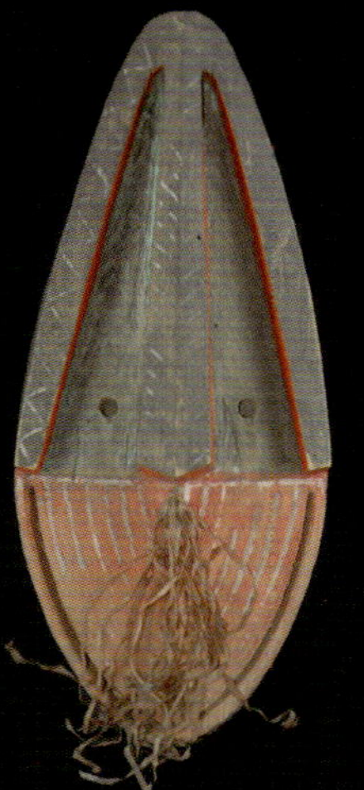
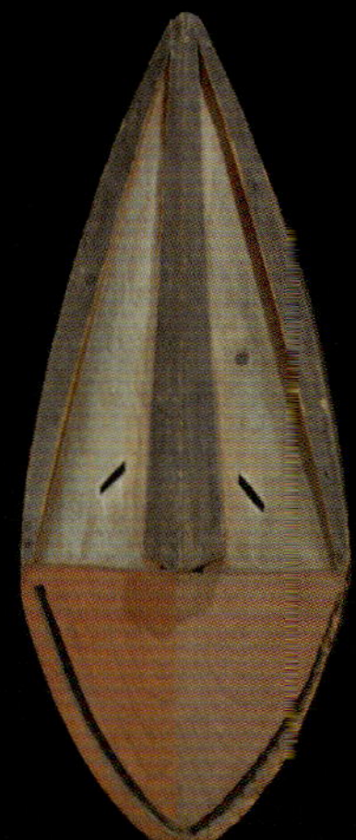

Figures 129, 130, 131, and 132 (LEFT TO RIGHT)
Portrait views of 988-2-189, 988-2-152, 988-2-190, and 988-2-159

Illustrations 129, 130, 131, et 132 (DE GAUCHE À DROITE)
Portraits de 988-2-189, 988-2-152, 988-2-190, et 988-2-159

One day another man arrived who was their brother. One of the two in the *qasgiq* seized him and said he was going to kill him. The other said he should not do it; that he was his natural brother. He made a vague reply then attempted to kill him again. The other, once more, reproached him. Since his brother could not make up his mind, he told him that if he really wanted to kill him, it would be better to take him by the sea and expose him. So they did. Having covered him with a parka they exposed him on a rock by the sea. The brother who was still very young started crying. Soon he heard a human voice asking him why he was crying. He turned around but did not see anyone and started crying again. Once again the voice spoke and asked why he was crying. He turned around again and saw a bird standing next to him. This bird was Kugulak who had turned into a bird. He asked him if he was hungry, then gave him a piece of seal. He told him he would take him as his companion and he would go with him where he lived in the North. Then he told him to put his head in a parka and made circles around him while blowing (a specific type of whistle used by shamans). They flew away and soon landed at the top of a mountain. There he gave him some food. They went on like this until they reached the settlement where Kugulak lived. There he saw his dwelling, a large rock filled with various animal skins. There they [word unclear]. When the summer returned Kugulak said that he should now go back to his settlement. Then they flew to the first mountain and Kugulak told his companion to pick some wild raspberries, because he said, "Here it is summer but where we are going it is fall." They flew like this from mountain to mountain, resting at each. Then they reached a mountain near the settlement where the brother and uncle who had tried to kill him lived. There they saw on the sea a number of baidarkas. It was the season of games and they were about to dance with the masks mentioned above. Kugulak told his companion that his brother and uncle who had meant to kill him lived there. Then they seized a bow and arrows that he [word unclear], and he told him, "Now you are going to fly over the *qasgiq*. Your brother is on the right side of the door, your uncle on the left side."

When they heard the first sounds of the drum, he took off and landed on the *qasgiq*. The *qasgiq* shook instantly and the two inside were startled and stopped moving. Then he entered the *qasgiq* through the upper hole and started dancing. As soon as he reached the *qasgiq* floor, the grass withdrew and the light went toward a corner. He danced around the *qasgiq* and at some point showed the raspberries he had brought. As he was asked where he lived, he replied "on the mountain." Then they shot some arrows at him, but he was invulnerable and the arrows glided over his body. He immediately took his bow and arrows and sent one straight to his brother's heart and another to his uncle.

The mentioned bird wearing a costume was the author *urcmpedu*.

The mentioned settlement is Agnalik on Afognak Island, facing Marmot Island.

The rock on which he was exposed is located between the two islands and is called Chashuarlik.

From there they flew over to the [word unclear] of Kodiak and there he started dancing with his mask on. His companion flew away and was never seen again.

A song and dance for Igyuyrtulik and Igyuyrtuliksiinaq appear above earlier in this appendix.

Kagukuak—Man Who Comes Back
No Known Mask

LEGEND. A man once was in a *baidarka* which capsized at sea. He had a mother. He lived at sea for so long that kelp started growing on his head. One day, while they danced in a settlement, he came out of the sea and brought this mask. He entered the *qasgiq* holding it in his hand. At once the grass crawled to the back of the *qasgiq* and the lamp to a corner. The air in the *qasgiq* was filled with the smell of the kelp from the beach (no one recognized him). In the *qasgiq* he saw his mother and father. Since they asked if he knew anything about their son who had capsized at sea a few years earlier, he set the mask on the floor near the lamp and went out, back to the sea.

Agiyashik—Translation Unknown

No Known Mask

LEGEND. They were two and had united their [word unclear] in the shape of lightning.

There were two poor young women who did not have anything to eat. The inhabitants of their settlement fed them in turns, but soon tired of it and sent them away. They wandered for a long time until on a stormy day, they flew out and met the thunder and lightning.

DANCE. When they enter the *qasgiq* everyone in the back wonders whom to give them. If someone has an inner illness, they are given away. The masks then lay him down on a bed of *lavtak*. Having prepared everything ahead of time inside their sleeves (blood, bowels, etc.), they pretend to open him up in different places. Then blood runs and they eat a little from the bowels and flesh hidden inside their sleeves. Soon after they leave. No singing, no drum.

Allayak—Different, Not Like Us or Stingy/ Greedy One (Male)

988-2-194

Allayak—Different, Not Like Us or Stingy/ Greedy One (Male)

71.1881.21.28

Allayak—Different, Not Like Us or Stingy/ Greedy One (Female)

988-2-193

LEGEND. (Associated with all three masks, collected in Karluk, February 6, 1872):

They say that at the beginning in the West there was a people which lived in evil. At the end the Llam Sua [supreme being] destroyed them and soon [word unclear] their appearance again, as bears [word unclear] the other men (they were men and women). As the animals were more and more necessary, he created them. And if the men killed them and considered them useful, then he made even more.

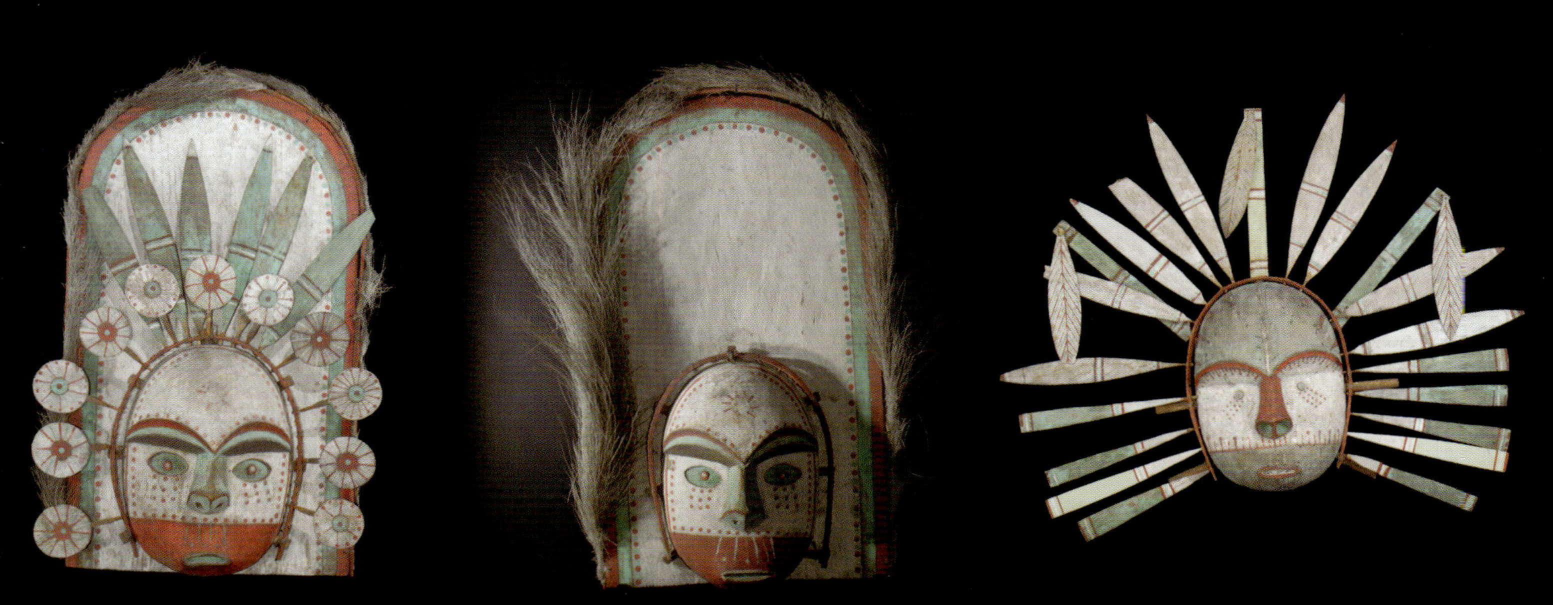

Figures 133, 134, and 135 (LEFT TO RIGHT)
Portrait views of 988-2-194, 71.1881.21.28, and 988-2-193.

Illustrations 133, 134, et 135 (DE GAUCHE À DROITE)
Portraits de 988-2-194, 71.1881.21.28, et 988-2-193.

Chants de masques

Traduction et transcription : Jeff Leer et Sven D. Haakanson Jr., aidés de Nick Alokli, Mary Haakanson et Florence Pestrikoff

Alphonse Pinart ne s'est pas contenté de collecter des masques sugpiat, il a aussi consigné les noms, les chants et les danses associés à certains d'entre eux[348]. Ses notes établissent le lien qui existait entre les sculptures et les croyances sugpiat, comme le font les rares informations dont nous disposons en langue alutiiq. Malheureusement, ses écrits s'avèrent très difficiles à déchiffrer et à traduire[349]. Pinart notait ses observations en plusieurs langues, le français, le russe, l'alutiiq, le latin et l'anglais. De plus, l'alutiiq étant une langue de tradition orale et non écrite, Pinart a transcrit les mots de vocabulaire alutiiq phonétiquement, en utilisant l'alphabet cyrillique russe pour reproduire les sons. La traduction de ses notes manuscrites effacées par le temps impliquait de maîtriser le français, le russe et l'alutiiq, et de faire appel à des personnes qui parlent couramment l'alutiiq pour interpréter le sens des mots. Certains mots alutiiq enregistrés par Pinart en 1872 sont soit inconnus de la langue courante alutiiq d'aujourd'hui, soit ils ont plusieurs sens possibles. Trois Anciens qui parlent couramment la langue alutiiq, Nick Alokli, Mary Haakanson et Florence Pestrikoff, ont travaillé avec nous avec toute leur énergie pendant plusieurs mois pour élaborer les traductions des chants, des danses et des légendes de masques que nous présentons ici, mais aussi pour donner des noms aux masques qui apparaissent dans

le catalogue et dans l'exposition « Giinaquq: Like a Face » *(voir chapitre 4)*. Nous avons soumis chacune des traductions à plusieurs relectures jusqu'à ce que toute l'équipe chargée du projet (locuteurs alutiiq, linguiste et anthropologues) soit satisfaite du résultat. En tant que traductrice, éducatrice et professionnelle de musée, Céline Wallace a fourni la transcription des notes françaises de Pinart, en reprenant ses propres mots sans apporter de correction à la langue française du XIXe siècle qu'il employait. Comme on le voit, les traductions présentées ici ne constituent pas une reprise de celles proposées par Desson[350], mais une nouvelle tentative d'interprétation des notes de Pinart.

Nous fournissons pour chaque masque toutes les informations disponibles *(tableau 1)*, comprenant généralement un nom et un chant. Ces textes traduisent en alphabet romain les mots de la langue alutiiq que Pinart a transcrits phonétiquement en utilisant l'alphabet cyrillique[351]. Les versions anglaise et française sont réalisées à partir de cette traduction alutiiq. Nous avons, à certains endroits, ajouté de la ponctuation pour faciliter la compréhension. Les mots qui apparaissent en italique sont ceux qui n'ont pu être traduits. Enfin, lorsque c'est possible, nous fournissons les versions anglaise et originale française des notes de Pinart concernant les danses et les légendes qui accompagnent certains masques. Pinart a généralement écrit ces notes en français, aussi nous ne proposons pas de traduction en alutiiq pour celles-ci.

Les textes associés aux masques, qui sont répertoriés ci-dessous, respectent l'ordre dans lequel les masques

Tableau 1. Textes qui accompagnent les masques selon les notes de terrain de Pinart

Nom alutiiq-Nom français	N° de catalogue	Chant	Légende	Danse
Shugashat-Traduction inconnue (F)[a]	988-2-179			
Shugashat-Traduction inconnue (M)[a]	988-2-185		1	2
Shugashat-Traduction inconnue (M)[a]	71.1881.21.31			
Payulik-Celui qui apporte la nourriture	988-2-169	1		1
Igyuyrtulik-Chercheur	988-2-190			
Igyuyrtuliksiinaq-Très grand chercheur	988-2-159	1	1	1
Unartuliq-Protecteur/Talismana[b]	988-2-199	1		1
Unnuyayuk-Voyageur nocturne	988-2-195	1	1	1
Chumliiq-Le premier[c]	988-2-172	1	1	1
Ingillagayak-Celui qui annonce le temps[c]	988-2-198	1	1	1
Agu'lik-Large masque	988-2-200	1	1	1
Shalgayak-Marchand	Aucun	1		1
Ashigik-L'idiot/Celui qui a de la chance	988-2-202	1		1
Nallumalik-Celui qui ne sait pas	988-2-204	1		1
Pugumalria-La Femme qui a pris	D47–13–75[d]	1		1
Nakirnalik-Celui au nez retroussé	988-2-171	1		1
Kuyauq-Celui au grand nez/Personne reconnaissante	988-2-175	1		1
Angalangyak-Bon Masque[e]	Aucun			
Chuyallik-Celui aux grosses lèvres[e]	Aucun	1		1
Angun-Vieil hommee	988-2-168	1		
Akrillria-Voyageur	988-2-205	1		
Ituryullria-Celui qui est arrivé	Aucun	1		1
Yuaulik-Chercheur[b]	988-2-201	1		1
Yuilria-Voyageur	Aucun	1	1	1
Agut'lik-Traduction inconnue	988-2-189			
Agut'liksiinaq-Très grand Agut'lik	988-2-152		1[f]	
Kagukuak-L'homme qui revient	Aucun		1	
Agiyashik-Traduction inconnue	Aucun		1	1
Allayak-Différent, pas comme nous (M)[g]	988-2-194			
Allayak-Différent, pas comme nous (M)[g]	71.1881.21.28		1	
Allayak-Différent, pas comme nous (F)[g]	988-2-193			

Notes:

(F) = Féminin ; (M) = Masculin

Le nombre de textes reportés dans ce tableau ne correspond pas au nombre total de textes que nous présentons, car certains masques partagent la même danse ou la même légende.

a. Ces masques partagent une légende.

b. Ces masques dansaient ensemble. Nous avons une seule danse pour les deux masques.

c. Ces masques faisaient leur entrée dans le *qasgiq* en même temps et dansaient ensemble. Ils partageaient une danse.

d. Ce numéro de catalogue plus ancien provient de l'inventaire de la collection Pinart réalisé au musée de l'Homme en 1947. Bien que Lot-Falck présente une illustration de ce masque dans son article publié en 1957 (planche 5), il est aujourd'hui introuvable.

e. Ces masques dansaient ensemble. Ils partageaient une danse.

f. Igyyrtulik-Chercheur partage cette légende.

g. Au dos de ces masques, Pinart a inscrit le mot « Allayak ». Selon sa prononciation, ce mot peut vouloir dire « différent, pas comme nous » en alutiiq ou « celui qui est pingre » ou « celui qui est cupide » (Haakanson). Les notes de Pinart associent aussi le mot « Kygumartaq » à la légende qui accompagne la version féminine de ce masque. En alutiiq, il signifie « qui a les jambes arquées ».

apparaissent dans le journal tenu par Pinart. Dans l'ensemble, cet ordre correspond à celui de la présentation des chants associés aux masques, transcrits par Pinart au cours de ses voyages dans les villages sugpiat, en particulier Eagle Harbor. Il convient de remarquer qu'il décrivit un certain nombre de danses et de légendes qui les accompagnent sous forme de notes prises de retour à Kodiak, après avoir visité des villages. Dans cette partie de son journal, il donne une seconde liste de chants associés aux masques, mais dans un ordre différent de celui où les couplets avaient été enregistrés auparavant[352]. Il complète cette liste à l'aide d'annotations qui résument les légendes et les descriptions de danses. Dans la présentation ci-dessous, nous réunissons les textes associés à chacun des masques. Lorsque nous la connaissons, nous indiquons l'origine des informations, c'est-à-dire le nom de la communauté auprès de laquelle Pinart les a collectées.

Lorsque c'est possible, nous présentons aussi les textes associés aux masques en même temps que leurs numéros de catalogue *(tableau 1)*. Le tableau montre que nous avons pu relier les textes à un ou plusieurs masques de la collection du Château-Musée, en nous appuyant sur les inscriptions placées au dos de certains masques par Pinart, ainsi que sur les informations fournies par le catalogue. À l'inverse, les textes qui n'ont pas de numéro de catalogue ne sont associés à aucun masque connu qui nous soit parvenu (ex. : Chuyallik-Celui qui a de grosses lèvres). Il est possible que le texte soit associé à un masque non identifié de la collection, ou bien à un masque que Pinart n'a pas collecté. Dans certains cas il semblerait que Pinart ait collecté des textes de masques sans y avoir associé aucun objet.

Le lecteur remarquera que certains masques sont associés à plusieurs groupes de légendes et de danses *(tableau 1)*. Dans ce cas nous indiquons quel groupe de textes présente des informations associées aux masques. Enfin, certains masques portent des noms identiques. Bien que chaque masque possède un nom alutiiq distinct, deux des masques portent un nom alutiiq qui signifie « Chercheur », et deux autres un nom qui signifie « Voyageur ». Ces répétitions du même nom ne sont pas surprenantes si l'on considère que ce sont des noms qui évoquent les thèmes du voyage et de la chasse, récurrents dans les chants de masques sugpiat. Les noms attribués aux masques sur ces thèmes étaient probablement très répandus. Il se peut aussi que ces noms indiquent une relation qui existe entre les masques, ou représentent un personnage précis récurrent dans le panthéon sugpiaq. Comme le souligne Desson, il arrive que des masques de style similaire portent le même nom dans la collection Pinart, pour indiquer qu'il existait des liens entre deux personnages, l'un masculin et l'autre féminin[353].

Pour conclure nous ajouterons que malgré les difficultés rencontrées lors de la traduction de ces textes en plusieurs langues, ce processus a contribué à redécouvrir leur signification alutiiq. Un exemple nous en est donné par l'interprétation que proposent les Anciens du mot *ikayuqa*. En russe ce mot est d'abord devenu *d'yavol*, soit diable. Cependant, les Anciens et le Dr. Leer l'ont traduit de l'alutiiq à l'anglais par *helper spirit* (esprit bénéfique). Cette différence change considérablement le sens du chant dans lequel *ikayuqa* apparaît et l'interprétation que nous pouvons en faire aujourd'hui.

Shugashat—Signification inconnue
988-2-179 (F), 988-2-185 (M), 71 1881 21 31 (M)

Danse 1. Quand l'individu qui le porte entre dans la casine [*qasgiq*]³⁵⁴ il tient en mains avec les castagnettes un javelot à baleine la pointe duquel est formée d'un os humain ; il avance jusqu'au milieu de la casine et menace ceux qui assistent quand le kashak se lève et s'interpose. Celui qui porte ce masque est considéré comme une espèce de diable ; il ne mange rien après pour vingt jours ; il porte une parka faite de peaux de perroquets de mer [macareux].

Danse 2. (associée à la légende ci-dessous, collectée sur l'île d'Afognak le 25 janvier 1872) :

Large masque qui était supposé venir de la mer : l'individu qui le portait arrivait dans la casine avec un (flapper) dans la bouche.

Il présente le coude premièrement du côté droit puis du côté gauche mettant la main sur le rein opposé, puis court en avant.

Pendant ce temps deux hommes et une femme battaient le [tambour] et l'homme portant le masque chantait.

U-gu-u, o-go, ugu-u. Ils le craignaient beaucoup.

Légende. (associée aux deux danses ci-dessus, collectée sur l'île d'Afognak le 25 janvier 1872) : La légende pour ce masque court ainsi : un jour pendant qu'ils étaient à danser dans la casine une femme qui ne craignaient pas demanda pourquoi durant les jeux ils n'allaient pas sur le rivage : seule alors elle alla en tenant à la main une lance de bois (une pour sécher le poisson) et aussitôt elle vit sur la mer une couleur rouge comme du feu et de cela apparurent deux hommes et une femme : les deux hommes avaient sur la tête Kaddaka et la femme seulement ses cheveux. La femme tenait dans la bouche une main humaine. Ils s'approchaient de plus en plus et bientôt étaient sur la berge : la femme qui était sortie de la cabine tenait en avant cette lance de bois se disposant à se défendre : les trois personnages sortirent de l'eau se dirigeant vers les montagnes : ils tombèrent et à leur place ne fut plus trouvées que des squelettes : des ventres seulement était encore [mot illisible] et gonflé comme une vessie. Peu après ils se relevèrent et volèrent vers les montagnes : un homme alors sortit de la casine après eux et bientôt retourna et les trois formes aussi : ils ne restèrent pas longtemps à la casine et bientôt disparurent entièrement.

Payulik—Celui qui apporte la nourriture
988-2-169

Chant.

Payulik

Ikayuqa alingenilu unani.
Agutamken ugwit puyuatni.
Unani agutamken.

Celui qui apporte la nourriture

Toi qui m'aides, n'aies pas peur là en bas.
Je vais grimper jusqu'à la fumée des rochers aux phoques.
Je t'y emmène.

Danse. Ce masque arrivant dans la casine tient un large kantag Beruske de chikcha et sarana (lys sauvage) : durant le temps que le chant dure il danse en tenant ce large kantag : quand le chant cesse il passe le kantag aux vieillards d'abord et les invite à manger : ensuite aux jeunes etc.

Igyuyrtulik—Chercheur
988-2-190

Igyuyrtuliksiinaq—Très grand chercheur
988-2-159

Chant.

Igyuyrtulik

Nani imna sun'arausqaq nani imna iwa'anaaqa.
Piani-kiq iwa'inaaqa wiyullriani iwa'inaaqa imna.

Chercheur

Où est-il ce jeune, ce petit, où est celui que je tente de chercher ?

Peut-être que, tout là-haut, celui que j'essaye de trouver est
parmi ceux qui tourbillonnent de-ci de-là.
C'est celui-là que j'essaye de trouver.

Danse. Il entre dans la *barabara*[355] recherchant dans tous
les rangs et sans trouver ce qu'il désire : après avoir regardé
partout et la chanson terminée il sort.

Une légende pour ces masques est présentée plus bas,
qu'ils partagent avec Agut'lik et Agut'liksiinaq.

Unartuliq—Protecteur/Talisman
988-2-199

Chant.

Unartuliq

Qaiciina-gua ikayuaqa unani cing'urcaa unani cing'unilnga
kia'ut agutamken llam ima'i iquanun.
Natgun maagun ag'it iluakun agumuukuk cauyang'arpetek
kiugna (takuyaru).

Protecteur/Talsiman

Pourquoi celui qui aide poussait-il là en bas ? Je ne poussais
pas.
Il t'emmène vers le Nord au bout de l'univers.
D'où part-on ? Par ici. Rentre les deux sont en train de
jouer.
Même si tu joues de la musique, réponds-moi et vas vérifier
où ça en est.

Danse. Les deux[356] dansent assis sur les genoux et font mouvements de droite à gauche, se tournant tantôt d'un sens
tantôt de l'autre : pendant la seconde partie ils se lèvent et
dansent avec un lourd mouvement et se [mot illisible] autour
de la casine.

Unnuyayuk—Voyageur nocturne
988-2-195

Chant.

Unnuyayuk

Qai-ciin ikayuqa, qai-ciin ulurakllua ?

ugwini pitarkirnaya'amken.
Agellrianga llam iluakun ; ikayuma kat'um tayatannga.
Aciqallrianga lliilerwiatnum gui.

Voyageur nocturne

Comment cela se fait-il, esprit bénéfique, comment se fait-il
que tu sois appréhensif envers moi sur les rochers aux
phoques ?
Je t'apporterai du gibier à capturer.
J'ai traversé les antres de l'univers ; toi mon aide, ça ça m'a
fait peur.
Je suis descendu là où ils créent du mouvement.

Légende. Ils disent que ce masque dans un voyage regarda
sur le diable et que la moitié de son visage fut brûlé à cette
vue.

Danse. Il entre dans la casine et se place dans le coin gauche,
le dos tourné à l'audience et danse assis sur ses genoux durant
la première partie du Chant. quand le second chant commence il se lève et toujours le dos tourné il se place au milieu
et saute par bonds et disparaît.

Chumliiq—Le premier
988-2-172

Chant.

Chumliiq

Engluqa pia'i, llam'i pia'i engluqa pia'i nallumaan.
Macam-qaa pik'um tunua pia'i ?
Ikayuqa, ulla'amken piaken tailaryaaqamken.
Ikayuqa, nunam pik'um waamestainek.

Le premier

Ma maison là-haut, dans l'univers là-haut, tu ne le sais pas.
Est-elle derrière le soleil ? Est-elle derrière celui qui est
là-haut ?
Mon aide, je viens vers toi depuis là-haut. Je continue à
essayer de venir.
Mon aide, les terres de celui-là n'ont pas besoin d'acteurs.

Légende. La légende dit que un homme un jour désirant se faire chaman se retira dans les bois et là il commença à devenir inspiré et vit le diable et se transforma en ce masque.

Danse. Ils arrivent à deux avec le masque suivant : le suivant se place dans le coin gauche caché par une *Kamlak* : celui-ci le veille et danse sur ses genoux pendant le premier chant. À la fin du premier chant, il se lève et tenant les castagnettes il danse par bonds autour de la casine tantôt tombant, se relevant et dansant à nouveau.

Ingillagayak—Celui qui annonce le temps
988-2-198

Chant.

Ingillagayak

Naken-gwa ikayuqa tailuni itrumaakut ikaymta
Ug'um itrumaakut.
Ikayuqa ugna wiiyuhnaarpet.
Unani ken'ami ken'am puyuani ikayuqa
Tan'rniq'gkia nani tang'rniq'gkia pitarkirnaamken tawamia.

Celui qui annonce le temps

De là où vient mon aide à l'instant, il entre et arrive sur
    nous notre aide
Il est entré et venu sur nous.
Mon aide devrions-nous faire tournoyer celui-ci ?
Là [dehors] en bas dans les replats sablonneux de la marée
    basse, dans la fumée du replat de la marée basse mon
    esprit bénéfique
Regarde-moi, quelque part, regarde-moi je vais capturer du
    gibier par là-bas.

Légende. Ils disent que quand le précédent[357] était dans le bois, celui-ci (le diable) le vit de loin et se mit à rire : et ce masque le représente.

Danse. Il danse autour, prend les castagnettes danse et se met à rire : il danse autour s'arrêtant au milieu entre les quatre coins et saute : pendant ce temps l'autre masque s'en va.

Agu'lik—Large Masque
988-2-200

Chant.

Agu'lik

Awalaryaaqaqua ken'ami gui.
awalaryaaqaqua, puyulegnun gui.
Ikayuqa aguhnaamken utakinermen ?
tus'uhnaamken pitarkanun ?
tuqumallriamun aguhnaamken ?

Large Masque

Je regarde maintenant où dans les replats sablonneux de la
    marée basse.
Je regarde maintenant où dans la fumée.
Mon esprit bénéfique devrais-je te mener au lieu d'attente ?
Devrais-je te mener auprès du gibier qui va être capturé ?
Devrais-je te mener auprès de ceux qui sont morts ?

Légende. Ils parlent de *rep hodyporu* (diables) [mots illisibles] ces masques là, dit le diable, sont les morts.

Danse. Celui qui porte ce masque entre dans la casine avec une parka d'*monopurka* [peau de macareux] les bras à l'intérieur de la parka et une manche sur la couche de devant et une autre sur le derrière : ainsi il danse sur place durant la première partie et ensuite il sort et quand il rentre il danse de nouveau, mais cette fois autour dansant lourdement et sur place à chaque avance qu'il fait.

Shalgayak—Le marchand
(on ne lui connaît pas de masque)

Chant.

Shalgayak

Piaken ima aciwartua qiuryat pingkut nunaqlliitnek
    iiyurwimnek aciwartua.
Lliilerwim sun'arai iiyuryuklluki aciwartua.

Le marchand

Je descends des aurores boréales, le territoire où ils vivent,
je tournoie lors de ma descente.
Je descends de là où vous mettez les petits, qui pensaient
qu'ils tournoient de-ci de-là.

Danse. (Chasseur de l'aurore boréale) Il arrive en scène avec une *kamleïka* les manches retroussées et les bras couverts de sang : la partie basse du masque est aussi couverte de sang : il danse autour de la casine en se retournant vivement.

Ashigik—L'idiot/Celui qui a de la chance
988-2-202

Chant.

Ashigik

Ikayuqa-gua taigua llam keg'um nallumasqaan-gua
tuuyaraaten.
Nallumasam pik'um ullakengama puyulget unkut neryugai.

L'idiot/Celui qui a de la chance

J'arrive mon esprit bénéfique. Celui qui vient de l'Univers
ne sait pas, veut te prendre.
Celui-là là-bas, celui-là, même s'il vient me voir, ceux là-bas
dans la fumée, il les veut.

Danse. Ce masque est longtemps avant d'entrer et on chante la première partie pendant qu'il n'est pas encore entré : il entre avec un aide auquel la figure est couverte et qui chante la seconde partie.

Nallumalik—Celui qui ne sait pas
988-2-204

Chant.

Nalylgalan

Taingama taiqua ken'aq kan'a kewegluku.
Taiwimkun taigua tawa'i.
Qasgimen iterngama giinaruama uniqaqaanga.

Celui qui ne sait pas

Je suis venu, je suis venu, qui est-ce, soulève-le.
D'où je suis venu, je suis venu. Alors voilà.
Quand je suis entré dans la maison des hommes, mon
masque me quitte sans arrêt.

Danse. L'homme entre sans masque avec seulement des plumes d'aigle sur la tête : le masque est suspendu et va d'une partie de la casine à l'autre : au moment donné il saisit le masque avec les dents, mais la ficelle qui le tient n'est pas détaché et après avoir dansé pour quelques moments, le masque s'envole de nouveau et vole de tout côté, tantôt tombant sur le sol, etc.

Pugumalria—La Femme qui a pris
D47-13-75[358]

Chant.

Pugumalria

Agwika ageng'arpet ikayuqa agwika
Nallumaan imam ima'i tagirnaa pugumawika.
Agellrianga llam iluakun ikayuqa tang'rhniqia.

La femme qui a pris

Où je vais, tu vas esprit bénéfique.
Tu ne sais pas d'où je viens, de la mer ou de la terre.
Pendant mon voyage à travers l'univers, esprit bénéfique
protège-moi.

Danse. Quand il arrive dans la casine il s'agenouille sur le seuil de la porte : il a une petite *ypupunkd* [lampe à huile]. On le couvre d'un large sac fait de peau d'ours : durant le temps qu'il est couvert il brûle à l'intérieur des racines de bouleau (la jeune racine) et aussitôt une fumée intense se fait dans la casine : on ôte le sac et il se tient toujours sur les genoux, le visage peint et sur la tête des plumes d'aigle : dans une main il tient la lampe sur le devant et les castagnettes de l'autre sur le derrière : il sort et quand on chante la seconde partie il saute sur le masque et danse lourdement autour de la casine.

Nakirnalik—Celui au nez retroussé

988-2-171

Chant.

Nakirnalik

Atra'aqama atraryukua imam ima'i iluakun maagun.
Cagua kat'um ikayuma unani qia'utek'agu ?
Giinaruaqa pitarkanun uulegtuq.

Celui au nez retroussé

À chaque fois que je descends je veux m'immerger dans
　l'eau de l'océan.
Pourquoi donc celui-là, mon aide, pleure-t-il par là-bas ?
Mon masque tremble pour le gibier qui va être capturé.

Danse. Il entre avec le masque dans la casine et se tient
pendant la première partie sur les genoux près de la porte
et danse tenant dans la main les castagnettes : quand la
seconde partie commence il se lève tournant le dos à l'audi-
toire : quand les paroles de la seconde partie commencent il
se retourne et fait le tour de la casine regardant chaque personne séparément : il se tourne [mot illisible] elle la porte
et fait le tour de nouveau en dansant lourdement à chaque
place et sort.

Kuyauq—Celui au grand nez/Personne reconnaissante

988-2-175

Chant.

Kuyauq

Naryam giinarua'a kana'I puyulegnun caulartuq.
Llam'ek gui aciwa'aqama amigenitua.
Man'a-kiq atkuk all'uku.
tugca'aryukua (aimqaryukua)

Celui au grand nez/Personne reconnaissante

Masque *Naryam*, sous le volcan tourné de façon à lui faire
　face.
De l'Univers je descends sans peau.

Ce manteau mets-le.
Je croyais que quelqu'un m'avait agrippé.

Danse. Il danse pendant la première partie le dos tourné à
l'audience ; dans la seconde partie il fait face à l'audience se
retournant de temps en temps et fait le tour de la casine.

Angalangyak—Bon Masque

On ne lui connaît pas de masque

Chuyallik—Celui qui a de grosses lèvres

On ne lui connaît pas de masque
Chant (collecté à Eagle Harbor, le 25 mars 1872) :

Angalangyak

Nani una mingraka agayulluku kananisuq c'iami
　agaiullaku ?
Nanai una agayuka nani una agayulluk kaninituk c'iami
　pitarkanun Agayulluku ?
Ayrutam aguya agauni yulara anguiagnun.

Bon Masque

Où est ton masque que tu portais par le dessous avec lequel
　tu as dansé sur les replats sablonneux de la marée basse ?
Où sont ces deux masques avec lesquels tu as dansé pour
　faire capturer le gibier ?
Depuis les étoiles il ne cesse d'ôter son masque pour les
　guerriers.

Danse. Ils dansent ensemble avant. [. . .] Ils entrent ensemble. [Chant]

Angun—Vieil homme

988-2-168

Akrillria—Voyageur

988-2-205

Chant 1.

Angun

Nani una ikayuqa ?

Aguhnaaqa, kanani ?
Ken'ami pitarkanun aguhnaaqa ?

Vieil homme

Où est mon aide ?
Vais-je le trouver ici bas ?
À qui devrais-je apporter la prise que j'ai faite ?

Chant 2.

Akrillria

Nallumawimnek llang'arcama (nuyarat) quagkut
    kayakuwanka.
(Cayami) Ken'ami tuqumawimni inarngawimni agellrianga
    gui ken'am puyuakun
unaagun.

Voyageur

Je ne savais pas où je me trouvais au réveil.
    Ils se cachent ceux-là dont j'ai vraiment peur.
Les replats de sable laissés par la marée où il était mort,
    Je me suis allongé.
J'ai traversé la fumée des replats de sable là en bas.

Ituryullria—Celui qui est arrivé

On ne lui connaît pas de masque

Chant.

Ituryullria

Kana'i taiwika ikayuqa takuyaru imam ima'i ketllia
    takuyaru taiwika.
Ageng'arpet ikayuqa agwika nallumaan kena'm kat'um
    ul'urwia kan'a.
Naken ikayuma ug'um agutakut (?) Itert'shnaarpet qunga-
    hnaarpet ciinuna kiugna.
Qungaquraarluten qangiq augkut lliilertet qayait
    ketgwartai.
Naken ikayuma taitakut lliilert'hnek iiyullrianek.

Celui qui est arrivé

Esprit bénéfique regarde le chemin que tu as emprunté
    pour venir, l'océan est face à toi.
Esprit bénéfique si tu vas où tu as l'intention d'aller, tu ne
    sauras pas qui est celui qui est venu ici.
Esprit bénéfique où nous emmènent-ils ? Quand ils sont
    entrés ils se sont habillés comme ceux-là là-bas.
Ces danseurs étaient habillés depuis longtemps et ont
    appelé pour qu'on les mette devant.
Esprit bénéfique où les danseurs qui tournoyaient par là
    nous ont-ils emmenés ?

Danse. Dans cette danse sur le fond de la casine sont assis les deux qui jouent sur le [tambour] dans un coin : entre eux est assis un homme vêtu d'une *kamleïka* [en intestin] d'ours, autour de la tête il a une auréole de peau de renne : quand ils chantent la première partie de la chanson il vole retenu par la corde et toujours revient à la même place : à un moment donné il saute de la pente supérieure de la casine et sort : pendant ce temps on chante le second chant et quand il est terminé il apparaît avec le masque. Dans le coin attenant à la porte se trouvent deux hommes ayant aussi l'auréole et ils dansent tous les trois ensemble.

Yuaulik—Chercheur

988-2-201

Chant.

Yuaulik

Qaiciina-gua ikayuaqa unani cing'urcaa unani cing'unilnga
kia'ut agutamken llam ima'i iquanun.
Natgun maagun ag'it iluakun agumuukuk cauyang'arpetek
    kiugna (takuyaru)

Chercheur

Pourquoi l'esprit bénéfique me poussait-il là en bas ? Je ne
    poussais pas.
Il t'emmène vers le Nord au bout de l'univers.
D'où part-on, par ici, rentre les deux sont en train de jouer.
    Même si vous jouez tous les deux du tambour répondez-
    moi et allez voir.

Danse. Les deux[359] dansent assis sur les genoux et font mouvements de droite à gauche, se tournant tantôt d'un sens tantôt de l'autre : pendant la seconde partie ils se lèvent et dansent avec un lourd mouvement et se [mot illisible] autour de la casine.

Yuilria—Voyageur

On ne lui connaît pas de masque

Chant.

Yuilria

Atagwa ikayuqa engluqa takuyaru
Imam ima'I tangirnaa pitarkanun sulalarwika.
Una'I ken'am asgurt'stai tang'rhniq'gki
Pitarkanun sulalaquut pitarkirnia'amken.

Voyageur

Mon bon aide va voir si tout va bien chez moi.
Près de l'océan où ils obtiennent la nourriture, où ils en
    demandent,
Il a surveillé ceux-là qui allaient contre le courant.
Continue de demander où ils obtiennent leur nourriture et
    je continuerai à t'en apporter.

Légende. Ce masque disent-ils, durant le sommeil de cet homme parlé plus haut, lui dit : si tu ne peux rien tuer, ne t'en inquiète pas, je te fournirai de [la] chasse.

Danse. Celui qui porte ce masque entre dans la casine et une auréole autour de la face et il danse durant le premier Chant. durant ce temps le masque est suspendu par une ficelle et oscile d'un côté de la casine à l'autre : il s'avance en demandant où se trouve le masque et au moment où ils commencent le second chant il saisit le masque avec ses dents et danse.

Agut'lik—Traduction inconnue

988-2-189

Agut'liksiinaq—Très grand Agut'lik

988-2-152

Igyuyrtulik—Chercheur

988-2-190

Igyuyrtuliksiinaq—Très grand chercheur

988-2-159

Légende. (associée à quatre masques, collectée sur l'île d'Afognak le 10 avril 1872) :

Les deux masques ils disent sont des hommes qui vivaient très loin là où le courant est très fort et dans une caverne.

Un homme nommé Kugulak dans un voyage arriva à cet endroit (dans le nord), là où vivent un grand nombre d'hommes : il retourna souvent et pendant un certain temps il passait là l'hiver, et à d'autres endroits l'été : un jour il eut l'idée de rapporter ces deux masques pour montrer à ses concitoyens comment étaient les hommes se [mots illisibles] : arrivant chez lui il tua les hommes qui se trouvaient dans la première *baïdarka* [mots illisibles] qu'il rencontra et [mots illisibles]. De même il tua deux hommes qu'il rencontra dans le bois : de là sur le masque était un homme et une *baïdarka*.

Il y avait dans une grande casine deux hommes frères naturels là où ils dessinaient les masques : ils étaient là pour quelques années : un jour arriva un autre homme frère des précédents. L'un des deux dans la casine le saisit et dit à l'autre qu'il allait le tuer : celui-ci dit qu'il ne devait pas le faire, qu'il était son frère naturel : il fit une vague réponse et de nouveau il voulait le tuer : l'autre de nouveau fit le même reproche et comme l'autre ne se décidait pas il lui dit que s'il désirait fortement le tuer il vaudrait mieux le prendre et l'exposer sur le bord de la mer. Ainsi ils firent et l'ayant revêtu d'une parka ils l'exposèrent sur un roc près de la mer. Le frère qui était encore très jeune se mit à crier : il entendit bientôt une voix humaine lui demandant pourquoi il pleurait : il se retourna et ne vit personne et se remit de nouveau à pleurer : de nouveau la voix parla et lui demanda pourquoi il pleurait il se retourna de nouveau et vit un oiseau se tenant près de lui : (cet oiseau était Kugulak) qui s'était transformé en oiseau et il lui demanda s'il avait faim : il lui donna alors un morceau de phoque et il lui dit qu'il le prendrait avec lui comme compagnon et qu'avec lui il irait là où il vivait dans le nord : il lui dit alors de mettre la tête dans une parka et tournant autour de lui et soufflant (une espèce particulière de sifflet employé par les chamans) il s'envola avec lui et bientôt il se reposa sur le sommet d'une montagne et là même il lui donna à manger : ils allèrent ainsi jusqu'au settlement où Kugulak vivait : là il vit la demeure était un large roc rempli de différentes peaux d'animaux. Là ils [mots illisibles] : quand l'été revint Kugulak dit qu'il devait maintenant retourner à son settlement : ils volèrent alors sur une première montagne et Kugulak dit à son compagnon de recueillir des baies de framboises sauvages car dit-il ici il est été mais là où nous allons il est automne. Ils volèrent ainsi de montagne en montagne se reposant quand ils arrivèrent à la montagne près du settlement où le frère et l'oncle qui avait voulu le tuer vivaient là ils virent sur la mer un nombre de *baïdarkas* : c'était le temps des jeux et ils étaient sur le point de danser avec ces masques ci-dessus. Kugulak dit à son compagnon que là vivait son frère et son oncle qui avaient voulu le tuer : ils prirent alors un arc et des flèches qu'il [mots illisibles] et il lui dit alors : tu vas maintenant t'envoler sur la casine : ton frère se trouve sur le côté droit de la porte, ton oncle sur le côté gauche : quand ils entendirent les premiers sons du tambour il s'envola et vint se poser sur la casine : aussitôt la casine trembla et les deux l'intérieur furent saisis et cessèrent tout mouvement : il entra alors dans la casine par le trou supérieur et se mit à danser : aussitôt qu'il arriva sur le terrain de la casine, l'herbe qui s'y trouvait se retira d'elle-même et la lumière dans un coin : il dansa autour de la casine et à un certain moment il montra les framboises qu'il avait apportées et comme on lui demandait où il vivait il répondit, sur la montagne : ils alors tirèrent sur lui des flèches, mais il était invulnérable les flèches glissèrent sur son corps : aussitôt il prit son arc et ses flèches et envoya une droit au cœur de son frère et l'autre à son oncle.

L'oiseau parlé comme déguisement était l'auteur (*urcmpedu*)

Le settlement parlé est [Agnalik] sur l'île d'Afognak vis-à-vis de [Marmot Island]

Le roc sur lequel il fut exposé est situé entre les deux îles et s'appelle [Chasuarlik]

De là ils s'envolèrent sur la [mots illisibles] de Kodiak et là il se mit à danser avec son masque : son compagnon s'envola et plus jamais il ne le revit.

Un chant et une danse qui se rapportent à Igyuyrtulik et Igyuyrtuliksiinaq apparaissent plus haut dans cette Annexe.

Kagukuak—L'homme qui revient
On ne lui connaît pas de masque

Légende. Un homme un jour étant dans une *baïdarka* chavira en mer : il avait une mère. Il vécut longtemps à la mer et sur sa tête poussèrent le varech – un jour, pendant qu'ils étaient à danser dans un settlement il sortit de la mer et rapporta ce masque : il entra dans la casine le tenant à la main : aussitôt l'herbe se retira sur le fond de dans la casine et la [lampe] dans un coin. L'air dans la casine devint empreint aussi de cette odeur que répand le varech sur la plage (personne ne le reconnut). Il vit dans la casine sa mère et son père et comme ils demandaient s'il savait quelque chose de leur fils qui avait chaviré en mer quelques années auparavant il déposa le masque près de la lampe et sortit et retourna à la mer.

Agiyashik—Traduction inconnue
On ne lui connaît pas de masque

Légende. Ils étaient deux et avaient uni les [mot illisible] en forme de la foudre.

Étaient deux jeunes filles, elles étaient pauvres et n'avaient rien à manger : les différents habitants du settlement les nourrissaient à leur tour : mais bientôt ils se fatiguèrent et les mirent à la porte : ils errèrent longtemps et un jour par une tempête elles s'envolèrent et trouvèrent le tonnerre et les éclairs.

Danse. Quand ils arrivent dans la casine chacun dans le fond se demande qui donner : alors quelqu'un s'il a quelque maladie intérieure ils le donnent : les masques alors l'étendent sur un lit de *lavtak* et ayant d'avance le tout préparé dans leur manche (sang, boyaux etc.) ils font semblant de l'ouvrir en différentes places, alors le sang coule et ils mangent un peu de boyaux et des chairs qu'ils tiennent cachés dans leur manche – et peu après ils s'en vont : point de chant, point de tambourin.

Allayak—Différent, pas comme nous ou Celui (celle) qui est pingre/cupide (masculin) 988-2-194

Allayak—Différent, pas comme nous ou Celui (celle) qui est pingre/cupide (masculin) 71.1881.21.28

Allayak—Différent, pas comme nous ou Celui (celle) qui est pingre/cupide (masculin) 988-2-193

Légende. (associée aux trois masques, collectée à Karluk le 6 février 1872) : Au commencement disent-ils il y avait dans l'Ouest un peuple qui vivait dans le mal : à la fin le *Llam Sua* [Être suprême] les détruisit et bientôt [mots illisibles] de nouveau furent leurs apparences, d'ours [mots illisibles] les autres hommes (ils étaient hommes et femmes) – au fur et à mesure que les animaux étaient nécessaires il les créait et si les hommes les tuaient et regardaient comme utiles, alors il en faisait davantage.

Notes

Chapter 1

1   Throughout this volume we use the term *Sugpiaq* (pl. Sugpiat) to refer to the Native people of the central Gulf of Alaska coast—including Prince William Sound, the outer Kenai Peninsula, the Kodiak archipelago, and the Alaska Peninsula. In contrast, we use the term *Alutiiq* to refer to their language. The word *Sugpiaq* comes from the Alutiiq language. It is a traditional self-designator meaning "real person" or "just like a person." The word *Alutiiq* comes from the word *Aleut*, a term broadly applied to Alaska Natives by Russian traders meaning "coastal dweller." In their language, the Native people of Kodiak say the word *Aleut* as "Alutiiq." This is now a common designator for the language of the Sugpiaq people, which is also known as Sugt'stun or Pacific Yupik (Clark 1984:195–196; Leer 1982:4; Woodbury 1984:53).

2   Black 1992.

3   Crowell 1992:20.

4   Knecht 1995.

5   Crowell et al. 2001.

6   Knecht 2000; Pullar 1992.

7   Desson 1995.

8   Pinart 1871–1872.

9   Lot-Falck 1957.

10   Today, masks collected by Alphonse Pinart in Alaska are part of two French museum collections. The largest portion of Pinart's assemblage, with seventy Sugpiaq masks, belongs to the Château-Musée of Boulogne-sur-Mer. An additional seven Sugpiaq masks are part of the collections of the Musée du quai Branly in Paris. Together, these seventy-seven pieces are the subject of this publication. There were once additional Sugpiaq masks in Pinart's assemblage (Lot-Falck 1957), but an incomplete initial inventory has obscured the total number and a few have been lost. We do not consider the fourteen masks Pinart collected from the Aleutian Islands held by the Château-Musée, or a potential Sugpiaq mask in the Musée du quai Branly collections whose provenance we consider uncertain (71.1959.29.1) (Musée du quai Branly 2007).

11   Pinart 1871–1872.

12   Birket-Smith 1953; Davydov 1977; Gideon 1989; Lisianski 1968; Merck 1980; Shelikhov 1981; Voznesenskii in Liapunova 1994.

13   Archaeological data on late prehistoric Sugpiaq culture come predominantly from the well-preserved collection of the Karluk One site, a settlement at the mouth of the Karluk River that yielded wooden artifacts (Donta 1994; Knecht 1995).

14   Birket-Smith 1953:72; Davydov 1977:164.

15   Today, Sitka spruce (*Picea sitchensis*) covers Shuyak and Afognak islands and the northern tip of Kodiak Island. Biologists believe these forests began growing about one thousand years ago (Heusser 1960:55).

16   Knecht 1995:554–555.

17   Birket-Smith 1953:73.

18   Knecht 1995:439.

19   Birket-Smith 1953:73; Knecht 1995:452, 461.

20   When Pinart visited Kodiak, Sugpiaq carvers were working with crooked-knives, implements fitted with a curved steel blade (Birket-Smith 1953:73–74; Crowell and Lührmann 2001:41).

21   Knecht 1995:661.

22   Knecht 1995:430–431.

23   The following description focuses on carved wooden masks. See Black 1991 for a discussion of bentwood hunting hats as a form of masks and Liapunova (1994:187–188) for examples of

Sugpiaq masks created with woven rings of grass. Additionally Desson (1995:70–71) notes that festival face painting was a form of masking.

24 Knecht 1995:665.

25 This piece is part of the Koniag, Inc. collection from Karluk One stored at the Alutiiq Museum.

26 Liapunova 1994:Figure 10-4.

27 Knecht 1995:675.

28 Jordan 1994:157; Liapunova 1994:198–199.

29 Davydov 1977:111; Liapunova 1994:192–196.

30 Davydov 1977:154–155; Gideon 1989:40; Merck 1980:100; Shelikhov 1981:56.

31 Knecht 1995:671.

32 Desson 1995:397–398; Krech 1989:Figure 44; Liapunova 1994:192, 193.

33 Knecht 1995:668.

34 Jordan 1994:164.

35 Knecht 1995:668.

36 Liapunova 1994:Figures 10-6 through 10-11.

37 Davydov 1997:110; Pinart 1871–1872.

38 Merck 1980:103–104; Russell 1995.

39 Davydov 1977:153, 187; Merck 1980:104.

40 Knecht 1995:545. See Desson 1995 for an analysis of the colors used in Sugpiaq mask design.

41 The antiquity of masks on Kodiak is not known, although archaeological assemblages from settlements dating to the Late Kachemak tradition include examples over one thousand years old (Clark 1970:111; Jordan and Knecht 1988:253; Steffian 1992:163).

42 Pinart, 1871–1872.

43 Jordan 1994:163.

44 Fienup-Riordan 1996:59.

45 Fienup-Riordan 1996:69–70.

46 Birket-Smith 1953:124; Crowell and Leer 2001:196.

47 Crowell and Leer 2001:Figure 195; Krech 1989:Figure 44a; Liapunova 1994:Figure 10-8.

48 Crowell and Leer 2001:196.

49 Jordan 1994:Figure 9-7c; Knecht 1995:667–668.

50 Masks also represented other kinds of spirits—including both devils and helping spirits as suggested by some of the original mask names in the Pinart collection (Crowell and Leer 2001:196).

51 Birket-Smith 1953:120; Crowell and Leer 2001:191–192.

52 Birket-Smith 1953:34.

53 Hunt 2000:55.

54 Birket-Smith 1953:42.

55 Birket-Smith 1953:108; Davydov 1977:107–111; Gideon 1989:94; Merck 1980:100; Shelikhov 1981:55.

56 Davydov 1977:154; Gideon 1989:40; Merck 1980:100; Shelikhov 1981:55.

57 Chechenev in Desson 1995:130.

58 Davydov 1977:109. See Desson (1995:136–158) for a discussion of the duties of a *kas'aq* and how these duties differed significantly from those of a shaman.

59 Gideon 1989:45; Holmberg 1985:60.

60 Davydov 1977:108, 184; Desson 1995:176.

61 Shelikhov 1981:55.

62 Davydov 1977:107.

63 Gideon 1989:45.

64 Gideon 1989:46; Merck 1980:101.

65 Desson 1995:177–178.

66 Gideon 1989:46.

67 Davydov 1977:184; Shelikhov 1981:55.

68 Birket-Smith 1953:109; Crowell and Leer 2001:204; Shelikhov 1981:81.

69 Liapunova 1994:176.

70 Pinart 1871–1872; Desson 1995:540–544 also summarizes this festival.

71 Crowell 1992:20. British collector Hugh Cecil Lowther, the Fifth Earl of Lonsdale, collected two Sugpiaq masks at the close of the nineteenth century. Lowther traveled on the Alaska Peninsula and Kodiak Island in the winter of 1888–1889 but took few notes. The provenance of these masks and the context from which he collected them is unknown (Krech 1989:124–125, and Figure 44a,b).

72 Crowell 1992:21.

73 Black 2004:256.

74 Partnow 2001:86–88, 90.

75 Partnow 2001:164.

76 Mishler 2003:119; J. Mulcahy 2001:23; Partnow 2001:163.

77 Mishler 2003:119.

78 Crowell and Leer 2001:216.

79 Mishler 2003:112–116.

80 Mishler 2003:117.

81   J. Mulcahy 2001:25–26.

82   Knecht 1995:658; Mishler 2003:117.

83   Mishler 2003:119.

84   J. Mulcahy 2001:26; Crowell and Leer 2001: 215–218.

85   Mishler 2003:119.

86   Mishler 2003:119; J. Mulcahy 2001:99.

87   Koniag, Inc. 2008.

88   Haakanson 2002.

89   Koniag, Inc 2008:90.

90   Laronde's position as curator of the Château-Musée is equivalent to that of a museum director in the United States.

91   Steffian 2006.

92   Lot-Falck 1957; Rousselot et al. 1991.

93   *Two Journeys: A Companion to the Giinaquq: Like a Face Exhibition*, a publication created jointly by Koniag, Inc. and the Alutiiq Museum for the opening of the exhibition in Kodiak, tells the story of the artists' trip to France (Koniag, Inc. 2008).

94   On his way back to Alaska in 2006, Haakanson stopped in Paris to visit the Musée du quai Branly with Will Anderson and Perry Eaton. Here they were able to photograph seven additional Sugpiaq masks collected by Pinart. These photographs appear in Chapter 4 with the gracious permission of the Musée du quai Branly.

95   See Crowell et al. 2001 for a summary of the *Looking Both Ways* project—a community-based, multivocal approach to interpreting Sugpiaq identity with museum collections.

96   Rousselot et al. 1991.

97   Koniag, Inc. 2008.

98   Pullar 1992.

99   Davis 1984:201. Additionally, Davis notes that cultural anthropologists did not begin studying Sugpiaq life ways until 1960.

100   Birket-Smith 1953.

101   Crowell et al. 2001; Steffian 2006.

102   See discussion of defining sacredness in Haakanson and Steffian 2004:156.

Chapter 2

103   Désveaux 2002; Desson 1995; Lot-Falck 1957:5–44 and plates I–IX.

104   This article is the synthesis of the research led by Géraldine Bouterin and Anne-Laure Gerbert, both Master I students at the Ecole du Louvre (Ministère de la Culture, Palais du Louvre, Paris): Bouterin 2007 and Gerbert 2007. These studies have received help and support from Sarah Frioux-Salgas and Angèle Martin, in charge of the Archives of the Musée du Quai Branly, to whom we are very grateful. In this article they are presented with the addition of annotations and invaluable corrections by Sarah Froning, doctor in Anthropology and Gwénaël Guigon, commissionned by the Musée du Quai Branly to research the history of their Arctic collections. In addition, this research as a whole has benefited from the priceless help and availability of the Alutiiq Museum and from the work group from the Kodiak archipelago involved in the preparation of the exhibition *Giinaquq: Like a Face*. We are particularly grateful to Helen Simeonoff, the team at the Alutiiq Museum gathered around its director Sven Haakanson Jr., his colleague Amy Steffian, and Perry Eaton, artist and important player in the Alutiiq cultural renewal, for their helpful hypotheses, information, and readiness to share archives.

105   Leunens 2003:74, thanks to Edmond Truffaut's indication, a member of the office of the friends of the Château-Musée of Boulogne-sur-Mer.

106   Boulogne-sur-Mer is currently the number-one fishing port in France and is one of the top European centers of seafood processing and trading (350,000 tons of seafood pass in transit through it each year, consiting mainly of salmon). Its fishing activity is particularly focused on herring.

107   Around the same period Boulogne-sur-Mer was also the birthplace of other intellectuals who marked the research and museum fields in France: Egyptologist Auguste Mariette (1821–1881); ethnologist Ernest-Théodore Hamy (1842–1908), founder of the Musée d'Ethnographie du Trocadéro; literary critic Charles-Augustin Sainte-Beuve (1804–1869); and curator and medievalist Désiré Louis Camille Enlart (1862–1927) to name a few. Most of these researchers have also given collections to the museum of their city of birth, today's Château-Musée (cf. Lottin 1983:198).

108   Bancroft n.d. 39:622. Americanist, archaeologist, ethnologist, historian, and linguist Charles-Etienne Brasseur de Bourbourg (1814–1874) was one of the founders of Americanism in France in the nineteenth century. For more information, see Dias 1991:230.

109   Alphonse Louis Pinart Archives, BANC MSS Z-Z 17:10.

110   During this first trip he collected objects that never made it back to France because the train transporting his packages was robbed by a group of Apache Indians (Pinart, July 4, 1872).

111   On April 27, 1871, Pinart boarded the schooner *Amanda Ager* in the direction of the Aleutian Islands, then fared from Nushagak to the Yukon River on board the schooner *John Bright*. Later his journey from Unalaska to Kodiak lasted two months and was

completed by *qayaq*. He returned via Sitka to San Francisco on May 21, 1872.

A variety of sources, archives, and scientific works enable us to go over the stages of Pinart's Alaskan journey:

- Pinart's own accounts and notes: Pinart 1873b:561–570; Pinart 1871–1872.

- Summaries of Pinart's archives: Gerbert 2007:11–15 and Appendix LIV:140–141); Robert-Lamblin 1976:19–27; Torres 2002:25–30.

- On the American side after the essential study by Parmenter 1966, Dominique Desson's works (Desson 1995) and Helen Simeonoff's personal research (Simeonoff 2007:2) have contributed to today's new development of some differing views about the visited places and the means of transportation.

Anne-Laure Gerbert covers Pinart's journey in detail. Here is the list of places mentioned chronologically in her work: Shumagin Islands, Unalaska, Bristol Bay, Ugashik Bay, Kuichak Bay, Iliamna Lake, Nushagak Lake, Walrus Islands, Hagemeister Island, Kuskokwim Bay, Nunivak Island, Bering Strait (to the Siberian shores), Norton Sound (Fort St. Michael), Unalaska, Unga, Illiuliuk, Belkofski, Unga, Port Delaroff (visit to the funerary cave of Aknanh), Shumagin Islands, Cape Kuprianoff, Archipelago Thiers [*sic*] Pinart Bay, Chignik Bay, Cape Kouniliun [*sic*], Cape Nunakhalkhak [*sic*], Katmai, Shelikhoff Strait, Kodiak Island (St. Paul Harbor, winterage), visit to Afognak and Shuyak Islands, journey back to Unalaska, San Francisco, trip along the United States Pacific Coast and from Canada to Sitka, Alaska.

112   Pinart, July 4, 1872.

113   Cf. Pinart 1873. Traveling with his own funds, Pinart did not receive any support from the "official" collecting system set up in 1874 by the Travel and Scientific and Literary Missions Commission of the Public Instruction Ministry. This commission offered grants aimed at encouraging travelers and promoting the shipping of regular reports and collected material packages (see also Dias 1991:163). Starting in 1882, Ernest-Théodore Hamy as the director of the new Musée d'Ethnographie du Trocadéro, founder of the *Revue d'Ethnographie*, and vice president of the Société d'Anthropologie de Paris, was in charge of the management of some of these teams and their shipments, collecting the reports, and organizing their transmission to various research societies in Paris (Dias 1991:61–63). As for Pinart he joined this system in 1878, when he received a grant from the ministry for an expedition with Léon de Cessac to Mexico and California, during which he acquired an important collection of American objects for the Musée d'Ethnographie (see Riviale 2001:351–362).

114   The spellings of the mentioned places are the ones used by Alphonse Pinart in his 1873 article (Pinart 1873c). See also Desson 1995:7–8.

115   The photographs taken by Pinart during his stay in Alaska are conserved at the Bibliothèque Nationale de France, in Paris (Département des cartes et plans, fonds de la Société Française de Géographie): reference BN C.Pl. Sg Wf 159. Forty-eight in number, they inform us on the way Pinart elected to organize his trip to the Aleutian Islands and the Kodiak archipelago. The pictures are of poor quality but they show landscapes, groups of people (indigenous, Creoles, and colonizers), and official and religious buildings. The original documents are available for consultation by appointment only, while the microfilms are available to any library user.

The same archival repository also conserves the only known photographic portraits of Pinart in France (microfilm references: Département des cartes et plans, fonds de la Société française de Géographie, reference number in the paper register of portraits under the name "Pinart": # 181, 1158, 1529, 1530).

The Musée du quai Branly conserves a group of photographs, donated by Pinart to the French State, representing Alaskan masks exhibited at the end of the nineteenth century at the Musée de l'Académie Impériale of St. Petersburg (masks called "Kaniagmiut Eskimo," "Koloche," and "Atka"). Sixteen frames are registered and are reproduced on the museum's website (reference numbers: PP0025992, PP0025995 to PP0026001, PP00260004, PP0026007, PP0026008, PP0026010).

116   Regarding the collection of Aleutian objects at the Château-Musée, see Pinart 1873c:573 and Pinart 1875. The second article presents some very beautiful etched illustrations of some of the collected objects.

See also the article synthesizing the scientific research led by Salabelle (2001:87–97).

The catalog of the 2002 exhibition of the Pinart collection by the Musée du quai Branly provides a detailed description of this collection composed of thirty pieces (Rousselot and Grahammer 2002:207–243).

See also the recent study by Géraldine Bouterin (2007:30–31).

117   St. Paul is the former name of the town now known as Kodiak on Kodiak Island.

118   The third chapter of Desson's doctoral thesis provides some analysis and interpretation of these songs, dances, and legends collected by Pinart at Kodiak (Desson 1995:126–265).

119   Contrary to his method when collecting immaterial elements, Pinart did not document the conditions of his collecting of Sugpiaq objects. Recent studies both in the United States and

in France were unable to identify any source from Pinart giving information regarding the exact date, place, and means of his object collecting. See notably Desson 1995:12 and Bouterin 2007:60.

120 Robert-Lamblin 1976:19. On this occasion or later on, Pinart put his Alaskan field notes in the custody of Hubert Bancroft. They remained the latter's property and are currently conserved by the University of California Berkeley library.

121 Pinart, July 4, 1872.

122 Regarding the story of Pinart's return to France and his processes as a traveler and collector according to French sources, see Rousselot and Grahammer 2002:201–205 and Gerbert 2007. These studies are notably based on the archives relating to Pinart that are conserved in various Parisian public institutions (letters and notes written by Pinart). Since the present article was written, Anne-Laure Gerbert wrote a second dissertation, focused on Pinart's career (Gerbert 2008).

123 Pinart's visits to other Alaskan collections in Europe in 1873 and 1874, (Pinart 1860–1877). He visited an ethnographic museum in Copenhagen, Denmark, in January 1873. He made a series of drawings of Alaskan objects at the Museum of Dorpta (now called Tarpu, in Estonia) in January 1873. He also made a series of drawings of Alaskan objects at St. Petersburg, Russia, at the archives of the Russian Academy of Sciences. There he drew and researched documents relating to the history of Alaska and the local languages. He also visited the Siberian Museum of the University of Helsinki in Finland and the Etholen collection in March 1873 at the Public Museum of Moscow, where he studied the Aleutian pieces. He then returned to the archives in St. Petersburg until January 1874 at least.

124 To this end, he notably purchased libraries on this theme, including one belonging to Americanist Abbé Brasseur de Bourbourg (Gerbert 2007:39). Pinart was also planning to publish three volumes about his trip to Alaska (Gerbert 2007:65). Only part of the first volume was published, covering the natural environment of Alaska; see Pinart 1873b. Regarding his published material about American languages, see Gerbert 2007:67–69.

125 Pinart communicated this to the Ministry of Public Education in a letter dated February 11, 1878, conserved in the Archives Nationale, F17 22997, piece #1, Paris. Contrary to what was sometimes assumed, Pinart's travels, publishing, and expenses would not be the cause of his family's bankruptcy (Parmenter 1966:18).

126 In 1877, Pinart traveled for seven months on the ship *Le Seignelay*, whose mission was to collect information related to social sciences in order to prepare the world exhibition about to take place the following year in Paris. Pinart thought he would thus reach Alaska, but the destination of the ship changed and put him on the way to Oceania. A man named Paul Emile Lafontaine shared part of this journey and painted his portrait in unforgiving terms: "we learnt that this gentleman was a famous traveling professor, who had made some important discoveries in Alaska, where he had gone twice, traveling by himself on a pirogue, with Laps or Eskimo savages, feeding like them on whale oil. As for us, we could only judge his originality by the length of his hair and nails, which was indeed extraordinary. But our commander let himself be convinced of this character's merit, and he offered to take him with us to Tahiti, food and shelter provided. Mister Pinart would not accept, being obligated to go to Europe for the publication of his numerous pieces of work; but he offered the commander to take him the following year to discover the polar seas." Lafontaine's descriptions are numerous and detailed. We learn among other things that Pinart had great difficulties using a camera and that he pretended to be able to speak many languages (Lafontaine 2006).

127 Zelia Maria Magdalena Nuttal (San Francisco 1857–Mexico 1933). She married Pinart in 1880. Together they went to the West Indies, France, and Spain. Their daughter was born in 1882 in San Francisco. The couple separated in 1884, then divorced in 1885. She then started a brilliant career as an anthropologist and Mexican archaeologist, which she spent between Europe, the United States, and Mexico (Gerbert 2007:62).

128 Regarding the story of the Sugpiaq masks in the Pinart collection of the Château-Musée, see Bouterin 2007. This research notably establishes the fact that the number of Sugpiaq masks donated by Pinart to the Château-Musée in 1875 is impossible to determine based on the archival written sources explored to this day.

129 The catalog of this exhibition counts 198 numbers registered in the part "Ethnography and collections exhibited under the flat showcase glass" ("Ethnographie et collections exposées sous la vitrine plate"); 37 numbers are related to the Sugpiaq masks. Several masks can be registered under the same number (see number 183 described as a "series of masks"). It is impossible to know the exact number of Sugpiaq masks exhibited based on this document (Pinart 1872a).

130 See the transcription of Pinart's letter to the mayor of Boulogne, Auguste Huguet, "Séance du Conseil Municipal du 16 février 1875," in *Registre des délibérations du Conseil Municipal de la ville de Boulogne-sur-Mer*, conserved in the town archives of Boulogne-sur-Mer. Pinart stipulates at this occasion two conditions to his donation: "that the collection enters as such without the possibility of any single piece to be later extracted to be exchanged for anything else," and "that the objects may not be loaned for study without due permission granted by myself or by any other

authorized individual." He also gave the instruction that he might extract temporarily some objects from this collection to appear in the book about Russian America that he had started writing. The mayor accepted his donation and expressed the wish to reorganize the museum and expand its galleries to better fit the collection (transcription of the letter from the mayor of Boulogne to Alphonse Pinart, Séance du Conseil Municipal du 16 février 1875," in *Registre des délibérations du Conseil Municipal de la ville de Boulogne-sur-Mer*, conserved in the town archives of Boulogne-sur-Mer. The museum commission also gave a favorable opinion and thanked "the country's son who picked the administrative capital of his neighborhood to conserve the result of his labor-intensive research and important discoveries" (transcription of the letter from Pinart to the mayor of Boulogne, Auguste Huguet, "Séance du Conseil Municipal du 16 février 1875," in *Registre des délibérations du Conseil Municipal de la ville de Boulogne-sur-Mer*, conserved in the town archives of Boulogne-sur-Mer). Later on, the curator of the museum of Boulogne, in a letter to the mayor, brought information regarding the future of the collection received "from Mister Alphonse Pinart, an ethnographic collection, brought back by himself from Russian America (today Alaska territory). This collection, composed of about 280 pieces, was placed temporarily in the mineralogy department and catches the attention of all the connoisseurs. I must not omit to mention that the Eskimo pieces of clothing made of skin, which are part of this collection, were infested by mites and that prior to their registration M. Duburquoy made them undergo a preparation fitting their conservation ("Séance du Conseil Municipal du 18 septembre 1976," in *Registre des délibérations du Conseil Municipal de la ville de Boulogne-sur-Mer*, conserved in the town archives of Boulogne-sur-Mer).

131   Although Félix Torres states that this donation was effected "thanks to Hamy," and the former curator of the Château-Musée, Françoise-Camille Halley-des-Fontaines-Poiret, states on her side that the tie of "mutual esteem" between the two men "resulted in" the donation by Pinart (see Torres 2002:25; Halley-des-Fontaines-Poiret 2002:187), the specific part played by Hamy in this event remains uncertain. It is true that Pinart and Hamy were tied to each other by a professional relationship, which might have been enhanced by the fact that they were from the same region. However, Hamy had similar professional relationships with many travelers and researchers at the time (Dias 1991:215; see also Sibeud 2001:187).

132   The letter of donation written by Pinart in 1875 stipulated that the collection should not be divided without the agreement of the donor, who was Pinart himself. Pinart gave this authorization at the end of 1886, but under the condition that the Trocadéro give an equal number of pieces in exchange. This exchange took over two years to be completed. It was first approved by the Château-Musée one year after Hamy's original request in August 1887. Then, the Château-Musée had to address a series of letters to Mayor Auguste Huguet asking him to authorize the decision. Huguet never did so. It was not until mid-1888 and the arrival of a new mayor, Jules Baudelocque, that the collections were finally exchanged between the two institutions, shortly after Hamy resigned from the board of the Château-Musée (Halley-des-Fontaines-Poiret 2002:189–90). We do not know to this day the exact nature of the exchanged pieces (which may have been of origin other than Alaskan).

133   The Château-Musée is currently conserving seventy Sugpiaq masks from the Pinart collection.

134   Here is the list of the various inventories of the Pinart collection of the Château-Musée of Boulogne-sur-Mer that we have identified in France:

- Alphonse Pinart, *Catalogue des collections rapportées de l'Amérique Russe (aujourd'hui territoire d'Aliaska), exposées dans l'une des galeries du Museum d'histoire naturelle de Paris (section d'Anthropologie)*, 1872.

- A mention of some masks numbered D47.13 in the *Cahier d'inventaire II des dépôts (1938-1972)* of the Ethnology research laboratory of the Musée de l'Homme (notebook accessible in digital format in the Musée du Quai Branly collections archives and documentation database).

- Descriptive index cards of the Alaskan objects turned in to the Musée de l'Homme between 1947 and 1950, compiled in 1949 by Evelyne Lot-Falck (in charge of the arctic collections at the Musée de l'Homme). They were used to put together work piece files in 1988, at the time of B. Coutancier's museum collection verification (see above). Those files are now conserved at the Château-Musée of Boulogne-sur-Mer.

- Photographic campaign in black-and-white, organized by the Musée de l'Homme, at the Château-Musée of Boulogne-sur-Mer, in 1976 (photographer: José Oster). Those photographs were later used to put together work piece files in 1988 (see below). Those files are now conserved at the Château-Musée.

- Inventory register 988.2 of the Château-Musée, compiled by the curator's assistant, Benoît Coutancier, in 1988, conserved at the Château-Musée of Boulogne-sur-Mer.

- Rousselot and Grahammer 2002:207–243.

- "Inventaire des masques sugpiat de la collection Alphonse Pinart conservés au Château-Musée de Boulogne-sur-Mer," in Bouterin 2007:Appendix VIII, pp. 17–61.

- Digitalized inventory index cards by Céline Ramio, Château-Musée, 2008.

Other inventories cover the collections donated by Pinart to the Musée d'Ethnographie du Trocadéro (now conserved at the Musée du quai Branly):

- Handwritten list by Alphonse Pinart, dated May 22, 1878, conserved at the Centre de documentation of the Musée du quai Branly: a list of the objects Pinart deposited at the Muséum d'Histoire Naturelle.

- List of objects brought back by Pinart, donated to the Musée d'Ethnographie du Trocadéro, referenced in the *Inventaire des collections du Musée d'Ethnographie (numéros 5600 à 9999)* under the numbers 81.21 (D000557).

- Descriptive index cards of the Alaskan objects in the Pinart collections conserved at the Musée de l'Homme, compiled in 1949 by Evelyne Lot-Falck (in charge of the Arctic department at the Musée de l'Homme), conserved at the Musée du quai Branly.

135   List of the temporary exhibitions the masks were loaned to since their arrival in France:

- World Exhibition of 1878 in Paris. Loan of "the whole Russian American collection" according to the "Town Council Session of December 18, 1878," in *Registre des délibérations du Conseil Municipal de la ville de Boulogne-sur-Mer*, conserved at the town archives of Boulogne-sur-Mer.

- In 1947, seventy Sugpiat, Aleutian, and Oceania masks from Boulogne were deposited, restored, and exhibited at the Musée de l'Homme in Paris (previously the Musée d'Ethnographie du Trocadéro founded by Ernest Hamy) at the occasion of the International Americanist Congress (see Letter of September 29th, 1947, File 988-FC 5 3 C, archives of the Château-Musée of Boulogne-sur-Mer). The masks in question received a deposit number ("D47.13"). They returned to Boulogne in 1950. Today, only four Sugpiaq masks in Boulogne do not bear this number.

- Other Parisian exhibitions: loan of twelve masks for the exhibition entitled *Masks*, in the annex of the Musée National des Arts asiatiques Guimet, in 1959; see diverse letters op. cit. and Perrin Olivier, *Masques* (Paris: R.M.N., 1965); exhibition *Kodiak, Alaska: The Pinart Collection Masks*, organized by the Musée du quai Branly at the Musée des Arts Africains et Océaniens, in 2002.

- Series of exhibitions of lesser extent organized in different regions of France (loan of a few masks each time): Maison de la Culture of Bourges (Region Centre) in 1964; museum of Tourcoing (Region Nord-Pas-de-Calais) in 1967; Maison de la Culture of Rennes (Region Brittany) in 1980; Château-Musée of Dieppe (Region Normandy) in September of 1980.

- Exhibition at Boulogne-sur-Mer: *Masks of Alaska (Alphonse Pinart collection)*, at the Château-Musée of Boulogne-sur-Mer, in 1970 (according to an invitation card kept in the archives of the Château-Musée of Boulogne-sur-Mer).

- The mask numbered D47.13.44 was loaned for the exhibition *Primitivism in 20th Century Art, Affinity of the Tribal and the Modern*, at the Museum of Modern Art in New York in 1984.

See also Bouterin 2007:41, 46–47, 51–52.

136   List of the restorations the masks have undergone since their arrival in France:

- In 1947, masks deposited at the Musée de l'Homme in Paris: nature of the interventions unspecified.

- Restoration carried out by restorers registered at the Musées de France: about thirty-six masks are thought to have been restored in 1958 by Jacques Bousquet, well-known restorer (in Boulogne, he notably intervened on the second most important collection of the museum, the Greek antique ceramics), in his workshop of Troyes (Region Champagne-Ardenne). The Château-Musée currently owns two gouache paintings on paper representing masks of the collection by this restorer who is giving back the objects their original colors (the masks are numbered 988-2-185 and 988-2-196). Later on two restorers, specialized in anthropological collections, who are still working today, consolidated the polychromy of a wide majority of the masks: Alain Renard in 1988, then Frédérique Vincent in 2002.

Sources: *Registre des délibérations du Conseil Municipal de la ville de Boulogne-sur-Mer*, conserved at the town archives of Boulogne-sur-Mer, and various letters extracted from the files 988-FC 5 3 F and L, archives of the Château-Musée of Boulogne-sur-Mer. See also Bouterin 2007:46, 49, 53.

Chapter 3

137   Miller 1981:1.

138   Wood Island village was a very short *qayaq* trip from Kodiak and would have been passed on Pinart's trip from Kodiak to Eagle Harbor. Ouzinkie would have been passed on Pinart's trip from Kodiak to Afognak.

139   Donald Clark, personal communication, November 24, 2008.

140   Case and Voluck 2002:47.

141   The 1867 Kodiak Parish Russian Orthodox Church records listed forty-nine Russians (Lührmann 2000:166). By 1870, the year before Pinart's arrival in Kodiak, the number of Russians listed was eleven (Lührmann 2000:167). It is possible that there were a very small number of Russians in Kodiak who were not Orthodox.

142   Case and Voluck 2002:47; Golovin lists 871 Creoles in the "Kodiak Department" in 1860 (Dmytryshyn and Crownhart-Vaughan 1979:140).

143   Black 1990:145.

144 Lührmann 2000:167.

145 Oleksa 1992:145–146.

146 Huggins 1981:41, 48.

147 Gibson 1976:93–111.

148 Holmberg 1985:41.

149 Wrangell 1980:18.

150 *Sugt'stun* means literally "to speak like a person."

151 Dauenhauer 1990:155.

152 Black 2001:60.

153 Crowell and Lührmann 2001:48; Petroff 1884:139; Holmberg 1855–1863:40.

154 Davydov 1977:151.

155 Petroff 1884:139; Holmberg 1985:39.

156 Crowell and Lührmann 2001:47.

157 Holmberg 1985:40.

158 Holmberg 1985:39.

159 Oleksa 1990:188–189.

160 *Llam Sua* literally translated means "person of the universe" (Crowell and Leer 2001:192). Birket-Smith describes *Llam Sua* as the being that had power over "not only the universe, but also the weather, the air, and even the great mystic power that permeates the world" (1953:121). Pinart recorded his perception of *Llam Sua* and translated it to "Man of Light" (Pinart 1871–1872 ms., translated by L. T. Black, August 15, 1981).

161 Oleksa 1992:124.

162 Oleksa 1992:125. The late Father Peter Kreta also explained the belief in this parallel to the author in 1991.

163 Davydov 1977:109.

164 Huggins 1981:1–2.

165 Huggins 1981:1. The Smithsonian naturalist referred to by Huggins was William H. Dall.

166 Hagan 1988:53.

167 Prucha 1975:136.

168 Case and Voluck 2002:44–46.

169 Kan 1988:510.

170 Petroff 1884:138; Holmberg 1985:38

171 Bancroft 1886:681.

172 Crowell 1997:14.

173 Davydov 1977:193.

174 Black 1988:79.

175 Fedorova 1973:193; Dilliplane 1990:131–143.

176 Fedorova 1973:196.

177 Portions of this wooden plume are still visible today.

178 Stevens 1990:193; Fedorova 1973:196.

179 Fedorova 1973:196.

180 Dall 1970:346; Black 2004:264.

181 Stevens 1990:195.

182 Dall 1970:349.

183 Gibson 1976:42.

184 Watrous 2001.

185 Black 1992:165. *Awa'uq* means "to become numb" in the Sugpiaq language. Called Refuge Rock in English, it is located just off the coast of Sitkalidak Island near the present-day village of Old Harbor.

186 Black 1992:172–173.

187 Solovjova and Vovnyanko 2002:9.

188 Black 1992:165–177.

189 Tikhmenev 1978:7.

190 Roppel 1986:4.

191 Roppel 1986:5.

192 Roppel 1986:4.

193 Hinckley 1972:126.

194 Lührmann 2000:56.

195 Naske and Slotnick 1979:62.

196 Naske and Slotnick 1979:61.

197 The Alaska Commercial Company records are housed in the University of Alaska Fairbanks, Rasmuson Library Archives.

198 Aron Crowell, Director, Alaska Office of the Arctic Studies Center, Smithsonian Institution. Personal communication, November 24, 2008.

199 Dmytryshyn and Crownhart-Vaughan 1979:153.

200 Lührmann 2000:141.

201 Mishler 2003:31–34.

202 Black 1992:165.

203 Black 2004:216.

204 Oleksa 1990:185; Elliott 1886:108.

205 Black 2004:215.

206 Oleksa 1990:185.

207 Oleksa 1990:185.

208 Oleksa 1992:145.

209   Lührmann 2000:167.

210   Lührmann 2000:51.

211   Black 1990:146.

212   Fedorova 1973:165.

213   Dmytryshyn and Crownhart-Vaughan 1979:17.

214   Elliott 1886:108.

215   Khlebnikov 1994:73.

216   Khlebnikov 1994:73.

217   Khlebnikov 1994:74.

218   Khlebnikov 1994:74.

219   Armstrong 1979:178.

220   Dall 1970:44.

221   Dmytryshyn and Crownhart-Vaughan 1979:17.

222   Black 1988:79.

223   Fedorova 1973:213.

224   Fedorova 1973:212.

225   Dmytryshyn and Crownhart-Vaughan 1979:17.

226   Dmytryshyn and Crownhart-Vaughan 1979:17–18.

227   Oleksa 1992:146.

228   It should be emphasized that there was more than one way for a person to become a Creole. One was to be of mixed Russian and Sugpiaq blood, and the other was to be educated in Russia and return to Alaska.

229   Wood 1943:204.

230   Wood 1943:204.

231   While the term "Creole" may have been on official records, many Kodiak Sugpiat were unaware of the term by the late twentieth century and were surprised to find it on the birth records of their parents and grandparents, as they had always considered themselves totally Native.

232   Wood 1943:206.

233   During the enrollment period for benefits under the Alaska Native Claims Settlement Act (ANCSA) of 1971, applicants were required to prove at least one-quarter Alaska Native blood quantum to be eligible. Most Creoles could meet this requirement but had been referring to themselves as Russians for many years in an attempt to maintain their elevated social status and to escape job and other forms of discrimination commonly practiced against Natives. Thus, when they were accepted under ANCSA many of those who had always claimed their "Nativeness" did not believe it was fair that people who had been referring to themselves as Russian should be eligible to share in the benefits. The phrase "He was never a Native until 1971" and the designation "land claims Native" became popular when referring to those who had not openly identified as Native prior to ANCSA. As time went on, however, many of the Creoles distinguished themselves in Native leadership positions and are widely accepted today as legitimate members of the Sugpiat community.

234   Khlebnikov 1973:105.

235   Khlebnikov 1994:9.

236   Fortuine 1989:200.

237   Fortuine 1989:201.

238   Fortuine 1989:201–202.

239   Khlebnikov, 1994:357–358.

240   Dall 1970:352.

241   Tikhmenev 1978:198–199.

242   Fortuine 1989:233.

243   Fortuine 1989:237. Dall claims there were seventy-five villages consolidated into seven in 1844 (1970 [1870]:341).

244   Hrdlička 1975:19.

245   Pullar 1992:186.

246   Tikhmenev 1978:200.

247   Fortuine 1989:194.

248   Fortuine 1989:207.

249   Fortuine 1989:203–204.

250   Fortuine 1989:199–208, 241, 255.

251   Fortuine 1989:203–204.

252   Russian word for "bath." On Kodiak Island it is more commonly spelled "*banya*." The traditional name is *maqiq* (Crowell et al. 2001:243).

253   Partnow 2001:257.

254   J. Mulcahy 2001:69.

255   Mishler 2003:141–147.

256   Partnow 2001:257; Davydov 1977:154–155; Knecht 1995:327–331.

257   Partnow 2001:257–258.

258   Davydov 1977:190; Crowell et al. 2001:43; Armstrong 1979:176.

259   The *qasgiq* is called a *kashim* or *Kazhim* in Russian (Gideon 1989:152).

260   Gideon 1989:40–41.

261   Morseth 1998:16.

262   Davydov 1977:190; Crowell 1997:70.

263   Lührmann 2000:49.

264   Petroff 1884:137–138.

265   Kodiak Area Native Association 1987:1; Oleksa 1987:396; L. Mulcahy 2003:86–88. *Staristaq* is the indigenized form of the Russian word *Starosta*.

266   Kodiak Area Native Association 1987:1–2.

267   Pullar 1997:173–174.

268   Only the village of Karluk on Kodiak Island chose to reorganize under the IRA. Even then they maintained much of the prior system in practice.

269   Pullar 1997:56.

270   Elliott 1886:107.

271   Gibson 1976:96.

272   Gibson 1976:97.

273   Gibson 1976:97.

274   Gibson 1976:96.

275   Petroff 1884:24–25.

276   Lührmann 2000:51.

277   Elliott 1886:115.

278   This is clearly erroneous, as records show that many tons of ice were shipped from Woody Island to San Francisco.

279   Elliott 1886:105.

280   Elliott 1886:106.

281   Elliott 1886:115.

282   Elliott 1886:106–107.

283   Gibson 1886:106–107.

284   The French word for employees, *employés*, is used in the original.

285   Porter 1893:73–74.

286   Porter 1893:74.

287   Petroff 1884:24.

288   Simon and Steffian 1994:93; Holmberg 1985:53.

289   Dall 1878:31.

290   Dall 1878:27.

291   Holmberg 1985:49.

292   Pullar 1994:18–19.

293   Dall 1878:27.

294   Dall 1878:27.

295   Dall 1878:27.

296   Dall 1878:28.

297   Dall 1875:439.

298   Dall 1878:28.

299   Dall 1875:439.

300   Desson 1995:9. The exact date of Pinart's departure from Kodiak is unknown, but his surviving diaries show that he was still there on April 11, 1872 (Desson 1995:12).

301   Desson 1995:9.

Chapter 4

302   Dzeniskevich and Pavlinskaia 1988:83–84.

303   Varjola 1988:10.

304   Crowell 1992:20; Crowell et al. 2001.

305   Birket-Smith 1941; Corey 1987; Krech 1989.

306   Haakanson and Laronde 2008.

307   Liapunova 1994:175.

308   Although located in the greater Uyak Bay region, the precise site of Uyak village is unknown. It may have been a seasonal settlement until the 1880s, when a cannery was built in adjoining Larsen Bay (Luerhmann 2008:26, 62, 104).

309   Pinart 1871–1872.

310   Château-Musée 2008. See Chapter 2 for a discussion of the history of the collection in France and the transfer of some pieces to the Trocadéro museum (now the Musée de l'Homme). Additionally, Desson's research indicates that some specimens made their way into private collections (1995:280).

311   Pinart collected one Alutiiq object—a knife blade—from the Alaska Peninsula (Château-Musée 2008). We concur with Desson (1995:279–315) regarding the provenance of Pinart's Sugpiaq mask collection. Although Lot-Falck (1957:6) proposes that some of the masks are from Prince William Sound, based on a pointed head shape, like Desson we believe that documentary evidence, stylistic data, and cultural information all confirm a Kodiak origin for the masks. There is no indication that Pinart traveled to Prince William Sound or that he obtained materials from this part of the Sugpiaq world. Moreover, a pointed head symbolizes a malevolent spirit in Sugpiaq cosmology (Crowell and Leer 2001:196), a fact that Pinart himself published (Pinart 1873a:678). Thus, this head shape is a widely used stylistic convention, not a regional trait.

312   The size of the mask assemblage and the prevalence of ceremonial items in Pinart's collection increase if the Musée du quai Branly's seven Sugpiaq masks are included in these considerations.

313   An *angyaq* is a large, open skin boat used for traveling in groups

and transporting loads (Crowell and Laktonen 2001:152–153).

314   Desson 1995:272.

315   Pinart 1871–1872. See summary in Desson 1995:540–543.

316   Desson 1995:281.

317   White oak is not indigenous to the Kodiak region, but was commonly used in the construction of sailing ships. Indeed, the pieces in the Pinart collection made of this material are all a relatively similar size, suggesting that they originated from a similar-sized plug—as if a mast or a beam was cut into sections and recycled into masks.

318   Lot-Falck (1957:29) suggests that these smaller masks were elements of plank masks, designed for attachment to a large backing board. Like Desson (1995:67), however, we do not agree with this idea. These masks are finished pieces and many have bite bars, identical to larger specimens.

319   Pinart 1875; see also discussions of Pinart's collecting from caves in Chapters 2 and 3 of this book.

320   Lisianskii 1968:174.

321   See Pinart in Desson 1995:89–90.

322   Desson 1995:9.

323   For the Château-Musée specimens, indicated by catalog number starting with 988-2, all measurements represent the maximum dimensions of the mask carving, not including attachments. For this collection, we omit dimensions in a few cases where damage precluded meaningful measurement. For the Musée du quai Branly specimens, indicated by catalog numbers starting with 71–1881–21, we took dimensions from a museum inventory (Musée du quai Branly 2007). Here missing information indicates that the inventory did not provide dimensions.

324   Compare the mask images presented by Lot-Falck (1957:plates 2 and 5) with those presented here. See also Desson 1995:288.

325   The opportunity to reexamine the thirty-four masks that came to Kodiak for the *Giinaquq* exhibition led to the revision of wood types for some pieces. As such, the wood types offered here supersede those published in *Two Journeys*, the 2008 exhibition guide (Koniag, Inc. 2008).

326   Desson 1995:293. During installation of the *Giinaquq* exhibition at the Anchorage Museum at Rasmuson Center in October of 2008, Haakanson discovered an additional mask name written in Pinart's hand on the bite bar of mask 988-2-205. Contemporary Elders named this piece *Aningua'at*—Boils. We now know that its original name was *Akrillria*—Voyager. As such, the information on mask names presented in this volume supersedes that presented in the 2008 exhibition guide (Koniag,

Inc. 2008).

327   Desson 1995:292.

328   Pinart 1872a.

329   Désveaux 2002; Rousselot et al. 1991.

330   Désveaux 2002; Koniag, Inc. 2008; Rousselot et al. 1991.

331   Lot-Falck 1957; Desson 1995.

332   This mask, currently exhibited at the Musée du Louvre in the Pavillon des Session (galleries dedicated to non-European art), where it was deposited by the Château-Musée, had to be photograph through glass.

333   Sugpiaq elders chose not to name this mask in Alutiiq due to its powerful appearance.

Chapter 5

334   Pullar 1992:182–183.

335   Dzeniskevich and Pavlinskaia 1988.

336   Varjola 1988.

337   Lot-Falck 1957; Desson 1995; Désveaux 2002.

338   Crowell 1992; Crowell et al. 2001.

339   Desson 1995.

340   Lot-Falck 1957.

341   No relation to Jacob Simeonoff.

342   Koniag, Inc. 2008:20.

343   Steffian 2001:201.

344   Koniag, Inc. 2008:74.

345   Koniag, Inc. 2008:49.

346   Steffian 2006:27–31.

347   Johnson and his Sugpiaq wife, Alisha Drabek, collaborate on jewelry design.

Appendix

348   Pinart 1871–1872.

349   Haakanson in press.

350   Desson 1995:187–240.

351   We present Alutiiq words with the modern Alutiiq orthography, cf. Leer 1982, 1990; Counceller and Steffian 2004.

352   The notes Pinart took in Kodiak following his trips to Sugpiaq communities include texts associated with the following masks, in the following order, with some repetition: Angun—Old Man, Akrillria—Voyager, Angun—Old Man, Akrillria—Voyager, Ituryulria—One Who Arrived, Unartuliq—Protector, Pugumalria—Woman Who Took, Nakirnalik—Snub-Nosed

One, Kuyauq—Big-Nosed One, Agu'lik—Large Mask, Chumliiq—First One, Yuilria—Voyager, Agu'lik—Large Mask, Shalgayak—Trader, Ashigik—Fool/Lucky One, Nallumalik—One Who Doesn't Know.

353   Desson 1995:280–281, 545.

354   A *qasgiq* was a large, single-room community house where men met to discuss politics, repair tools, and prepare for war (Chechenev in Desson 1995:130). In the winter, this building became a ceremonial center where people of all ages gathered to sing, dance, and feast (Davydov 1977:154; Gideon 1989:40).

355   *Barabara* is the Russian term for a Sugpiaq sod house—known in the Alutiiq language as a *ciqlluaq*. This general reference to a Sugpiaq structure is probably to a *qasgiq* or community house, however, not a dwelling.

356   This song is associated with two masks that dance together, Yuaulik—Searcher and Unartuliq—Protector.

357   This refers to the previous mask, Chumliiq—First One.

358   An image of this mask, missing from the Château-Musée collections, appears in Lot-Falck 1957:Plate 5.

359   This song is associated with two masks that dance together, Yuaulik—Searcher and Unartuliq—Protector.

Notes

Chapitre 1

1   L'utilisation du terme *sugpiaq* (pluriel : *sugpiat*) tout au long de cet ouvrage fait référence au peuple autochtone de la région du golfe situé au centre de la côte d'Alaska (y compris le Prince William Sound, l'extérieur de la péninsule de Kenaï, l'archipel de Kodiak et la péninsule d'Alaska). Le terme fait, lui, référence à leur langue. Le mot « sugpiaq » est issu de la langue alutiiq. C'est un mode traditionnel d'autoréférence qui signifie « personne réelle » ou « tout comme une personne ». Le mot « alutiiq » vient du mot « aléoute », un terme général appliqué aux autochtones d'Alaska par les marchands russes, qui signifie « habitant côtier ». Dans leur langue, les autochtones de Kodiak disent pour dire le mot « aléoute ». De nos jours, ce mot désigne aussi la langue du peuple sugpiaq, également connue comme *sugt'stun* ou *yupik* du Pacifique (Clark 1984, p. 195–196 ; Leer 1982, p. 4 ; Woodbury 1984, p. 53).

2   Black 1992.

3   Crowell 1992, p. 20.

4   Knecht 1995.

5   Crowell et al. 2001.

6   Knecht 2000 ; Pullar 1992.

7   Desson 1995.

8   Pinart 1871–1872.

9   Lot-Falck 1957.

10   Aujourd'hui, les masques collectés par Alphonse Pinart en Alaska font partie des collections de deux musées français. Soixante-dix de ces masques, qui forment presque l'ensemble collecté par Pinart, appartiennent au Château-Musée de Boulogne-sur-Mer. Sept masques supplémentaires font partie des collections du musée du Quai-Branly, à Paris. Réunies, ces soixante-dix-sept pièces sont l'objet de la présente publication. D'autres masques sugpiat faisaient autrefois partie de l'ensemble collecté par Pinart (Lot-Falck 1957), mais un premier inventaire incomplet a semé le doute sur leur nombre total et quelques-uns ont été perdus. Nous n'incluons pas les quatorze masques collectés par Pinart dans les îles Aléoutiennes, détenus aussi par le Château-Musée, ni le masque dit sugpiaq des collections du musée du Quai-Branly, dont la provenance reste incertaine (71.1959.29.1, musée du Quai-Branly 2007).

11   Pinart 1871–1872.

12   Birket-Smith 1953 ; Davydov 1977 ; Gideon 1989 ; Lisianski 1968 ; Merck 1980 ; Shelikhov 1981 ; Voznesenskii in Liapunova 1994.

13   Les données archéologiques concernant la culture sugpiaq préhistorique la moins ancienne viennent en majeure partie de la collection bien préservée du site de Karluk One, un campement à l'embouchure de la rivière Karluk qui a révélé des artefacts en bois (Donta 1994, Knecht 1995).

14   Birket-Smith 1953, p. 72 ; Davydov 1977, p. 164.

15   Aujourd'hui, l'épicéa de Sitka (*Picea sitchensis*) recouvre les îles de Shuyak et d'Afognak, ainsi que la pointe nord de l'île de Kodiak. Les biologistes pensent que ces forêts ont commencé à pousser il y a environ mille ans (Heusser 1960, p. 55).

16   Knecht 1995, p. 554–555.

17   Birket-Smith 1953, p. 73.

18   Knecht 1995, p. 439.

19   Birket-Smith 1953, p. 73 ; Knecht 1995, p. 452, 461.

20   Quand Pinart a visité Kodiak, les sculpteurs sugpiat travaillaient avec des couteaux tordus, des outils munis d'une lame d'acier recourbée (Birket-Smith 1953, p. 73–74 ; Crowell et Lührmann 2001, p. 41).

21   Knecht 1995, p. 661.

22   Knecht 1995, p. 430–431.

23 La description suivante concerne les masques en bois sculpté. Se reporter à Black 1991 pour des informations sur les chapeaux de chasse en bois courbé considérés comme une forme de masque, et Liapunova (1994, p. 187–188) pour des exemples de masques sugpiat fabriqués avec des anneaux d'herbe tressée. Par ailleurs, Desson (1995, p. 70–71) remarque que les visages peints lors des festivals sont une forme de masques.

24 Knecht 1995, p. 665.

25 Cette pièce appartient à la collection Koniag, Inc. issue du site de Karluk One, conservée à l'Alutiiq Museum.

26 Liapunova 1994, ill. 10-4.

27 Knecht 1995, p. 675.

28 Jordan 1994, p. 157 ; Liapunova 1994, p. 198–199.

29 Davydov 1977, p. 111 ; Liapunova 1994, p. 192–196.

30 Davydov 1977, p. 154–155 ; Gideon 1989, p. 40 ; Merck 1980, p. 100 ; Shelikhov 1981, p. 56.

31 Knecht 1995, p. 671.

32 Desson 1995, p. 397–398 ; Krech 1989, ill. 44 ; Liapunova 1994, p. 192, 193.

33 Knecht 1995, p. 668.

34 Jordan 1994, p. 164.

35 Knecht 1995, p. 668.

36 Liapunova 1994, ill. 10-6 à 10-11.

37 Davydov 1977, p. 110 ; Pinart 1871–1872.

38 Merck 1980, p. 103–104 ; Russell 1995.

39 Davydov 1977, p. 153, 187 ; Merck 1980, p. 104.

40 Knecht 1995, p. 545. Cf. Desson 1995 pour une analyse des couleurs utlisées dans la conception des masques sugpiat.

41 On ne sait pas jusqu'à quelle date remonte la tradition des masques à Kodiak, mais des assemblages issus de fouilles archéologiques sur les sites de campements qui datent de la dernière période de la tradition Kachemak comprennent des exemples d'il y a plus de mille ans (Clark 1970, p. 111 ; Jordan et Knecht 1988, p. 253 ; Steffian 1992, p. 163).

42 Pinart 1871–1872.

43 Jordan 1994, p. 163.

44 Fienup-Riordan 1996, p. 59.

45 *Ibid.*, p. 69–70.

46 Birket-Smith 1953, p. 124 ; Crowell et Leer 2001, p. 196.

47 Crowell et Leer 2001, ill. 195 ; Krech 1989, ill. 44a ; Liapunova 1994, ill. 10-8.

48 Crowell et Leer 2001, p. 196.

49 Jordan 1994, ill. 9-7c ; Knecht 1995, p. 667–668.

50 Les masques représentaient aussi d'autres sortes d'esprits, y compris des diables et des esprits bénéfiques comme le suggèrent les noms originels de certains masques de la collection Pinart (Crowell et Leer 2001, p. 196).

51 Birket-Smith 1953, p. 120 ; Crowell et Leer 2001, p. 191–192.

52 Birket-Smith 1953, p. 34.

53 Hunt 2000, p. 55.

54 Birket-Smith 1953, p. 42.

55 Birket-Smith 1953, p. 108 ; Davydov 1977, p. 107–111 ; Gideon 1989, p. 94 ; Merck 1980, p. 100 ; Shelikhov 1981, p. 55.

56 Davydov 1977, p. 154 ; Gideon 1989, p. 40 ; Merck 1980, p. 100 ; Shelikhov 1981, p. 55.

57 Checenev, in Desson 1995, p. 130.

58 Davydov 1977, p. 109. Cf. Desson (1995, p. 136–158) au sujet des tâches que devait remplir le *kas'aq* et leur différence significative avec celles d'un chaman.

59 Gideon 1989, p. 45 ; Holmberg 1985, p. 60.

60 Davydov 1977, p. 108, 184 ; Desson 1995, p. 176.

61 Shelikhov 1981, p. 55.

62 Davydov 1977, p. 107.

63 Gideon 1989, p. 45.

64 *Ibid.*, p. 46 ; Merck 1980, p. 101.

65 Desson 1995, p. 177–178.

66 Gideon 1989, p. 46.

67 Davydov 1977, p. 184 ; Shelikhov 1981, p. 55.

68 Birket-Smith 1953, p. 109 ; Crowell et Leer 2001, p. 204 ; Shelikhov 1981, p. 81.

69 Liapunova 1994, p. 176.

70 Pinart 1871–1872 ; Desson 1995, p. 540–544, résume aussi ce festival.

71 Crowell 1992, p. 20. Le collecteur britannique Hugh Cecil Lowther, cinquième comte de Lonsdale, collecta deux masques sugpiat vers la fin du xixe siècle. Lowther voyagea le long de la péninsule d'Alaska et sur l'île de Kodiak durant l'hiver 1888–1889, mais il prit peu de notes. On ne connaît ni la provenance de ces masques ni le contexte dans lequel il les a collectés (Krech 1989, p. 124–125 et ill. 44a, b).

72 Crowell 1992, p. 21.

73 Black 2004, p. 256.

74 Partnow 2001, p. 86–88, 90.

75 *Ibid.*, p. 164.

76 Mishler 2003, p. 119 ; J. Mulcahy 2001, p. 23 ; Partnow 2001, p. 163.

77 Mishler 2003, p. 119.

78 Crowell et Leer 2001, p. 216.

79 Mishler 2003, p. 112–116.

80 *Ibid.*, p. 117.

81 J. Mulcahy 2001, p. 25–26.

82 Knecht 1995, p. 658 ; Mishler 2003, p. 117.

83 Mishler 2003, p. 119.

84 J. Mulcahy 2001, p. 26 ; Crowell et Leer 2001, p. 215–218.

85 Mishler 2003, p. 119.

86 *Ibid.*, p. 119 ; J. Mulcahy 2001, p. 99.

87 Koniag, Inc. 2008.

88 Haakanson 2002.

89 Koniag, Inc 2008, p. 90.

90 Le poste de conservatrice de Mme Laronde au Château-Musée est équivalent à celui d'un directeur de musée aux États-Unis.

91 Steffian 2006.

92 Lot-Falck 1957, Rousselot et al. 1991.

93 *Two Journeys: A Companion to the Giinaquq: Like a Face Exhibition*, une publication créée en association avec Koniag, Inc. et l'Alutiiq Museum pour l'ouverture de l'exposition à Kodiak, raconte l'histoire du voyage des artistes en France (Koniag, Inc. 2008).

94 Sur le chemin du retour vers l'Alaska, en 2006, Haakanson fit un arrêt à Paris pour visiter le musée du Quai-Branly avec Will Anderson et Perry Eaton. Ils purent y photographier les sept autres masques collectés par Pinart. Ces photographies sont reproduites dans le chapitre 4, avec l'aimable autorisation du musée du Quai-Branly.

95 Cf. Crowell et al. 2001 pour un résumé du projet « Looking Both Ways », une approche qui repose sur la communauté et l'expression de voix multiples pour interpréter l'identité sugpiaq au sein des collections de musées.

96 Rousselot 1991.

97 Koniag, Inc. 2008.

98 Pullar 1992 et al.

99 Davis 1984, p. 201. Par ailleurs, Davis remarque que les anthropologues ne commencèrent à étudier la culture sugpiaq qu'à partir de 1960.

100 Birket-Smith 1953.

101 Crowell et al. 2001 ; Steffian 2006.

102 Pour une discussion de la définition du sacré, cf. Haakanson et Steffian 2004, p. 156.

Chapitre 2

103 Désveaux 2002 ; Desson 1995 ; Lot-Falck 1957, p. 5–44 et pl. I-IX.

104 Le présent article est la synthèse des recherches de Géraldine Bouterin et Anne-Laure Gerbert, étudiantes en master I à l'école du Louvre (ministère de la Culture, palais du Louvre, Paris) : Bouterin 2007 et Gerbert 2007. Ces travaux de recherche ont bénéficié de l'aide et du soutien de Sarah Frioux-Salgas et d'Angèle Martin, du service des archives du musée du Quai-Branly, que nous remercions chaleureusement. Dans le présent article, ils sont complétés des annotations et précieuses corrections de Sarah Froning, docteur en anthropologie, et de Gwénaël Guigon, missionnée par le musée du Quai-Branly sur l'histoire de leurs collections arctiques. En outre, l'ensemble de ces recherches a bénéficié de l'aide et de la disponibilité précieuse de l'Alutiiq Museum et du groupe de travail de l'archipel de Kodiak investi dans la préparation de l'exposition « Giinaquq: Like a Face ». Nous tenons tout particulièrement à remercier Helen Simeonoff, l'équipe de l'Alutiiq Musuem autour de son directeur Sven Haakanson Jr., sa collaboratrice Amy Steffian et Perry Eaton, artiste et acteur du renouveau culturel alutiiq, pour leurs précieuses hypothèses, informations et partage d'archives.

105 Leunens 2003, p. 74, sur les précieuses indications d'Edmond Truffaut, membre du bureau des Amis du Château-Musée de Boulogne-sur-Mer.

106 Boulogne-sur-Mer est aujourd'hui le premier port de pêche français, l'un des premiers centres européens de transformation et d'échange des produits de la mer (trois cent cinquante mille tonnes y transitent chaque année, principalement de saumon).

107 Boulogne-sur-Mer est également la ville natale d'autres intellectuels qui marquèrent la recherche et les musées français : l'égyptologue Auguste Mariette (1821–1881), l'ethnologue Ernest-Théodore Hamy (1842–1908), fondateur du Musée d'ethnographie du Trocadéro, le critique littéraire Charles-Augustin Sainte-Beuve (1804–1869) et le conservateur et médiéviste Désiré Louis Camille Enlart (1862–1927), entre autres. La plupart de ces chercheurs ont aussi donné des collections au musée de leur ville, l'actuel Château-Musée. Cf. Lottin 1983, p. 198.

108 Bancroft, tome 39, p. 62 Américaniste, archéologue, ethnologue, historien et linguiste, Charles-Étienne Brasseur de Bourbourg (1814–1874) est l'un des fondateurs de l'américanisme en France au xixe siècle. Sur ce personnage, cf. Dias 1991, p. 230.

109 Archives d'Alphonse Louis Pinart, BANC MSS Z-Z 17, p. 10.

110 Lors de ce premier voyage, il collectionne des objets qui n'arriveront jamais en France, car le train qui convoyait ses caisses a été attaqué par un groupe d'Apaches. Pinart, 4 juillet 1872.

111 Le 27 avril 1871, Pinart embarque sur la goëlette *Amanda Ager* en direction des îles Aléoutiennes, puis il navigue de Nushagak à la rivière Yukon à bord de la goélette *John Bright*. Plus tard, le voyage d'Unalaska à Kodiak dure deux mois et est effectué en umiak. Il rentre, *via* Sitka, à San Fransisco le 21 mai 1872. Tout un ensemble de sources, archives et ouvrages scientifiques permettent de retracer les étapes du voyage alaskien de Pinart :

- les récits et notes de Pinart lui-même : « Voyage à la côte nord-ouest d'Amérique, d'Ounalashka à Kadiak (les Aléoutiennes et péninsule d'Aliaska) », in *Bulletin de la Société de géographie*, 6e série, tome VI, Paris, juillet-décembre 1873, p. 561–570 ; *Trip Around Afognak and Shouiak from March 24th to April 10th*, carnet de voyage, archives de la Bancroft Library, cote Z-Z 17, v.3, université de Berkeley (Californie, US) ;

- des synthèses des archives de Pinart : Gerbert 2007, p. 11–15, et annexe LIV, p. 140–14 ; Robert-Lamblin 1976, p. 19–27 ; Torres, in Désveaux 2002, p. 25–30 ;

- côté américain, après l'étude fondamentale de Parmenter 1966, les travaux de Dominique Desson (Desson 1995) et les recherches personnelles d'Helen Simeonoff (Simeonoff 2007, p. 2) ont apporté quelques précisions quant aux lieux visités et aux modes de transport utilisés.

Anne-Laure Gerbert retrace de façon très détaillée le parcours de Pinart. Voici la liste des lieux mentionnés par ordre chronologique dans son ouvrage : îles Shumagin, Unalaska, baie de Bristol, baie d'Ougachik, baie de Kouitchak, lac Iliamna, lac de Noushagak, îles Morses, îles de Hagenmeister, baie de Kuskokwin, île de Nunivak, détroit de Béring (jusqu'à la rive sibérienne), golfe de Norton (Fort Saint-Michel), Unalaska, Unga, Illiouliok, Bellkoffsky, Unga, port Delaroff (visite de la grotte funéraire d'Aknanh), îles Shumagin, cap Kouprianoff, archipel Thiers, baie Pinart, baie Chignik, cap Kounilioun, cap Nounakhalkhak, Katmay, détroit de Shelikhoff, île de Kodiak (Port Saint-Paul, hivernage), visite des îles d'Afognak et de Shouiak, retour à Unalaska, San Francisco, voyage sur la côte Pacifique des États-Unis et du Canada jusqu'à Sitka (Alaska).

112 Pinart, 4 juillet 1872.

113 Pinart, « Voyage à la côte nord-ouest d'Amérique, d'Ounalashka à Kadiak », 1873. Voyageant à ses propres frais, Pinart ne bénéficie pas encore du système de collecte « officiel » mis en place à partir de 1874 par la commission des voyages et missions scientifiques et littéraires du ministère de l'Instruction publique. Cette commission proposait des bourses afin d'encourager les voyageurs et promouvoir des envois de rapports réguliers et de caisses de matériels collectés (cf. Dias 1991, p. 163). À partir de 1882, Ernest-Théodore Hamy, en tant que directeur du nouveau Musée d'ethnographie du Trocadéro, fondateur de la *Revue d'ethnographie* et vice-président de la Société d'anthropologie de Paris, se charge de la gestion de certaines de ces équipes et de leurs envois, recueillant les rapports et organisant leur communication aux sociétés de recherche à Paris (Dias 1991, p. 61–63). Quant à Pinart, il fera partie de ce système à partir de 1878, quand il obtiendra une bourse du ministère pour une expédition avec Léon de Cessac au Mexique et en Californie, lors de laquelle il constituera une collection importante d'objets américains pour le Musée d'ethnographie (cf. Riviale 2001, p. 351–362).

114 L'orthographe des lieux cités est celle utilisée par Alphonse Pinart dans son article de 1873 (Pinart 1873c). Cf. également Desson 1995, p. 7–8.

115 Les photographies prises par Pinart lui-même, lors de son séjour en Alaska, sont conservées à la Bibliothèque nationale de France (département des Cartes et Plans, fonds de la Société française de géographie, cote BN C.Pl.Sg Wf 159), à Paris. Au nombre de quarante-huit, elles renseignent sur la façon dont Pinart a choisi d'organiser son voyage dans les îles Aléoutiennes et dans l'archipel de Kodiak. Les clichés sont de bien mauvaise qualité, mais ils montrent des paysages, des groupes de personnes (autochtones, métis et colons), des édifices civils et religieux. Les documents originaux peuvent être consultés sur rendez-vous et les microfilms sont accessibles à la consultation de tous les lecteurs de la bibliothèque.

Le même fonds d'archives conserve aussi les seuls portraits photographiques connus de Pinart à ce jour en France (références des microfilms : département des Cartes et Plans, fonds de la Société française de géographie, cote dans le fichier manuel des portraits sous l'entrée « Pinart », nos 181, 1158, 1529, 1530).

Le musée du Quai-Branly conserve de son côté un fonds de photographies, données par Pinart à l'État français, qui représentent des masques d'Alaska exposés à la fin du xixe siècle au musée de l'Académie impériale de Saint-Pétersbourg (masques dits « Eskimo Kaniagmiout », « Koloche », « Atka »). Seize clichés sont répertoriés et communicables à ce jour (cotes : PP0025992, PP0025995 à PP0026001, PP00260004, PP0026007, PP0026008, PP0026010) et sont reproduits sur le site Internet du musée.

116 Au sujet de la collection d'objets aléoutiens du Château-Musée de Boulogne-sur-Mer, cf. Pinart 1873c, p. 573, et, surtout, Pinart 1875, qui offre de très belles planches illustrées lithographiées de certains des objets collectés. Cf. aussi l'article de synthèse de l'étude scientifique Salabelle 2001, p. 87–97.

Le catalogue de l'exposition de la collection Pinart en 2002 publié par le musée du Quai-Branly donne une description détaillée de cette collection composée de trente pièces : Rousselot et Grahammer, in Désveaux 2002, p. 207–243. Cf. aussi l'étude récente de Géraldine Bouterin (Bouterin 2007, p. 30–31).

117 Saint-Paul est l'ancien nom de l'actuelle commune dénommée Kodiak, sur l'île de Kodiak.

118 Le troisième chapitre de la thèse de Dominique Desson (Desson 1995, p. 126–265) fournit des analyses et des interprétations de chants, danses et légendes de Kodiak collectés par Pinart.

119 Contrairement à ce qu'il fait lors de ses collectes immatérielles, Pinart ne documente pas les conditions de sa collecte d'objets sugpiat. À ce jour, les récentes études menées aux États-Unis comme en France n'ont pu identifier aucune source émanant de Pinart renseignant sur la date, le lieu et les moyens exacts de ces collectes d'objets. Cf. notamment Desson 1995, p. 12, et Bouterin 2007, p. 60.

120 Robert-Lamblin 1976, p. 19. À cette occasion ou par la suite, Alphonse Pinart a confié les carnets de terrain de son séjour en Alaska à Hubert Bancroft. Restés en la possession de ce dernier, ils sont aujourd'hui conservés à la bibliothèque de l'université de Berkeley.

121 Pinart, 4 juillet 1872.

122 Pour l'histoire d'Alphonse Pinart, de son retour en France et de sa démarche de voyageur et de collectionneur à partir des sources françaises, cf. principalement Rousselot et Grahammer, « Le fonds Pinart à la Bancroft Library », in Désveaux 2002, p. 201–205, et Gerbert 2007. Ces études exploitent notamment les archives relatives à Pinart conservées dans différentes institutions parisiennes publiques (correspondances et écrits de Pinart). Depuis la rédaction de cet article, Anne-Laure Gerbert a écrit un second mémoire, centré sur la carrière de Pinart (Gerbert 2008).

123 Visites de Pinart à d'autres collections alaskiennes en Europe en 1873 et 1874 (source : lettres de A. Pinart à E. Hamy, correspondance Ernest Hamy, tome I, 1860–1877) : Musée ethnographique de Copenhague (Danemark), janvier 1873, où il réalise une série de dessins d'objets alaskiens ; musée de Dorpta (ville universitaire nommée aujourd'hui Tarpu, Estonie), janvier 1873, où il réalise également une série de dessins d'objets alaskiens ; Saint-Pétersbourg (Russie), musée et archives de l'Académie des sciences, où il dessine et effectue des recherches de documents sur l'histoire de l'Alaska et les langues locales ; séjour en Sibérie ; musée de l'Université d'Helsinki (Finlande), collection Etholén, mars 1873 ; Musée public de Moscou (Russie), mars 1873, où il étudie les pièces aléoutes ; puis retour aux archives de Saint-Pétersbourg, au moins jusqu'en janvier 1874.

124 Pour cela, il achète notamment des bibliothèques sur cette

thématique, dont celle de l'abbé Brasseur de Bourbourg (cf. Gerbert 2007, p. 39). Pinart avait aussi le projet de publier trois volumes sur son voyage en Alaska, Gerbert 2007, p. 65. Seule une partie du premier volume a été publiée, portant sur l'environnement naturel de l'Alaska, cf. Pinart, *Voyages à la côte nord-ouest de l'Amérique exécutés durant les années 1870–1872*, volume I, partie I, Histoire naturelle, Paris, éd. Ernest Leroux, 1875. Sur ses publications à propos des langues américaines, cf. Gerbert 2007, p. 67–69.

125 Pinart en fait part au ministère de l'Instruction publique dans une lettre datée du 11 février 1878, conservée aux Archives nationales, F17 22997, pièce n° 1, Paris. Contrairement à ce qui a pu être parfois avancé, ce ne serait donc pas Alphonse Pinart qui aurait causé par ses voyages, publications et achats, la ruine de sa famille (cf. Parmenter 1966, p. 18).

126 En 1877, Alphonse Pinart embarque sept mois sur le navire *Le Seignelay*, qui a notamment pour mission de collecter des informations dans le domaine des sciences humaines en vue de la préparation de l'Exposition universelle qui doit se tenir l'année suivante à Paris. Pinart pensait rejoindre ainsi l'Alaska, mais la destination du navire change : il fait désormais route vers l'Océanie. Un certain Paul Émile Lafontaine partage une partie de son voyage et en croque un portrait sans concession : « Nous apprîmes que ce monsieur était un illustre savant voyageur, qui avait fait des découvertes importantes à l'Alaska, où il était allé deux fois, voyageant seul dans une pirogue, avec des sauvages lapons ou esquimaux, et se nourrissant comme eux d'huile de baleine. Quant à nous, nous ne pouvions juger son originalité que par la longueur de ses cheveux et de ses ongles, qui étaient en effet extraordinaires. Mais notre commandant se laissa convaincre du mérite de ce personnage, et lui proposa de venir avec nous à Tahiti, lui offrant la table et le logement. Monsieur Pinart ne voulut pas accepter, étant obligé de se rendre en Europe pour publier ses nombreux travaux ; mais il proposa au commandant de le conduire l'année suivante en découverte dans les mers polaires. » Les descriptions de Lafontaine sont nombreuses et détaillées. On y apprend notamment que Pinart a bien du mal à se servir d'un appareil photographique et qu'il prétend savoir parler de nombreuses langues (Lafontaine 2006).

127 Zelia Maria Magdalena Nuttal (San Francisco, 1857-Mexique, 1933) épouse Pinart en 1880. Ensemble, ils partiront aux Antilles, en France et en Espagne. Leur fille naît en 1882, à San Francisco. Les époux se séparent en 1884 et divorcent en 1885. Elle commence alors une brillante carrière d'ethnologue et d'archéologue mexicaniste entre l'Europe, les États-Unis et le Mexique. Cf. Gerbert 2007, p. 62.

128 Pour l'histoire des masques sugpiat de la collection Pinart du Château-Musée de Boulogne-sur-Mer, cf. principalement

Bouterin 2007. Cette étude établit notamment que le nombre de masques sugpiat donnés par Alphonse Pinart au Château-Musée de Boulogne-sur-Mer en 1875 est impossible à déterminer à partir des sources écrites archivistiques françaises dépouillées à ce jour.

129 Le catalogue de cette exposition répertorie 198 numéros d'inventaire dans la partie « Ethnographie et collections exposées sous la vitrine plate », 37 numéros concernent les masques sugpiat. Sous un même numéro peuvent être inventoriés plusieurs masques (voir le numéro 183 qualifié de « série de masques »). Il nous est impossible de connaître le nombre exact de masques sugpiat exposés alors à partir de ce document. Pinart 1872.

130 Voir la retranscription de la lettre d'Alphonse Pinart adressée au maire de Boulogne, Auguste Huguet, « Séance du conseil municipal du 16 février 1875 », in *Registre des délibérations du conseil municipal de la ville de Boulogne-sur-Mer*, conservé aux Archives municipales de Boulogne-sur-Mer. Alphonse Pinart y stipule deux conditions à son don : « que la collection entre telle quelle sans qu'aucune pièce puisse par la suite en être distraite pour échange ou tout autre chose » ; « que les objets ne pourront être prêtés pour étude que sur ma permission fournie par moi ou toute autre personne autorisée ». Il précise aussi qu'il pourra retirer momentanément des objets de cette collection pour qu'ils figurent dans l'ouvrage sur l'Amérique russe qu'il a entrepris de rédiger. Le maire accepte son don et souhaite réaménager le musée, étendre ses galeries pour mieux accueillir la collection. La commission du musée émet elle aussi un avis favorable à ce don et remercie « l'enfant du pays qui a choisi le chef-lieu de son arrondissement pour conserver les dépôts de ses laborieuses recherches et de ses importantes découvertes ». Plus tard, le conservateur du musée de Boulogne, écrivant au maire, apporte des informations quant au devenir de la collection reçue « de Monsieur Alphonse Pinart, une collection ethnographique, rapportée par lui de l'Amérique Russe (aujourd'hui territoire de l'Alaska). Cette collection, composée d'environ 280 pièces, a été placée provisoirement dans la galerie de minéralogie et appelle l'attention de tous les amateurs. Je ne dois pas omettre de signaler que les vêtements d'Esquimaux en peaux, faisant partie de cette collection, ont été envahis par les mites et que, préalablement à leur classement, M. Duburquoy leur a fait subir une préparation propre à leur conservation » (« Séance du conseil municipal du 18 septembre 1876 », in *Registre des délibérations du conseil municipal de la ville de Boulogne-sur-Mer*, conservé aux Archives municipales de Boulogne-sur-Mer).

131 Si Félix Torres constate que cette donation se fait « grâce à Hamy » et si l'ancien conservateur du Château-Musée, Mme Halley-des-Fontaines-Poiret, constate pour sa part que le lien « d'estime mutuelle » entre les deux hommes « aboutit » au don fait par Pinart (cf. Torres, in Désveaux 2002, p. 25 ; Halley-des-Fontaines-Poiret, in Désveaux 2002, p. 187), le rôle spécifique de Hamy dans cet événement demeure incertain. Il est certes vrai que Pinart et Hamy étaient liés l'un à l'autre par une relation professionnelle qui était peut-être renforcée par le fait d'être originaire de la même région, mais Hamy avait également de telles relations professionnelles avec de nombreux voyageurs et chercheurs à l'époque (cf. Dias 1991, p. 215). Cf. également Sibeud, in Blanckaert 2001, p. 187.

132 La lettre de donation écrite par Pinart en 1875 stipulait que la collection ne devrait pas être divisée sans la permission du donateur, c'est-à-dire Pinart lui-même. Ce dernier donne cette permission avant la fin de l'année 1886, sous condition que le Trocadéro donne un nombre équivalent de pièces en échange. Cet échange met plus de deux ans à se réaliser. Il est d'abord approuvé par le musée de Boulogne un an après la demande originale de Hamy, en août 1887. Ensuite, le musée a dû adresser une série de lettres au maire, Auguste Huguet, lui demandant d'officialiser la décision. Huguet ne le fera jamais : il fallut attendre la mi-1888 et l'arrivée du nouveau maire, Jules Baudelocque, pour que les collections soient enfin échangées entre les deux institutions. Peu après, Hamy démissionne de la commission du musée de Boulogne (Halley-des-Fontaines-Poiret, in Désveaux 2002, p. 189–190). Nous ne connaissons pas à l'heure actuelle la nature des objets échangés (qui ont pu être de provenance autres qu'alaskienne).

133 Le Château-Musée de Boulogne-sur-Mer conserve actuellement soixante-dix masques sugpiat de la collection Pinart.

134 Voici la liste des différents inventaires de la collection Pinart du Château-Musée de Boulogne-sur-Mer que nous avons identifiés en France :

- Pinart (Alphonse), *Catalogue des collections rapportées de l'Amérique russe (aujourd'hui territoire d'Alaska), exposées dans l'une des galeries du Museum d'histoire naturelle de Paris (section d'Anthropologie)*, 1872 ;

- mention de masques numérotés D47.13 dans le Cahier d'inventaire II des dépôts (1938–1972) du Laboratoire d'ethnologie du musée de l'Homme (cahier accessible en version numérisée sur la base de donnée des archives et de la documentation des collections du musée du Quai-Branly) ;

- fiches descriptives des objets alaskiens déposés au musée de l'Homme de 1947 à 1950, rédigées en 1949 par Évelyne Lot-Falck (chargée des collections arctiques au musée de l'Homme). Elles ont été utilisées pour constituer des dossiers d'œuvres en 1988, lors du récolement de B. Coutancier (cf. *supra*), dossiers conservés au Château-Musée de Boulogne-sur-Mer ;

- campagne de photographies en noir et blanc organisée par le musée de l'Homme au Château-Musée de Boulogne-sur-Mer, en 1976 (photographe : José Oster), photographies qui ont été utilisées ensuite pour constituer des dossiers d'œuvres en 1988 (cf. *infra*), dossiers conservés au Château-Musée de Boulogne-sur-Mer ;

- registre d'inventaire 988.2 du Château-Musée de Boulogne-sur-Mer, rédigé par le conservateur-adjoint Benoît Coutancier en 1988, conservé au Château-Musée de Boulogne-sur-Mer ;
- Rousselot et Grahamer, in Désveaux 2002, p. 207–243 ;
- « Inventaire des masques sugpiat de la collection Alphonse Pinart conservés au Château-Musée de Boulogne-sur-Mer », in Bouterin 2007, annexe VIII, p. 17–61 ;
- fiches informatisées d'inventaire, par Céline Ramio, Château-Musée, 2008.

  D'autres inventaires concernent les collections que Pinart a données, non pas à Boulogne-sur-Mer, mais au Musée ethnographie du Trocadéro (aujourd'hui conservées au musée du Quai-Branly) :

- liste manuscrite d'Alphonse Pinart, datée du 22 mai 1878, conservée au Centre de documentation du musée du Quai-Branly : liste des objets que Pinart dépose au muséum d'Histoire naturelle ;
- liste des objets rapportés par Pinart, donnés au Musée d'ethnographie du Trocadéro, référencés dans l'Inventaire des collections du Musée d'ethnographie (numéros 5600 à 9999), sous les numéros 81.21 (D000557) ;
- fiches descriptives des objets alaskiens des collections Pinart conservées au musée de l'Homme, rédigées en 1949 par Évelyne Lot-Falck (chargée du département Arctique au musée de l'Homme), conservées au musée du Quai-Branly.

135 Liste des expositions temporaires auxquelles les masques ont été prêtés depuis leur arrivée sur le sol français :

- Exposition universelle de 1878 à Paris : prêt de « toute la collection de l'Amérique Russe » selon la « Séance du conseil municipal du 18 décembre 1878 », in *Registre des délibérations du conseil municipal de la ville de Boulogne-sur-Mer*, conservé aux Archives municipales de Boulogne-sur-Mer ;
- en 1947, soixante-dix masques sugpiat, aléoutes et océaniens de Boulogne sont déposés, restaurés et exposés au musée de l'Homme, à Paris (l'ancien Musée du Trocadéro fondé par Ernest Hamy), à l'occasion du Congrès international des américanistes (voir *Lettre du 29 septembre 1947*, dossier 988-FC 5 3 C, archives du Château-Musée de Boulogne-sur-Mer). Les masques concernés reçoivent alors un numéro de dépôt (« D47.13 »). Ils rentreront à Boulogne en 1950. Aujourd'hui, seuls quatre masques sugpiat de Boulogne ne portent pas ce numéro ;
- autres expositions parisiennes : prêt de douze masques à l'exposition intitulée « Masques », dans l'annexe du Musée

national des arts asiatiques Guimet, en 1959 (voir diverses lettres, *op. cit.*, et Perrin 1965) ; exposition « Kodiak, Alaska. Les masques de la collection Alphonse Pinart », organisée par le musée du Quai-Branly au musée des Arts africains et océaniens, en 2002 ;

- série d'expositions, de moins grande ampleur, organisées dans différentes régions de France (prêt de quelques masques à chaque opération) : maison de la Culture de Bourges (Région Centre) en 1964, musée de Tourcoing (Région Nord-Pas-de-Calais) en 1967, maison de la Culture de Rennes (Région Bretagne) en 1980, Château-Musée de Dieppe (Région Normandie) en septembre 1980 ;
- exposition à Boulogne-sur-Mer : « Masques de l'Alaska (collection Alphonse Pinart) », au Château-Musée de Boulogne-sur-Mer, en 1970 (selon un carton d'invitation imprimé conservé dans les archives du Château-Musée de Boulogne-sur-Mer) ;
- le masque D47.13.44 a été prêté à l'exposition intitulée « Primitivism in 20th Century Art, Affinity of the Tribal and the Modern », au Museum of Modern Art à New York en 1984.

  Cf. aussi : Bouterin 2007, p. 41, 46–47, 51–52.

136 Liste des restaurations auxquelles les masques ont été soumis depuis leur arrivée sur le sol français :

- en 1947, masques déposés au musée de l'Homme, à Paris. Nature des interventions : indéterminée ;
- restaurations de consolidation effectuées par des restaurateurs agréés par les Musées de France : en 1958, environ trente-six masques auraient été restaurés par Jacques Bousquet, restaurateur réputé (à Boulogne, il est notamment intervenu sur la seconde collection d'importance du musée, les céramiques grecques antiques), dans son atelier de Troyes (Région Champagne-Ardenne). Le Château-Musée possède aujourd'hui deux gouaches sur papier représentant des masques de la collection par ce restaurateur qui y restitue les coloris initiaux de l'objet (il s'agit des masques 988-2-185 et 988-2-196). Puis deux restaurateurs spécialisés dans les collections ethnologiques, encore en activité actuellement, ont consolidé la polychromie d'une grande partie des masques : Alain Renard en 1988, puis Frédérique Vincent en 2002.

  Sources : *Registre des délibérations du conseil municipal de la ville de Boulogne-sur-Mer*, conservé aux Archives municipales de Boulogne-sur-Mer et lettres diverses extraites des dossiers 988-FC 5 3 F et L, archives du Château-Musée de Boulogne-sur-Mer. Cf. aussi Bouterin 2007, p. 46, 49, 53.

Chapitre 3

137 Miller 1981, p. 1.

138 Le village de Wood Island était à une distance facilement

franchissable en depuis Kodiak. Pinart a dû y passer sur son chemin lors de son voyage entre Kodiak et Eagle Harbor. Il a aussi dû passer par Ouzinkie, entre Kodiak et Afognak.

139 Donald Clark, communication personnelle du 24 novembre 2008.

140 Case et Voluck 2002, p. 47.

141 Les archives de l'église orthodoxe russe de Kodiak datant de 1867 comptent quarante-neuf Russes (Lührmann 2000, p. 166). En 1870, l'année précédant l'arrivée de Pinart à Kodiak, le nombre de Russes inscrits était de onze (Lührmann 2000, p. 167). Il est possible qu'il y ait eu un très petit nombre de Russes non orthodoxes à Kodiak.

142 Case et Voluck 2002, p. 47 ; Golovin enregistre 871 créoles dans le « Département de Kodiak » en 1860 (Dmytryshyn et Crownhart-Vaughan 1979, p. 140). Notons que le mot « créole » employé dans ces pages est le terme historique utilisé en Alaska depuis la colonisation russe et que son sens diffère quelque peu de son sens habituel en français.

143 Black 1990, p. 145.

144 Lührmann 2000, p. 167.

145 Oleksa 1992, p. 145–146.

146 Huggins 1981, p. 41, 48.

147 Gibson 1976, p. 93–111.

148 Holmberg 1985, p. 41.

149 Wrangell 1980, p. 18.

150 *Sugt'stun* signifie littéralement « parler comme une personne ».

151 Dauenhauer 1990, p. 155.

152 Black 2001, p. 60.

153 Crowell et Lührmann 2001, p. 48 ; Petroff 1884, p. 139 ; Holmberg 1855–1863, p. 40.

154 Davydov 1977, p. 151.

155 Petroff 1884, p. 139 ; Holmberg 1885, p. 39.

156 Crowell et Lührmann 2001, p. 47.

157 Holmberg 1985, p. 40.

158 *Ibid.*, p. 39.

159 Oleksa 1990, p. 188–189.

160 *Llam Sua* signifie littéralement « personne de l'univers » (Crowell et Leer 2001, p. 192). Birket-Smith décrit *Llam Sua* comme l'Être qui a non seulement pouvoir « sur l'univers, mais aussi sur le temps qu'il fait, sur l'air, et même cet immense pouvoir mystique omniprésent dans le monde » (1953, p. 121). Pinart relate sa perception du *Llam Sua* qu'il traduit par « Homme fait de lumière. » (Pinart 1871–72 ms, traduction de L.T. Black, 15 août 1981).

161 Oleksa 1992, p. 124.

162 *Ibid.*, p. 125. Feu le Père Kreta expliquait également la croyance en ce parallélisme à l'auteur en 1991.

163 Davydov 1977, p. 109.

164 Huggins 1981, p. 1–2.

165 *Ibid.*, p. 1. Le spécialiste en sciences naturelles auquel Huggins fait référence était William H. Dall.

166 Hagan 1988, p. 53.

167 Prucha 1975, p. 136.

168 Case et Voluck 2002, p. 44–46.

169 Kan 1988, p. 510.

170 Petroff 1884, p. 138 ; Holmberg 1855–1863, p. 38

171 Bancroft 1886, p. 681.

172 Crowell 1997, p. 14.

173 Davydov 1977, p. 193.

174 Black 1988, p. 79.

175 Fedorova 1973, p. 193 ; Dilliplane 1990, p. 131–143.

176 Fedorova 1973, p. 196.

177 Des morceaux de cette plume en bois sont encore visibles aujourd'hui.

178 Stevens 1990, p. 193 ; Fedorova 1973, p. 196.

179 Fedorova 1973, p. 196.

180 Dall 1970, p. 346 ; Black 2004, p. 264.

181 Stevens 1990, p. 195.

182 Dall 1970, p. 349.

183 Gibson 1976, p. 42.

184 Watrous 2001

185 Black 1992, p. 165. *Awa'uq* signifie « devenir engourdi » dans la langue sugpiaq. Connu sous le nom anglais de Refuge Rock, ce lieu est situé juste au large de l'île de Sitkalidak, près du village d'aujourd'hui de Old Harbor.

186 Black 1992, p. 172–173.

187 Solovjova et Vovnyanko 2002, p. 9.

188 Black 1992, p. 165–177.

189 Tikhmenev 1978, p. 7.

190 Roppel 1986, p. 4.

191 *Ibid.*, p. 5.

192 *Ibid.*, p. 4.

193 Hinckley 1972, p. 126.

194 Lührmann 2000, p. 56.

195 Naske et Slotnick 1979, p. 62.

196 *Ibid.*, p. 61.

197 Les archives de la Compagnie commerciale d'Alaska sont conservées à l'université d'Alaska, à Fairbanks (Rasmusson Library Archives).

198 Aron Crowell, directeur de l'Alaska Office of the Arctic Studies Center, à la Smithsonian Institution. Communication du 24 novembre 2008.

199 Dmytryshyn et Crownhart-Vaughan 1979, p. 153.

200 Lührmann 2000, p. 141.

201 Mishler 2003, p. 31–34.

202 Black 1992, p. 165.

203 Black 2004, p. 216.

204 Oleksa 1990, p. 185 ; Elliott 1886, p. 108.

205 Black 2004, p. 215.

206 Oleksa 1990, p. 185.

207 *Ibid.*

208 Oleksa 1992, p. 145.

209 Lührmann 2000, p. 167.

210 *Ibid.*, p. 51.

211 Black 1990, p. 146.

212 Fedorova 1973, p. 165.

213 Dmytryshyn et Crownhart-Vaughan 1979, p. 17.

214 Elliott 1886, p. 108.

215 Khlebnikov 1994, p. 73.

216 *Ibid.*

217 *Ibid.*, p. 74.

218 *Ibid.*

219 Armstrong 1979, p. 178.

220 Dall 1970, p. 44.

221 Dmytryshyn et Crownhart-Vaughan 1979, p. 17.

222 Black 1988, p. 79.

223 Fedorova 1973, p. 213.

224 *Ibid.*, p. 212.

225 Dmytryshyn et Crownhart-Vaughan 1979, p. 17.

226 *Ibid.*, p. 17–18.

227 Oleksa 1992, p. 146.

228 Il convient de souligner qu'il existait plus d'une façon d'être créole. Une première façon était d'être le descendant d'un Russe et d'une Sugpiaq, tandis qu'une autre consistait à être éduqué en Russie avant d'être renvoyé en Alaska.

229 Wood 1943, p. 204.

230 *Ibid.*

231 Bien que le terme « créole » ait pu figurer sur les registres officiels, de nombreux Sugpiat de Kodiak ignoraient ce terme à la fin du xxe siècle et furent surpris de le découvrir sur les certificats de naissance de leurs parents et grands-parents, car ils s'étaient toujours considérés comme complètement autochtones.

232 Wood 1943, p. 206.

233 Durant la période d'inscription pour bénéficier de l'*l'Alaska Native Claims Settlement Act* (ANCSA) de 1971, les candidats devaient, pour y avoir droit, apporter la preuve qu'ils avaient au moins un quart de sang autochtone d'Alaska. La plupart des créoles remplissaient cette condition, mais depuis des années ils s'étaient définis comme Russes pour tenter de préserver leur statut social et échapper aux emplois et autres formes de discriminations couramment réservées aux autochtones. Aussi, lorsqu'ils furent acceptés par l'ANCSA, beaucoup de gens qui avaient toujours clamé leur « autochtonie » trouvèrent injuste que des personnes qui se considéraient jusque-là comme Russes aient droit à une part des allocations. L'expression « il n'était pas autochtone jusqu'à 1971 » et le qualificatif d'« autochtone de la loi de compensation pour les terres » devinrent populaires pour désigner ceux qui ne s'identifiaient pas ouvertement comme autochtones avant l'ANCSA. Au fil du temps, cependant, de nombreux créoles se sont distingués en tant que leaders autochtones et sont aujourd'hui largement acceptés comme membres légitimes de la communauté sugpiaq.

234 Khlebnikov 1973, p. 105.

235 Khlebnikov 1994, p. 9.

236 Fortuine 1989, p. 200.

237 *Ibid.*, p. 201.

238 *Ibid.*, p. 201–202.

239 Khlebnikov, 1994, p. 357–358.

240 Dall 1970, p. 352.

241 Tikhmenev 1978, p. 198–199.

242 Fortuine 1989, p. 233.

243 *Ibid.*, p. 237. Dall affirme que soixante-quinze villages furent transformés en sept en 1844 (1970 [1870], p. 341).

244 Hrdlička 1975, p. 19.

245 Pullar 1992, p. 186.

246 Tikhmenev 1978, p. 200.

247 Fortuine 1989, p. 194.

248 *Ibid.*, p. 207.

249 *Ibid.*, p. 203–204.

250 *Ibid.*, p. 199–208, 241, 255.

251 *Ibid.*, p. 203–204.

252 Mot russe pour « bain. » Sur l'île de Kodiak, le mot s'écrit généralement « banya ». Le nom traditionnel est *maqiq* (Crowell et al. 2001, p. 243).

253 Partnow 2001, p. 257.

254 J. Mulcahy 2001, p. 69.

255 Mishler 2003, p. 141–147.

256 Partnow 2001, p. 257 ; Davydov 1977, p. 154–155 ; Knecht 1995, p. 327–331.

257 Partnow 2001, p. 257–258.

258 Davydov 1977, p. 190 ; Crowell et al. 2001, p. 43 ; Armstrong 1979, p. 176.

259 Le *qasgiq* est appelé *kashim* ou *kazhim* en russe (Gideon 1989, p. 152).

260 Gideon 1989, p. 40–41.

261 Morseth 1998, p. 16.

262 Davydov 1977, p. 190 ; Crowell 1997, p. 70.

263 Lührmann 2000, p. 49.

264 Petroff 1884, p. 137–138.

265 Kodiak Area Native Association 1987, p. 1 ; Oleksa 1987, p. 396 ; L. Mulcahy 2003, p. 86–88. est la forme indigénisée du mot russe *starosta*.

266 Kodiak Area Native Association 1987, p. 1–2.

267 Pullar 1997, p. 173–174.

268 Seul le village de Karluk, sur l'île de Kodiak, a choisi de se réorganiser selon l'IRA. Même après cela, il a maintenu la plus grande partie du système précédent en fonctionnement.

269 Pullar 1997, p. 56.

270 Elliott 1886, p. 107.

271 Gibson 1976, p. 96.

272 *Ibid.*, p. 97.

273 *Ibid.*

274 *Ibid.*, p. 96.

275 Petroff 1884, p. 24–25.

276 Lührmann 2000, p. 51.

277 Elliott 1886, p. 115.

278 Cette affirmation est clairement erronée, puisque des archives montrent que des tonnes de glace ont été expédiées de Woody Island à San Francisco.

279 Elliott 1886, p. 105.

280 *Ibid.*, p. 106.

281 *Ibid.*, p. 115.

282 *Ibid.*, p. 106–107.

283 Gibson 1976, p. 106–107.

284 Le mot « employés » est utilisé en français dans le document original.

285 Porter 1893, p. 73–74.

286 *Ibid.*, p. 74.

287 Petroff 1884, p. 24.

288 Simon et Steffian 1994, p. 93 ; Holmberg 1985, p. 53.

289 Dall 1878, p. 31.

290 *Ibid.*, p. 27.

291 Holmberg 1985, p. 49.

292 Pullar 1994, p. 18–19.

293 Dall 1878, p. 27.

294 *Ibid.*

295 *Ibid.*

296 *Ibid.*, p. 28.

297 Dall 1875, p. 439.

298 Dall 1878, p. 28.

299 Dall 1875, p. 439.

300 Desson 1995, p. 9. On ne connaît pas la date exacte du départ de Pinart de Kodiak mais, selon le journal qu'il tenait qui nous est parvenu, il s'y trouvait encore le 11 avril 1872 (Desson 1995, p. 12).

301 Desson 1995, p. 9.

Chapitre 4

302 Dzeniskevich et Pavlinskaia 1988, p. 83–84.

303 Varjola 1988, p. 10.

304 Crowell 1992, p. 20 ; Crowell et al. 2001.

305 Birket-Smith 1941 ; Corey 1987 ; Krech 1989.

306 Haakanson et Laronde 2008.

307 Liapunova 1994, p. 175.

308 Bien qu'on le sache situé dans la vaste région d'Uyak Bay, on ne connaît pas le site précis du village d'Uyak. Il peut s'agir d'un campement saisonnier utilisé jusque dans les années 1880, avant qu'une conserverie soit construite au bord de la baie voisine de Larsen (Luerhmann 2008, p. 26, 62, 104).

309 Pinart 1871–1872.

310 Château-Musée 2008. Se reporter au chapitre 2 pour lire l'histoire

de la collection en France et le transfert de certaines pièces du Musée du Trocadéro (aujourd'hui musée de l'Homme). Les recherches de Desson indiquent par ailleurs que certains spécimens ont rejoint des collections privées (1995, p. 280).

311 Pinart a collecté un objet alutiiq (une lame de couteau) sur la péninsule d'Alaska (Château-Musée 2008). Nous partageons la conclusion de Desson (1995, p. 279–315) concernant la provenance de la collection des masques sugpiat de Pinart. Contrairement à Lot-Falck (1957, p. 6), qui suggère que certains des masques proviennent de Prince William Sound, au regard de la forme pointue de leur tête, nous pensons, comme Desson, que les preuves documentaires, les données stylistiques et les informations culturelles confirment l'origine des masques à Kodiak. Il n'existe aucune indication que Pinart ait voyagé dans le Prince William Sound ni qu'il ait obtenu des objets de cette partie du territoire sugpiaq. D'autre part, une tête pointue symbolise un esprit malfaisant dans la cosmologie sugpiaq (Crowell et Leer 2001, p. 196), un fait que Pinart lui-même a publié (Pinart 1873a, p. 678). Aussi cette forme de tête est-elle une convention stylistique répandue, et non une caractéristique régionale.

312 La taille du groupe de masques et la prévalence d'objets cérémoniels dans la collection Pinart sont encore plus importants si l'on ajoute à ces considérations les sept masques du musée du Quai-Branly.

313 Un *angyaq* est un large bateau en peau de forme ouverte utilisé pour transporter des groupes de personnes ou des charges importantes (Crowell et Laktonen 2001, p. 152–153).

314 Desson 1995, p. 272.

315 Pinart 1871–1872. Cf. le résumé de Desson, in Desson 1995, p. 540–543.

316 Desson 1995, p. 281.

317 Le chêne blanc n'est pas une essence indigène de la région de Kodiak, mais il était couramment utilisé dans la construction des navires. En effet, les pièces de la collection Pinart fabriquées à partir de ce matériau sont de tailles relativement similaires, ce qui suggère qu'elles sont issues d'un tronçon de même taille, comme si un mât ou une poutre avaient été recyclés sous forme de masques.

318 Lot-Falck (1957, p. 29) suggère que ces plus petits masques étaient des éléments des masques-planches, destinés à être attachés à un grand panneau. Cependant, à l'instar de Desson (1995, p. 67), nous réfutons ce point de vue. Ces masques sont des pièces finies, et beaucoup d'entre elles sont munies d'un mors identique à ceux des spécimens de grande taille.

319 Pinart 1875. Cf. aussi les références aux collectes de Pinart dans des grottes aux chapitres 2 et 3 de cet ouvrage.

320 Lisianskii 1968, p. 174.

321 Pinart, in Desson 1995, p. 89–90.

322 Desson 1995, p. 9.

323 Les spécimens du Château-Musée sont présentés dans l'ordre de leurs numéros de catalogue, qui commencent par 988-2. Toutes les mesures des masques indiquent leurs dimensions maximales, accessoires exclus. Dans le cas de cette collection, nous avons omis les dimensions lorsque les masques présentaient des dommages empêchant toute mesure pertinente. Concernant les spécimens du musée du Quai-Branly, répertoriés suivant leur numéro de catalogue en commençant par 71-1881-21, nous avons reproduit les dimensions fournies par un inventaire du musée (musée du Quai-Branly 2007). Les informations manquantes indiquent que l'inventaire ne fournissait pas de dimensions.

324 Comparer les images de masques présentées par Lot-Falck (1957, plaques 2 et 5) avec celles qui sont présentées dans cet ouvrage. Cf. aussi Desson 1995, p. 288.

325 L'opportunité de réexaminer les trente-quatre masques transportés à Kodiak à l'occasion de l'exposition « Giinaquq » nous a conduit à redéfinir l'essence de bois utilisé pour certaines pièces. Ainsi, les essences de bois proposées ici sont-elles mises à jour par rapport au guide de l'exposition « Two Journeys », publié en 2008 (Koniag, Inc. 2008).

326 Desson 1995, p. 293 Au cours de l'installation de l'exposition « Giinaquq » à l'Anchorage Museum, au Rasmuson Center, en octobre 2008, Haakanson a découvert un nouveau nom de masque écrit à la main par Pinart sur le mors du masque 988-2-205. Les Anciens avaient donné un nom contemporain à cette pièce : *Aningua'at* (pustules). Nous savons maintenant que son nom d'origine était *Akrillria* (Voyageur). En conséquence, les informations concernant les noms de masques présentées dans cet ouvrage remplacent celles qui figuraient dans le guide de l'exposition de 2008 (Koniag, Inc. 2008).

327 Desson 1995, p. 292.

328 Pinart 1872a.

329 Désveaux 2002 ; Rousselot et al. 1991.

330 Désveaux 2002 ; Koniag, Inc. 2008 ; Rousselot et al. 1991.

331 Lot-Falck 1957 ; Desson 1995.

332 Ce masque, actuellement déposé par le Château-Musée au musée du Louvre, à Paris, au sein du pavillon des Sessions, département dédié à l'art extra-européen, a dû être photographié à travers une vitrine.

333 Les Anciens de culture sugpiaq ont choisi de ne pas donner de nom alutiiq à ce masque en raison de son apparence puissante.

Chapitre 5

334 Pullar 1992, p. 182–183.

335 Dzeniskevich et Pavlinskaia 1988.

336 Varjola 1988.

337 Lot-Falck 1957 ; Desson 1995 ; Désveaux 2002.

338 Crowell 1992 ; Crowell et al. 2001.

339 Desson 1995.

340 Lot-Falck 1957.

341 Sans lien de parenté avec Jacob Simeonoff.

342 Koniag, Inc. 2008, p. 20.

343 Steffian 2001, p. 201.

344 Koniag, Inc. 2008, p. 74.

345 *Ibid.*, p. 49.

346 Steffian 2006, p. 27–31.

347 Johnson et son épouse sugpiaq Alisha Drabek collaborent à la conception des bijoux.

Annexes

348 Pinart 1871–1872.

349 Haakanson, sous presse.

350 Desson 1995, p. 187–240.

351 Nous présentons les mots en alutiiq selon leur orthographe alutiiq moderne, cf. Leer 1982, 1990 ; Counceller et Steffian 2004.

352 Les notes que Pinart a rédigées à Kodiak après son voyage auprès des communautés sugpiat comprennent des textes associés aux masques suivants, dans l'ordre : *Angun* (Vieil Homme), *Akrillria* (Voyageur), *Angun* (Vieil Homme), *Akrillria* (Voyageur), *Ituryullria* (Celui qui est arrivé), *Unartuliq* (Protecteur), *Pugumalria* (La femme qui a pris), *Nakirnalik* (Celui au nez retroussé), *Kuyauq* (Celui au grand nez), *Agu'lik* (Large Masque), *Chumliq* (Le premier), *Yuilria* (Voyageur), *Agu'lik* (Large Masque), *Shalgayak* (Marchand), *Ashigik* (L'idiot/Celui qui a de la chance), *Nallumalik* (Celui qui ne sait pas).

353 Desson 1995, p. 280–281, 545.

354 Un *qasgiq* était un grand bâtiment commun d'une seule pièce, où les hommes discutaient de politique, réparaient les outils et préparaient les guerres (Chechenev, in Desson 1995, p. 130). En hiver, ce bâtiment devenait un centre cérémoniel où les personnes de tous âges se rassemblaient pour chanter, danser et festoyer (Davydov 1977, p. 154 ; Gideon 1989, p. 40). Dans ses notes, Pinart transcrit ce terme par « casine ».

355 *Barabara* est le terme russe pour désigner une maison sugpiaq recouverte de terre, appelée *ciqlluaq* dans la langue alutiiq. Cette référence à une structure sugpiaq désigne en revanche probablement le *qasgiq* ou bâtiment commun, plutôt qu'une habitation.

356 Ce chant est associé à deux masques qui dansent ensemble, *Yuaulik* (Chercheur) et *Unartuliq* (Protecteur).

357 En référence au masque précédent, *Chumliiq* (Le premier).

358 Une image de ce masque, disparu des collections du Château-Musée, apparaît dans Lot-Falck 1957, pl. 5.

359 Ce chant est associé à deux masques qui dansent ensemble, *Yuaulik* (Chercheur) et *Unartuliq* (Protecteur).

References
Références

Armstrong, Karl

1979 The Koniagmiut. *Alaska Geographic* 6(3). The Alaska Geographic Society, Anchorage.

Bancroft, Hubert Howe

n.d. Literary Industries, tome 39.

1886 History of Alaska: 1730–1885. In *The Works of Hubert Howe Bancroft*, Vol. XXXIII. A. L. Bancroft and Co., San Francisco.

Birket-Smith, Kaj

1941 Early Collections from the Pacific Eskimo. *Nationalmuseets Skrifter, Etnografisk Raekke* 1:121–163.

1953 The Chugach Eskimo. *Nationalmuseets Skrifter, Etnografisk Raekke*, Vol. VI, Copenhagen.

Black, Lydia T.

1988 The Story of Russian America. In *Crossroads of Continents: Cultures of Siberia and Alaska*, edited by W. W. Fitzhugh and A. Crowell, pp. 24–30. Smithsonian Institution Press, Washington, D.C.

1990 Creoles in Russian America. *Pacific* 2(2):142–155.

1991 *Glory Remembered: Wooden Headgear of Alaska Sea Hunters*. Alaska State Museums, Juneau.

1992 The Russian Conquest of Kodiak. *Anthropological Papers of the University of Alaska* 24(1–2):165–182.

2001 Forgotten Literacy. In *Looking Both Ways: Heritage and Identity of the Alutiiq People*, edited by Aron L. Crowell, Amy F. Steffian, and Gordon L. Pullar, pp. 60–61. University of Alaska Press, Fairbanks.

2004 *Russians in Alaska: 1732–1867*. University of Alaska Press, Fairbanks.

Bouterin, Géraldine

2007 *Les Masques Sugpiaq de la collection Alphonse Pinart conservés au Château-Musée de Boulogne-sur-Mer*. Mémoire d'étude de Master I. Ecole de Louvre, Paris.

Case, David S., and David A. Voluck

2002 *Alaska Natives and American Laws*, 2nd ed. University of Alaska Press, Fairbanks.

Château-Musée

2008 Collection Pinart du Château-Musée de Boulogne-sur-Mer. Unpublished inventory, Château-Musée, Boulogne-sur-Mer, France.

Clark, Donald W.

1970 The Late Kachemak Tradition at Three Saints and Crag Point, Kodiak Island, Alaska. *Arctic Anthropology* 6(2):73–111.

1984 Pacific Eskimo: Historical Ethnography. In *Arctic*, edited by David Damas, pp. 185–197. Handbook of American Indians, Vol. 5, W. C. Sturtevant, general editor, Smithsonian Institution, Washington, D.C.

Corey, Peter

1987 *Faces, Voices & Dreams: A Celebration of the Centennial of the Sheldon Jackson Museum Sitka, Alaska 1888–1988*. Division of Alaska State Museums and the Friends of the Alaska State Museum, Sitka.

Counceller, April G. L., and Amy F. Steffian (editors)

2004 *Sharing Words—Lessons in Alutiiq Language*. Alutiiq Museum, Kodiak.

Crowell, Aron

1992 Postcontact Koniag Ceremonialism on Kodiak Island and the Alaska Peninsula: Evidence from the Fisher Collection. *Arctic Anthropology* 29(1):18–37.

1997 *Archaeology and the Capitalist World System: A Study from Russian America*. Plenum Press, New York.

Crowell, Aron L., Amy F. Steffian, and Gordon L. Pullar (editors)
2001   *Looking Both Ways: Heritage and Identity of the Alutiiq People*. University of Alaska Press, Fairbanks.

Crowell, Aron L., and April Laktonen
2001   Súgucihpet—"Our Way of Living." In *Looking Both Ways: Heritage and Identity of the Alutiiq People*, edited by Aron L. Crowell, Amy F. Steffian, and Gordon L. Pullar, pp. 137–187. University of Alaska Press, Fairbanks.

Crowell, Aron L., and Jeff Leer
2001   Ukgwepet—"Our Beliefs." In *Looking Both Ways: Heritage and Identity of the Alutiiq People*, edited by Aron L. Crowell, Amy F. Steffian, and Gordon L. Pullar, pp. 189–221. University of Alaska Press, Fairbanks.

Crowell, Aron L., and Sonja Lührmann
2001   Alutiiq Culture: Views from Archaeology, Anthropology and History. In *Looking Both Ways: Heritage and Identity of the Alutiiq People*, edited by Aron L. Crowell, Amy F. Steffian, and Gordon L. Pullar, pp. 21–72. University of Alaska Press, Fairbanks.

Dall, William H.
1870   *Alaska and Its Resources*. Boston: Lee and Shepard. Facsmilie reprint, New York.
1875   Alaskan Mummies. *The American Naturist* (IX) 6 (August).
1878   *On the Remains of Later Pre-Historic Man: Obtained from the Caves in the Catherina Archipelago, Alaska Territory*. Smithsonian Institution, Washington, D.C.
1970   *Alaska and Its Resources*. Lee and Shepard, Boston. 1970
[1870] facsmile ed. Arno and the New York Times, New York.

Dauenhauer, Richard L.
1990   Education in Russian America. In *Russian America: The Forgotten Frontier*, edited by Barbara Sweetland Smith and Redmond J. Barnett, pp. 155–163. Washington State Historical Society, Tacoma.

Davis, Nancy Yaw
1984   Contemporary Pacific Eskimo. In *Arctic*, edited by David Damas, pp. 198–204. Handbook of North American Indians, Vol. 5, W. C. Sturtevant, general editor, Smithsonian Institution, Washington, D.C.

Davydov, G. I.
1977   *The Two Voyages to Russian America, 1802–1807*. Limestone Press, Kingston, Ontario.

Desson, Dominique
1995   Masked Rituals of the Kodiak Archipelago. Unpublished Ph.D. Dissertation, University of Alaska Fairbanks.

Désveaux, Emmanuel
2002   *Kodiak, Alaska: Les masques de la collection Alphonse Pinart*. Adam Biro, Paris.

Dias, Nélia
1991   *Le Musée d'Ethnographie du Trocadéro*. Editions du CNRS, Paris.

Dilliplane, Timothy
1990   Industries in Russia America. In *Russian America: The Forgotten Frontier*, edited by Barbara Sweetland Smith and Redmond J. Barnett, pp. 131–143. Washington State Historical Society, Tacoma.

Dmytryshyn, B., and E. A. P. Crownhart-Vaughan
1979   *The End of Russian America: Captain P. N. Golovin's Last Report, 1862*. Oregon Historical Society, Portland.

Donta, Christopher
1994   Continuity and Function in the Ceremonial Material Culture of the Koniag Eskimo. In *Reckoning with the Dead: The Larsen Bay Repatriation and the Smithsonian Institution*, edited by T. L. Bray and T. W. Killion, pp. 122–136. Smithsonian Institution Press, Washington, D.C.

Dzeniskevich, G. I., and L. P. Pavlinskaia
1988   Treasures by the Neva: The Russian Collections. In *Crossroads of Continents*, edited by W. W. Fitzhugh and A. Crowell, pp. 83–88. Smithsonian Institution Press, Washington, D.C.

Elliott, Henry W.
1886   *Our Arctic Province*. Charles Scribner's Sons, New York.

Fedorova, Svetlana G.
1973   *The Russian Population in Alaska and California: Late 18th Century–1867*. Limestone Press, Kingston, Ontario.

Fienup-Riordan, Ann
1996   *Agayuliyararput—Our Way of Making Prayer: The Living Tradition of Yup'ik Masks*. University of Washington Press, Seattle.

Fortuine, Robert

1989 *Chills and Fevers: Health and Disease in the Early History of Alaska.* University of Alaska Press, Fairbanks.

Gerbert, Anne-Laure

2007 *Alphonse Pinart (1852–1911), Voyageur, collectionneur, érudit, éditeur.* Mémoire d'étude de Master I. Ecole du Louvre, Paris.

2008 *Voyage d'étude d'un Français en Alaska: étude comparative du voyage d'Alphonse Pinart en Alaska et de ses apports avec les voyages de ses prédécesseurs et ses contemporains.* Mémoire d'étude de Master II. Ecole du Louvre, Paris.

Gibson, James R.

1976 *Imperial Russia in Frontier America.* Oxford University Press, New York.

Gideon, Hiermonk

1989 *The Round the World Voyage of Hiermonk Gideon.* Translated by Lydia Black, edited by Richard A. Pierce. Limestone Press, Kingston, Ontario.

Haakanson, Sven D.

2002 Nouvelle vie des masques a Kodiak Aujourd'hui. In *Kodiak, Alaska: Les masques de la collection Alphonse Pinart*, edited by Emmanuel Désveaux, pp. 124–131. Adam Biro, Paris.

In press Collections and Cultural Discovery: A Never-Ending Journey. In *La Collection*, edited by Yves Le Fur. Flammarion, Paris.

Haakanson, Sven D., and Anne-Claire Laronde

2008 A Shared History: Alphonse Pinart, the Alutiiq People and the Château-Musée. In *Two Journeys: A Companion to the Giinaquq: Like A Face Exhibition*, Koniag, Inc., pp. 3–4. Alutiiq Museum, Kodiak.

Haakanson, Sven D., and Amy F. Steffian

2004 The Alutiiq Museum's Guidelines for the Spiritual Care of Artifacts. In *Stewards of the Sacred*, edited by Lawrence E. Sullivan and Alison Edwards, pp. 155–166. American Association of Museums, Washington, D.C.

Hagan, William T.

1988 United States Indian Policies, 1860–1900. In *History of Indian-White Relations*, edited by W. E. Washburn, pp. 51–65. Handbook of North American Indians, Vol. 4, W. C. Sturtevant, general editor, Smithsonian Institution, Washington, D.C.

Halley-des-Fontaines-Poiret, Françoise-Camille

2002 Le destin de la collection Pinart, 1871–2001. In *Kodiak, Alaska: Les masques de la collection Alphonse Pinart*, edited by Emmanuel Désveaux, pp. 186–199. Adam Biro, Paris.

Heusser, C. J.

1960 *Late-Pleistocene Environments of North Pacific North America.* American Geographical Society Special Publication 35. New York.

Hinckley, Ted C.

1972 *The Americanization of Alaska, 1867–1897.* Pacific Books, Palo Alto, California.

Holmberg, Heinrich Johan

1985 *Holmberg's Ethnographic Sketches.* Translated by F. Jaensch, edited by M. W. Falk. The Rasmuson Library Historical Translation Series, Vol. 1. University of Alaska Press, Fairbanks.

Hrdlička, Aleš

1975 *The Anthropology of Kodiak Island.* AMS Press, New York.

Huggins, Eli Lundy

1981 *Kodiak and Afognak Life, 1868–1870.* Limestone Press, Kingston, Ontario.

Huguet, Auguste

1875 Retranscription de la lettre d'Alphonse Pinart adressée au maire de Boulogne, Séance du Conseil Municipal du 16 février 1875. Boulogne-sur-Mer, Archives municipales. Registre des délibérations du Conseil Municipal de la ville de Boulogne-sur-Mer.

1875 Retranscription de la lettre du maire de Boulogne adressée à Alphonse Pinart, Séance du Conseil Municipal du 16 février 1875, Boulogne-sur-Mer, Archives municipales. Registre des délibérations du Conseil Municipal de la ville de Boulogne-sur-Mer.

1875 Séance du Conseil Municipal du 18 septembre 1876, Boulogne-sur-Mer, Archives municipals. Registre des délibérations du Conseil Municipal de la ville de Boulogne-sur-Mer.

Hunt, Dolores Cecelia

2000 The Ethnography of Alutiiq Clothing: Comparative Analysis of the Smithsonian's Fisher Collection. Unpublished master's thesis, San Francisco State University, San Francisco.

Jordan, Richard H.

1994 Qasqiluteng: Feasting and Ceremonialism Among the Traditional Koniag of Kodiak Island. In

Anthropology of the North Pacific Rim, edited by W. W. Fitzhugh and V. Chaussonnet, pp. 147–173. Smithsonian Institution Press, Washington, D.C.

Jordan, Richard H., and Richard A. Knecht

1988   Archaeological Research on Western Kodiak Island, Alaska: The Development of Koniag Culture. In *Late Prehistoric Development of Alaska's Native People*, edited by Robert D. Shaw, Roger K. Harritt, and Don E. Dumond, pp. 225–306. Aurora, Vol. IV, Alaska Anthropological Association, Anchorage.

Kan, Sergei

1988   The Russian Orthodox Church in Alaska. In *History of Indian-White Relations*, edited by W. E. Washburn, pp. 506–521. Handbook of North American Indians, Vol. 4, W. C. Sturtevant, general editor, Smithsonian Institution, Washington, D.C.

Khlebnikov, K. T.

1973   *Baranov: Chief Manager of the Russian Colonies in America.* Limestone Press, Kingston, Ontario.

1994   *Notes on Russian America: Parts II–V: Kad'iak, Unalaska, Atkha, the Pribylovs.* Limestone Press, Kingston, Ontario.

Knecht, Richard A.

1995   The Late Prehistory of the Alutiiq People: Culture Change in the Kodiak Archipelago from 1200–1750 AD. Unpublished Ph.D. dissertation, Bryn Mawr College.

2000   Archaeology and Alutiiq Cultural Identity on Kodiak Island. In *Working Together: Native Americans and Archaeologists*, edited by Kurt E. Dongoske, Mark A. Aldenderfer, and Karen Doehner, pp. 147–153. Society for American Archaeology, Washington, D.C.

Kodiak Area Native Association

1987   The History of the Traditional Native Village of Old Harbor and Its Government. Ms. on file at the Kodiak Area Native Association, Kodiak.

Koniag, Inc.

2008   *Two Journeys: A Companion to the Giinaquq: Like A Face Exhibition.* Alutiiq Museum, Kodiak.

Krech, Shepard III

1989   *A Victorian Earl in the Arctic. The Travels and Collections of the Fifth Earl of Lonsdale 1888–89.* University of Washington Press, Seattle.

Lafontaine, Paul-Emile

2006   *Campagne des Mers du Sud.* Mercure de France, Paris.

Liapunova, R. G.

1994   Eskimo Masks from Kodiak Island in the Collections of the Peter the Great Museum of Anthropology and Ethnography in St. Petersburg. In *Anthropology of the North Pacific Rim*, edited by W. W. Fitzhugh and V. Chaussonnet, pp. 175–203. Smithsonian Institution Press, Washington, D.C.

Lisianskii, U.

1968   *Voyage Round the World in the Years 1803, 1804, 1805, and 1806.* Bibliotheca Australiana 42. N. Israel, Amsterdam and De Capo Press, New York.

Leer, Jeff

1982   *A Conversational Dictionary of Kodiak Alutiiq.* Alaska Native Language Center, University of Alaska Fairbanks.

1990   *A Classroom Grammar of Kodiak Alutiiq, Kodiak Island Dialect.* Alaska Native Language Center, University of Alaska Fairbanks.

Leunens, Daniel

2003   *Biographie de Léon Pinart (1809–1859), La Métallurgie en Boulonnais (1810–2003).* Association A.M.A., Boulogne-sur-Mer.

Lot-Falck, Evelyne

1957   Les masques eskimo et aléoutes de la collection Pinart. *Journal de la Société des Américanistes* 46:5–42.

Lottin, Alain

1983   *Histoire de Boulogne sur Mer.* Presses Universitaires, Lille.

Luehrmann, Sonja

2008   *Alutiiq Villages Under Russian and U.S. Rule.* University of Alaska Press, Fairbanks.

Lührmann, Sonja

2000   *Alutiiq Villages Under Russian and U.S. Rule.* Unpublished master's thesis, Johann Wolfgang Goethe University, Frankfurt.

Merck, Carl Heinrich

1980   *Siberia and Northwestern America 1788–1792.* Translated by Fritz Jaensch, edited by Richard A. Pierce. Limestone Press, Kingston, Ontario.

Miller, David Hunter

1981   *The Alaska Treaty.* The Limestone Press, Kingston, Ontario.

Mishler, Craig

2003   *Black Ducks and Salmon Bellies: An Ethnography of Old Harbor and Ouzinkie, Alaska.* Donning Company Publishers, Virginia Beach, Virginia.

Morseth, Michelle

1998   *Puyulek Pu'irtuq! The People of the Volcanoes.* Aniakchak National Monument and Preserve Ethnographic Overview & Assessment. National Park Service, Anchorage.

Mulcahy, Joanne B.

2001   *Birth and Rebirth on an Alaskan Island.* University of Georgia Press, Athens.

Mulcahy, Laurie

2003   The Native Village of Old Harbor and Its Traditional Government. In *Black Ducks and Salmon Bellies: An Ethnography of Old Harbor and Ouzinkie, Alaska,* pp. 80–89. Donning Company Publishers, Virginia Beach, Virginia.

Musée du quai Branly

2007   Alutiiq collections at present in the Musée du quai Branly. Unpublished inventory, Musée du quai Branly, Paris.

Naske, Claus-M., and Herman E. Slotnick

1979   *Alaska: A History of the 49th State.* William B. Eerdmans Publishing Company, Grand Rapids, Michigan.

Oleksa, Michael J. (editor)

1987   *Alaskan Missionary Spirituality.* Paulist Press, New York.

1990   The Creoles and Their Contributions to the Development of Alaska. In *Russian America: The Forgotten Frontier,* edited by Barbara Sweetland Smith and Redmond J. Barnett, pp. 185–195. Washington State Historical Society, Tacoma.

1992   *Orthodox Alaska: A Theology of Mission.* St. Vladimir's Seminary Press, Crestwood, New York.

Parmenter, Ross

1966   *Explorer, Linguist and Anthropologist: A Descriptive Bibliography of the Published Works of Alphonse Louis Pinart, With Notes on His Life.* South West Museum, Los Angeles.

Partnow, Patricia H.

2001   *Making History: Alutiiq/Sugpiaq Life on the Alaska Peninsula.* University of Alaska Press, Fairbanks.

Petroff, I.

1884   *Report on the Population, Industries and Resources of Alaska.* Department of the Interior, Census Office. Government Printing Office, Washington, D.C.

Pinart, Alphonse Louis

1860–   Lettres d'A. Pinart à E. Hamy, Paris. Archives du Muséum

1877   National d'Histoire Naturelle (salle des Vélins). Archives des correspondances d'Ernest Hamy, Tome I.

1871–   Trip around Afognak and Shouiak from March 24th to

1872   April 10th. University of California Berkeley, Bancroft Library Archives, Z-Z 17, v.3.

1872a   *Catalogue des collections rapportées de l'Amérique Russe (aujourd'hui territoire d'Aliaska), exposées dans l'une des galeries du Museum d'histoire naturelle de Paris (section d'Anthropologie).* J. C. Claye, Paris.

1872b   Lettre à Ernest Hamy, 4 juillet 1872, Marquette (Michigan, U.S.), d'A. Pinart à E. Hamy, Correspondance Ernest Hamy, Paris. Archives du Muséum National d'Histoire Naturelle (salle des Vélins). Archives des correspondances d'Ernest Hamy, Tome I.

1873a   Eskimaux et Koloches: idées religieuses et traditions des Kaniagmioutes. *Revue d'Anthropologie* 2:673–680.

1873b   *Voyages à la côte nord-ouest de l'Amérique exécutés durant les années 1870–1872, Histoire naturelle,* Vol. I, part I. Ernest Leroux, Paris.

1873c   Voyage à la Côte Nord-ouest d'Amérique, d'Ounalashka à Kadiak (Les Aléoutiennes et Péninsules d'Aliaska). *Bulletin de la Société de Géographie,* 6th ser., 6(July–December): 561–570.

1875   *La caverne d'Aknanh, île d'Ounga (archipel Shumagin, Alaska).* Ernest Leroux, Paris.

Porter, Robert P.

1893   Report on Population and Resources of Alaska at the Eleventh Census: 1890. Government Printing Office, Washington, D.C.

Prucha, Francis Paul

1975   *Documents of United States Indian Policy.* University of Nebraska Press, Lincoln.

Pullar, Gordon L.

1992   Ethnic Identity, Cultural Pride, and Generations of Baggage: A Personal Experience. *Arctic Anthropology* 29(2):186.

1994   The Qikertarmiut and the Scientist: Fifty Years of Clashing World Views. In *Reckoning with the Dead: The Larsen Bay Repatriation and the Smithsonian Institution*, edited by T. L. Bray and T. W. Killion, pp. 15–25. Smithsonian Institution Press, Washington, D.C.

1997   Indigenous culture and organizational culture: A case study of an Alaska Native organization. Unpublished Ph.D. dissertation, Union Institute, Cincinnati, Ohio.

Riviale, Pascal

2001   Eugène Boban ou les aventures d'un antiquaire au pays des américanistes, *Journal de la Société des Américanistes* (87):351–362.

Robert-Lamblin, Joëlle

1976   Exploration de l'archipel aléoute (Alaska) par le Français Alphonse-Louis Pinart, en 1871–72, Suisse. *Bulletin de la Société Suisse des Américanistes.*

Roppel, Patricia

1986   *Salmon from Kodiak: History of the Salmon Fisheries of Kodiak Island*. Alaska Historical Commission, Anchorage.

Rousselot, J.-L., B. Abel, J. Pierre, and C. Bihl

1991   *Masques Eskimo d'Alaska*. Éditions Amez, Routelle, France.

Rousselot, Jean-Louis, and Veronika Grahammer

2002   Catalogue raisonné de la collection du Château-Musée de Boulogne-sur-Mer. In *Kodiak, Alaska: Les masques de la collection Alphonse Pinart*, edited by Emmanuel Désveaux, pp. 207–243. Adam Biro, Paris.

Russell, Priscilla

1995   Kodiak Alutiiq Plantlore. Unpublished manuscript, produced for the Kodiak Area Native Association, on file Alutiiq Museum, Kodiak.

Salabelle, Marie-Amélie

2001   La caverne aux masques, la collection Pinart du musée de Boulogne-sur-Mer. *Gradhiva* (29):87–91.

Shelikhov, Grigorii I.

1981   *A Voyage to Russian America, 1783–1786*. Translated by Marina Ramsey, edited by Richard A. Pierce. Limestone Press, Kingston, Ontario.

Sibeud, Emmanuelle

2001   La Fin du Voyage: De la pratique coloniale à la pratique ethnographique, 1878–1913. In *Les Politiques de l'Anthropologie : Discours et Pratiques en France 1860–1940*, edited by Claude Blanckaert. l'Harmattan, Paris.

Simeonoff, Helen

2007   Unpublished family group sheet in the files of the author. Anchorage, Alaska.

Simon, James J. K., and Amy F. Steffian

1994   Cannibalism or Complex Mortuary Behavior? An Analysis of Patterned Variability in the Treatment of Human Remains from the Kachemak Tradition of Kodiak Island, Alaska. In *Reckoning with the Dead: The Larsen Bay Repatriation and the Smithsonian Institution*, edited by T. L. Bray and T. W. Killion, pp. 75–100. Smithsonian Institution Press, Washington, D.C.

Solovjova, Katerina G., and Aleksandra A. Vovnyanko

2002   *The Fur Rush: Essays and Documents on the History of Alaska at the End of the Eighteenth Century*. Phoenix Press, Anchorage.

Steffian, Amy F.

1992   Fifty Years After Hrdlicka: Further Investigations at the Uyak Site, Kodiak Island, Alaska. *Anthropological Papers of the University of Alaska* 24(1&2):141–164.

2001   An Alutiiq Mask Maker. In *Looking Both Ways: Heritage and Identity of the Alutiiq People*, edited by Aron L. Crowell, Amy F. Steffian, and Gordon L. Pullar, pp. 201. University of Alaska Press, Fairbanks.

2006   Teaching Traditions: Public Programming at the Alutiiq Museum. In *Living Homes for Cultural Expression*, edited by K. C. Cooper and N. I. Sandoval, p. 27–41. National Museum of the American Indian, Washington, D.C.

Stevens, Gary

1990   The Woody Island Ice Company. In *Russia in North America: Proceedings of the 2nd International Conference on Russian America*, edited by R. A. Pierce, pp. 192–212. Limestone Press, Kingston, Ontario.

Tikhmenev, P. A.

1978   *A History of the Russian American Company.* Translated and edited by R. A. Pierce and A. S. Donnelly. University of Washington Press, Seattle.

Torres, Félix

2002   Un Français en Alaska. In *Kodiak, Alaska: Les masques de la collection Alphonse Pinart*, edited by Emmanuel Désveaux, pp. 24–31. Adam Biro, Paris.

Varjola, Pirjo

1988 *ALASKA Russian American*. National Board of Antiquities, Finland.

Watrous, Stephen

2001 Outpost of an Empire: Russian Expansion to America. In Fort Ross, Fort Ross Interpretive Association. Electronic document, http://www.fortrossstatepark.org/Russian%20American%20Company.htm. Retrieved July 6, 2007.

Wood, Margaret Mary

1943 The Russian Creoles of Alaska as a Marginal Group. *Social Forces* 22(2), December. University of North Carolina Press.

Woodbury, Anthony C.

1984 Eskimo and Aleut Languages. In *Arctic*, edited by David Damas, pp. 49–63. Handbook of American Indians, Vol. 5, W. C. Sturtevant, general editor. Smithsonian Institution, Washington, D.C.

Wrangell, Ferdinand Petrovich Von

1980 *Russian America: Statistical and Ethnographic Information*. Translated by M. Sadouski, edited by R. A. Pierce. Limestone Press, Kingston, Ontario. Distributed by University of Alaska Press.

Index

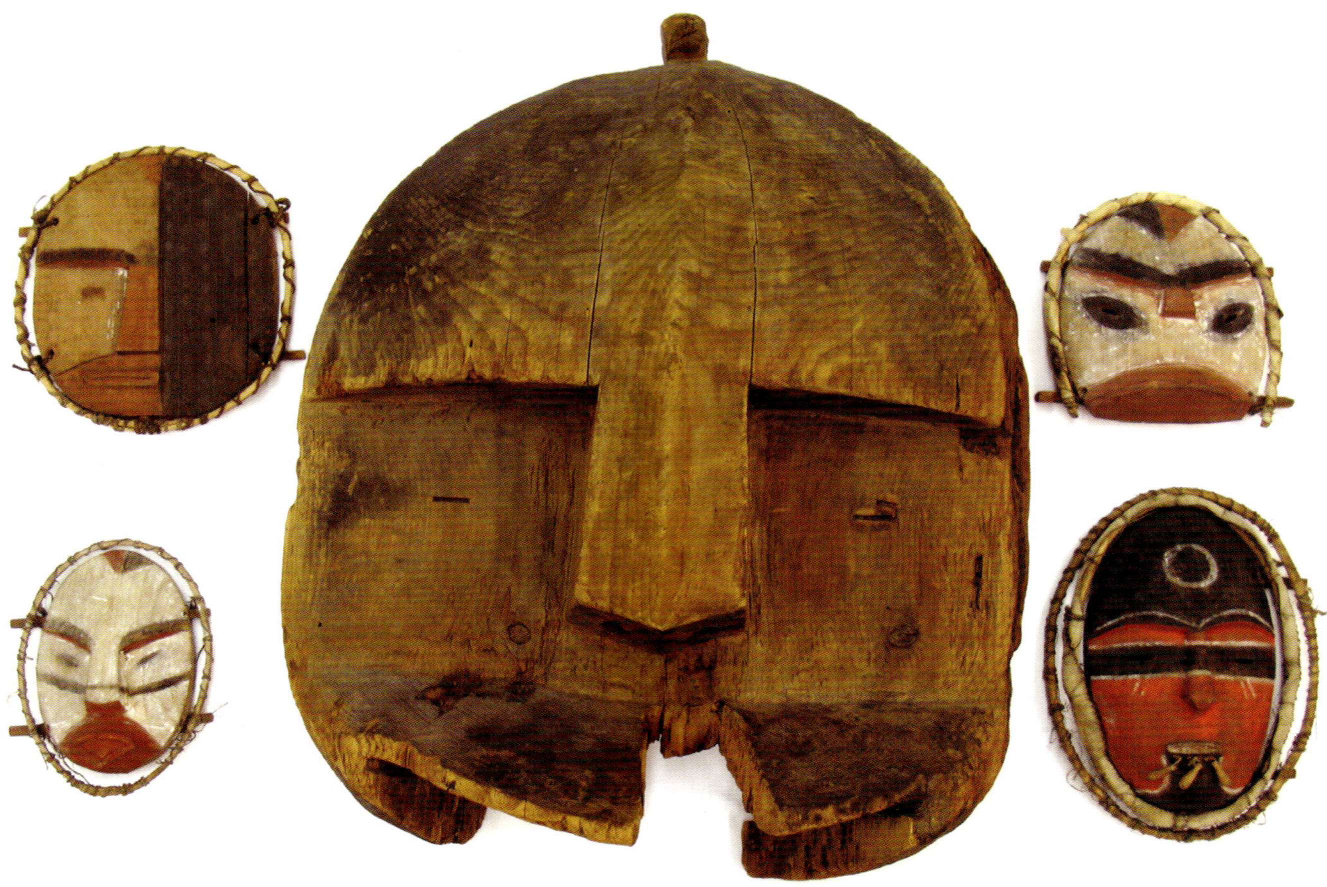

Figure 136. Many of the ornately painted masks collected by Pinart are smaller in comparison with unpainted masks in the collection.

PHOTO BY SVEN HAAKANSON JR.

Illustration 136. De nombreux masques peints collectés par Pinart sont de petite taille, comparés aux masques sans peinture de la collection.

PHOTO DE SVEN HAAKANSON JR.

About the Editors

Sven D. Haakanson Jr., Ph.D., project director and curator of the *Giinaquq: Like a Face* exhibition, is the executive director of the nationally acclaimed Alutiiq Museum and Archaeological Repository. A member of the Old Harbor Alutiiq tribe, Haakanson works to share Native American perspectives with museums and museum practices with Native people. For the past decade he has made collections more accessible to Native communities by researching objects in the world's museums and developing traveling exhibits and educational resources around the information they hold. In 2007 the MacArthur Foundation honored his work with their prestigious fellowship. Haakanson maintains an active research program. He is systematically documenting Kodiak's prehistoric petroglyphs and continues to publish his research on the Nenets culture of Siberia. In addition, he is an accomplished artist, known for his carvings and photography. His doctoral degree is from Harvard University.

Amy F. Steffian, M.A., a member of the *Giinaquq: Like a Face* exhibition team, serves as deputy director of Kodiak's Alutiiq Museum and Archaeological Repository. A professional archaeologist who joined the museum's staff at its inception, Steffian works to develop educational programs, create exhibits and publications, and lead anthropological research. Steffian's current research focuses on tracking the changing relationships between fishing, food storage, and settlement in Kodiak prehistory. Museums Alaska honored Steffian's contributions to the Alutiiq Museum with a career achievement award in 2005. She holds a master's degree from the University of Michigan.

À propos des directeurs de la publication

Sven D. Haakanson Jr., docteur en anthropologie, directeur de projet et conservateur de l'exposition « Giinaquq: Like a Face », est le directeur exécutif de l'Alutiiq Museum & Archaeological Repository. Membre de la tribu alutiiq d'Old Harbor, Haakanson œuvre à faire connaître le point de vue amérindien auprès des musées, et les pratiques muséales auprès des Amérindiens. Depuis une dizaine d'années, il a facilité l'accès des communautés amérindiennes aux collections muséales grâce à ses recherches concernant des objets conservés dans des musées à travers le monde et à l'élaboration d'expositions itinérantes et de matériel pédagogique basé sur les informations que ces musées contiennent. En 2007, la Fondation MacArthur a récompensé son travail en lui attribuant sa bourse prestigieuse. Haakanson anime un programme actif de recherches. Il documente systématiquement les pétroglyphes préhistoriques de Kodiak et continue à publier ses recherches sur la culture Nenet de Sibérie. Il est par ailleurs un artiste talentueux, connu pour ses sculptures et photographies. Il a obtenu son diplôme de doctorat à l'université de Harvard.

Amy F. Steffian, titulaire d'un master et membre de l'équipe de projet de l'exposition « Giinaquq: Like a Face », occupe le poste de directrice adjointe de l'Alutiiq Museum & Archaeological Repository de Kodiak. Archéologue professionnelle, elle a rejoint le personnel du musée à son ouverture, où elle développe des programmes éducatifs, des expositions et des publications, tout en menant des recherches anthropologiques. Ses recherches actuelles s'intéressent à l'évolution des liens entre la pêche, la conservation de la nourriture et les campements préhistoriques à Kodiak. L'organisation Museums Alaska a mis à l'honneur en 2005 le travail de Steffian à l'Alutiiq Museum en lui remettant un prix qui récompense sa carrière. Elle a obtenu son diplôme de master à l'université de Michigan.

Dépôt légal : juin 2009

Published by
University of Alaska Press
PO Box 756240
Fairbanks, Alaska 99775-6240
USA

Printed by
Everbest Printing Company Ltd., China

ISBN 978-1-60223-049-1